P9-CMO-489

EXPLORER'S GUIDE

CAPE COD MARTHA'S VINEYARD & NANTUCKET

EXPLORER'S GUIDE

CAPE COD MARTHA'S VINEYARD & NANTUCKET

ELEVENTH EDITION

KIM GRANT

with photographs by the author

THE COUNTRYMAN PRESS
A division of W. W. Norton & Company
Independent Publishers Since 1923

Copyright © 2017, 2014, 2011, 2009, 2007, 2005, 2003, 2001, 1999, 1997, 1995 by Kim Grant

All rights reserved
Printed in the United States of America

For information about permission to reproduce selections from this book, write to
Permissions, The Countryman Press, 500 Fifth Avenue, New York, NY 10110

For information about special discounts for bulk purchases, please contact
W. W. Norton Special Sales at specialsales@wwnorton.com or 800-233-4830

The Countryman Press
www.countrymanpress.com

A division of W. W. Norton & Company, Inc.
500 Fifth Avenue, New York, NY 10110
www.wwnorton.com

978-1-68268-011-7 (pbk.)

1 0 9 8 7 6 5 4 3 2 1

*Special thanks to Laurie Yankowitz,
the book's biggest online fan,
a continuous print supporter for 20 years,
and for this edition, the best researcher ever.*

EXPLORE WITH US!

Welcome to the 11th edition of the most comprehensive guide to Cape Cod, Martha's Vineyard, and Nantucket. I have been highly selective but broadly inclusive, based on years of repeated visits, cumulative research, and ongoing conversations with locals. All entries—attractions, inns, and restaurants—are chosen on the basis of personal experience.

I hope that the organization of this guide makes it easy to read and use. The layout has been kept simple; the following pointers will help you get started.

WHAT'S WHERE In the beginning of the book you'll find an alphabetical listing of special highlights and important information that you can reference quickly. You'll find advice on everything from where to find the best art galleries and lighthouses to where to take a whale-watching excursion.

LODGING Prices: Since prices, seasons, and specials are so variable, I have used "abstract" pricing to give you a general idea of the relative rates between lodging places. Please also see Lodging in "What's Where on Cape Cod, Martha's Vineyard, and Nantucket." Double room rate designations for high season are as follows:

$ = $1–199
$$ = $200–299
$$$ = $300–399
$$$$ = $400–499
$$$$$ = $500–599
$$$$$+ = $600+

RESTAURANTS In most sections, I make a distinction between Dining Out and Eating Out. Restaurants listed under Eating Out are generally inexpensive and more casual; reservations are often suggested for restaurants in Dining Out. A range of prices for main dishes is included with each entry. Main dish designations are as follows:

$ = $1–9
$$ = $10–19
$$$ = $20–29
$$$$ = $30+

THINGS TO SEE & DO Prices: The Web is much better suited to offering up-to-the-minute pricing than print. To give you a general idea about how much things cost per person:

$ = $1–9
$$ = $10–19
$$$ = $20–29
$$$$ = $30–39
$$$$+ = $40+

GREEN SPACE In addition to trails and walks, "green space" also includes white and blue spaces, that is, beaches and ponds.

KEY TO SYMBOLS

❄ The "off-season" icon appears next to appealing year-round lodging or attractions.

🏵 The "special-value" icon appears next to lodging entries, restaurants, and activities that combine exceptional quality with moderate prices.

🐾 The "pet-friendly" icon appears next to lodgings where pets are welcome.

✎ The "child and family interest" icon appears next to lodging entries, restaurants, activities, and shops of special appeal to youngsters and families.

☂ The "rainy-day" icon appears next to things to do and places of interest that are appropriate for foul-weather days.

🍸 The "martini glass" icon appears next to restaurants and entertainment venues with good bars.

♿ The "handicap" symbol indicates lodging and dining establishments that are truly wheelchair accessible.

WHERE TO START Start with the aptly named "What's Where." Seriously. It gives a big picture, contextual overview of everything on the Cape and the islands.

This guidebook remains *the* go-to source for the most comprehensive guidance to Cape and island travel. For a real-time, on-the-ground *supplement* please dip into the guidebook's highlights on my website BinduTrips.com/destination/cape-cod.

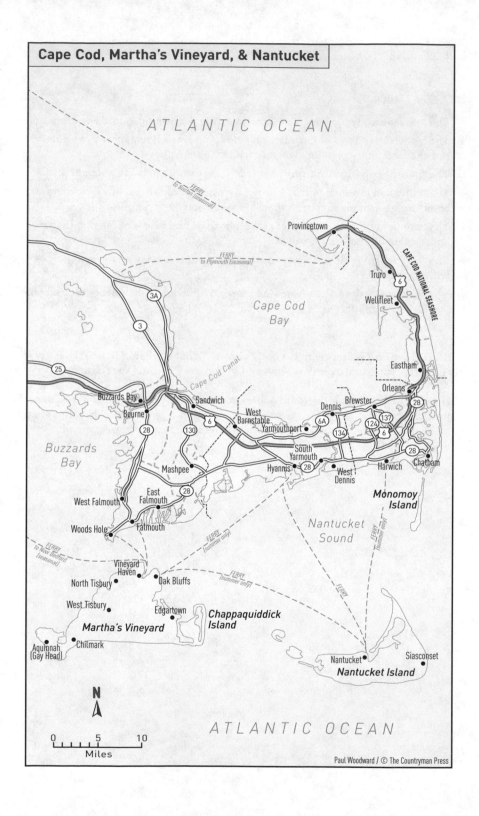

Cape Cod, Martha's Vineyard, & Nantucket

ATLANTIC OCEAN

FERRY to Boston (seasonal)

FERRY to Plymouth (seasonal)

Provincetown

Truro

Wellfleet

Cape Cod Bay

CAPE COD NATIONAL SEASHORE

6

Eastham

Orleans

28

Dennis   Brewster

137

6A

124

134

6

West Barnstable

Yarmouthport

South Yarmouth

Sandwich

Cape Cod Canal

6

130

Bourne

Buzzards Bay

25

28

Buzzards Bay

28

Mashpee

Hyannis   28

West Dennis

Harwich   Chatham

28

Monomoy Island

East Falmouth

West Falmouth

28

Woods Hole   Falmouth

Nantucket Sound

FERRY (summer only)

FERRY (summer only)

FERRY to New Bedford (seasonal)

FERRY

Vineyard Haven

North Tisbury   Oak Bluffs

FERRY (summer only)

West Tisbury

Edgartown   *Chappaquiddick Island*

Martha's Vineyard

Aquinnah (Gay Head)   Chilmark

Nantucket   Siasconset

Nantucket Island

N

0   5   10

Miles

ATLANTIC OCEAN

Paul Woodward / © The Countryman Press

CONTENTS

MAPS

INTRODUCTION

Welcome to the 11th edition of *Cape Cod, Martha's Vineyard & Nantucket: An Explorer's Guide.*

My highest objective is saving you time and money by helping you make the best decisions for your trip. Having trustworthy content all in one place is integral to that goal.

With the Web, you have infinite information at your fingertips. But information without context and comparisons is simply a commodity and not worth that much. We all Google dozens of places to stay and eat on the Web, top 10 lists of things to see and do. But that information is written by thousands of people. Who are they? Do they travel or eat out much? Are they friends of the proprietors? Do they know the big picture about a place?

The average traveler visits 38 websites while planning a trip. You can reduce that number considerably by dipping into this book first.

This guide provides a reasoned assessment of all your Web choices. Its pages are devoted to why you should visit one place over another, why one place is right for you and not for your sister. I see my job as providing "decision assistance," as my colleague Tom Brosnahan likes to say.

I have personally visited every place in this guide, so these reviews are all written from the perspective of someone who has been there and done practically everything.

In every town, I pop into 85 percent of the restaurants, lodging places, shops, and attractions. So what I choose not to review is just as important as what I include. You don't need a hundred places to eat; you just need the best (for a family, a romantic evening, on a budget, etc.). Curation is key.

In my position, I ferret out the great from the good. I assess those intangible qualities that make experiences memorable. I look for how personable the innkeepers are; how service-oriented the staff is; if an afternoon would be better spent doing this or that. Those factors can't be measured through surfing Web pages.

This guide differs from others in that I alone have researched and written it since 1994. What that means to you is that when I say a place is the best clam shack on the Cape, you know that I have visited them all. Many other guidebooks dispatch a team of researchers to various parts of the Cape; when these authors write that a place is the best clam shack on the Cape, what they really mean is, "This is the best clam shack in the territory I was assigned for this edition." Furthermore, because I have written every edition of this book since its inception, you will benefit from insights I have gained over the course of more than 20 years of research.

This guidebook is intended to be many things to many people. It is written for people who live close enough, or are fortunate enough, to be able to make many short trips to the Cape throughout the year—people who know that the region takes on a whole different character from Labor Day weekend to Memorial Day weekend.

It's proven invaluable to year-rounders who must give advice to a steady stream of summer guests. It's for Cape residents who may live on the Upper Cape but don't know much about the Lower Cape.

It's for people whose only trip to the Cape or the islands is their annual summer holiday—people who have always vacationed in Wellfleet, let's say, but are ready to explore other places.

My highest hope, though, is to introduce the *other* Cape and islands to that segment of the traveling public that assumes traffic jams, crowded beaches, and tacky souvenir shops define the region.

About 100,000 cars cross the Cape Cod Canal daily in July and August, and island ferries transport more than 2 million people each summer. So it would be a stretch of the imagination to say that these fragile parcels of prized real estate are unexplored. In fact, sometimes it seems there isn't a grain of sand that hasn't been written about.

But just when I think I've seen it all, a ray of bright, clear sunlight will hit the Provincetown dune shacks in such a way as to make them seem new again. I'll strike up a conversation with a historical society curator, and she'll regale me with stories about town affairs at the turn of the 19th century. I'll walk down a trail in October that I previously walked in May and hear different birds and see different plants.

This book is the result of years of research, conversation, observation, pleasure reading, and personal exploration. I am a Bostonian who spent youthful summer vacations on Cape Cod, bicycling at the Cape Cod National Seashore, eating saltwater taffy in Provincetown, and camping on Martha's Vineyard. My introduction to Nantucket came later, in the mid-1980s; by then I was old enough to appreciate the island's sophisticated culinary treats and rich history all the more.

I am also pleased to supplement my written observations with a visual portrait. I have intentionally emphasized the region's tranquility, since conventional wisdom already associates the Cape with masses of humanity.

Traveling, and writing about it, is a nice lifestyle; and I'm grateful for the opportunity. But it is work. The book wouldn't have been possible without the guidance and firsthand experience of many people who appreciate the Cape and the islands from many different perspectives.

As much as I love both four-star dining and a bucket of fried clams from a shack on the pier, I just can't eat everywhere for every edition. I have called upon my innkeeper friends, who benefit from the collective opinions of dozens of guests who eat in dozens of places night after night and then discuss their experiences the next morning over breakfast.

As with all editions, this one benefits from the accumulated knowledge fellow explorers have shared with me through letters and over breakfast at B&Bs. Specifically I would like to thank Laurie Yankowitz, who has written "Why Buy This Book" below.

The folks at The Countryman Press (a division of W. W. Norton) epitomize everything that's good about the print and ebook publishing industry. I appreciate their responsiveness to and respect for writers, as well as their commitment to providing a quality guidebook to the book-buying public.

I welcome readers' thoughtful comments, criticisms, and suggestions for the next edition of *Cape Cod, Martha's Vineyard & Nantucket: An Explorer's Guide*. Feel free to e-mail me (kim@kimgrant.com); please use the subject header "Explorer's Guide" so I notice it better.

And add your up-to-the-minute contributions and suggestions to BinduTrips.com/destination/Cape-Cod. It's a real-time supplement. As always, this guidebook remains the go-to source for the most comprehensive guidance.

—Kim Grant

WHY BUY THIS BOOK?

ecause it will be a profoundly rewarding and sound investment, immeasurably enhancing your vacation for you and your travel companions for years to come! It certainly has for me.[1]

Believe it or not, even in 2017, not every business and resource has a website. Many special places have eschewed the Web altogether or decided that maintaining a website is not worth the expense. Trust me, you don't want to miss out on those hidden gems who've opted out of cyber marketing. You *will* find them here.

Do you really want to spend hours of screen time curating your vacation plans? Kim has done that for you and then some (as have I, her No. 1 fan and diligent assistant). This guide is masterfully organized to make it easy to find what interests you and every member of your party. Succinct descriptions provide discerning highlights for efficient decision making on your part. When planning is minimal, enjoying becomes maximal.

From the normal Cape Cod experiences (beaches, seafood, splurge-dining, and cheap eats) and wide-ranging recreational pursuits (golf, bicycling, water sports, and nature trails) to cultural activities (bookstores, concerts, historic sites, and art galleries) and places to pick up treasures (thrift shops, upscale boutiques, and one-of-a-kind finds), Kim's recommendations steer you to the best of the Cape and islands. (Careful readers will note and avoid her omissions as well.)

Want to speak to a live person on the Cape? More and more businesses push for digital-only contact, but many of the telephone numbers in this guide predate the Web and still work!

Read any chapter and I dare you *not* to find at least one activity, shop, resource, or event that you would not have known about otherwise. But now that you do, your Cape Cod experience will have an additional dimension—one that less fortunate folks will miss out on—such as an exceptional high tea, a breathtaking scenic drive, or a Friday night lobster roll dinner at a local historic church. This guide is filled with off-the-beaten-path temptations that add depth and flavor not likely to be found through cyber searches.

Kim's introductory town narratives and dining and lodging reviews are highly instructive, offering essentials for making discerning choices. On top of that, she is witty and entertaining. Her lauded photographer's eye whets your appetite for the region's wide-ranging visual delights. Kim also enjoys ongoing relationships with locals who keep her informed of what's new, what's the best. The guide is permeated with inside scoops.

---

[1] I contacted Kim years ago through social media to express gratitude for the countless ways the guide enhanced my enjoyment of the Cape. Following a meet-up in New York City when Kim was in town for a travel writer's conference, and through much subsequent correspondence, I was hired to help update this edition. I tackled the assignment with diligence born of great loyalty to the readers and the high standards set by Kim. Every phone number, website, address, and name mentioned was verified as close to the publication date as possible.

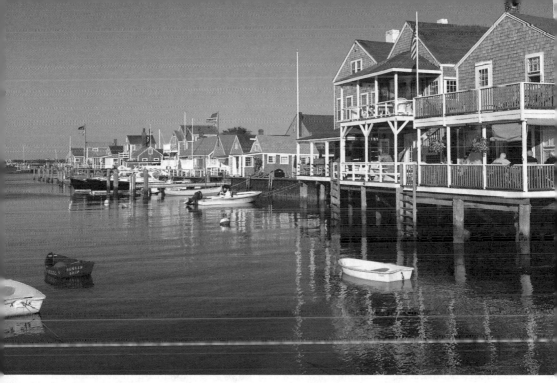

NANTUCKET HARBOR

There is also something for every budget. Kim knows value and quality at every price point. Her recommendations are proudly featured by proprietors who appreciate her prized seal of approval.

I have used each edition of this guide extensively for more than 20 years, and I remain amazed by her consistently infallible suggestions. The result? Always. The. Happiest. Cape Cod. Vacation. Ever.

This guide is so jam-packed with places to go and things to do, it would take a life-time to explore them all. Stick to a town or two or follow an interest (antiques, historic houses, bookstores, nature trails) from Sandwich to Provincetown and the islands. Spend more time doing and less time clicking!

If you have decided to buy this book, I am happy for you! Use it in good health. Enjoy the Cape and islands to the hilt.

—H. Laurie Yankowitz

SUGGESTED ITINERARIES

IF YOU HAVE 3 DAYS Special thanks for buying this book. It contains far more information than you'll ever be able to use. We hope you will pass this book along to a friend after it serves you well. For sure, as a starting point, check out the "A Perfect Day In . . ." for each town.

IF YOU HAVE 5 DAYS You'll need to be efficient. Visit the village of Sandwich, poke around antiques and artisan shops on Route 6A, and drive down scenic bayside roads north of Route 6A, spending two nights mid-Cape. On the third morning, pop down to Main Street and the lighthouse in Chatham, and then head to the Outer Cape and the famed Cape Cod National Seashore beaches, stopping at the Salt Pond Visitor Center in Eastham. Spend two nights on the Outer Cape (or in Orleans): Visit galleries in Wellfleet, walk the Atlantic beaches and short nature trails, and take a day trip to Provincetown.

IF YOU HAVE 7 DAYS You'll end up with a very enjoyable trip. Spend three nights mid-Cape and three on the Outer Cape. Do all of the above, plus linger longer in Sandwich, visiting the Glass Museum and/or Heritage Museums & Gardens. Add a beach walk at Barnstable's Sandy Neck Beach and/or Nauset Beach in Orleans. Visit the Cape Cod Museum of Natural History in Brewster and/or the Wellfleet Bay Wildlife

MARTHA'S VINEYARD

Sanctuary. Spend a day and a half in Provincetown—watching people, walking Commercial Street, ducking into art museums and the informative Provincetown Museum, taking in a sunset from Race Point or Herring Cove, heading out on a whale-watching excursion.

IF YOU HAVE 10 DAYS You'll be very happy. Allot the entire three additional days (from the above plan) to Martha's Vineyard. (Trying to see the Vineyard in a day borders on silliness.) Or add a night or two in the diverse Falmouth and Woods Hole area and a day trip to Nantucket. Back on the Cape, get out on the water with a trip to Monomoy Island in Chatham or some other boat tour. Add a couple of whistle-stops at the Cape's small, sweet, historic museums.

IF YOU HAVE 2 WEEKS You're really lucky. Allot three days to one of the islands. Add a quiet canoe or kayak paddle somewhere. Take a leisurely bike ride or an aerial sight-seeing flight. Get tickets to summer stock and cheer on the home team at a free baseball game. Slip into a parking space at the Wellfleet Drive-In. Investigate an old cemetery. Take an art class. Visit Mashpee's South Cape Beach State Park.

IF YOU LIVE ON THE CAPE & ISLANDS You're the luckiest of all. Scribble comments in the margins of this book and lend it to visiting friends so you don't have to keep repeating yourself. Explore something new at least once a week. Isn't that one reason you live here?

A PERFECT DAY IN . . . These town-by-town, hour-by-hour tours will get you started on how best to dip into a town. But a word of caution: If you try to do everything mentioned, you might not feel like you're on a vacation. Use them merely as a guide.

WHAT'S WHERE ON CAPE COD, MARTHA'S VINEYARD, & NANTUCKET

✳ General Information

AREA CODE The area code for the region of Cape Cod, Martha's Vineyard, and Nantucket is **508**.

AIRPORTS & AIRLINES There is regularly scheduled air service from Boston to Provincetown. Hyannis is reached by air from Boston, Providence, and New York. Nantucket and Martha's Vineyard enjoy regularly scheduled year-round service; **Cape Air** (508-771-6944; capeair .com) offers the most flights. Sight-seeing by air is best done in Chatham, Barnstable, Provincetown, and Martha's Vineyard.

ATTIRE The Cape and the islands are casual for the most part; a jacket is required at only one or two places. At the other end of the spectrum, you'll always need shoes and shirts at beachfront restaurants.

BUS SERVICE The **Plymouth & Brockton bus line** (508-778-9767; p-b.com) serves some points along Route 6A and the Outer Cape from Boston. **Bonanza/Peter Pan** (888-751-8800; peterpanbus .com) serves Bourne, Falmouth, Woods Hole, and Hyannis from Boston, Providence, and New York City.

✏ **CHILDREN, ESPECIALLY FOR** Within this guide a number of activities and sites that have special "child appeal" are identified by the crayon symbol.

EMERGENCIES Call **911** from anywhere on Cape Cod. Major hospitals are located in Falmouth (508-548-5300) and Hyannis (508-771-1800). And of course the Vineyard (508-693-0410) and Nantucket (508-825-8100).

EVENTS The largest annual events are listed within each chapter of this book. Otherwise, invest in the *Cape Cod Times* (capecodonline.com). It features a special section about the day's events and a Friday calendar supplement.

FERRIES There are fast and slow ferries to Provincetown from Boston and a day-tripper from Plymouth. To reach Martha's Vineyard, the car ferry departs from Woods Hole, and passenger ferries depart from Woods Hole, Falmouth, Hyannis, and New Bedford. There is a seasonal inter-island ferry. There are high-speed and regular ferries to Nantucket from Hyannis (car and passenger) and Harwich (passenger). See the appropriate chapter for details on schedules.

HIGH SEASON Memorial Day weekend in late May kicks things off, then there is a slight lull until school lets out in late June. From then on, the Cape is in full swing through Labor Day (early September). There are two exceptions to this, though, and they're the best-kept secrets for planning a Cape Cod vacation: The Cape is

relatively quiet during the week following the July Fourth weekend and the week prior to Labor Day weekend. You will find B&B vacancies and no lines at your favorite restaurant. As a rule, traveling to the Cape or the islands without reservations in high season is not recommended. Accommodations—especially cottages, efficiencies, and apartments—are often booked by January for the upcoming summer. The Cape and islands are also quite busy from Labor Day to Columbus Day (mid-October). It's fairly common for B&Bs to be booked solid on every autumn weekend.

HIGHWAYS Route 6, also called the Mid-Cape Highway, is a speedy, four-lane, divided highway until Exit 9 1/2, when it becomes an undivided two-laner. After the Orleans rotary (Exit 13), it becomes an undivided four-lane highway most of the way to Provincetown.

Scenic Route 6A, also known as Old King's Highway and Main Street, runs from the Sagamore Bridge to Orleans. It is lined with sea captains' houses, antiques shops, bed & breakfasts, and huge old trees. Development along Route 6A is strictly regulated by the Historical Commission. Route 6A links up with Route 6 in Orleans. Without stopping, it takes an extra 30 minutes or so to take Route 6A instead of Route 6 from Sandwich to Orleans.

Route 28 can be confusing. It's an elongated, U-shaped highway that runs from the Bourne Bridge south to Falmouth, then east to Hyannis and Chatham, then north to Orleans. The problem lies with the Route 28 directional signs. Although you're actually heading north when you travel from Chatham to Orleans, the signs will say ROUTE 28 SOUTH. When you drive from Hyannis to Falmouth, you're actually heading west, but the signs will say ROUTE 28 NORTH. Ignore the north and south indicators and look for towns that are in the direction you want to go.

INFORMATION For those coming from the Boston area, Cape-wide information can be obtained at the tourist office on Route 3 (Exit 5) in Plymouth. There is also a year-round **Cape Cod Chamber of Commerce Welcome Center** at Exit 6 off Route 6 (CapeCodChamber.org).

INTERNET Free wireless Internet is readily available at most lodging places, libraries, and chambers of commerce. In addition, many towns are experimenting with service that blankets part of their downtowns. You should have little trouble getting online for free almost everywhere.

LODGING There are many choices—from inns and bed & breakfasts to cottages, apartments, and efficiencies. Rates quoted are for two people sharing one room in the inn's definition of high season. $ means $1–199, $$ means $200–299,

shorelines that look interesting on the map and always finding scenic roads that I didn't expect.

MEDIA Print publications are charming on the Cape and really give you insight into the local scenes. The *Cape Cod Times* (capecodonline.com), with Cape- and islandwide coverage, is published daily. Also look for these local weeklies: the *Cape Codder* (focusing on the Lower and Outer Cape), *Falmouth Enterprise*, and the *Provincetown Banner* (provincetown.wickedlocal.com). And on the islands: the *Vineyard Gazette* (mvgazette.com), the *Martha's Vineyard Times* (mvtimes.com), and Nantucket's the *Inquirer and Mirror* (ack.net).

In addition to its bimonthly magazine, *Cape Cod Life* publishes an annual guide and a "Best of the Cape & Islands" within its June edition.

$$$ means $300–399, and $$$$ means $400+. Cottages are generally rented from Saturday to Saturday. Most inns and bed & breakfasts don't accept children under 10 to 12 years of age. All accept credit cards unless otherwise noted. None allows smoking unless otherwise noted. Pets are not accepted unless otherwise noted by our 🐾 icon in the margin. So many places require a two-night minimum stay during the high season that I have not included that information unless it deviates significantly. Holiday weekends often require a three-night minimum stay. And then there are a whole host of options on airbnb.com and TripAdvisor's equivalent, flipkey.com. Good youth hostels (usahostels.org/cape) are located on **Martha's Vineyard** and **Nantucket** and in **Eastham** and **Truro**.

MAPS I love the out-of-print *Cape Cod Street Atlas (Includes Martha's Vineyard and Nantucket)* (DeLorme). I'm forever searching out bodies of water or

❄ **OFF-SEASON** In an attempt to get people thinking about visiting the Cape and the islands off-season, I have put the ❄ symbol next to activities, lodging, and restaurants that are open and appealing in the off-season.

🐾 **PETS** Look for the 🐾 icon to find lodgings where your pet is welcome. But always call ahead; there may be additional fees associated with bringing your pet, and there may be special rooms reserved for pets and their owners.

PHOTOGRAPHY For tips about how and where to take perfect photos, pick up a copy of *The Photographer's Guide to Cape Cod & the Islands* by Chris Linder. As you'll see, it *is* possible to shoot in places that are not overrun with tourists in the summertime.

POPULATION More than 220,000 people live year-round on the Cape and the islands. No one has a truly accurate count of how many people visit in summer, but it is well into the millions.

RADIO WOMR (92.1 FM) in Provincetown has diverse and great programming. Tune in to National Public Radio with WCCT (90.3 FM). On the Vineyard tune to WMVY (92.7 FM); on Nantucket, WNAN (91.1 FM); and on the Cape try WCOD (106.1 FM), WFCC (107.5 FM), and WQRC (99.9 FM).

☂ RAINY-DAY ACTIVITIES Chances are, if it were sunny every day we would start taking the sunshine for granted. So when the clouds move in and the raindrops start falling on your head, be appreciative of the sun and look for the ☂ icon in this book, which tells you where to head indoors.

ROTARIES When you're approaching a rotary, cars already within the rotary have the right-of-way.

SMOKING Smoking in bars and restaurants is not permitted in the state of Massachusetts.

SWIMMING POOLS For a fee, you can swim at **Willy's Gym** in Eastham, the **Nantucket Community Pool**, and at the **Mansion House** in Vineyard Haven on the Vineyard. Swimming at the **Provincetown Inn** is free.

TRAFFIC It's bad in July and August no matter how you cut it. It's bumper-to-bumper on Friday afternoon and evening, when cars arrive for the weekend. It's grueling on Sunday afternoon and evening when they return home. And there's no respite on Saturday, when all the weekly cottage renters have to vacate their units and a new set of renters arrives to take their places.

TRAINS The **Cape Cod Central Railroad** runs between Sandwich and Hyannis, alongside cranberry bogs and the Sandy Neck Great Salt Marsh.

🐚 VALUE The 🐚 symbol appears next to entries that represent an exceptional value.

WEATHER You really can't trust Boston weather reports to provide accurate forecasts for all the microclimates between Routes 28 and 6A, from the canal to Provincetown. If you really want to go to the Cape, just go. There'll be plenty to do even if it's cloudy or rainy. When in doubt, or when it really matters, consult capecodweather.net.

WEBSITES Web addresses are listed throughout.

✳ Arts & Culture

ANTIQUARIAN BOOKS Among the many shops on Route 6A, two are great: **Titcomb's Book Shop** in Sandwich and **Parnassus Book Service** in Yarmouth Port. I also highly recommend **Isaiah Thomas Books & Prints** in Cotuit.

ANTIQUES Antiques shops are located all along **Route 6A**, on the 32-mile stretch from Sandwich to Orleans, but there is an especially dense concentration in **Brewster**, often called Antique Alley. You'll also find a good concentration of antiques shops in **Barnstable**, **Dennis Port**, **Chatham**, and **Nantucket**. (It's never made sense to me to buy antiques on an island, but folks do!)

AQUARIUMS The **Woods Hole Science Aquarium** is small, but it's an excellent introduction to marine life. There is also the small **Maria Mitchell Association Aquarium** on Nantucket.

ART GALLERIES **Wellfleet** and **Provincetown** are the centers of fine art on the Cape. Both established and emerging artists are well represented in dozens of diverse galleries. Artists began flocking to Provincetown at the turn of the 20th century, and the vibrant community continues to nurture creativity. The islands also attract large numbers of artists, some of whom stay to open their own studios and galleries. **Chatham, Nantucket**, and **Martha's Vineyard** also have many fine galleries. Look for the outstanding color booklet **"Arts & Artisans Trails of Cape Cod, Martha's Vineyard and Nantucket"**—and then don't leave home without it.

AUCTIONS Estate auctions are held throughout the year. Great benefit auctions include the **Fine Arts Work Center Annual Benefit Auction**, the **AIDS Support Group's Annual Silent and Live Auction** in Provincetown, and the celebrity-studded **Possible Dreams Auction** on Martha's Vineyard.

BASEBALL The 10-team **Cape Cod Baseball League** (capecodbaseball.org) was established in 1946. Only players with at least one year of collegiate experience are allowed to participate. Wooden bats are supplied by the major leagues. In exchange for the opportunity to play, team members work part time in the community, live with a community host, and pay rent. Carlton Fisk and the late Thurman Munson are just two alumni of the Cape Cod League who succeeded in the majors. Currently, about 250 major-league players are former

league players. A whopping 13 Cape League players were in the 2016 World Series between the Cubs and Indians. Games are free and played from mid-June to mid-August; it's great fun. In relevant chapters, baseball venues are listed under *To Do*.

CLASSES & WORKSHOPS Want to "improve" yourself on vacation or brush up on some long-lost creative artistic urges? There are more programs in **Provincetown**, the **Vineyard**, and **Nantucket** than I can list here; see *To Do* under each town or region. Also see the sidebar "Artistic Outlets during Vacation" in "Truro" for offerings at the **Truro Center for the Arts at Castle Hill**. The other Outer Cape sidebar, "Trails, Birds, Seals & Classes" in "Wellfleet," discusses the **Wellfleet Bay Wildlife Sanctuary Adult Field School**.

COUNTRY STORES Old-fashioned country stores still exist on Cape Cod and the islands. Aficionados can seek out **The Brewster Store** in Brewster and **Alley's General Store** in West Tisbury on the **Vineyard**.

CRAFTS Craftspeople have made a living on the Cape and the islands since they began making baskets, ships, and furniture 300 years ago. The tradition continues with artists emphasizing the aesthetic as well as the functional. Today's craftspeople are potters, jewelers (particularly in Dennis), scrimshaw and bird carvers, weavers, glassblowers, clothing designers, and barrel makers. Look for the highly coveted (and pricey) lightship baskets in Nantucket and glass objects in Sandwich, Bourne, and Brewster. There are too many artisans in Provincetown, Chatham, Nantucket, and Martha's Vineyard to detail here. Look for the outstanding color booklet, **"Arts & Artisans Trails of Cape Cod, Martha's Vineyard and Nantucket"**—and then don't leave home without it.

FLEA MARKETS **Wellfleet Flea Market** (at the Wellfleet Drive-In) is the biggie.

GOLF There are about 50 courses on the Cape and the islands, and because of relatively mild winters, many stay open all year (although perhaps not every day). **Highland Golf Links** in **Truro** is the Cape's oldest course; it's also very dramatic.

HISTORIC HOUSES Every town has its own historical museum or house, but some are more interesting than others. Among the best are **Hoxie House** in **Sandwich**; **Centerville Historical Museum** and **Osterville Historical Society Museum**, both in **Barnstable**; and the **Truro Historical Museum**. The center of **Nantucket** has been designated a historic district, so there are notable houses everywhere you turn; the oldest is the **Jethro Coffin House**. The **Nantucket Historical Association** publishes a walking guide to its properties. Don't miss the **Martha's Vineyard Museum** on Martha's Vineyard.

LIBRARIES The Cape and the islands boast a few libraries with world-class maritime collections and works pertaining to the history of the area: **Sturgis Library** in **Barnstable**; **William Brewster Nickerson Memorial Room** at Cape Cod Community College in **West Barnstable**; the **Atheneum** and **Nantucket Historical Association Research Library**, both in **Nantucket**; and the

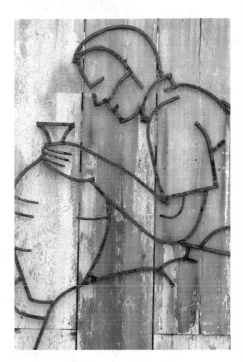

Martha's Vineyard Museum in Edgartown on Martha's Vineyard. In addition to being great community resources, libraries also make great rainy-day (*) destinations.

LIGHTHOUSES It's a toss-up as to whether the most picturesque lighthouse is **Nobska Light** in **Woods Hole** or **Great Point Light** on **Nantucket**. (Nobska is certainly more accessible.) But there are also working lighthouses in **Chatham**, **Eastham**, **Truro**, and **Provincetown**. **Nantucket** and **Martha's Vineyard**, too, have their share of working lighthouses. For a really unusual trip, the lighthouse at **Race Point** in **Provincetown** is available for an overnight stay by advance reservation.

MOVIES In addition to the standard multiplex cinemas located across the Cape, the **Wellfleet Drive-In** remains a much-loved institution. The **Cape Cinema** in **Dennis** is also a special venue; check it out. The **Nantucket Film Festival** and the **International Film Festival**

in **Provincetown**, both held in mid-June, are relatively new "must-see" events for independent-film buffs. And not to be outdone is the **Martha's Vineyard Film Festival**, since 2001. Because moviegoing is a popular vacation activity, I have listed mainstream movie theaters under *Entertainment*.

MUSEUMS People who have never uttered the words *museum* and *Cape Cod* in the same breath don't know what they're missing. Don't skip the **Glass Museum** and **Heritage Museums & Gardens**, both in Sandwich; **Museums on the Green** in Falmouth; **Aptucxet Trading Post and Museum** in Bourne Village; **Cahoon Museum of American Art** in Cotuit; **John F. Kennedy Hyannis Museum**; **Cape Cod Museum of Art** in Dennis; **Cape Cod Museum of Natural History** in Brewster; **Provincetown Art Association & Museum**, the **Pilgrim Monument & Provincetown Museum**, and the **Old Harbor Lifesaving Station**, all in Provincetown; **Martha's Vineyard Museum** in Edgartown on Martha's Vineyard; and the **Nantucket Whaling Museum** and **Shipwreck and Lifesaving Museum** on Nantucket.

Children will particularly enjoy the **Railroad Museum** in Chatham.

MUSIC Outdoor summertime band concerts are now offered by most towns, but the biggest and oldest is held in Chatham at **Kate Gould Park**. Sandwich offers a variety of outdoor summer concerts at **Heritage Museums & Gardens**.

The **Nantucket Musical Arts Society** and the **Vineyard's Chamber Music Society** are also excellent, albeit with much shorter seasons.

The 85-member **Cape Symphony Orchestra** (508-362-1111; capesymphony .org) performs classical, children's, and pops concerts year-round.

There are a couple of regular venues for folk music, including the **Woods Hole Folk Music Society** and the **First Encounter Coffee House** in Eastham.

This edition lists many more venues with live music; see the *Entertainment* headings under each town.

SHOPPING **Chatham** and **Falmouth's** Main Streets are well suited to walking and shopping. Commercial Street in **Provincetown** has the trendiest shops. **Mashpee Commons** features a very dense and increasingly fine selection of shops. Shopping on the **Vineyard** and **Nantucket** is a prime activity.

THEATER Among the summer-stock and performing arts venues are **Cape Playhouse** in Dennis; **Cape Repertory Theatre** in Brewster; **Monomoy Theatre** in Chatham; **Academy Playhouse** in Orleans; **Wellfleet Harbor Actors Theater**; **Provincetown Repertory Theatre** and **Provincetown Theatre Co.**; **College**

Light Opera Company in Falmouth; Barnstable Comedy Club; Harwich Junior Theatre; the Theatre Workshop of Nantucket; and the Vineyard Playhouse on Martha's Vineyard.

❋ Food & Drink

Y BARS Look for the Y symbol next to restaurants and entertainment venues that have more than a few bar stools.

CRANBERRIES The cranberry is one of only three major native North American fruits (the other two are Concord grapes and blueberries). Harvesting began in Dennis in 1816 and evolved into a lucrative industry in Harwich Port. Harvesting generally runs from mid-September to mid-October, when the bogs are flooded and ripe red berries float to the water's surface. Before the berries are ripe, the bogs look like a dense green carpet, separated by 2- to 3-foot dikes. Nantucket has two bogs, but most of her bog acreage lies fallow due to a glut in supply. Harwich, which lays claim to having the first commercial cranberry bog, celebrates with a Cranberry Harvest Festival (harwichcranberryfestival.org) in mid-September. Most on-Cape bogs are located on the Mid- and Lower Cape.

DINING Perhaps the biggest surprise to visitors is the high quality of cuisine on the Cape these days. Modernity and urbane sophistication are no longer rare breeds once you cross the canal bridges. Indeed, locals are so supportive that many fine restaurants stay open through the winter. During the off-season, many chefs experiment with creative new dishes and offer them at moderate prices.

With the exception of July and August (when *practically* all places are open nightly), restaurants are rarely open every night of the week. The major problem for a travel writer (and a reader relying on the book) is that this schedule is subject to the whims of weather and foot traffic.

As a result, for each restaurant I have only indicated which meals are served—not which days—because I do not want to lead you astray. To avoid disappointment, phone ahead before setting out for a much-anticipated meal.

Expect to wait for a table in July and August. Always call for reservations at *Dining Out* establishments. Remember that many restaurants are staffed by college students who are just learning the ropes in June and who may depart before Labor Day weekend, leaving the owners shorthanded. Smaller seasonal establishments don't take credit cards.

Main dish price designations are $ ($1–9), $$ ($10–19), $$$ ($20–29), and $$$$ ($30+).

WINERIES The Cape and islands are not Napa and Sonoma, but you could drop in for tastings at Truro Vineyards of Cape Cod in Truro and the Cape Cod Winery in East Falmouth. The Nantucket Vineyard (are you confused?) imports grapes to make wine.

❋ Nature & Outdoors

BEACHES Cape Cod National Seashore (CCNS; nps.gov/caco) beaches are the stuff of dreams: long expanses of dune-backed sand. In fact, you could walk with only a few natural interruptions (breaks in the beach), as Henry David Thoreau did, from Chatham to the tip of Provincetown. My favorites on the Cape include **Sandy Neck Beach** in West Barnstable; **Nauset Beach** in Orleans; **Old Silver Beach** in North Falmouth; **Chapin Memorial Beach** in Dennis; **West Dennis Beach**; **Craigville Beach** near Hyannis; and all the **Outer Cape** ocean beaches. Practically all of **Nantucket's** beaches are public, and although the same cannot be said for **Martha's Vineyard**, there are plenty of places to lay your towel.

A daily parking fee ($–$$) is enforced from mid-June to early September; many of the smaller beaches are open only to residents and weekly cottage renters. CCNS offers a seasonal parking pass for its beaches. There is no overnight parking at beaches. Four-wheel-drive vehicles require a permit, and their use is limited. Open beach fires require a permit. Greenhead biting flies plague non–Outer Cape beaches in mid- to late July; they disappear with the first high tide at the new or full moon in August, when the water level rises, killing the eggs.

Generally, beaches on **Nantucket Sound** have warmer waters than the **Outer Cape Atlantic Ocean** beaches, which are also pounded by surf. **Cape Cod Bay** beaches are shallower than **Nantucket Sound** beaches, and the bay waters are a bit cooler. Because of the proximity of the warm Gulf Stream, you

can swim in Nantucket Sound waters well into September.

BICYCLING The Cape is generally flat, and there are many paved, off-road bike trails. The 26-mile **Cape Cod Rail Trail** runs along the bed of the Old Colony Railroad from Route 134 in **Dennis** to **Wellfleet**; bike trails can be found along both sides of the **Cape Cod Canal**; the **Shining Sea Bike Path** runs from **Falmouth** to **Woods Hole**; and bike trails can be found within the **CCNS** in **Provincetown** and **Truro**. **Nantucket** is ideal for cycling, with six routes emanating from the center of town and then circling the island. Bicycling is also great on the **Vineyard**, but stamina is required for a trip up-island to Aquinnah. For super specifics, consult *Backroad Bicycling on Cape Cod, Martha's Vineyard, and Nantucket* by Susan Milton and Kevin and Nan Jeffrey.

Rubel Bike Maps (bikemaps.com) are the most detailed maps available for the Cape and islands. Rubel produces a combination Nantucket and Vineyard map, as well as another that includes the islands, Cape Cod, and the North Shore.

BIRD-WATCHING The **Bird Watcher's General Store** in Orleans is on every birder's list of stops. Natural areas that are known for bird-watching include

Monomoy National Wildlife Refuge off the coast of Chatham; **Wellfleet Bay Wildlife Sanctuary** (massaudubon.org); **Felix Neck Wildlife Sanctuary** in Vineyard Haven; **Ashumet Holly and Wildlife Sanctuary** in East Falmouth; and on Nantucket, **Coatue–Coskata Great Point**. The **Maria Mitchell Association** and **Eco Guides**, both in Nantucket, offer bird-watching expeditions, as do **Wellfleet Bay Wildlife Sanctuary** and **Monomoy National Wildlife Refuge**. Scheduled bird walks are also offered from both CCNS visitors centers: **Salt Pond Visitor Center** in Eastham and **Province Lands Visitor Center** in Provincetown. The **Cape Cod Museum of Natural History** in Brewster is always an excellent source of information for all creatures within the animal kingdom residing on the Cape.

CAMPING No camping is permitted on **Nantucket**, but there is still one campground on **Martha's Vineyard**. The Cape offers dozens of private campgrounds, but only those in natural areas are listed; the best camping is in **Nickerson State Park** in Brewster and in **Truro**.

CANOEING & KAYAKING For guided naturalist trips and lessons there is no better outfitter than **Goose Hummock** in Orleans (508-255-0455; goose.com). Also look for the book *Paddling Cape Cod: A Coastal Explorer's Guide* by Shirley and Fred Bull. There are also very good venues and outfitters in **Falmouth** and **Wellfleet**, and on **Martha's Vineyard** and **Nantucket**.

CAPE COD NATIONAL SEASHORE Established on August 7, 1961, through the efforts of President John F. Kennedy, the CCNS (nps.gov/caco) stretches more than 40 miles through Eastham, Wellfleet, Truro, and Provincetown. It encompasses more than 43,500 acres of land and seashore. Sites within the CCNS that are listed in this guide have been identified with "CCNS" at the beginning of the entry. The **Salt Pond Visitor Center** in **Eastham** and **Province Lands Visitor Center** in **Provincetown** are excellent resources and offer a variety of exhibits, films, and ranger-led walks and talks. The CCNS is accessible every day of the year, although you must pay to park at the beaches in summer.

ECOSYSTEM This narrow peninsula and these isolated islands have a delicate ecosystem. Remember that dunes are fragile, and beaches serve as nesting grounds for the endangered piping plover. Avoid the nesting areas when you see signs directing you to do so. Residents conserve water and recycle, and they hope you will do likewise.

FISHING Procure freshwater and saltwater fishing licenses and regulations online, or try your luck at various town halls or bait and tackle shops.

Charter boats generally take up to six people on four- or eight-hour trips. Boats leave from the following harbors on Cape Cod Bay: Barnstable Harbor in **West Barnstable**; Sesuit Harbor in **Dennis**; Rock Harbor in **Orleans**; **Wellfleet Harbor**; and **Provincetown**. On Nantucket Sound, head to Hyannis Harbor, Saquatucket Harbor in **Harwich Port**, and **Chatham**. You can also fish from the banks of the Cape Cod Canal and surf-fish on the Outer Cape. There are also plenty of opportunities for fishing off the shores of **Nantucket** and the **Vineyard**. **Goose Hummock** (goose.com) in Orleans offers lots of very good trips, as does **Chatham Family Charters** (chatham familycharters.com).

HORSEBACK RIDING There are a surprising number of riding facilities and trails on the Cape. Look for them in **Falmouth**, **Brewster**, and on **Martha's Vineyard**.

LYME DISEASE Ticks carry this disease, which has flulike symptoms and may result in death if left untreated. Immediately and carefully remove any ticks that might have migrated from dune grasses to your body. Better yet, wear long pants, tuck pants into socks, and wear long-sleeved shirts whenever possible when hiking. Avoid hiking in grassy and overgrown areas of dense brush.

NATURE PRESERVES There are walking trails—around salt marshes, across beaches, through ancient swamps and hardwood stands—in every town on the

Cape and the islands, but some traverse larger areas and are more "developed" than others. For a complete guide, look for the excellent *Walks and Rambles on Cape Cod and the Islands* by Ned Friary and Glenda Bendure. Watch for poison ivy and deer ticks; the latter carry Lyme disease. And pick up a copy of *Wildflowers of Cape Cod and the Islands* by Kate Carter to help make the most of any walk.

To find some Upper Cape green space, head to **Green Briar Nature Center & Jam Kitchen** in Sandwich; **Lowell Holly Reservation** in Mashpee; and **Ashumet Holly and Wildlife Sanctuary** and **Waquoit Bay National Estuarine Research Reserve**, both in East Falmouth. In the mid-Cape area, you'll find **Sandy Neck Great Salt Marsh Conservation Area** in West Barnstable. The Lower Cape offers **Nickerson State Park** in Brewster and **Monomoy National Wildlife Refuge** off the coast of Chatham. The **CCNS** has a number of short interpretive trails on the Outer Cape, while Wellfleet has the **Wellfleet Bay Wildlife Sanctuary** and **Great Island Trail**.

On Martha's Vineyard you can escape the crowds at **Felix Neck Wildlife Sanctuary** in Vineyard Haven; **Cedar Tree Neck Sanctuary** and **Long Point Wildlife Refuge**, both in West Tisbury; and **Cape Pogue Wildlife Refuge** and **Wasque Reservation** on

Chappaquiddick.

Nantucket boasts conservation initiatives that have protected 45 percent of the land from development, including the areas of **Coatue–Coskata–Great Point, Eel Point, Sanford Farm, Ram Pasture**, and the **Woods**.

PONDS Supposedly there are 365 freshwater ponds on Cape Cod, one for every day of the year. As glaciers retreated 15,000 years ago and left huge chunks of ice behind, depressions in the earth were created. When the ice melted, "kettle ponds" were born. The ponds are a refreshing treat, especially in August, when salty winds kick up beach sand.

tides vary considerably from one spot to another, it's best to stop in at a local bait-and-tackle shop for a tide chart. For **Cape Cod Canal** tide information, log on to boatma.com/tides/Cape-Cod .html.

WALKING **Cape Cod Pathways** (cape codcommission.org/pathways/) is a growing network of trails linking open space in all 15 Cape Cod towns from Falmouth to Provincetown. Also consult cctrails.org.

And pick up *Walks & Rambles on Cape Cod and the Islands* by Ned Friary and Glenda Bendure.

WHALE-WATCHING Whale-watching trips leave from **Provincetown**, including the excellent **Dolphin Fleet Whale Watch** (508-240-3636), but you can also catch the **Hyannis** *Whale Watcher* **Cruises** (508-362-6088) out of **Barnstable Harbor.**

SEAL CRUISES A colony of seals lounges around Monomoy, and there is no shortage of outfits willing to take you out to see them. See listings in **Chatham** and **Wellfleet** for detailed information.

SHELLFISHING Procure licenses and regulations online, or try your luck at local town halls. Sometimes certain areas are closed to shellfishing due to contamination; it's always best to ask.

SURFING & SAILBOARDING Surfers should head to **Nauset Beach** in **Orleans**, **Coast Guard** and **Nauset Light** beaches in **Eastham**, and **Marconi Beach** in **Wellfleet**. Sailboarders flock to **Falmouth**. **Vineyard** beaches are also good for sailboarding.

TIDES Tides come in and go out twice daily; times differ from day to day and from town to town. At low tide, the sandy shore is hard and easier to walk on; at high tide, what little sand is visible is more difficult to walk on. Because

✳ Recommended Reading

ABOUT CAPE COD Henry Beston's classic *The Outermost House: A Year of Life on the Great Beach of Cape Cod* recounts his solitary year in a cabin on the ocean's edge. Cynthia Huntington's marvelous *The Salt House* updates Beston's work with a woman's perspective in the late 20th century. Also look for *The House on Nauset Marsh* by Wyman Richardson (The Countryman Press). Henry David Thoreau's naturalist classic *Cape Cod* meticulously details his mid-1800s walking tours. Josef Berger's 1937 Works Progress Administration (WPA) guide, *Cape Cod Pilot*, is filled with good stories and still-useful information. I devoured the excellent *Nature of Cape Cod* by Beth Schwarzman, as well as everything by poet Mary Oliver. Pick up anything by modern-day naturalists Robert Finch (including *The Primal Place*) and John Hay. Finch also edited a volume of writings by others about the Cape, *A Place Apart* (with a black-and-white cover photo by yours truly). Another collection of writings about Cape Cod is *Sand in Their Shoes*, compiled by Edith and Frank Shay. Look for *Cape Cod, Its People & Their History* by Henry Kittredge (alias Jeremiah Digges) and *The Wampanoags of Mashpee* by Russell Peters. Mary Heaton Vorse, a founder of the Provincetown Players, describes life in Provincetown from the 1900s to the 1950s in *Time and the Town: A Provincetown Chronicle*. And for children, Kevin Shortsleeve has written an illustrated history book, *The Story of Cape Cod*. Look also for Admont Clark's *Lighthouses of Cape Cod, Martha's Vineyard, and Nantucket: Their History and Lore* and photographer Joel Meyerowitz's *A Summer's Day* and *Cape Light*.

ABOUT MARTHA'S VINEYARD Start with the *Vineyard Gazette Reader*, a marvelous "best-of" collection edited by Richard Reston and Tom Dunlop; it will give you an immediate sense of the island. *On the Vineyard II* contains essays by celebrity island residents, including Walter Cronkite, William Styron, and Carly Simon, with photographs by Peter Simon (Carly's brother). *Martha's Vineyard* and *Martha's Vineyard, Summer Resort*, are both by Henry Beetle Hough, Pulitzer Prize–winning editor of the *Vineyard Gazette*. Photographer Alfred Eisenstaedt, a longtime summer resident of the Vineyard, photographed the island for years. Contemporary *Vineyard Gazette* photographer Alison Shaw has two Vineyard books to her credit: the black-and-white

Remembrance and Light and the color collection *Vineyard Summer*. Also look for her new *Photographer's Guide to Martha's Vineyard*.

ABOUT NANTUCKET Edwin P. Hoyt's *Nantucket: The Life of an Island* is a popular history, and Robert Gambee's *Nantucket* is just plain popular. Architecture buffs will want to take a gander at *Nantucket Style* by Leslie Linsley and Jon Aron, and the classic *Early Nantucket and Its Whale Houses* by Henry Chandler Forman. Photography lovers will enjoy *On Nantucket*, with photos by Gregory Spaid.

THE UPPER CAPE

BOURNE

SANDWICH

FALMOUTH & WOODS HOLE

MASHPEE

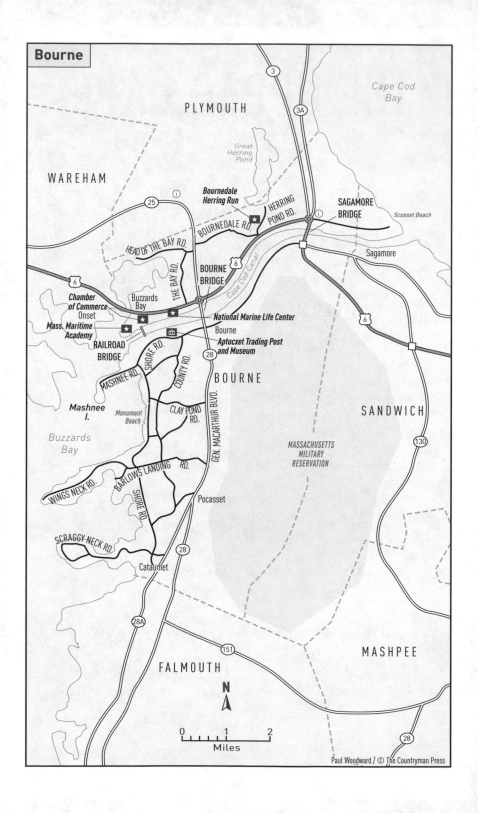

Bourne

PLYMOUTH

WAREHAM

Cape Cod Bay

Great Herring Pond

Scusset Beach

Bournedale Herring Run

HERRING POND RD.

SAGAMORE BRIDGE

BOURNEDALE RD.

HEAD OF THE BAY RD.

Cape Cod Canal

Sagamore

BOURNE BRIDGE

THE BAY RD.

Chamber of Commerce
Onset

Buzzards Bay

National Marine Life Center

Mass. Maritime Academy

Bourne

RAILROAD BRIDGE

Aptucxet Trading Post and Museum

SHORE RD.

COUNTY RD.

MASHNEE RD.

Mashnee I.

Monument Beach

CLAY POND RD.

GEN. MACARTHUR BLVD.

BOURNE

SANDWICH

Buzzards Bay

MASSACHUSETTS MILITARY RESERVATION

BARLOWS LANDING RD.

WINGS NECK RD.

SHORE RD.

Pocasset

SCRAGGY NECK RD.

Cataumet

FALMOUTH

MASHPEE

N

0   1   2
Miles

Paul Woodward / © The Countryman Press

BOURNE

Despite summertime traffic tie-ups approaching the Sagamore and Bourne Bridges, there's something magical about the first glimpse of them, a sure sign that you're entering a place separate from where you've been. All travelers, except those arriving by plane or boat, must pass through Bourne, over the bridges and the Cape Cod Canal.

Bourne straddles the canal, nips at the heels of Sandwich on the Cape Cod Bay side, and follows the coastline south toward Falmouth along Route 28, a.k.a. Cranberry Highway. (All the land to the immediate east of Route 28 belongs to the Massachusetts Military Reservation.) Bourne is often completely bypassed as travelers head south to catch the Vineyard ferry from Falmouth or Woods Hole. Indeed, there is some justification for not spending a monthlong holiday here.

Bourne is predominantly inhabited by year-rounders, enjoying a quiet, rural, unhurried existence and tending their gardens and lives. But perhaps of the entire Cape, Bourne remains the most unexplored area. The back roads off County and Shore Roads are lovely for bicycling, as are the peninsulas reached by Scraggy Neck Road and Wings Neck Road. Fishing, walking, and bicycling are prime activities along the Cape Cod Canal. In fact, there are more than 1,700 acres of protected land along the canal for your enjoyment.

When Sandwich refused to grant Bourne its independence, the state legislature incorporated it in 1884. Originally known for its fishing wharves, shipbuilding, and factories, Bourne quickly attracted prominent vacationers to its sandy shores. Named for an affluent resident who made his fortune during the whaling heyday, Bourne encompasses 40 square miles and consists of many tiny villages.

Sagamore, on both sides of the canal and on Cape Cod Bay, has more in common with Sandwich; it even has a renowned glassmaking factory. **Bournedale**, on the "mainland" and wedged between the two bridges, has a diminutive old red schoolhouse and a picturesque herring pond. And although **Buzzards Bay**, north and west of the Bourne Bridge, is the region's commercial center, it also offers some lovely glimpses of Buttermilk Bay. (Buzzards Bay, by the way, was misnamed by inexperienced birders. If the original settlers had gotten it right, it would be called Osprey Bay today.) On the western end of the canal, the Massachusetts Maritime Academy affords nice views of the canal and handsome summer homes on the other side.

Across the 2,384-foot Bourne Bridge (almost twice as long as the Sagamore Bridge), the Cape villages of **Monument Beach**, **Bourne Village**, **Gray Gables**, **Pocasset**, and **Cataumet** are tranquil in summer and downright sleepy in winter. In total, about 19,000 people live in these villages year-round.

The first "Summer White House" was in Gray Gables, where President Grover Cleveland spent the season fishing during the 1890s. Monument Beach, Cataumet, and Pocasset are pleasant, residential, seaside towns with old houses, just west of Route 28. Residents don't take much notice of visitors; they just go about their business, fishing, shopping, raising children, and commuting to work. Cataumet Pier was the site of the nation's first labor strike, when dockworkers demanded a 100 percent pay raise in 1864, from 15¢ per hour to 30¢.

GUIDANCE ✻ **Cape Cod Canal Region Chamber of Commerce** (508-759-6000; cape codcanalchamber.org), 70 Main Street, Buzzards Bay. Office open year-round. On-site information center open late May to mid-October. Another center, the Cape Cod Canal Visitor Center (774-413-7475), 1 Meetinghouse Lane, Sagamore Beach, is open late April to mid-November.

Herring Run Visitor Center (a.k.a. **Cape Cod Canal Visitor Center**; 508-833-9678), Route 6 on the mainland side of the canal, about a mile south of the Sagamore Bridge. Open late April to early October.

GETTING THERE *By car:* To reach Sagamore, take Exit 1 onto Route 6A from the Sagamore Bridge. To reach Bournedale and Buzzards Bay, take Route 6 west at the Sagamore Bridge. To reach the other villages, take the Bourne Bridge across the canal, and at the rotary take Shore Road. You can also whiz down Route 28 and head west to Pocasset, Cataumet, and Monument Beach.

By bus: **Bonanza/Peter Pan** (888-751-8800; peterpanbus.com) operates buses from Bourne to Boston as well as Providence, New York City, and other points south and west of the Cape. The bus stops at the convenience store (105 Trowbridge Road) at the Bourne Bridge rotary.

GETTING AROUND Bourne is quite spread out, so you'll need a car. The Cape Cod Canal has a great bicycle trail (see *To Do*).

PUBLIC RESTROOMS Located at the chamber office and at the Herring Run Visitor Center/Cape Cod Canal Visitor Center.

PUBLIC LIBRARY ✻ ✐ ✞ **Jonathan Bourne Public Library** (508-759-0644; bourneli brary.org), 19 Sandwich Road, Bourne. Book clubs, art displays, story hour, and children's programs.

MEDICAL EMERGENCY Call 911.

It's not an "emergency" (the kind you'd expect under this category, anyway), but many area water wells have been contaminated by years of training with grenades and other live munitions at the Massachusetts Military Reservation. I drink bottled water on the Upper Cape.

✻ To See

Massachusetts Maritime Academy (508-830-5000; maritime.edu), 101 Academy Drive, Taylors Point, off Main Street, Buzzards Bay. The academy's presence explains why you'll see so many young men with close-cropped hair jogging along the canal bicycle trail. Call ahead for a campus tour, or arrange to tag along on a weekday tour for prospective merchant mariners. Not only will you see the oldest continuously operating maritime academy in the country (established in 1891) from an insider's perspective, but, if you're lucky, you'll also get to tour the cadets' training ship and eat in the cadets' dining hall overlooking the canal.

Aptucxet Trading Post and Museum (508-759-9487; bournehistoricalsociety.org/ aptucxet-museum), 24 Aptucxet Road, Bourne. From the Cape-side Bourne Bridge, follow signs for Mashnee Village, then Shore Road and Aptucxet Road. Open late May to mid-October. English settlers thought this location, near two rivers, was perfect for a post to promote trade with their neighbors, the Wampanoag Indians and the Dutch

OUR VERY OWN PANAMA CANAL

The Cape Cod Canal (7.5 miles long) separates the mainland from Cape Cod. The canal, between 480 and 700 feet wide at various points, is the world's widest ocean-level canal. In 1623 Captain Myles Standish, eager to facilitate trade between New Amsterdam (New York City) and Plymouth Colony, was the first to consider creating a canal, which also would eliminate the treacherous 135-nautical-mile voyage around the tip of the Cape. George Washington brought up the idea again in the late 18th century as a means to protect naval ships and commercial vessels during war, but the first serious effort at digging a canal was not attempted until 1880 by the Cape Cod Canal Company.

For a few months, the company's crew of 500 immigrants dug with hand shovels and carted away the dirt in wheelbarrows. Then, in 1899, New York financier Augustus Belmont's Boston, Cape Cod, and New York Canal Company took over the project with more resolve. They began digging in 1909, and the canal opened to shipping five years later, on July 30, 1914. (It beat the Panama Canal opening by a scant 17 days.) On hand at the opening was then Assistant Secretary of the Navy Franklin D. Roosevelt. But the enterprise wasn't a financial success because the canal was too narrow (it could handle only one-way traffic) and early drawbridges caused too many accidents. In 1928 the federal government purchased the canal, and the U.S. Army Corps of Engineers (USACE) built the canal we know today. The USACE has overseen the canal ever since. The canal provides a north–south shortcut for some 30,000 vessels each year, hundreds daily in summer. Water currents in the 32-foot-deep canal change direction every six hours.

The **Cape Cod Canal Vertical Lift Railroad Bridge** (western end of the canal at the **Buzzards Bay Recreation Area**) is the third longest vertical railway bridge in the world. It stands 270 feet high and 540 feet long, but those in Chicago, Illinois, and on Long Island, New York, beat it. The railroad bridge was completed the same year as the Sagamore and Bourne Bridges. When trains approach, it takes two or three minutes for the bridge to lower and connect with the tracks on either side of it. The most reliable times (read: it's not so reliable) to witness this event are at 9:30 AM and 5 PM (more or less), when trains haul trash off-Cape. You might see the morning lowering at 7 AM too. Free parking.

This is a good place to start the bicycle trail on this side of the canal.

There is great bicycling, fishing, boating, and walking from the canal shores. See the appropriate sections under *To Do.*

CANAL RAILROAD BRIDGE

from New Amsterdam. Furs, sugar and other staples, tools, glass, tobacco, and cloth were bought and sold; wampum (carved quahog shells made into beads) served as currency. Cape Cod commerce was born.

The trading post you see today was built in 1927 by the Bourne Historical Society on the foundations of the original; a few bricks from the fireplace date to the Pilgrims. The hand-hewn beams and wide floor planks came from a 1600s house in Rochester, Massachusetts. On the grounds a small Victorian railroad station was used solely by President Grover Cleveland when he summered at his Gray Gables mansion in Monument Beach. You'll also find a Dutch-style windmill (which was intended merely "to add interest and beauty to the estate"), an 18th-century saltworks, an herb garden, a gift shop, and a shaded picnic area. Admission $.

✒ **Bournedale Herring Run** (508-759-4431), Route 6, about a mile south of the Sagamore Bridge. Open late May to early June. After the canal destroyed the natu-

BOURNEDALE HERRING RUN

ral herring run into Great Herring Pond, local engineers created an elaborate artificial watercourse to allow mature herring to migrate back to their birthplace. Each twice-daily tide brings thousands of the bony fish slithering upstream, navigating the pools created by wooden planks. In total, hundreds of thousands of herring pass through the Bournedale run annually. Kids really get a kick out of this spring ritual.

✒ **National Marine Life Center** (508-743-9888; nmlc.org), 120 Main Street, Buzzards Bay. Open late May to early September. In late 2008 a marine-animal rehabilitation hospital opened to aid whales, dolphins, sea turtles, and seals that wash ashore on Cape Cod and require medical attention before they can be set free again. There are several interactive exhibits, various kids' programs in July and August, and a small science museum where one learns about the impact of humankind on the ocean.

Briggs McDermott House & Blacksmith Shop (508-759-6120), 522 Sandwich Road, Bourne. Generally open mid-June to late September. This early-19th-century Greek Revival home—complete with period gardens, a carriage house with quite a collection of carriages, and a granite-walled

BRIGGS MCDERMOTT HOUSE

barn—is maintained by the Bourne Society for Historic Preservation. Inquire about guided tours, on which docents might discuss local architecture or former neighbor Grover Cleveland. Blacksmiths operate a restored forge on-site—complete with artifacts, tools, and a wagon—where President Cleveland's horses were shod.

Mashnee Island. From the Cape side of the Bourne Bridge, take Shore Road and follow signs for Mashnee Island. From the 2-mile-long causeway, there are lovely views of summer homes dotting the shoreline, sailboats on the still waters, and the distant railroad bridge and Bourne Bridge. Parking is nonexistent in summer, and as the island is private, you'll have to turn around at the end of the causeway.

Massachusetts Military Reservation (Otis Air National Guard Base) (508 968-4003), off the rotary at Routes 28 and 28A. The 21,000 acres east of Route 28 are a closed installation that contains Camp Edwards Army National Guard Training Site, Otis Air National Guard Base, the

MASHNEE ISLAND

U.S. Coast Guard Air Station, the State Army Aviation complex, and the PAVE PAWS radar station. The last detects nuclear missiles and tracks satellites (it was established during the Cold War).

Although you won't read about it in most guidebooks, the MMR has been designated by the Pentagon as a federal environmental Superfund site since 1989. Most experts agreed that it would take decades to clean up the toxic Cold War–era pollutants that are contaminating the groundwater. Others suggested it may be impossible to clean up all the underground chemical plumes that resulted from various training exercises, landfill leaks, and oil spills.

✳ To Do

BICYCLING & RENTALS ⚓ **Cape Cod Canal.** The canal is edged by level, well-maintained service roads perfect for biking; each side is about 6.5 to 7 miles long. Access points along the mainland side of the canal include Scusset State Park off Scusset Beach Road; the Sagamore Recreation Area off Canal Road at the Sagamore Bridge; near the Bournedale Herring Run in Bournedale; and beneath the Bourne Bridge. On the Cape side of the canal, there are access points

from the Sandcatcher Recreation Area off Tupper Road in Sandwich; from Pleasant Street in Sagamore; and from the Bourne Bridge. If you want to cross the canal with your bike, use the Sagamore Bridge—its sidewalk is safer.

❋ **Sailworld Cape Cod** (508-759-6559; sailworld.com), 139 Main Street, Buzzards Bay. Talk to the helpful owners, Jim and Pam. $$ hourly, $$$ for 3 hours, $$$$ daily.

BOAT EXCURSIONS & RENTALS ✇ **Cape Cod Canal Cruises** (508-295-3883; hyline cruises.com), off Routes 6 and 28 at the Onset Bay Town Pier (a few miles west of the mainland-side Bourne Bridge rotary), Onset. Operated by Hy-Line Cruises, these two- and three-hour tours—with running commentary—depart from May to mid-October. $$. There are also sunset cocktail, live music, and jazz cruises, as well as discounted family trips. These tours fill up, so book in advance.

FISHING For saltwater fishing, the banks of the Cape Cod Canal provide plenty of opportunities for catching striped bass, bluefish, cod, and pollock. Just bait your hook and cast away; no permits are required if you're fishing with a rod and line from the shore. Lobstermen pull traps from the shoreline. But there is no fishing, lobstering, or boat trolling permitted in the canal.

Maco's Bait and Tackle (508-759-9836; macosbaitandtackle.com), 3173 Cranberry Highway, Wareham. This mainstay for the area fishing community is just down the street from its former location of 45 years. Open April through October.

See also **Bournedale Herring Run** under *To See*.

FOR FAMILIES ✇ **Water Wizz Water Park** (508-295-3255; waterwizz.com), 3031 Cranberry Highway, Routes 6 and 28, a few miles west of the Bourne Bridge, Wareham. Open mid-June to early September. Southern New England's largest and Cape Cod's only water park has it all: a 50-foot-high water slide with tunnels, tube rides, a hanging rope bridge, a wave pool, three kiddie water areas, and a river ride. You can let kids run around without too much worry, and because the park is well-staffed with lifeguards, it feels safe for kids older than 5 or 6. Lastly, it's less expensive than larger parks, and the food selection and quality are good. If you're taller than 4 feet, tickets $$$$; otherwise, it's $$$.

✇ **Cartland of Cape Cod** (508-295-8360; cartlandofcapecod.com), 3022 Routes 6 and 28, East Wareham. Open daily in summer, weekends in spring and fall. Bumper boats, go-carts, boxing robots, batting cages, mini-golf, and an obvious place for birthday parties, especially given its ice cream menu.

❋ ✇ **Ryan Family Amusements** (508-759-9892; ryanfamily.com), 200 Main Street, Buzzards Bay. Bowling, a game room, and facilities for birthday parties.

See also **Cataumet Arts Center** under *Selective Shopping*.

HORSEBACK RIDING ❋ **Grazing Fields Farm** (508-759-3763; grazingfields.com), 201 Bournedale Road, off Head of the Bay Road, Buzzards Bay. Private and semiprivate lessons are offered. $$$$+.

ICE-SKATING **John Gallo Ice Arena** (508-759-8904; galloarena.com), 231 Sandwich Road, Buzzards Bay. The public skating schedule is highly variable.

JUNIOR RANGER PROGRAMS ✇ **The Cape Cod Canal Visitor Center** (**U.S. Army Corps of Engineers**; 508-833-9678), 60 Ed Moffitt Drive, Sandwich. Free programs for kiddos in July and August; no preregistration is required.

SCENIC DRIVE See Mashnee Island, under *To See*.

TENNIS Public courts are located at the old schoolhouse, County Road in Cataumet; at Chester Park, across from the old railroad station in Monument Beach; behind the Town Hall on Perry Avenue in Buzzards Bay; at the community center off Main Street in Buzzards Bay; and behind the fire station on Barlows Landing Road in Pocasset Village.

✳ Green Space

BEACHES (Department of Natural Resources; 508-759-0621, ext. 504; townofbourne .com). The canal moderates considerable differences in tides between Buzzards Bay (4 feet) and Cape Cod Bay (9¼ feet on average). Because of heavy boat traffic and the swift currents caused by tides, swimming is prohibited in Cape Cod Canal.

    Scusset and Sagamore beaches, Cape Cod Bay, Sagamore. Both beaches are located near the Sagamore Bridge via Scusset Beach Road. Facilities include changing areas, restrooms, and a snack bar. (Note that in season, Sagamore parking is reserved for residents.) Scusset is a state-run beach and has floating beach wheelchairs available at no charge, although reservations are recommended. Parking $$. Scusset does not require a town-issued parking sticker

    Monument Beach, Buzzards Bay, on Emmons Road off Shore Road, Monument Beach. The warm waters of Buzzards Bay usually hover around 75 degrees in summer. This small beach has restrooms, a snack bar, and a lifeguard. Nonresident beach sticker $$$$+/week.

WALKS ⚓ **Cape Cod Canal**. The U.S. Army Corps of Engineers (508-833-9678 or 508-759-4431, ext. 622; nac.usace.army.mil), 60 Ed Moffitt Drive, Sandwich, offers

CATAUMET MARINA

numerous and excellent one- and two-hour guided walks and talks from early July to mid-October. There is also biking and hiking along the canal. Call for meeting place.

Red Brook Pond (Bourne Conservation Trust; 508-563-2884; bourneconservation trust.org), Thaxter Road off Shore Road, Cataumet. With 40 acres of wooded conservation land, Red Brook Pond offers a number of hiking trails that traverse pine woods and hug a cranberry bog. The Bourne Conservation Trust offers a well-marked 0.75-mile trail.

See also **Cape Cod Canal** under *To Do*.

✳ Lodging

There really aren't many places to stay in this quiet corner.

CAMPGROUNDS 🐾 **Bayview Campgrounds** (508-759-7610; bayviewcamp ground.com), 260 MacArthur Boulevard, Route 28 (1 mile south of the Bourne Bridge). Open May to mid-October. RVers make up the majority of guests in these 325-plus sites. Services include a dog park, pools, baseball, volleyball, an ice cream parlor, and more.

🐾 **Bourne Scenic Park Campground** (508-759-7873; bournescenicpark.com), 370 Scenic Highway, Route 6 on the mainland side of the canal, Buzzards Bay. Open late March to late October. Camping is practically underneath the pylons of the Bourne Bridge. The same is true for the five rustic cabins. Facilities include a basketball court, playground, and a pool; campfires are allowed. Reservations accepted starting late March; required for cabins.

✳ Where to Eat

Despite the region's drive-through feel, there are a number of places to sit down.

🍸 **Chart Room** (508-563-5350; char troomcataumet.com), 1 Shipyard Lane off Shore Road at the Cataumet Marina. Open L, D May to October. It's bustling and boisterous and the wait is long, but the Chart Room epitomizes summertime dining on the Cape to many (despite rising prices), with a great salty

atmosphere and a cast of regulars. For the best sunset views from picturesque Red Brook Harbor, get a table on the edge of the outer dining room. The Chart Room serves killer mudslides and reliable sandwiches and seafood standards, including lobster salad and lobster rolls (ask for it even if it's not on the menu), broiled scallops, and swordfish. You won't find any fried seafood on the menu here. Live piano and bass duo nightly in summer. L $$–$$$, D $$–$$$$.

🐾 🐶 ✳ **Sagamore Inn** (508-888-9707; sagamoreinncapecod.com), 1131 Route 6A, Sagamore. Open B, L, D, mid-April to mid-December. This iconic institution, resurrected under the watchful eyes of Michael and Suzanne, successfully walks that tightrope of drawing in new patrons while not alienating longtime ones like previous, longtime owner Shirley Pagliarani, who still drops in for dinner. Inside the shuttered green-and-white building are signs of "old Cape Cod": shiny wooden

CHART ROOM

floors, captain's chairs at round tables, and a white tin ceiling. I recommend skipping the Italian dishes and heading straight to the seafood choices: jumbo lump crabcake, broiled seafood platter, baked stuffed shrimp, or lobster casserole. A side order of homemade, thin-cut fries is big enough to share. Shirley's pot roast remains a classic! L $–$$, D $$$.

❋ **Stir Crazy** (508-564-6464; stircrazyrestaurant.com), 570 MacArthur Boulevard, Route 28, Pocasset. Open D. This small, welcoming Asian restaurant gets consistently good reviews and features homemade Cambodian noodle dishes with fresh spices and vegetables. Everything is prepared from scratch here, and the veggies are fresh, thanks to owner Bopha Samms. L $, D $$.

❋ ⌔ **Lobster Trap** (508-759-7600; lobstertrap.net), 290 Shore Road, Bourne. Open L, D. Every town has one restaurant that overlooks water and has the requisite nautical paraphernalia; this is Bourne's. The menu (take-out or sit down) features daily specials, fried seafood, seafood rolls, and seafood plates. There's a fish market attached, so you're pretty sure it's all going to be fresh! $–$$$.

❋ Selective Shopping

❋ Unless otherwise noted, all shops are open year-round.

Pairpoint Crystal (800-888-2344; pairpoint.com), 851 Sandwich Road, Route 6A, Sagamore. "America's oldest glassworks," this place has existed under one name or another since 1837. Many Pairpoint pieces are found in Boston's MFA and New York City's Metropolitan Museum of Art. Thomas Pairpoint, a glass designer in the 1880s, used techniques created by Deming Jarves, and master craftspeople still employ these techniques here today. Clear or richly colored glass is handblown, hand sculpted, or hand pressed on a 19th-century press. Through large picture windows you can watch the master glassblowers working on faithful period reproductions and candlesticks or more modern lamps, paperweights, and vases.

⌔ **Cataumet Arts Center** (508-737-8261; cataumet-arts.org), 76 Scraggy Neck Road, off County Road and Route 28A, Cataumet. This community arts center has ever-changing exhibits, classes, and galleries. It's a beloved resource.

🕯 **Christmas Tree Shops** (508-888-7010; christmastreeshops.com), on the Cape side of the Sagamore Bridge, Exit 1 off Route 6; open daily. This may be the first Christmas Tree Shop you see, but it won't be the last—there are five more on the Cape. This is the place where "everyone loves a bargain," and they've gone all out to get your attention: You can't miss the revolving windmill and thatched roof—made from Canadian marsh grass and so authentic that thatchers come from England and Ireland every other year to make repairs. As for the merchandise, it has little to do with Christmas. It revolves around inexpensive housewares, random gourmet food items, or miscellaneous clothing accessories. By the way, it's been owned by Bed Bath & Beyond since 2003.

PAIRPOINT CRYSTAL

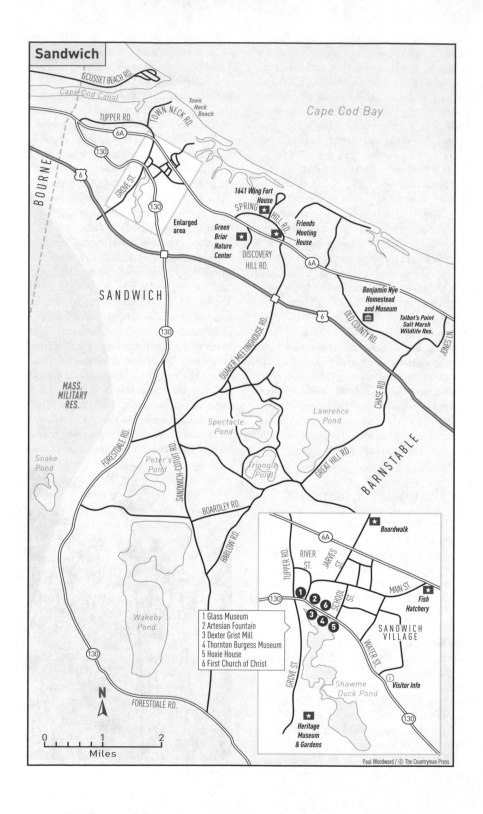

Sandwich

SCUSSET BEACH RD.

Cape Cod Canal

TUPPER RD.

Town Neck Beach

Cape Cod Bay

6A

130

6

BOURNE

TOWN NECK RD.

GROVE ST.

130

130

Enlarged area

1641 Wing Fort House ★

SPRING HILL RD.

Green Briar Nature Center ★

DISCOVERY HILL RD.

Friends Meeting House ★

6A

SANDWICH

Benjamin Nye Homestead and Museum 🏛

6

OLD COUNTY RD.

Talbot's Point Salt Marsh Wildlife Res.

JONES LN.

QUAKER MEETINGHOUSE RD.

MASS. MILITARY RES.

130

Spectacle Pond

Lawrence Pond

CHASE RD.

Snake Pond

Peter's Pond

Triangle Pond

GREAT HILL RD.

BARNSTABLE

FORESTDALE RD.

SANDWICH-COTUIT RD.

BOARDLEY RD.

HARLOW RD.

Wakeby Pond

6A

Boardwalk ★

TUPPER RD.

RIVER ST.

JARVES ST.

SCHOOL ST.

MAIN ST.

130

1
2
6
3
4
5

Fish Hatchery ★

SANDWICH VILLAGE

WATER ST.

1 Glass Museum
2 Artesian Fountain
3 Dexter Grist Mill
4 Thornton Burgess Museum
5 Hoxie House
6 First Church of Christ

GROVE ST.

ℹ Visitor Info

Shawme Duck Pond

130

130

N

FORESTDALE RD.

Heritage Museum & Gardens ★

0   1   2
Miles

Paul Woodward / © The Countryman Press

SANDWICH

Sandwich is calm, even in the height of summer. Many visitors whiz right by it (which is a shame), eager to get farther away from the "mainland." Even people who know about delightful Sandwich Village often hop back onto Route 6 without poking around the rest of Sandwich—the back roads and historic houses off the beaten path. Those who take the time to explore will find that Sandwich is a real gem.

You could spend a day wandering the half-mile radius around the village center, a virtual time capsule spanning the centuries. Antiques shops, attractive homes, and quiet, shady lanes are perfect for strolling. **Shawme Duck Pond**, as idyllic as they come, is surrounded by **historic houses** (including one of the Cape's oldest), an **old cemetery** on the opposite shore, a **working gristmill**, swans and ducks, and plenty of vantage points from which to take it all in.

Sandwich's greatest attraction lies just beyond the town center: **Heritage Museums & Gardens**, a 76-acre horticulturist's delight with superb collections of Americana and antique automobiles.

Beyond the town center, the **Benjamin Nye Homestead** is worth a visit; have a look-see, even if it's closed, because it sits in a picturesque spot. East of town on Route 6A, past densely carpeted cranberry bogs (harvested in autumn), you'll find a few farm stands, antiques shops, artisans' studios, and the **Green Briar Nature Center & Jam Kitchen**, paying homage to naturalist Thornton W. Burgess, a town resident and the creator of Peter Cottontail.

At the town line with Barnstable, you'll find one of the Cape's best beaches and protected areas: **Sandy Neck Beach** (see the "Barrier Beach Beauty" sidebar in "Barnstable") and **Sandy Neck Great Salt Marsh Conservation Area** (see *Green Space* in "Barnstable").

The **marina**, off Tupper Road, borders the Cape Cod Canal with a recreation area. The often-overlooked town beach is nothing to sneeze at, either, and there are numerous conservation areas and ponds for walking and swimming.

Although a surprising number of Sandwich's 20,675 year-round residents commute to Boston every morning, their community dedication isn't diminished. A perfect example took place after fierce storms in August and October 1991 destroyed the town boardwalk, which had served the community since 1875. To replace it, townspeople purchased more than 1,700 individual boards, each personally inscribed, and a new boardwalk was built within eight months.

The oldest town on the Cape, Sandwich was founded in 1637 by the Cape's first permanent group of English settlers. The governor of Plymouth Colony had given permission to "tenn men from Saugust" (now Lynn, Massachusetts) to settle the area with 60 families. Sandwich was probably chosen for its close proximity to the Manomet (now Aptuxcet) Trading Post (see *To See* in "Bourne") and for its abundant salt-marsh hay, which provided ready fodder for the settlers' cows. Agriculture supported the community until the 1820s, when Deming Jarves, a Boston glass merchant, decided to open a glassmaking factory. The location couldn't have been better: There was a good source of sand (although more was shipped in from New Jersey), sea salt was plentiful, salt-marsh hay provided packaging for the fragile goods, and forests were thick with scrub pines to fuel the furnaces. But by the 1880s, midwestern coal-fueled glassmaking factories and a labor strike shut down Sandwich's factories. The story is told in great detail at the excellent Sandwich Glass Museum. Today, glassblowers work in a few studios in town.

Sandwich was named, by the way, for the English town, not for the sandwich-creator earl, as many think. (That Earl of Sandwich was born 81 years after this town was founded.)

PUMP THE HANDLE

Artesian fountain, between the gristmill and Town Hall. Join residents by filling water jugs with what some consider the Cape's best water, reportedly untainted by the plume of pollution that affects Upper Cape tap water.

GUIDANCE ❋ **Sandwich Chamber of Commerce** (508-833-9755; sandwichchamber .com), 510 Route 130. Information booth open mid-May to mid-October. Pick up the good village walking guide at this booth (and at many shops in town).

Cape Cod Canal Visitor Center (508-833-9678; capecodcanal.us), 60 Ed Moffit Drive, east of the Sandwich Marina. Open mid-May to late October. This office dispenses information about boating, fishing, camping, and other canal activities. Highlights of the center include historic photos, interactive monitors, and a small theater showing films on canal history, critters, and wildflowers. Inquire about their hikes, lectures, and other programs.

GETTING THERE *By car:* Take the Sagamore Bridge to Route 6 east to Exit 2 (Route 130 North) and travel 2 miles to Main Street. From Exit 1 and Route 6A, you can take Tupper Road or Main Street into the village center.

By bus: There is no bus service to Sandwich proper, but **Plymouth & Brockton** (508-778-9767; p-b.com) buses bound for Boston stop at the Sagamore Bridge, behind McDonald's in the commuter parking lot. For points south and west, **Bonanza** (888-751-8800; peterpanbus.com) buses stop nearby in Bourne.

GETTING AROUND Sandwich Village is perfect for strolling, but you'll have to get back in your car to reach the marina and Heritage Museums & Gardens (see *To See*).

PUBLIC RESTROOMS Seasonal restrooms are located across from Town Hall and at Russell's Corner.

PUBLIC LIBRARY ❋ ✑ ⚐ **Sandwich Public Library** (508-888-0625; sandwichpublicl brary.com), 142 Main Street.

MEDICAL EMERGENCY Call **911**.

It's not an "emergency" (the kind you'd expect under this category, anyway), but many area water wells are closed due to contamination caused by years of training with grenades and other live munitions at the Massachusetts Military Reservation. I drink bottled water on the Upper Cape.

❋ To See

IN SANDWICH VILLAGE

✑ **Dexter Grist Mill** (508-888-4910), on Shawme Duck Pond, Water Street. Open mid-June to mid-October. The circa-1640 mill has had a multiuse past, and the site wasn't always as quaint as it is now. The mill was turbine powered during Sandwich's glass making heyday; it then sat idle until 1920, when it was converted into a tearoom. After adjacent mills were torn down in the late 1950s, it was opened to tourists in 1961, with the cypress waterwheel you see today. You can also purchase stone-ground cornmeal here—great for muffins, Indian pudding, and polenta. $.

🏛 **Hoxie House** (508-888-1173), 18 Water Street. Open mid-June to mid-October. For a long time this circa-1640 structure was thought to be the Cape's oldest saltbox, but it's impossible to know definitively because the Barnstable County Courthouse deeds were lost in a fire. Nonetheless, the house has a rare saltbox roofline, small diamond-shaped leaded windows, and a fine vantage above Shawme Duck Pond. Thanks to loaner furniture from Boston's Museum of Fine Arts, the restored interior looks much as it did during colonial times. One of the most remarkable facts about this house is that it was occupied without electricity or indoor plumbing until the 1950s. The house was named for Abraham Hoxie,

DEXTER GRIST MILL

who purchased it in 1860 for $400. The Reverend John Smith lived here in 1675 when he came to be minister of the First Parish Church. The rather fun tours include more of a social historical view rather than emphasizing dates.

HOXIE HOUSE

HOXIE HOUSE WINDOWS

8:15	Grab a great bite at Café Chew.
9:30	Locate 17th-century gravestones at the Old Town Cemetery.
10:30	Fill glass containers with clear water from the artesian fountain.
10:45	Feed ducks, geese, and swans at Shawme Pond.
11:15	Visit one of a remarkable trio of houses dating to the mid–17th century: Wing Fort House, Hoxie House, or Benjamin Nye Homestead.
12:45	Gather bread, cheese, and wine from the Brown Jug.
2:00	Peruse used, rare, and new tomes at Titcomb's Book Shop.
3:00	Learn about the process of glassmaking, and see stunning examples of antique glass, at the fine Sandwich Glass Museum.
6:30	Dine at Belfry Bistro.
8:30	Indulge in a hot fudge sundae from Twin Acres Ice Cream.

First Church of Christ (508-888-0434; firstchurchsandwich.org), 136 Main Street. This Christopher Wren–inspired church with a tall white spire was built in 1847, but its brass bell, cast in 1675, is thought to be the country's oldest.

Town Hall (508-888-5144; sandwichmass.org), 130 Main Street. Sandwich has certainly gotten its money's worth out of this Greek Revival building. It was constructed at a cost of little more than $4,000 in 1834 and still serves as the center for town government.

Old Town Cemetery, Grove Street, on the shore opposite the Hoxie House. You'll recognize the names on many gravestones (including those of Burgess, Bodfish, and Bourne) from historic houses and street signs around town. Although the oldest marker dates to 1683, most are from the 1700s; many are marked with a winged skull, a common Puritan design.

ELSEWHERE AROUND TOWN

❋ ❦ **Heritage Museums & Gardens** (508-888-3300; heritagemuseumsandgardens .org), 67 Grove Street. Open early April to late October. Established in 1969 by Josiah K. Lilly III, a descendant of the founder of the pharmaceutical firm Eli Lilly and Company, this place is an oasis for garden lovers, antiques and vintage-car buffs, and Americana enthusiasts. These 100 acres are planted with outstanding collections of rhododendrons, including the famous Dexter variety, which blooms from late May to early June. (Charles O. Dexter was the estate's original owner, and he experimented with hybridizing here.) There are also impressive collections of holly bushes, heathers, hostas, hydrangeas, and more than 1,000 daylilies, which bloom from mid-July to early August. Don't miss the **labyrinth** or the Hart family **maze garden**. The estate is equally pleasant for an autumn walk. Or have a go at their zip line (see *To Do*).

SAND TRANSFORMED

♦ ⚡ ☂ **Sandwich Glass Museum** (508-888-0751; sandwichglassmuseum.org), 129 Main Street. Open year-round except January. If you're in the habit of skipping town historical museums, break the habit this time; you won't be disappointed. During the 19th century, Sandwich glass-making flourished at Deming Jarves's Boston & Sandwich Glass Company (1825–1888) and the Cape Cod Glass Works (1859–1869). Today this internationally known museum, operated by the Sandwich Historical Society, chronologically displays more than 6,000 pieces of decorative and functional glass objects, which became increasingly more elaborate and richly colored as the years progressed. Many displays are dramatically backlit by natural light streaming through banks of windows. Check out the elaborate table setting featuring Hannah Rebecca Burgess's late-1800s collection; a 20-minute multimedia presentation that describes the first 200 years of Sandwich's history; and lots of changing seasonal exhibits. You'll also enjoy glassblowing demonstrations and the contemporary gallery with changing exhibits. $.

Inquire about the museum's excellent 90-minute village walking tours (mid-June through October).

The **American History Museum** features an extensive collection of bird carvings by Elmer Crowell in addition to a large array of hand-painted miniatures, while the J. K. Lilly III **Antique Automobile Museum**, in the replica **Shaker Round Barn**, houses the museum's outstanding vintage-car collection. A 1930 Duesenberg built for Gary Cooper and President Taft's White Steamer (the first official auto of the White House) are two of the mint-condition classics.

The **Art Museum** features folk art, scrimshaw, cigar-store figures, weather vanes, and Currier & Ives lithographs. Also on the grounds you'll find an 1800 windmill, an operational Coney Island–style 1912 carousel, and a **café**. The alfresco café has a menu of overstuffed sandwiches, salads, and desserts. There is golf cart transportation for those who may need assistance. Keep your eyes peeled for museum special events, including plant sales, a rhododendron festival (see *Special Events*), concerts, and car shows. Gift and garden shop at the entrance. $$.

Benjamin Nye Homestead and Museum (508-888-4213; nyefamily.org), 85 Old County Road, East Sandwich. Open mid-June to mid-October. Off Route 6A, this 1685 homestead belonged to one of Sandwich's first settlers and has undergone many structural changes over the years. Although it began life as a small, narrow house with a central chimney, an addition turned it into a saltbox. A second floor created the full Colonial you see today. Although the interior is hardly a purist restoration, you'll see some of the original construction, early paneling, 18th-century wallpaper, a rosewood melodeon built by the Nye family in the 1850s, a spinning wheel, and handwoven sheets. $.

1641 Wing Fort House (508-833-1540; wingfamily.org), 63 Spring Hill Road (off Route 6A), East Sandwich. Open mid-June to September. The Wing house is the country's oldest home continuously inhabited by the same family. This circa-1646 house began as a one-room cottage when Stephen Wing, descendant of the Reverend John Wing, arrived with his new bride. In the mid-1800s, a second house was added to it to create the current three-quarter Colonial. $.

Friends Meeting House (508-398-3773), 6 Quaker Road, off Spring Hill Road (from Route 6A), East Sandwich. Meetings every Sunday. The building standing today was

FRIENDS MEETING HOUSE

built in 1810, the third Quaker meetinghouse on this site. The congregation has been meeting since 1657, which makes it the oldest continuously used meeting house in North America. The interior is simple, with pews and a wood-burning stove stoked in winter for 25 or so congregants.

❀ ✿ **Sandwich Fish Hatchery** (508-888-0008; masswildlife.org), 164 Route 6A at Old Main Street. Open daily. More than 200,000 trout at various stages of development are raised to stock the state's ponds. Throw in pellets of food (bring quarters for the vending machines) and watch 'em swarm.

✿ **Boardwalk**, Harbor Street off Factory Street. The boardwalk crosses marshland, Mill Creek, and low dunes to connect to Town Neck Beach (see *Green Space*). Depending on the season, you might see teens jumping into the creek (1½ hours before and after high tide, when the water is theoretically deep enough) or blue heron poking around the tidal pools and tall grasses. There are expansive views at the end of the 1,350-foot walkway.

❉ To Do

BLUEBERRY PICKING **The Blueberry Bog** (508-888-1560), 92 Spring Hill off Route 6A. In the 1940s, this former cranberry bog was turned into a blueberry farm. Today there are about 400 bushes on more than 4 acres. Pick your own from late-July to August.

BICYCLING **Ecotourz** (508-888-1627; ecotourz.net), 20 Jarves Street. In addition to bikes, these folks offer kayak rentals and estuary tours. Open mid-April to early November. Bike rentals by the hour ($), day ($$), or multiday ($$$–$$$$).

CANOEING & KAYAKING **Shawme Duck Pond**, Water Street (Route 130), is actually linked to two other ponds, so you can do a lot of canoeing here.

Scorton Creek. Head east on Route 6A, turn right onto a gravel road before reaching the Scorton Creek Bridge. This is a good place for picnics, too.

Wakeby Pond, off Cotuit Road, South Sandwich.

FARMERS' MARKET On the village green, 164 Route 6A, June through October (Tuesday 9 AM-1 PM).

FISHING Procure freshwater and saltwater fishing licenses and regulations online.

Sandcatcher Recreation Area and **Scusset Beach State Reservation** pier (off Scusset Beach Road from the rotary on the mainland side of the canal) are good places to cast a line into the canal.

GOLF ❊ **Holly Ridge Golf Club** (508-428-5577; hollyridgegolf.com), off Route 130, South Sandwich. An award-winning, 18-hole, 3,000-yard, par-54 course.

❊ **Sandwich Hollows Golf Club** (508-888-3384; sandwichhollows.com), Exit 3 off Route 6, East Sandwich. An 18-hole, par-71 course.

MINI-GOLF ✐ **Sandwich Mini Golf** (508-833-1905; sandwichminigolf.net), 159 Route 6A. Open mid-May to mid-October and daily in summer. This course is set on a cranberry bog and boasts a floating raft for a green. An honest-to-goodness stream winds around many of the 35 holes. $-$$.

SCENIC RAILROAD ✐ **Cape Cod Central Railroad** (888-797-7245 for tickets; capetrain.com), 70 Main Street, Buzzards Bay. Late May through late October. The relaxing 48-mile trip takes two hours and passes alongside cranberry bogs and the Sandy Neck Great Salt Marsh. (I always try to have "beginner's eyes" on this trip, seeing it as a first-timer would, but honestly, the scenery is a tad . . . shall we say, uneventful.) On certain days in July and August, when there are two trains daily, you can take the first one from Hyannis, hop off in Sandwich, walk around Sandwich center for three hours, and then catch the next train back to Hyannis. The best part of this trip is the local narration—unless you've never been on a train before, in which case the simple act of taking a train will tickle you more. Oh, and the dinner part of the dinner train? They serve a pretty decent meal. $$$.

TENNIS Public courts are located at **Wing Elementary School** on Route 130; **Oak Ridge School** and **Sandwich High School**, both off Quaker Meetinghouse Road; and **Forestdale School** off Route 130.

ZIP LINE ✐ **The Adventure Park at Heritage Museums and Gardens** (508-866-0199), 67 Grove Street. This aerial obstacle course and zip line has been fun for the whole family since it opened in 2015. Open daily in summer, weekends in fall. $$$-$$$$.

❊ Green Space

✐ **Shawme Duck Pond**, Water Street (Route 130), in the village center. Flocks of ducks, geese, and swans know a good thing when they find it. And even though this idyllic spot is one of the most easily accessible on the Cape, it remains a tranquil place

SHAWME POND

for humans and waterfowl alike. Formerly a marshy brook, the willow-lined pond was dammed prior to the gristmill operating in the 1640s. It's a nice spot to canoe.

❄ 🚲 🚣 **Shawme-Crowell State Forest** (877-422-6762 reservations; reserveamerica .com), Route 130. You can walk, bicycle, and camp at almost 300 sites on almost 750 acres. When the popular Nickerson State Park (see the sidebar "A Supreme State Park" in "Brewster") is full of campers, there are often dozens of good sites still available here. There are also a few yurts; reservations required.

❄ 🚲 🚣 **Scusset Beach State Reservation** (877-422-6762 reservations; reserveam erica.com), on Cape Cod Bay, off Scusset Beach Road from the mainland side of the canal. The 380-acre reservation offers about 100 campsites (primarily used by RVers) in-season (early May to mid-October), bicycling, picnicking, and walking opportunities. Facilities include camping, in-season lifeguard, restrooms, changing rooms, and a snack bar. Parking $.

See also **Giving Tree Gallery and Sculpture Gardens** under *Selective Shopping*.

BEACHES **Town Neck Beach**, on Cape Cod Bay, off Town Neck Road and Route 6A. This pebble beach extends 1.5 miles from the Cape Cod Canal to Dock Creek. Visit at high tide if you want to swim; at low tide it's great for walking. $. The lot rarely fills up.

See also **Scusset Beach State Reservation**, above.

PONDS **Wakeby Pond** (off Cotuit Road), South Sandwich, offers freshwater swimming and picnicking.

IT IS A WONDERFUL THING TO SWEETEN THE WORLD

✍ **Green Briar Nature Center & Jam Kitchen** (508-888-6870; thorntonburgess.org), 6 Discovery Hill Road off Route 6A, East Sandwich. Trails open year-round. Jam-cooking demonstrations most days April to December. Even in an area with so many tranquil spots, Green Briar rises to the top. It's run by the Thornton W. Burgess Society "to re-establish and maintain nature's fine balance among all living things and to hold as a sacred trust the obligation to make only the best use of natural resources." Located on Smiling Pond and adjacent to the famous Briar Patch of Burgess's stories, this big patch of conservation land has many short interpretive nature trails (less than a mile long), a lovely wildflower garden, and a veritable Noah's Ark of resident animals. The society hosts natural history classes, lectures, nature walks, and other programs for children and adults.

The Jam Kitchen was established in 1903 by Ida Putnam, who used her friend Fanny Farmer's recipes to make jams, jellies, and fruit preserves. Step inside the old-fashioned, aromatic, and homey place to see mason jars filled with apricots and strawberries, and watch fruit simmering on vintage-1920 Glenwood gas stoves. Two-hour workshops (sign up in advance) on preserving fruit and making jams and jellies are also held. About this place, Burgess said to Putnam in 1939, "It is a wonderful thing to sweeten the world which is in a jam and needs preserving." Berry festivals are held throughout summer: look for strawberries in June, blueberries in August, and cranberries in September.

GREEN BRIAR JAM KITCHEN

GREEN BRIAR JAM TRAILS

GIVING TREE GALLERY

WALKS Talbot's Point Salt Marsh Wildlife Reservation, off Old County Road from Route 6A. This little-used, 1.5-mile (round-trip) hiking trail winds past red pines, beeches, and a large salt marsh.

See also **Green Briar Nature Center & Jam Kitchen** and **Shawme-Crowell State Forest**.

✳ Lodging

🍴 Sandwich's historic hostelries provide great diversity and something for everyone—from an incredibly impressive church conversion to a large motor inn.

RESORT MOTOR INN ✳ 🎣 **Dan'l Webster Inn & Spa** (508-888-3622; danlwebsterinn.com), 149 Main Street. Modeled after an 18th-century hostelry where Revolutionary patriots met, today's motor inn has a certain colonial charm that's vigilantly maintained by the Catanias, owners since 1980. Most of the 48

traditionally decorated rooms and suites are of the top-notch motel/hotel variety. A minority are more distinctively innlike and found in two separate older houses. Touring motor coaches are part of the parking lot landscape. $$–$$$.

INNS ✳ **Belfry Inn** (508-844-4542; belfryinn.com), 8 Jarves Street. Innkeeper Chris Wilson presides over the center of town (and the town's wedding business) with the circa-1900 **Abbey**, the circa-1879 **Painted Lady**, and the 1830s Federal-style **Village House**. Between the three, there are 23 guest rooms appointed with fine antiques and tasteful furnishings. Abbey rooms are downright spectacular: outfitted with stained glass, flying buttresses, fancy linens, bold colors, beds made from pews, gas fireplaces, Jacuzzis, and balconies. Chris and his architect deserve awards for this spectacular conversion, which consistently wins rave reviews. Most Painted Lady rooms have whirlpools, while Village House rooms are relatively modest with hardwood floors (some bleached) and down comforters. The Belfry also offers dining to the public (see *Dining Out*). Full breakfast included. $–$$$.

BED & BREAKFASTS ❀ **Isaiah Jones Homestead** (508-888-9115; isaiahjones .com), 165 Main Street. This Victorian gem in the middle of the village deserves your full attention. Filled with killer antiques and showing lots of elegant decorating prowess (they're not as fussy as the website photos suggest), there isn't one single room I'd hesitate to recommend. For more privacy, though, choose the adjacent carriage house with whirlpool tubs, robes, and upscale amenities. Presiding since 2007, the delightful innkeepers Katherine and Donnie Sanderson (he grew up in Chatham) serve a three-course breakfast (think French toast that's more akin to soufflé) and wonderful special-occasion dinners. They've also outfitted each of their seven rooms with either a fireplace or gas stove. $$.

❀ **1750 Inn at Sandwich Center** (508-888-6958; innatsandwich.com), 118 Tupper Road. Expert hospitality is a watchword at this five-room inn operated by lovely innkeepers Jan and Charlie Preus. They serve delicious breakfasts (like macadamia nut French toast or quichettes served in individual ramekins) in the keeping room—complete with a beehive oven—or on the patio. And they set out brandy and chocolates in the evening. Guests gather in the living room surrounded by period architectural details and are regaled with vivid stories about the inn's history. The two

choice guest rooms, painted in soothing colors, are the upper floor front rooms. Come off-season to best enjoy the fireplaces (in most rooms). $–$$.

COTTAGES & MOTELS **Spring Garden Inn** (508-888-0710), 578 Route 6A, East Sandwich. Open April through October. Reserve early if you can; this is one of the best motels on Route 6A. Although modest from the street, the bilevel motel overlooks a salt marsh and the Scorton River, particularly beautiful at sunset. The peaceful backyard is dotted with lawn chairs, grills, and picnic tables. Owner Steve Lang has eight carpeted rooms with knotty-pine paneling, two double beds, and refrigerator. In addition, there are two efficiencies and a two-room suite with a private deck. $.

ISAIAH JONES HOMESTEAD

1750 INN AT SANDWICH CENTER

CAMPGROUND 🐾 **Peters Pond Park** (508-477-1775; peterspond.com), 185 Cotuit Road. Open mid-April to mid-October. Call for current status. At last look the RV resort offered more than 450 well-groomed campsites, cottages, yurts, walking trails, summertime children's activities, a ball field, two beaches, a campfire ring, and a popular spring-fed lake for trout and bass fishing, boating, and swimming. Rental rowboats, paddleboats, and kayaks were also available. $.

See also **Shawme-Crowell State Forest** and **Scusset Beach State Reservation** under *Green Space*.

RENTAL HOUSES & COTTAGES
Beach Realty (508-888-4998; beachrealtycapecod.com), 133 North Shore Boulevard, East Sandwich.

✳ Where to Eat

Sandwich eateries run the gamut, from fine dining in a former church to casual eating in a tiny tea shop.

DINING OUT ✳ 🍷 ♿ **Belfry Bistro** (508-888-8550; belfryinn.com), 8 Jarves Street. Open L, D. The quiet setting (inside a converted church) is divinely dramatic—with soaring beadboard ceilings, stained glass, interior flying buttresses, a confessional converted into a tasteful bar, and a former altar set with tables. It's also elegant—with candlelight, damask-covered tables, high-backed leather chairs, and a wood-burning fireplace. Tasteful alfresco terrace dining is available, but it seems a waste not to sit indoors here. Chef Toby offers a menu ranging from simple (like clam chowder or fish-and-chips) to sophisticated (like tuna carpaccio nicoise or briochecrusted codfish). The experience is as much about the food as the setting. L $$, D $$–$$$$.

✳ 🐾 ✐ 🍷 **Amari** (508-375-0011; amarirestaurant.com), 674 Route 6A, East Sandwich. Open D. On the town line with Barnstable and near Sandy Neck Beach, Bob and Maureen Hixon's upscale but comfortable eatery has a little something—with big portions—for

BELFRY BISTRO

flair. Best bets include wood oven pizza and fried calamari. $$.

✴ ✎ **Dan'l Webster Inn** (508-888-3622; danlwebsterinn.com), 149 Main Street. Open B, L, D. Just so you're not wondering, this kitchen serves classic American dishes (think prime rib and filet mignon) in comfortable dining rooms. The sunlit Conservatory resembles a greenhouse; the Music Room is more traditional; and the casual Tavern has lighter fare. B $, L $–$$, D $$–$$$.

EATING OUT ✴ **Café Chew** (508-888-7717; cafechew.com), 4 Merchant's Road. Open B, L, D. Dubbed "Sandwich's Sandwichery," the delightful Chew offers sandwiches from a blackboard menu, a full line of fair trade organic coffees, and artsy tables at which to dine. There are plenty of reasons owners Tobin and Bob win tons of awards: Their renowned German breakfast sandwich features eggs with melted Gruyère cheese and ham encased in a Bavarian pretzel roll. The Midwestern lunch sandwich boasts homemade meat loaf with cheddar cheese, bacon, and

everyone. Dine within sight of an open kitchen, surrounded by lots of mahogany, on Italian cooking with a contemporary

CAFÉ CHEW

BROWN JUG

tomato relish on ciabatta bread. And don't even get me started about their mint chocolate brownie. For kids, the peanut butter is paired with all-natural preserves. Soups, specialty salads, and daily specials, too. $.

✳ **The Brown Jug** (508-888-4669; thebrownjug.com), 1 Jarves Street. Proprietor Michael Johnston tastes everything he sells at his specialty food-and-wine-shop-cum-café. And what taste he has! Bostonians and New Yorkers whizzing to points elsewhere have all the reason they need to detour in Sandwich: artisan cheese, pâtés, dozens of kinds of salt, caviar, pastas, gravlax, breads, and more. Furthermore, the wine store is one of the best I've wandered, with bottles in the $10–$100 range; they even carry my favorite and little-known Gruet champagne from New Mexico. Check out

the Friday night wine tastings and the cappuccino bar. Miss The Brown Jug at your peril.

✳ **Dunbar Tea Room & Gift Shop** (508-833-2485; dunbarteashop.com), 1 Water Street. Open L. I always want to love this tiny English tearoom, set in a slightly rustic, American-style country setting. But in my experience, service can be "relaxed" and less than friendly, and the portions small. Still, if you want, try the authentic ploughman's lunch or scones and Scottish shortbread. Afternoon English tea includes scones, finger sandwiches, and desserts. In summer, garden tables are an oasis; in winter, the fireplace makes it cozy indoors. L $–$$.

✳ 🐾 🍷 **Marshland Restaurant** (508-888-9824; marshlandrestaurant.com), 109 Route 6A. Open B, L, D. It's primarily locals who frequent this small, informal roadside place for coffee and a breakfast muffin—or lunch specials like homemade meat loaf, quiche with great salads, and chicken club sandwiches. They serve real mashed potatoes for dinner, too, along with large portions of *out-of-this-world* good stuffed quahogs. Eat at one of the Formica booths or on a swiveling seat at the U-shaped counter. B $, L $–$$, D $–$$.

✳ **Beth's Bakery** (508-888-7716; bethsbakery.net), 16 Jarves Street. Beth and Joe, lifetime residents of Sandwich, offer light breakfasts, scones and such, soups, salads, and sandwiches. Patio and indoor seating and local Beanstock coffee, too. Dishes $.

🐾 🍷 ♿ **Seafood Sam's** (508-888-4629; seafoodsams.com), 6 Coast Guard Road. Open L, D, early March to mid-November. This casual spot near the marina serves fried and broiled seafood, seafood sandwiches, and seafood salad plates. L $, D $$.

DRINKS 🍸 **Horizons** (508-888-0060; hoizonsonthebay.com), 98 Town Neck Road. Open seasonally. This is a nice place for an afternoon drink on the deck; views are spectacular.

ICE CREAM ✎ **Twin Acres Ice Cream Shoppe** (508-888 0566, twinacresicecreamshoppe.com), 21 Route 6A. Open April to mid-October. The best in the area. The shop also boasts a lush lawn, a little oak grove, and plenty of tables and chairs. (It sure beats standing in a parking lot!) It's lit at night, too. My only complaint: There's so much colorful signage describing the offerings that it's overwhelming. To compensate, I've returned often enough to memorize the menu. Generous servings; banana boats, hot fudge sundaes, and an ample grill menu at lunchtime through late September.

✳ Entertainment

✎ **Band concerts**, at the Wing School off Route 130, are given by the Sandwich Town Band on Thursday evenings at 7:30 in July and August.

✳ Selective Shopping

✳ Unless otherwise noted, all shops are open year-round. (Still, don't expect many to be open midweek during the winter.)

ANTIQUES **Sandwich Antiques Center** (508-833-3600), 131 Route 6A. A multidealer shop worth your time . . . if you treasure the hunt.

   Maypop Lane (508-888-1230), Route 6A at Main Street. With many dealers under one roof, there's a broad selection: decoys, quilts, jewelry, sterling, copper, brass, glass, furniture, and other collectibles and antiques.

AUCTIONS **Sandwich Auction House** (508-888-1926; sandwichauction.com), 15 Tupper Road. Consignment estate sales are held once a week. Call about their

BROWN JUG

TITCOMBS BOOK SHOP

staffed the shop since 1969 and, with the help of their eight children, have made hundreds of yards of shelves. It's a charming place, promoting browsing. By the way, owner Nancy Titcomb helped resurrect interest in Thornton W. Burgess, and, as you might imagine, she offers a great selection of his work. Titcomb's was recently selected by the International Booksellers Federation as one of 50 unique bookshops around the world. Check the website for book signings and other special events.

SPECIAL SHOPS 🖌 **Giving Tree Gallery and Sculpture Gardens** (508-888-5446), 550 Route 6A, East Sandwich. Open March to December. The fabu gallery's motto might as well be "Where Art and Nature Meet." It's a wonderful and aesthetically pleasing place. Outdoor sculpture is exhibited on acres of marshland with nature paths, perennial gardens, and a bamboo grove. And the rope suspension bridge out to the marsh is fun for kids. But don't overlook the indoor gallery, featuring mainly the work of hundreds of jewelry artists.

   Glass Studio (508-888-6681; capecod glass.net/the-studio), 470 Route 6A, East Sandwich. Open April through December. Artist Michael Magyar offers a wide selection of glass made with modern and centuries-old techniques. He's been glassblowing since 1980, and you can watch him work most weekends in season. Choose from graceful Venetian goblets, square vases, bud vases, handblown ornaments, and "sea bubbles" glassware, influenced by the water around him.

   The Weather Store (508-888-1200; theweatherstore.com), 146 Main Street. If it relates to measuring or predicting weather, it's here: weather vanes, sundials, and weather sticks to indicate when a storm is headed your way.

   Home for the Holidays (508-888-4388), 154 Main Street. Each room of this 1850 house is filled with decorations and gifts geared to specific holidays or

monthly super-duper Oriental rug auction.

BOOKSTORE 🐾 🖌 ⚜ **Titcomb's Book Shop** (508-888-2331; titcombsbookshop .com), 432 Route 6A, East Sandwich. Book enthusiasts won't be disappointed; rare-book lovers will be even happier; and online shoppers in heaven. This three-story barn is filled with more than 30,000 new, used, and rare books for adults and children, a good selection of Cape and maritime books, educational toys and puzzles, and cards by Tasha Tudor. Personalized service is exceptional: The Titcombs have owned and special occasions. Items in one room are changed every month, so there's always a room devoted to the current holiday.

Horsefeathers (508-888-5298), 454 Route 6A, East Sandwich. This small shop sells linens, lace, Victoriana, teacups, and vintage christening gowns.

Collections Unlimited (508-833-0039; collectionsgallery.com), 23a Jarves Street. Handcrafted items—wood objects, pottery, baskets, stained glass, and the like—from members of the Cape's longest-running cooperative (since 1990).

Mrs. Mugs (508-362-6462; mrsmugs .com), 680 Route 6A, East Sandwich. Reader Janet Grant (no relation) and my mother (relation) write enthusiastically about this place, which has mugs (of course) but also funky T-shirts, unique watches, locally made jewelry, and what has to be the largest selection of Crocs on the Cape. The beloved owner, Lori Simon, offers gifts for all price ranges.

Crow Farm (508-888-0690; crow farmcapecod.com), 192 Route 6A, East Sandwich. Open May to December. In addition to jams, jellies, corn, summer squash, native peaches, and bread, Paul Crowell's farm stand also offers cornmeal ground at the local gristmill.

See also **Green Briar Nature Center & Jam Kitchen** under *Green Space* and The Brown Jug under *Eating Out*.

✳ Special Events

Late June: **Sandwich Fest** (sandwichfest .com). This sandwich contest was hugely popular when it debuted in 2009.

Mid- to late May: **Annual Rhododendron Festival** (508-888-3300; heritage museumsandgardens.org). Includes a

GIVING TREE GALLERY

rhododendron canopy walk, photography and other workshops, on-site flower experts, and more. And for families: scavenger hunts, nature detectives, and other games.

Late November through December: **Holly Days** (508-833-9755; sandwich hollydays.com). A chamber-sponsored festival with caroling, hot cider served at open houses, trolley tours, and crafts sales. The full calendar is listed on the chamber's website.

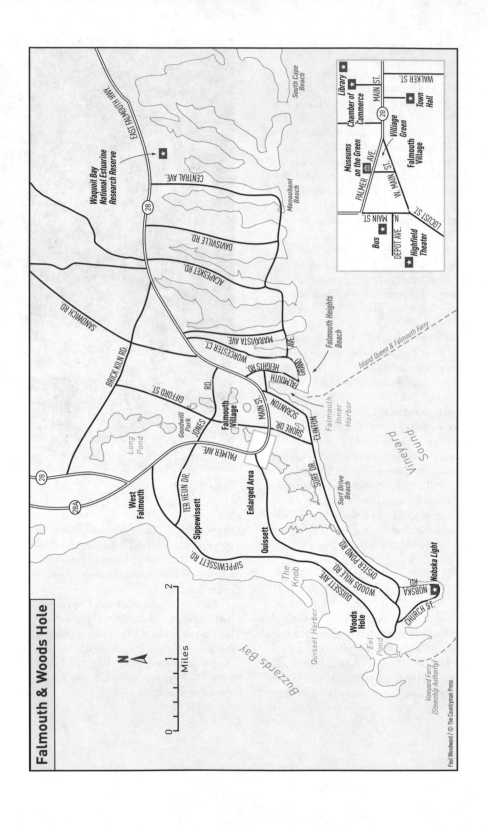

Falmouth & Woods Hole

Paul Woodward / © The Countryman Press

FALMOUTH &
WOODS HOLE

The Cape's second largest town, Falmouth has more shore and coastline than any other town on the Cape. In fact, it has 14 harbors, 12 miles of public beaches, and more than 30 ponds. Saltwater inlets reach deep into the southern coastline, like fjords—only without the mountains. Buzzards Bay laps at the western shores of quiet North and West Falmouth and bustling **Woods Hole**. Falmouth's eight distinctive villages accommodate about 101,000 summer people, which about triples the year-round population of 33,000.

The villages differ widely in character. Quiet, restful lanes and residents who keep to themselves characterize **Sippewissett** and both **North** and **West Falmouth**. The **West Falmouth Harbor** (off wooded, scenic Route 28A) is tranquil and placid, particularly at sunset. Although **Falmouth Heights** is known for its opulent, turn-of-the-20th-century shingled houses on Vineyard Sound, its beach is a popular gathering spot for 20-somethings—playing volleyball, sunbathing, flying kites, and enjoying the relatively warm water and seaside condos that line Grand Avenue and Menauhant Road. Falmouth Heights has early ties to the Kennedys: Rose Fitzgerald was vacationing here with her family when Joe Kennedy came calling.

East Falmouth is a largely residential area. There are several motels and grand year-round and summer homes lining the inlets of Green Pond, Bourne's Pond, and Waquoit Bay. Historic **Danville** was once home to whaling-ship captains and has a strong Portuguese and Cape Verdean fishing community and farming heritage.

The **center of Falmouth**, with plentiful shops and eateries, is busy year-round. And the village common, picture-perfect with historic houses (converted to beautiful bed & breakfasts) encircling the tidy green space, is well worth a stroll. Falmouth's Inner Harbor is awash with restaurants, boatyards, a colorful marina, and moderate nightlife. Two passenger ferries to Martha's Vineyard operate from here.

Four miles south of Falmouth, **Woods Hole** is more than just a terminus for the **Steamship Authority** auto and passenger ferries to the Vineyard. It is also home to three major scientific institutions: the **National Marine Fisheries Service** ("the Fisheries"), **Woods Hole Oceanographic Institution** (or WHOI, pronounced *hooey*), and the **Marine Biological Laboratory** (MBL).

Woods Hole, named for the "hole" or passage between Penzance Point and Nonamesset Island, was the site of the first documented European landing in the New World. Bartholomew Gosnold arrived here from Falmouth, England, in 1602.

GUIDANCE ❊ **Falmouth Chamber of Commerce** (508-548-8500; falmouthchamber .com and woodshole.com), 20 Academy Lane, Falmouth. This knowledgeable office also has Woods Hole information, good foldout street maps, and a historical walking-tour brochure.

GETTING THERE *By car:* Via Route 28 South, Falmouth is 15 miles from the Bourne Bridge and 20 miles from the Sagamore Bridge. Route 28 turns into Main Street. In

FALMOUTH PUBLIC LIBRARY

northern Falmouth, Route 28A parallels Route 28 and is much more scenic. Route 28 leads directly to Locust Street and Woods Hole Road for Woods Hole.

The directional signposts for Route 28 are a tad confusing from this point on. Although Hyannis and Chatham are east of Falmouth, the signpost from Falmouth to Chatham says Route 28 South. This is because Route 28 originates in Bourne and does indeed head south to Falmouth before jogging east.

By bus: **Bonanza/Peter Pan** (888-751-8800; peterpanbus.com) has service to Falmouth (Peter Pan bus terminal) and Woods Hole (Steamship Authority) from New York, Providence, Connecticut, western Massachusetts, and Boston. Some Logan Airport buses connect with Vineyard ferries, although the ferry won't wait for a late bus. The round-trip fare from Boston to Woods Hole is $$$$$.

WHOOSH TROLLEY

GETTING AROUND **Cape Cod Regional Transit Authority** (508-385-1430; cape codtransit.org), whose Whoosh trolleys are equipped with bike racks, travels between Falmouth and Woods Hole. Tourists can hop on and off downtown and at shops and beaches; flag it down when you see it. The trolley operates about late May to early September; $. Look for schedules and route maps at the chamber, the Steamship Authority, and some local

A PERFECT DAY IN FALMOUTH

8.00	Down a double espresso at "Coffee O" with other groove-meisters.
8:45	Appreciate one person's generosity at the waterfront Spohr Gardens.
10:00	Find the Punch Bowl kettle pond at Beebe Woods and take a dip.
11:45	Learn a little something at the Museums on the Green.
1:00	Enjoy lunch from the harborfront Clam Shack.
2:30	Kayak around Waquoit Bay and over to Washburn Island.
6:00	Drive the back roads to Quissett Harbor and walk around the Knob.
8:00	Enjoy a fab meal at The Glass Onion.
10:00	Sing along at Liam Maguire's Irish Pub.

shops. Parking is extremely limited in Woods Hole, and roads are congested, so use this service if you're just visiting for the afternoon.

GETTING TO MARTHA'S VINEYARD There is year-round automobile and passenger ferry service to Martha's Vineyard from Woods Hole; there are two seasonal passenger ferry services to the Vineyard from Falmouth Harbor. See *Getting There* in "Martha's Vineyard."

MEDIA *The Falmouth Enterprise* (508-548-4700; capenews.net), 50 Depot Avenue, Falmouth, published every Tuesday and Friday, has local news and gossip.

The Falmouth Visitor (508-548-3047; falmouthvisitor.com), geared toward repeat and long-term visitors, is a great and free publication that gets beneath Falmouth's outer shell.

PUBLIC RESTROOMS *In Falmouth:* Chamber of Commerce on Academy Lane; Peg Noonan Park on Main Street; and the library.

In Woods Hole: At the Steamship Authority.

PUBLIC LIBRARIES ❄ ✆ ☂ The area has multiple branches (falmouthpubliclibrary. org), but the biggest and downright greatest is **Falmouth Public Library** (508-457-2555), 300 Main Street.

Woods Hole Public Library (508-548-8961; woodsholepubliclibrary.org), 581 Woods Hole Road, Woods Hole. As you might imagine, there are lots of scientists and NPR *Science Friday* types at this branch.

MEDICAL EMERGENCY **Falmouth Hospital** (508-548-5300; capecodhealth.org), 100 Ter Heun Drive (off Route 28), Falmouth.

8:30	Enjoy pastry and java from Pie in the Sky.
9:30	Watch the Eel Pond drawbridge go up and down.
9:45	Support local artists at Woods Hole Handworks.
10:30	Take a walking tour with WHOI or MBL.
12:30	Dine waterfront at Water Street Kitchen.
2:30	Contemplate quietude from St. Mary's Garden after climbing to the top of St. Joseph's Bell Tower.
4:00	Ride the Shining Sea Bike Path out to Nobska Light and beyond.
6:30	Head back to Falmouth for dinner or enjoy a waterfront picnic here.

✳ To See

IN FALMOUTH

Village Green. The green is bordered by Colonial, Federal, Italianate, and Greek Revival homes, many built for wealthy ship captains and then converted to B&Bs. Designated as public land in 1749 and now on the National Register of Historic Places, this large triangle of grass is enclosed by a white fence, surely as pastoral a sight today as it was more than 250 years ago. It's not difficult to imagine local militiamen practicing marches and drills, and townspeople grazing horses—in fact, a local militia reenacts maneuvers on July Fourth. Walking tours around the green and old cemetery depart June through October on Tuesday and Thursday mornings from the Hallett Barn Visitor Center at the **Falmouth Historical Society**. The tour returns by a secret back route. Call 508-548-4857 to make the recommended reservations. $.

    First Congregational Church, 68 Main Street, on the green. This quintessential New England church—with its high steeple and crisp white lines—is graced by a bell (which still rings) commissioned by Paul Revere. The receipt for the bell—from 1796—is on display; the inscription on the bell reads: THE LIVING TO THE CHURCH I CALL, AND TO THE GRAVE I SUMMON ALL. Today's church was built on the foundations of the 1796 church

🐾 🖎 **Museums on the Green** (508-548-4857; falmouthhistoricalsociety.org), 55–65 Palmer Avenue, just off the village green. Open mid-May to early October; archives open by appointment year-round. Operated by the Falmouth Historical Society. **The Conant House** (a circa 1760 structure) contains sailors' valentines, scrimshaw, and old tools. One room honors Katharine Lee Bates, a Wellesley College professor and author of the lyrics for "America the Beautiful," who was born nearby in 1859 at 16 Main Street (not open to the public). I suspect most Falmouth residents would lend support to the grassroots movement in the United States to change the national anthem from "The Star-Spangled Banner" to Bates's easier-to-sing, less militaristic song.

Next door, look for a formal Colonial-style garden and a cannon from HMS *Nimrod*; the replicated 100-year-old **Hallett Barn**, with an educational center with hands-on exhibits; and the late-18th-century **Julia Wood House**, home to Dr. Francis Wicks, known for his work with smallpox inoculations. $. If it's a Friday during July and August and your pod constitutes a family, head here for tailor-made, well-done, hands-on history activities.

The Dome (woodsholemuseum.org), Woods Hole Road, Woods Hole. When Buckminster Fuller was teaching at MIT, he patented the geodesic dome design in 1954. One of his domes, which epitomizes doing more with less, is just north of town.

Cape Cod Winery (508-457-5592; capecodwinery.com), 4 Oxbow Road, East Falmouth. Open early May to mid-December. Weekend tours in July and August. Come for tastings of fruity wines, a blanc de blancs blend, cabernet, pinot grigio, merlot, and more. During harvest time in late September and early October, visitors may pick grapes in exchange for a gift certificate redeemable for that particular vintage. Once the wine is bottled, it includes a custom label that indicates the names of the harvesters.

See also **Highfield Hall** and **Bourne Farm**, both under *Green Space*.

IN WOODS HOLE

❄ 🐾 🖎 **Woods Hole Science Aquarium** (508-495-2001; aquarium.nefsc.noaa .gov), Water Street. When it opened in 1871, this was the first aquarium in the country. Today it's a fun place to learn about slippery fish, living shellfish (rather than the empty shells we're all accustomed to seeing), and other lesser-known creatures of the deep. Visitors delight in observing and interacting with lobsters, hermit crabs, and other crawling sea critters in a several tanks, including two touch tanks, a seal pool (feedings at 11 AM and 4 PM most days), and shallow pools of icy-cold bubbling seawater.

🐾 **Woods Hole Oceanographic Institution (WHOI) and Ocean Science Exhibit Center** (508-289-2663; 508-289-2252 for tour reservations; whoi.edu), 15 School Street. Open mid-April through

WOODS HOLE SCIENCE AQUARIUM

December. A Rockefeller grant of $2.5 million got WHOI off the ground in 1930, and since then its annual budget has grown to about $220 million. It is the largest independent oceanography lab in the country. About 1,000 students and researchers from all over the world are employed here year-round. During World War II, WHOI worked on underwater explosives and

WOODS HOLE OCEANOGRAPHIC INSTITUTE

submarine detection. Today scientists study climate issues, undersea volcanoes, ocean and coastal pollution, deep-sea robotics and acoustics, and large and small marine life. Relatively unpolluted waters and a deep harbor make Woods Hole an ideal location for this work

WHOI buildings cover 200 acres. One-hour guided walking tours are offered weekdays at 10:30 AM and 1:30 PM during July and August. The tour covers a lot of ground and is geared to adults and teenagers. The small exhibit center shows excellent videos and has an interactive display with marine-mammal sounds and a fascinating display of *Alvin*, the tiny submarine that allowed WHOI researchers to explore and photograph the *Titanic* in 1986. While you're at it, don't miss the exhibit on the *Titanic*. $; walking tour free, but reservations required.

✳ **Marine Biological Laboratory (MBL)** (508-289-7623 tour reservations; mbl.edu), 127 Water Street. Tours, weekdays from late June through August, are very popular and restricted in size, so reservations are required at least a week in advance. Visitor center open May through October. Founded in 1888 as "a nonprofit institution devoted to research and education in basic biology," the MBL, affiliated with the University of Chicago, studies more than fish. It studies life at its most basic level, with an eye toward answering the question, "What is life?" Marine creatures tend to be some of the most useful animals in that quest. MBL scientists (including 49 Nobel laureates over the years) study the problems of infertility, hypertension, Alzheimer's, AIDS, and other diseases. It's not hyperbole to say there's no other institution or academy like it in the world. Guides lead excellent tours that include a video about what goes on at the MBL. History buffs will be interested to note that one of the MBL's granite buildings was a former factory that made candles with spermaceti (whale oil).

St. Joseph's Bell Tower, Millfield Street (north shore of Eel Pond). To encourage his colleagues not to become too caught up in the earthly details of their work and lose their faith in the divine, an MBL student designed this pink-granite Romanesque bell tower in 1929. He arranged for its two bells to ring twice a day to remind the scientists and townspeople of a higher power. (One bell is named for Gregor Mendel, the 19th-century botanist, the other for Louis Pasteur.) Nowadays the bells ring three times: at 7 AM, noon, and 6 PM. But really, do we need that much more reminding these days? The meticulously maintained **St. Mary's Garden** surrounds the tower with flowers, herbs, a bench, and a few chairs. Right on the harbor, this is one of the most restful places in the entire area.

Church of the Messiah (508-548-2145; churchofthemessiahwoodshole.org), 22 Church Street. Nine Nobel Prize winners are buried in the churchyard. This 1888 stone Episcopal church is admired by visiting scientists, tourists, and townsfolk alike. The herb meditation garden is a treasure. Classical music lovers will enjoy the "noontunes" concert series on Wednesdays in July.

🏺 ⚓ **Woods Hole Historical Museum** (508-548-7270; woodsholemuseum.org), 579 Woods Hole Road. Museum open mid-June to September; archives open year-round by appointment. This is a little gem. Located at the end of Woods Hole Road, near the

Woods Hole Library, this museum has two galleries with changing exhibits of local historical interest. It also maintains a good library on maritime subjects, more than 500 local oral histories, and a scale model of Woods Hole in the late 1800s. Dr. Yale's actual 1890s workshop is in a separate building. The adjacent Swift Barn exhibits small historic boats that plied these local waters long ago. Inquire about a free 60-minute **walking tour** around Eel Pond once weekly in July and August. And if you're around on Saturday mornings, drop by to watch volunteers help restore boats in the collection.

WOODS HOLE HISTORICAL COLLECTION

✳ To Do

BASEBALL 𝒶 **Fuller Field**, 790 Main Street, Falmouth. The **Commodores**, one of 10 teams in the Cape Cod Baseball League, play in July and August. Check online (falmouthcommodores.com) for schedules and team information.

BICYCLING & RENTALS ✳ **Corner Cycle** (508-540-4195; cornercycle.com), 115 Palmer Avenue, Falmouth, rents a variety of bicycles. It's a couple of hundred yards from the Shining Sea Bike Path. Ask for details about the **23-mile Sippewissett route**.
See also **Shining Sea Bike Path**.

BOAT EXCURSIONS & RENTALS ✳🐾 **Patriot Party Boats** (508-548-2626; patriotpartyboats.com, theliberte.com), 227 Clinton Avenue at Scranton Avenue, Falmouth. This excellent outfit operates sunset and two- and three-hour sails from late June to early September on the *Liberté*, a 74-foot, three-masted schooner that carries 49 passengers; $$$. The Tietje (pronounced *teegee*) family has been chartering boats since the mid-1950s, and they know the local waters like the backs of their hands. Patriot also has a year-round **ferry shuttle service** to Oak Bluffs on Martha's Vineyard. Although they primarily service commuters, you can hitch an inexpensive ride.

CAPE COD KAYAK

CANOEING & KAYAKING ✳🐾 **Cape Cod Kayak** (508-563-9377; capecodkayak.com), 802 MacArthur Blvd., Pocasset. Exploring salt marshes, tidal inlets,

WATERFRONT BEAUTIES

Nobska Light, Church Street, off Woods Hole Road. Although there are no regular tours, visits can be arranged for groups of 15 or more by calling 508-457-3210. Built in 1828, rebuilt in 1876, and automated in 1985, the beacon commands a high vantage point on a bluff. The light is visible from 17 miles out at sea. It's a particularly good place to see the "hole" (for which Woods Hole was named), the Elizabeth Islands, and the north shore of Martha's Vineyard, and to watch the sunset. Some 30,000 vessels—ferries, fully rigged sailing ships, and pleasure boats—pass by annually, as does the internationally regarded Falmouth Road Race.

SPOHR GARDENS, WOODS HOLE

❄ **Spohr Gardens** (508-548-0623; spohr-gardens.org), 45 Fells Road off Oyster Pond Road from Woods Hole Road or Surf Drive; park on Fells Road. Thanks to Charles and Margaret Spohr, this spectacular 6-acre private garden is yours for the touring. More than 100,000 daffodils bloom in spring, followed by lilies, azaleas, magnolias, and hydrangeas. (You'll share the wide path with geese and ducks.) Don't miss the iris garden by the water; remarkably, it's maintained by only two people! Free.

Consider bicycling here via the **Shining Sea Bike Path** (see *To Do*), which also has great water views.

A VIEW FROM THE SHINING SEA BIKE PATH TO NOBSKA LIGHT

SCENIC DRIVE

Take Route 28A to Old Dock Road to reach placid West Falmouth Harbor. Then double back and take Route 28A to Palmer Avenue, to Sippewissett Road, to hilly and winding Quissett Avenue, and to equally tranquil **Quissett Harbor**. At the far edge of the harbor you'll see a path that goes up over the hill of the **Knob**, an outcrop that's half wooded bird sanctuary and half rocky beach. Walk out to the Knob along the water and back through the woods. It's great for picnicking and sunset watching. Sippewissett Road takes you past **Eel Pond** and **Woods Hole** via the back way. Surf Drive from Falmouth to **Nobska Light** is also picturesque.

freshwater ponds, and the ocean shoreline from the vantage point and speed of a one- or two-seater kayak is a great way to experience the Cape. If you want to go kayaking but don't know where to go, they will recommend spots or locations suited to your interests and level of ability. They also organize small tours; $$$$+.

See also **Waquoit Bay National Estuarine Research Reserve** under *Green Space*.

FISHING & SHELLFISHING Procure freshwater and saltwater fishing licenses and regulations online (mass.gov/eea/agencies/dfg/licensing).

❋ **Eastman's Sport & Tackle** (508-548-6900; eastmanstackle.com), 783 Main Street. Head to this knowledgeable shop for regulations, local fishing information, and rod and reel rental, too.

𝒮 **Patriot Party Boats** (508-548-2626; patriotpartyboats.com), departing from Falmouth Charterboat Marina, 180 Scranton Avenue. Sport- and bottom-fishing from mid-June to early September. $$$$+.

Susan Jean (508-548-6901), Eel Pond, off Water Street, Woods Hole. From late May to mid-October, Capt. John Christian's 22-foot Aquasport searches for trophy-sized striped bass. This trip is for the serious angler—John usually departs in the middle of the night because of the tides.

Fish for trout, smallmouth bass, chain pickerel, and white perch at the town landing on **Santuit Pond** and on the **Quashnet River**. Surf casting is great on **Surf Drive** (after beach hours is best).

The chamber of commerce (see *Guidance*) publishes a very good visitor's fishing guide.

AMERICA (IS) THE BEAUTIFUL ALONG THIS TRAIL

Shining Sea Bike Path. The easygoing 10.7-mile (one-way) trail is one of Falmouth's most popular attractions. Following the old Penn Central Railroad line between Falmouth and Woods Hole, the path parallels unspoiled beaches, marshes, and bird sanctuaries. It was named in honor of Katherine Lee Bates, composer of "America the Beautiful." The last line of her song—"from sea to shining sea"—is a fitting description of the trail, which offers lovely views of Vineyard Sound, Martha's Vineyard, and Naushon Island.

The trail connects with several other routes: from Falmouth to Menauhant Beach in East Falmouth, and from Woods Hole to Quissett and Sippewissett. There is a trailhead and parking lot on Locust Street (at Mill Road) and another at Depot Avenue in Falmouth, as well as access points at Elm Road and Oyster Pond Road. Park here; it's very difficult to park in Woods Hole. Pick up a bike map at the chamber's office.

SHINING SEA BIKE PATH

GOLF ❊ **Ballymeade Country Club** (508-540-4005; ballymeade.com), 125 Falmouth Woods Road, North Falmouth. A tough semiprivate course; reservations required a week in advance.

❊ **Cape Cod Country Club** (508-563-9842; capecodcountryclub.com), 48 Theater Drive, off Route 151, North Falmouth. A scenic course with great variety.

❊ **Paul Harney Golf Club** (508-563-3454; paulharneygolfcourse.com), 74 Club Valley Drive, off Route 151, East Falmouth. This par-60 course offers somewhat narrow fairways but is generally within the ability of weekend golfers.

❊ **Falmouth Country Club** (508-548-3211; falmouthcountryclub.com), 630 Carriage Shop Road off Route 151, East Falmouth. An 18-holer, par 72, with a good mix of moderate and difficult pars, and a nine-holer, par 37.

HORSEBACK RIDING ❊ 🐎 **Haland Stable** (508-540-2552; halandstable.com), 878 Route 28A, West Falmouth. Reservations absolutely necessary. Haland offers excellent English instruction, individual and group lessons, and guided trail rides through pine wood groves, fields, a bird sanctuary, cranberry bogs, and salt-marsh land. Pony rides by appointment.

ICE-SKATING 🐎 **Falmouth Ice Arena** (508-548-0275; falmouthicearena.com), 9 Technology Park Drive, off Palmer Avenue, Falmouth. Call for public skating times; $.

PICK-YOUR-OWN 🐾 **Tony Andrew's Farm** (508-548-4717), 394 Old Meeting House Road, East Falmouth. Open mid-June through October, since 1935. Strawberries, strawberries everywhere, and other produce, too, all reasonably priced (especially if you pick your own). From the looks of it, East Falmouth was once the strawberry center of the world! Strawberry season runs from early June to early July, more or less. You can also pick your own peas in June, tomatoes in August, sunflowers from July to October, and pumpkins in late September and October. Lots of other family activities, too. Call ahead for availability.

SAILBOARDING **Cape Cod Windsurfing** (508-801-3329; capecodwindsurfing.com), 350 Quaker Road, North Falmouth, (off Route 28A, North Falmouth) on Old Silver Beach. Open seasonally. Old Silver Beach gets a good, predominantly southwestern wind, so there is good sailboarding here. You can take lessons or rent nonmotorized vessels like kayaks, canoes, and windsurfers. Or take a guided Jet Ski tour. This outfit also has radio communication helmets for students so instructors can be in constant touch with them. Also available for rental: paddleboards, pedal boats, and bicycles. Because the Sea Crest Hotel only offers parking to hotel guests and the nearby public (fee) lot fills up quickly, get there early.

TENNIS ❋ The following courts are public: the **elementary school**, Davisville Road, East Falmouth; **Lawrence School**, Lakeview Avenue, Falmouth; the **high school**, Gifford Street Extension, Falmouth (call for reservations); **Nye Park**, North Falmouth; **Blacksmith Shop Road**, behind the fire station, West Falmouth; and **Taft's Playground**, Bell Tower Lane, Woods Hole.

    Ballymeade Country Club (508-540-4005; ballymeade.com), 125 Falmouth Woods Road, North Falmouth. Outdoor Har-Tru and hard courts; lessons and clinics.

    Falmouth Sports Center (508-548-7433), 33 Highfield Drive, Falmouth. Indoor and outdoor courts.

❋ Green Space

Ashumet Holly Wildlife Sanctuary (508-362-7475; massaudubon.org), 286 Ashumet Road (off Route 151), East Falmouth. Crisscrossed with self-guided nature trails, this 45-acre Massachusetts Audubon Society sanctuary overflows with holly: There are more than eight species, 65 varieties, and 1,000 trees (from America, Europe, and Asia). More than

ASHUMET HOLLY WILDLIFE SANCTUARY

130 bird species also have been sighted here: Since 1935, nesting barn swallows have made their home in the rafters of the barn from mid-May to late August. Other flora and fauna thrive as well. Rhododendrons and dogwoods bloom in spring. Large white franklinia flowers (named for Benjamin Franklin) make a show in autumn, and in the summer Grassy Pond might overflow (depending on water levels) with rare wild-flower blossoms. Pick up the informative trail map before setting out. By the way, local philanthropist Josiah K. Lilly III (of Heritage Museums & Gardens fame; see *To See* in "Sandwich") purchased and donated the land in 1961 after the death of Wilfred Wheeler, who cultivated most of these plants and had been very concerned about holiday overharvesting of holly. $.

Waquoit Bay National Estuarine Research Reserve (508-457-0495; waquoitbayre serve.org), 131 Waquoit Highway, East Falmouth. Part of a national system dedicated to research and education regarding coastal areas and estuaries, Waquoit Bay has four components: **South Cape Beach State Park** (see also *Green Space* in "Mashpee"), **Washburn Island**, **Quashnet River Property**, and the **headquarters**, which houses watershed exhibits. More than 3,000 acres of delicate barrier beaches, pine barrier beaches, and marshlands surround lovely Waquoit Bay. Stop in at the headquarters for a trail map and schedule of guided walks in July and August. In summer look for "Evenings on the Bluff" talks as well as other activities like the Watershed Block Party in August, with hands-on activities and demonstrations about the bay that are per-fect for kids and families. Within South Cape Beach State Park is the little-used, mile-long **Great Flat Pond Trail** (accessible year-round). It winds past salt marshes, bogs, and wetlands and along coastal pine forests. Pine-filled, 330-acre, Washburn Island is accessible year-round if you have a boat. The 11 primitive island campsites require reservations.

Falmouth Moraine Trail. These 10 miles of trails are part of Cape Cod Pathways (capecodcommission.org), "a growing network of walking paths linking open space in

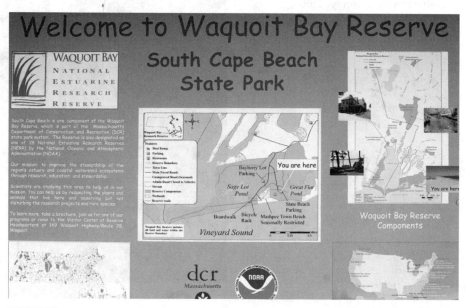

WAQUOIT BAY

FALMOUTH BEACHES

all 15 Cape Cod towns." I'm honestly at a loss as to what else to say besides directions and details are confusing.

See also the **Knob** under *To See*.

BEACHES Along Buzzards Bay and Vineyard Sound, 12 miles of Falmouth's 68 mile shoreline are accessible to the public via four beaches. (There are eight additional town beaches.) Generally, waters are a bit warmer off Falmouth than off northside beaches because of the Gulf Stream. Weeklong cottage renters qualify to purchase a beach sticker, obtainable at the Surf Drive Beach Bathhouse daily in summer. The permit costs $$$$+ for one week. Some innkeepers provide beach stickers. Otherwise, you may pay a daily fee to park at the following beaches. (The **Falmouth Beach Department** [508-548-8623] has further details.)

Menauhant Beach, on Vineyard Sound, off Route 28 and Central Avenue, East Falmouth. The best Sound beach, by far. Waters are less choppy on Vineyard Sound than they are on the Atlantic. Facilities include restrooms, lifeguard, and snack bar. Parking $.

✐ **Old Silver Beach**, on Buzzards Bay, off Route 28A and Quaker Road, North Falmouth. One of the sandiest beaches in town, this is a good one for children, as an off-shore sandbar creates shallow tidal pools. Facilities include a lifeguard and a snack bar. Parking $$.

Surf Drive Beach, on Vineyard Sound, on Surf Drive, off Main and Shore Streets, Falmouth. This beach attracts sea kayakers, walkers, and swimmers who want to escape "downtown" beach crowds. It's accessible via the Shining Sea Bike Path (see *To Do*); by foot it's 15 minutes from the center of Falmouth. Facilities include a bathhouse, snack bar, and lifeguard. Parking $$.

Falmouth Heights Beach, on Vineyard Sound, Grand Avenue, Falmouth Heights. Although there is no public parking, the beach is public and popular. Facilities include restrooms, a lifeguard, and lots of snack bars.

A WALK IN THE WOODS

🐾 **Beebe Woods**, access from Ter Heun Drive off Route 28A or Highfield Drive off Depot Avenue, behind the College Light Opera Company (see *Entertainment*), Falmouth. The Beebes, a wealthy family originally from Boston, lived in Falmouth from the late 1870s to the early 1930s. Generous town benefactors, they were among the first to purchase land in Falmouth. The 1878 Highfield Hall (508-495-1878; highfieldhallandgardens.org) was the centerpiece of the property and has been magnificently restored with the vision of Friends of Highfield. (They hold concerts, exhibits, and workshops here, all with marvelous acoustics. If you have an opportunity to get inside, seize it!) The 383 acres around it contain miles of public trails for walking, mountain biking, dog walking, and bird-watching. In autumn especially it seems like the whole town takes the trail to the **Punch Bowl** (a kettle pond). It's particularly pretty in May when the lady's slippers bloom.

HIGHFIELD HALL, FALMOUTH

PONDS ✎ **Grews Pond**, off Route 28 at Goodwill Park, Route 28, West Falmouth. Lifeguard in-season, as well as picnic and barbecue facilities and a playground. There are also hiking trails all around the pond.

WALKS **Waterfront Park**, Water Street near the MBL in Woods Hole, with shaded benches and a sundial from which you can tell time to within 30 seconds.

Eel Pond, off Water Street in Woods Hole. The harborlike pond has a drawbridge that grants access to Great Harbor for fishing boats, yachts, and research vessels moored here. (The walk around the shore is lovely.) The little bridge goes up and down on demand; in summer boats line up to pass through.

🐾 **Bourne Farm** (508-548-8484; saltpondsanctuaries.org), Route 28A, North Falmouth. Bucolic grounds open year-round; house open by appointment. Owned by the nonprofit Salt Pond Areas Bird Sanctuaries, Inc., this 1775 historic landmark includes a

EEL POND, WOODS HOLE

restored and furnished farmhouse, a bunkhouse (now a private residence), a barn, and 49 acres of orchards, fields, and wooded trails. It's a perfectly tranquil spot overlooking **Crocker Pond**, complete with a picnic area under a grape arbor. It's about as relaxing as it gets anywhere on the Cape! The property and barn are available for wedding rentals.

See also **Spohr Gardens** under the sidebar "Waterfront Beauties" and **Ashumet Holly and Wildlife Sanctuary**, **Grews Pond**, and **Waquoit Bay National Estuarine Research Reserve** under *Green Space*.

✳ Lodging

Falmouth boasts as wide a variety of places to stay as anywhere on the Cape but, unfortunately, many of its family motels have been converted to time-share units. Generally, your lodging dollars will go a long way around here.

BED & BREAKFASTS

IN FALMOUTH HEIGHTS

✳ 🐾 **Inn on the Sound** (508-457-9666; innonthesound.com), 313 Grand Avenue. Without exaggeration, as good as it gets anywhere on Cape Cod, Howard Grosser's place welcomes with contemporary grace, sophistication, and warmth. And it's waterfront to boot! He (and his niece Whitney Tynan) have a perfectly attuned

sense of what people want: Fabrics are fashionable but not overdone; sitting areas are comfortable and substantial but seaside-breezy; and the turn-of-the-20th-century B&B is elegantly upscale

INN ON THE SOUND

yet casual. Eight of the 10 bedrooms, each with an utterly tasteful aesthetic, have direct and expansive ocean views. Five have a private deck with those same ocean views. A lavish breakfast (served at individual tables) includes an artful array of breads, fruits, and perhaps an egg dish like *huevos oceaneros*. When you need a dose of relaxation, you might even find yourself visiting the website simply to listen to its ocean soundtrack. $$–$$$$.

⚓ **Bailey's by the Sea** (508-548-5748; baileysbythesea.com), 321 Grand Avenue. Open mid-May through October. The accommodating innkeepers offer six rooms with fabulous views at this nicely renovated waterfront B&B. The first-floor living space helps, too: It boasts a wraparound porch with a dozen picture windows and plenty of rocking chairs. In the comfortable guest rooms (with flat-screen TVs), decor ranges from Victorian to Japanese to traditional. Families should inquire about adjoining rooms at special rates. Third-floor rooms are particularly spacious. A full breakfast, served on the porch, might include poached peaches with white cheese mousse, a rolled omelet, and freshly baked bread. Bailey's blended juice drinks are a specialty. $$–$$$.

ON OR NEAR THE FALMOUTH GREEN

❄ **Captain's Manor Inn** (508-388-7336; captainsmanorinn.com), 27 Main Street. Well, well, well: This place continues to amaze me by raising the bar higher with each passing year. If you want to be close to downtown but a world away, this Georgian plantation-style house—the only one of its kind on Cape Cod—is set back from the road in the heart of the historic district. Innkeepers Trish and Kevin Robinson are the proud and hospitable hosts of this elegant B&B. Guest rooms are large enough not to be overwhelmed by tall, shuttered casement windows, while the living room,

CAPTAIN'S MANOR INN

with its impressively high ceilings, is casually elegant. The backyard parklike gardens and a gazebo are visible from the wraparound porch. Full breakfast at individual tables included. (As a footnote: Thinking of eloping? They have a package for that.) $$–$$$.

❄ 🐾 **The Palmer House Inn** (508-548-1230; palmerhouseinn.com), 81 Palmer Avenue. Innkeepers Pat and Bill O'Connell run an upscale Victorian B&B that's chock-full of period appointments and fanciful decor right in the middle of town. The main house is a Queen Anne beauty with stained-glass windows, shiny hardwood floors, and front-porch rockers. I particularly like the rooms, many with gas fireplace, in the adjacent guest house because they afford greater privacy. In all, the O'Connells preside over 16 "bedchambers" and one cottage suite, all with robes, lots of lace, flowers, triple sheeting, and turndown service. Breakfast is elaborate and full, served at individual tables. Loaner bikes are available. $$–$$$.

✒ 🐾 **Captain Tom Lawrence House Inn** (508-548-9178; captaintomlawrence .com), 75 Locust Street, Open February through December. This 1861 former sea captain's home is a pleasant and friendly B&B operated by Anne Grebert and Jim Cotter. The inn, set back from the road, offers six comfortable rooms with mini-fridges, showers (as opposed to bath tubs), and carpeting (to keep down the noise). A few of the bathrooms are small, so if you are large, inquire. Families might appreciate the efficiency apartment with private entrance. A full breakfast is served at two tables in the combo living/dining room. $–$$.

IN WOODS HOLE

❄ ✒ **Woods Hole Passage** (508-548-9575; woodsholepassage.com), 186 Woods Hole Road. On the road connecting Woods Hole and Falmouth, Julie and Martha's quiet B&B has a delightful feel. Its 2 acres of gardens are best enjoyed from the hammock or from the plentiful lounge chairs. The attached barn has five renovated guest rooms; second-floor rooms are more spacious, with vaulted ceilings and exposed beams. Decor is crisp country-modern, and each room has a bold splash of color. A full breakfast (served on the relaxing back patio) is included, as are loaner bikes, beach chairs, beach towels, and use of the outdoor shower. The owners have three kids of their own, so families feel right at home here. The B&B is within walking distance of a beach. $$.

OTHER PLACES TO STAY **Sands of Time** (508-548-6300; sandsoftime.com), 549 Woods Hole Road, Woods Hole. Open April to mid-November. This motel has been in Susie Veeder's family since the mid 1960s, and you'd be hard pressed to find as much family pride elsewhere. Who stays? Some guests missed the last ferry; others know it's a convenient place for exploring Woods Hole (a five-minute walk away). And the rooms? There are 20 air-conditioned motel units (most with a delightful view of Little Harbor and two with kitchenettes), an apartment (eh), and 15 nice and large innlike rooms in an adjacent 1870s house, many with a harbor view and working fireplace. Fresh flowers, morning coffee and doughnuts, a small heated pool, and morning newspapers set this place apart. It's also a short walk to the

WOODS HOLE PASSAGE

beach and is adjacent to the Shining Sea Bikeway. $–$$.

✻ ✐ ☀ ♟ **Seaside Inn** (508-540-4120; seasideinnfalmouth.com), 263 Grand Avenue, Falmouth Heights. Across from Falmouth Heights Beach (see *Green Space*) and playing fields, this way-above-average, family-oriented motel has 23 rooms. Rates vary widely and are based on the degree of water view and amenities; whether the room has access to a deck, full kitchen, or kitchenette; and if the deck is shared or private. Rooms in the back building are the nicest, but the reservation folks won't guarantee a particular room. Too bad, because the third-floor rooms are the best. $–$$.

By the way, the Falmouth branch of the **British Beer Company** (508-540-9600; britishbeer.com) is on the premises. It's a fine place for an authentic stout or ale on tap. (Note I didn't mention the food.) Live music on weekends and most summer nights.

✐ **Mariner's Point Resort** (508-457-0300; marinerspointresort.com), 425 Grand Avenue, Falmouth. Open mid-April to late October. This bilevel time-share offers 37 efficiency studios and apartments within a short stroll of Falmouth Heights Beach (see *Green Space*). Most of the four-person units overlook the pool area; a few have unobstructed views of Vineyard Sound and a town-owned park popular with kite fliers. $–$$.

RENTAL HOUSES & COTTAGES
Real Estate Associates (capecodhouses .com) in North Falmouth (508-563-7173), West Falmouth (508-540-3005), Falmouth (508-548-0200), or Pocasset (508-563-5266).

CAMPGROUNDS ☀ **Sippewissett Campground & Cabins** (508-548-2542; sippewissett.com), 836 Palmer Avenue, Falmouth. Open mid-May to mid-October. This well-run, private campground has cabins, tepees, and 100 large campsites for tents, trailers, and RVs;

clean, large bathrooms and showers; free shuttles in July and August to Chapoquoit Beach and year-round to the Martha's Vineyard ferry. $.

See also **Waquoit Bay National Estuarine Research Reserve** under *Green Space*.

✻ Where to Eat

Falmouth and Woods Hole restaurants satisfy all palates and budgets through upscale bistro dining, waterfront fish houses, taverns, and diners.

DINING OUT

IN FALMOUTH

✻ **The Glass Onion** (508-540-3730; the glassoniondining.com), 37 North Main Street. Open D. Dining in Falmouth (and the Upper Cape for that matter) hasn't been the same since The Onion burst onto the scene in 2010. Utilizing market-fresh ingredients from start to finish, the chef-owners sure know how to please. I've been known to dine here three nights over a 10-day period, but I moderate in other ways by selecting lobster strudel only once per trip. No reservations. $$$$.

THE GLASS ONION

❋ 🍴 **La Cucina Sul Mare** (508-548-5600; lacucinasulmare.com), 237 Main Street. Open L, D. This Northern Italian and Mediterranean eatery with outdoor seating offers portions so large that you should think about sharing dishes. To make matters even better, the husband and wife team of Cynthia and Mark Cilfone do a super job of making it feel like one giant dinner party here (reservations only for parties of five or more). Intimate, charming, and villa-like, La Cucina has been offering fresh, Old World pasta and seafood specials since 2002. Live music on Sundays. L $–$$, D $$–$$$.

Anejo Mexican Bistro & Tequila Bar (508-388-7631; anejomexicanbistro.com), 188 Main Street. Open L, D. This place excels in adventurous Mexican dishes, tequila cocktails, and outside dining. It's almost impossible to go wrong with any of their house specials (like chile rellenos, carne asada, or pork carnitas), but don't overlook their excellent cod. I always judge places like this on their house margaritas and guacamole: the latter as a side dish would feed a small army, while the house version of the classic drink rules.

Osteria La Civetta (508-540-1616; osterialacivetta.com), 133 Main Street. Open L, D. When you want to linger, this Old World and family-style trattoria has few equals—partly because service is so "relaxed" and partly because that's the way things are done in the home country. (That didn't change when the Osteria doubled in size and a little something was lost in translation.) All of the six or seven main dishes (including the gluten-free pasta) are made completely from scratch. Come hungry and do it up with all four courses: antipasti, primi, secondi, and contorni. Or eat lighter at the little bar. L $$ (weekends only), D secondi $$$.

❋ 🍷 🍸 **Chapoquoit Grill** (508-540-7794; chapoquoitgrill.com), 410 West Falmouth Highway, West Falmouth. Open D. From the moment this eclectic New American bistro opened in the early 1990s, it was a success. Still run by the original owners with their loyal chef overseeing the kitchen, "Chappy's" has a Grateful Dead kind of cult following (i.e., regulars who would follow them anywhere no matter what). You can spot the neighborhood folks who appreciate the low-key atmosphere: They order from the nightly specials menu. Pasta dishes are always superb. The popular wood-fired, super-thin-crust pizzas are also excellent. No reservations are taken, so get there when it opens at 5 PM or be prepared for a wait in the convivial bar. $$.

IN WOODS HOLE

❋ **Water Street Kitchen and Public House** (508-540-5656; waterstreetkitchen.com), 56 Water Street. Open D. Housed within the former Fishmonger, the casually romantic Kitchen offers upscale waterfront dining, plenty of seafood dishes, and fresh-from-the-farm seasonal fare. The ever-changing expressive menu might include pan-fried shishito peppers with lime ponsu; sea scallops with truffled beets and cauliflower purée; or a flat iron steak with lobster-bacon hash. The mint-lemonade soda is rather refreshing for a change, but as you can imagine, they have an ample selection of wines, sake, and a creative cocktail list. D $$$.

EATING OUT

IN FALMOUTH

❋ **Parkside Market** (774-763-2066; parksidemarket.com), 281 Main Street. Open B, L, D. When you want a quick meal with very good food (and *huuuge* portions) at very good prices, think Parkside. It's nothing fancy inside (although the food is fancier than you'd think), but you can feed a family of four without mortgaging your future. From burgers and delicious fish-and-chips to a three-cheese sandwich with avocado and light and creamy (superb) clam chowder, you'll be pleased with this friendly joint. $–$$$.

Clam Shack (508-540-7758), 227 Clinton Avenue. Open L, D, late May to early September. There is rarely enough room inside this old-time and favored shack, but it's just as well—head to the back deck to munch on fried clams, scallops, and fish while watching pleasure boats and fishing boats come and go. No credit cards. $–$$.

Simply Divine Pizza (508-548-1222; divinepizza.com), 271 Main Street. This might be the Cape's best pizza: stone-fired Neapolitan with a thin and crispy crust. The whole package comes together here: creative offerings (like fig and bacon), relaxing atmosphere, and good service. There are pasta dishes, too. I bet you'll be tempted to eat here more than once.

Pies a la Mode (508-540-8777; piesalamode.com), 352 Main Street #4, near White Hen Pantry. Open B, L. I love this hidden gem, which makes everything from scratch and on premises. Take their amazing chicken pot pies (!!) and Cornish pasties to the beach, to the green, or home, and count yourself lucky to have found them! Excellence continues with dessert pies and gelato. $$–$$$.

Golden Swan (508-540-6580), 323 Main Street. Open L, D. When you tire of New American cuisine or seafood, you won't be disappointed with the Indian cuisine here—unless you hail from Bangalore. Too bad the interior is so dark. $$.

Peking Palace (508-540-8204; pekingpalacefalmouth.com), 452 Main Street. Open L, D. If you're hankering for take-out from your favorite suburban-style Chinese restaurant at home, the Peking Palace is your place. Along with a sushi bar, there must be 200 Mandarin, Szechuan, and Cantonese dishes on the menu. L $, D $–$$.

Betsy's Diner (508-540-0060), 457 Main Street, East Falmouth. Open B, L, D. The old-fashioned 1957 Mountain View Diner was transported in 1992 from Pennsylvania to Main Street, where it was placed on the site of another diner. The boxy addition isn't historic, just

CLAM SHACK

functional. Folks come for inexpensive fare: club sandwiches, breakfast specials, and the famous roast turkey dinner. Specials are generally very good and portions large. Breakfast is served all day to tunes from the '60s. $.

Mary Ellen's Portuguese Bakery (508-540-9696), 829 Main Street. Open B, L. In addition to traditional Portuguese offerings like kale soup and malasadas, these super-friendly (and family-friendly) folks offer breakfast omelets throughout the day and cheeseburgers, too. It's small, but it's a find. No credit cards. $.

Dana's Kitchen (508-540-7900; danas-kitchen.com), 881 Palmer Avenue. Open B, L. This overgrown farm stand with outdoor seating offers sandwiches, salads, and pastries in a tranquil, country-style setting. If only the ordering system were so tranquil . . . $.

Casino Wharf FX (508-540-6160; casinowharffx.com), 286 Grand Avenue. Open L, D, March to January. When this two-story upscale place supplanted one hosting wet T-shirt contests, everyone breathed a sigh of relief—the stunning waterfront location was accessible to all once again. I go only because of the views at lunch from one of two beach-front decks; the interior has soaring ceilings but rather conservative decor. The bar plays a central role in the dining room. Check out the weekend evening entertainment on the deck. L $-$$, D $$-$$$.

The Flying Bridge (508-548-2700; flyingbridgerestaurant.com), 220 Scranton Avenue. Open D. The only reason I'm including this is because of its prominent harborfront location. If that persuades you, the only thing I recommend is lobster. $$.

See also **Liam Maguire's** and **Boathouse** under *Entertainment*.

IN WOODS HOLE

❋ ✐ **Quicks Hole Tavern** (508-495-0048; quicksholewickedfresh.com), 29 Railroad Avenue. Open L, D. Part taqueria, part tavern, part farm-to-table fine dining, the bustling Quicks Hole has an enviable perch right across from the ferry terminal for the Vineyard. Nothing like watching your ship come in—but please get in line way before that! L $-$$, D $$-$$$.

❋ ✐ ϒ **Captain Kidd** (508-548-8563; thecaptainkidd.com), 77 Water Street. Both the tavern and fancier waterfront section overlooking Eel Pond are open L, D. This local watering hole is named for the pirate who supposedly spent a short time in the environs of Woods Hole on the way to his execution in England. As such, a playful pirate mural hangs above barrel-style tables across from the long, hand-carved mahogany bar. The Kidd offers specialty pizzas, burgers, sandwiches, fish-and-chips, scrod, steaks, and blackboard fish specials. The glassed-in patio with a woodstove is a cozy place to be in winter. The only drawback here: The staff is at times more attentive to the TV at the bar than they are to patrons. Still, it's an institution, with bouncers. Tavern $$, waterfront dining $$-$$$. No credit cards.

❋ **Pie in the Sky** (508-540-5475; woodshole.com/pie), 10 Water Street. Open 364 days a year ("at least 5 AM–10 PM"). This funky—in a good way—institution has strong coffee (they roast

PIE IN THE SKY

it themselves), strong WiFi, good handmade pastries, hearty sandwiches, and homemade soups. There are a few tables inside and garden/streetside. In summer, frequent patio entertainment packs a crowd that extends up the hillside. It's inevitably my first and last stop in Woods Hole. $-$$.

COFFEE, ICE CREAM, & MARKETS

❋ **Coffee Obsession** (508-540-2233; coffeeobsession.com), 110 Palmer Avenue, Falmouth; and 38 Water Street in Woods

COFFEE OBSESSION

Hole Village. Caffeine addicts flock to "Coffee O" for bracing espressos, a slice of coffee cake, and a smidgen of counter-culture à la Falmouth and Woods Hole. Eggnog, apple cider, and other seasonal beverages, too. A retail shop serves all your chai- and coffee-related needs.

Smitty's Ice Cream (508-457-1060; smittysic.com), 326 East Falmouth Highway, Route 28, East Falmouth. My dear friend Jan loved this place and so do I—by extension and on its own merits. (Also in Barnstable on Route 6A, in Mashpee at the rotary of Routes 28 and 151, and in North Falmouth on Route 28A.)

✴ **West Falmouth Market** (508-548-1139), 623 Route 28A, West Falmouth. A great neighborhood place to stop for light groceries, deli sandwiches, and wine.

✴ **Windfall Market** (508-548-0099; windfallmarket.com), 77 Scranton Avenue, Falmouth. Prepared foods, a deli section, lobsters, and homemade breads are baked fresh daily.

✴ **Ben & Bill's Chocolate Emporium** (508-548-7878; benandbills.com), 209 Main Street, Falmouth. This old-fashioned sweets shop is lined with walls of confections, some made on the premises. But the store's best offering? Excellent store-made ice cream served in abundant quantities.

See **Pie in the Sky**, too.

✴ Entertainment

🎵 **Band concerts**, July and August. The **Falmouth Town Band** performs at **Marine Park**, on the west side of the Inner Harbor, on Thursday evenings. Bring a chair or a blanket and watch the kids dance to simple marches and big-band numbers. Or wander around and look at the moored boats. There are also free Friday concerts at 6 PM at **Peg Noonan Park** on Main Street in July and August.

🎵 **Movies Under the Stars** (falmouth villageassociation.com), Peg Noonan Park on Main Street, Falmouth. Late June through August. Family-friendly movie starts at dusk every Wednesday. It's a charming way to spend the evening—rather like a drive-in of yore, except without the car!

College Light Opera Company (508-548-0668; collegelightoperacompany .com), 58 Highfield Drive, Depot Avenue, Falmouth. Performances late June to late August. Founded in 1969, this talented and energetic company includes music majors and theater arts students from across the country. Reserve early, as these performances sell out quickly. $$$$.

Highfield Hall (508-495-1878; high fieldhall.org). After a $6.5 million labor of love, this magnificently restored 1878 manse opened as a community cultural center. It holds concerts, exhibits, and workshops, all with marvelous acoustics. April to November.

Woods Hole Folk Music Society (508-540-0320; arts-cape.com/whfolk music), Community Hall, 68 Water Street, Woods Hole. Well-known folkies generally play on the first and third Monday of each month, except December. $$.

The Cape Cod Theatre Project (508-457-4242; capecodtheatreproject.org), Falmouth Academy, 7 Highfield Drive, Falmouth. Established by two New York actors who were vacationing in Woods Hole in 1994, the project stages readings of new American plays in July. $$$.

See also **Highfield Hall** in the "A Walk in the Woods" sidebar under *Green Space*.

MOVIES

✴ 🐾 ⚲ **Regal (Hoyts) Cinemas Nickelodeon 5** (844-462-7342), 742 Nathan Ellis Highway, North Falmouth. Art house, independent, and first-run flicks.

⚲ NIGHTLIFE

✴ **Liam Maguire's Irish Pub & Restaurant** (508-548-0285; liammaguire.com),

LIAM MAGUIRE'S IRISH PUB & RESTAURANT

273 Main Street, Falmouth. It doesn't get any more fun than this unless you go to South Boston or Dublin. Irish students serve shepherd's pie, Irish beef stew, or fish-and-chips in beer batter ($$ at L, D). Food is average, the sandwiches a bit better, and the quinoa salad pretty darn good. Come for beer (Guinness on draft) and live entertainment year-round (including sing-alongs). Liam himself plays some nights.

Shuckers World Famous Raw Bar & Café (508-540-3850; shuckerscapecod .com), 91A Water Street. When you're in the mood for beer in plastic cups, this place has a seat with your name on it.

Pier37 Boathouse (508-388-7573; falmouthpier37.com), 88 Scranton Avenue, Falmouth. Open late April to mid-October. The Boathouse jumps with live music and lively crowds.

✳ Selective Shopping

✳ Between the quality of its shops and the strollability of the street, you can easily pass a couple of very pleasant hours on Falmouth's Main Street.

ART GALLERY **Falmouth Artists Guild** (508-540-3304; falmouthart.org), 137 Gifford Street at the corner of Dillingham Avenue. This nonprofit guild (active since the 1950s) holds eight to 13 exhibitions annually, a few of which are juried; classes; and various fund-raising auctions. See *Special Events* for the sand sculpture contest.

ARTISANS **Woods Hole Handworks** (508-540-5291), 68 Water Street, Woods Hole. Open mid-June to mid-October.

SHOPPING ON MAIN STREET, FALMOUTH

WOODS HOLE HANDWORKS

This tiny artisans cooperative, perched over the water near the drawbridge to Eel Pond, has a selection of fine hand-made jewelry, scarves, weaving, and beadwork.

Under the Sun (508-540-3603; underthesunwoodshole.com), 22 Water Street, Woods Hole. An eclectic selection of handcrafted jewelry, pottery, glass, and wood. Although the quality is somewhat uneven, the very good far outweighs the all right.

BOOKSTORES 🐦 ✐ **Eight Cousins Children's Books** (508-548-5548; eightcousins.com), 189 Main Street. Long before it won the equivalent of the Pulitzer Prize for children's bookstores in 2002, this excellent shop enjoyed broad and deep roots in the community. Named for one of Louisa May Alcott's lesser-known works, Eight Cousins stocks more than 17,000 titles and is a great resource, whether you're a teacher, a gift buyer, or entertaining a child on a rainy afternoon.

It continues to excel with kids' programs, regular story times, and great service. Don't miss artist Sarah Peters's Alphabet Chair metal sculpture in front of the store. It's a favorite with kids *and* adults, who love to sit on it and feel the different textures of the individual letters that make up the throne.

CLOTHING **Maxwell & Co.** (508-540-8752; maxwellandco.com), 200 Main Street. Absolutely fine men's and women's clothing.

Liberty House (508-548-7568; libertyhousecapecod.com), 89 Water Street, Woods Hole; 119 Palmer Avenue (508-548-3900), Falmouth. Falmouth store open mid-April to January; Woods Hole store open mid-April to December. Good taste and reasonable prices for linen shorts and slacks, sundresses, stacks of cotton T-shirts, and gifts.

FARMERS' MARKET At Falmouth Marine Park on Scranton Avenue, every Thursday mid-June to mid-October.

MALL **Falmouth Mall** (508-790-2844; falmouth-mall.com), 137 Teaticket Highway. A smaller version of the nearby Cape Cod Mall in Hyannis.

SPECIAL SHOPS **Rosie Cheeks** (508-548-4572), 233 Main Street. Women's clothing and home accents.

Twigs (508-540-0767), 178 Main Street. Practical, decorative, and functional accessories for the home and garden.

✷ Special Events

Early–mid-July: **Arts and Crafts Street Fair**. Main Street fills with crafts, artisans, and food stalls.

Late July–early August: **Woods Hole Film Festival** (508-495-3456; woodsholefilmfestival.com). This is the oldest independent film festival in Cape Cod. About 50 films by established and new

⚓ FAIRS AND POWWOWS

Early July: Powwow (508-477-0208, Wampanoag Tribe; mashpeewampanoagtribe.com), 483 Great Neck Road South, Mashpee. The People of the First Light's Mashpee Wampanoag Powwow has been open to the public since before 1924, and the Mashpee Wampanoag Tribal Council has sponsored it since 1974. The powwow attracts Native Americans in full regalia from nearly every state as well as Canada, Mexico, and some Central and South American countries. These traditional gatherings provide an opportunity for tribes to exchange stories and discuss common problems and goals. Dancing, crafts demonstrations, storytelling, pony rides, a "fire ball," a clambake, and vendor booths. Kids are encouraged to join in the dancing and nearly constant percussive music. $$.

Late July: Barnstable County Fair (508-563-3200; barnstablecountyfair.org), 1220 Nathan Ellis Highway, East Falmouth. A popular weeklong family tradition. Local and national musical acts, a midway, livestock shows, and horticulture, cooking, and crafts exhibits and contests. $.

filmmakers have been screened at various locations since the early 1990s.

Mid-August: **Annual Antiques Show**, Falmouth Historical Society; since 1970.

Falmouth Road Race (508-540-7000; falmouthroadrace.com). The event of the year in Falmouth: an internationally renowned 7-mile seaside footrace, limited to about 12,800 participants. Get your registration in before early May or you won't have a chance of running. Reserve your lodging ASAP—like when you send in your registration!

Mid- to late September: **Cape Cod Scallop Fest**, Cape Cod Fairgrounds, East Falmouth (capecodscallopfest.com). A weekend celebration with games, concerts, and restaurants and vendors offering dishes that celebrate—what

else?—the scallop. Rain or shine, as the eating takes place under a big tent; since 1969. $.

Early October: **JazzFest** (artsfalmouth .org), Arts Foundation of Cape Cod, Marina Park.

Late October: **Cape Cod Marathon** (508-540-6959; capecodmarathon.com). A high-spirited event, beginning and ending on Falmouth's village green and attracting more than 2,000 long-distance runners and relay teams. Commit by September or you'll be disappointed.

Early December: **Christmas by the Sea**. Tree lighting, caroling at the lighthouse and town green, and a significant Christmas parade. Popular house tours are operated by the West Falmouth Library (508-548-4709).

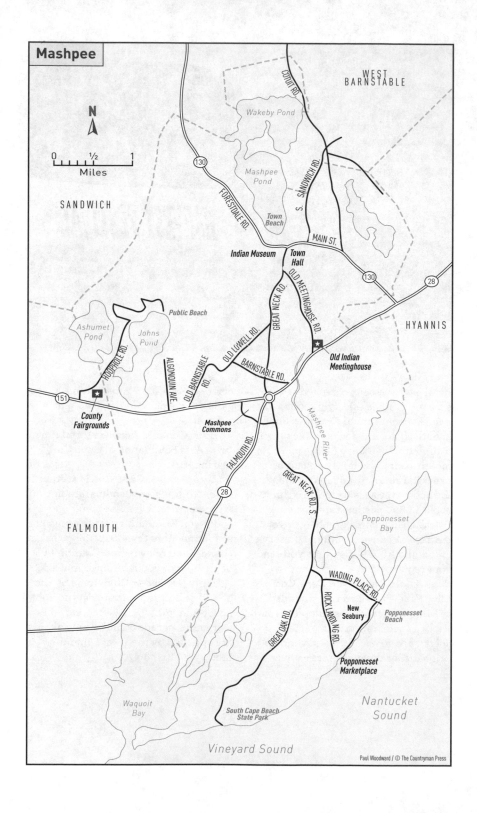

MASHPEE

Just east of Falmouth, fast-growing Mashpee (which means "land near the great cove") is one of two Massachusetts towns administered by Native Americans (the other is Aquinnah on Martha's Vineyard).

The largest developed area of Mashpee is **New Seabury**, a 2.5-square-mile enclave of homes, condos, restaurants, golf courses, shops, and beaches. When developers won their lengthy legal battle with the Wampanoag, the tribe—and the town—lost much of its prettiest oceanfront property. The only noteworthy beach is **South Cape Beach**, a relatively pristine barrier beach with several miles of marked nature trails and steady winds that attract sailboarders. Compared with its neighbors, Mashpee is a quiet place, with a year-round population of 14,000, plenty of commuters into Boston, and an upscale outdoor mall, **Mashpee Commons**.

When the *Mayflower* arrived at Plymouth, the Wampanoag population was an estimated 30,000; there are about 1,600 Wampanoag in Mashpee today.

For 1,000 years prior to the colonists' arrival, native Wampanoag Indians had established summer camps in the area, but with the settlement of Plymouth Colony they saw larger and larger pieces of their homeland taken away from them and their numbers decimated by imported disease.

MASHPEE PUBLIC LIBRARY

In 1617, three years after Capt. John Smith explored the area, six Native Americans were kidnapped and forced into slavery. By 1665, the missionary Rev. Richard Bourne appealed to the Massachusetts legislature to reserve about 25 square miles for the Native Americans. The area was called Mashpee Plantation (or Massapee or Massipee, depending on who's doing the translating), in essence the first Native American reservation in the U.S. In 1870 the plantation was incorporated as the town of Mashpee.

Mashpee wasn't popular with wealthy 19th-century settlers, so there are few stately old homes here. The Wampanoag maintain a museum and church, both staffed by knowledgeable tribespeople. In the 1930s classic *Cape Cod Ahoy!* Arthur Wilson Tarbell observed something about Mashpee that could still be said today: it's "retiring, elusive, scattered, a thing hidden among the trees."

GUIDANCE ❋ **Mashpee Chamber of Commerce** (508-477-0792; mashpeechamber. com), 5 N. Market Street within Mashpee Commons, Mashpee.

GETTING THERE *By car:* From the Sagamore Bridge, take Route 6 east to Route 130 south to North Great Neck Road to the Routes 151/28 Mashpee rotary. The Mashpee Commons shopping area at the rotary acts as Mashpee's hub.

MEDIA *The Mashpee Enterprise* (capenews.net) dishes up the local scene.

PUBLIC RESTROOMS Mashpee Commons (see *Selective Shopping*).

PUBLIC LIBRARY ❋ ✎ ☂ **Mashpee Public Library** (508-539-1435; friendsofmashpeelibrary.org), 64 Steeple Street, off Route 151 and adjacent to Mashpee Commons. One of the best on Cape Cod. Period.

MEDICAL EMERGENCY **Mashpee Family Medicine** (508-477-4282), Mashpee Health Center, 5 Industrial Drive at Route 28.

It's not an "emergency" (the kind you'd expect under this category, anyway), but many area water wells have been contaminated by years of training with grenades and other live munitions at the Massachusetts Military Reservation. I drink bottled water on the Upper Cape.

❋ To See and Do

HISTORIC HOUSES **Mashpee Indian Meetinghouse** (508-477-0208, Wampanoag Tribal Council; mashpeewampanoagtribe.com), 410 Meetinghouse Road off Route 28. Completely restored and located on the edge of what was once a Wampanoag-only cemetery ("They even took our burial ground away from us and made it theirs," laments a volunteer guide), this is the Cape's oldest surviving meetinghouse. It was built in 1684 by the descendants of Massasoit and moved to its current spot in 1717.

Mashpee Wampanoag Museum (508-477-9339; mashpeewampanoagtribe.com), 414 Main Street, on Route 130 across from Lake Avenue. This small, early-19th-century

MASHPEE INDIAN MEETINGHOUSE

house was built by Richard Bourne, minister and missionary to the Mashpee Wampanoag. (Check out the herring run at the end of the parking lot.)

FISHING & SHELLFISHING Procure freshwater and saltwater fishing licenses and regulations online (http://www.mass.gov/eea/agencies/dfg/licensing). That said, the town clerk's office will be happy to answer pertinent questions (508-539-1418), Town Hall, 16 Great Neck Road North.

Fish for trout, smallmouth bass, chain pickerel, and white perch at **Mashpee–Wakeby Pond** and the **Mashpee River** (access from Quinnaquisset Avenue). Surf casting is great at **South Cape Beach State Park** (see *Green Space*).

FOR FAMILIES ❋ ♂ ⬆ **Cape Cod Children's Museum** (508-539-8788; capecod-childrensmuseum.org), 577 Great Neck Road South. Toddlers love the castle, puppet theater, and 30-foot pirate ship; younger kids enjoy arts and crafts. Older kids I know . . . not so much. Check out the Starlab Planetarium and high-tech submarine with a working periscope, too. $.

WAMPANOAG INDIAN MUSEUM

GOLF ❋ **Quashnet Valley Country Club** (508-477-4412; quashnetvalley.com), 309 Old Barnstable Road, off Great Neck Road. This semiprivate course winds around woods and cranberry bogs; ponds and marshes surround 12 of 18 holes. Par 72, 18 holes. $$$$+.

PADDLEBOARDING **Mocean Cape Cod** (508-477-1774; moceancapecod.com), 34 Steeple Street, Mashpee Commons. Arrange your own group paddleboarding lesson, join a scheduled tour, or shop for top-quality water sport gear that enjoys raves from enthusiasts. $$$–$$$+.

TENNIS **Mashpee High School**, 500 Old Barnstable Road (off Route 151), has public courts.

✳ Green Space

BEACH **South Cape Beach State Park** (508-457-0495; waquoitbayreserve.com), on Vineyard Sound, Great Neck Road. Open late May to early September. The 432-acre state park boasts a lovely mile-long, dune-backed barrier beach, boardwalks, and nature trails. In-season facilities include restrooms and a handicap ramp onto the beach. Parking $ in-season; free off-season.

PONDS **Mashpee** and **Wakeby Ponds**, off Route 130. Combined, these ponds create the Cape's largest freshwater body (729 acres), wonderful for swimming, fishing, and boating. This area was a favorite fishing spot of both patriot Daniel Webster and President Grover Cleveland.

✳ WALKS **Lowell Holly Reservation** (508-636-4693; thetrustees.org), off South Sandwich Road from Route 130. Open year-round. Donated by Harvard University President Abbott Lawrence Lowell to the Trustees of Reservations in 1942, this tranquil 135-acre preserve contains an untouched forest of native American beeches and

SOUTH CAPE BEACH

more than 100 varieties of wild hollies, as well as white pines, rhododendrons, and wildflowers. There is a small bathing beach (no lifeguard) and 4 miles of walking trails and former carriage paths. $ parking fee late May to early September.

Mashpee River Woodlands/South Mashpee Pine Barrens. Parking on Quinnaquisset Avenue (off Route 28 just east of the rotary) and at the end of River Road off Great Neck Road South. The 8-mile hiking trail winds along the Mashpee River, through a quiet forest, and along marshes and cranberry bogs. Put in your canoe at the public landing on Great Neck Road.

Jehu Pond Conservation Area. Established in late 1990s, there are almost 5 miles of trails here on almost 80 acres encompassing woodlands, marshes, an abandoned cranberry bog, two islands, and Atlantic white cedar swamplands. Take Great Neck Road South toward South Cape Beach and follow the CONSERVATION AREA signs.

Great Flat Pond Trail, at South Cape Beach State Park. This easy-grade trail, a little less than a mile long, winds through woodland and wetland.

The Mashpee Environmental Coalition (mashpeemec.us) is a good source for trails.

See also **South Cape Beach State Park** under *Beach*.

LOWELL HOLLY RESERVATION

✳ Lodging

Family-style accommodations rule in Mashpee.

✳ ♦ **New Seabury Resort** (508-477-9400; newseabury.com), 20 Red Brook Road. This self-contained resort fronting Nantucket Sound consists of 13 "villages" of small, gray-shingled buildings that offer a variety of rental accommodations. Your best bet is to check VRBO and similar platforms. Facilities are de rigueur: restaurants, tennis courts, private golf courses, health club, outdoor pools, miles of private beach on Nantucket Sound, a small shopping mall, and mini-golf. You needn't leave the grounds, although that would be a shame. $$$–$$$$.

✳ ♦ **Cape Cod Holiday Estates** (508-477-3377; capecodholidayestates.com), 97 Four Seasons Drive. These 34 upscale time-share houses consist of airy one-, two-, and three-bedroom units with a full modern kitchen, Jacuzzi (except one-bedroom units), central air-conditioning, separate living and family room, and private patio. On-premise activities and facilities include an indoor heated pool, shuffleboard, game room, tennis, basketball, and a putting green. $$$ nightly but inquire about weekly rates.

RENTAL HOUSES & COTTAGES I can't recommend one agency over another in Mashpee; you'll be best served by an Internet search.

✳ Where to Eat

There aren't many choices in Mashpee, but the ones here are good. If you're not satisfied with these, stop at Mashpee Commons shopping area to see if any new restaurants opened recently.

DINING OUT ✳ ⌀ **Bleu** (508-539-7907; bleurestaurant.com), 10 Market Street at the Mashpee Commons. Open L, D; B on wintertime Sundays. I really love Bleu—from the very cool blue interior to the cushy seats where you could sit all afternoon to the side-alley alfresco dining. It's upscale but casual and definitely stylin', with a smart waitstaff decked out in all black. French chef-owner Frederic Feufeu excels in both inspired bistro and contemporary cuisine, from regional French classics like *cassoulet* with duck confit to seafood specialties. You'd almost be certifiably nuts not to save room for their caramel arborio rice pudding. In fact, let's just start and end with that. There's a nice wine selection, too. L $–$$, D $$$–$$$$.

✳ ⌀ **Siena Italian Bar & Grill** (508-477-5929; siena.us), 17 Steeple Street at the Mashpee Commons. Open L, D. Graham Silliman's spacious Italian ristorante features a contemporary, sophisticated menu that has been dishing from an open kitchen since 2006. In general, I always expect the quality of the cuisine to be a tad higher for the prices. That said, the skewered seared scallops are absolute perfection! If you cannot live by scallops alone, consider their addictive Caesar salad, thin-crust pizzas, or the Cotuit oysters and clams that hail from waters less than 3 miles away. As an added bonus, Siena offers discounted movie tickets to patrons heading to a flick at Mashpee Commons. Although I like the buzz and the booths in the dining room, there is also popular patio dining in the summer (when service can hit some rough patches). Either way, the bartender is known for margaritas and pomegranate martinis; wines are poured liberally. L $–$$, D $$–$$$.

EATING OUT **Marketplace Raw Bar** (508-539-4858; therawbar.com), 252 Shore Drive, Popponessett Marketplace, New Seabury. Open mid-June to mid-October. You know this tiny place has something going for it because locals outnumber tourists. Part Cape Cod, part Caribbean, the raw bar boasts loyal staff and fresh seafood.

BLEU

MASHPEE COMMONS

Since 1985, Bob Weekes' little joint has been offering casual fare from hot dogs to lobster. In fact, the lobster salad may be the best on Cape Cod! Grab a picnic table outside and chow down. $–$$$$.

Wicked (508-477-7422; wickedrestaurant.com), 680 Falmouth Road, in the South Cape Village shopping area. Open L, D. Wicked takes the traditional slice one step further. The dozen adventurous "fire-kissed pizza" offerings include organics, gluten-free, fig and prosciutto, scallop BLT, and BBQ chicken and pineapple. You gotta love TVs and loud music to enjoy the experience here. L $–$$, D $–$$$.

Popponeset Marketplace (popponessetmarketplace.com), New Seabury. If you're staying in the neighborhood, this little collection of shacks and seashell-lined pathways also has a good coffee joint, pizza place, and an Emack & Bolio's.

✿ ✍ **Cooke's Seafood** (508-477-9595; cookesseafood.com), 7 Ryan's Way, off Great Neck Road North adjacent to Mashpee Commons. Open L, D

seasonally. The area's best fried clams, along with other seafood, of course, and lighter fare. L $–$$, D $$.

✳Entertainment

Mashpee Commons (508-477-5400; mashpeecommons.com), Routes 151 and 28, Mashpee. Dozens of performances, including some free concerts, take place here. Keep your eyes peeled for current listings.

✳ ✿ ☂ **Regal Mashpee Commons** (844-462-7342), Mashpee Commons, 15 Steeple Street (Routes 151 and 28). With six movie screens.

✳Selective Shopping

✳ **Mashpee Commons** (508-477-5400; mashpeecommons.com), Routes 151 and 28. Open daily. If you're familiar with Seaside, the planned community of architectural note in Florida, you might recognize elements of this 30-acre outdoor shopping mall–cum–new town center. It's located at what the Wampa-noag used to call "pine tree corner," back when Mashpee was quieter than it is today. Developers have won numerous awards for transforming a strip mall into a veritable downtown commercial district. It's one of the most concentrated shopping venues on the Cape, boasting several good clothing stores, specialty boutiques, a movie theater, restaurants, cafés, and free outdoor entertainment in summer. Shops range from the Gap, Coldwater Creek, Origins, Pottery Barn, and Starbucks to more one-off shops like **Market Street Bookshop** (an excellent independent; 508-539-6985) and **McDermott Glass Studio** (with one-of-a-kind pieces; 508-477-0100).

❋Special Events

See the "Fairs and Powwows" sidebar in "Falmouth and Woods Hole."

MID-CAPE

■

BARNSTABLE

HYANNIS

YARMOUTH

DENNIS

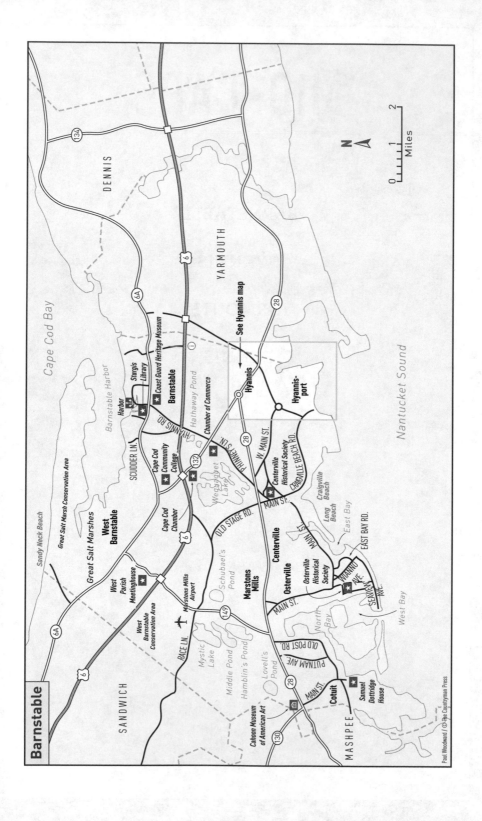

Barnstable

Cape Cod Bay

Nantucket Sound

DENNIS

YARMOUTH

SANDWICH

MASHPEE

134

6A

6

6

6A

6

28

28

28

28

149

130

1

132

See Hyannis map

Hyannis

Hyannis-port

W. MAIN ST.

CRAIGVILLE BEACH RD.

Craigville Beach

Long Beach

East Bay

East Bay

West Bay

North Bay

Centerville Historical Society

MAIN ST.

OLD STAGE RD.

PHINNEY'S LN.

HYANNIS RD.

SCUDDER LN.

Chamber of Commerce

Coast Guard Heritage Museum

Stargis Library

Harbor

Barnstable

Barnstable Harbor

Great Salt Marshes

West Barnstable

Sandy Neck Beach

Great Salt Marsh Conservation Area

West Barnstable Conservation Area

West Parish Meetinghouse

Cape Cod Chamber

Cape Cod Community College

Weyaquppet Lake

Hathaway Pond

Schubael's Pond

Marstons Mills Airport

Marstons Mills

RACE LN.

Mystic Lake

Middle Pond

Hamblin's Pond

Lovell's Pond

Centerville

Osterville

Osterville Historical Society

MAIN ST.

MAIN ST.

WIANNO AVE.

SEAVIEW AVE.

Cotuit

Samuel Dottridge House

Cahoon Museum of American Art

PUTNAM AVE.

OLD POST RD.

MAIN ST.

N

0 1 2

Miles

Paul Woodward / © The Countryman Press

BARNSTABLE

The Cape's largest town covers 60 square miles and is home to 48,000 year-round souls. It's also the Cape's second-oldest town, incorporated two years after Sandwich, in 1639. Barnstable actually comprises seven distinct villages—Cotuit, Marstons Mills, Osterville, Centerville, and Hyannis along Route 28, and West Barnstable and Barnstable along Route 6A. (Barnstable is sometimes referred to as Barnstable Village to distinguish it from Barnstable County, which embraces the whole of the Cape.)

On the bayside, Route 6A (also called Old King's Highway and Main Street) winds through **West Barnstable** and **Barnstable Village**. Development—or lack thereof—is rigidly controlled by the Old King's Highway Historical Commission, which regulates signage and does not allow gas stations, chain stores, or unconventional restorations within sight of the road. **Sandy Neck**, a haven for naturalists and beachgoers, is located off Route 6A, as are stately homes now converted into B&Bs.

On the southside, off Route 28 you'll find **Centerville**, **Osterville**, and **Cotuit**—parts of which front Nantucket Sound. Centerville's Main Street is full of handsome old homes built during the 19th century by affluent sea captains and businessmen. Osterville boasts some of the Cape's largest summer mansions, all with **Nantucket Sound** as their front yard. Osterville's Main Street is lined with upscale shops. At the turn of the 20th century, Cotuit was dubbed "Little Harvard," as it was home to many academicians. Cotuit's Main Street is lined with impressive Federal, Greek Revival, and Queen Anne houses, with American flags and Adirondack chairs dotting the lawns. The popular **Craigville Beach** dominates this side of Barnstable.

Landlocked and wedged between Routes 28 and 6, **Marstons Mills** is tiny, quiet, and residentially developed. It was founded by the Marston family, who built and ran the mills driven by the Goodspeed River.

Barnstable was founded by English Congregationalist minister John Lothrop and a small band of religious renegades who found Plymouth Colony a bit too settled for them. The neighborhood of Oysterville, as it was called, was purchased from the Native Americans in 1648 for "two copper kettles and some fencing." The area then was called Mattakeese, which translates as "plowed fields"—indeed, the land had already been cleared—but the settlers eventually named it for a similar harbor in Barnstaple, England.

GUIDANCE ❋ **Hyannis Area Chamber of Commerce** (508-775-2201; hyannis.com), 397 Main Street, Hyannis. The visitor center is located at the JFK Hyannis Museum, and the Hyannis chamber has information about all Barnstable villages.

GETTING THERE *By car:* Barnstable is 15 miles from the Cape Cod Canal. Take Route 6 to Exit 5 for West Barnstable (Route 149 North) and Marstons Mills, Cotuit, and Osterville (Route 149 South). Take Exit 6 for Barnstable Village (Route 132 West) and Centerville (Route 132 East).

By bus: The **Plymouth & Brockton** bus line (508-778-9767; p-b.com) connects Barnstable with other Cape towns, as well as with Boston's Logan Airport. The bus stops at the big commuter parking lot behind Burger King, Exit 6 off Route 6 at Route 132.

8:00	Break bread with fellow guests at your B&B.
9:30	Wander the dunes at Sandy Neck Beach.
11:15	Pore over centuries-old primary sources of Cape Cod history at the Nickerson Memorial Room at Cape Cod Community College.
12:30	Duck into the Anglicized and Japanese-style St. Mary's Church garden.
1:15	Enjoy a casual lunch at the Barnstable Tavern.
2:30	Pop into Route 6A antiques and specialty stores like West Barnstable Tables.
7:00	Dine on seafood with the locals at Five Bays Bistro.
9:00	Appreciate seasonal, fleeting beach plum ice cream from Four Seas.

GETTING AROUND *By shuttle:* The **Barnstable Villager** (800-352-7155; capecodtransit.org) connects Barnstable's Route 6A (at the courthouse) with the malls in Hyannis on Route 132, the Hyannis Transportation Center bus terminal, and the Barnstable harbor.

MEDIA The weekly *Barnstable Patriot* (508-771-1427; barnstablepatriot.com) has local news and gossip.

PUBLIC LIBRARIES Osterville Village Library (508-428-5757; ostervillevillageli brary.org), 43 Wianno Avenue, Osterville.
    Also see **Sturgis Library** under *To See and Do.*

MEDICAL EMERGENCY Cape Cod Hospital (508-771-1800; capecodhealth.org), 27 Park Street, Hyannis.

To See

ALONG OR NEAR ROUTE 6A

West Parish Meetinghouse (508-362-4445; westparish.org), 2049 Meetinghouse Road, off Route 149, West Barnstable. Open late May to early September. This fine example of early Colonial architecture is the second oldest surviving meetinghouse on Cape Cod. Don't miss it. (The oldest, the 1684 Old Indian Meetinghouse, is in Mashpee.) Its members belong to the oldest Congregationalist church fellowship in America, established in 1639 and descended from London's First Congregational Church. Founding pastor John Lothrop and his small band of followers erected their first meetinghouse in 1646. By 1715 the Congregational church had become so popular that Barnstable split into two parishes; the building you see today was constructed in 1717. Its bell tower, topped by a gilded rooster, holds a bell cast in Paul Revere's foundry in 1806; it still rings. Until 1834 the meetinghouse doubled as a town hall—so much for separation of church and state! In the 1950s, the meetinghouse was fully restored to its original modest, neoclassical beauty. Donations.

West Barnstable Cemetery, Routes 6A and 149. Near the stone wall along Route 6A, look for a large granite memorial bearing the following inscription: IN THIS CEMETERY LIE THE MORTAL REMAINS OF CAPT. JOHN PERCIVAL KNOWN AS "MAD JACK." BORN APRIL 3, 1779. DIED SEPTEMBER 17, 1862 IN COMMAND OF *OLD IRONSIDES* AROUND THE WORLD 1844–1846.

※ ⬆ **William Brewster Nickerson Memorial Room at Cape Cod Community College** (508-362-2131, ext. 4445; capecod.edu), 2240 Route 132, West Barnstable. Rainy day or not, visitors with more than a passing interest in the social

WEST PARISH MEETINGHOUSE

history, literature, institutions, and people of the Cape and islands owe it to themselves to stop at the "4 C's." Students voted in 1966 to set up this collection to honor the college's second president's son, a Vietnam War hero and *Mayflower* descendant. The significant collection contains more than 5,000 documents: religious treatises, biographies, autobiographies, oral histories, letters by dune poet Harry Kemp, scrimshaw, ship registers and logs, early diaries, U.S. Lifesaving Service reports, telephone directories from 1886 on, and aerial photographs. The place is a treasure trove for researchers; several excellent books have been written solely using these materials.

※ ✐ ⬆ **Sturgis Library** (508-362-6636; sturgislibrary.org), 3090 Main Street, Route 6A, Barnstable Village. Researchers from all over the U.S. (including entrepreneurs looking for information about shipwrecks) visit the country's oldest public library. It boasts one of the finest collections of genealogical records, dating to the area's first European settlers; more than 200 oral histories; an original 1605 Lothrop Bible; more than 1,500 maps and charts; and archives filled with other maritime material. William Sturgis, by the way, was born in the original part of the building, went off to sea at age 15 when his father died, and returned four years later as a ship's captain. Although he received no formal education, this self-made man obtained reading lists from a Harvard-educated friend and deeded the building to the town as a library. Use of the collections is free, though donations are welcome. The library also has a very good children's area.

Barnstable County Courthouse (508-362-2511), 3195 Main Street, Route 6A, Barnstable Village. Built in 1831–32, this imposing granite Greek Revival building is one of few reminders that tranquil Barnstable is the county seat for the Cape (and has been since 1685). Look for original murals and a pewter codfish in the main courtroom. On

LOTHROP HILL CEMETERY

the front lawn, a bronze sculpture commemorates James Otis Jr., a West Barnstable "patriot" who wrote the famous 1761 Writs of Assistance speech. President John Adams said Otis was the "spark by which the child of Independence was born." And on the side lawn, a memorial stands to Mercy Otis Warren, who self-published her Revolutionary War memoirs.

Lothrop Hill Cemetery, Route 6A, just east of Barnstable Village. Slate headstones are scattered across this little hillock, where John Lothrop and other Barnstable founders rest.

Barnstable Harbor, Mill Way Road off Route 6A. Fishing charters and whale-watching trips depart from this small harbor.

✎ ⌕ **Coast Guard Heritage Museum (Old Customs House)** (508-362-8521; coastguardheritagemuseum.org), 3353 Main Street, Route 6A, Barnstable Village. Open early May to early November. Before Barnstable Harbor filled with silt around 1900, it was the Cape's busiest port. The Old Customs House was built in 1856 to oversee the enormous stream of goods passing through the harbor. When harbor activity diminished, the brick Italian Renaissance Revival building served as a post office until the Barnstable Historical Commission made it its headquarters in 1959. The commission restored the beautiful building, painted it deep red, and opened this museum complex. On the grounds you'll find the Coast Guard Heritage Museum (showcasing the history of the Coast Guard and the lighthouse service), a blacksmith shop, and a circa-1690 jail cell (the oldest in the U.S. but closed because of a fire), complete with colonial "graffiti." $.

OFF ROUTE 28

✳ ✎ ⌕ **Cahoon Museum of American Art** (508-428-7581; cahoonmuseum.org), 4676 Falmouth Road, Route 28, Cotuit. This magnificent 1775 Georgian Colonial farmhouse was once a stagecoach stop on the Hyannis-to-Sandwich route. Today it houses a permanent collection of 19th- and early-20th-century American art, and features the whimsical and often humorous paintings of the late neoprimitive artists Martha and Ralph Cahoon. The building's low ceilings, wide floorboards, fireplaces, and wall stenciling provide an intimate backdrop for the artwork. Don't miss it. The museum also offers summer workshops and classes. $.

✎ ⌕ **Centerville Historical Museum** (508-775-0331; centervillehistoricalmuseum .org), 513 Main Street, Centerville. Open May to mid-December. The 1850s Mary

Lincoln House (no relation to Abraham) was built by Mary's father, Clark, a local tin-smith. Then along came Charles Ayling, a wealthy Cape businessman and philanthropist, who endowed a wing and assembled an entire Cape Cod colonial kitchen, complete with large open fireplace and dozens of iron utensils. The 14 rooms are filled with rare Sandwich glass, Civil War artifacts, maritime artifacts, historic quilts, costumes from 1750 to 1950, children's toys and games, perfume bottles, and A. E. Crowell's miniature duck carvings. Exhibits change throughout the season. $

✲ **The 1856 Country Store** (508-775-1856; 1856countrystore.com), 555 Main Street, Centerville. With the exception of the original wooden floors, the store is more picturesque outside than inside. Crowds do flock here for the selection of cutesy country and perfumed things.

Osterville Historical Museum (508-428-5861; ostervillemuseum.org), 155 West Bay Road, Osterville. Open late May to mid-September. The museum comprises three properties, well worth a visit for local history buffs. The **Captain Jonathan Parker House**, built circa 1824, contains period art, antiques, furniture, and dolls, as well as paintings and porcelain from the China trade. The one-room-deep **Cammett House**, a simple Cape Cod farmhouse built circa 1790, is furnished with period pieces. And the **Boat Shop Museum** showcases the famous Crosby-designed catboat *Cayuga*, built in 1928, and the *Wianno Senior* and *Junior*. Half models, tools, and historic Osterville waterfront photographs are also displayed. Don't miss the period colonial gardens maintained by the Osterville Garden Club.

Samuel B. Dottridge House (508-428-0461; cotuithistoricalsociety.org), 1148 Main Street, Cotuit. Open late May to early September. Owned by the Historical Society of Sansuit and Cotuit, this 1790 house contains historical but otherwise fairly unremarkable objects pertaining to daily 19th-century life. $.

SPECIAL PROGRAMS ✲ **Tales of Cape Cod (at the Olde Colonial Courthouse)** (talesofcapecod.org), 3046 Main Street, Route 6A and Rendezvous Lane, Barnstable

OLD CUSTOMS HOUSE

SCENIC DRIVES

From the center of Centerville, take South Main Street toward Osterville. Turn left on East Bay, which will wind around and become Seaview; follow that to the end. Double back and turn left on Eel River, then turn left onto Bridge. You will not be able to go very far on this road (it empties into a gated community), but it does cross a sparkling waterway. After turning around, follow West Bay back to Main Street.

You can also take Main Street off Route 28 in Santuit (as you head toward Falmouth on Route 28, turn left onto Main Street just before the Mashpee town line). Follow Main Street through Cotuit center, jog left onto Ocean View overlooking Nantucket Sound, then jump back onto Main Street and follow it to the end for more pond and Sound views.

Village. This simple, white-clapboard building served as the Barnstable County Courthouse from 1772 to 1832, when the "new" granite structure down the road was built. The secular Olde Colonial Courthouse then became a Baptist church until it was purchased in 1949 by Tales of Cape Cod, a nonprofit organization that preserves Cape folklore and oral histories. The organization sponsors an excellent summertime lecture series delivered by knowledgeable townspeople. (Refreshments alone are worth the price of admission.) $.

See also **Barnstable Comedy Club** under *Entertainment*.

✳To Do

AIRPLANE RIDES ✳ **Cape Cod Airfield** (508-428-8732; capecodairfield.com), Marstons Mills Airport, Route 149, Marstons Mills. These scenic tours, from the Cape's only grass-strip airport, can go virtually anywhere on the Cape. Reservations recommended. $$$$+.

BASEBALL ✺ The **Cotuit Kettleers** (kettleers.org) play at Lowell Park in Cotuit from mid-June to mid-August.

BICYCLING If you don't have a friend with a summer place in the exclusive Wianno section of town, the best way to enjoy the village of Osterville is to cycle or drive along Wianno Avenue to Seaview Avenue, then turn right onto Eel River Road to West Bay Road and head back into town.

FISHING & SHELLFISHING Procure freshwater and saltwater fishing licenses and regulations online (mass.gov/eea/agencies/dfg/licensing).

Wequaquet Lake in Centerville has plenty of largemouth bass, sunfish, and northern pike to go around. Limited parking along Shootflying Hill Road. Marstons Mills has three ponds stocked with smallmouth bass, trout, and perch: **Middle Pond**, Race Lane; **Hamblin's Pond**, Route 149; and **Schubael's Pond**, off Race Lane.

FOR FAMILIES ✳ ✺ **Cape Cod YMCA** (508-362-6500; ymcacapecod.org), Route 132, West Barnstable. In addition to a fitness and cardiovascular center, the YMCA offers tons of programs for adults and kids that are open to short-term visitors. Open swims daily. Drop off the children and go out to dinner while they do arts and crafts. The Y also has a summer camp with weekly sessions.

BARRIER BEACH BEAUTY

Sandy Neck Beach, on Cape Cod Bay, off Route 6A in West Barnstable, is one of the Cape's most stunning beaches. The entrance to this 6-mile-long barrier beach is in Sandwich. Encompassing almost 4,500 acres, the area is rich with marshes, shellfish, and bird life. Sandy Neck dunes protect Barnstable Harbor from the winds and currents of Cape Cod Bay. Sandy Neck was the site of a Native American summer encampment before the colonists purchased it in 1644 for three axes and four coats. Then they proceeded to harvest salt-marsh hay and boil whale oil in tryworks on the beach. Today a private summertime cottage community occupies the far eastern end of the beach. Known locally as the Neck, the former hunting and fishing camps, built in the late 19th century and early 20th, still rely on water pumps and propane lights.

Beach facilities include restrooms, changing rooms, and a snack bar. You can purchase four-wheel-drive permits at the gatehouse (508-362-8300). But six items must be in your car when the permit is issued: a spare tire, jack, ¾-inch board, shovel, low-pressure tire gauge, and something to tow the car. Parking $$.

SANDY NECK BEACH

GOLF ❄ **Cotuit Highground Country Club** (508-428-9863; cotuithighground.com), 31 Crocker Neck Road, Cotuit. Nine holes. $$–$$$.

Olde Barnstable Fairgrounds Golf Course (508-420-1141; barnstablegolf.com), 1460 Route 149, Marstons Mills. So close to the airport that you can see the underbellies of approaching planes from the driving range. $$$$+.

TENNIS Public courts are located at the **Centerville Elementary School** on Bay Lane; at the **Cotuit Elementary School** on Old Oyster Road; at the **Marstons Mills East Elementary School** on Osterville–West Barnstable Road; and at the **Barnstable–West Barnstable Elementary School** on Route 6A.

WHALE-WATCHING ⚓ **Hyannis Whale Watcher Cruises** (508-362-6088; whales .net), Mill Way off Route 6A, Barnstable Harbor. Daily departures, April to mid-October. A convenient mid-Cape location and a fast boat make this a good choice for whale-watching. An on-board naturalist provides commentary. Summertime sunset clambake cruises, too. $$$$+.

HYANNIS WHALE WATCHER CRUISES

✳Green Space

BEACHES **Millway Beach**, just beyond Barnstable Harbor. Although a resident parking sticker is needed in summer, you can park here and look across to **Sandy Neck Beach** (see the "Barrier Beach Beauty" sidebar) in the off-season.

⚓ **Craigville Beach**, on Nantucket Sound, Centerville. This crescent-shaped beach—long and wide—is popular with teens and college crowds. Facilities include restrooms, changing rooms, and outdoor showers. Parking $$.

Long Beach, on Nantucket Sound, Centerville. Centerville residents favor Long Beach, at the western end of Craigville Beach; walk along the water until you reach a finger of land between the Sound and the Centerville River. Long Beach is uncrowded, edged by large summer shore homes and a bird sanctuary on the western end. Although a resident sticker is required, I include it for my nonresident readers because it's the nicest beach, and Explorers can check it out off-season.

CRAIGVILLE BEACH

PONDS **Hathaway Pond**, Phinney's Lane, Barnstable Village, is a popular freshwater spot with a bathhouse and lifeguard. The following freshwater locations require a resident sticker: **Lovell's Pond**, off Newtown Road from Route 28, Marstons Mills; **Hamblin's Pond**, off Route

149 from Route 28, Marstons Mills; and **Wequaquet Lake**, off Shootflying Hill Road from Route 132, Centerville.

WALKS Sandy Neck Great Salt Marsh Conservation Area (508-362-8300), West Barnstable; trailhead at the parking lot near the gatehouse off Sandy Neck Road. First things first: Hike off-season when it's not so hot. It takes about six hours to do the whole circuit. The 12-mile (round-trip) trail to Beach Point winds past pine groves, wide marshes, low blueberry bushes, and 50- to 100-foot dunes. It'll be obvious that this 3,295-acre marsh is the East Coast's second largest. Beginning in June, be on the lookout for endangered piping plovers nesting in the sand. Eggs are very difficult to see and, therefore, easily crushed. If you're into camping they have a **primitive campground** open May to mid-October with four sites (first-come, first-served). Hike in the 3.3 miles with your gear; they provide wood, water (free), and bathroom facilities. Parking $$.

✎ **Long Pasture Wildlife Sanctuary** (508-362-1426; massaudubon.org), 345 Bone Hill Road. These 100 acres include wooded trails, tidal flats, and incredible views of Sandy Neck dunes. Dip into their guided hikes, children's programs, or kayaking and paddleboarding. $.

St. Mary's Church Gardens (508-362-3977; stmarys-church.org), Route 6A (across from the library), Barnstable Village. Locals come to these peaceful, old-fashioned gardens to escape summer traffic swells on Route 6A. In spring, the gardens are full of crocuses, tulips, and daffodils. A small stream, crisscrossed with tiny wooden bridges, flows through the property; the effect is rather like an Anglicized Japanese garden.

Tidal flats, Scudder Lane, off Route 6A, West Barnstable. At low tide you can walk onto the flats and almost across to the neck of Sandy Neck.

West Barnstable Conservation Area, Popple Bottom Road, off Route 149 (near Route 6), West Barnstable. Park at the corner for wooded trails.

Armstrong-Kelley Park, Route 28 near East Bay Road, Osterville. This lovely 8½-acre park has shaded picnic tables, flowers blooming throughout the summer, wooded walking trails with specimens identified, and wetland and woodland walkways. Look for rare trees like the umbrella magnolia and the Camperdown elm. This park claims to be the oldest and largest private park on the Cape.

SANDY NECK GREAT SALT MARSH CONSERVATION AREA

ST MARY'S CHURCH GARDENS

✳Lodging

While a number of historic B&Bs line Route 6A, I've included only a select few because each offers exceptional hospitality and are all quite different.

BED & BREAKFASTS ✳ **Honeysuckle Hill** (508-362-8418; honeysucklehill.com), 591 Route 6A, West Barnstable. Among the most welcoming innkeepers on the Cape (since Day One when they began in 2013), Nancy and Rick have applied their considerable talents to making this 1810 farmhouse a favorite. Their four rooms and two-bedroom suite (an extremely good value) have feather bedding, robes, fine English toiletries, flat-screen TVs, and marble baths. Friendly, elegant, and modestly furnished with a mix of white wicker and antiques, they're a breath of fresh air. I particularly like Wisteria, the largest, with a king bed, blue toile decor, and its own entrance. What's not to love—from the garden that boasts woodland walks and sitting areas to the spa tub with outdoor shower and a large screened-in porch. Nancy and Rick indulge guests with concierge services (they are a font of local information) and bountiful breakfasts. $–$$.

✳ 🐾 🦮 **Lamb and Lion Inn** (508-362-6823; lambandlion.com), 2504 Route 6A, Barnstable. Although it's the kind of place where guests are left alone if they want, proprietors Alice Pitcher and Tom Dott know a little something about service and hospitality: They operated a Relais & Châteaux restaurant in the

Hudson Valley before coming here. This transformed inn consists of 10 guest rooms (including the Lamb's Retreat cottage and the most excellent Barn-Stable that can accommodate families) surrounding an open-air heated swimming pool and hot tub. Long hallways are brightened with sky murals, and the diverse rooms are pleasant, with wicker and antiques. I particularly like Room 9, which gets great afternoon sun, and the suite with a private deck, hot tub, and kitchenette. Although rooms are quite different, most have a fireplace, half have a kitchenette, and most have a spiffy motel-style bathroom. Before leaving, ask to see the rare, triple-sided fireplace in the original 1740 house. A fine expanded continental breakfast is included, and for $5 extra you can order a hot breakfast. $$–$$$.

RENTAL HOUSES 🌊 **Craigville Realty** (508-775-3174; craigvillebeach.com), 648 Craigville Beach Road, West Hyannisport.

✳ Where to Eat

Barnstable isn't overflowing with dining options, but it does have two fine ones, a waterfront restaurant, an excellent local tavern, and the best homemade ice cream on the Cape. In the end, what more do you really need?

DINING OUT ✳ **Five Bays Bistro** (508-420-5559; fivebaysbistro.com), 825 Main Street, Osterville. Open D. Named for the five bodies of water that surround Osterville, this buzzy (or noisy, depending on your sensibilities) little place is urban and stylish—befitting a neighborhood awash with patrons sizing each other up and keeping up with the Joneses. As for the sophisticated fusion cuisine, it gets very good reviews across the board. Local seafood (perhaps done with an Asian twist) and lobster mac and cheese are always a good bet. $$$.

✳ 🌊 ♈ **Dolphin** (508-362-6610; the dolphincapecod.com), 3250 Main Street,

HONEYSUCKLE HILL

LAMB AND LION INN

Route 6A, Barnstable. Open L, D. This reliable and friendly watering hole, in chef-owner Nancy Jean Smith's family for three generations, features extensive seafood selections. At midday you'll find everything from crabcakes and oysters to salads, specialty sandwiches, and baked and fried seafood. At dinner it's a bit more elaborate. The Dolphin, complete with a long bar separated from the main dining room, is heavily patronized by locals who've been coming for years (and staffed by the same). L $–$$, D $$–$$$.

EATING OUT ❈ ⅋ **Barnstable Restaurant and Tavern** (508-362-2355; barnstablerestaurant.com), 3176 Main Street, Route 6A, Barnstable Village. Open L, D. Thanks to Bob Calderone and Susan Finegold, this old tavern in Barnstable's historic district is a decent choice—whether for a burger and beer in the tavern or a more substantial meal of fried seafood (or daily specials like sautéed sea scallops) in the main dining room. I

prefer the tavern, which attracts a slightly younger clientele. Salads are always a good bet. $$.

❈ **Craigville Pizza & Mexican Restaurant** (508-775-2267; craigvillepizza.com), 618 Craigville Beach Road, Centerville. Open L, D. Although this is a no-frills place, you can't beat it for these parts. $–$$.

DOLPHIN

SINFUL SCOOPS

♨ 🍴 **Four Seas Ice Cream** (508-775-1394; fourseasicecream.com), 360 South Main Street, at Centerville Four Corners. Open mid-May to mid-September. Founded in 1934, Four Seas is owned by Dick Warren, who took over from his father—who had owned it since 1960, when he bought it from the folks who had given him a summer job as a college student. Got that? The walls of this funky place, a former blacksmith's shop, are lined with photos of preppy summer crews, newspaper articles about Four Seas (it wins national ice cream awards every year), and poems penned in honor of past anniversaries. You can see that this place really inspires folks! It's named for the four "seas" that surround the Cape: Buzzards Bay, Cape Cod Bay, the Atlantic Ocean, and Nantucket Sound. Oh yes, about that ice cream: The Cape's best is made almost daily, using the freshest ingredients. The only downside: Every time I stopped by this past summer, it was way too melty and I had to gobble it down too quickly. Try the coconut or black raspberry. Lobster salad sandwiches are great, too. Really great.

❀ **Cotuit Fresh Market** (508-428-6936; cotuitfreshmarket.com), 737 Main Street, Cotuit. This old multiuse building would go unnoticed in Vermont, but on the Cape it's an anomaly. It's a convenience store–wine shop–grill–fruit and veggie market. $.

Nirvana Coffee Company (508-744-6983), 3206 Route 6A, Barnstable Village. What more can you ask for: strong coffee or green tea, a comfy vibe with pleasant service, breakfast sandwiches or gluten-free bagels, and some Adirondack chairs on the main drag when the weather is warm. Some people (no names, please) have been known to patronize this place daily when researching back-and-forth along Route 6A.

🍸 **Kettle Ho Restaurant & Tavern** (508-428-1862), 12 School Street, Cotuit. Open L, D. When you want to hang out with locals for a beer or mixed drink (and a great burger!), this friendly place is *the* place. Blink and you'll miss it because Cotuit only consists of four or five

BARNSTABLE RESTAURANT AND TAVERN

buildings. Even though it's been refurbished, it still feels divey—in a good way.

✳ Entertainment

Barnstable Comedy Club (508-362-6333; barnstablecomedyclub.org), 3171 Route 6A, across from the Barnstable Restaurant and Tavern, Barnstable Village. Performances November through May. Let's get something straight right off the bat: This is not an actual comedy club! Founded in 1922, the state's oldest amateur theater group performs more than comedies in this 200-seat theater—look for musicals and straight (though not heavy or provocative) theater. Since 1922 its motto has been "To produce good plays and remain amateurs." (Kurt Vonnegut got his feet wet here and was the club's first president.) $$$. No credit cards.

✳Selective Shopping

✳ All shops are open year-round unless otherwise noted. Osterville center, with a number of upscale shops, is good for a short stroll.

ANTIQUES **Harden Studios** (508-362-7711; hardenstudios.com), 3264 Main Street, Route 6A, Barnstable Village. This late-17th-century house was beautifully restored by Charles M. Harden in the mid-1990s and now functions as an antiques shop and gallery. It's a true family affair: Harden's son, Charles, operates an etching press and art gallery in the adjacent shed, and son Justin researches the fine antiques collection. The collection includes American antiques from the early 1700s to the 1840s; Empire and Federal pieces; Oriental rugs, lamps, and chandeliers.

Sow's Ear Antiques (508-428-4931; sowsearantiqueco.com), 4698 Falmouth Road, Route 28 at Route 130, Cotuit. Americana and primitive folk art and furniture sold from an 18th-century house; some garden antiques, too.

Cotuit Antiques (508-420-1234), 70 Industry Road, behind Cotuit Landing off Route 28, Cotuit. Henry Frongillo enjoys people and keeping his shop folksy. Since he buys whole estates, you never know what you'll find. Primarily, though, he offers fine furniture, collectibles, some art, pottery, and lots of great old signage and advertising memorabilia.

ART GALLERIES **Cape Cod Art Association** (508-362-2909; capecodartassoc.org), 3480 Route 6A, Barnstable Village. This nonprofit was founded in 1948 and displays a fine range of juried art and artists in a beautiful and airy gallery. Shows change monthly. Indoor and outdoor classes and workshops are offered.

Tao Water Art Gallery (508-375-0428; taowatergallery.com), 1989 Route 6A, West Barnstable. The offerings of this contemporary Asian gallery, representing more than 35 artists from post–Cultural Revolution China and the States, run the gamut from exceptional abstract painting to landscapes, sculpture, and Chinese contemporary art. At more than 5,600 square feet, one of the largest galleries on the Cape.

See also **Harden Studios** under *Antiques*.

BOOKSTORES ✳ **Books by the Sea** (508-420-9400; booksbythesea.net), 874 Main St. Head here to indulge in the strong local book selection; it's small but great. Look for special events by Cape Cod authors, too.

✳ **Isaiah Thomas Books & Prints** (508-428-2752; isaiahthomasbooks.com), 4632 Falmouth Road, at Routes 28 and 130, Cotuit. Jim Visbeck offers more than 70,000 antiquarian, first-edition, and slightly used books, including books for children. They're divided by age group and interest. He also offers appraisals, search services, and archival materials. The Cape's only antiquarian bookseller is simply marvelous; you could easily spend an afternoon here. (Well, I have.)

WEST BARNSTABLE TABLES

SPECIAL SHOPS West Barnstable Tables (508-362-2676; westbarnstablet ables.com), 2454 Meetinghouse Way, Route 149, West Barnstable. This showroom features the work of a dozen or so master craftsmen and artists, including that of Dick Kiusalas. Because it's difficult (not to mention prohibitively expensive) to find antique tables anymore, Dick makes tables using salvaged 18th- and 19th-century wood. His creations are exquisite and worth admiring, even if you don't have a couple thousand dollars to spare. Less expensive pieces include primitive cupboards made with old painted wood and found objects, and Windsor and thumb-back chairs.

Margo's (508-428-5664; margoshome .com), 27 Wianno Avenue, Osterville. Unusual picture frames, serving pieces, furniture, home accessories, bed linens, gifts, and interior design services.

✳ Special Events

Mid-July: **Osterville Village Day** (talk to Gail at 508-420-4590). Third Saturday; includes a crafts and antiques fair, a road race, children's events, and a parade.

July 4: **Hyannis Village Parade**, Main Street, Hyannis.

Early July: **Fireworks** over Lewis Bay at dusk (usually the Saturday of Fourth of July weekend); view from Veterans Beach. The Cape Symphony Orchestra plays at Aselton Park before the display.

✤ Late July: **Barnstable County Fair** (508-563-3200; barnstablecountyfair .org), Route 151, East Falmouth. Local and national music acts, a midway, livestock shows (including horse, ox, and pony pulls), and horticulture, cooking, and craft exhibits and contests. A weeklong tradition, especially for teens and families. $$

Early-August: **Centerville Old Home Week** (centervilleoldhomeweek.com). Main Street open houses, art auctions, live music, and bonfire gatherings; until it was resurrected in the mid-1990s, this event hadn't been held for 90 years.

Mid-October: **Osterville Village Fall Festival Day** (508-420-4590). Wine tasting, entertainment, an antiques show, a dog show, and food. Typically held the Saturday after Columbus Day.

Mid-December: **Osterville Christmas Open House and Stroll** (508-420-4590). Since 1972, the village has gussied itself up with traditional decorations for New England's second oldest stroll. Upward of 2,000 to 3,000 participate in Friday-evening festivities, which include music, hayrides, trolley rides, wine tastings, and more.

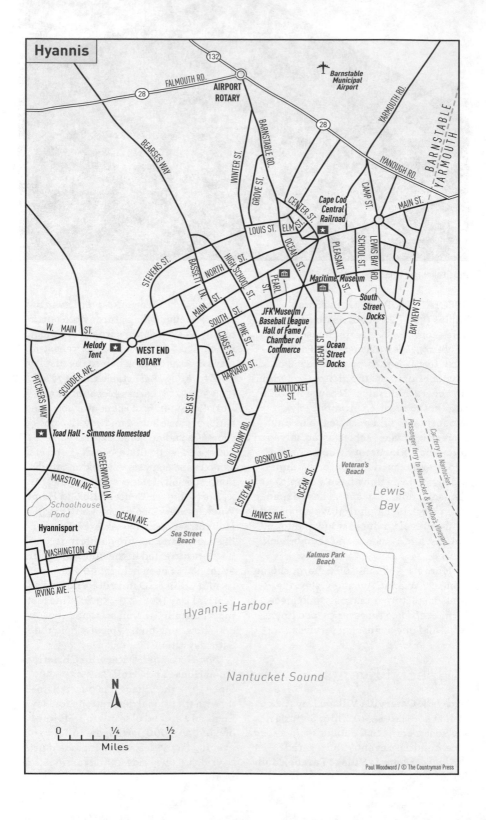

Hyannis

Paul Woodward / © The Countryman Press

HYANNIS

Hyannis is the Cape's commercial and transportation hub: Just under 1 million people take the ferry from Hyannis to Nantucket every year. Most Cape visitors end up in Hyannis at some point, whether by choice or by necessity.

Among Cape visitors, Hyannis seems to be everyone's favorite whipping post: A sigh of sympathy is heard when someone mentions he "has" to go into Hyannis in July or August. Yes, traffic is gnarly and Route 28 is overbuilt, but those same Cape residents and off-Cape visitors who moan about congestion in Hyannis couldn't live as easily without its services, including many fine restaurants. They come to buy new cars, embark to the islands, visit doctors, and shop at malls. Thus, because it is so distinct from the rest of Barnstable, I have given it its own chapter even though Hyannis is technically one of Barnstable's seven villages.

Hyannis's **harborfront and Main Street** began to be revitalized in the 1990s, thanks in part to the encouragement of the late Ben Thompson, architect of Boston's Quincy Market shopping complex and other successful urban waterfront development projects. And it's received additional, phased face-lifts ever since. It's a downright pleasant place these days. Boating activity on Lewis Bay is active. Main Street is a study in contrasts: Lined with benches and hanging flower baskets in an attempt to attract strollers, it also has lots of T-shirt shops, some vacant storefronts, and a growing crop of congregating youth and shops geared to them. (Hyannis is, after all, the closest thing to a "city" that the Cape has.) Look for the **Walkway to the Sea**—a nice, spiffy link between Main Street and the waterfront—and harborfront "shacks" from which artists sell their goods.

HYANNIS PORT YACHT CLUB

Hyannis has a bit of everything: discount outlets, upward of 50 eating establishments *in the waterfront district alone*, some quiet cottages and guest houses, plenty of motels geared to overnight visitors waiting for the morning ferry, harbor tours, and lots of lively bars and nightlife.

Then there's the Kennedy mystique. **Hyannisport**—a neighborhood within Hyannis but quite distinct from Hyannis— will forever be remembered as the place where, in the early 1960s, President John F. Kennedy and his wife, Jacqueline, sailed offshore and played with Caroline and

John. Visitors who come in search of the "Kennedy compound," or in hopes of somehow experiencing the Kennedy aura, will find only an inaccessible, residential, Yankee-style community of posh estates.

Lastly, let's talk historical perspective for a paragraph or two. Hyannis's harbor area was inhabited about 1,000 years ago by ancestors of the Eastern Algonquian Indians, who set up summer campsites south of what is now Ocean Street. The first European to reach Cape Cod, Bartholomew Gosnold, anchored in the harbor in 1602. Shortly thereafter, settlers persuaded Native American sachem Yanno to sell them what is now known as Hyannis and Centerville for £20 and two pairs of pants.

Main Street was laid out in 1750, and by the early 1800s Hyannis was already known as the Cape's transportation hub. The harbor bustled with two- and three-masted schooners. When the steam-train line was extended from Barnstable in 1854, land-based trade and commerce supplanted the marine-based economy. Tourists began arriving in much greater numbers by the end of the 19th century. Yachts filled the harbor by the 1930s and continued to do so until John Kennedy (who tied up at the Hyannisport Yacht Club) renewed interest in traditional local sailboats, known as catboats, in the 1950s.

GUIDANCE ❋ **Hyannis Area Chamber of Commerce** (508-775-2201; hyannis.com), 388 Main Street, Hyannis.

A PERFECT DAY IN HYANNIS

9:00	Go for an early-morning swim at Veterans Beach.
10:45	Relive or discover Camelot at the JFK Hyannis Museum.
1:00	Eat harborside at Baxter's or more sublimely at Pain D'Avignon.
2:30	See kettle chips roll off the assembly line at CC Potato Chip Factory.
4:00	Get out on the water with Hyannisport Harbor Cruises.
6:00	Order a sublime seafood dish at the Naked Oyster.
8:00	Take in an outdoor concert at the Cape Cod Melody Tent.
10:30	Sit beneath a rare 200-year-old weeping beech tree.

🎵 Cape Cod Melody Tent (508-775-5630; melodytent.org), 21 West Main Street. Shows June through early September. When this big white tent with a revolving stage was erected in 1950, entertainment was limited to Broadway musicals. Today, despite the occasional, less-than-perfect sound and acoustics, it's the Cape's biggest and best venue for top-name musicians. Look for the likes of Chicago, Bonnie Raitt, ZZ Top, Shawn Colvin, Melissa Etheridge, Tony Bennett, Julio Iglesias, and Lyle Lovett. It's only "big" by Cape standards; you'll be surprised how close you are to your favorite stars here—about 20 rows max. That translates to about 50 feet.

GETTING THERE *By car:* To reach Hyannis, about 30 minutes from the Cape Cod Canal, take Exit 6 off Route 6; follow Route 132 south to the airport rotary (at the junction of Routes 28 and 132). Take the second right off the rotary onto Barnstable Road, which intersects with Main, Ocean, and South Streets (for the harbor).

By bus: The **Plymouth & Brockton** bus line (508-746-0378; p-b.com) connects Hyannis with other Cape towns, as well as with Boston's Logan Airport. **Bonanza/Peter Pan** (888-751-8800; peterpanbus.com) connects Hyannis to Providence, T. F. Green Airport, and New York City. Both buses operate out of the Hyannis Transportation Center at Center and Main Streets.

☀ *By air:* **Barnstable Municipal Airport** (508-775-2020), at the rotary junction of Route 28 and Route 132, Hyannis. Small carriers serving Hyannis include **Cape Air** (508-771-6944; capeair.com) and **Nantucket Air** (800-227-3247; nantucketairlines.org)

GETTING AROUND *By car:* Hyannis suffers from serious summer traffic problems. Parking on Main Street is free if you can get a space. If not, try North Street, one block north of Main Street and parallel to it. Main Street (one-way) is geared to strolling, but it's a long walk from end to end.

For rentals, call the big agencies based at the airport: **Hertz** (508-775-5825; hertz.com), **Avis** (508-775-2888; avis.com), and **Budget** (508-771-4734; budget.com). **Thrifty** (508-771-0450; thrifty.com) is across from the airport. **Trek** (508-771-2459; trekrentacar.com) is near the bus terminal, but they'll pick you up from the airport.

Hyannis Area Trolley (508-385-1430; 800-352-7155; capecodtransit.org). Operating daily from late June through early September; daily except Sunday in the winter. The summertime beach trolley makes a loop down Main Street to Sea Street, the beaches, and South Street. $.

The **Sealine** connects Hyannis to Barnstable, Mashpee, Falmouth, and Woods Hole. Pick up a schedule at the chamber of commerce (see *Guidance*) or Hyannis Transportation Center. $.

GETTING TO THE ISLANDS From Hyannis, there is year-round auto and passenger service to Nantucket and seasonal passenger service to Martha's Vineyard. For complete information, see *Getting There* in "Martha's Vineyard" and "Nantucket." You can also fly to the islands.

MEDIA The daily *Cape Cod Times* (508-775-1200; capecodonline.com) is published in Hyannis (319 Main Street).

PUBLIC RESTROOMS At beaches (see *Green Space*), behind the JFK Hyannis Museum on Main Street, and at the Ocean Street Docks (Bismore Park).

PUBLIC LIBRARY ❄ ✎ ⍦ **Hyannis Public Library** (508-775-2280; hyannislibrary.org), 401 Main Street. This charming little house has a much larger facility tacked onto the rear.

MEDICAL EMERGENCY **Cape Cod Hospital** (508-771-1800), 27 Park Street. Open 24/7.

❄ To See

John F. Kennedy Hyannis Museum (508-790-3077; jfkhyannismuseum.org), 397 Main Street. Open mid-February through December. This museum opened in the early 1990s to meet the demands of visitors making the pilgrimage to Hyannis in search of JFK. People wanted to see "something," so the chamber gave them a museum that focuses on JFK's time in Hyannisport and on Cape Cod. The museum features more than 100 photographs of Kennedy from 1931 to 1963, arranged in themes: JFK's friends, JFK's family, JFK the man. He said, "I always go to Hyannisport to be revived, to know the power of the sea and the master who rules over it and all of us." (If you want to *really* learn something about the president and his administration, head to the JFK Museum in Boston.) A statue of JFK, sculpted by native Cape Codder David Lewis, graces the front of the museum. $–$$.

   Baseball League Hall of Fame (508-790-3077), ground floor of the John F. Kennedy Hyannis Museum. Hours same as museum above. Celebrating the 10 teams in the Cape Cod Baseball League, the museum displays autographed bats and balls, old photos, baseball cards of players drafted by the majors, and other memorabilia. If you're

JFK MEMORIAL

KENNEDY COMPOUND

a *real* fan of America's favorite pastime, this will be of interest to you. If you're more interested in peanuts and Cracker Jack, go to a game instead. $.

JFK Memorial, Ocean Street. The fountain, behind a large presidential seal mounted on a high stone wall, is inscribed: I BELIEVE IT IS IMPORTANT THAT THIS COUNTRY SAIL AND NOT SIT STILL IN THE HARBOR. There is a nice view of Lewis Bay from here.

Kennedy compound. Joe and Rose Kennedy rented the Malcolm Cottage in Hyannisport from 1926 to 1929 before purchasing and remodeling it to include 14 rooms, nine baths, and a private movie theater in the basement. (It was the first private theater in New England.) By 1932 there were nine children scampering around the house and grounds, which included a private beach, dock, tennis court, and pool. In 1956, then Sen. John Kennedy purchased an adjacent house at the corner of Scudder and Irving Avenues, which came to be known as the "Summer White House." Bobby bought the house next door, which now belongs to his widow, Ethel. Sen. Edward Kennedy's former house (it now belongs to his ex-wife, Joan) is on private Squaw Island. Eunice (Kennedy) and Sargent Shriver purchased a nearby home on Atlantic Avenue.

It was at Malcolm Cottage that JFK learned he'd been elected president; at Malcolm Cottage that Jacqueline and the president mourned the loss of their infant son; at Malcolm Cottage that the family mourned the deaths of the president and Bobby Kennedy; at Malcolm Cottage that Sen. Edward Kennedy would annually present his mother with a rose for each of her years; at Malcolm Cottage that matriarch Rose Kennedy died in 1995 at the age of 104; and at Malcom Cottage in 2009 where the clan gathered to transport Senator Kennedy's body from his beloved Cape Cod to services at the JFK Library in Boston (before he was interred in Arlington Cemetery in Washington, D.C., next to his brothers). In 2012 the Marchant house was donated to the Edward M. Kennedy Institute for the U.S. Senate, with plans to open it to the public.

Although Kennedy sightings are rare, the Kennedys are still Hyannis's No. 1 "attraction."

If you drive or walk around this stately area, you'll see nothing but high hedges and fences. Those who can't resist a look-see will be far better off taking a boat tour (see *To Do*); some boats come quite close to the shoreline and the white frame houses.

St. Francis Xavier Church, 347 South Street. Members of Rose Kennedy's clan worshiped here when they were in town. The pew used by JFK is marked with a plaque, while the altar is a memorial to JFK's brother, Lt. Joe Kennedy Jr., killed during World War II.

❊ **Cape Cod Maritime Museum** (508-775-1723; capecodmaritimemuseum.org), 135 South Street. Open mid-March to mid-December. This harborfront museum offers interactive exhibits, lectures, and classes in ship model making, maritime archaeology, and boatbuilding. It also displays boats that illuminate the region's past, present, and forthcoming connections with the sea. After the traditional catboat *Sarah* was built on

Weeping beech trees. In the courtyard behind 605 Main Street (Hyannis) and in the front yard of an inn on Route 6A (Barnstable; pictured here). To the town of Hyannis' knowledge, these specimens represent two of the seven remaining weeping beech trees in the entire country. They are awesome, magnificent, 200-plus-year-old beauties.

the premises (quite a production), she was launched in Lewis Bay in 2007 and set out on excursions from ports between Chatham and Woods Hole. Don't miss a chance to go on 90-minute cruises with her (Thursday through Saturday, $$$). Museum $.

✳ ⊘ ↑ **Cape Cod Potato Chip Factory** (888-881-2447; capecodchips.com), 100 Breed's Hill Road, Independence Park, off Route 132. After Chatham resident Steve Bernard began the company in 1980 and parlayed it into a multimillion-dollar business, he sold it to corporate giant Anheuser-Busch and moved on to the business of purveying Chatham Village Croutons. But in the mid-1990s, when Anheuser-Busch wanted to sell or close it, Bernard bought the company back, saving about 100 year-round jobs. (Now it's owned by Lance, Inc., another snack manufacturer.) Take the 15-minute self-guided tour of the potato-chip-making process, then sample the rich flavor and high crunchability resulting from all-natural ingredients cooked in small kettles. Free.

Cape Cod Beer (508-790-4200; capecodbeer.com), 1336 Phinneys Lane. This microbrewery bills itself as a community space; think Friday farmers' market meets local happy hour. It has super informative tours and tastings, live music at times, fun games all the time, and a beer garden (i.e., a roped-off section of a parking lot when it's not indoors during inclement weather). All in all, people enjoy themselves here.

TOAD HALL

⊘ **Cape Cod Central Railroad** (508-771-3800; capetrain.com), 252 Main and Center Streets. Trips late May to late October. The 48-mile trip takes two hours and passes cranberry bogs, the Sandy Neck Great Salt Marsh, and the Cape Cod Canal. Because there are typically two trains daily, you take the first one, hop off in Sandwich, walk into the picturesque village (it's about a 10-minute walk), and then catch the next train back to Hyannis. The best part of this trip is the local narration—unless you've never been on a train before, in which case, the simple act of taking a train will tickle you more. The scenery isn't all that interesting, actually. $$$

Town green, adjacent to the JFK Hyannis Museum. Note the life-sized bronze of the sachem Iyanough, chief of the Mattakeese tribe of Cummaquid and friend to the Pilgrims, created by Osterville sculptor David Lewis.

❊ **Toad Hall—Classic Sports Car Collection at the Simmons Homestead Inn** (508-778-4934; toadhallcars.com), 288 Scudder Avenue. Bill Putman relishes his quirkiness, and it's on full display here with an impressive collection of classic red sports cars—45 at last count. They're packed into a low-slung, garage-style barn, complete with fake Oriental carpets lining the gravel pathways between the cars. $.

SCENIC DRIVE Hyannisport is by far the loveliest section of Hyannis, but don't come expecting to see the Kennedys. The "compound" is wedged between Scudder and Irving Avenues. From Main Street, turn left onto Sea Street, right onto Ocean Avenue, left onto Hyannis Avenue, left onto Iyanough Road (Route 132), right onto Wachusett Avenue, and left onto Scudder Avenue.

❊ To Do

BASEBALL ✐ The **Hyannis Harbor Hawks of the Cape Cod Baseball League** (capecodbaseball.org) plays from mid-June to early August under the lights at McKeon Park. (Take South Street to High School Road and turn right.)

BICYCLING & RENTALS ❊ **Bike Zone** (508-775-3299; bikezonecapecod.com), 323 Barnstable Road. Tim and Ryan's shop is one of the best on the Cape. Rent by the hour ($), return the same day ($$), or dig into the area with multiple-day packages and weekly rates ($$–$$$$+).

BOAT EXCURSIONS & RENTALS ✐ **Hyannisport Harbor Cruises** (508-790-0696; hylinecruises.com), 220 Ocean Street. Mid-April to mid-October. Lewis Bay and Hyannis Harbor are beautiful, and the best way to appreciate them is by water. Also, if you're like 85,000 other visitors each season and you want the best possible view of the Kennedy compound, take this hour-long Hy-Line excursion. The boat comes within 500 feet of the shoreline compound—which is closer than you can get by foot or car. During the height of summer, there's a Sunday afternoon family cruise with Ben & Jerry's ice cream sundaes. Oh, and kids ride free on morning summertime trips. $$.

Cape Cod Duckmobiles (508-790-2111; capecodduckmobile.com), 437 Main Street. Mid-June to early September departures every 30 minutes. These amphibious tours last 45 minutes, go splashing around Hyannis Harbor, and then roll along the street, rather like ducks out of water. $$.

✐ **Pirate Adventures** (508-394-9100; capecodpirateadventures.com), 180 Ocean Street. Trips mid-June to early September. Particularly fun for children, this swashbuckling trip begins with face painting on the dock. Then kids sign on to the pirate ship as crew, take a pirate oath, search for sunken treasure, and fire water cannons against renegade pirates. On the return voyage, the booty is shared and pirates celebrate with song and dance. $$$.

Cat Boat (508-775-0222; catboat.com), 146 Ocean Street. Late May to mid-October. Look for the big cat on the sail. Eventide has a full complement of trips, including 90-minute excursions and private charters; head down to the dock to see what they offer. $$$$.

HYANNIS PORT

FISHING & SHELLFISHING Procure freshwater and saltwater fishing licenses and regulations online (mass.gov/eea/agencies/dfg/licensing)

❄ **Sports Port** (508-775-3096; sportsport.us), 149 West. Main Street. Surely you've seen the statue of a yellow guy in a red rowboat? That means the store is open. References for charters and tours; supplies for freshwater, saltwater, and fly-fishing; shellfish permits; and ice-fishing details, too.

Hy-Line Fishing Trips (508-790-0696; hylinecruises.com), Ocean Street Docks. Bottom-fishing "Captain's Choice" for fluke and blues from mid-June to early September. Half-day trips. $$$$.

❄ The supercruiser *Helen-H* (508-790-0660; helenh.com), Pleasant Street Docks, goes in search of big fish, too. You'll find cod all year long, bottom fish in the spring, and blues in summer.

GOLF ❄ **Hyannis Golf Club** (508-362-2606; barnstablegolf.com), Route 132.

❄ **Twin Brooks Golf Course** (508-862-6980; twinbrooksgolf.net), 35 Scudder Avenue, West End Circle. At the Resort and Conference Center at Hyannis.

ICE-SKATING **Kennedy Memorial Skating Rink** (508-790-6345), 141 Bassett Lane off Bearses Way.

SPECIAL PROGRAMS ❄ **Eastern Mountain Sports (EMS)** (508-362-8690; ems.com), 1513 Route 132. In addition to renting kayaks (great for navigating herring rivers, creeks, and inlets), the Cape's largest purveyor of outdoor gear offers free instructional clinics periodically. Topics range from outdoor cooking to mastering compass skills.

TENNIS Public courts are located at **Barnstable High School** off West Main Street.

❄ Green Space

BEACHES Weekly cottage renters can purchase beach stickers at the Kennedy Memorial Skating Rink at the Hyannis Youth & Community Center (508-790-6345), 141 Bassett Lane, Bearses Way.

Kalmus Park Beach, at the end of Ocean Street on Nantucket Sound. This beach is good for sailboarding. The land, by the way, was donated by Technicolor inventor Herbert Kalmus, who also owned the Fernbrook estate in Centerville. Facilities include a restroom, picnic area, lifeguards, snack bar, and bathhouse. Parking $$.

✔ **Veterans Beach**, on Hyannis Harbor (Lewis Bay), off Ocean Street. This is a good beach for children because the waters are fairly shallow and calm, and it's a fine place to watch harbor sailboats (because the Hyannis Yacht Club is next door). Facilities include a restroom, bathhouse, lifeguards, a snack bar, swings, grills, and a big wooded area with picnic tables. Parking $$.

Sea Street/Orrin Keyes Beach, on Nantucket Sound, Sea Street. Facilities include a restroom, lifeguards, snack bar, and bathhouse. Parking $$.

✳ Lodging

Hyannis has hordes of nondescript motels and many good family-oriented cottages. If you want a good B&B, stay in one of Barnstable's other villages.

RESORT MOTOR INN ✳ ✔ **Cape Codder Resort & Spa** (508-771-3000; capecodderresort.com), 1225 Route 132 at Bearses Way. About 2 miles from the center of town, this two-story destination property is owned by the Catania family (the Catanias have long owned the Dan'l Webster Inn in Sandwich and the family-style Hearth & Kettle restaurants), and they have poured millions into the Cape Codder. This ultra-family-friendly resort has 257 rooms, an indoor wave pool (complete with 2½-foot waves and waterslides), an indoor/outdoor water park with a 10,000-square-foot wave pool, a three-story medi-spa, two restaurants, a wine bar, a large fitness center, a game room, and tennis. Fractional ownership residences are also available. $$.

COTTAGES & TOWNHOUSES 🐾 ✔ **Harbor Village** (508-775-7581; harborvillage.com), 160 Marstons Avenue, Hyannisport. Open May to mid-October. Delightfully off the beaten path but still centrally located, these one- to four-bedroom cottages can sleep up to nine people. They're set on a private, wooded, 17-acre compound within a two-minute walk of Quahog Beach. It doesn't get

much better than this. Each of the 13 cottages has a living room, dining area, fully equipped kitchen, individual heat, a fireplace, a deck or patio with grill, and cable TV. A few have central air and washer/dryer; most have a dishwasher. You'll need to bring your own beach towels and chairs, though. Weekly rates in-season. $$–$$$.

✳ ✔ **Capt. Gosnold Village** (508-775-9111; captaingosnold.com), 230 Gosnold Street. In a residential area near the harbor, the family-friendly Capt. Gosnold's is a short walk to three beaches. Children also will enjoy the wooded and grassy grounds with a fenced-in pool and lifeguard, lawn games, and a play area. All rooms have been redecorated, and most of the 24 cottages are spacious and have a private deck and a gas grill. Request a newer cottage with three bedrooms and you'll also get three bathrooms and four TVs. While you can expect maid service Monday through Saturday and fully equipped kitchens, you'll have to bring your own beach towels. $–$$$$.

✳ ✔ **The Yachtsman** (508-771-5454; yachtsmancondo.com), rental office at 500 Ocean Street, Apt. 14. These privately owned townhouse condominiums, with their own private stretch of beach between Kalmus and Veterans Beaches (see *Green Space*), are right on Lewis Bay. During the summer, about 40 of the 125 units are available for rent. Although the decor varies from one unit to another, all meet certain standards. Multilevel

CAPTAIN GOSNOLD COTTAGES

units have a full kitchen, 2½ baths, private sundeck, sunken living room, and two to four bedrooms. About half have water views; half overlook the heated pool. No credit cards. $$$$.

❋ Where to Eat

With more than 150 eateries around town, Hyannis offers everything from mod seafood to romantic Italian. Unless otherwise noted, all restaurants are open year-round.

DINING OUT ❋ ⍭ **Naked Oyster** (508-778-6500; nakedoyster.com), 410 Main Street. Open L, D. This cosmopolitan and sophisticated bistro offers palate-pleasing seafood and steaks complemented by a wonderful selection of wines by the glass. In addition to excellent raw bar choices, try appetizers like Thai shrimp, tuna tartare, lobster salad, and an oyster sampler. Mains like halibut with lobster meat, swordfish chops, and filet mignon take center stage at night. Whatever you do, don't miss their silk chocolate martini (at their stylin' bar)

and chocolate crème brûlée (arguably the best on the Cape) . . . or their basil strawberries and chocolate bark. Hip and hopping hats off to Florence Lowell, owner since 2006. L $–$$, D $$–$$$$.

❋ **Pain D'Avignon** (508-778-8588; paindavignon.com), 15 Hinckley Road. Open B, L, D. A delightful surprise! Try rustic French breads, bagels, and home-baked crackers from the oh-so-French-style boulangerie. And from the café,

PAIN D'AVIGNON

try tantalizing sandwiches like a (warm and open-faced) *croque monsieur* with ham and Gruyère cheese. (The *croque madame* offers the same ingredients topped with an egg.) The French dinner fare—coquilles St. Jacques, steak frites, and crème brûlée—is pretty darn excellent too. It's a bit off the beaten path, but totally worth seeking out, even if the outdoor dining is adjacent to the parking lot. B $–$$, L $$–$$$, D $$$–$$$$.

❋ ⚓ **Pizza Barbone** (508-957-2377; pizzabarbone.com), 390 Main Street. Open L, D. This wood-fired Neapolitan pizza place deserves all the high praise it consistently receives. $–$$.

❋ ⚓ **Alberto's Ristorante** (508-778-1770; albertos.net), 360 Main Street. Open L, D. Thanks to chef-owner Felis Barreiro, Alberto's has been consistently fabulous, catering to a loyal following since 1984. Elegant and romantic, done up with faux marble and off-white colors, it may look formal, but it doesn't project an ounce of stuffiness. The service is delightfully professional. The extensive Northern Italian menu features large portions of homemade pasta and regional specialties. Nightly seasonal additions are surprising in their breadth and execution. Despite not having room, I still top off my meal with a rich cappuccino and a decadent dessert sampler. Sidewalk tables are pleasant in the summer, and a jazz pianist draws diners on Friday and Saturday nights year-round. D $$–$$$$.

❋ ⵝ **Roadhouse Café** (508-775-2386; roadhousecafe.com), 488 South Street. Open D. This charming and pleasant place—with polished floors, Oriental carpets, hanging plants, tongue-and-groove ceilings with paddle fans, candlelight, and two fireplaces—is also dependable (if uninspired), thanks to the long tenure of owner Dave Colombo. Come for a romantic interlude or with a group for some fun. The extensive Italian and seafood menu features large portions. Consider splitting a simple main dish and pairing it with a couple of appetizers. Creative, thin-crust pizzas are offered in the Back Door Bistro (see *Entertainment*), which has a clubby feel with dark paneling and a mahogany piano bar. It also has a large selection of wine by the glass and 22 brands of beer. D $$$–$$$$.

ROADHOUSE CAFÉ

✳ **Colombo's** (508-790-5700; colomboscafe.com), 544 Main Street. Open L, D. This spacious and mainstream eatery, brought to you by the owner of the Roadhouse Café, has a little something for everyone: from outside dining to an indoor bar and gelato case, from lunchtime sandwiches and salads to intermediate offerings like pizza and pasta to more hefty nighttime selections like grilled salmon and chicken Parmesan. They run a tight ship here. $–$$$.

✳ **Black Cat Tavern** (508-778-1233; blackcattavern.com), 165 Ocean Street. Open L, D. Local restaurateur Dave Colombo runs the Black Cat, which offers a casual waterfront feel and quite good fried and baked seafood staples—fish-and-chips, scallops, seafood platter—while kicking casual up a notch with the likes of pan-seared scallops with strawberry pineapple risotto and lobster ravioli. Gourmet burgers and salads, too. Stick around for a drink in the piano lounge. L $–$$, D $$–$$$.

EATING OUT **Spanky's Clam Shack** (508-771-2770; spankysclamshack.com), 138 Ocean Street. Open L, D, mid-April to mid-October. Right on the harbor near where the sight-seeing boats launch, this casual seafood place is the best of the fry bunch. Portions are huge, the prices are right, and you have a choice of inside or outside dining. Service can be the toughest thing to digest here. The kitschy tune introducing Spanky's website reflects the good-time atmosphere on site. $$–$$$.

🍸 **Baxter's Boathouse Club and Fish 'n Chips** (508-775-7040; baxterscapecod.com), 177 Pleasant Street. Open L, D, mid-April to mid-October. It's as much about location as it is food here, and even though they serve the same menu throughout the day, I prefer going at lunchtime. Built on an old fish-packing dock near the Steamship Authority terminal, Baxter's has attracted a crowd since 1956, from beautiful people tying up at the dock to singles meeting at the bar, from families to folks who don't

HYANNIS

mind eating on paper plates on a harborfront picnic table. It's really the best waterfront table in town. The fried and broiled seafood is consistent, too, if not exemplary. $$–$$$.

❋ **Brazilian Grill** (508-771-0109; braziliangrill-capecod.com), 680 Main Street. Open L, D. You'd have to fly to Rio for more authentic *churrascaria rodizio*, a traditional, elaborate all-you-can-eat barbecue buffet of skewered meats. Come hungry or don't bother. And then don't bother eating for the rest of the week. The servers sure are friendly here, and the setting is airy at lunchtime. Buffet $$$–$$$$.

❋ ✿ **Ying's** (508-790-2432; yings .net), 59 Center Street. Open L, D. Ying's boasts very good pad Thai, Japanese and Korean dishes, noodles, and sushi. The atmosphere here is tranquil, rather like an indoor garden. Maki sushi is half price on Fridays. L $, D $$.

❋ ✿ **Common Ground Café** (508-778-8390; hyanniscommonground.com), 420 Main Street. Open L, D. When you step inside, let your eyes adjust to the darkness for a minute: You'll find hand-hewn booths resembling hobbit houses and an old-fashioned community (a religious collective, actually) of folks serving honest food. The menu includes a few wholesome sandwiches and wraps, soups, salads, and daily specials. Everything is made from scratch. There is also a juice bar upstairs. $.

❋ ✿ **Sam Diego's** (508-771-8816; sam diegos.com), 950 Route 132. Open L, D. Decorated with colored lights, colorful serapes, toucans, and sombreros, this huge and hopping place is often full of families. They come for decent southwestern- and Mexican-inspired fare like chicken fajitas, barbecued ribs, burritos, enchiladas, and daily blackboard specials. In warm weather, dine on the large outdoor patio. $–$$.

❋ ✿ **Spoon and Seed** (774-470-4634; spoonandseed.com), 12 Thornton Drive. Open B, L. Have you heard folks raving about these breakfasts and this little family-run, out-of-the-way place? Their "spudnut" (a doughnut made with potatoes) might just make you skip breakfast at your B&B. From the hash and grits to cheesy biscuits and eggs Benny, you really can't go wrong. For lunch I totally recommend the hippie burger. Hats off to the owners, the Tropeanos. Dishes $.

❋ ✿ **Tumi Ceviche Bar & Ristorante** (508-534-9289; tumiceviche.com), 592 Main Street. Open L, D. I didn't get a chance to try the tuna ceviche and paella, but I heard great reviews. They offer both Peruvian and Italian dishes, with indoor and patio dining. $$–$$$.

ICE CREAM **Katie's Ice Cream** (508-771-6889; katiesicecreamcapecod.com), 570 Main Street. Open mid-April to early September. Everyone seems to end up at this little shop sometime during the day or night for homemade scoops.

DINNER TRAIN ✿ **Cape Cod Dinner Train** (508-771-3800; capetrain.com), 252 Main Street. Operates early May through December with a highly variable schedule. I include this just so you know I haven't overlooked it; I recommend checking around for its current reputation.

❋ Entertainment

✿ **Cape Symphony Orchestra** (508-362-1111; capesymphony.org). Performances September through May. The orchestra performs about 15 concerts for children and adults at the 1,400-seat Barnstable High School, 744 West Main Street in Hyannis.

❋ ✿ ⌕ **Regal Cape Cod Mall Stadium 12** (508-771-7872), 793 Route 132 at intersection with Route 28, at the Cape Cod Mall.

⌕ **Back Door Bistro** at the Roadhouse Café (508-775-2386; roadhousecafe.com), 488 South Street. Check the website for which nights feature jazz and piano

CAPE COD DINNER TRAIN

throughout the year. It's de rigueur for Hyannis repeat visitors.

♈ See also **Cape Cod Beer** under *To Do*.

Free concerts (hyannismainstreet .com) on Thursday and Friday summer evenings on Main Street.

✳ Selective Shopping

✳ Unless otherwise noted, all shops are open year-round.

ART GALLERIES & CRAFTS **Artist Shanties** (508-862-4678; hyartsdistrict .com), Bismore Park, on the waterfront. Open late May through September. Taking a page out of the playbook of Nantucket's waterfront area, these little shacks are occupied by 15 juried artists, including one revolving one. Mediums vary from watercolors and pastels to tapestries and jewelry to calligraphy and photography. It really livens up the area, whether or not you're waiting for a ferry.

Red Fish Blue Fish (508-775-8700; redfishbluefish.com), 374 Main Street. The most fun and whimsical "gallery" in town carries unusual gifts and crafts. When it's not too busy, you can watch owner Jane Walsh making handblown glass jewelry in the store.

Guyer Art Barn (508-790-6370; hyartsdistrict.com), 250 South Street. Part of the Harbor Your Arts scheme (see **Artist Shanties**, above). The Barnstable Arts and Humanities Council established this art gallery in 1986, now a showcase for emerging and established local artists in a wide variety of genres.

BOOKSTORES **Barnes & Noble** (508-862-6310), Cape Cod Mall, Route 132, north of the airport rotary.

CLOTHING **Plush & Plunder** (508-775-4467; plushandplunder.com), 605 Main Street. Vintage and eccentric used clothing adorns those marching to an offbeat drummer, including fabled customers like Cyndi Lauper, Joan Baez, and Demi

Moore. You don't have to be an entertainer to shop here, although you'll end up entertained and entertaining (if you purchase something) while searching for gold lamé, a boa, or other retro accessories. Don't miss this place.

FACTORY OUTLETS **Christmas Tree Shops** (508-778-5521; christmastreeshops.com), between 655 Route 132, next to the Cape Cod Mall. This is the largest of the six Christmas Tree Shops on the Cape.

MALL ✍ **Cape Cod Mall** (508-771-0201; simon.com), Routes 132 and 28. The Cape's only "real" mall—as distinguished from a plethora of strip malls—is anchored by big retailers and supplemented by more than 100 other stores, a huge food court, and an ultramodern movie theater. To keep kids occupied, there's a Venetian carousel, too.

SPECIAL SHOPS **Cellar Leather** (508-771-5458; cellarleather.com), 578 Main Street. Quality coats, vests, shoes, clogs, sandals, briefcases, hats, and wallets—if you have any money left over.

All Cape Cook's Supply (508-790-8908), 237 Main Street. Useful gadgets for pros and amateurs.

Kandy Korner Gifts (508-771-5313; kandykorner.com), 474 Main Street. Watch chocolates and fudge being made in the front windows before heading in to indulge your sweet tooth.

✳ Special Events

May: **Annual Figawi Sailboat Race Weekend** (figawi.com). The largest sailboat race in New England goes from Hyannis to Nantucket.

Late July: **Regatta** (hyannisyachtclub.org). At the Hyannis Yacht Club since the early 1940s.

Early August: **Pops by the Sea** (artsfoundationcapecod.org). Cape Cod's single largest cultural event features the Boston Pops Esplanade Orchestra on the town green playing to an audience of 15,000. In the past, guest conductors have included Mike Wallace, Julia Child, Olympia Dukakis, and Walter Cronkite. Reserved-seating and general-admission tickets.

Early December: **Harbor Lighting and Boat Parade** (capecodchamber.org), Bismore Park, Ocean Street. Parade of boats includes the arrival of Santa; entertainment with a holiday theme.

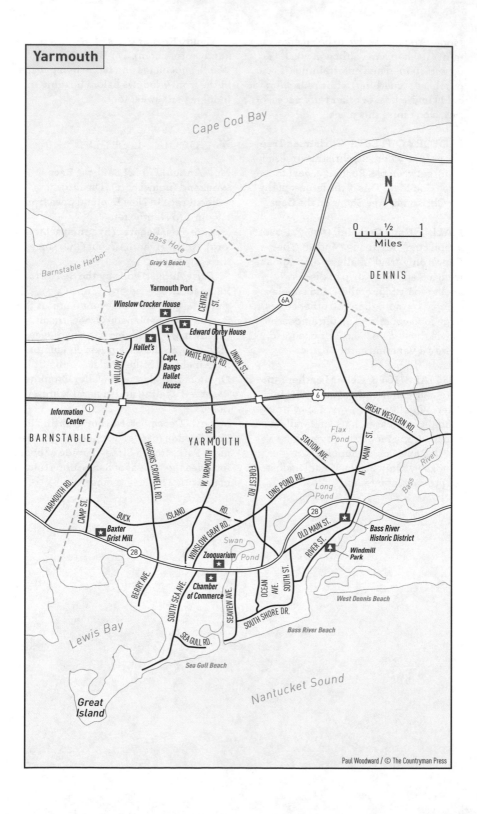

YARMOUTH

Yarmouth, like neighboring Dennis, stretches from Cape Cod Bay to Nantucket Sound; it unfolds along quiet Route 6A *and* congested Route 28. It's a family-oriented town, with golf courses, tennis courts, and town-sponsored sailing lessons, as well as quite a few southside oceanfront resorts.

Although Yarmouth's 5.3-mile section of **Route 28** was planted with more than 350 trees in 1989 (on its 350th birthday), the road is still a wall-to-wall sea of mini-golf courses, shops, fast-food places, and family-style attractions like a billiards emporium and boating on the Bass River. A larger-than-life plastic polar bear, a lunging shark, and an elephant epitomize the Cape's kitschier side. They're alternately viewed as icons and eyesores.

It's difficult to imagine that Route 28 was once open land dotted with small farms and that Yarmouth's ports bustled in the 19th century: Packets sailed to New York City and Newark from South Yarmouth at the Bass River. Today the scenic Bass River and South Yarmouth Historic District provide a delightful detour south of Route 28.

On the northside, **Route 6A** (a.k.a. Main Street) was settled in the 1600s, traveled by stagecoaches in the 1700s, and reached its height of prosperity in the 1800s, when it was lined with houses built for and by rope makers, sea captains, bankers, and shipbuilders. At one time, a mile-long section of Yarmouth Port was referred to as Captain's Row, as it was home to almost 50 sea captains. Many former sea captains' houses are now attractive B&Bs.

Stephen Hopkins, a *Mayflower* passenger, built the first house in Yarmouth in 1638 (off Mill Lane), and the town was incorporated just one year later. Today Yarmouth is the third most populous town on the Cape, with 24,000 year-round residents. Meander along tranquil Route 6A and you'll find crafts and antiques shops, a quiet village green, a couple of fine historic houses open to the public, walking trails, and an antiquarian bookstore. Take any lane off Route 6A to the north, and you'll find picturesque residential areas and the bay, eventually.

GUIDANCE ❄ **Yarmouth Area Chamber of Commerce** (508-778-1008; yarmouthcapecod.com), 424 Route 28, West Yarmouth. Along with a helpful chamber staff, the office has two self-guided historical tours of Yarmouth and Old South Yarmouth.

GETTING THERE *By car:* Yarmouth is 26 miles from the Cape Cod Canal; take Route 6 to Exit 7 for the northside (Yarmouth Port and Route 6A). For points along Route 28 on the southside, take Exit 7 south to Higgins Crowell Road for West Yarmouth. Take Exit 8 south for South Yarmouth and the Bass River.

GETTING AROUND *By bus:* If you need public transportation, inquire at the chamber about a bus that runs along Route 28 between Hyannis and Orleans, with stops in Yarmouth.

MEDIA The weekly *Register* (508-375-4945; wickedlocalcapecod.com) lists local happenings.

A PERFECT DAY IN YARMOUTH

8:30	Order an Irish farmhouse breakfast from the Keltic Kitchen.
10:00	Cruise Route 28 for mini-golf at Pirate's Cove Adventure Golf or bowling at Ryan Family Amusement Center.
12:00	Satisfy everyone in your party at Skipper's or Jack's (depending on what side you are on).
1:30	Get in touch with your quirky side at the Edward Gorey House.
3:00	Buy inflatable beach toys on Route 28 and head to Sea Gull Beach.
6:30	Have a relaxing and unusual dinner at the creative Inaho.

ENTERING INC. 1639 YARMOUTH

PUBLIC RESTROOMS On Route 6 between Exits 6 and 7; at the town hall, 1146 Route 28, South Yarmouth; and at Gray's Beach (open seasonally, off Centre Street from Route 6A).

PUBLIC LIBRARIES ❋ ❂ ⇑ Call ahead to the small branches in South Yarmouth (508-760-4820) and West Yarmouth (508-775-5206) or visit yarmouthlibraries.org.

MEDICAL EMERGENCY Call **911**.
  Bass River Chiropractic (508-394-1353; bassriverhealthcare.com), 833 Route 28, South Yarmouth. Dr. Reida, an extraordinary chiropractor, dispenses healing when you are in pain on a holiday.

❋ To See

❋ ❂ **Edward Gorey House** (508-362-3909; edwardgoreyhouse.org), 8 Strawberry Lane, Yarmouth Port. Open mid-April to late December. *Curious, surreal, bizarre, whimsical,* and *quirky*: These have all been used to describe Gorey. His masterful pen-and-ink illustrations, as well as his offbeat sense of humor, endeared him to a wide audience. And the reputation he earned by doing the introductory credit for PBS's *Mystery* propelled him even further. So did the Tony Award he won for costume design for the Broadway production of *Dracula*. Closer to home, when Gorey moved to the Cape full time in the early 1980s, he contributed greatly to local theater productions. The restored house contains exhibits celebrating this marvelous artist, who lived here until his death in 2000. $.
  ☙ ⇑ **Hallet's** (508-362-3362), 139 Main Street, Route 6A, Yarmouth Port. Open April through December. Hallet's has been a community fixture since it was built as an apothecary in 1889 by Thacher Taylor Hallet. It's the oldest family-owned, old-fashioned soda fountain in the U.S. Today, great-grandson Charles owns and operates the store, which boasts an old-fashioned oak counter and a marble-topped soda fountain. As time stands still, sit on a swivel stool or in one of the wrought-iron,

EDWARD GOREY HOUSE

heart-shaped chairs beneath the tin ceiling and relax over an ice cream soda (the food's not much to write home about). The second floor has been turned into something of a museum, documenting Yarmouth's history as seen through one family's annals and attic treasures. In addition to being a pharmacist (old medicine bottles are on display), T. T. Hallet was a postmaster (during his tenure, only 15 families had mail slots), selectman (the second floor was used as a meeting room from 1889 to the early 1900s), and justice of the peace. The charming displays include store posters from the past 100 years and historical photographs. Tours $.

Village pump, Route 6A near Summer Street, Yarmouth Port. This wrought-iron pump has served the community since 1886. It's located just west of the Old Yarmouth Inn, the oldest inn (and stagecoach stop) on the Cape, dating from 1696. The pump's iron frame, decorated with birds, animals, and a lantern, is supported by a stone trough from which horses drank. Horse-drawn carriages traveling from Boston to Provincetown stopped here.

⬥ **Captain Bangs Hallet House** (508-362-3021; hsoy.org), 11 Strawberry Lane (park behind the post office on Route 6A), Yarmouth Port. Tours June to

HALLET'S

VILLAGE PUMP

mid-October. The original section of this Greek Revival house was built in 1740 by town founder Thomas Thacher, but it was substantially enlarged by Capt. Henry Thacher in 1840. Captain Hallet and his wife, Anna, lived here from 1863 until 1893. The house, maintained by the Historical Society of Old Yarmouth, is decorated in a manner befitting a prosperous sea captain who traded with China and India. Note the original 1740 kitchen, and don't miss the lovely weeping beech behind the house or the 1850 **Gorham Cobbler Shop**, which serves an archival research center. $.

🐾 ⛵ **Winslow Crocker House** (617-994-6661; historicnewengland.org), 250 Main Street, Route 6A, Yarmouth Port. Tours June to mid-October. Set back from Route 6A, this two-story Georgian home was built in 1780 with 12-over-12 small-paned windows and rich interior paneling. The house was constructed for a wealthy 18th-century trader and land speculator and moved to its present location in 1936 by Mary Thacher, a descendant of Yarmouth's original land grantee and an avid collector of 17th-, 18th-, and 19th-century furniture. She used the house as a backdrop for her magnificent collection. $.

Whydah Pirate Museum (508-534-9571, discoverpirates.com), 674 Route 28, West Yarmouth. This is more of an interactive science museum than the main Whydah museum in Provincetown (see *To Do*).

⛵ **Baxter Grist Mill**, 151 Route 28, West Yarmouth. Call Town Hall (508-398-2231, ext. 1292; hsoy.org) for opening hours. The original mill was built in 1710 with an exterior waterwheel. But in 1860, when water levels in Mill Pond became so low that the wheel froze, an indoor water turbine was added. (This is the Cape's only mill with an indoor water turbine.) Kids can help grind corn with "the Mill Man." Free.

Windmill Park, off River Street from Old Main Street, South Yarmouth. This eight-sided windmill on the Bass River was built in 1791 and moved here in 1866. This scenic spot also has a small swimming beach.

✱ To Do

BASEBALL ⛵ The Cape League (ydredsox.pointstreaksites.com) sponsors the **Yarmouth–Dennis Red Sox**. Games are held from mid-May to early August, typically at 5 PM at the Dennis-Yarmouth Regional High School, Station Avenue, South Yarmouth.

FISHING & SHELLFISHING Procure freshwater and saltwater fishing licenses and regulations online (mass.gov/eea/agencies/dfg/licensing).

CAPTAIN BANGS HALLET HOUSE

WINSLOW CROCKER HOUSE

❋ **Riverview Bait & Tackle** (508-394-1036), 1273 Route 28, South Yarmouth. Among other services, the staff will direct you to local fishing spots, including the Bass River and High Bank Bridges, Sea Gull Beach at Parker's River off South Shore Drive, and Smugglers Beach off South Street.

Shark Shark Tuna (774-212-0016; sharksharktuna.com), 17 Neptune Lane, South Yarmouth. Highly recommended fishing excursions.

Ship Shops (508-398-2256; shipshops.com/rentals), 130 Pleasant Street, Bass River. For all your powerboat rental needs when you know where to fish on your own.

FOR FAMILIES ✐ **A playground** is on Center Street in South Yarmouth; another is in **Old Townhouse Park** on Old Townhouse Road in South Yarmouth.

❋ ✐ ⌂ **Ryan Family Amusement Center** (508-394-5644; ryanfamily.com), 1067 Route 28, South Yarmouth. When rain strikes, head indoors to bowl away the blues. Ten-pin and candlepin. $$$.

✐ **Cape Cod Inflatable Park** (508-771-6060; capecodinflatablepark.com), 518 Route 28, West Yarmouth. I didn't get a chance to experience this place personally, but check out the website's activities and decide for yourself if your kids would have fun here. $$–$$$.

GOLF **King's Way** (508-362-8870; yportgolf.com), off Route 6A, Yarmouth Port. Open March to mid-November. A challenging Cornish and Silva course.

❋ **Bayberry Hills** (508-394-5597; golfyarmouthcapecod.com), off West Yarmouth Road, West Yarmouth. Also with a driving range.

SCENIC DRIVES

South Yarmouth and the Bass River Historic District, on and around Old Main Street (off Route 28), South Yarmouth. The Pawkannawkut Indians (a branch of the Wampanoag tribe) lived, fished, and hunted on a tract of land Yarmouth set aside for them along Long Pond and the Bass River in 1713. But by the 1770s, a smallpox epidemic wiped out most of the Native population. In 1790 David Kelley, a Quaker, acquired the last remaining Pawkannawkut land from the last surviving Pawkannawkut, Thomas Greenough. Quakers then settled the side streets off Old Main Street near Route 28 and built handsome homes. The Historical Society of Old Yarmouth publishes a walking-tour brochure to Old South Yarmouth, which you can get at the chamber of commerce (see *Guidance*). Note the simple traffic rotary at River and Pleasant Streets; it's thought to be the oldest in the country.

Yarmouth Port. From Route 6A, turn onto Church Street across from the village green. Follow it around to Thacher Shore Drive and Water Street. When Water Street turns left, head right down a dirt road for a wide-open view of marshland. Continue on Water Street across Keveney Bridge, which crosses Mill Creek; Keveney Lane takes you back to Route 6A. Turn left to head east, back into Yarmouth Port. This scenic loop is nice for a quiet walk, a bicycle ride, or an early-morning jog.

❊ **Bass River Golf Course** (508-398-9079; golfyarmouthcapecod.com), 62 Highbank Road, South Yarmouth. Great views of the Bass River.

❊ **Blue Rock Golf Course** (508-398-9295; bluerockgolfcourse.com), 48 Todd Road, off Highbank Road, South Yarmouth. A short course.

KAYAKING ✐ **Great Marsh Kayak Tours** (508-328-7064; greatmarshkayaktours. com), West Yarmouth. Unsure of where or how to kayak or unfamiliar with local tides? Check out these wonderful three-hour tours of Nauset Marsh (see Orleans), tidal marshes, and the Parker River (here in town).

MINI-GOLF ✐ **Pirate's Cove Adventure Golf** (508-394-6200; piratescove.net), 728 Route 28, South Yarmouth. Open early April through October. At the granddaddy of all Cape mini-golf courses, kids have their choice of two 18-hole courses complete with lavish pirate-themed landscaping, extravagant waterfalls, and dark caves. Kids receive eye patches, flags, tattoos, and a jaunty pirate hat.

✐ **Skull Island Sports World** (508-398-6070; skullislandcapecod.com), 934 Route 28 at Long Pond Road, South Yarmouth. Open April to early October. In addition to a "Swiss Family Treehouse" adventure mini-golf, Bass River lures families with baseball and softball batting cages, soccer cages, a game room, go-carts, and a driving range.

TENNIS The public can play at **Flax Pond** (off North Main Street from Route 28 in South Yarmouth); at **Sandy Pond** (from Route 28 in West Yarmouth, take Higgins Crowell Road to Buck Island Road); and at **Dennis-Yarmouth Regional High School** (from Route 28, take Station Avenue to Regional Avenue in South Yarmouth). All are free.

PIRATE'S COVE ADVENTURE GOLF

✳ Green Space

BEACHES Some lodging places offer discounted daily beach stickers; don't forget to ask. Weekly stickers for cottage renters are available at Town Hall (508-398-2231), 1146 Route 28, South Yarmouth.

Sea Gull Beach, off South Sea Avenue from Route 28, West Yarmouth. This is the longest, widest, and nicest of Yarmouth's southside beaches, which generally tend to be small, narrow, and plagued by seaweed. The approach to the beach is lovely, with views of the tidal river. (The blue boxes you see, by the way, are fly traps—filled with Octenol, a synthetic version of ox breath, they attract the dreaded biting greenhead flies that terrorize sunbathers in July.) Facilities include a bathhouse, restrooms, and food service. Parking $$.

WALKS Botanical Trails of the Historical Society of Old Yarmouth, behind the post office and Captain Bangs Hallet House, off Route 6A, Yarmouth Port. This 1.5-mile trail, dotted with benches and skirting 60 acres of pines, oaks, and a pond, leads past rhododendrons, holly, lady's slippers, and other delights. The trail begins at the gatehouse, which has a lovely herb garden. A spur trail leads to the profoundly simple Kelley Chapel, built in 1873 as a seaman's bethel (a sacred space for sailors) by a father for his daughter, who was mourning the untimely death of her son. The interior contains a few pews, an old woodstove, and a small organ. It may be rented (508-360-9796) for small weddings and special events.

Taylor-Bray Farm, Bray Farm Road South, off Route 6A near the Dennis town line, Yarmouth Port. Open dawn to dusk. The Bray brothers purchased this land in the late 1800s and created a successful shipyard and farm. Now town-owned conservation

BOARDWALK, NOT PARK PLACE

⚓ **Bass Hole (or Gray's) Beach**, off Centre Street from Route 6A, Yarmouth Port. The small, protected beach is good for children, but the real appeal lies in the **Bass Hole Boardwalk**, which extends across a marsh and a creek. From the benches at the end of the boardwalk you can see across to Chapin Memorial Beach in Dennis. It's a great place to be at sunset, although you won't be alone. The 2.5-mile **Callery-Darling Trail** starts from the parking lot and crosses conservation lands to the salt marsh. As you walk out into the bay, a mile or so at low tide, recall that this former harbor used to be deep enough to accommodate a schooner shipyard in the 18th century. Free parking; handicap ramp.

BASS HOLE BEACH AND BOARDWALK

land, this working farm offers a short walking trail and tidal-marsh views. It's a nice place for a picnic. You can't help but take a deep breath of fresh air here.

Captain's Mile. The Historical Society of Old Yarmouth has printed a booklet (look for it at the chamber of commerce or Captain Bangs Hallet House) that covers three walking tours of local sea captains' houses along Route 6A. It's an informative brochure and gives some perspective about the area.

Meadowbrook Road Conservation Area, off Route 28, West Yarmouth. This recommendation originally came from Joseph Molinari, a longtime explorer from New Jersey. A peaceful place to relax, this area has a 310-foot boardwalk with an observation deck that overlooks a swamp and salt marsh. Take Winslow Gray Road north from Route 28 in West Yarmouth. After a few miles, take Meadowbrook Lane to the right and park at the end.

See also **Bass Hole (or Gray's) Beach** in the sidebar "Boardwalk, Not Park Place." And, don't forget about the **walking-tour** brochure published by the Historical Society of Old Yarmouth (see *Guidance*).

✳ Lodging

Route 6A is lined with lovely B&Bs, while the southside generally appeals to families (with a couple of notable exceptions).

RESORT 🏊 **Red Jacket Beach Resort** (508-760-9220; redjacketresorts.com), 1 South Shore Drive, South Yarmouth. Open early April to mid-October. Occupying 7 acres wedged between Nantucket Sound and the Parker's River, this extensive complex courts families. Amenities include a large private beach, heated indoor and outdoor pools, a golf course, kiddie pool with water features, supervised children's program, tennis, parasailing, kayaks, and Jet Skis. A family-style restaurant serves all three meals. All accommodations (150 rooms and 14 cottages) have their own deck or patio and in-room fridge. Rates vary considerably, according to view: near the hotel entrance, riverside or poolside, ocean view, and oceanfront (from least to most expensive). $$$–$$$$.

BED & BREAKFASTS ✳ 🍴 **Liberty Hill Inn** (508-362-3976; libertyhillinn.com), 77 Main Street, Route 6A, Yarmouth Port. Innkeepers John Hunt and Kris Srihadi offer the best bang for the buck in Cape Cod lodging. (Even more so now that they also rent a gloriously renovated house nearby! It's perfect for a romantic weeklong stay or family reunions.) The former 1825 whaling tycoon's home is nicely set back from Route 6A on a knoll. It features five comfortable rooms in the elegant main house and four in the adjacent post-and-beam-style carriage house. Light and airy rooms in the main inn benefit from

LIBERTY HILL INN

THE INN AT CAPE COD

lofty ceilings, floor-to-ceiling windows, a dramatic spiral staircase, and restored bathrooms. Crisp linens, triple sheeting, and arrival snack baskets are the norm. Next door, rooms might have a whirlpool, fireplace, or canopy bed. A sumptuous breakfast (served at individual tables) is included. $$.

❋ **The Inn at Cape Cod** (508-375-0590; innatcapecod.com), 4 Summer Street, Yarmouth Port. Helen and Mike Cassels, innkeepers since the mid-2000s, have brought this 1820s gem back to life through keen decorating skills and quintessential British hospitality. I love being surprised, and their attention to this Southern Plantation-style inn is a delight. The seven guest rooms and two suites (the latter with a separate sitting room and private balcony) are lovely and elegant. Each is equipped with a flat-screen TV and gas fireplace, and each features spacious, high ceilings and expertly renovated bathrooms. A four-course breakfast is served at individual tables in the sunny breakfast room or terrace. As you might expect, afternoon tea served fireside with homemade treats is worth returning for. There's plenty of additional guest space, including elegant gardens, porches, and a sitting room with fireplace. $$–$$$.

❋ **The Belvedere** (508-619-7639; the-belvedere-inn.com), 167 Old Main Street, South Yarmouth. Matt and Sara Fitzsimmons may only be three antique-filled rooms and a carriage house suite here, but what rooms they are: The early-19th-century house has been outfitted with the luxuries of the 21st century. They (and the whole house) have been completely renovated and restored with a casual elegance and historical charm that's hard to match. A full breakfast is typically served on the screened-in porch. $$.

The King's Inne (508-375-9109; kingsinne.com), 112 Main Street, Route 6A, Yarmouth Port. Open April through November. Completely renovated in 2010 by Carina and Paul Lewis, a lovely British couple, the King's Inne offers three fancily decorated suites in a circa 1830s house. $–$$.

🍴 🛈 **Village Inn** (508-362-3182; thevillageinncapecod.com), 92 Main Street, Route 6A, Yarmouth Port. Open May to mid-October. If you want to understand genuine hospitality, stay with Robin and Claire, an Irish brother-and-sister team who took over this historic, colonial landmark in 2015. They provide a modest but spick-and-span, 10-room place for travelers to relax and interact, then toss in a few modern conveniences. When you're looking for value, look no further. And when you're here, walk five minutes down the adjacent lane to the old wharf on the water. $–$$.

Captain Farris House (508-760-2818; captainfarris.com), 308 Old Main Street, South Yarmouth. Open mid-February to early January. Located within a small pocket of historic homes off Route 28, the 1845 Captain Farris House offers understated elegance and luxurious modern amenities. Lovely window treatments, antiques, fine linens, and Jacuzzi tubs fill the guest rooms. Of the 10 rooms, four are suites, five have a fireplace, a few have a private deck, and most have a private entrance. A fancy three-course breakfast is served at individual tables in the courtyard or at one formal dining room table. $$.

COTTAGES & MOTOR INNS ✍ **Seaside** (508-398-2533; seasidecapecod.com), 135 South Shore Drive, South Yarmouth. Open May to late October. These 41 one- and two-room cottages, built in the 1930s but nicely upgraded and well maintained, are very popular for their oceanfront location. Reserve by mid-March if possible; otherwise, cross your fingers. Sheltered among pine trees, the shingled and weathered units are clustered around a sandy barbecue area and sit above a 500-foot stretch of private beach. (A playground is next door.) Kitchens are fully equipped and linens are provided, as is daily maid service. Many of the tidy units have a working fireplace. The least-expensive units (without views) are decorated in 1950s style. Don't bother with the motel efficiencies. $$–$$$.

🍴 ✍ **Beach House at Bass River** (508-394-6501; beachhousecapecod.com), 73 South Shore Drive, Bass River. Open early April to late October. This tasteful bilevel motor inn, built in the 1970s by Cliff Hagberg (who still operates it), sits on a 110-foot stretch of private Nantucket Sound beach. Each of the 26 rooms in the tidy complex is decorated differently with country antiques and wicker; generally the oceanfront rooms are a bit spiffier, with country-pine furnishings. All rooms have a private balcony or patio and a refrigerator. An expansive buffet breakfast is included. $$.

✍ **Ocean Mist** (508-398-2633; ocean mistcapecod.com), 97 South Shore Drive, South Yarmouth. Open mid-May to mid-October. This shingled three-story complex fronting a 300-foot private Nantucket Sound beach offers 32 rooms and 32 loft suites. Each of the contemporary rooms has a wet bar or full efficiency kitchen, two double beds, and air-conditioning. Loft suites feature an open, second-floor sitting area—many of the rooms have ocean views, all have a sofa bed, many have skylights and two private balconies. Mixed reviews are warranted but it's hard to beat the location for families. There's also an indoor pool on the premises. $$–$$$.

RENTAL HOUSES ✍ **Great Island Ocean Club** (508-775-0985; greatisland oceanclub.com), off South Sea Avenue, West Yarmouth. Open April through November. This gated residential community has about 30 rental homes, fully equipped houses with one to six bedrooms. Best of all, they're located on or within ¼ mile of a private Nantucket Sound beach. Off by itself, it's a real find, perfect for families. Shared facilities include tennis courts and a pool. Reservations by mail only, from December until February. $$$.

✍ **Century 21—Sam Ingram Real Estate** (508-362-8844; summerrentals capecod.com).

✳ Where to Eat

Route 6A has a couple of excellent restaurants, and while Route 28 is lined with dozens, most are not discernible from one another. I have reviewed only the few that are. If you're staying on the southside and want more choice, check the entries in "Dennis."

DINING OUT ✳ 🍴 **Inaho** (508-362-5522; inahocapecod.com), 157 Main Street, Route 6A, Yarmouth Port. Open D. Year in and year out, this remains on my Top 10 Cape Cod list. Inaho continues to give patrons plenty of reason to remain loyal, offering some of the most sophisticated and authentic Japanese cuisine east of Tokyo. While fearless diners are handsomely rewarded with specials, the less adventurous revel in traditional tofu, teriyaki (the best I've had), bento box combinations, and miso soup. Then there is tempura, an exemplary metaphor for life: Wait too long to partake and the fleeting, perfect moment passes by. Meanwhile, over at the bar, intense concentration is focused on the Zen of sushi preparation. Save room for banana tempura or ginger ice cream. The only downside: You often have to wait because service can be slow. Reservations recommended. $$–$$$.

❋ ♪ **Old Yarmouth Inn** (508-362-9962; oldyarmouthinn.com), 223 Main Street, Route 6A, Yarmouth Port. Open L, D. You have a choice to make at this 1696 inn, the oldest on the Cape: casual pub dining or fine dining in one of three dining rooms. The fireplaces and white linens in the main dining rooms create a cozy elegance, but I often end up at the low-key tavern, a former stagecoach stop. It's just the perfect place for a grilled chicken Caesar, a cup of clam chowder, or a great burger. Lobster (baked, stuffed, in a roll, or whatever) is always a terrific choice. And the extensive Sunday buffet brunch is popular. L $–$$, D $$–$$$.

❋ **Gerardi's Café** (508-394-3111; gerardiscafe.com), 902 Route 28, South Yarmouth. Open L, D. This cute and casual place, with wooden booths, wooden chairs, a gas fireplace, and Oriental carpets, packs a big punch relative to its size. Thanks to chef Diego Gerardi, raised by restaurateurs in Boston's North End and trained at the Costigliole d'Asti at the Italian Culinary Institute for Foreigners, you can look with assurance for authentic Italian dishes like chicken Marsala and fettuccine Alfredo. You gotta love a place that knows what it is, doesn't overreach, and executes with aplomb. D $$–$$$.

EATING OUT ❋ 🍴 ♪ **Keltic Kitchen** (508-771-4835; keltickitchen.com), 415 Route 28, West Yarmouth. Open B (until

INAHO

OLD YARMOUTH INN

2 pm). Chef-owner and Irishman Dave Dempsey and his staff still sport thick brogues from the old country when they take your orders. How about an Irish farmhouse breakfast with rashers and black and white pudding or Keltic Bennys with poached eggs on an English muffin and corned beef hash? And despite having no ties to Ireland, the cranberry French toast, made with Portuguese bread, is a favorite. Lemon ricotta blueberry pancakes get raves as well. Come once to this friendly and cozy place and I bet you'll come back again. Try the beef and barley soup for lunch. And dine outside in fine weather. $.

Skipper Chowder House (508-394-7406; skipperrestaurant.com), 152 South Shore Drive, South Yarmouth. Open L, D, mid-April to mid-October. With a name like this, the "chowdah's" gotta rock—and it does! For a nice twist on two perennial faves, try the fried clam chowdah, which is fabu. Appetizers run the gamut from raw bar delicacies and Portuguese mussels to potato skins and buffalo wings; main dishes revolve around wicked awesome lobster variations, fish-n-chips and classic seafood rolls. Dine on the enclosed upper deck or on the patio, all the better to drink in the ocean. Save room for a little somethin' somethin' at their ice cream shack. Dishes $$.

❀ ♪ **Oliver's & Planck's Tavern** (508-362-6062; oliverscapecod.com), 960 Main Street, Route 6A, Yarmouth Port. Open L, D. Oliver's offers generous portions in cozy, tavernlike surroundings (or on the outdoor deck in summer). Oliver's attracts an older crowd at lunchtime; longtime Cape residents who like to keep things simple; and families who need to satisfy everyone. Specialties include seafood flatbread and broiled seafood, but hearty sandwiches, steak tips, and fettuccini are also quite popular. Live entertainment on weekends. L $-$$, D $$-$$$.

❀ ♪ **Royal II Restaurant and Grill** (508-362-2288; royalpizzagrill.com) 715 Route 6A, Yarmouth Port. Open L, D. Don't let the non-descript exterior fool you. This simple but pleasant family-friendly place offers fancy and traditional pizzas, classic Italian pasta dishes, some Mediterranean specialties like gyros and moussaka, and lots of requisite cheap eats like grinders, burgers, and fried seafood. (They also have a location on Lower Country Road in Dennis Port.) Dishes $$.

❀ ♞ ♪ **Jack's Outback** (508-362-6690), 161 Main Street, Route 6A, Yarmouth Port. Open B, L. Classic American down-home cooking is served from an exposed, dinerlike kitchen. Get there early for fluffy omelets, pancakes, and popovers or be prepared to wait. $-$$.

♞ ♪ **Seafood Sam's** (508-394-3504; seafoodsamsyarmouth.com), 1006 Route 28, South Yarmouth. Open L, D February to mid-November. Sam's offers reliable, informally presented, reasonably priced fried or broiled seafood. L $-$$, D $-$$$.

❀ Entertainment

♪ **Band concerts** (508-778-1008), Mattachesse Middle School band shell, Higgins Crowell Road, West Yarmouth.

A BREED APART

Parnassus Book Service (508-362-6420; parnassusbooks.com), 220 Main Street, Route 6A, Yarmouth Port. Deliberately avoiding signs and categories, the Muse family (proprietors since forever) wants people to browse and dig around, perhaps finding a first edition James or Melville among the stacks. Specializing in maritime, Cape Cod, and ornithology, the Muses have been selling new, used, and rare books since the mid-1950s. Shelves line the wall outside, where the books are available for browsing or purchase on a 24/7 honor system. In its former incarnations, this 1840 building served as a general store and a church. This really is one unique shop.

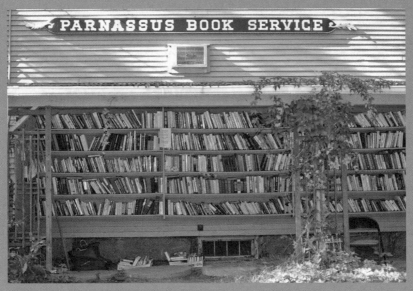

PARNASSUS BOOK SERVICE

Monday night at 7 PM in July and August since 1970.

❋ ☙ ⚲ **Entertainment Cinemas** (508-760-1633), 2–6 Enterprise Road, South Dennis.

❋ Selective Shopping

❋ Unless otherwise noted, all shops are open year-round.

SPECIAL SHOPS **Bass River Boatworks** (508-398-4883), 1361 Route 28, South Yarmouth. Barely west of the Bass River, this crammed shop will satisfy nautical fanatics. Look for copper weather vanes, lightship baskets, marine antiques, custom-made glass display cases, lighthouse models, and ship-model kits. They also do lots of ship-model restoration. In fact, that's their specialty.

Design Works (508-362-9698; designworkscapecod.com), 159 Route 6A, Yarmouth Port. Scandinavian country antiques, home furnishings, and accessories like throws, pillows, and linens.

Wilma's Eclectic Finds for You (508-778-0123; wilmaseclectic.com), 618 Route 28, West Yarmouth. Wilma, and her eclectic consignment and thrift shop, are a treasure.

✳ Special Events

Late May–late September: **Art shows** (yarmouthartguild.org). The Yarmouth Art Guild sponsors outdoor shows at the Cape Cod Cooperative Bank (Route 6A in Yarmouth Port) on many Sundays (10 AM–5 PM).

Mid-October: **Seaside Festival** (yarmouthseasidefestival.com). Begun in 1979, this festival features jugglers, clowns, fireworks, field games, a parade, sand castle competitions, arts and crafts, and bicycle, kayak, and road races.

Mid-November: **Trolley Tour Taste of Yarmouth** Join the local culinary tour trend with this (new) annual event. More than a dozen restaurants participate, offering a variety of appetizer-sized dishes at each stop. Festivities are hosted at different venues each year.

🎵 *Early December:* **Yarmouth Port Christmas Stroll** (hsoy.org). Tree lighting on the village common, caroling, and special children's activities; wreaths for sale.

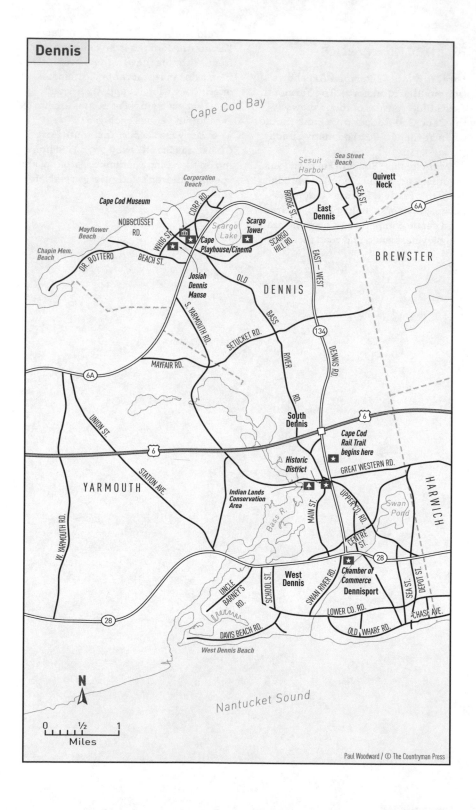

Dennis

Cape Cod Bay

Sesuit Harbor

Sea Street Beach

Quivett Neck

Corporation Beach

Cape Cod Museum

NOBSCUSSET RD.

Mayflower Beach

Chapin Mem. Beach

CORP. RD.

WHIG ST.

BEACH ST.

DR. BOTTERO

Scargo Lake

Cape Playhouse/Cinema

Scargo Tower

SCARGO HILL RD.

BRIDGE ST.

SEA ST.

East Dennis

6A

EAST – WEST

BREWSTER

Josiah Dennis Manse

S. YARMOUTH RD.

OLD

BASS

DENNIS

SETUCKET RD.

MAYFAIR RD.

6A

RIVER RD.

134

DENNIS RD.

UNION ST.

STATION AVE.

6

South Dennis

6

Cape Cod Rail Trail begins here

GREAT WESTERN RD.

YARMOUTH

W. YARMOUTH RD.

Historic District

Indian Lands Conservation Area

Bass R.

MAIN ST.

UPPER CO. RD.

Swan Pond

HARWICH

CENTRE ST.

28

SCHOOL ST.

West Dennis

SWAN RIVER RD.

Chamber of Commerce

Dennisport

SEA ST.

DEPOT ST.

28

UNCLE BARNEY'S RD.

DAVIS BEACH RD.

LOWER CO. RD.

OLD WHARF RD.

CHASE AVE.

West Dennis Beach

Nantucket Sound

N

0   ½   1
Miles

Paul Woodward / © The Countryman Press

DENNIS

Located at the Cape's geographic center, Dennis is a convenient base for day trips. Some visitors are drawn to Dennis for fine summer theater; others come for family-style attractions along Route 28. Indeed, to outsiders (including the 40,000 or so summer visitors), Dennis suffers from a split personality. Luckily, the 14,000 year-round residents have long since reconciled the village's conflicting natures.

On the **northern side of town**, Route 6A (a.k.a. Main Street) continues along its scenic way, governed by a historical commission. Skirting Dennis and **East Dennis**, Route 6A is lined with a smattering of antiques shops, crafters, and sea captains' gracious homes. (During the 19th century, more than 400 sea captains called Dennis home.) Colonial side roads off Route 6A lead to beach communities, **Quivett Neck** (settled in 1639), and Sesuit Marsh and **Sesuit Harbor**, where the fishing industry once flourished and fishing charters now depart. Note the streets in this area, named for methods of preserving fish: Cold Storage Road and Salt Works Road.

The Cape's oldest cranberry bog is also off Route 6A; Dennis resident Henry Hall cultivated the first cranberries in 1807. He discovered that the berries grow much better when covered with a light layer of sand. His brother, Isaiah, a cooper, patented the barrels used to transport the harvest. It wasn't until the 1840s, when sugar became more readily available, that anyone could do much with these tart berries, though.

The center of Dennis has a quintessential white steeple church, town green, and bandstand.

On the **southern side of town**, the 6-mile-long **Bass River** is the largest tidal river on the eastern seaboard. It serves as a natural boundary between Yarmouth and Dennis, offering numerous possibilities for exploration, fishing, and birding. Although it has never been proved, it's widely believed that Viking explorer Leif Eriksson sailed up the Bass River about 1,000 years ago, built a camp, and stayed awhile. Follow Cove Road off Route 28 and Main Street for nice views of the Bass River and sheltered Grand Cove. (The villages of **South Dennis** and **West Dennis** were once connected by a bridge here.) In **Dennis Port**, kids will enjoy the smaller **Swan River** in a paddleboat.

Each side of Dennis has its own nice, long beach: **Chapin Memorial Beach** on Cape Cod Bay and **West Dennis Beach** on Nantucket Sound. Head to **Scargo Tower** for an expansive view.

GUIDANCE ❋ **Dennis Chamber of Commerce** (508-398-3568; dennischamber.com), 238 Swan River Road (near Routes 134 and 28), West Dennis. Chamber staff are quite knowledgeable.

GETTING THERE *By car:* From the Cape Cod Canal, take Exit 9 off the Mid-Cape Highway (Route 6). Head north on Route 134 to Route 6A for Dennis and East Dennis. Head south on Route 134 to Route 28 for West Dennis and Dennis Port. The tiny historic district of South Dennis is just west of Route 134 as you head south. Depending on traffic, it takes 20 to 30 minutes to get to various points in Dennis from the canal.

GETTING AROUND As the crow flies, Dennis is only about 7 miles wide from Cape Cod Bay to Nantucket Sound. When navigating, keep a couple of things in mind:

South Dennis is actually the geographic center of Dennis, and Dennis Port (the southeastern portion of town) doesn't have a harbor on the ocean as you might expect (given its name!). In general, there isn't much to interest travelers between Routes 6A and 28. Year-rounders make their homes here, visit doctors' and lawyers' offices, and buy food and gardening supplies. Concentrate your meandering north of Route 6A and around the tiny historic district on Main Street in South Dennis.

PUBLIC RESTROOMS Sesuit Harbor in East Dennis; Town Hall, Main Street, South Dennis; Dennis Port Public Library, 5 Hall Street, Dennis Port.

PUBLIC LIBRARIES ❋ ❧ ⸙ There are five small village libraries, but the biggest is **Dennis Public Library** (508-760-6219; dennispubliclibrary.org), 5 Hall Street.

MEDICAL EMERGENCY Call **911**.

❋ To See

❧ **Scargo Tower**, Bass Hill Road, Dennis. (Bass Hill Road is just off Scargo Hill Road from Route 6A.) The 30-foot stone tower sits 160 feet above sea level atop the area's tallest hill, and on a clear day the panoramic view extends all the way to Provincetown. Even on a hazy day you can view the width of the Cape from Nantucket Sound to Cape Cod Bay. **Scargo Lake** (see *Green Space*), a glacial kettle pond, is directly below the tower.

❧ **Josiah Dennis Manse Museum** and **Old West Schoolhouse** (508-385-2232; 385-3528 for tours), 77 Nobscusset Road at Whig Street, Dennis. Open late June through August. This 1736 saltbox was home to the Reverend Mr. Dennis, for whom the town is named. Today it's set up much as it would have been during the reverend's time, with a keeping room, child's room, maritime wing, and spinning exhibit in the attic. Costumed

LOCAL SIGNAGE

SCARGO TOWER

7:30	Wax nostalgic over breakfast at the old-fashioned waterfront Lighthouse Inn.
9:30	Rent an electric paddleboat (or a kayak) from Cape Cod Waterways.
1:00	Chow down on a lobster roll aboard a lobster boat at Sesuit Harbor Café.
2:45	Tour the Cape Cod Museum of Art, featuring important area artists.
4:45	Climb Scargo Tower on a clear day to see Provincetown.
5:15	Skip stones on Scargo Lake, a freshwater kettle pond.
7:30	Immerse yourself in garlic with any dish at Gina's by the Sea.
10:00	Order a mocha chip ice cream cone at the Ice Cream Smuggler.

interpreters are on hand to answer questions. The 1745 one-room schoolhouse, filled with wooden and wrought-iron desks, was moved to its present location in the mid-1970s.

Congregational Church of South Dennis (508-394-5992, congregationalchurchof southdennis.org), 216A Main Street, South Dennis. The staff will let you into this 1835 church on weekday mornings. What's there? The chapel features a chandelier made with Sandwich glass and a 1762 Snetzler pipe organ, the country's oldest, which is still in use during services. The church is also called the Sea Captains Church because more than 100 of its founding members were sea captains.

❋ ♪ **Jericho House and Barn Museum**, 90 Old Main Street and Trotting Park Road, West Dennis. Open by appointment (when there are enough volunteers). The 1801 full Cape-style house contains period furnishings, and the 1810 barn is filled with antique

JOSIAH DENNIS MANSE

A WORTHY CULTURAL STOP

✳ ✎ ⛫ **Cape Cod Museum of Art** (508-385-4477; ccmoa.org), 60 Hope Lane, off Route 6A, Dennis. Open May to mid-October. The museum is a winner, with eight exhibition spaces, a glassed-in sculpture court, and the Weny Education Center. At the CCMA, Cape Cod's important, historical, and contemporary artists—both living and dead—are represented by almost 2,000 works on paper and canvas as well as sculpture. It should definitely be at the top of your list of things to do. The museum also sponsors lectures and art classes for adults and children, and features first-run independent and foreign films in their Screening Room. Stop in to the Artful Hand Gallery museum shop before leaving. $.

CAPE COD MUSEUM OF ART

tools, carriages, and a fanciful collection of folk art animals (a veritable "driftwood zoo") crafted in the 1950s by Sherman Woodward.

✳ To Do

BICYCLING & RENTALS The **Cape Cod Rail Trail** is a well-maintained asphalt bikeway that follows the Old Colony Railroad tracks for 26 miles from Dennis to Wellfleet. The trail begins off Route 134 in South Dennis across from Hall Oil.

Parking and bikes are available at the trailhead from **Barbara's Bike Shop** (508-760-4723; barbsbikeshop.com), 430 Route 134. Rentals daily $$. The shop stays open from April through November.

BOAT EXCURSIONS & RENTALS ✐ **Starfish Water Safaris** (508-362-5555; capecod kayaking.com), 109 Main Street, Route 28, West Dennis. These worthwhile 90-minute narrated trips of the Bass River, the largest tidal river on the East Coast, operate late May through September. Along the shoreline you'll see windmills, luxurious riverfront estates, sea captains' homes, and lots of birds. The flat-bottomed aluminum boat (which has an awning) accommodates almost 50 people. Boat trips $$; kayak rentals $$–$$$.

SCENIC DRIVES

The **South Dennis Historic District**, on and around Main Street from Route 134, gets wonderful afternoon light and relatively little traffic. Escape the crowds and head for this little gem; it's worth a short drive or quiet walk. Note the South Dennis Free Public Library (circa 1858) on Main Street, a cottage-style building covered with wooden gingerbread trim. Liberty Hall is also noteworthy; it was used for concerts, fairs, lectures, and balls when the second story was added in 1865. Edmond Nickerson, founder of the Old South Dennis Village Association, deserves much of the credit for initiating fund-raising drives and overseeing restoration projects.

For a pleasant alternative to Route 134, which also connects the north- and southsides, take Old Bass River Road, which turns into Main Street in the South Dennis Historic District.

✍ **Cape Cod Waterways** (508-398-0080; capecodwaterways.com), 16 Main Street, Dennis Port. Open daily mid-April to mid-October. The small and winding Swan River heads about ¾-mile north to the 200-acre Swan Pond and 2 miles south to Nantucket Sound. Cape Cod Waterways rents electric and manual paddleboats, canoes, and kayaks that can accommodate a family with two small children.

FISHING & SHELLFISHING Freshwater fishing for smallmouth bass and trout is good at **Scargo Lake**. Procure freshwater and saltwater fishing licenses and regulations online (www.mass.gov/eea/agencies/dfg/licensing).

Bass River Bridge, Route 28, West Dennis. Park on one side and try your luck; or just stop and watch. Although fishing is officially not allowed here, the rule is not enforced (they'll get you more for the parking on the bridge than they will for the fishing). A number of competitively priced, seasonal fishing charters depart from Sesuit Harbor, off Route 6A in East Dennis. But it's best to contact the chamber for specifics.

FOR FAMILIES ✍ **Cartwheels** (508-394-6755; capecodcartwheels.com), 11 South Gages Way, across from Tony Kent Arena, South Dennis. Open in the summer. "Indy-style" go-carts, batting cages, an arcade, moon walk, Italian ice, and ice cream.

"PUTTING IN" AT CAPE COD WATERWAYS

GOLF ❋ **Dennis Highlands** (508-385-8347; dennisgolf.com), 825 Old Bass River Road, Dennis. Wider and more forgiving than most; great driving range and practice putting greens.

❋ **Dennis Pines** (508-385-8347; dennisgolf.com), off Route 134 at the end of Golf Course Road, East Dennis. Tight and flat, and more competitive than Highlands.

ICE-SKATING ❋ **Tony Kent Arena** (508-760-2415; tonykentarena.com), 8 South Gages Way, South Dennis. Located off Route 134, this rink served as Olympic silver medalist Nancy Kerrigan's training ground back in the early 1990s.

MINI-GOLF ✑ **Holiday Hill** (508-398-8857), 352 Main Street, Dennis Port. Open late April to mid-October. Route 28 is lined with mini-golf courses similar in quality, but can others claim that they plant more than 10,000 flowers annually, as Holiday Hill can?

❋ Green Space

BEACHES Cottage renters may purchase a weekly parking pass at Town Hall (508-394-8300), 485 Main Street, South Dennis. Day-trippers pay ($$$) to park at the following beaches:

✑ **West Dennis Beach** (off Lighthouse Road) on Nantucket Sound is the town's finest and longest beach (it's more than a mile long). Like many Nantucket Sound beaches, though, it's also rather narrow. While there's parking for more than 1,300 cars, the lot rarely fills. If you drive to the western end, you can usually find a few yards of beach for yourself. The eastern end is for residents only. Facilities include 10 lifeguard stations, a snack bar at the eastern end, showers, and restrooms. It's difficult to imagine that fishing shanties, fish weirs, and dories once lined the shores of West Dennis Beach. But they did.

BREWSTER FLATS

CHAPIN MEMORIAL BEACH

Chapin Memorial Beach, off Chapin Beach Road on Cape Cod Bay, is open to four-wheel-drive vehicles. It's a nice, long, dune-backed beach. As you drive up to Chapin, you'll probably notice an incongruous-looking building plunked down in the marshes and dunes. In fact, it's the headquarters for the Aquaculture Research Corporation (known as the Cultured Clam Corp.), the only state-certified seller of shellfish seed. Begun in 1960, the company is a pioneer in the field of aquaculture. There's no better place to study shellfish. Facilities at the beach include portable restrooms.

Corporation Beach, off Corporation Road on Cape Cod Bay, is backed by low dunes and was once used as a packet-ship landing by a group of town residents who formed the Nobscusset Pier Corporation (hence its name). The crescent-shaped beach has concession stands, a playground and picnic area, lifeguards, and restrooms.

✍ **Mayflower Beach**, off Beach Street on Cape Cod Bay, has a boardwalk, restrooms, and a concession stand. **Sea Street Beach**, off Sea Street, and **Howes Street Beach**, off Howes Street, are backed by low dunes; both have boardwalks. The Sea Street parking lot fills up by noon. These three beaches are relatively small and good for families with young children because the water is shallow. As at Corporation and Chapin Memorial beaches, at low tide you can walk a mile out into the bay.

There are seven other public beaches on Nantucket Sound, but all are quite small.

PONDS & LAKES **Scargo Lake**, a deep, freshwater kettle hole left behind by retreating glaciers, has two beaches: **Scargo Beach** (off Route 6A) and **Princess Beach** (off Scargo Hill Road). Princess Beach has a picnic area; bathers at Scargo Beach tend to put their beach chairs in the shallow water or on the narrow, tree-lined shore. There are two legends concerning the lake's creation—you decide which you prefer: Did an Indian princess have the lake dug for fish that she received as a present? Or did a giant named Maushop dig the hole as a remembrance of himself to the local Native Americans?

Swan Pond Overlook, off Centre Street from Searsville Road and Route 134. A small overlook best for bird-watching.

WALKS **Indian Lands Conservation Area**, behind Town Office on Main Street, South Dennis. This easy, 2-mile round-trip walk skirts the banks of the upper Bass River. In

SCARGO LAKE (AND CAPE COD BAY) FROM SCARGO TOWER

winter you'll see blue herons and kingfishers; lady's slippers bloom in May. From the northern end of the Town Hall parking lot on Main Street, follow the power line right-of-way path for half a mile to the trailhead. The adjacent cemetery near the parking lot offers gravestones of Dennis' ancestors from the 1690s.

❋ Lodging

🦞 Dennis lodging establishments represent very good values. One place off Route 6A *really* stands out on the northside, while the southside is loaded with family places (with one noteworthy exception). Most southside places are on or quite close to the beach.

RESORT ✐ **Lighthouse Inn** (508-398-2244; lighthouseinn.com), Lighthouse Inn Road, West Dennis. Open mid-May to mid-October. They don't make them like this anymore. This classic Cape Cod, family-friendly resort on Nantucket Sound has 68 rooms and tidy cottages on 9 grassy, waterfront acres. The resort, expertly operated by the Stones since 1938, has lots of amenities: supervised children's activities, special children's dinners, a heated pool, tennis, shuffleboard, mini-golf, volleyball, and the Sand Bar Club and Lounge. On rainy days guests gather in the common rooms of the lodge-style main building, stocked with games, books, and a TV. Oriental carpets lend it a delightful, old-shoe, Adirondack-camp feel. And a staff of more than 100 hustle around, keeping guests happy. A full breakfast is included. Its Bass River Lighthouse is the only privately owned working lighthouse in the country. $$–$$$.

BED & BREAKFASTS ❋ ✐ **Isaiah Hall Bed and Breakfast Inn** (508-385-9928; isaiahhallinn.com), 152 Whig Street, Dennis. On a quiet street off Route 6A, innkeepers Jerry and Judy Neal's rambling 1857 farmhouse is one of the most comfortable and welcoming places on Cape Cod. It feels like one big nonstop social event here, with guests lingering in the pass-through kitchen and hanging around in the "great room." Main inn guest rooms are furnished with country-style antiques, while rooms in the attached carriage house are newer, each decorated with stenciling, white wicker, and knotty pine paneling. Check out the newer Isaiah Hall Suite, a jewel of a two-bedroom suite with a fireplace. All 12 rooms are air-conditioned and equipped with flat-screen TVs, DVDs, and 600–thread count sheets. There is plenty of indoor and outdoor common space, including that cathedral-ceilinged great room (with a guest computer), a delightfully relaxing garden, and a deep lawn that leads to the Cape's oldest cranberry bog. A full breakfast is served at one long, extraordinarily convivial table. $–$$.

❄ **Shady Hollow Inn** (508-694-7343; shadyhollowinn.com), 370 Main Street, South Dennis. This off-the-beaten-path B&B, with a tranquil side garden, is a graciously renovated sea captain's house that dates to 1839. Beth and Gary Albert's three guest rooms, with Mission-style furnishings and quilts, are outfitted with a hefty dose of attention,

soothing color palettes, and tasteful bathroom renovations. $.

✎ **An English Garden B&B** (508-398-2915; anenglishgardenbb.com), 32 Inman Road, Dennis Port. Open late April through October; guest house and suites open year-round. This is a very good, comfortable, contemporary choice. Within a two-minute walk of the beach, this B&B has nine tasteful rooms, two suites, and a three-bedroom guest house. Each boasts hardwood floors, quilts, and a deck or small balcony; some have a whirlpool or ocean view. Both airy living rooms are perfect for reading on a rainy afternoon. A full breakfast is served at individual tables in a spacious and bright breakfast room. $$.

✎ **By the Sea Guests B&B** (508-398-8685; bytheseaguests.com), 57 Chase Avenue at Inman Road, Dennis Port. Guest house open late April through September, while suites are available year-round. You can't get closer to Inman Beach than this. Each of the 12 large rooms, with refrigerator and cable TV, is basically but pleasantly outfitted. Look for well-maintained 1950s-style cottage

ISAIAH HALL B&B INN

furniture, white cotton bedspreads, and white curtains. It's all very summery, charming, and breezy. On rainy days, guests can head to the enclosed porch overlooking the private beach (just steps away) or to the large living room with books, games, and a ready supply of snacks. There are also five contemporary, fully equipped one- and two-bedroom suites for weekly stays. Full breakfast included with B&B rooms: $$–$$$.

COTTAGES 🐚 **Dennis Seashores** (508-778-8108; dennisseashores.com), 20 Chase Avenue, Dennis Port. Open May through October. These 35 housekeeping cottages are some of the best on Nantucket Sound; make reservations a year in advance. The two-, three-, and four-bedroom shingled cottages, with knotty-pine paneling and fireplaces, are decorated and furnished in a "Cape Cod Colonial" style. Cottages, with fully equipped kitchens, towels, and linens, are either beachfront or nestled among pine trees; each has a grill and picnic table. The resort's private stretch of beach is well tended. $$$–$$$$+.

RENTAL HOUSES 🐚 **Foran Realty** (508-385-1355; capecodproperties.com), 585 Main Street, Route 6A in Dennis.

❋ Where to Eat

Dennis has embarrassing riches of good and great restaurants to satisfy every budget and whim. Surrounding towns should be so lucky.

DINING OUT **Red Pheasant Inn** (508-385-2133; redpheasantinn.com), 905 Main Street, Route 6A, Dennis. Open D. Chef-owner Bill Atwood and his wife, Denise, have been going strong here since 1980 and still receive consistently glowing reviews. Low ceilings, wood floors, exposed beams, and linen-draped tables set a rustic and romantic tone. Located in a 200-year-old renovated barn (actually, a former ship chandlery on Corporation Beach), the elegant restaurant enjoys a fine reputation for attentive service, first-rate cuisine, and a well-chosen (and a very well-priced) wine list. Prime portions of sole and duck with regional American influences are offered. Lobster and other seafood are always popular, and their rack of lamb could compete head-to-head anywhere! In a nod to changing palates, they've added a bistro bar menu. $$$–$$$$.

Fin (508-385-2096; fincapecod.com), 800 Main Street, Route 6A, Dennis. Open D, mid-February through December. This upscale-ish contemporary seafood bistro (intimate and housed in a two-story antique Cape building) has been all the rage since it opened. Don't miss the dayboat sea scallops or flounder (a house specialty)—most is locally sourced. And the chef-owner, Martha Kane, hails from the acclaimed Brewster Fish House. Oh, and hubby Jonathan Smith is an oyster grower, so don't miss the oyster chowder or Nobscussett oysters. $$$.

🦞 🍸 **Ocean House** (508-394-0700; oceanhouserestaurant.com), 425 Old Wharf Road, at the end of Depot Street, Dennis Port. Open B, D, mid-March to early January. Everyone loves the Ocean House, but don't let appearances deceive you: The boxy brick building belies the ocean views that await. Go before sunset to drink in the views; it's half the fun. The other half is artful chef Anthony Silvistri, who prepares seasonal, contemporary, New American dishes with a local influence. Look for fusion dishes like cedar-roasted teriyaki salmon, grilled Hawaiian tuna steak, or a 12-ounce Wolfneck's Farm rib eye. If you don't have reservations, dine at the bar on gourmet pizzas and appetizers. Definitely save room for distinctive desserts, and consider starting with a signature martini. $$–$$$$.

❋ 🐚 🍸 **The Oyster Company Raw Bar & Grille** (508-398-4600; theoystercompany.com), 202 Depot Street, Dennis Port. Open L, D. This is one hip

THE RED PHEASANT

and happening place to nosh with pals. And to think, you don't have to drive to Wellfleet to enjoy magnificently fresh oysters anymore. Although the Oyster Company offers other fishy temptations besides briny delicacies, the $1.25 oysters (available from 5 to 6:30) really pack 'em in. Oysters are harvested daily from Quivet Neck in Dennis. Try summertime oysters barely broiled in cilantro and butter. The regular menu is fairly limited because the chef relies on the daily catch for inspiration. $$–$$$.

♈ **Gina's by the Sea** (508-385-3213), 134 Taunton Avenue, Dennis. Open D, April through November. Gina's is a very friendly and fun place, with a low-key bar, knotty-pine walls, a fireplace, and exposed beams. A fixture in this beachside enclave since 1938, Gina's really is as consistently good as everyone says. Its Northern Italian menu features signature dishes like garlicky shrimp scampi, mussels marinara, and chicken "gizmonda." Because the restaurant is small, very popular, and doesn't take reservations, arrive early or wait until after 9 PM. Otherwise, put your name on the waiting list and take a walk on nearby Chapin Memorial Beach,

or have a drink and watch the sunset. Gina's epitomizes the essence of summer. $$–$$$.

❄ ✆ ♪ **Scargo Café** (508-385-8200; scargocafe.com), 799 Main Street, Dennis. Open L, D. The friendly staff here are particularly adept at getting patrons (most of whom are older) to Cape Playhouse shows (see *Entertainment*) on time without hurrying them. If you're really late, light bites and finger foods such as shrimp martini and calamari are served in the pleasant bar. Otherwise, dependable specials include seafood

GINA'S BY THE SEA

CHAPIN'S

strudel, a vegetable-and-Brie sandwich, rack of lamb, and lobster risotto. As for the atmosphere, the bustling, renovated former sea captain's house is awash in wood: paneling, wainscoting, and floors. Brothers Peter and David Troutman have presided over the extensive and well-executed menu since 1987. It's hard to beat the prices and quality here. L $–$$, D $$–$$$$.

Clean Slate Eatery (508-292-8817; cleanslateeatery.com). 702 Route 28, West Dennis. Open D. The entrepreneurs behind Clean Slate (in the "pop-up" dining business prior to opening this brick-and-mortar place in 2016) are putting a fresh and adventurous spin on the local dining scene with two prix-fixe seatings at two different price points. Choose from traditional and vegetarian tasting menus, which might include roasted blue hubbard squash with apple cider–braised kale dumplings in a sweet onion tarragon veloute; halibut romesco with pickled dragon beans, cherry tomatoes, and roasted eggplant; or olive oil cake with ginger ice cream and vanilla compressed

peaches. Proclaiming this "dinner as an event" is about right. $$$$+.

❄ ✐ **Chapin's** (508-385-7000; chapinsrestaurant.com), 85 Taunton Avenue, Dennis. Open L, D. Near the beach, this casual eatery has something for everyone, which generally means the food isn't gourmet quality, but it also means that most folks will walk away fairly happy. There's a lot to be said for that. From a salad bar to a raw bar, Chapin's also offers chicken, local seafood, lobster, steaks, sandwiches, prime rib, and pasta dishes. See what I mean? This noisy place is wildly popular in the winter, when they offer value-laden specials to keep locals coming back. The outdoor deck is pleasant. Music fans, check out their entertainment calendar. $–$$$.

✐ **Lighthouse Inn** (508-398-2244; lighthouseinn.com), 1 Lighthouse Road, off Lower County Road, on the road to West Dennis Beach. Open B, L, D, mid-May to mid-October. The decor and cuisine here are decidedly old-fashioned; it's the kind of place you might expect in the Catskills, à la 1950. Except this is seaside. Along with peaked ceilings and knotty-pine paneling, the large and open dining room features a full wall of windows overlooking the ocean. B $, D $$–$$$.

EATING OUT 🍴 🚣 **Sesuit Harbor Café** (508-385-6134; sesuit-harbor-cafe.com), 357 Sesuit Neck Road, Dennis. Open B, L, D, April through October. Wildly, wildly popular with good reason, this café offers excellent lobster rolls and trips aboard a retrofitted lobster boat (508-385-1686; lobsterrollcruises.com). If you prefer to keep your feet on terra firma, make a beeline through the marina and boatyard for their simple harborfront shack. It's nothing to look at, but the raised herb beds augur well for quality ingredients. Order off the blackboard menu and eat at picnic tables, inside or outside, with mismatched umbrellas. Baked goods are also now available: Try breakfast treats like spinach-feta croissants and desserts like red velvet cupcakes. BYOB. Cash only. B, L $–$$, D $–$$$.

🍷 ❄ **Harvest Gallery Wine Bar** (508-385-2444; harvestgallerywinebar.com), 776 Main Street, Route 6A, Dennis. Open D. From the live music and art everywhere you look to the wine bar and convivial atmosphere, this place rocks. (As do the late hours it keeps.) $$.

🍴 🚣 **Captain Frosty's** (508-385-8548; captainfrosty.com), 219 Main Street, Route 6A, Dennis. Open L, D, mid-April through September. This no-frills roadside clam shack uses premium ingredients like hooked (not gillnetted) Chatham cod, Gulf shrimp, native clams, lobster, and small sea scallops, so you'll want to look for daily specials. If you're tired of fried seafood, the lobster rolls are pretty darn good. And rest assured that the seafood and onion rings are deep-fried in 100 percent canola oil. Choose between the casual dining room or outdoor seating at a brick patio surrounded by rhododendrons. Save room for the Cape's best soft-serve ice cream. $–$$.

🚣 **Swan River Restaurant and Fish Market** (508-394-4466; swanriverrestaurant.com), 5 Lower County Road, Dennis Port. Open L, D, mid-May to mid-October. Family owned and operated, this casual restaurant's appeal is fresh, fresh hook-caught fish, thanks to the attached fish market. Keep it simple with lobster, clams, oysters, and the catch of the day. Arrive early to secure a table overlooking a river, a marsh, Nantucket

SESUIT HARBOR CAFÉ

Sound, and a windmill. Outdoor dining, too. L $–$$, D $$–$$$.

Wee Packet (508-394-6595; wee packetrestaurant.com), 79 Depot Street, Dennis Port. Open B, L, D, early May to late October. Since 1949, this small and sweet place has been serving full Irish breakfasts, tons of egg dishes, clam chowder, great scallops, and fish-and-chips (but not at the same time of day!). The outdoor patio and summer cocktails are a nice addition. $–$$.

❄ **Lost Dog Pub** (508-385-6177; lost dogpubs.com), 1374 Route 134, East Dennis. Open L, D; kids menu for lunch only. I wouldn't waste good daylight hours at this tavern at lunchtime, but it makes a cozy spot after dark—when you just want something homey and decent, with good service. Their burgers and pizza are good; seafood, fishcakes, and clam chowder are specialties. L $, D $$.

❄ 𝒫 **The Breakfast Room** (508-398-0581; thebreakfastroomcapecod.com), 675 Route 28, West Dennis. Open B, L, mid-March through December. This place is classic, a local fixture. In addition to griddlecakes, you can order no-nonsense egg dishes or go whole hog and chow down on steak, eggs, and potatoes. They have cran-nut pancakes, eggs Benedict, and French toast, too. Lunch features salads, sandwiches, and burgers. $.

𝒫 **Kream 'n' Kone** (508-394-0808; kreamnkone.com), 961 Main Street, West Dennis. Open L, D, mid-February to mid-October. This place dishes honest-to-goodness kitsch, not kitsch imported from any consultant who says kitsch is cool. Come for self-serve fried seafood (fresh, never frozen), ice cream, and clams. Although it's campy, it's not necessarily cheap; a family can easily spend $60 here. $–$$.

🍴 **The Dog House** (508-398-7774; doghousedennis.com),189 Lower County Road, Dennis Port. Open L, D, mid-May to mid-October. This old-fashioned hot dog stand dispenses dogs with sauerkraut or bacon and cheese or lots of other combos. Lemonade aficionados take note: They serve it fresh squeezed here. After you've ordered from the take-out window, have a seat at one of a few covered picnic tables.

COFFEE & SWEETS ❄ 🍴 **Buckies Biscotti** (508-398-9700; buckiesbiscotti .com), 681 Route 28, Dennisport. Open B, L. For excellent espresso, authentic Italian cookies, biscotti, and cannoli, and savory sandwiches and panini, it's tough to beat Buckies. Long live entrepreneurs like baker Alyson Bucchiere. (They also have a location at Harwich Port.)

❄ **Stage Stop Candy** (508-394-1791; stagestopcandy.com), 411 Main Street, Dennisport. Ray and Donna Hebert originated the ultimate chocolate-covered cranberry. You gotta try it. They'll make chocolates in any shape, including computer boards and TV remote controls.

Sundae School Ice Cream Parlor (508-394-9122; sundaeschool.com), 381 Lower County Road, Dennisport. Open mid-April to mid-October. This

ICE CREAM SMUGGLER

HEAVENLY SCREENINGS

✳ **Cape Cinema** (508-385-2503; capecinema.com), 35 Hope Lane, off Route 6A, Dennis. Built in 1930 as a movie theater, Cape Cinema continues to bring fine art films, foreign films, and independent productions to Cape audiences. The exterior was designed after the Congregational church in Centerville, while the interior ceiling was designed by Rockwell Kent to represent his view of heaven, filled with comets and constellations. When Kent refused to set foot in Massachusetts because he was protesting the 1921 verdict in the Sacco and Vanzetti trial, Jo Mielziner supervised the painting and installation of the 6,400-square-foot art deco mural, which was done by the Art Students League in a New York theater and shipped by train to the Cape. There are about 300 seats in this theater, which was chosen to premiere *The Wizard of Oz* in 1940. Don't miss catching a flick here.

old-fashioned parlor is replete with a marble soda fountain, marble tables, tin signage, and a nickelodeon. Some confections are delightfully modern, though: Frozen yogurt and ice cream are made with two-thirds less fat. I refuse to take a stand, by the way, in the Sundae School versus Smuggler debate of which is better. You can't make me walk the plank on that one.

P&D Fruit, 349 Lower County Road, Dennis Port. Open mid-May to mid-September. Who says the southside of Cape Cod is so commercialized that you can't find a decent farm stand? Look no further.

Ice Cream Smuggler (508-385-5307; icecreamsmuggler.com), 716 Main Street, Dennis. Open April to mid-October. Homemade ice cream—including a great mocha chip and black raspberry—and frozen yogurt.

✳ Entertainment

🐾 ✎ ⍟ **Cape Playhouse** (508-385-3911; capeplayhouse.com), 820 Main Street, Dennis. Shows mid-June to early September. The Cape Playhouse was established in 1927 by Californian Raymond Moore, who initially went to Provincetown to start a theater company but found it too remote. Moore's attitude when he purchased this former 1830s Unitarian meetinghouse for $200 was, "If we fix it up, they will come." Sure

enough, the playhouse proudly claims the title of the country's oldest continuously operating professional summer theater and the Cape's only full Equity theater. Basil Rathbone starred in the company's first production, *The Guardsman*. Over the years, the playhouse has featured the likes of Helen Hayes, Julie Harris, Olivia de Havilland, and Jessica Tandy, when they were already "stars." Henry Fonda, Bette Davis, Humphrey Bogart, and Gregory Peck acted here before they were "discovered." Check the summertime schedule for worthwhile

CAPE COD PLAYHOUSE

WHIMSY IN THE WOODS

❄ **Scargo Pottery** (508-385-3894; scargopottery.com), 30 Dr. Lord's Road South, off Route 6A, Dennis. Down a path through the woods, Harry Holl's four daughters (Tina, Kim, Mary, and Sarah) make whimsical and decidedly untraditional birdhouses, fountains, and architectural sculptures, among other things. The "gallery" is a magical world that you won't want to miss: Pieces hang from tree branches and sit on tree stumps. The work isn't cheap, but it isn't run-of-the-mill, either. There's no question that this is pottery as art.

SCARGO POTTERY

children's theater. If you make it to only one summer production, let it be here. $$$–$$$$+.

❄ ☙ ⚲ **Entertainment Cinemas 12** (508-394-4700; entertainmentcinemas .com), Patriot Square Plaza, Route 134, South Dennis. Take Exit 9 off Route 6.

❄ **O'Shea's Olde Inne** (508-398-8887; osheasoldeinne.com), 348 Main Street, West Dennis. It's too packed to deal with in the summer, the food portions are smallish, and screaming kids can ruin the experience for some, but I recommend O'Shea's off-season for deeply authentic, serious Irish music on weekends. The smell of whiskey shots fills the air.

See also **Cape Cinema** in the "Heavenly Screenings" sidebar and **Cape Cod Museum of Art** under *To See.*

✳ Selective Shopping

❄ Unless otherwise noted, all shops are open year-round.

Ross Coppelman and Kate Nelson (508-385-7900; rosscoppelman.com and katenelson.com), 1439 Main Street, East Dennis. Ross has been fashioning stunning gold designs for more than 20 years. His shop is a special-occasion kind of place, and his creations have lots of zeros on the price tags. Kate's work is some of the most sophisticated abstraction I've seen on the Cape. Her nonrepresentational paintings and prints are extraordinary and, as she says, "ever-changing, like the path to the outgoing tide on the Brewster flats." She continues to fuse the experience of exterior landscape with the "inscape," the inner landscape of psyche and spirit.

Fritz Glass (508-394-0441; fritzglass .com), 36 Upper County Road, Dennis Port. Fritz Lauenstein creates and sells his colorful, striking, extraordinarily decorative, and functional glass pieces here. Watch him work and check out the inventory of fun and intricate marbles (sold in museums around the country) and sand dollars, honey pots and bud vases. Chances are that Fritz's wife, June, and daughter Coco will be in the shop, too.

Eden Hand Arts (508-385-9708; eden handarts.net), corner of Dr. Lord's Road and Route 6A, Dennis. This is an unusual place. They make such limited amount of their jewelry, Majolica and pottery that they require (free) tickets and don't take credit cards.

A Touch of Glass (508-398-3850; atouchofglasscapecod.com), 711 Route 28, West Dennis. These stained-glass lamps and lampshades are created using the same techniques employed by Tiffany.

Dennis Port center is a quiet place for year-round antiques browsers. Chief among the half-dozen shops "downtown" is the **Main Street Antique Center** (508-760-5700), 691 Main Street. With more than 20 dealers, it's just one of many retailers trying to revitalize the little district.

Antiques Center of Cape Cod (508-385-6400; antiquecenterofcapecod.com), 243 Main Street, Route 6A, Dennis. With more than 250 dealers, this two-story (former) building supply store is the Cape's largest cooperative, offering curios large and small. Don't miss it or the giant warehouse next door. Most objects sell for under $200 and are classified as "old," "vintage," or "collectible" rather than "antique."

Eldred's Auctions (508-385-3116; eldreds.com), 1483 Main Street, Route 6A, East Dennis. This high-end auction house—the Cape's largest—moves magnificent collections. In July the weekly auctions concentrate on books, collectibles, marine items, and paintings. During August there is an Americana auction the first week; contemporary Cape Cod art auction the second week; and a weeklong Asian art auction late in the month. In spring and fall, call about the monthly specialty auctions.

Tobey Farm, (508-385-2930), Main Street, Route 6A, Dennis. This colorful farm has been in the same family since 1681, when it was given to Thomas Tobey for his service during King Philip's War.

✍ **Pizazz** (508-760-3888), 633 Main Street, Dennis Port. Specializing in giant blowup beach toys and summer novelties, this shop is similar to dozens of others which just lack the, errrr, pizazz of this place.

✳ Special Events

✍ *Mid-August:* **Sandcastle Contest** (508-398-3568), on Mayflower Beach in the morning. Free.

THE LOWER CAPE

■

BREWSTER

HARWICH

CHATHAM

ORLEANS

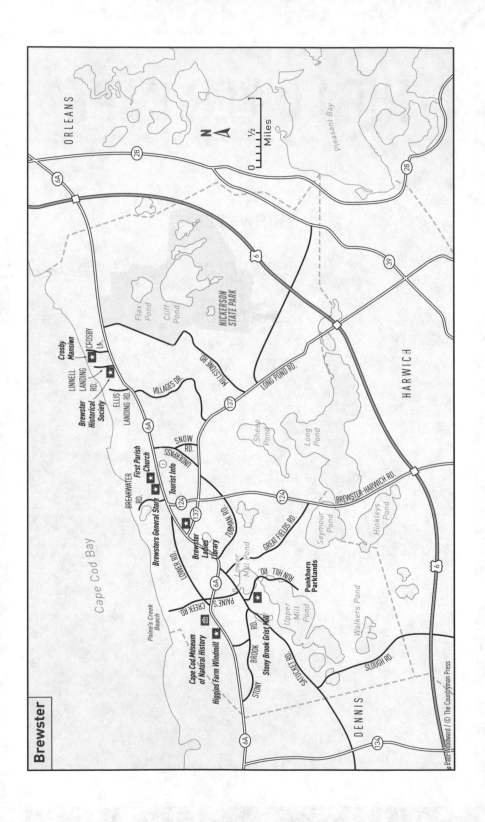

BREWSTER

You could spend a charmed week in Brewster with plenty to occupy you. While the 2,000-acre Nickerson State Park boasts facilities for a dozen outdoor activities, there is also Punkhorn Parklands, an undeveloped, 800-acre parcel of conservation land in town. Although Brewster has only 10,000 year-round residents, it has more than its share of attractions, including two good golf courses, horseback-riding trails, an outstanding museum of natural history, and exceptional dining choices.

Brewster's section of Route 6A is a vital link in the 80-square-mile Old King's Highway Historic District. Known for its selection of fine antiques shops, Brewster also attracts contemporary artists, who are drawn to a landscape more evocative of the countryside than the seaside—the land south of Route 6A is dotted with ponds, hills, and dales.

Brewster, settled in 1659 and named for *Mayflower* passenger Elder William Brewster, wasn't incorporated until 1803, when it split from Harwich. By then the prosperous sea captains who'd built their homes on the bay side wanted to distance themselves from their less-well-off neighbors to the south. Between 1780 and 1870, 99 sea captains called Brewster home (although they sailed their clipper ships out of Boston and New York), a fact that even Henry David Thoreau commented on during his 1849 trip. Many of these beautiful houses on Route 6A have been converted to B&Bs and inns.

In the early 1800s, Breakwater Beach was a popular landing for packet ships, which transported salt and vegetables to Boston and New York markets and brought tourists to the area. Salt making was big business in 1837, when more than 60 saltworks dotted Brewster beaches. Windmills pumped seawater into 36-by-18-foot vats, where it was left to evaporate (this process was developed in Dennis). During the late 18th and early 19th centuries, Brewster's Factory Village sold cloth, boots, and food to people all over the Cape.

GUIDANCE ❊ **Brewster Chamber of Commerce** (508-896-3500; brewster-capecod .com), 2198 Route 6A, about half a mile east of Route 124, in Town Hall. Staff are very friendly and quite knowledgeable.

GETTING THERE *By car:* Brewster is 30 minutes from the Cape Cod Canal (take Route 6 east to Exit 9, to Route 134, to Route 6A); it is 45 minutes from Provincetown, at the tip of the peninsula.

GETTING AROUND It's very easy to get around in Brewster. There's no real "center" to the town; places of interest are strung along Route 6A.

PUBLIC RESTROOMS Nickerson State Park and the Visitor Information Center, both on Route 6A.

PUBLIC LIBRARY See **Brewster Ladies' Library** under *To See.*

MEDICAL EMERGENCY Call **911**.

✳ To See

✳ ♪ **Cape Cod Museum of Natural History** (508-896-3867; ccmnh.org), 869 Route 6A. Founded by naturalist John Hay (along with seven local educators) in 1954, this is a terrific resource for learning about the Cape's natural world. The museum takes its mission seriously: to "inspire and foster an understanding and appreciation of our environment through education, and a means to sustain it." Check out marine tanks (containing rotating displays with native crabs, lobsters, mollusks, turtles, eels, frogs, and mesmerizing moon jellies), a live "osprey cam" which shows a bird family nesting

CAPE COD MUSEUM OF NATURAL HISTORY

nearby, whale displays, a natural history library, as well as many interactive, hands-on exhibits for children. The gift shop is packed with fun and educational toys, books, and games. The Wing's Island Trail—just one trail traversing the museum's 80 acres of marshes, beaches, and woodland—begins from here (see *Green Space*). $. (Also see **Summer camps** under *For Families*.)

STONY BROOK GRIST MILL

Stony Brook Grist Mill and Museum and Herring Run (508-896-1734), 830 Stony Brook Road. Open July and August; inquire about corn grinding on Saturdays and corn meal for sale. This millside pond is one of the Cape's most picturesque places, especially during the spring migration (mid-April to early May), when the herring are "running" and the natural "ladders" are packed with the silver-backed fish. In 1663 America's first water-powered mill stood on this location. The present gristmill, constructed on 1873 woolen mill foundations (part of the 19th-century Factory Village), contains old milling equipment and an antique loom. The museum includes early American artifacts and Native American stone tools.

✳ ♪ ♟ **Brewster Ladies' Library** (508-896-3913; brewsterladieslibrary.org), 1822 Route 6A. In 1852 two teenage Brewster girls established this "library," which began as a shelf of books lent from the girls' houses. After local sea captains donated funds in 1868, the ever-expanding library moved to a handsome red Victorian building. The two original front-parlor rooms—each with a fireplace, stained-glass windows, and armchairs—are still filled with portraits of sea captains

8:00	Read the morning paper on the front porch of The Brewster Store.
9:30	Traverse marshland, beaches, and woodlands at the Cape Cod Museum of Natural History (or Nickerson State Park).
12:30	Dine outdoors at Cobie's or Guapo's.
2:00	Poke around the Stony Brook Grist Mill and Herring Run.
3:30	Discover shallow tidal pools and abstractions on the Brewster flats.
5:30	Arrive early for chowder bisque and scallops at Brewster Fish House.
8:00	Lick a fast-melting ice cream cone from Brewster Scoop.
10:00	Star gaze in Drummer Boy Park.

ENTERING

INC. 1803

BREWSTER

and ships. Not just for ladies, the modern library has a large children's area, DVDs, CDs, periodicals, newspapers, and computers. Call for details about lectures and art exhibits.

❊ **The Brewster Store** (508-896-3744; brewsterstore.com), 1935 Route 6A at Route 124. Purveying groceries and general merchandise since 1866, this quintessentially Cape Cod store was built in 1852 as a Universalist church. As always, locals and visitors sit outside on old church pews, sip coffee, read the morning newspaper, eat penny candy and ice cream, and watch the world go by. Upstairs has been re-created with memorabilia from the mid-1800s to the mid-1900s; downstairs has a working antique nickelodeon and often-used peanut roaster.

BREWSTER LADIES' LIBRARY

Brewster Historical Society Museum (508-896-9521; brewsterhistoricalsociety.org), 739 Lower Road at the Captain Elijah Cobb House. Open late June through August. Highlighting Brewster's rich heritage, this small museum has an 1884 barbershop, a 1830s sea captain's room, dolls and toys, the old East Brewster Post Office, and antique gowns. Special summertime exhibits feature little-known aspects of Brewster history. The society also maintains the **Higgins Farm Windmill, Harris-Black House, and Hopkins Blacksmith Shop**, located at Drummer Boy Park, 773 Route 6A, in West Brewster. Volunteer members of the BHS are on hand to regale you with historic anecdotes, like how a family raised 10 children in the one-room house (possibly the "last remaining primitive one-room house on the Cape"). The 1795

THE BREWSTER STORE

windmill is known for its octagonal design, while its top resembles a boat's hull. A walking trail originates from the house (see Spruce Hill Conservation Area under *Green Space*).

Crosby Mansion (508-896-1744; crosbymansion.com), 163 Crosby Lane off Route 6A. Call for opening months. This Colonial Revival structure, once the elegant home of Albert and Matilda Crosby, sits on 19 acres of bayside property. Massachusetts acquired the land (and the house by default) by eminent domain in 1985 so that the public could access Cape Cod Bay from Nickerson State Park. Because the state couldn't afford to maintain it (the 28-room mansion requires millions in repairs), a volunteer group, the Friends of Crosby Mansion, stepped in. They've done an impressive job repairing the worst structural damage and much of the interior.

Once upon a time, Albert Crosby owned the Chicago Opera House and fell in love with one of the showgirls, Matilda. When she came to live in Albert's modest turn-of-the-20th-century house, she was so unhappy that Albert had a mansion built for her—around his original four-room house! (Kids compare stepping into the smaller house to what Alice must have felt like in Wonderland.) Matilda is said to have entertained in the larger mansion while Albert stayed in his interior boyhood home.

⚓ **First Parish Church** (508-896-5577; firstparishbrewster.org), 1969 Route 6A, on the town green (a.k.a. "The Egg" because of its shape and natural depression). Gothic windows and a bell tower mark the church's 1834 clapboard exterior, while interior pews are marked with names of prominent Brewster sea captains. Wander around the graveyard behind the church, too.

✳ To Do

BASEBALL ⚓ The **Brewster Whitecaps** (508-896-7442; brewsterwhitecaps.com), who joined the Cape Cod Baseball League in 1988 as an expansion team, play behind the school, 384 Underpass Road, from mid-June to early August. The Whitecaps also sponsor weeklong clinics and a baseball camp in June and July.

BICYCLING & RENTALS Because the Cape Cod Rail Trail runs through Brewster, and Nickerson State Park (see the "A Supreme State Park" sidebar) has its own network of bicycle trails linked to the trail, plenty of places rent bicycles. Look for **Cape Cod Rail Trail Bike & Kayak** (508-896-8200; railtrailbikeshop.com), 302 Underpass Road, which rents and sells bikes. As the name implies, they also rent kayaks for use on the kettle ponds, sandy lake beaches, and salt marshes along the trail. **Brewster Bike** (508-896-8149; brewsterbike.com), 442 Underpass Road, is open March through November. Both shops also offer parking, sales, and repairs. Rentals $$. Pick up their excellent, free Nickerson trail map.

If you brought your own bikes, there is rail-trail parking on Route 137, on Underpass Road off Route 137, and at Nickerson State Park on Route 6A.

✇ Trailers and alleycats (rented above) for hauling kids are great for this stretch because it's shady and fairly flat. Nickerson trails go up and down and around, roller-coaster style.

TIDAL FLATS

At low tide, you can walk 2 miles out onto the tidal flats of Cape Cod Bay. During Prohibition, townspeople walking on the flats would often stumble onto cases of liquor thrown overboard by rumrunners. But encounters are tamer these days: Kids discover tidal pools, play in channels left by receding tides, and marvel at streaked "garnet" sand. On a clear day you can gaze from the Pilgrim Monument to Sandwich. You can reach the flats from any bay beach.

CAPE COD RAIL TRAIL

BOATING & PADDLEBOARDING RENTALS See the "A Supreme State Park" sidebar below and Cape Cod Rail Trail Bike & Kayak under *Bicycling/Rentals* above.

SUPfari Adventures (508-205-9087; supfariadventures.com), multiple locations in Brewster and Orleans. Stand-up paddleboarding brought from Maui to the Cape by Brewster's former harbormaster. Great multigenerational fun. $$$$.

FISHING & SHELLFISHING Brewster has almost 70 freshwater ponds, and a state fishing license is required. The following ponds are stocked: **Sheep Pond**, off Route 124, **Upper Mill** (off Run Hill Road), and **Flax, Little Cliff**, and **Higgins Ponds** within Nickerson State Park. For shellfishing permits (and specifics about where and when to find the creatures), head to Town Hall (508-896-3500), 2198 Route 6A. In July and August shellfishing is permitted only on Thursday and Sunday. Shellfish beds at **Saint's Landing Beach** (off Lower Road from Route 6A) are seeded in summer. Quahogs and sea clams are harvested in July and August on Thursday and Sunday; steamers are harvested October to mid-April. Nonresident permits cost $$ weekly. Oyster beds are open October to late November on Sunday at the rock beds at Ellis Landing (off Route 6A).

FOR FAMILIES ✇ **Summer camps** (508-896-3867; ccmnh.org), 869 Route 6A, at the Cape Cod Museum of Natural History (see *To See*). Got an extra two hours or five days? Got children age 3 to 12? Classes explore "Mudflat Mania," "Extreme Science," tidal

NICKERSON STATE PARK

flats, archaeology, and Monomoy's barrier beach. The emphasis is on fun, outdoor adventure, and education.

✐ **Playground by the Bay**, Drummer Boy Park, Route 6A. Shaped like a packet ship to honor Brewster's seafaring history, this play structure has separate areas for toddlers and older children. Picnic tables, too.

See also **Cape Repertory Theatre** under *Entertainment* and **First Parish Church** under *To See*.

GOLF ❋ **The Captains Golf Course** (508-896-1716 pro shop; captainsgolfcourse.com), 1000 Freemans Way off Route 6A. A highly rated public course.

❋ **Ocean Edge Golf Club** (508-896-9000; oceanedge.com), Ocean Edge Resort, 8320 Villages Drive off Route 6A. A tournament-caliber course by the Nicklaus Design Group, for members and resort guests exclusively.

HORSEBACK RIDING ❋ ✐ **Woodsong Farm Equestrian Center** (508-896-5800; woodsongfarm.com), 121 Lund Farm Way. Open by appointment. Established in 1967, Woodsong offers riding instruction, boarding, training, coaching for competitive riders, children's day programs, horse shows, and an on-premises tack shop (woodsong tack.com).

SAILING **Cape Sail** (508-896-2730; capesail.com), out of Brewster's Upper Mill Pond and Harwichport's Saquatucket Harbor. Late May to mid-October. A Coast Guard–licensed captain since 1983, Bob Rice offers customized sailing lessons and an overnight sailing school, as well as sunset and moonlight cruises and custom charters. Call him to discuss your interests.

TENNIS Check the free public courts located behind the Fire Department near the town offices, Route 6A. There is a small court fee at the Brewster Community Tennis Courts (508-896-9430; brewsterrecreation.com), 384 Underpass Road.

❋ Green Space

BEACHES Brewster has 8 miles of waterfront on Cape Cod Bay and eight public beaches, none of which are particularly spacious and all of which are located off Route 6A. Daily ($$) nonresident parking permits are purchased at the Town Hall at 2198 Route 6A (508-896-3701). In other words, you cannot pay at the beach. No permit is required at any town beach after 3 pm.

Paine's Creek Beach, Paine's Creek Road off Route 6A. This is one of Brewster's most picturesque beaches because of the creek that feeds into it. Parking fee, restrooms, but no lifeguards.

A SUPREME STATE PARK

Nickerson State Park (508-896-3491; mass.gov/dcr), 3488 Route 6A. Open 8 AM–8 PM daily during camping season, dawn to dusk off-season. This former estate of Chatham native Roland Nickerson, a multimillionaire who founded the First National Bank of Chicago, contains just under 2,000 acres of pine, hemlock, and spruce and 11 to 14 kettle ponds, depending on water levels. Nickerson and his wife, Addie, who entertained such notables as President Grover Cleveland, had a fairly self-sufficient estate, with their own electric generator, ponds teeming with fish, vegetable gardens, and game that roamed the land. When the mansion that Roland's father, Samuel, built for him burned down in 1906, a disconsolate Roland died two weeks later. (The "replacement" is now the Ocean Edge Conference Center.) Addie ultimately donated the land in 1934 to honor their son, who died in the 1918 influenza epidemic.

Nickerson State Park has been developed with walking trails, bicycling trails, jogging paths, more than 400 campsites—including yurt camping—picnic sites, boat launches, an amphitheater, and sandy beaches. Winter conditions often provide for ice skating and ice fishing and occasionally for cross-country skiing. (Snow rarely stays on the ground for more than a few days, though.) If you're at all interested in the out-of-doors, don't bypass Nickerson, one of the Cape's real treasures. Almost 500,000 people visit annually. In summertime, look for park programs like bayside strolls, night walks, campfires, and "kiddiescope" bird-watching. Parking $.

Jack's Cape Cod (508-896-8556; jackscapecod.com), located at Flax Pond, open mid-June to early September. Jack's rents canoes, kayaks, Sunfish, surf bikes, sea cycles, and pedal boats. Rentals $$$$.

Flax Pond and Cliff Pond. Flax has Nickerson's best public beach, a picnic area, and a bathhouse, but no lifeguard. Cliff Pond is ringed with little beaches, but bathers share the pond with motorized boats. (It's not really a problem, though.)

⚲ 🐾 ✐ **Camping** (877-422-6762 reservations; 508-896-3491 information; reserveamerica .com), mid-April to late October. Because Nickerson is very popular, summer reservations are absolutely essential. They're accepted six months in advance for all of the 400+ sites. There is a 14-day limit in summer.

See also *Bicycling/Rentals* and *Fishing/Shellfishing* under *To Do*.

NICKERSON STATE PARK

PONDS **Long Pond** and **Sheep Pond**, both off Route 124, have freshwater swimming and sandy beaches. Long Pond has a summertime lifeguard. Long and Sheep Ponds are among the best of Brewster's more than 50 ponds. Parking permits are required for residents and visitors. You'll find portable toilets at both.

See also the "A Supreme State Park" sidebar.

WALKS Famed nature writer John Hay lived in Brewster and certainly had plenty of places nearby to enjoy Mother Nature. You can follow in his footsteps.

Wing's Island Trail, **South Trail**, and **North Trail**, at the Cape Cod Museum of Natural History (see *To See*), 869 Route 6A. Named for Brewster's first settler, a Quaker forced to leave Sandwich due to religious persecution, the Wing's Island Trail (about 1.5 miles round-trip) meanders past sassafras groves and salt marshes, which provide habitat for diverse plants and animals. Traversing a tidal island, it ends on the dunes with a panoramic bay view. South Trail is on the opposite side of Route 6A and extends for about a mile past Stony Brook, a beech grove, and the remnants of a cranberry bog. The short North Trail wends around the museum's immediate grounds, crossing a salt marsh. Naturalist-led walks depart from the museum (508-896-3867) twice daily on weekdays in summer; free with museum admission.

Punkhorn Parklands, at the end of Run Hill Road, off Stony Brook Road. Miles of scenic trails on 880 acres—some overlooking kettle ponds—traverse oak and pine forests, meadows, and marshes. Trails are used by birders and mountain bikers, even coyotes and foxes. Pick up a detailed trail and off-road map from the Visitor Information Center (see *Guidance*).

Spruce Hill Conservation Area, behind the Brewster Historical Society Museum, 3171 Route 6A. This trail, and the uncrowded little beach at the end of it, is a secret treasure. The 20-minute, round-trip trail (¼ mile each way) follows an overgrown, old, clay dirt carriage road—probably used for off-loading fish and lumber and rumored to have been used by bootleggers during Prohibition—which runs from the museum to the bay and a private stretch of sandy beach. The Conservation Commission manages the 25-acre area.

See also the sidebar, "A Supreme State Park."

❋ Lodging

Brewster has it all, from first-class inns and homey B&Bs to resort condos and family cottages.

RESORT TOWNHOUSES ♫ **Ocean Edge Resort** (800-343-6074 booking agent; oceanedge.com), 2660 Route 6A. Town houses available seasonally. Once part of the vast Roland Nickerson estate (see the "A Supreme State Park" sidebar), this 380-acre complex includes a Gothic and Renaissance Revival stucco mansion (now mainly a conference and event center) and 11 private, contemporary condominium "villages." Rental units are configured as apartments, two-story town houses (with one, two, and three bedrooms), and Cape cottages. Some units are bayside; the majority overlook the golf course. Most have "real" backyards and are within walking distance of resort facilities. Resort facilities include indoor and outdoor pools, a private 1,000-foot bayside beach (for bayside rentals only), restaurants, a playground, and organized programs for children (for a fee). Golf packages, without instruction, are available through the resort on a "pay-as-you-play" basis. $$$–$$$$+.

INNS ❋ ☙ ♫ **Old Sea Pines Inn** (508-896-6114; oldseapinesinn.com), 2553 Route 6A. I'm always impressed anew when I visit this delightful, period-perfect hostelry. In 1907 the building housed the Sea Pines School of Charm and Personality for Young Women. When Michele and Steve Rowan renovated it in 1981, they combined 1920s and '30s nostalgia with modern but unfussy comforts to create palpable authenticity. Few innkeepers work harder. All 24 rooms and three suites are pleasant, furnished with old brass or iron beds and antiques. The less expensive "classrooms" are small and share baths—it will be easy to imagine yourself as a young girl at boarding school. The rear annex has less charm but still features the Rowans' attention to detail; family suites are quite economical. The inn is set on 3½ acres, and there's plenty of space to relax inside, too, including a large, comfy living room with fireplace that leads onto the wraparound porch set with rockers. On Sunday evenings in summer, the Cape Repertory Theatre holds a well-received Broadway musical dinner revue here (see *Entertainment*). And no matter the day, a buffet-style breakfast is always included in the rates. $.

Chillingsworth (508-896-3640; chillingsworth.com), 2449 Route 6A. Open late May to late November. Overnight in Europe without a passport? Sure, if you stay here. This 1689 house, believed to be Brewster's second oldest, rents three European-style guest rooms above the restaurant (see *Dining Out*). The antiques-filled Stevenson Room boasts a private entrance and four-poster double bed—it's the largest and nicest of the rooms. The Foster Room has views of the back gardens and gazebo. Although the Ten Eyck Room is small and without a view, it's charming nonetheless. All have private bath, TV, and air-conditioning. Rates include afternoon wine and cheese, a continental breakfast, access to a private beach at the end of the street, and privileges at a private club with an indoor/outdoor pool, tennis courts, and golf. $.

BED & BREAKFASTS ✴ **Captain Freeman Inn** (508-896-7481; captainfreemaninn.com), 15 Breakwater Road. This former gem has been resurrected with aplomb by veteran innkeepers Donna and Byron Cain (formerly of Brewster by the Sea fame). Sitting proudly on the town's oval-shaped green and next door to the iconic general store, the inn would do its namesake proud. Each of the 11 guest rooms are oh-so tasteful and tranquil. Some are distinguished by luxurious baths; others by private porches. Even the most humble (what they call "boutique rooms") might make other innkeepers envious. I particularly like the private third-floor rooms. Pack a bathing suit for the pool but leave your scale at home because of the indulgent breakfasts. $$–$$$.

✴ **Brewster by the Sea Inn & Spa** (508-896-3910; brewsterbythesea.com), 716 Route 6A. Nothing is ordinary here; everything is elevated to an art form. Let's start with the full breakfast served on the back deck (surrounded

CAPTAIN FREEMAN INN

BREWSTER BY THE SEA INN & SPA

by splendid gardens and a hydrangea-ringed pool): from a fruitini glass of melon and mint to goat cheese, Gruyère, and ham panini, Donna and Byron Cain (and their labradoodle mascot, Harrison) set the tone for a perfect day. They've been excelling since the early 2000s. Stay in the newer adjacent carriage house (a.k.a. the Old Orchard House) or the main Greek Revival farmhouse inn. Either way, you'll find English country decor in seven luxurious and spacious suites and stylish guest rooms. All feature flat-screen TVs and DVDs and luxurious amenities like thick towels, fine bedding, and nightly turndown with a truffle. One has a private deck; most have a fireplace; three have a whirlpool tub. Spa services (poolside in summer and fireside in winter) include a full range of massages, facials, reflexology, and body scrubs. Inquire about lots of packages and special weekends. (And enjoy the surprise contents of the departure goodie bag.) $$–$$$.

Sea Meadow Inn at Isaiah Clark House (508-896-2223; seameadowinn

.com), 1187 Route 6A. I didn't get a chance to see rooms here because they were booked when I dropped by, but trustworthy friends have stayed and have only stellar observations to report. The seven rooms are luxurious and cozy; bathrooms are modern; breakfast is full and "to die for." $$$.

The Ruddy Turnstone Inn (508-385-9871; 1-800-654-1995; theruddyturnstone .com), 463 Route 6A. Open April through October. This is one of only two B&Bs on Route 6A with a view of Cape Cod Bay and the salt marsh. And what a view it is! If the weather is good, you'll enjoy it from the garden, deck, under the fruit trees, or from a hammock. All three guest rooms at this early-19th-century Cape-style house boast private entrances and plenty of privacy and hospitality. Inquire about weekly rates; otherwise, nightly $$–$$$.

COTTAGES & APARTMENTS ❄ 🐾 ✏
Michael's Cottages (508-896-4025; michaelscapecodcottages.com) 618 Route 6A. I can't say enough complimentary things about Michael's (now

owned and run by Matthew). Set back from the road, these four tidy and crisp cottages (there's also a B&B in the main house) are a five-minute walk from a bay-side beach. They're a bargain; one is actually a small house that sleeps six and features a deck with a hot tub. Most others have a screened-in porch and fireplace; all have air-conditioning and include linen service. New little improvements take place every year. Ask about Michael's two B&B rooms. $–$$.

☀ **Ellis Landing Cottages** (508-896-5072; ellislandingcottages.com), off Ellis Landing Road. Open June to mid-October. Only dune grasses and sandy lanes separate these six cozy waterfront cottages from the bay. Most of the refurbished housekeeping cottages were built by Gil Ellis's father and grandfather in the 1940s and 1950s. Some of the pine-paneled cottages are more rustic than others. All have kitchens, linens, and cable TV. My favorite is the cozy Resthaven Cottage, once the East Brewster railroad station, with a private garden, screened-in porch, fireplace, and three bedrooms. Call for prices. No credit cards.

RENTAL HOUSES & COTTAGES
Stonecroft–Abbott Real Estate (508-896-2290), 16 White Swallow Cartway.

Kinlin Grover Vacation Rentals (508-896-7004; vacationcapecod.com), 1990 Route 6A.

See also **Ocean Edge Resort** under *Resort*.

CAMPGROUNDS See the sidebar "A Supreme State Park" under *To Do*.

Alternatives to Nickerson State Park include **Shady Knoll Campground** (508-896-3002; shadyknoll.com), 1709 Route 6A at Route 137, which offers tent sites from mid-May to mid-October, and **Sweetwater Forest** (508-896-3773; sweetwaterforest.com), off Route 124, which is open April through October and set on 75 acres abutting a freshwater lake. Both accept reservations, but I like Sweetwater's 250 wooded sites a bit better.

✳ Where to Eat

Brewster has a wide variety of great restaurants.

DINING OUT 🐾 ♟ **Brewster Fish House** (508-896-7867; brewsterfish.com), 2208 Route 6A. Open L, D, mid-February through December. This long-beloved, small roadside bistro doesn't look like much from the outside, but inside it's an intimate and pleasant place with fresh flowers, high ceilings, and a small bar. It's consistently excellent. Alongside creative and eclectic specials you'll find grilled and broiled seafood and fish served on mod plates; go for the catch of the day. Try the superlative chowder or lobster bisque, which has a nice, spicy kick to it. In season, arrive before 6 PM or expect to wait at least an hour (no reservations taken here). Put your name on the list and walk across the street to the beach; they'll honor your position on the list when you return. L $$, D $$–$$$.

BREWSTER FISH HOUSE

Chillingsworth (508-896-3640; chill ingsworth.com), 2449 Route 6A. Open L, D, mid-May to late November. If you can't fly to Paris for the weekend, you can at least dine at this special occasion restaurant. But you have to understand it to appreciate it. These small, candlelit dining rooms, filled with antiques, feel rather like European salons. The sophisticated service is well paced and discreet. Indulge in a six-course, prix fixe menu featuring superlative French/California-style haute cuisine—or dine more lightly at The Bistro, an airy greenhouse setting with a menu featuring grilled fish, pastas, cobblers, and chocolate bread pudding. Or dine alfresco. À la carte luncheons in the greenhouse (or on the terrace) are always relaxing. Chef "Nitzi" Rabin and his wife, Pat, proudly preside. The adjacent Chillingsworth Pastry Shop offers tasty pastries, rustic breads, and artisanal cheese to go (seasonal hours are similar to the restaurant). The wine cellar earns extraordinary marks. Bistro L $$, bistro D $$$, multicourse dinners $$$$+.

BRAMBLE INN

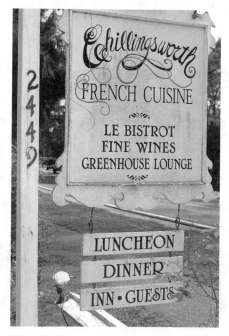

CHILLINGSWORTH

🦞 🍸 **Bramble Inn** (508-896-7644; brambleinn.com), 2019 Route 6A. Open D, mid-April through October. After all these years, chef-owner Ruth Manchester's place is still a treat. Look for New American and internationally inspired cuisine like parchment-roasted chicken with grilled lobster, rack of lamb, and seafood curry. Along with gracious service and intimate dining rooms (or courtyard dining), you'll find elegantly casual mix-and-match antique place settings. The broad, prix fixe menu changes every few weeks. (What doesn't change? It ain't cheap, but you can order a less expensive three-course menu if to the order reaches the kitchen by 6 PM.) Their hip little **Bayside Bistro Bar** is a bit of heaven, thanks to ceviche and pan-seared dayboat scallops with mushroom and truffle risotto. There's no entertainment, unless you consider Ruth's husband, Cliff; they've presided over the place since 1985. Bistro menu $$, four-course D $$$$–$$$$+.

❄ **Peddler's Restaurant** (508-896-9300; peddlersrestaurant.com), 67 Thad

Ellis Road. Open D, limited nights. Off Route 6A (turn at the Brewster Book Store), this small roadhouse completely covered in wisteria is an unlikely suspect in the local restaurant wars. And it's a winner. Chef Alain Hasson specializes in authentic Paris bistro cooking, offering dishes like sole meuniere, slow-roasted rustic duck, and steak au poivre. (Although I gravitate to the French plates, he also gives a respectful nod to Italian dishes.) Entrées are served in the skillet with potatoes and haricots verts. I've never met a blackboard special that didn't delight. No reservations. Cash and American Express only. $$$.

EATING OUT ✐ **Guapo's Tortilla Shack** (508-896-3338; guaposcapecod.com), 239 Underpass Road. Open L, D, March through November. (Orleans location open year-round with live music.) I'd be happy eating every meal at this authentic Baja-style taqueria. Try the chicken burrito: es muy bueno. As is the smoked street corn dip—wow. Look for all the usual Mexican dishes and look forward to them being a cut above. To boot: this place is on the rail trail. $.

❊ ✐ **Café Alfresco** (508-896-1741), Lemon Tree Village, 1097 Route 6A. Open B, L. This modest café offers breakfast (eggs any style and great muffins), lunch sandwiches, soups, and homemade bread, and specials like fish-and-chips, scallop rolls, and chicken salad. But I generally only come for the lobster roll ($$) at lunchtime. There are a few outdoor tables where you hear trickling water fountains, but most people sit inside.

✐ **Cobie's** (508-896-7021; cobies .com), 3260 Route 6A. Open L, D, May to mid-October. Owner Rob Slavin has operated this old-fashioned summertime seafood and ice cream shack since 1984, and his staff is quite loyal, which says a lot. I like the lobster rolls, onion rings, fried scallops, charbroiled burgers, and sweet potato fries (a healthified fast food indulgence). Enjoy it all seated at covered

GUAPOS

picnic tables near the pine trees. They also feature tasty all-natural smoothies and deeply yummy ice cream treats. Sure, you are eating with plastic in a parking lot, but it's summertime and the living is easy, right? Cobie's is convenient for rail trail cyclists (see *To Do*) and families just back from the beach. Some people prefer JT's across from Ocean Edge, but I'm a big Cobie's fan. L $, D $$.

❊ **Eat Cake 4 Breakfast Bakery** (508-896-4444; eatcake4breakfastbakery .com), 302 Underpass Rd. Life is short. What's in a name? It says it all at this fabu bakery. Fiendishly accessible on the rail trail, this killer place dispenses buttery croissants, mouth-tingling brownies, quiches, and more. Will you need to ride the entire rail trail and back to work off this stop? Yup. Oh, and you'll need some coffee for when you come off that carb and sugar high. $.

Brewster Coffee Shop (508-896-8224), 2149 Route 6A. Open B, L, April through November. If you're renting a house or cottage, you'll end up at this

COBIES

friendly joint once—if you can get in at breakfast, that is. The place is always packed to the gills in the morning. Order up a short stack of pancakes, share some eggs Benedict, and then go for a walk. $.

PICNICS, COFFEE, & ICE CREAM **Satucket Farm Stand** (508-896-5540; satucketfarm.com), 76 Route 124, just off Route 6A. Open late May to early September. An old-fashioned open-air stand with farm-fresh produce, including fantastic corn, pies, baked goods, jams, honey, and cheeses. It's a popular spot for local chefs.

Brewster Scoop (508-896-7824), 1935 Route 6A. Open late May to early September. Behind The Brewster Store, this small shop is a purveyor of Bliss Dairy's sugar-free ice cream and nonfat frozen yogurt. But lest this sound too limiting and dietary in nature, as a friend said, they also have decadent sugary offerings, too.

See also **Great Cape Herbs** under *Selective Shopping*, for coffee.

✳ Entertainment

Υ **The Woodshed** (508-896-7771; the brewsterwoodshed.com), 1993 Route 6A near The Brewster Store. Open late April to late November. Live acoustic rock nightly in summer, weekends in fall and spring. This answers the

BREWSTER SCOOP

SATUCKET FARMS

question: Where do all the summer workers go on their night off? With wooden rafters and well-worn wooden floors (reeking of stale beer), this dark joint jumps with locals.

🎵 **Band concerts**, Drummer Boy Park, 773 Route 6A, 2.5 miles west of Route 124. Summertime concerts at 6 PM Sunday during July and August at the gazebo. Bring a blanket and lawn chairs.

🎵 **Cape Repertory Theatre** (508-896-1888; caperep.org), 3299 Route 6A. On the grounds of the former Camp Monomoy in Nickerson State Park, this company presents performances at a 200-seat open-air theater in the woods and at a 129-seat indoor theater. There is also a popular summertime Broadway musical dinner revue at the Old Sea Pines Inn (see *Lodging*). Shows May through November; $$$. Children's productions in July and August; $.

✳ Selective Shopping

✳ Unless otherwise noted, all shops are open year-round.

The sweet **Lemon Tree Village** (1069 Route 6A; lemontreevillageshops.com) is a collection of eateries and shops worth poking around for gifts and souvenirs. Of note: **Lemon Tree Pottery**

CAPE REPERTORY THEATRE

(508-896-3065) for handcrafted wares; **Brewster Birdhouse** (508-896-1522) for fine feathered friend finds; the **Village Toy Store** (508-896-8185) for kids of all ages; and the **Cook Shop** (508-896-7698), featuring two well-organized floors of kitchen gadgets, gourmet treats, and high-quality cookware.

ANTIQUES Dozens of antiques shops line Route 6A; only a tiny sampling follows.

Wysteria Antiques (508-896-8650; wisteria-antiques.com), 1199 Route 6A. The lavender exterior, the scent of wisteria as you cross the threshold, and three rooms filled top to bottom with amethyst glassware and porcelain add up to one unusual establishment. The owners, in business since the early 1980s, have an eye for Limoges porcelain, mirrors, chandeliers, and Venetian glass, even if the presentation is over the top. Decide for yourself: if the stuff is good enough for Barbra Streisand (which it is), it might be right up your alley.

Countryside Antiques (508-896-1444), 2052 Route 6A. Look for English,

Irish, Scandinavian, European, and Chinese antiques and fine reproductions—as well as nautical and maritime antiques.

ART GALLERIES Underground Art Gallery (508-896-3757; undergroundartgallery.com), 673 Satucket Road. Amazingly, this working studio sits beneath 100 tons of soil and is supported by 10 tree trunks. The gallery features the work of watercolorist Karen North Wells, who also uses oil and acrylic for her seascapes and landscape florals. (Check the website for her classes and other events.) Karen's late husband, Malcolm Wells (malcomwells.com), designed earth-covered solar buildings like this one and wrote books on sustainable architecture.

Maddocks Gallery (508-896-6223; jamesmaddocksgallery.com), 1283 Route 6A. Open May through October; otherwise call for hours. James Maddocks paints nostalgic, traditional, and representational Cape Cod scenes.

Ruddeforth Gallery (508-255-1056; ruddeforthgallery.com), 3753 Route 6A. Open mid-May to mid-October; otherwise call for hours. Watercolors, oils,

LEMON TREE

ROUTE 6A'S ANTIQUES AND GALLERIES

and limited edition prints of Cape Cod scenes, florals, and still lifes by Debra Ruddeforth (a signature member of the Copley Society in Boston). Husband Tom Ruddeforth's color and black-and-white photographs are also displayed.

Struna Galleries (508-255-6618; strunagalleries.com), 3873 Route 6A. Working from copper plates to make dry-point engravings, artist Tim Struna creates sweet little renderings of Cape Cod scenes. They're a nice (and affordable) reminder of why life on the Cape is so special. Since his studio is here, you'll often find Tim hard at work, although there is also a gallery in Chatham. He also sells larger watercolors.

ARTISANS **Heart Pottery** (508-896-6189; dianeheartpottery.com), 1145 Route 6A. Specializing in functional and decorative porcelain and raku, Diane Heart spends most days at her wheel here in the shop. Her raku, using an ancient Japanese firing technique, is stunning. Diane's husband, Mark Preu, offers nature and scenic photographs.

Clayton's Clay Works (508-255-4937; claytonsclayworks.com), 3820 Route 6A. Clayton Calderwood makes large, stoneware fish platters, which can be used to serve food or be displayed, indoors or out.

BOOKSTORES ✏ **Brewster Book Store** (508-896-6543; brewsterbookstore.com), 2648 Route 6A. One of the Cape's better bookstores, this one features a large and excellent selection of children's books within a small space. Also Cape Cod titles, games, toys, book signings, and story time.

SPECIAL SHOPS **The Spectrum** (800-221-2472; spectrumamerica.com), 369 Route 6A. This two-story shop, which opened in 1966, represents high-quality arts and craftspeople from all over the country. I hesitate to itemize even a few of their pieces, because I don't want to limit your imagination.

Sydenstricker Galleries (508-385-3272; sydenstricker.com), 490 Route 6A. Glass-fusing demonstrations, using a technique developed by Brewster native Bill Sydenstricker (who died in 1994), are often given. Sydenstricker glass is

BREWSTER BOOK STORE

used in two American embassies and displayed in museum collections around the country.

Great Cape Herbs (508-896-5900; greatcape.com), 2624 Route 6A, East Brewster. With more than 170 varieties of Western and Chinese herbs in stock, this herbal apothecary may well be the largest retailer of its kind in New England. Look for all sorts of preparations, oils, balms, tinctures, and teas. Proprietor Stephan Brown, who opened the rustic shop in the early 1990s, also stocks a selection of New Age literature on health and well-being and many products from Thailand and China. Walk through the modest herb and community agricultural gardens and revive yourself with a cup of strong espresso before leaving.

✳ Special Events

Mid-April–early May: **Herring Run**. Hundreds of thousands of alewives (herring) return from the salt water to lay their eggs in the same freshwater ponds where they were born (see **Stony Brook Grist Mill** and **Herring Run** under *To See*).

Early May: **Brewster in Bloom** (brewsterblooms.com). A three-day scholarship fundraiser for local teens pursuing higher education, this festival features a golf contest, self-guided antiques and arts tour, 5K run, children's festival, juried fine arts and crafts show, and tour of historic inns.

Late June: **Open Air Antiques Fair** sponsored by the Brewster Historical Society (508-896-9521) at Drummer Boy Park. $.

SYDENSTRICKER GALLERIES

HARWICH

Harwich isn't nearly as developed as its westerly neighbors, although its stretch of Route 28 does have its share of bumper boats, mini-golf courses, and go-carts. In fact, the town exudes a somewhat nonchalant air. It's as if the 12,200 year-rounders are collectively saying, "This is what we have and you're welcome to come and enjoy it with us if you wish"—which is not to say that Harwich doesn't attract visitors. It boasts a wide range of places to stay and eat, from humble B&Bs to family-friendly cottages, from exceptional New American fare to roasted chicken-on-a-spit. At the same time, while Harwich has more saltwater and freshwater beaches than any other town on the Cape, only a few have parking for day-use visitors.

Harwich, mostly blue collar and middle class, comprises seven distinct villages and is blessed with one of the most picturesque harbors on the Cape, **Wychmere Harbor**. Nearby, lovely **Saquatucket Harbor** is reserved for fishing charters and ferry service to Nantucket. It's worth poking around the quiet center of **Harwich**, with its historic homes standing in marked contrast to the heavily developed areas just a mile or so away. Harwich, which bills its annual **Cranberry Harvest Festival** as "the biggest small-town celebration in the country," lays claims to cultivating the first commercial cranberry bog.

GUIDANCE ❋ **Harwich Chamber of Commerce** (508-430-1165; harwichcc.com) and **Harwich Information Center** (508-432-1600), Route 28, One Schoolhouse Road, Harwich Port. Pick up Harwich biking and walking trail maps, as well as their very helpful (free) street map.

GETTING THERE *By car:* From the Cape Cod Canal, take Route 6 to Exit 10 (Route 124 South and Route 39 South) to Route 28, or take Exit 11 to Route 137 for East Harwich. It takes 35 to 40 minutes to reach Harwich from the canal.

By bus: The **Plymouth & Brockton** bus line (508-746-0378; p-b.com) connects Harwich with Hyannis and other Cape towns, as well as with Boston's Logan Airport. The bus stops at the Park & Ride commuter lot near the intersection of Routes 6 and 124.

WYCHMERE HARBOR

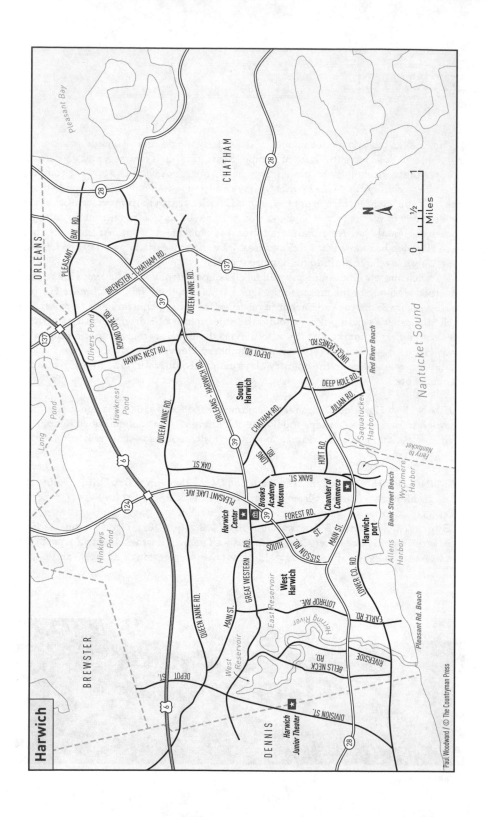

Harwich

BREWSTER

ORLEANS

CHATHAM

DENNIS

Pleasant Bay

Long Pond

Hinkleys Pond

Hawknest Pond

Olivers Pond

Round Cove Pond

PLEASANT BAY RD.

BREWSTER CHATHAM RD.

HAWKS NEST RD.

QUEEN ANNE RD.

QUEEN ANNE RD.

DEPOT RD.

South Harwich

CHATHAM RD.

ORLEANS - HARWICH RD.

DEEP HOLE RD.

JULIAN RD.

UNCLE VENIES RD.

Red River Beach

Nantucket Sound

Ferry to Nantucket

Saquatucket Harbor

Wychmere Harbor

Bank Street Beach

Allens Harbor

Harwich-port

MAIN ST.

HOYT RD.

LONG RD.

OAK ST.

BANK ST.

FOREST RD.

Chamber of Commerce

Academy Museum

Brooks

Harwich Center

PLEASANT LAKE AVE.

SISSON RD.

SOUTH ST.

GREAT WESTERN RD.

West Harwich

East Reservoir

West Reservoir

Herring River

LOTHROP AVE.

LOWER CO. RD.

EARLE RD.

RIVERSIDE

BELLS NECK RD.

Pleasant Rd. Beach

MAIN ST.

QUEEN ANNE RD.

DEPOT ST.

DIVISION ST.

Harwich Junior Theater

N

0   ½   1

Miles

Paul Woodward / © The Countryman Press

GETTING AROUND *By car:* Route 28 is also called Main Street. (This is not to be confused with the Main Street—a.k.a. Route 39—in the center of Harwich, which is inland.) Although most points of interest are located along or off developed Route 28, head inland to explore Harwich's ponds and conservation areas.

GETTING TO NANTUCKET There is seasonal passenger ferry service to Nantucket from Harwich Port. For many people, this service is more convenient than going into Hyannis to catch a boat. For complete information, see *Getting There* in "Nantucket."

PUBLIC RESTROOMS At the chamber (see *Guidance*).

PUBLIC LIBRARY ✳ ✐ ⍑ **Brooks Free Library** (508-430-7562; brooksfreelibrary.org), 739 Main Street, Harwich.

MEDICAL EMERGENCY **Fontaine Outpatient Center** (508-432-4100), 525 Long Pond Drive, off Route 137, Harwich.

✳ To See

⍑ **Brooks Academy Museum** (508-432-8089; harwichhistoricalsociety.org), 80 Parallel Street, Harwich Center. Open late June to early October. This imposing 1844 Greek Revival schoolhouse was home to one of the country's early vocational schools of navigation, established by Sidney Brooks. Now operated by the Harwich Historical Society, the museum features a history of cranberry farming, historical photographs, and changing exhibits on Harwich's past. There is also a permanent display of art by C. D. Cahoon, a gunpowder house used from 1770 to 1864, and a restored 1872 outhouse. Genealogical resources and a significant manuscript collection round out the research facility. $.

First Congregational Church, 697 Main Street, Harwich Center. Built in the mid-1700s, this church is surrounded by a white picket fence and anchors the tiny town center.

✳ ✐ **Harwich Jr. Theatre** (508-432-2002; capecodtheatrecompany.org), 105 Division Street, West Harwich. This semiprofessional theater—the country's oldest children's theater, established in 1951—produces up to 12 shows a year for both children and adults. In summer, children star in kids' roles, manage the sound and lighting, and sell refreshments. Whether your child is considering acting or you want to introduce him or her to theater, this is an imaginative alternative to another round of mini-golf. Classes or workshops are offered year-round. $$. Their **Harwich Winter Theatre** offers plays geared toward an older crowd off-season.

✳ To Do

All listings are in Harwich Center unless otherwise noted.

BASEBALL ✐ **The Harwich Mariners** (harwichmariners.org) play baseball from mid-June to mid-August at Whitehouse Field behind the high school in Harwich Center, off Oak Street from Route 39. They also host weekly clinics from late June to early August; $$$$+.

A PERFECT DAY IN HARWICH

8:30	Order a famous meltaway sweet bun at Bonatt's.
10:00	Find the quiet center of Harwich Center.
10:30	Swim in a glacial kettle pond.
12:30	Dine outdoors at Brax, overlooking Saquatucket Harbor.
1:45	Paddle up the Herring River with a kayak.
4:00	Play a round at Harbor Glen Miniature Golf.
5:00	Watch the light change on sailboats in Wychmere Harbor.
6:00	Have a romantic New American dinner at Cape Sea Grille.
8:00	Catch a Cape Cod League baseball game.
10:00	Enjoy an old-fashioned cone from the Sundae School.

BICYCLING & RENTALS About 5 miles of the Cape Cod Rail Trail run through Harwich; you can pick up the trail near the old Pleasant Lake General Store on Route 124 and off Great Western Road near Herring Run Road. The chamber of commerce publishes a good biking map.

BOATING Saquatucket Harbor (threeharbors.com), Route 28. With 200 berths, this is the largest municipal marina on the Cape. A few slips are reserved for transient visitors, who can launch at both Saquatucket and Allens Harbor.

ALONG THE CAPE COD RAIL TRAIL

SAQUATUCKET HARBOR

Wychmere Harbor, Harbor Road off Route 28. A fleet of sloops is often moored here, making it one of the Cape's most scenic (albeit human-made) harbors. In the late 1800s, Wychmere Harbor was simply a salt pond around which a racetrack was laid. But locals, disapproving of horse racing, convinced the town to cut an opening from the pond into Nantucket Sound. A harbor was born.

Allen Harbor, on Lower County Road, is the town's other picturesque, well-protected, and human-made harbor. Only seasonal ramp passes are available.

The **Herring River**, which runs north to a reservoir and south to Nantucket Sound, is great for kayaking.

See also **Herring River/Sand Pond Conservation Area/Bells Neck** under *Green Space*.

FISHING & SHELLFISHING Shellfishing permits ($$ daily for nonresident families) are obtained from the harbormaster (508-430-7532) at Saquatucket Harbor, June through September.

A number of charter fishing boats depart from Saquatucket Harbor, including the *Yankee* (508-432-2520).

Try your luck casting from a jetty at **Red River Beach** (see *Green Space*) or the **Herring River Bridge** in West Harwich. And rent equipment from **Sunrise Bait & Tackle** (508-430-4117), 431 Route 28.

FOR FAMILIES ♂ **Grand Slam Entertainment** (508-430-1155; capecodbumperboats .com), 320 Route 28. Open April to mid-September. Batting cages with varying degrees of difficulty and bumper boats for toddlers to teens. Also a zip line over the pool, a radar pitching cage, and one of the world's only (purportedly) Wiffle ball cages for kids.

♂ **Trampoline Center** (508-432-8717), 296 Route 28. Open late June to mid-September. There are no age or height restrictions; the only limit at this outdoor center is that kids can't do flips.

♂ **Bud's Go-Karts** (508-432-4964), 9 Sisson Road, at Route 28. Open mid-April to mid-October. Kids have to be more than 54 inches tall and at least 8 years old to drive without parents at this busy track.

⚓ **Castle in the Clouds**, behind the Harwich Elementary School, South Street. A fun playground.

Playground, Brooks Park, Route 39, Harwich.

GOLF **Cranberry Valley Golf Course** (508-430-5234; cranberrygolfcourse.com), 183 Oak Street, off Main Street, which turns into Route 39. Open March through December. An 18-hole, par-72 course with driving range and practice putting green.

❋ **Harwich Port Golf Club** (508-432-0250), 51 South Street. A nine-hole, par-34 course.

MINI-GOLF ⚓ **Harbor Glen Miniature Golf** (508-432-8240), 168 Route 28, West Harwich. Open April to mid-October. With fountains and imitation rocky waterfalls, this place packs 'em in, especially at night. Perhaps it's due to the adjacent restaurant, which offers kids' meals and ice cream. $.

SAILING See **Cape Sail** under *Sailing* in "Brewster."

TENNIS Free public courts are located at **Brooks Park** (508-430-7553), Route 39 and Oak Street. In summer there are morning programs for children.

❋ Green Space

BEACHES If you're renting a cottage, purchase a parking sticker at the Community Center (508-430-7568), 100 Oak Street, or at Earle Road Beach off Lower County Road.

Red River Beach, off Depot Road from Route 28, is one of the few beaches with daily parking; $$. Facilities include restrooms, concessions, and a lifeguard.

Pleasant Bay, off Route 28, is salt water, but calm, like a pond.

BUD'S GO-KARTS

NANTUCKET SOUND BEACHES

PONDS **Hinckleys Pond** and **Seymour Pond**, both off Route 124, are open to nonresidents. You can also swim at **Bucks Pond**, off Route 39. Limited parking; sticker required.

Long Pond has two beaches, although both require parking stickers ($$). One is located off Long Pond Drive from Route 124, the other off Cahoons Road from Long Pond Drive from Route 137.

Sand Pond is off Great Western Road.

WALKS The chamber of commerce (see *Guidance*) publishes a good walking-trail map.

Herring River/Sand Pond Conservation Area/Bells Neck (park off Bells Neck Road from Great Western Road) in West Harwich. These 200-plus acres of marshland, tidal creeks, reservoir, and riverway are great for birding and canoeing. You may see cormorants, ospreys, and swans.

❀ **Thompson's Field**, Chatham Road, south of Route 39. This 57-acre preserve, with dirt-road trails for you and your canine friends, is full of wildflowers in springtime. This gives you an idea of what the Cape probably looked like 100 years ago.

✳ Lodging

BED & BREAKFASTS ❋ **The Platinum Pebble Boutique Inn** (508-432-7766; platinumpebble.com), 186 Belmont Road, West Harwich. Decidedly different (in a good way) from most every other bed-and-breakfast or inn on Cape Cod, the Platinum Pebble will knock your socks off with its service, tickle your fancy with its mod décor, and pamper you silly with its luxe amenities. The centrally located boutique property features some rooms with private patios with direct access to the pool and others with soaking. All have fine linens and bedding. Schedule a time, and dine in your room or the lounge, poolside or in the garden on a sumptuously sweet or savory full breakfasts. $$-$$$.

Winstead Beach Resort (508-432-4444; winsteadinn.com), 4 Braddock

Lane, Harwich Port. Open mid-January to early November. You'll pay dearly for this privileged perch because there's nothing between the decks and the ocean except a private beach. Just so you know: Gregg Winston has transformed this modest beachfront house into an upscale establishment with 18 simple but deluxe rooms and four suites. All rooms are off a central hallway; two offer a direct beach view and some have a private deck and Jacuzzi. The back porch, sheltered by *Rosa rugosa*, leads to multilevel decks set with lounge chairs. Extensive continental breakfast buffet included. $$$–$$$$$.

MOTELS & MORE 🐾 ✍ **Commodore Inn** (508-432-1180; commodoreinn.com), 30 Earle Road, West Harwich. Open April

WINSTEAD BEACH RESORT

through October. For the money and more, this is the best value in Harwich. At first glance, the complex looks like just another cluster of motel rooms set around a pool. But the delightful place is so much more than that. The large pool is heated; an excellent full breakfast buffet (at the in-house **Raspberries**) is included in summertime; and the 27 rooms are nicely outfitted with wicker furniture and white cotton bedspreads. There is real attention to detail here. Some rooms have a Jacuzzi, gas fireplace, and a wet bar; all have microwaves; many can sleep four. Ask for a room with a vaulted ceiling; they feel much more spacious. Located on 2½ acres in a quiet residential area, the Commodore is 75 yards from the beach, and there's a play area. Tour groups stay here in the fall, but don't let that dissuade you; there are too many other things going for it—including the best scones on the planet. $$.

❄ ✍ **Tern Inn** (508-432-3714; theterninn.com), 91 Chase Avenue, West Harwich. Hands-on owners Sue and Dan run a spotless operation, and it pays off. A 10-minute walk from the beach, these six nicely maintained and renovated cottages and efficiencies (one of which is shaped like a gazebo) are set on a 2-acre wooded lot. They also rent eight guest rooms in a half-Cape house, where a bountiful breakfast buffet is included. A pool, swings, and basketball court are on the premises, perfectly oriented toward weeklong family stays. $$$.

RENTAL HOUSES **New England Vacation Rentals** (508-432-0900; newenglandvacationrentals.com), 565 Main Street, Route 28, Harwich Port.

❋ Where to Eat

Harwich has one of the Cape's best restaurants, a great hole-in-the-wall, and a bunch of places in between: You won't go hungry here.

DINING OUT **Cape Sea Grille** (508-432-4746; capeseagrille.com), 31 Sea Street, Harwich Port. Open D, April to mid-December. This contemporary bistro offers well-prepared, creative New American cuisine with a French Mediterranean influence. Because it's also served by twinkling candlelight in a lovely old sea captain's home, it's more like a grand slam. Outstanding signature dishes include pan-seared lobster with pancetta and asparagus and duck confit. Dishes change seasonally, but preparations always play with the classics. You'd better save room for strawberry shortcake or silky ginger crème brûlée. The three-course sunset menu is a steal. Jennifer Ramler and her chef husband Doug have (thankfully) presided since the day it opened in the early 2000s. $$$–$$$$.

Viera (774-408-7492; vieracapecod .com), 11 Route 28. Open D. The cuisine here is often described as "exquisite" and I resoundingly agree. Locals Ben and Angela Porter have brought a degree of sophistication worthy of every accolade they have received since opening in 2014. Their place highlights seasonal cuisine paired in inventive but accessible ways. My reviews usually highlight worthy house specialties, but honestly the whole menu, on every visit, has been consistently perfect. To boot, the quality of service matches the quality of cocktails. $$$–$$$$.

❋ **Buca's Tuscan Roadhouse** (508-432-6900; bucasroadhouse.com), 4 Depot Road. Open D. You might be hard-pressed to know which continent you're on at this cozy little trattoria. Both romantic and relaxing, with high-backed booths and red-and-white-checked tablecloths, they serve authentic and excellent *gamberetti alla Toscana* (Tuscan herbed shrimp, goat cheese risotto, lemon butter sauce, and kale), fresh mozzarella, seafood stew, as well as classic eggplant *Parmigiana*. Furthermore, portions are generous, desserts are homemade by the owner, and there's a good selection of wines by the glass. $$$. Check out their fast food cart, **Depot**

CAPE SEA GRILLE

BUCA'S TUSCAN ROADHOUSE

Dogs (depotdogs.net), parked in their lot. You can't miss it.

❄ **L'Alouette Bistro** (508-430-0405; frenchbistrocapecod.com), 787 Route 28, Harwich Port. Open D. Alan and Gretchen Champney's French country cuisine is simple but splendid, as rich as you might expect, but it's always a winner. Try the roast duck breast and duck confit in elegant but relaxed surroundings. Look for their bargain three-course dinner with wine in June, estate-grown wines, and after-dinner tarts. $$$–$$$$.

EATING OUT ✿ ⍷ **Brax** (508-432-5515; braxlanding.com), 705 Route 28, Harwich. Open L, D, April through December. Bar open year-round. Overlooking Saquatucket Harbor, this not particularly deservedly popular and casual tavernlike restaurant has a varied menu. Look for fish and chicken sandwiches, fried seafood, seafood stew, and lobster rolls. For sure, their steamers are particularly renowned. A few indoor seats have choice views, but the real draw is outdoor seating by the tranquil harbor. A bountiful brunch buffet packs 'em in on Sunday. Regardless of the time of day, there is often a 45-minute wait. L $–$$, D $$.

❄ **Hot Stove Saloon** (508-432-9911; hotstovesaloon.com), 551 Route 28, Harwich Port. Open L, D. Offering good-value pub grub since the mid-2000s, this place sports the requisite low lighting and boisterous quality you want in a (primarily) sports bar. The cheeseburgers are great, but you could also go for a thin-crust pizza, fish-and-chips, or any number of sandwiches (BLT, cheesesteak, or hot pastrami, for instance). A couple of picnic tables out front provide good watching on Main Street. $.

❄ ✿ ✿ **Bonatt's Bakery & Restaurant** (508-432-7199; bonattsbakeryrestaurant .com), 537 Route 28 at Sea Street, Harwich Port. Open B, L. A Harwich landmark since they created the meltaway sweet bun in 1939, Bonatt's is still hanging in there. $–$$.

❄ **The Mason Jar** (508-430-7600; masonjarcapecod.com), 544 Route 28,

Harwich Port. Open L. Look for fine specialty sandwiches, homemade soups, prepared meals to go, and desserts. Patio seating. $.

SNACKS & COFFEE **Sundae School Ice Cream Parlor** (508-430-2444; sundae school.com), 606 Route 28, Harwich Port. Open mid-May to late September. This "olde"-fashioned "shoppe" is the place to go for homemade ice cream concoctions.

✳ Entertainment

✦ **Band concerts** are held Tuesday evening at 7 in Brooks Park, Route 39 and Oak Street.

Jazz Festival (wequassett.com/jazz). Tuesdays and Wednesdays in summer at the Wequassett Resort, on the Harwich-Chatham border.

See also **Harwich Jr. Theatre** under *To See*.

✳ Selective Shopping

✳ All establishments are open year-round unless otherwise noted.

SPECIAL SHOPS **Cape Cod Tileworks** (508-432-7346; capecodtileworks.com), 705 Main Street, Harwich Center. This colorful shop sells nothing but tile: ceramic, marble, limestone, and hand-painted. They do custom designs and installation, too.

Monahan & Co. Jewelers (508-432-3302; monahanjewelers.com), 540 Main Street, Harwich Port. Prices for high-end jewelry (manufactured, purchased from estate auctions, and left on consignment) range from the double digits to six digits. The largest jewelry shop on the Cape and America's oldest family-owned jewelry store (established in 1815), it has been in Michael Monahan's family for generations.

BRAX

MONAHAN JEWELERS

✳ Special Events

Mid-May: **Fooding Around Harwich. Formerly the Toast of Harwich,** this trolley tasting tour of the town's chefs includes (for VIPs) a reception with wine and bourbon tastings at the Wequassett Resort on the Harwich-Chatham town line. $$$$$.

July through September: **Guild of Harwich Artists** (guildofharwich-artists.com) sponsors Monday "Art in the Park" programs at Doane Park, off Lower County Road. (Rain date is Wednesday.)

Mid-September: **Fall for Harwich** (harwichcranberryfestival.org) at the Harwich High School off Oak Street. Community spirit prevails at this popular celebration, which boasts an attendance of almost 40,000 people. Events include fireworks, a parade, a carnival, and hundreds of top-notch crafts displays.

Early December: **Christmas Weekend in the Harwiches** (harwichcc.com) includes hayrides, strolling minstrels, a choral group, and merchant open houses.

CRANBERRY BOGS BEFORE HARVESTING

CHATHAM

Although Chatham is less accessible from Route 6 than are its neighbors, even the most hurried Cape visitors stop here. Occupying the tip of Cape Cod's elbow, the town offers a good mix of archetypal Cape Cod architecture, a classic Main Street, a refined sensibility, plenty of excellent beaches and shops, and a rich seafaring history.

Chatham is known for its calm, genteel, independent spirit. The town's vigilant zoning commission has kept tourist-trap activity to a minimum. Bordered on three sides by water, the town is populated by descendants of its oceangoing founders, many of whom continue in their ancestors' footsteps. Despite the difficulty in navigating the surrounding waters, Chatham sustains an active fleet of fishermen and leisure-time sailors. Fishermen, sailors, shop owners, and an increasing number of retirees live quietly in this delightfully traditional village.

Chatham, along with the spectacularly desolate **Monomoy National Wildlife Refuge**, boasts 65 miles of shoreline. As such, Chatham's **beaches** are varied: Some are hit by pounding surf, sandbars shelter others; some are good for shell collecting, others are wide and sandy. A walk along the shore reveals gentle inlets and beautiful seafront homes. An inland drive or bicycle ride takes you past elegant shingled cottages and stately white houses surrounded by picket fences and boasting primroses and tidy lawns.

In the center of Chatham, **Main Street** is chock-full of upscale shops, offering everything from tony antiques and nautically inspired gifts to jewelry, clothing, and culinary supplies. This central part of town has excellent restaurants and inns and some of the Cape's finest bow houses (so named because they're shaped like the bow of a ship turned upside down). North Chatham, primarily residential, is dotted with several picturesque inlets. West and South Chatham border the beaches; you'll find lots of rental houses, summer cottages, and piney woods here. Chatham's year-round population of 6,600 balloons to about 35,000 in the summer.

As for a snippet of history, to place Chatham in context with its neighboring towns: When Samuel de Champlain and his party tried to land at Stage Harbor in 1606, they were met with stalwart resistance from the Native inhabitants. Fifty years later, though, Yarmouth's William Nickerson purchased a great deal of land from Chief Mattaquason. By 1712, the permanent "settlers" had incorporated the town.

GUIDANCE ❊ **Chatham Chamber of Commerce and Visitor Information Center** (508-945-5199; chathaminfo.com), 2377 Main Street, in the historic Bassett House. The map-lined walls come in handy when you're planning an itinerary or looking for a specific place—as does the walking guide. There is also a summertime downtown welcome booth at 533 Main Street, with the same hours as the main office.

GETTING THERE *By car:* From the Cape Cod Canal, take Route 6 east to Exit 11 (Route 137 South) to Route 28 South. The center of Chatham is 3 miles from this intersection, about 45 minutes from either bridge.

GETTING AROUND Chatham is crowded in July and August, and you'll be happiest exploring Main Street on foot. It's about a 15-minute walk from mid–Main Street to the lighthouse, and another 15 minutes from the light to the pier (one-way). There is free

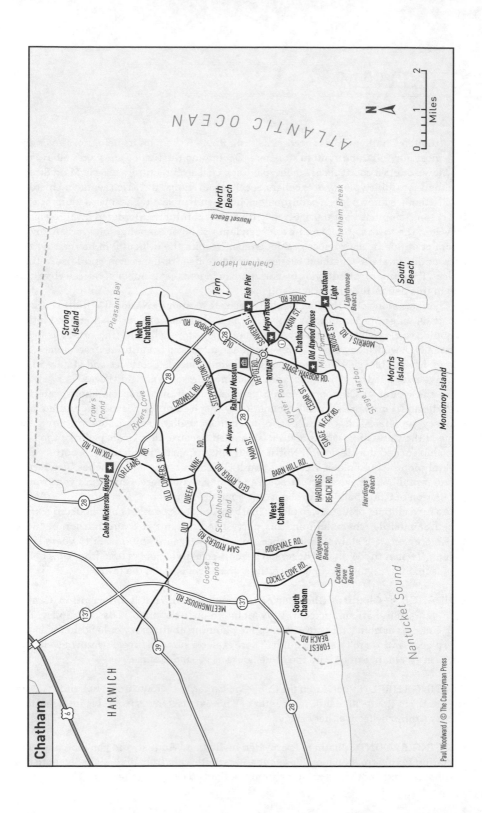

Chatham

Paul Woodward / © The Countryman Press

A PERFECT (JAM-PACKED) DAY IN CHATHAM

7:30	Have breakfast at the Lazy Lobster.
9:00	Drive back roads overlooking Pleasant Bay, Oyster Pond, and Stage Harbor.
10.00	Chase seagulls and peer through telescopes at the Chatham Break and lighthouse.
10:30	Stroll Main Street and duck into Odell's Studio.
12:30	Take a chicken potpie or bumbleberry pie from Marion's to Chase Park. Or spare a bit more time (and money) to dine oceanfront at the Outer Bar & Grille or Beach House Grill.
1:30	Count personable seals on a Beachcomber cruise.
4:00	Find your rhythm on a front-porch rocker at the Chatham Bars Inn.
5:30	Create memories with sophisticated cuisine at Twenty-eight Atlantic (or save some cash and enjoy bistro-y Pisces).
8:00	Listen to crickets and catch the second half of a baseball game.

parking at Town Hall (off Main Street), the Colonial Building (off Stage Harbor Road), one block west of the rotary at the elementary school, and on Chatham Bars Avenue behind the Impudent Oyster restaurant off Main Street.

PUBLIC RESTROOMS Year-round facilities are located at the town offices on Main Street, at the Fish Pier on Shore Road, and the parking lot behind St. Christopher's Church on Main Street. Summertime restrooms are located behind Kate Gould Park (off Main Street).

PUBLIC LIBRARY ✳ ✎ ☂ **Eldredge Public Library** (508-945-5170; eldredgelibrary .org), 564 Main Street. One of the Cape's best libraries.

MEDICAL EMERGENCY Call **911**.

✳ To See

Chatham Light (newenglandlighthouses.net), Main Street and Bridge Street. Built in 1808 and rebuilt in 1877, the lighthouse has a beacon visible 23 miles out to sea. The U.S. Coast Guard–operated lighthouse is open in the afternoon on most/many Wednesdays, May to mid-October. Climbing the lighthouse requires some exertion, as there are 44 steps followed by eight steps up a ladder. Parking limit of 30 minutes during the summer.

    Fish Pier, Shore Road at Bar Cliff Avenue. Chatham's fleet of fishing boats returns— from as far away as 100 miles—to the pier from about 2 PM to 4 PM each afternoon (depending on the tides). From the pier's second-floor observation deck you can watch fishermen unloading their catch of haddock, lobster, cod, halibut, flounder, and pollock. While you're at the pier, take a gander at the **Fisherman's Monument**. A 1992 call for designs attracted nearly 100 applicants from around the world. The committee chose Sig Purwin, a Woods Hole sculptor, to memorialize the town's fishermen. In recent years, as stocks have begun to dwindle, fishermen have increasingly turned to shellfish harvesting. (Local bay scallops harvested in late fall are like nothing you've ever tasted.) In fact, more commercial licenses are purchased yearly in Chatham than anywhere else on the Cape.

CHATHAM LIGHT

✍ ⚲ **Chatham Railroad Museum**, (508-945-5100; chathamrailroadmuseum .com), 153 Depot Road. Open mid-June to mid-September. This carefully restored 1887 depot—on the National Register of Historic Places—features decorative "railroad gothic" architecture (unique to the U.S.) from its turret to its gingerbread trim. In fact, this is such a good example of this architecture that students of architectural history come to Chatham to study it. On the track in front of the station, you will find a 1910 New York Central train caboose (visitors are free to climb on the caboose and explore its interior); inside the museum are such treasures as photos, models, and equipment pertaining to the Cape's railroad history.

CHATHAM FISH PIER

RAILROAD MUSEUM

✎ ⚲ **Atwood House Museum** (508-945-2493; chathamhistoricalsociety.org), 347 Stage Harbor Road. Open June through October. This gambrel-roofed house, built by a sea captain in 1752, has been maintained by the Chatham Historical Society since 1926. (Note the low doorways and how much we've grown over the past two centuries by eating our vegetables!) The museum complex includes a gallery devoted to the history of fishing on Cape Cod and seven additional galleries that display antique dolls, tools, toys, portraits of sea captains, seashells from around the world, Sandwich glass, and other Chatham seafaring artifacts. The adjoining train barn features a three-panel mural by Alice Stallknecht that depicts more than 130 townspeople with a "modern Christ." $.

Mayo House (508-945-6098; chathamconservationfoundation.org), 540 Main Street. Open limited weekdays and hours, late June to early September. Built in 1818 by Josiah Mayo (who served for 40 years as Chatham's first postmaster) and filled with period antiques, the Mayo House is owned and maintained by the Chatham Conservation Foundation. The tiny, gray-with-red-shutters, three-quarter Cape isn't the "best this" or the "oldest that"; it's just a nice little old house.

Caleb Nickerson House (508-945-6086; nickersonassoc.org), 1107 Orleans Road (Route 28). Open mid-June to late September. This near pristine full-Cape home, which dates to 1772, is a "jewel box of authentic Colonial architecture." Don't miss it. Although the house was moved from its original location overlooking Oyster River, it ended up on homestead land that originally belonged to the great-great-great-great-grandfather of the founder of Chatham, William Nickerson.

SCENIC DRIVES Chatham is one of the most scenic Cape towns. Route 28 toward Orleans offers some of the loveliest scenery, with views of Pleasant Bay to the east. Shore Road passes handsome cedar-shingled houses. The causeway to Morris Island affords harbor views as well as views of the open ocean beyond tall grasses and sandy

CHATHAM BREAK

Coin-operated telescopes across from the lighthouse allow visitors to take a closer look at the Chatham Break. The main break was the result of a ferocious nor'easter on January 2, 1987. During the historic storm, the barrier beach (the lower portion of Nauset Beach) that had previously protected Chatham Harbor from the open ocean was breached. As a result, low dunes were flattened, tidal waters rose, and waves and high winds forced a channel through Nauset Beach. Over the next few years, many expensive waterfront homes were destroyed by the ensuing, unrestrained pounding of the fierce Atlantic Ocean. Although fishermen now have a more direct passage through the (formerly) long barrier beach, boating around the harbor's strong currents is more difficult than ever.

In a matter of hours in 1987 (rather than over the natural course of 50 years), the break altered Chatham's way of life—as do new breaks. The effects are still felt and debated today. But ocean currents have a mind of their own; in 1846 a previous break in South Beach repaired itself. That hasn't happened to this breach yet. But some beachfront is returning, and some of it belongs to folks who saw their lots washed away in the late 1980s. Sand, like birds, migrates south; Wellfleet's and Eastham's beach losses are Chatham's gain. Lighthouse Beach is directly below the lookout area; South and North Beaches are visible across the harbor (see *Green Space*). Enjoy the view; it's a work in progress.

Sure enough, the work continues: In April 19, 2007, another break developed in North and South Beach. Eight cottages washed into the sea, some were moved, and others could not be moved because of nesting piping plovers. Stay tuned.

And as if on cue (unfortunately), another South Beach breach was created in the February 2013 Nemo blizzard. Look for "impressive" aerial video footage online. One side note about the protected piper plovers: this local environmental point of contention has prompted the brisk sale of bumper stickers that read PIPING PLOVER TASTES LIKE CHICKEN.

shores. And the road to Cockle Cove Beach from Route 28 in South Chatham runs along a picturesque salt marsh and tidal river.

❋ To Do

AIRPLANE RIDES ❋ 🐾 **Stick'n Rudder Aero Tours** (508-945-2563; chathamairport .com), Chatham Municipal Airport, 240 George Ryder Road. To really appreciate Chatham's shoreline and the fragility of the Outer Cape landscape, head 900 feet above it in a four-seater Cessna. These wonderful sight-seeing rides are pricey but special. Prices are per ride, whether it's for one person or three (maximum). Walk-ups are welcome, but reservations are wiser ($$$$+).

🐾 **Chatham Family Charters** (508-237-2628; chathamfamilycharters.com). Captains Story and Annie Fish (in Chatham since the 1980s and for a lifetime, respectively) know the waters of Pleasant Bay like your back lawn on a riding mower. They specialize in tours for kids with fishing gear that is sized just for them. My friend Jean's young nephew had a ball pulling in a blue fish with a tiny little "fish harness" around his waist—just like the big boys! Custom cruises at sunrise and sunset also available. $$$$+.

ART CLASSES ❋ **Creative Arts Center** (508-945-3583; capecodcreativearts.org), 154 Crowell Road. The center offers classes during July and August in pottery, drawing, photography, painting, jewelry making, and other fine arts. Work is shown at the

OUTERMOST ADVENTURES, CHATHAM

center's on-site **Edward A. Bigelow Gallery**, alternating student/teacher work with regional shows by other artists. Since 1971, the center has held an annual art festival in August (see *Special Events*), where you may meet the artists and purchase their work.

BASEBALL 𝒮 **The Chatham Anglers** (508-945-5511; chathamanglers.com), one of 10 teams in the Cape Cod Baseball League, usually play ball at 7 PM from mid-June to early August at Veterans Park, Route 28, just west of the rotary. The information booth (see *Guidance*) has schedules. The A's sponsor weekly clinics for youngsters from mid-June to July. Inquire about particulars and bring your own glove.

BICYCLING & RENTALS With gentle inclines, quiet lanes, and a well-marked 2.75-mile route around town, Chatham is nice for bicycling. Laurie, a leisure bicycling enthusiast, enjoys a 10-mile route around Chatham, detailed in *Short Bike Rides on Cape Cod*, as among her favorites. An extension of the Cape Cod Rail Trail to Chatham also makes for family-friendly pedaling. For rentals, stop in at **Chatham Hood Bikes** (508-469-0210; chathamhoodbikes.com), 284 Commerce Park North, which has free area pickup and delivery (and bike trailers for rent).
See **Rail Trail Bike & Kayak** under *Bicycling* in "Brewster."

BOAT EXCURSIONS & RENTALS **Outermost Adventures** (508-945-2030; outermost harbor.com), 83 Seagull Road, Outermost Harbor Marine, off Morris Island Road. Late June to mid-September. This outfit offers continuous shuttles to pristine South Beach and Monomoy Island. Round-trip $$ (kids); $$$ (adults).
Rip Ryder (508-237-0420; monomoyislandferry.com), Stage Harbor Marine, 80 Bridge Street. Boats run April through November; make reservations the night before. Regular launches to South Monomoy. When the captain drops you off, tell him what time you want to be picked up. Inquire about fly-fishing, birding, and seal trips ($$$).
Beachcomber (508-945-5265; sealwatch.com), 174 Crowell Road; reservations required. Boats leave from the Fish Pier on Shore Road. Beach and fishing shuttles to

North Beach. Like most other outfits, they also offer 90-minute seal trips ($$$), but they use a faster boat so you spend more time watching seals and less time traveling. In this case it's the destination, not the journey. Beach shuttle $$ (kids); $$$ (adults).

Down Cape Charters and Boat Rentals (508-430-6893; downcapeboating.com), at the Wequassett Resort, Route 28. You can rent kayaks, catamarans, powerboats, and Sunfish from mid-June to early September. Make reservations for lessons. Cocktail and hors d'oeuvre cruises through Pleasant Bay and Chatham Harbor are offered on Friday and Saturdays evenings for $$$$+.

FISHING & SHELLFISHING Freshwater permits can be obtained from the Goose Hummock on Route 6A in Orleans. Saltwater permits can be obtained at the mass.gov website.

✎ **The Fishin' Bridge.** Follow Stage Harbor Road to Bridge Street, where Mill Pond empties into Stage Harbor. You'll haul in crabs, small flounder, eels, and perhaps even a bluefish. Locals will certainly be there with long rakes, harvesting shellfish. Stop even if you don't fish; it's picturesque.

South Beach offers the best opportunity for surf casting for striped bass, but **North Beach** is a close second.

Schoolhouse Pond (reached via Sam Ryders Road) and **Goose Pond** (off Fisherman's Landing) offer freshwater fishing for rainbow trout. In-season there is resident-only parking at Schoolhouse (visitors can park along Sam Ryders Road).

For sportfishing charters (May through November), try Bob Miller's Headhunter (508-237-6626; capecodfishingcharters.com) out of Stage Harbor Marine.

For custom tackle, supplies, rod rentals, and more charter information, stop in at **Top Rod Fly & Surf Tackle Shop** (508-945-2256; capefishingcharters.com), 1082 Orleans Road, next to Ryders Cove in North Chatham. Owner/captain Joe Fitzback also offers charters aboard the *Top Rod* and *Teresita*. May through October.

See also **Beachcomber** under *Boat Excursions*.

FOR FAMILIES *✎* There's a great **playground** next to the Chatham Community Center on Depot Road.

GENEALOGY Nickerson Family Association (508-945-6086; nickersonassoc.org), 1107 Orleans Road. Chatham's founder, William Nickerson, has more than 350,000 descendants. Think you're one of them? This genealogical research center will help you find out. In addition to mapping the Nickerson family tree, the volunteer association casts a wide net, compiling information on folks associated with the Nickersons and original settlers of Cape Cod and Nova Scotia.

GOLF ❋ **Chatham Seaside Links** (508-945-4774; chathamseasidelinks.com), 209 Seaview Street, next to the Chatham Bars Inn. A nine-holer, open March through November.

KAYAKING For rentals see **Monomoy Sail & Cycle** under *Sailboarding*.

SAILBOARDING Monomoy Sail & Cycle (508-945-0811; chathambikeshop.com), 275 Orleans Road, North Chatham. Rents sailboards and kayaks. Pleasant Bay enjoys easterly and northeasterly winds, while Forest Beach receives southwesterly winds.

SEAL CRUISES See the "Monomoy National Wildlife Refuge" sidebar under *Green Space*.

TENNIS Free public courts are located on **Depot Road** by the Railroad Museum and at **Chatham High School** on Crowell Road.

Chatham Bars Inn (508-945-6759; chathambarsinn.com), 297 Shore Road. Courts open mid-April to mid-November. CBI has waterfront courts made of synthetic "classic-clay" (they play like clay but are much easier to maintain) which they rent to nonguests ($$$/hour). Summertime lessons, too.

❊ Green Space

Chase Park and **Gristmill**, on Cross Street, is a tranquil vest pocket of parkland just a couple of blocks from the summertime madness on Main Street. It's perfect for a picnic lunch and overlooks a tranquil gristmill built in 1797 and most recently renovated in fall of 2010. Public access to the mill is under review.

HYDRANGEA WALKWAY

Hydrangea Walkway. Heading north on Shore Road from Main Street, the road is lined with stately private homes overlooking the ocean. One house on the left, in particular, is really eye-catching from mid-June to September, when its front walkway is awash with more than 50 blooming hydrangea plants.

BEACHES Cottage renters purchase weekly beach stickers for Hardings, Ridgevale, and Cockle Cove beaches (see below). Otherwise, from late June to early September, parking (508-945-5158) is $$ daily.

CHATHAM BEACHES

MONOMOY NATIONAL WILDLIFE REFUGE

North and South Monomoy Islands (fws.gov/refuge/monomoy), acquired by the federal government as part of a wildlife refuge in 1944, comprise a 7,600-acre habitat for more than 285 species of birds. Birds and seaside animals rule the roost; there are no human residents, no paved roads, no vehicles, and no electricity. (Long ago the island did support a fishing community, though.) It's a quiet, solitary place. Monomoy, one of four remaining "wilderness" areas between Maine and New Jersey, is an important stop for shorebirds on the Atlantic Flyway—between breeding grounds in the Arctic and wintering grounds in South America. Conditions here may well determine whether the birds will survive the journey. Some beaches are closed from April to mid-August to protect threatened nesting areas for piping plovers and terns. The lovely old lighthouse, built in 1823 and not used since 1923, was restored in 1988.

In the mid-1990s, the U.S. Fish and Wildlife Service embarked on a long-term management project to restore avian nesting diversity to Monomoy NWR by creating habitat for terns, which historically numbered in the thousands. Restoring the nesting space was controversial because the government considered it necessary to "remove" (with bread chunks laced with poison) about 10 percent of the aggressive seagulls that also nested here. As a result, by the late 1990s, the number of nesting terns, including 18 pairs of roseate terns, increased dramatically. Some protesters still maintain that the Fish and Wildlife Service took this action under pressure from off-road-vehicle drivers, who are often banned from driving on mainland

Hardings Beach, on Nantucket Sound. From Route 28, take Barn Hill Road to Hardings Beach Road. One Explorer e-mails: "Hardings Beach is great mostly because it has a channel into a salt pond and marsh. You can tube or float in the channel depending on the tides, and the water's warm." Look for small dunes, restrooms, and lifeguards.

Ridgevale Beach, on Nantucket Sound. Take Ridgevale Road off Route 28. Restrooms and lifeguards.

✪ **Cockle Cove Beach**, protected from Nantucket Sound by Ridgevale Beach. Take Cockle Cove Road off Route 28. Gentle waves and soft sand make this a good choice for families. Lifeguards and portable toilets.

✪ **Pleasant Bay Beach**, Route 28, North Chatham. The 7,000-acre inlet and bay have been called breathtakingly beautiful, and they are. This beach is narrow but great for children because the water is so shallow.

North Beach, on the Atlantic Ocean. North Beach, which is actually the southern end of Nauset Beach, is accessible only by boat (see *To Do* for water taxi services). It's well worth the effort to get here.

Lighthouse Beach and **South Beach**, below the lighthouse, on the Atlantic Ocean. Parking is limited to 30 minutes, but you can bicycle or walk to the lane off Morris Island Road just beyond the lighthouse; a sign points the way to South Beach. It's a bit of a walk, but try parking on Bridge Street; from the lighthouse, keep going on Bridge Street until there are no more signs saying NO PARKING ON EITHER SIDE OF STREET. (You'll notice lots of other cars parked here, too.) If you're day-tripping to Chatham, pay to park at the Eldredge Taxi parking lot, 365 Main Street, and take its taxi to the beach. The most desolate part of the beach requires quite a long walk, but the early sections are very nice, too. Many ferries (see *To Do*) take passengers to the farthest, most remote reaches of the beach. One of the best aspects of this beach is that you've got surf on the east side and calm bay waters on the west.

POND ✪ **Oyster Pond Beach**, off Stage Harbor Road, near the rotary. This inland saltwater pond is connected to Nantucket Sound by way of Oyster Creek and Stage

beaches because of nesting endangered birds. But by the late 1990s, Monomoy had become the second largest tern-nesting site on the East Coast, and the biggest between here and the Canadian Maritimes. In 1998 the refuge was dogged by another controversy: Dens of coyotes (and their pups) were feasting on newborn chicks. Management "removed" them as well. These days commercial clammers and crabbers are sparring with the refuge over the issuance (or lack thereof) of permits.

Monomoy was attached to the mainland until a 1958 storm severed the connection; a storm in 1978 divided the island in two. The islands are accessible only by boat (see *To Do*) and only under favorable weather conditions. Guided tours are available from the Wellfleet Bay Wildlife Sanctuary (508-349-2615; massaudubon.org; see the "Trails, Birds, Seals & Classes" sidebar in "Wellfleet") late May through September. Call to reserve because space is limited. Since the early 1980s, about 300 gray and harbor seals have been frolicking off the shores of Chatham in the summertime; about 10 times that rally here in winter. Monomoy has been a haven only since the 1991 hurricane created a break in the barrier beach.

The 40-acre Morris Island is accessible by car and foot: head south from Chatham Light and turn left onto Morris Island Road, then take your first right and continue on Morris Island Road to the end.

The visitor center is staffed with very helpful volunteers, and there are trails from here through dunes and along the beach. Restrooms and parking to boot!

Harbor. Good for families, its shores are calm and its waters are the warmest in town. Free parking. Lifeguard, bathhouse, and restrooms.

WALKS **Chatham Conservation Foundation** (508-945-4084; chathamconservation foundation.org). With more than 645 acres, the foundation has created three distinct walking areas traversing marshes, wetlands, and meadows. Contact the town information booth on Main Street (see *Guidance*) for directions to Frost Fish Creek, Barclay Pond, and Honeysuckle Lane.

🐾 **The Dog Runs**, as it's known locally. Walk 10 minutes along Bridge Street away from the lighthouse to find this forested coastal trail along Stage Harbor. Enjoy a picnic in the cattail marshes.

See also the "Monomoy National Wildlife Refuge" sidebar under *Green Space*.

✲ Lodging

Generally, Chatham is one of the more expensive places to stay on Cape Cod. Its motels, though, are some of the best on Cape Cod. Two-night minimum stays in July and August are normal, and many of Chatham's most notable places are booked for July and August well before July 4. Unless otherwise noted, all lodging is in Chatham proper.

RESORTS & HOTELS ❄ ✐ **Chatham Bars Inn** (508-945-0096; chathambarsinn.com), 297 Shore Road. This grande dame's gracious elegance is rivaled by only a handful of places in New England. Built in 1914 as a hunting lodge, it's now the quintessential seaside resort. And after extensive million-dollar renovations, it's better than ever—with spiffed up guest rooms, landscaping, dining and public facilities, and a fleet of sportfishing vessels. Grounds are lushly landscaped, and the seaside setting nearly perfect. Scattered over 25 acres, the main inn and cottages have a total of 217 rooms and suites comfortably decorated

CHATHAM BARS INN

in a traditional Cape Cod style—with wicker, hand-painted furniture, and understated florals. Some ocean-view rooms have private balconies or decks. The complex includes a private beach, a heated outdoor pool, a spa, gift shop, three tennis courts, croquet, a health and wellness center, a nine-hole golf course, launch service to Nauset Beach, sailing lessons, seal and whale tours, Orvis fly-fishing lessons, and a full and complimentary children's program. Although prices don't normally include meals, B&B packages offer a lavish buffet every morning (which is otherwise $$$). A 10-minute walk from town, the hotel also has an expansive veranda and very comfortable, grand living rooms. $$$$+.

✄ **Wequassett Resort and Golf Club** (508-432-5400; wequassett.com), 2173 Route 28. Open April through November. The Wequassett (10 minutes north of Chatham on picturesque Pleasant Bay)—known for an attentive staff, exceptional service, and understated elegance—consists of 23 buildings set on 22 beautifully landscaped acres. It also boasts an excellent restaurant, **Twenty-eight Atlantic** (see *Dining Out*), four tennis courts, sailing, and an oh-so-suave pool renovated with aplomb with cabanas, a Jacuzzi,

and a waterfront bar, LiBAY-tion. (There isn't a more perfectly situated pool on the Cape.) Other resort amenities include a fitness center, boat rentals, launch service to an uncrowded section of the National Seashore, baby-sitting, and summertime children's programs. The resort also offers guests playing privileges on the otherwise private Cape Cod National Golf Course, a challenging Silva course (golf packages available). As for the 116 rooms, some have cathedral ceilings and their own decks, though not all have views of boat-studded Round Cove. Triple sheeting, morning delivery of the newspaper, and turndown service

WEQUASSETT RESORT

are standard. Light lunches are served at the pool; nightcaps are soothing at the charming **Thoreau's**. $$$$–$$$$$+.

❋ **Chatham Wayside Inn** (508-945-5550; waysideinn.com), 512 Main Street. Dominating Main Street, this historic 1860 hostelry (which now looks brand new) has 46 guest rooms and five suites furnished with flair and a decorator's touch. Triple sheeting, thick towels, and top-notch bathroom amenities are standard. Some rooms have a canopy or four-poster bed and reproduction period furniture, a fireplace, a whirlpool tub, or a private patio or balcony. As for views, choose between the town green, golf course, or parking lot. Whether in summer or winter, cocktails are served fireside in the pub. Swimming pool. $$–$$$$+.

BED & BREAKFASTS ❋ **The Captain's House Inn** (508-945-0127; captainshouseinn.com), 369–377 Old Harbor Road. The epitome of traditional elegance, this Greek Revival inn enjoys a privileged position—with plenty of good reasons. Jill and James Meyer, innkeepers since the mid-2000s, preside over an enthusiastic British hotel management staff, 2 acres of well-tended gardens, 12 handsome rooms, and four sumptuous suites. It's easily among the top 10 places to stay in New England. The Captain's Cottage contains one particularly historic room with wood-burning fireplace, walnut-paneled walls, and pumpkin-pine flooring; a hideaway attic suite; and a honeymoon-style room with a double whirlpool. Antiques-filled inn rooms are more traditional, but all have triple sheeting, luxe amenities, contemporary bathrooms, and flat-screen TV/DVD. Full breakfasts are served on linen, china, and silver in a wonderfully airy room. Smoked salmon graces the sideboard every morning; an authentic English tea is offered every afternoon; cookies always seem to be baking throughout the day; and the DVD library always has port in the evening. The inn also has an oh-so-exclusive-feeling swimming pool

CAPTAIN'S HOUSE INN OF CHATHAM

and a small but expert fitness room. Check for minimum stays, even outside of high season. $$–$$$$.

❄ **Carriage House Inn** (508-945-4688; thecarriagehouseinn.com), 407 Old Harbor Road. This superlative six-room B&B on the edge of town (and at a busy intersection) gets rave reviews—with good reason—from travelers across the board. Jim and Val offer sophisticated and contemporary decor with clean lines. I prefer the slightly pricier rooms in the adjacent carriage house because they have fireplaces, private outdoor sitting areas, and separate entrances. Lots of upscale amenities are included, making this an even better value than it already is. Don't miss the lemon blueberry crepes (if you're lucky) at breakfast. $$–$$$.

❄ **Chatham Inn at 359 Main** (508-945-9232; 359main.com), 359 Main Street. This two-story, 18-room boutique hotel (a 10-minute walk from Chatham Light and the beach and a five-minute walk from the heart of downtown) was recently completely renovated with aplomb. Upscale guest-room furnishings—blending a light quasi-cottage feel offset by polished wood floors—might have a fireplace, private balcony (overlooking the parking lot), and wet bar. All have top-notch amenities and "soft goods." All enjoy solicitous service you might expect. Behind the inn a little nature trail and an unharvested cranberry bog beckon, but most guests enjoy rocking in chairs on the long veranda. A full breakfast is enjoyed at individual tables. Come late afternoon (and for Sunday brunch); their **Chatham Wine Bar and Restaurant** (chathamwinebar.com) is open to the public. $$–$$$.

COTTAGES **Metters Cottages** (508-432-3535; chathambeach.com), 94 Chatharbor Lane, West Chatham. Open late May through October. These three waterview cottages are more like homes than cottages. Talk with George and Donna Metter about your needs when reserving;

CHATHAM TIDES

there's probably a cottage with your name on it. $$–$$$.

MOTELS 🦞 **Chatham Tides** (508-432-0379; chathamtides.com), 394 Pleasant Street, South Chatham. Open mid-May to mid-October. I can't say enough about this favored place, maintained with impressive care. Delightfully off the well-trodden path and about 4 miles from the center of town, this quiet beachfront complex of 24 rooms and suites is a real find. It stands out for its view—alone worth the price. After staying here once, you'll probably return again and again. Try booking in February after the repeat guests get their pick of the litter in January. $$–$$$.

🦞 **Hawthorne Motel** (508-945-0372; thehawthorne.com), 196 Shore Road. Open mid-May to mid-October. Not wanting to sound like a broken record, I can't say enough about this place either, which is all about location, location, location. Every time I stop in, it feels like coming home. A 10-minute walk from Main Street, this motel is popular because nothing stands between it and the ocean except grass and a path to the private beach. *Nothing.* The simple complex consists of 16 motel rooms and 10 efficiencies and cottages (with kitchens). They all provide delightfully easy access to sunning, swimming, and lazing on the beach. I particularly like the corner rooms, as they're much larger. $$–$$$.

♂ **Pleasant Bay Village Resort Motel** (508-945-1133; pleasantbayvillage.com), 1191 Orleans Road, Route 28. Open May through October. Three miles from town, this tranquil place will forever change your opinion of a motel complex. It's a horticulturalist's delight. The 6 acres of lush, Japanese-style landscaping and the tasteful heated pool with a Jacuzzi are reason enough to recommend it—as is the extensive selection of 58 well-maintained rooms. Some have a sundeck, others overlook a cascading waterfall; some are spacious, others are snug; some have grills, some have fully equipped kitchens with stainless appliances; most have fabulously tiled bathrooms. The spacious lobby is filled with Oriental carpets and is a great place to hang out on a rainy day, as is the airy breakfast room. Walk across the street and down Route 28 to Pleasant Bay Beach (see *Green Space*). Don't make the mistake of guests who book for two or three days and want to stay for five or six (and can't because of limited availability.) Hats off to Howard Gamsey, owner since 1953. $$–$$.

♀ ♂ **Chatham Highlander** (508-945-9038; chathamhighlander.com), 946 Route 28. All rooms open April to mid-November; a few available year-round. An excellent choice for budget-minded travelers, this favored motel is just a stone's throw from the center of town. The two adjacent buildings sit on a little knoll above a well-traveled road. Each of the 29 rooms has a TV, small refrigerator, newly tiled bathroom, and air-conditioning; the one-bedroom apartment has a bona fide kitchen. The cheery rooms are sparkling white; other aspects are charmingly retro. There are also two heated pools. $$–$$.

RENTAL HOUSES & COTTAGES **Sylvan Vacation Rentals** (508-945-7222;

HAWTHORNE MOTEL

sylvanrentals.com), 1715 Route 28, West Chatham.

Chatham Home Rentals (508-945-9444; chathamhomerentals.com), 1370 Route 28.

❋ Where to Eat

Dining options in Chatham run the gamut, from elegant to child-friendly places. Reserve ahead in summer (especially at *Dining Out* eateries) or be prepared for a lengthy wait.

DINING OUT ✍ ♈ **twenty-eight Atlantic** (508-430-3000; wequassett.com), at Wequassett Resort and Golf Club, 2173 Route 28, Chatham (just over the Harwich town line, actually). Open B, D, April through November. Who says some places are reserved only for "special occasions"? Not me. Not this place. At the Wequassett Resort's signature restaurant, I can't decide whether it's the water views (come before sunset to enjoy the view through floor-to-ceiling windows) or the food that reigns supreme. Hard to say, since they both rise above lofty expectations. Executive chef James Hackney oversees the regional and contemporary American menu, full of artfully presented dishes packed with great flourishes and flavors. The seasonal menu is served ever-so-graciously on Limoges china in a genteel, understated, open, and elegant dining room—which has a nice buzz to it as the evening wears on. Lengthy recitations by an-oh-so professional waitstaff accompany and elevate each course. Service is seamless. Seafood is a specialty, of course, and everything we tried was spirited and ambitious. D $$$–$$$$$.

Pisces (508-432-4600; piscesofchatham.com), 2653 Main Street, South Chatham. Open D, late April to mid-October. A deserved foodie's delight (since it opened in the early 2000s) lies tucked inside an inconspicuous yellow cottage. This charming and contemporary bistro offers Mediterranean and coastal cuisine dishes like local cod sautéed in a spiced cornmeal crust with lemon caper aioli, toasted orzo pasta, and summer vegetables. The simple decor features local art on the walls, but the plates are anything but simple. It's always crowded here, and if they had twice the space, twice as many people would be salivating. Start with a mouthwatering cosmo, a signature cocktail. $$$–$$$$.

❋ ✍ ♈ **Impudent Oyster** (508-945-3545), 15 Chatham Bars Avenue. Open L, D. Ask around in Chatham, and this place is still at the top of everyone's list—even though it's been around since the mid-1970s. The atmosphere is certainly pleasant and almost rustic: peaked ceiling with exposed beams, skylights, and hanging plants. And the extensive menu highlights internationally inspired fish and shellfish dishes. Try the deservedly popular spicy Portuguese mussels, Nantucket scallop sandwich, or beer-battered fish-and-chips for lunch. Otherwise, follow the regulars (of which there are many) and order from the daily specials. Or have a burger at the everybody-knows-your-name lower bar. L $–$$, D $$$.

❋ ♈ **Bistro on Main and Chatham Raw Bar** (508-945-5033; bistroonmainchatham.com), 595 Main Street. Open L in summer, D year-round (but per usual, check the days open). What a brilliant transformation from Steve Vining, who operated his second-floor institution since the early 1990s. The new bistro has kept its soul as one of the area's more adventurous eateries, specializing in wood grilling while still roaming the world. In addition to moving to the ground floor with a lovely patio, Steve has expanded to include an excellent raw bar with specialty cocktails. Perhaps surprisingly, it's the only raw bar in town. Not surprisingly, the bistro still has a great vibe. $$$

❋ ✍ ♈ **Chatham Bars Inn** (508-945-0096; chathambarsinn.com), Shore Road. Open B, D. CBI offers a number of dining options. The grand hotel's veranda, overlooking the ocean, makes a picture-perfect setting for a late-afternoon drink and/or a light meal. As for the other draws, panoramic ocean views and grand Sunday-night buffets ($$$$+) in the main dining room are legendary. (Long pants and collared shirt are requested at dinner.) If you normally avoid buffets, break that rule here. The family-friendly tavern serves fireside lunches and dinners daily in a more casual atmosphere—think panini, sandwiches, and salads. ($$). Otherwise, breakfast buffet $$$; D $$–$$$$$.

♈ See also **Chatham Wine Bar and Restaurant** (chathamwinebar.com) at the **Chatham Inn at 359 Main**, under Lodging.

EATING OUT ☻ ❄ ✐ ♈ **Chatham Squire** (508-945-0945 restaurant; 508-945-0942 tavern; thesquire.com), 487 Main Street. Open L, D. A friendly place, Chatham's best family restaurant offers something for everyone—from burgers and moderately priced daily seafood specials to a raw bar, multiethnic dishes, and excellent chowder. Paisley carpeting, low booths, captain's chairs at wooden tables, exposed beams, and pool tables (off-season only) add to the family-den feel of the place. Drop in for a drink in the busy and colorful tavern (a rowdy

CHATHAM SQUIRE

watering-hole haven for 20-somethings in summer until locals take it back for the off-season). They offer lots of entertainment options, including karaoke on Tuesday evenings. L $$, D $$–$$$.

♈ **Outer Bar & Grille** (508-432-5400; wequassett.com), Pleasant Bay Road, Route 28, North Chatham (just over the Harwich town line, actually). Open L, D, mid-June to mid-September. The main reason to come is unrivaled ocean views. At the Wequassett Resort, this sophisticated and "smart casual" eatery is one of the Cape's few oceanside eateries, and its porch is a great place to enjoy a lunchtime lobster roll, salad, grilled pizza, panini, or sandwich. But be careful or prices can add up quickly and it might not be worth it. Still, those views . . . $$–$$$.

✐ **Beach House Grill** (508-945-0096; chathambarsinn.com), 297 Shore Road. Open L, D, mid-June to mid-September. One of the Cape's few alfresco oceanside eateries, the grill's deck is anchored in the sand, overlooking a wide, golden beach. Settings rarely get better than

OUTER BAR & GRILLE

this. The overpriced menu features upscale seaside standards: burgers, summer salads, lobster rolls ($25), peel-and-eat shrimp, and fried seafood platters. Popular dinners revolve around family-friendly themes like clam and lobster bakes or Caribbean night (where folks dress up in pirate garb). There's live music nightly. L $$–$$$.

❊ ◕ **Marion's Pie Shop** (508-432-9439; marionspieshopofchatham.com), 2022 Main Street. Open B, L. Cindy and Blake Stearns's pies are a delicious alternative. (Marion's gone, but the recipes are better than ever—no offense to Marion.) You can't go wrong with the savory potpies (chock-full of chicken), seafood pies, beefsteak pies, sweet fruit pies (the bumbleberry knocks my socks off, while the razzleberry dazzles Laurie), or any of the breakfast baked goods. This humble but humming little house only has take-out. Careful with the children; misbehaving ones "will be made into pies."

❊ ◔ **Wild Goose Tavern** (508-945-5590; wildgoosetavern.com), 512 Main Street. Open L, D. Because of its prominent in-town location and a constant parade of strollers-by, this pleasant room really packs in visitors. The streetside patio is pleasant. Sandwiches, salads, pizzas, and panini dominate the midday menu. The indoor bar has a flat-screen TV when you need to catch a game or some breaking news. B, L $–$$, D $$–$$$.

❊ **The Corner Store** (508-432-1077; freshfastfun.com), 1403 Old Queen Anne

CORNER STORE

Road. Sit on the front benches (or take to the beach because there's nowhere else to sit) and partake in grilled panini (turkey, cheddar, bacon, sun-dried tomato aioli, and baby spinach), burritos (built to order), sandwiches, soups, desserts, and coffees. $.

❊ ◔ **Carmine's** (508-945-5300), 595 Main Street. Open L, D. Quick and inexpensive, Carmine's offers very good traditional and gourmet pizzas (slices and whole pies).

❊ **Chatham Village Café** (508-945-3229; 508-945-2525; chathamvillagecafe.com), 69 Crowell Road. Relocated from its former location at 400 Main Street, this upscale deli offers creative sandwiches from $7 and excellent cranberry muffins. There are a couple of picnic tables in front.

❊ **New England Pizza** (508-945-9070; newenglandpizzachatham.com), 1200 Route 28, heading toward West Chatham. Open L, D. Most people think this is the best pizza place in town, and I have no reason to disagree. $$.

Lazy Lobster (508-945-0032; lazy-lobster.com), 247 Orleans Road (heading north on Route 28 toward the rotary). Open B, L, April to late October. If you're renting a house and don't feel like cooking, this casual eatery has some of the best breakfasts in town. $–$$.

WELL BEHAVED
CHILDREN
WELCOME.

THE REST WILL BE
MADE INTO PIES.

MARION'S PIE SHOP

See also **Concerts** (lobster roll suppers) under *Entertainment*.

SPECIALTY OUTLETS **High Tea at The Captain's House Inn** (508-945-0127; captainshouseinn.com), 369–377 Old Harbor Road. This inn **serves an** exceptional afternoon tea to nonguests by reservation. With a vast assortment of savories and sweets, all beautifully presented, it's well worth it. $$.

   Chatham Pier Fish Market (508-945-3474; chathampierfishmarket.com), at the Fish Pier on Shore Road. Open May to mid-October. Without going out on the dayboats yourself, it's hard to get fresher fish! You'll also find excellent take-out like lobster rolls, fish-and-chips, chowder, and fried seafood at reasonable prices.

   ❋ **Chatham Fish & Lobster Company** (508-945-1178; chathamfishandlobster.com), 1291 Route 28, Cornfield Market Place. For those of you with cooking facilities: They hook 'em, you cook 'em. They also rightfully proud of a well-rounded menu featuring healthy choices for most tastes and diets.

   ❋ **Cape Cod Natural Markets** (508-945-4139; capecodnaturalmarkets.com), 1218 Route 28. Organic and whole food, vitamins, and other natural products and literature.

HIGH TEA AT THE CAPTAIN'S HOUSE

❋ Entertainment

Monomoy Theatre (508-945-1589; monomoytheatre.org), 776 Main Street. Performances mid-June through August. Operated by Ohio University, the Monomoy is among the Cape's better-known and oldest (1930) playhouses. A new production—anything from a

MONOMOY THEATRE

NOSTALGIA REIGNS

✒ **Band concerts at Kate Gould Park** (chathamband.com), off Main Street. Every Friday night at 8 PM, late June to early September, this brass-band concert is the place to be. Upward of 6,000 lighthearted visitors enjoy music and people-watching as they have for the past 60 years. Dance and swing to Sousa marches, big band selections, and other standards. Between the bandstand, balloons tied to strollers, bags of popcorn, blankets on the grass (set yours out at 10 AM for the best position), and the "Star-Spangled Banner" finale—it hasn't changed a "whit" since it began. (Except that beloved Whit Tileston, who led the band for almost 50 years, passed away in 1995. The bandstand was renamed in his honor.)

KATE GOULD PARK

Rodgers and Hammerstein musical to Shakespeare—is staged every week. There isn't a bad choice among the 263 seats.

🦞 ✒ **Concerts and lobster roll suppers**, (508-945-0474; chathammethodist .org), First United Methodist Church, 569 Main Street at Cross Street. The church sponsors free choral, jazz, big band, light classical, and a cappella concerts Sunday summer evenings. Since the mid-1960s, the church has also held popular Friday lobster roll suppers at 4:30 PM. Lobster prices vary with market conditions.

Chatham Orpheum (508-945-0874; chathamorpheum.org), 637 Main Street. This beloved and community-driven,

early-20th-century cinema reopened to great appreciation in 2013.

Bands. Locals flock to the **Chatham Squire** (see *Eating Out*) to hear live music off-season.

✳ Selective Shopping

✳ Although merchants and visitors loyal to Provincetown's Commercial Street may have something to say about it, Chatham's Main Street might be the Cape's best shopping street. Instead of organizing shops by category as I usually do, I list them here in the order you'll encounter them while strolling. Unless otherwise noted, all shops are open year-round. (*Note, though, that many places listed as open year-round are open only on weekends in winter.*)

WEST OF THE ROTARY

Chatham Glass Company (508-945-5547; chathamglass.com), 758 Main Street. James Holmes designs and creates unique, colorful glass items—candlesticks, platters, bud vases, and marbles—which are sold at Barneys, Neiman Marcus, and Gump's. The working studio is just behind the brilliantly lit displays, so you can watch the creative process of glassblowing.

Munson Gallery (508-237-5038; munsongallery.net), 1455 Main Street. Open April through December. In the Munson family for four generations, this space is the oldest gallery in New England and has been showing fine paintings and sculpture by contemporary artists since 1955. The collection, with something for everyone in both price and taste, is housed in a wonderfully restored barn. Even the horse stalls are hung with art.

Chatham Pottery (508-430-2191; chathampottery.com), 2058 Route 28, South Chatham. Gill Wilson and Margaret Wilson-Grey's large studio offers a wide array of functional, decorative stoneware—hand-thrown pots, pitchers, sinks, plates, bowls, tiles, and tables.

Chatham Jam and Jelly Shop (877-526-7467; chathamjamandjellyshop.com), 16 Seaquanset Road (and many other locations found on their website). This colorful shop sells dozens of varieties of homemade jams and jellies. Feel free to taste them before committing. Try the wild beach plum, elderberry, or damson plum.

Maps of Antiquity (508-945-1660; mapsofantiquity.com), 1409 Main Street. These folks carry rare antique and reproduction maps of the 19th century and earlier from around the world. If you want to know what the Cape or a specific town looked like 100 years ago, this shop will have a reproduction map that will tell you. It's a treasure trove.

EAST OF THE ROTARY

Main Street Pottery (508-945-0128; mainstreetpotterychatham.com), 645C Main Street. Barbara Parent works here, so you can watch her making pots similar to the one you're purchasing.

Yankee Ingenuity (508-945-1288; yankee-ingenuity.com), 525 Main Street. This eclectic assortment of "cool things" extends from glass and jewelry to clocks and lamps. Prices run $2 to $1,500. If you don't get something here the day you see it, it may be gone tomorrow.

Yellow Umbrella Books (508-945-0144; yellowumbrellabooks.net), 501 Main Street. Owner Eric Linder has gathered a fine selection of Cape Cod titles and some used books, too, for all ages and interests. "Long live the independents!"

CHATHAM POTTERY

YELLOW UMBRELLA BOOKS

Mark August Designs (508-945-4545; markaugust.com), 490 Main Street. Functional and fun, creative and artsy decorative items for your house. Jewelry, too.

Chatham Candy Manor (508-945-0825; candymanor.com), 484 Main Street. They've been making hand-dipped chocolate, fudge, and liqueur-flavored truffles since 1955.

🐚 **The Mayflower** (508-945-0065; the-mayflowershop.com), 475 Main Street. Established in 1885, this venerable, old-time variety store has joined the modern era (almost) on swanky Main Street.

Artful Hand Gallery (508-945-5681; artfulhandgallery.com), 459 Main Street. This is one of the best artistic craft galleries in New England.

Demos Antiques, Ltd. (508-945-1939), 447 Main Street. You can't miss this place; a trove of funky treasures spill out onto the front lawn. Run by Peter and Cynthia Demos, the shop has been a family-owned business since 1956. If they don't have it, you don't need it.

Odell Studio and Gallery (508-945-3239; odellarts.com), 423 Main Street. Tom and Carol Odell, metalsmith and painter, respectively, have lived and worked in their lovely old home since 1975. Carol does colorful nonobjective, multimedia paintings, monotypes, oils, and encaustic. Her work complements Tom's jewelry and sculpture, which he fashions from precious metals and alloys. Tom's recent work shows evidence of a Japanese aesthetic. This remains my favorite shop in town.

🐚 **Mermaids on Main** (508-945-3179), 410 Main Street. Open late May through December. Kids love this colorful place, bursting at the seams with purple- and aquamarine-colored playthings. Books, bubble bath, candles, mobiles, mermaids, and stuffed and rubber creatures.

🐚 **Where the Sidewalk Ends** (508-945-0499; booksonthecape.com), 432 Main Street. Open daily. This mother-and-daughter led bookstore is one of the best independents I've encountered in years. From outdoor and fireside seating and children's story hours to coffee-with-the-author book signings and a great staff, this airy place has it all.

✳ Special Events

July 4: **Independence Day Parade** (cha thamparade.com), from Main Street to Veterans Field. **Strawberry Festival**

ODELL STUDIO

ARTFUL HAND

WHERE THE SIDEWALK ENDS

with shortcake at the First United Methodist Church (16 Cross Street) after the parade.

July: **Antique Show**. Since the mid-1950s; held at the Chatham Elementary School, Depot Road. $.

Mid-August: **Chatham Festival of the Arts**, Chase Park. Since 1970. On the third weekend in August, the Creative Arts Center sponsors more than 100 exhibitors, from painters to quilters to sculptors (see *To Do*).

December: **Christmas by the Sea and Christmas Stroll** (chathaminfo .com). This annual event includes a tree-lighting ceremony, candy-cane-making demonstrations, caroling, mulled cider served at the Mayo House (see *To See*), hayrides, open houses, and much more.

New Year's Eve: **First Night Celebration** (firstnightchatham.com). Fireworks over Oyster Pond. Chatham limits the number of buttons sold to residents and visitors so the town won't be overrun.

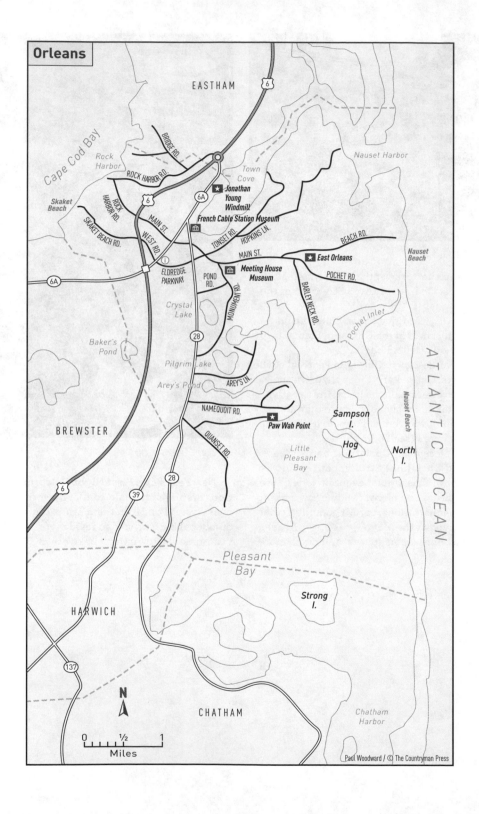

Orleans

EASTHAM

Cape Cod Bay

Rock Harbor

Skaket Beach

Rock Harbor Rd.

ROCK HARBOR RD.

SKAKET BEACH RD.

WEST RD.

MAIN ST.

Town Cove

★ Jonathan Young Windmill

French Cable Station Museum

Nauset Harbor

TONSET RD.

HOPKINS LN.

MAIN ST.

BEACH RD.

★ East Orleans

POCHET RD.

Nauset Beach

ELDREDGE PARKWAY

POND RD.

Meeting House Museum

MONUMENT RD.

BARLEY NECK RD.

Crystal Lake

Baker's Pond

Pilgrim Lake

Arey's Pond

AREY'S LN.

Pochet Inlet

Nauset Beach

NAMEQUOIT RD.

★ Paw Wah Point

Sampson I.

Hog I.

North I.

QUANSET RD.

Little Pleasant Bay

ATLANTIC OCEAN

BREWSTER

Pleasant Bay

HARWICH

Strong I.

Chatham Harbor

CHATHAM

N

0   ½   1
Miles

Paul Woodward / © The Countryman Press

ORLEANS

Many could argue, with some success, that Orleans's biggest draw is **Nauset Beach (in East Orleans)**, an Atlantic Ocean barrier beach more than 9 miles long. It can accommodate hundreds of sun seekers and sand-castle builders in summer. But in the off-season, you'll be practically alone, walking in quiet reflection, observing shorebirds and natural rhythms. It's a beautifully haunting place during a storm—so long as it's not a huge storm. Nauset Beach also has historical significance. Gosnold explored it in 1602 and Champlain in 1605. It was the location of the first recorded shipwreck on the eastern seaboard, in 1626, when the Sparrow Hawk ran aground near Pochet. It is the only place in the continental U.S. to be fired upon in the War of 1812 (by the British) and in World War I (in 1918 it was shelled by a German submarine). More recently, two Englishmen set off from nearby Nauset Harbor to row successfully across the Atlantic Ocean.

The real charm of Orleans, which has few historical sights, lies not in the sand but in the waters that surround the town. A large number of fingerlike inlets creep into the eastern shoreline from aptly named **Pleasant Bay**, dotted with tiny islands. And most of these quiet inlets are accessible via back roads and town landings. Excursion boats explore the rich habitat of **Nauset Marsh** to the north, while bayside, **Rock Harbor** is home to the Cape's most active charter fishing fleet.

Because Routes 6, 6A, and 28 converge in Orleans, traffic is heavy in summer; getting anywhere takes time. But Orleans straddles the two distinct worlds of the Outer Cape and the Lower Cape. On the one hand, Orleans serves as a year-round commercial and retail center for the area. It offers plenty of activities and a variety of dining and lodging options. On the other hand, Orleans has its share of exclusive residential areas and plenty of quiet, waterside spots. In the summer, Orleans balloons to a population of about 22,000 from its year-round count of 6,700.

Orleans is the only Cape town without a Native American or English name. Incorporated in 1797 after separating from Eastham, Orleans was named for Louis-Philippe de Bourbon, Duke of Orléans (and later king of France), who sojourned here in 1797 during his exile.

GUIDANCE ✳ **Orleans Chamber of Commerce Information Booth** (508-255-1386; orleanscapecod.com), 8 Eldredge Park Way (Exit 12 off Route 6A). Booth open late May to mid-October. The administrative office, at 44 Main Street, is open year-round. Orleans publishes a helpful booklet and an excellent free map.

GETTING THERE *By car:* Take Route 6 east from the Cape Cod Canal for about 48 miles to Exit 12. Route 6A East takes you directly into town.

By bus: The **Plymouth & Brockton** bus line (508-746-0378; p-b.com) connects Orleans with Hyannis and other Cape towns, as well as with Boston's Logan Airport. It only stops at the CVS on Main Street.

GETTING AROUND East Orleans Village and Nauset Beach are 3 miles east of Orleans center (which stretches along Route 6A); Rock Harbor and Skaket Beach are 1.5 miles west of the center.

8:00	Get buttery delights from Cottage St. Bakery or the Hot Chocolate Sparrow.
9:00	Kayak around Pleasant Bay or Nauset Marsh.
12:00	Order a simple fish feast at Cap't Cass Rock Harbor Seafood.
1:00	Read a trashy novel (or existential poetry) at the 9-mile-long Nauset Beach on the Atlantic Ocean.
5:30	Enjoy a highly sophisticated, creative dinner at ABBA.
8:00	Listen to twilight at Rock Harbor while watching the fishing fleet return for the day.
10:00	Enjoy a nightcap at the convivial Joe's Beach Road Bar & Grille.

By shuttle: The **H2O** (800-352-7155; capecodrta.org), used more by locals than visitors, travels Route 28 between the Hyannis Transportation Center and Orleans daily in the summer.

PUBLIC RESTROOMS At the information booth and 44 Main Street.

PUBLIC LIBRARY ❋ ✎ ⛨ **Snow Library** (508-240-3760; snowlibrary.org), 67 Main Street at Route 28.

MEDICAL EMERGENCY Orleans Medical Center (508-255-9577; 508-255-8825; orleansmedicalcenter.org), 204 Main Street or Exit 12 off Route 6.

❋ To See

⛨ **Meeting House Museum** (508-240-1329; orleanshistoricalsociety.org), 3 River Road at Main and School Streets. Open July and August. Built in 1833 as a Universalist meetinghouse, and now operated by the Orleans Historical Society, the museum contains artifacts documenting Orleans's early history. Among the items are an assessor's map of Orleans homes in 1858, photographs, Native American artifacts, and a bicentennial quilt. The building itself is a fine example of Greek Revival Doric architecture. Down at Rock Harbor, the museum also has a Coast Guard rescue boat that was used during a 1952 shipwreck off the Chatham coast. That 32 people piled into this tiny boat is beyond belief. You can board the boat; in fact, following restoration it now once again travels the waters on Cape Cod and beyond. A tour schedule is posted on-site. Free.

⛨ **French Cable Station Museum** (508-240-1735; frenchcablestationmuseum.org), Route 28 at Cove Road. Open June through September. Before the advent of the information superhighway and wireless communications, there was the French Cable Station. Direct transmissions from Brest, France (via a 3,000-mile underwater cable), were made from this station between 1890 and 1941, at which time transmissions were automated. Among the relayed news items: Charles Lindbergh's successful crossing

FRENCH CABLE STATION

of the Atlantic and his 1927 Paris landing, and Germany's invasion of France. Much of the original equipment and instruments are still set up and in working order. (Alas, the cable is no longer operational.) The displays, put together with the help of the Smithsonian Institution, are a bit intimidating, but someone is on hand to unravel the mysteries. Free.

JONATHAN YOUNG WINDMILL

Jonathan Young Windmill (508-240-1329), 27–33 Route 6A at Windmill Park Conservation Area. Open July and August. This circa-1720 gristmill was built in South Orleans, transported to the center of town in 1839, moved to Hyannisport in 1897, and returned to Orleans in 1987. Although it's no longer operational, the windmill is significant because of its intact milling machinery. Inside you'll find interpretive exhibits, including a display of a 19th-century miller's handiwork, as well as a guide who might explain the origins of "keep your nose to the grindstone." (Because grain is highly combustible when it's ground, a miller who wasn't paying close attention to his grain might not live to see the end of the day.) The setting, overlooking Town Cove, provides a nice backdrop for a picnic. Free.

ROCK HARBOR

Rock Harbor, on Cape Cod Bay, at the end of Rock Harbor Road from Main Street. This protected harbor, the town's first commercial and maritime center, served as a packet landing for ships transporting goods to Plymouth, Boston, and Maine. When the harbor filled with silt, several old houses in the area were built from the lumber of dismantled saltworks. During the War of 1812, Orleans militiamen turned back Britain's HMS *Newcastle* from Rock Harbor. And what about those dead trees in the water? They mark the harbor channel that is dredged annually for the charter fishing fleet. This is a popular sunset spot for watching the boats come in, if you can tolerate the bugs.

✳ To Do

BASEBALL ✐ **The Orleans Firebirds** (508-255-0793; orleansfirebirds.com) play ball at Eldredge Park Field, off Route 28 at Eldredge Park Way, from mid-June to early August. Their clinics for boys and girls begin in late June. As many as 60 or 70 young sluggers might show up, but there is always a good ratio of instructors to children. $$$$$+ for the first week, or $$$ per day.

BICYCLING & RENTALS ✐ **The Cape Cod Rail Trail** runs near the center of town, right past **Orleans Cycle** (508-255-9115; orleanscycle.com), 26 Main Street, which is open April through December. $$ for four hours.

BOAT EXCURSIONS ✿ ✐ **Nauset Marsh Cruise** (508-349-2615; wellfleetbay. org), Town Cove, behind Goose Hummock, off Route 6A. Mid-June to mid-October.

Sponsored by the Wellfleet Bay Wildlife Sanctuary, these two-hour pontoon voyages do not depart daily, so it's best to call for departure times and days. Adult trips focus on birding and the natural history of the marsh and depart with high tides; kids' trips are synced with low tide, all the better for interactive exploration. Along with informative on-board interpretation, kids haul traps, unearth worms and steamers, and participate in scavenger hunts. $$$$$.

BOWLING ❋ ✇ ⼂ **Orleans Bowling Center** (508-255-0636; orleansbowlingcenter .com), 191 Route 6A. OK, so you didn't come to the Cape to go bowling, but if it's raining and you've got kids in the car, it's an idea.

FISHING & SHELLFISHING Procure freshwater and saltwater fishing licenses and regulations online (www.mass.gov/eea/agencies/dfg/licensing). Then head to **Crystal Lake**, off Monument Road (see *Green Space*), which has perch, trout, and bass. There are also a dozen fresh- and saltwater town landings in Orleans.

❋ **Goose Hummock** (508-255-0455; goose.com), Town Cove, 15 Route 6A at the rotary. This outfitter fulfills all fishing-related needs, including rod rentals, fishing

GOOSE HUMMOCK

SCENIC DRIVES

Pleasant Bay, Little Pleasant Bay, Nauset Harbor, and Town Cove creep deep into the Orleans coastline at about a dozen named inlets, ponds, and coves. With the detailed centerfold map from the Orleans Chamber of Commerce guide in hand (see *Guidance*), head down the side roads off Tonset Road, Hopkins Lane, Nauset Heights Road, and Barley Neck Road to the town landings. After passing beautifully landscaped residences, you'll be rewarded with serene, pastoral scenes of beach grass and sailboats. Directly off Route 28 heading toward Chatham there are two particularly lovely ponds with saltwater outlets: **Arey's Pond** (off Arey's Lane from Route 28) and **Kescayogansett Pond** (off Monument Road from Route 28). There's a little picnic area with limited parking at **Kent's Point** near here, off Frost Fish Lane from Monument Road.

trips, instruction, and wintertime fly-tying seminars. Shellfishing equipment, too. The great staff offers lots of free advice and information.

 ✍ **Rock Harbor Charter Fleet** (508-255-9757; rockharborcharters.com), Rock Harbor. Trips daily mid-May to early October. These 13, U.S. Coast Guard–licensed captains and boats make up the largest charter fleet in New England. All offer four- and eight-hour trips for groups in search of bluefish and striped bass.

FITNESS CLUB ❊ ✍ **Willy's Gym** (508-255-6826; 508-255-6370; willysgym.com), 21 Old Colony Way, off West Road from Route 6A, Orleans Marketplace. One of the Cape's best fitness centers, Willy's has an extensive array of cardiovascular machines, free weights, sauna and steam rooms, classes, a juice bar, and supervised childcare. Lap swimmers will appreciate the indoor unheated pool. $$.

MINI-GOLF ✍ **Cape Escape** (508-240-1791; capeescapeadventures.com), 14 Canal Road, off Route 6A near the Orleans rotary. Open April to mid-October.

MODEL RAILROADING ✍ **Nauset Model Railroad Club** (nausetmodelrailroad-club.com), Hilltop Plaza (around the back), 180 Route 6A. And now for something

CANOEING AND KAYAKING

The protected, calm waters of northern Pleasant Bay offer delightful paddling opportunities. And the folks at Goose Hummock (508-255-2620; goose.com), off Route 6A on Town Cove, are the experts in this neck of the bay. Talk to them about Southern Pleasant Bay, for instance; it can be tricky for the uninitiated. Pick up the Nauset Harbor tide chart and rent a canoe or recreational kayak ($$$ for three hours). Parking is limited at the town landings, but it's free. If you're new to kayaking, take their three-hour introductory course ($$$$$+) to learn basic paddle strokes and skills. Otherwise, they have a huge array of other courses and specialty tours: intro to kayaking, tidal currents and navigation, open-water kayaking, sunrise tours, kids in kayaks, and more.

completely different, head to this open house (Wednesdays and Fridays) as an alternative to more common Cape Cod activities for kiddos and aficionados of any age. Free.

PADDLEBOARDING **SUPfari Adventures** (508-205-9087; supfariadventures.com), multiple locations in Brewster and Orleans. Stand-up paddleboarding brought from Maui to the Cape by Brewster's former harbormaster. Great multigenerational fun. $$$$.

SAILING ⌀ **Arey's Pond Boat Yard** (508-255-0994, sailing school; areyspondboatyard.com), 43 Arey's Lane off Route 28, South Orleans. June through September. They offer 10 hours of beginning and intermediate sailing instruction to groups of kids, July through August, over the course of five weekdays. Private lessons by appointment.

SKATEBOARDING ⌀ **Jean Finch Skateboard Park**, located at the middle school fields, 70 Route 28. Helmets required. $.

SKATING ❄ ⌀ **Charles Moore Arena** (508-255-5902; charlesmoorearena.org), 23 O'Connor's Way; look for signs near the information booth (see *Guidance*). Although this big arena is reserved most of the year, public skating times are set aside (including Friday nights when it's strobe lit for kids).

SUPFARI ADVENTURES

SHARK AWARENESS FLAGS: RECENT ARRIVALS TO CAPE COD

Purple flags emblazoned with a distinctive solid white shark shape debuted in 2016 on the Atlantic Coast beaches. The first time I spotted one (at Head of the Meadows), I didn't understand why people were still in the water and there were August crowds along the shore.

Conversations with lifeguards, tour guides, and locals provided highly useful intel. Apparently flags are not necessarily up because of a shark sighting on any particular day, but to heighten awareness that these enormous, mammal-eating creatures are becoming more frequent visitors to Cape Cod waters. Why? The seal population has exploded in recent years; you'll see them sunning on sand bars and exchanging wide-eyed stares with humans.

Cape Cod's sharks are becoming better known to its resident researchers; apparently lone sharks (pardon the pun) have adopted particular neighborhoods. Large Marge has staked out Orleans, while Mary Lee has aligned herself with upscale Chatham. It's reassuring that a contingent of dedicated experts are spotting, tagging, and monitoring these sea giants, gaining knowledge about their behavior, and have a ready system for communication if and when their presence becomes a threat.

The newly formed Atlantic White Shark Conservancy (atlanticwhiteshark.org), working to "increase knowledge of Atlantic white sharks and change public perception to conserve the species and ensure biologically diverse marine ecosystems," has developed an app called Sharktivity. It allows users to follow shark whereabouts and receive beach-specific notifications of sightings. Beach managers will replace purple flags with red ones and visitors will be kept out of the water for at least one hour following a sighting.

Sharks, I am glad to report, are not especially interested in dining on Homo sapiens. They will, however, "gum" a person who crosses their path to investigate palatability, resulting in potential severe injury (or worse), given dimensions averaging 15 feet in length and a ton in poundage. Still, if you mind the flags and respect these creatures' space on the still-rare occasions when they happen by, your safety is assured.

—H. Laurie Yankowitz

SPECIAL PROGRAMS ✳️ 𖣘 **Academy of Performing Arts** (508-255-5510; 508-255-1963; apacape.org), 5 Giddiah Hill Road. The academy offers instruction (to all ages) in dance, fitness, music, and theater. Their weekly July and August sessions (concentrating on musical theater, ballet, and drama production) culminate with a performance. Inquire about children's summertime matinees.

SURFING **Nauset Surf** (508-255-4742; nausetsports.com), Jeremiah Square, Route 6A at the Orleans rotary. Open April through January, but rentals are only provided in-season: surfboards, paddleboards, skimboards, boogie boards, and wet suits.

TENNIS You'll find three public courts at **Eldredge Park** (off Route 28 at Eldredge Park Way) and three at the **elementary school** (off Eldredge Park Way), both with seasonal fees.

✳️ Green Space

BEACHES 𖣘 ♿ **Nauset Beach** (508-240-3780), on the Atlantic Ocean, off Beach Road, beyond the center of East Orleans. It doesn't get much better than this: good

NAUSET BEACH

bodysurfing waves and 7 miles of sandy Atlantic shoreline backed by a low dune. (Only about a half-mile stretch is covered by lifeguards; much of the rest is deserted.) A gently sloping grade makes this a good beach for children. Facilities include an in-season lifeguard on weekends, restrooms, a snack bar, a boardwalk over dunes, outside showers, chairs and umbrellas for rent, and plenty of parking (parking is rarely a problem). Parking $–$$, depending on the day/month.

Four-wheel-drive vehicles with permit are allowed onto Nauset Beach. Certain areas, though, may be restricted during bird breeding and nesting periods. Obtain permits at the Nauset administrative offices, Parks and Beaches Department (508-240-3775), 18 Bay Ridge Lane.

✎ ♿ **Skaket Beach** on Cape Cod Bay, off West Road. Popular with families, as you can walk a mile out into the bay at low tide; at high tide the beach grass is covered. The parking lot often fills up early, creating a 30-minute wait for a space. Parking $$ in season. (The parking fee is transferable to Nauset Beach on the same day.) Facili-

ties include an in-season lifeguard, a bike rack, restrooms, a boardwalk, outside showers, and a snack bar.

Pleasant Bay Beach, Route 28, South Orleans. A saltwater bayside inlet beach with limited roadside parking.

PONDS **Crystal Lake** (off Monument Road and Route 28) and **Pilgrim Lake** (off Herring Brook Road from Route 28) are both good for swimming. Pilgrim Lake has an in-season lifeguard, restrooms, changing rooms, picnic tables, a dock, and a small beach; parking stickers only. At Crystal Lake, parking is free but limited; no facilities.

WALKS & PICNICS **Paw Wah Point Conservation Area**, off Namequoit Road from Eldredge Park Way, has a loop trail leading to a nice little beach with picnic tables.

Rhododendron Display Garden, Route 28 and Main Street. A nice place for a picnic.

Sea Call Farm, Tonset Road, just north of the intersection with Main Street. Overlooking Town Cove, this is another fine picnic spot.

✳ Lodging

🐚 Lodging in Orleans is a very good value. You'll find everything from super-stellar and friendly B&Bs to almost-beachfront motels and family motor inns.

RESORT MOTOR INN ✳ 🌊 **The Cove** (508-255-1203; thecoveorleans.com), 13 South Orleans Road. This modest complex of 47 rooms and suites is situated on the waterfront along Town Cove and close to bike paths. Pluses include a free boat tour of Town Cove and Nauset Beach; an outdoor heated pool; a dock for sunning and fishing; and picnic tables and grills that are well situated to exploit the view. Deluxe rooms have a sitting area and sofa bed; most waterfront rooms have a shared deck overlooking the water; two-room suites have a kitchen (some with a fireplace and private deck); and inn rooms have a bit more decor (some also have a fireplace and private deck). $–$$.

BED & BREAKFASTS **A Little Inn on Pleasant Bay** (508-255-0780; alittlein nonpleasantbay.com), 654 South Orleans Road. Open May to late October. I affectionately dub my favorite place to stay, marvelously and tastefully renovated, "a little slice of heaven on high." The European innkeepers (Sandra, Pamela, and Bernd) have transformed this 1798 house into a priceless diamond with commanding views of Pleasant Bay and a thoroughly contemporary aesthetic. No other B&B on the Cape comes close to matching their bountiful, European buffet breakfast—especially when it's taken outside in summer. Formerly a stop on

A LITTLE INN ON PLEASANT BAY

NAUSET HOUSE INN

the Underground Railroad, the main house has plenty of common space, including a big living room with windows all around. It's all quite conducive to luxuriating. Guest rooms feature whitewashed barn board and lovely bathroom tilework; some have private decks or patio. Blue stone patios grace the front and back yards, which are beautifully landscaped. The Bay Rooms (carved from a former paddock) and the carriage house have also been renovated with similar doses of grace and style. Late-afternoon sherry and access to a private beach and dock are all included. $$$.

Nauset House Inn (508-255-2195; 800 771-5508; nausethouseinn.com), Beach Road, East Orleans. Open mid-April through October. These 14 rooms (eight with private bath) have so very much going for them: The inn has genuinely hospitable hosts; it's half a mile from Nauset Beach; guest rooms are thoughtfully and tastefully appointed; afternoon drinks and cheese are a treat; and a greenhouse conservatory is just one of the many quiet places to relax. Oh, and it's the only B&B on the Cape where you order from among an array of breakfast entrées! You'll have Diane Johnson, her daughter Cindy,

and son-in-law John to thank: They've owned and constantly upgraded the 1810 farmhouse since the early 1980s. Rooms in the carriage house are generally larger than inn rooms, while the rustic cottage, with peaked ceiling, is quite private and cozy. There's immense attention to detail here. $–$$.

❋ **The Parsonage Inn** (508-255-8217; 888-422-8217; parsonageinn.com), 202 Main Street, East Orleans. Guests are quite happy here, as are innkeepers Jo-Anne and Richard Hoad. This

PARSONAGE INN

pleasant, rambling, late-18th-century house has eight guest rooms comfortably furnished with a blend of contemporary furnishings and country antiques. (Only two rooms have adjoining walls, so there is plenty of privacy.) Wide-pine floors, canopy beds, and newly redone bathrooms are common. Willow, the studio apartment, has a kitchenette and private entrance, while the roomy Barn, with exposed beams and eaves, has a sitting area and sofa bed. $$.

✳ **Orleans Inn** (508-255-2222; 800-863-3039; orleansinn.com), 3 Old County Road. Near the Orleans rotary and with a crisp mansard roof, this inn commands a prominent position as you enter town. You can't miss it. Ed and Laurie Maas's 11 rooms and suites are a pleasant surprise, made more so by the inn's friendly policies: There is no cancellation fee, no deposit required, and they accept one-nighters in the summer. That might lead you to believe that there's something wrong with the rooms, but there isn't. Rooms are located off a long hallway, and they're quite pleasant. Half overlook Nauset Bay; for $50 more, you obviously want one of these, which also have a fireplace! Full breakfast included. Rooms $$, suites $$$–$$$$.

MOTELS & **Nauset Knoll Motor Lodge** (508-255-2364; nausetknollmotorlodge.com), 237 Beach Road, East Orleans. Open mid-April to mid-October. Nauset Knoll, a few steps from Nauset Beach, is often booked long before other places because of the expansive views of dune and ocean. You can watch the sun as it rises over the ocean from lawn chairs atop the lodge's namesake knoll. The 12 simply furnished rooms (à la 1950s) with large picture windows are in three separate units, distinctively modeled after a barn, shed, and Cape-style cottage. $–$$.

RENTAL HOUSES & COTTAGES
The Rental Company at William Raveis (508-240-2222; capecodvacation.com), 213 Main Street, East Orleans.

✳ Where to Eat

Orleans has an excellent variety of restaurants.

DINING OUT ✳ ☂ & **ABBA** (508-255-8144; abbarestaurant.com), 89 Old Colony Way. Open D. Serving contemporary and sophisticated Mediterranean food (with a Thai flair), this lively bistro (read loud with tightly spaced tables) would be perfectly at home in Boston's South End. Since it burst onto the scene in 2001, it's taken this part of the Cape by storm. Chef-owner Erez Pinhas and his front-of-the-house partner, Christina Bratberg, have a flair for creating mod spaces and inviting plates. The urbane menu changes often, but look for the luscious likes of black sea bass with fava beans, grilled foie gras with creamy lentils, or an ab-fab falafel with Israeli salsa in a tahini amba sauce. House specialties include a sublime shrimp, curries, or organic tofu pad thai. The wine list is impressive and desserts are lovely: the poached strawberries and rhubarb in a shredded phyllo is killer. $$–$$$$.

✳ 🍴 ⚓ ☂ & **Joe's Beach Road Bar & Grille (Barley Neck Inn)** (508-255-0212; barleyneck.com), 5 Beach Road, East Orleans. Open D. Joe's *gets it*—both for atmosphere *and* cuisine. Joe's has a delightful split personality: One side has almost-formal dining, one is almost reserved for families, and the other is a hopping (upscale-ish) bar-happy place with barn-board walls and a large fieldstone fireplace. All you really need to know, though, is that locals continue to flock here even as the summer crowds swell. It's packed for good reason. Look for a variety of lobster dishes, lots of New American seafood dishes prepared with flair, as well as dishes featuring veggies from their organic garden. Chef Will Hollinger knows how to please his patrons. For lighter appetites and thinner wallets, there's pizza, pasta, soup, and main-course salads. $$–$$$.

JOE'S

❊ **Nauset Beach Club** (508-255-8547; nausetbeachclub.com), 222 Main Street, East Orleans. Open D. Neither a club nor on the beach, this buzzy bistro has a warm and welcoming feeling, thanks to proprietor Arthur Duquette. For Northern Italian cuisine, featuring local seafood, homemade pastas, and plenty of meat and game dishes, it has few rivals. On my last visit, the *ravioli di zuccaro et ricotta, risotto del giorno, carre d'agnello arrosto* (lamb), and daily special of sea bass were all executed with aplomb. Although tables are set with linens, crystal, and china, it has a relaxed atmosphere thanks to the warming fireplace and friendly service. The wine list is quite impressive. I enjoy this place more each season. $$$.

❊ ✐ ☿ **Mahoney's Atlantic Bar & Grill** (508-255-5505; mahoneysatlantic.com), 28 Main Street. Open D. Consistent and appealing across-the-board, this cozy storefront bistro serves a surprisingly sophisticated menu. It's firing on all cylinders (except maybe service). Expect contemporary New American dishes like pan-roasted lobster, tuna sashimi, and roasted chicken. During my last visit the striped bass tasted like it was just off the boat, as did the sashimi apps. Salads, creative pasta dishes, and a few veggie dishes round out the choices. It's hard to go wrong here. Their lively and upscale martini bar (where you can get lighter dishes) also sports a few satellite TVs, all the better to catch a Sox game. The place is packed in the winter, which is always a good sign. Watch for live entertainment intermittently throughout the year. Bar menu $, D $$–$$$.

❊ ✐ **Captain Linnell House** (508-255-3400; linnell.com), 137 Skaket Beach Road. Open D. For a truly lovely dining experience, let chef-owner Bill Conway's fine fare match the gracious ease of this former sea captain's mansion. The traditional dining is romantic, with candles, fine china, and linens. One dining room overlooks a small water garden; the salon overlooks the side garden. Start with fabulous chowder or lobster bisque and move to scrod in parchment with crab and shrimp or roasted pork tenderloin. Rack of lamb specials are always popular. Chef Conway will also dish out small portions for children with refined palates. If you're seated by 5:30 PM, you'll receive a complimentary lobster bisque or chowder and dessert with your dinner. It's one of the best deals in the land! Bill and his wife, Shelly, have owned and been restoring this gem since 1988. Prix fixe or à la carte, $$$.

❊ ✐ **The Beacon Room** (508-255-2211; beaconroom.com), 23 West Road. Open L, D. For casual fine dining on the way to Skaket Beach, this intimate bistro offers sizable portions of well-presented dishes at reasonable prices. Dinnertime dishes range from pasta and lamb (quite popular) to seafood and chicken saltimbocca. Sandwiches and burgers are offered at lunch. No reservations, but you can call ahead for dinner. L $–$$, D $$–$$$.

NAUSET BEACH CLUB

CAPTAIN LINNELL HOUSE

EATING OUT **Cap't Cass Rock Harbor Seafood**, 117 Rock Harbor Road. Open L, D, mid-April to mid-October. Straight out of a movie set, with everything except the prices preserved, this classic harborside lobster shack is adorned with colorful buoys on the outside and checkered table-cloths on the inside. As for the food, it's a cut above: The lobster roll hasn't a shred of lettuce or breading in it; the she-crab stew is outrageously delectable; and the home-made chowder and fish-and-chips are pretty darn good, too. The menu is posted on cardboard, as it has been since 1958. There really was an 80-something-year-old Captain Cass, by the way. But today the "shack" is run by the fish market next door. BYOB. No credit cards. L $$, D $$–$$$.

CAP'T CASS

✳ ✿ ✐ ♉ **Land Ho!** (508-255-5165; land-ho.com), 38 Main Street. Open L, D. A favorite local hangout since 1969 (with lines out the door in the summertime), John Murphy's place is very colorful (literally), from red-and-white-checked tablecloths, to old business signs hanging from the ceiling, to a large black-board menu. Newspapers hang on a wire to separate the long bar from the dining area. Beyond club sandwiches, fried sea-food dishes, and great burgers, look for specialties like fish-and-chips, BBQ ribs, stuffed clams, clam pie, and kale soup. With the addition of sashimi and grilled tuna, the menu is also going a bit upscale these days. But they always have draft beer. You'll find lots of families, col-lege students, and old-time locals here. There's live music Thursday through Saturday. $$.

✳ **Guapo's Tortilla Shack** (508-255-3338; guaposcapecod.com), Staples Plaza, off Route 6A. *See Eating Out in "Brewster."*

✳ ✿ ✐ **Sir Cricket's Fish 'n Chips** (508-255-4453; nausetfish.com/sir-cricket-fish-n-chips), 38 Route 6A. Love this place. This tidy hole-in-the-wall dishes out fast pints of fried seafood,

LAND HO

British-style fish-and-chips, and mixed platters (scallops, oysters, and clams are the most popular). Kids might prefer chicken tenders and hot dogs. After the beach, plan on take-out, as there are only a couple of tables. $$.

❋ ⵉ **Orleans Inn** (508-255-2222; orleansinn.com), 3 Old County Road. Open L, D. This waterfront eatery has really upped its offerings to the caliber of "decent" lately, and folks are flocking here because of the prime water views. Go easy with the expectations and you'll be thrilled. The traditional-feeling dining room offers surf and turf, sandwiches, fried seafood platters, and salads. Dine and have drinks on the deck and you'll be raving. Welcoming service is learned top down from the hands-on owners. $$.

𝒶 & **The Lobster Claw** (508-255-1800; lobsterclaw.com), 42 Cranberry Highway, near the Orleans rotary. Open L, D, daily April to mid-October. You want your basic broiled, grilled, fried seafood served up with that nautical-tourist look? Look no further. Since 1970 the Berig family has been dishing up seafood at their large, convenient, family-style restaurant. Proudly maintained and decorated with that requisite motif, The Lobster Claw serves straightforward preparations like delicately broiled

fisherman's platters, crabcakes, and fried clams. Lobster sandwiches and salads are popular at lunch. Early specials from 4 PM to 5:30 PM, and a "waiting lounge" upstairs. L $–$$, D $$–$$$.

❋ 𝒶 ⵉ & **Old Jailhouse Tavern** (508-255-5245; jailhousetavern.com), 28 West Road. Open L, D. Slightly boisterous by night, more sedate by day, the tavern is a decent choice when everyone in your party wants something different:

SIR CRICKETS

THE LOBSTER CLAW

nachos, soup and salad, fish-and-chips, or a broiled seafood sampler. Or when you have late-night munchies. How's that for a rousing endorsement? Eat in one of the booths, on the atriumlike terrace overlooking the garden, at the long oak bar, or within the rock walls of the old jail. In the early 1800s the town constable offered the use of his front bedroom, complete with bars on the windows, as an overnight lockup facility. No reservations are taken, but call ahead anyway, just in case. $$–$$$.

❄ ✒ ♿ **The Hole in One** (508-255-3740; theholecapecod.com), 98 Route 6A within Main Street Square. Open B, L. The Hole is a pleasant and airy place, a real local hangout for turkey subs or BLTs. It's packed at breakfast time, when eggs-your-way and a short stack of pancakes rule, and friendly all day. You gotta try their hand-cut doughnuts. $.

SNACKS, ICE CREAM, & COFFEE ❄ **The Hot Chocolate Sparrow** (508-240-2230; hotchocolatesparrow.com), 5 Old Colony Way, behind CVS on Route 6A. Open early to late. On the rail trail (with a convenient window for ice cream), this place is on my short list of never-miss-driving-by-without-stopping-in-for-something-anything! Proprietor Marje Sparrow sends her staff to "espresso lab" to make sure they know the hows and whys of making a consistent cup. Without a doubt, they make the best cappuccino, lattes, and hot chocolate

THE HOT CHOCOLATE SPARROW

between Beantown and Provincetown ... not to mention frozen espresso drinks like "Affogato" (with soft-serve ice cream), "The Bash" (with fresh raspberries), and old-fashioned freshly squeezed lemonade. Come at 7 AM, when the scones and croissants pour out of the ovens. Or come whenever, because all cookies are made on the premises. In addition to an overflowing blackboard menu, they also make luscious hand-dipped chocolates and sweet treats. The candy counter is filled with treats like "bark," chock-full of pecans and cranberries, or peppermint or myriad other temptations. Marje's big space is a terrific place to hang out (with de rigueur free WiFi).

❋ **Cottage St. Bakery** (508-255-2821; cottagestreetbakery.com), 5 Cottage Street near Routes 6A and 28. This European-style bakery, buttering up the community since 1984, has a number of oddly named specialties, including "Dirt Bombs," an old-fashioned French doughnut recipe that requires baking, not frying. Their breads are also great. Knead I say more? OK, I will: You can get homemade soups, lasagna, chicken pies, and sandwiches here, too. There are a few indoor and outdoor tables.

❋ **Village Farm Market** (508-255-1949), 199 Main Street, East Orleans. Not your average farm stand, you can assemble a gourmand's feast here with cold pastas, roasted chicken, sesame noodles, baked goods, and deli sandwiches. There's a salad bar and a full-service bakery, too.

❋ **Jo Mama's** (508-255-0255; jomamas capecod.com), 125 Route 6A. Bagel sandwiches, smoothies, health tonics, and fair trade coffee. This mod little space has a few tables.

❋ **Phoenix Fruit & Vegetable** (508-255-5306; capecodorganicproduce.com), 14 Cove Road. This tiny shop is a delight for foodies. If you have cooking facilities, you'll appreciate organic greens, locally made clam pies, and hearty Pain d'Avignon bread.

COTTAGE STREET BAKERY

Sundae School Ice Cream Parlor (508-255-5473; sundaeschool.com), 210 Main Street, East Orleans. Open late May to mid-September. Try the sublime black raspberry or Grape-Nuts ice cream.

See also **Orleans Whole Food Store** under *Selective Shopping*.

FISH MARKETS **Young's Fish Market** (508-255-3366; nausetfish.com/youngs -fish-market), Rock Harbor. Open late May to early September. If you don't like to cook lobster, place your order here by 4:30 PM (the earlier, the better) and they'll do it for you. Their lobster rolls are also good. The market, by the way, has been in the Harrison family since 1962, when they bought it from the Youngs.

❋ Entertainment

❋ **Academy Playhouse** (508-255-1963; apacape.org), 120 Main Street. This 162-seat playhouse, in the 1873 Old Town Hall, and its resident theater company (established in 1975) host 10 to 12

YOUNG'S FISH MARKET

dramas, comedies, and musicals each year. Think popular productions like *Grease, Cinderella,* and *Biloxi Blues.* Their eagerly awaited April event brings established and unknown Cape writers (who have been holed up working all winter) together with audiences. Thankfully (even if it's only needed for a couple of sweltering weeks) the playhouse is now air-conditioned. $$$.

Hog Island Beer Company (508-255-2337; hogislandbeerco.com), 28 West Road. Operated by and attached to the Old Jailhouse Tavern, Hog Island specializes in IPAs (and maybe 4 to 8 other beers on tap) and fun (in the form of a tons of indoor and outdoor games). It's a great place to hang with pals—and often lots of families. $-$$.

✳ Selective Shopping

✳ Unless otherwise noted, all shops are open year-round.

ANTIQUES **Pleasant Bay Antiques** (508-255-0930; pleasantbayantiques .com), 540 Route 28, South Orleans. Most of these high-quality, 18th- and

19th-century American antiques come from area residents rather than auctions. They're displayed in a lovely old barn.

Continuum (508-255-8513), 7 Route 28. Dan Johnson sells expertly restored antique lamps and fixtures from the Victorian to the art deco period.

ACADEMY PLAYHOUSE

IF YOU ONLY STOP AT ONE LOWER CAPE GALLERY, MAKE IT THIS ONE.

Addison Art Gallery (508-255-6200; addisonart.com), 43 Route 28. Helen Addison represents both new and established artists working in realistic and traditional realms. Look for oils, watercolors, limited-edition prints, egg tempuras, and sculpture. It's comfortable for browsing and buying, for serious collectors and novices. Saturday openings throughout the summer.

ADDISON ART GALLERY

ART GALLERIES **Left Bank Gallery** (508-247-9172; leftbankgallery.com), 8 Cove Road. One of the best galleries on the Cape, with ceramics, glass, jewelry, and furniture. The owner, Audrey Parent, has a good eye.

Tree's Place (508-255-1330; treesplace .com), 60 Route 6A at Route 28. Tree's offers a vast collection of unusual gifts (like kaleidoscopes and antique jewelry) displayed throughout nine small rooms; an excellent collection of representational New England painters; and a tile shop. Meet-the-artist champagne receptions.

ARTISANS **Nauset Lantern Shop** (800-899-2660; nausetlanternshop.com), 52 Route 6A. Michael Joly expertly handcrafts copper and brass Colonial- and

Early American–style lanterns. Most of the nautical and onion lanterns are for exterior use, but he also makes sconces and indoor accessories. Watch him work.

Kemp Pottery (508-255-5853; kemp pottery.com), 9 Cranberry Highway, near

KEMP POTTERY

the Orleans rotary. Father Steven and son Matt Kemp create unusual designs using Nauset Beach sand. They have functional porcelain and stoneware pieces like lamps, platters, mirrors, dinner sets, and bathroom sinks, as well as less common decorative objects for home and garden, like pagodas and torsos. They also make fountains and tile.

BOOKSTORES **Booksmith/Musicsmith of Orleans** (508-255-4590), Orleans Marketplace, 136 Route 6A. Paperbacks and best-sellers.

Main Street Books (508-255-3343; mainstreetbooksonline.com), 46 Main Street. The husband-and-wife team of Janis and Don have presided over a small but worthy selection of titles since 1975.

HONEY CANDLE CO

CLOTHING **Karol Richardson** (508-255-3944; karolrichardson.com), 47 Main Street. Stylish women's clothing.

FARMERS' MARKET **Orleans Farmers' Market** (orleansfarmersmarket.com), Old Colony Way near Depot Square. Pick up local produce 8 AM–noon every Saturday from mid-May to late November.

SPECIAL SHOPS **Bird Watcher's General Store** (800-562-1512; birdwatchers generalstore.com), 36 Route 6A near the Orleans rotary. If it pertains to birds or watchers of birds, this store has it: bird feeders in every size and shape, birdseed in barrels (a ton of seed is sold daily), bird note cards, bird kitchen magnets, bird playing cards. As important as commerce is, though, this place is an invaluable resource for news of where and when birds have been sighted or will be sighted. (This place isn't just for the birds!)

Honey Candle Co (508-255-7031; hon eycandle.com), 37 Main Street. The light is bright; the scent is natural and sweet. That's because Honey Candle offers candles made entirely from beeswax.

Oceana (508-240-1414; oceanacape cod.com), 1 Main Street Square. Carol Wright stocks lovely household items, watercolors, glass, and jewelry inspired by the sea and nature.

BIRD WATCHERS GENERAL STORE

ORLEANS WHOLE FOOD STORE

Orleans Whole Food Store (508-255-6540; orleanswholefoodstore.com), 46 Main Street, Orleans. Healthy foods, lunches-to-go, vitamins, books, and items that promote holistic living.

Cape Cod Photo & Art Supply (508-255-0476; capecodphotoandart.com), 60 Route 6A, inside Tree's Place. All things digital, one-hour film processing, and painting supplies if the wonderful Cape Cod light inspires you.

✳ Special Events

Annual: Because print guidebooks circulate for years, and because events are so changeable, I normally only include big annual events around which you'd want to plan. In this case, I suggest checking orleanscapecod.com.

THE OUTER CAPE

EASTHAM

WELLFLEET

TRURO

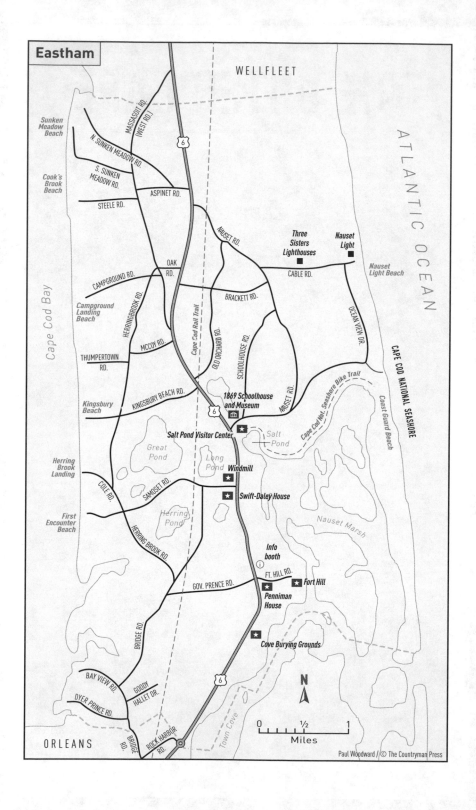

Eastham

WELLFLEET

ATLANTIC OCEAN

Sunken Meadow Beach

Cook's Brook Beach

MASSASOIT RD. (WEST RD.)

N. SUNKEN MEADOW RD.

S. SUNKEN MEADOW RD.

ASPINET RD.

STEELE RD.

NAUSET RD.

Three Sisters Lighthouses

Nauset Light

CABLE RD.

Nauset Light Beach

OAK RD.

CAMPGROUND RD.

HERRINGBROOK RD.

BRACKETT RD.

Cape Cod Bay

Campground Landing Beach

THUMPERTOWN RD.

MCCOY RD.

Cape Cod Rail Trail

OLD ORCHARD RD.

SCHOOLHOUSE RD.

NAUSET RD.

OCEAN VIEW DR.

CAPE COD NATIONAL SEASHORE

Kingsbury Beach

KINGSBURY BEACH RD.

1869 Schoolhouse and Museum

Salt Pond Visitor Center

Salt Pond

Cape Cod Nat. Seashore Bike Trail

Coast Guard Beach

Great Pond

Long Pond

Windmill

Herring Brook Landing

COLE RD.

SAMOSET RD.

Swift-Daley House

Nauset Marsh

First Encounter Beach

Herring Pond

HERRING BROOK RD.

Info booth

FT. HILL RD.

GOV. PRENCE RD.

Fort Hill

Penniman House

BRIDGE RD.

Cove Burying Grounds

BAY VIEW RD.

GOODY HALLET DR.

DYER PRINCE RD.

N

ORLEANS

ROCK HARBOR RD.

Town Cove

0   ½   1
Miles

Paul Woodward / © The Countryman Press

EASTHAM

Eastham is content to remain relatively undiscovered by 21st-century tourists. In fact, although almost 29,000 folks summer here, year-rounders (fewer than 5,500) seem perfectly happy that any semblance of major tourism development has passed them by. There isn't even a Main Street or town center per se.

What Eastham does boast, as gateway to the Cape Cod National Seashore (CCNS), is plenty of natural diversions. There are four things you should do, by all means. Stop in at **Salt Pond Visitor Center**, one of two CCNS headquarters, which dispenses a wealth of information and offers ranger-guided activities and outstanding nature programs. Consider taking a boat trip onto **Nauset Marsh**, a fragile ecosystem that typifies much of the Cape. Hop on a bike or walking trail; a marvelous network of paths traverses this part of the seashore, including the **Fort Hill** area. And of course, head to the beach.

The Cape's renowned, uninterrupted stretches of sandy beach, backed by high dunes, begin in earnest in Eastham and extend all the way up to Provincetown. One of them, Coast Guard Beach, is also where exalted naturalist Henry Beston spent about two years during the mid-1920s, observing nature's minute changes from a little cottage and recording his experiences in *The Outermost House*, which was published in 1928.

Eastham is best known as the site where the *Mayflower*'s Myles Standish and a Pilgrim scouting party met the Nauset Indians in 1620 at First Encounter Beach. The "encounter," in which a few arrows were slung (without injury), served as sufficient warning to the Pilgrims: They left and didn't return for 24 years. When the Pilgrim

SALT POND TRAIL AT THE VISITOR CENTER

7:30	Start the day simple: at The Sparrow (Orleans), a local hangout.
9:00	Bike the Cape Cod Rail Trail up to Wellfleet and down to Dennis.
12:30	Get a fabu lobster roll from the Friendly Fisherman and enjoy it with panoramic views atop Fort Hill; walk the 1.5-mile Red Maple Swamp Trail afterward; tour the Edward Penniman House.
2:00	Build sand castles at the shallow, bayside First Encounter Beach.
5:30	Enjoy unusually tasty cuisine at Karoo Restaurant.
8:00	Build a bonfire at the National Seashore (after having picked up a permit), or check what's scheduled at the First Encounter Coffee House.

settlers, then firmly entrenched at Plymouth, went looking for room to expand, they returned to Eastham. Led by Thomas Prence, they purchased most of the land from Native Americans for an unknown quantity of hatchets.

Although the history books cite these encounters as the beginning of Eastham's recorded history, the 1990 discovery of a 4,000-year-old settlement (see the "Coast Guard Beach" sidebar) is keeping archaeologists and anthropologists on their toes.

GUIDANCE **Eastham Information Booth** (508-240-7211 chamber; 508-255-3444 info booth; easthamchamber.com), 1700 Route 6, near Fort Hill. Open June to mid-October.

❋ ☙ ⚸ **Salt Pond Visitor Center** (508-255-3421; 508-771-2144; nps.gov/caco), 50 Nauset Road, off Route 6. In 1961 newly elected president John F. Kennedy, Sen. Leverett Saltonstall, and Rep. Hastings Keith championed a bill to turn more than 43,000 acres into the **Cape Cod National Seashore** (CCNS), protected forever from further development. (About 600 private homes remain within the park.) Today, more than 5 million people visit the CCNS annually. The excellent center shows short films on Thoreau's Cape Cod, Marconi, the ever-changing natural landscape, and the history of whaling and lifesaving. And the fine museum includes displays on the salt and whaling industries and the diaries of Captain Penniman's wife, Augusta, who accompanied him on several voyages. Rangers lead lots of activities during the summer, from sunset campfires on the beach to talks on tidal flats and bird walks. Two short loop trails depart from here around Salt Pond and are worth your time. Programs are also offered during spring and fall. Free.

GETTING THERE *By car:* Eastham is 40 miles from the Cape Cod Canal via Route 6.

By bus: The **Plymouth & Brockton** bus line (508-778-9767; p-b.com) connects Eastham with Hyannis and other Cape towns, as well as with Boston's Logan Airport. The bus stops across from Town Hall on Route 6 and at the Village Green Plaza at Bracket Road on Route 6 in North Eastham.

GETTING AROUND Eastham is only a few miles wide and 6 miles long. Most points of interest are well marked along or off Route 6. The CCNS is to the east of Route 6.

PUBLIC RESTROOMS Salt Pond Visitor Center, 50 Nauset Road off Route 6.

PUBLIC LIBRARY ✳ ✎ ☂ **Eastham Library** (508-240-5950; easthamlibrary.org), 190 Samoset Road. At press time Eastham's library was undergoing a major expansion; it is expected to open late summer 2017. Temporary digs are next to Town Hall on Route 6. Story time and summer events for children; audio books for everyone.

MEDICAL EMERGENCY Call **911**.

✳ To See

Edward Penniman House (508-349-3785), off Route 6 in the Fort Hill area, CCNS. Open early May to late October; inquire about tour times/days. At age 11 Penniman left Eastham for the open sea. When he returned as a captain 26 years later, he had this 1868 house built for him. Boasting indoor plumbing (the first in Eastham to make that claim) and a kerosene chandelier, this French Second Empire–style house has Corinthian columns, a mansard roof, and a cupola that once afforded views of the bay and ocean. Ever-helpful National Park Service guides dispense lots of historical information. Even if it's closed, peek in the windows. Free.

    Swift-Daley House and **Tool Museum** (508-240-1247; easthamhistoricalsociety .org), next to the post office at 2375 Route 6. Open July and August. In the late 1990s one of the seashore dune shacks (see **Dune shacks** under *To See* in "Provincetown") was moved to this site. Although it's difficult to imagine what dune-shack life might have

EDWARD PENNIMAN HOUSE

PLEIN-AIR PAINTING AT THE EDWARD PENNIMAN HOUSE

been like, this helps. As for the Swift-Daley House, it's a completely furnished full Cape Colonial built by ship's carpenters in 1741. It has wide floorboards, pumpkin-pine woodwork, narrow stairways, and a fireplace in every room on the first floor. The Tool Museum behind the house displays hundreds of old tools for use in the home and in the field. And the Olde Shop sells antiques and local arts and crafts. Donations.

1869 Schoolhouse and Museum (508-255-0788; easthamhistoricalsociety.org), 25 Schoolhouse Road off Route 6 across from the Salt Pond Visitor Center. Open July and August. During the time when this former one-room schoolhouse served the town (1869 until 1936), there were separate entrances for boys and girls. Inside you'll learn about Henry Beston's year of solitude spent observing natural rhythms on nearby Coast Guard Beach. Thanks to the Eastham Historical Society, you can also learn about the town's farming history, daily domestic life, Native Americans, offshore shipwrecks, and the impressive Lifesaving Service. Donations.

Oldest windmill (easthamhistoricalsociety.org), on Route 6 at Samoset Road. Open July and August. Across from Town Hall, the Cape's oldest working windmill was built in Plymouth in the 1680s and moved to Eastham in the early 1800s.

First Encounter Beach, off Samoset Road and Route 6. A bronze marker commemorates where the Pilgrims, led by Capt. Myles Standish, first met the Native Americans. The exchange was not friendly. Although arrows flew, no one was injured. The site goes

SWIFT DALEY HOUSE AND TOOL MUSEUM

1869 SCHOOLHOUSE AND MUSEUM

down in history as the place where the Native Americans first began their decline at the hands of European settlers. On a more modern note of warfare history, for 25 years the U.S. Navy used an offshore ship for target practice. Until recently, it was still visible on a sandbar about a mile offshore. The beach, with its westward vista, is a great place to catch a sunset. Seasonal parking $$.

Doane Homestead Site, between the Salt Pond Visitor Center and Coast Guard Beach, a mile down Nauset Road on the southside, CCNS. Only a marker remains to identify the spot where Doane, one of Eastham's first English settlers, made his home.

Cove Burying Grounds, Route 6 near Corliss Way. Many of these graves date back to the 1700s, but look for the memorial to the three *Mayflower* Pilgrims who were buried here in the 1600s.

Nauset Light (508-240-2612; nausetlight.org), at the corner of Cable Road and Ocean View Drive, CCNS. Inquire about tour times May through October. This light was originally built in Chatham in 1877, one of a twin, but was moved here shortly thereafter. In the mid-1990s, when Nauset Light was just 37 feet from cliff's edge, the large red-and-white steel lighthouse was moved—via flatbed truck over the course of three days—from the eroding shoreline. And a few years later, the keeper's house (which dates to 1875) was also moved back. For now, the cast-iron behemoth sits a respectable distance from the shoreline, its beacon still stretching 17 miles to sea. Free, but you

OLDEST WINDMILL

might have to pay to park at Nauset Light Beach (see *Green Space*).

Three Sisters Lighthouses (508-255-3421), inland from Nauset Light, CCNS. Inquire about tour times May through October. In 1838 this coastal cliff was home to three brick lighthouses that provided beacons for sailors. They collapsed from erosion in 1892 and were replaced with three wooden ones. When erosion threatened those in 1918, two were moved away; the third was moved in 1923. Eventually the National Park Service acquired all three and moved them to their current location, nestled in the woods far back from today's coastline. (It's a rather incongruous sight: lighthouses, surrounded by trees, unable to reach the water.) Head inland from the beach parking lot along the paved walkway. Free, but you'll have to pay to park at Nauset Light Beach (see *Green Space*).

THREE SISTERS LIGHTHOUSE

✳ To Do

BICYCLING & RENTALS **Cape Cod Rail Trail**. This scenic, well-maintained, 24-mile (one-way) paved path winds from Dennis to Wellfleet. Park at the Salt Pond Visitor Center (see *Guidance*).

Nauset Bike Trail, CCNS. This 1.6-mile (one-way) trail connects with the Cape Cod Rail Trail and runs from the Salt Pond Visitor Center, across Nauset Marsh via a boardwalk, to Coast Guard Beach. The trail passes large stands of thin, tall black locust trees not native to the area—they were introduced to return nitrogen to the soil after overfarming.

Rent from the family-owned **Little Capistrano Bike Shop** (508-255-6515; littlecapistranobikeshop.com), 30 Salt Pond Road. Open April to mid-November. A superb shop right on the rail trail and across the street from the Nauset Bike Trail. The owner, Melissa, is wonderful. The shop, across from the Salt Pond Visitor Center behind the Lobster Shanty, offers well-priced rentals, repairs, and sales.

LITTLE CAPISTRANO BIKE SHOP

BOAT EXCURSIONS & RENTALS **Castaways Marine** (508-255-7751; castawaysmarnescapecod.com), 4655 Route 6. Along with surfing and kayaking lessons and rentals, these folks include free local delivery to and from the water. You can't miss them across from Willy's Gym. Single and double kayak rentals $$$$+.

NATIONAL SEASHORE BONFIRES

A beach bonfire, with or without a clambake, defines the essence of summertime on the Outer Cape. That said, officials prefer the term campfire—nothing too big, just cozy and toasty compared to anything rip-roaring. Here's the process you need to follow to secure a permit: In July and August head to the Salt Pond Visitor Center (508-255-3421; nps.gov/caco) three days before you want a permit and request one. For instance, if you want it for Wednesday, go on Sunday. Be there when the center opens (9 AM). On the day of your big event, be at the visitor center by 3:30 PM or you'll lose your permit to someone waiting in line. In the off-season, you can call three days ahead of your desired date without a problem. There are limits on the number of permits given out: four at Coast Guard Beach, four at Nauset Light Beach, and four at Marconi Beach; there are also limitations on the sizes of the groups allowed to congregate. Beach rangers will check permits. BYOF—bring your own firewood and don't forget to extinguish the flames. Fires are permitted year-round from 5:30 to 11:30 PM.

SALT POND VISITOR CENTER

FISHING & SHELLFISHING Procure freshwater and saltwater fishing licenses and regulations online (www.mass.gov/eea/agencies/dfg/licensing). Then head to **Goose Hummock** (508-255-0455; goose.com), 15 Route 6A at the rotary in Orleans, and the stocked, spring-fed **Herring Pond** (see *Green Space*). Most of Eastham's shellfishing areas are open daily; however, shellfishing is only permitted at Salt Pond (Route 6) and Salt Pond River on Sunday.

FITNESS CLUB ❋ **Willy's Gym** (508-255-6370; willysgym.com), 4730 Route 6. Facilities include racquetball and squash courts, Nautilus and free weights, a lap pool, saunas and steam rooms, a whirlpool, six indoor tennis courts, four outdoor courts, a climbing rock wall, a three-story soft play structure, and aerobics, yoga, Pilates, and spinning classes. Daily pass $$$. They also offer movie nights and food.

COAST GUARD BEACH

This long National Seashore beach, backed by grasses and heathland, is perfect for walking and sunning. Facilities include changing rooms, restrooms, and in-season lifeguards. In summer a shuttle bus ferries visitors from a parking lot that fills by 10 AM; it's a mile from the beach and it's no use trying to drop off passengers at the beach *before* parking; the seashore banned it to control traffic and protect resources. Parking entrance fee per car $$ (good all day on any CCNS beach; no charge after 4 PM) from late June to early September and on shoulder season holidays.

At times during the winter, you might be lucky enough to spot gray seals and small brown harbor seals congregating at the southern tip of Coast Guard Beach. They feed on the ever-present sand eels. Take the walk at low tide and allow an hour to cover the 2 miles.

Henry Beston published his 1928 classic, *The Outermost House*, about the year he lived in a two-room bungalow on Coast Guard Beach. The book chronicles Beston's interaction with the natural environment and records seasonal changes. The cottage was designated a national literary landmark in 1964, but the blizzard of 1978 washed it into the ocean. Bundled up (tightly!) against the off-season winds, you'll get a glimpse of the haunting isolation Beston experienced.

After a brutal 1990 storm washed away a large chunk of beach, an amateur archaeologist discovered evidence of a prehistoric dwelling on Coast Guard Beach. It is one of the oldest undisturbed archaeological sites in New England, dating back 1,100 to 2,100 years to the Early and Middle Woodland cultures. Because Coast Guard Beach was then 5 miles inland, the site provided a safe encampment for hunters and gatherers. In response to the thousands of ships that were wrecked off this treacherous coast, the Life-Saving Service established in 1872 morphed into the U.S. Coast Guard. After the Cape Cod Canal was built in 1914 and ships could pass through instead of going around the Cape, fatalities off this coastline decreased dramatically. And as such, by 1958, the Coast Guard Station at the top of the cliff could be decommissioned. It now serves as a CCNS educational center.

COAST GUARD BEACH

FOR FAMILIES ♂ **Recreational programs** (508-240-5974) are held late June to mid-August. Visitors and summer residents are encouraged to bring their younger children to the playground at Nauset Regional High School (on Cable Road, North Eastham) for various programs. In the past they've included archery, arts and crafts, and soccer. Supervised swimming and instruction are also offered at Wiley Park (see *Green Space*). Fees vary.

♂ **Cedar Banks Links Adventure Golf** (508-255-2575; arnoldsrestaurant.com), 3580 Route 6. Open mid-May to mid-September. Forget T-Time and Poit's Place, this attractive and waterfall-filled place attached to Arnold's makes waiting at Arnold's worth your time! Some holes are challenging and many are replicated historical landmarks.

TENNIS **Nauset Regional High School** (nausetschools.org), Cable Road. The public can use these eight courts for free after school gets out.

See also *Fitness Club*.

✳ Green Space

BEACHES **Nauset Light Beach**, CCNS (nps.gov/caco), on the Atlantic Ocean. An idyllic, long, broad, dune-backed beach. Facilities include changing rooms, restrooms, and a lifeguard in-season. Parking $$; $ for pedestrians, bicyclists, and motorcycles (transferable to any CCNS beach; no charge after 4 PM); the lot fills by 10 AM in summer.

First Encounter Beach, **Campground Beach**, and **Cook's Brook Beach**. These bayside town beaches are well suited to kite flying and shelling. Because of the shallow water and gradual slope, they are also safe for children. At low tide, vibrant green sea grasses and rippled sand patterns are compelling. Parking $$. Weekly stickers are

NAUSET LIGHT BEACH

AN ABSOLUTE FAVORITE VIEW & WALK

Fort Hill area, CCNS; trailhead and parking off Route 6. The trail—one of my all-Cape favor-ites—is about 1.5 miles round-trip with a partial boardwalk, some log steps, and some hills. It offers lovely views of Nauset Marsh, especially from Skiff Hill, but also winds through the dense Red Maple Swamp and past the Edward Penniman House (see *To See*). Birders enjoy this walk year-round, but it is particularly beautiful in autumn when the maples turn color. Pastoral Fort Hill was farmed until the 1940s, and rock walls still mark boundaries.

FORT HILL TRAIL

available from the Town of Eastham's Sticker Office (508-240-5976), 555 Old Orchard Road (off Route 6 or Brackett Road). No credit cards. First Encounter Beach has a bath-house; the others are equipped with portable toilets. Parking $$.

PONDS **Herring Pond** and **Great Pond**, both west of Eastham center off Samoset, Great Pond, and Herring Brook Roads. Great Pond has a fair amount of parking, a big-gish beach, lifeguards, and two swimming areas (including Wiley Park, with a beach, playground, and bathhouse). Parking $$.

WALKS **Nauset Marsh Trail**, CCNS; trailhead behind the Salt Pond Visitor Center (see *Guidance*). About 1 mile round-trip; some log steps. This trail runs along Salt Pond and yields expansive vistas of Nauset Marsh, which was actually Nauset Bay when French explorer Samuel de Champlain charted it in 1605. As the barrier beach devel-oped, so did the marsh. Along those same lines, Salt Pond was a freshwater pond until the ocean broke through from Nauset Marsh. This complex ecosystem sustains all manner of ocean creatures and shorebirds.

   Buttonbush Trail, CCNS, trailhead at the Salt Pond Visitor Center. The trail is half a mile (round-trip), with some boardwalk, some log steps. It was specially designed with Braille markers for the blind and visually impaired.

❋ **Eastham Hiking Club.** The club meets on Wednesdays from September to late May for a vigorous two hour walk somewhere between Yarmouth and Provincetown. The contact person and phone number changes from year to year, so it's best to Google or ask around. Generally about 45 to 50 people gather for the 4- to 6-mile hike along wooded trails and ponds. Call for the meeting place. Free.

❋ Lodging

Route 6 is lined with cottage colonies, but there are a few quite notable alternatives.

BED & BREAKFASTS ♿ **Whalewalk Inn & Spa** (508-255-0617; whalewalkinn.com), 220 Bridge Road. Open April to December. This upscale 19th-century whaling captain's home has been run like a tight ship by Elaine and Kevin Conlin since the mid-2000s. Expect a range of accommodations, including a romantic cottage, four suites, a luxuriously renovated carriage house, and the most romantic room, the spa penthouse. (Book it now!) Carriage house rooms are outfitted with four-poster beds and gas fireplaces; all have a small private deck or balcony, and some have a large whirlpool. Inn rooms are decorated with country sophistication, a smattering of fine antiques, and breezy floral fabrics. I particularly like the brick patio, where a full breakfast (mesclun salad with pecans, Gorgonzola, and pear slices, followed by a killer Grand Marnier oatmeal pie with vanilla yogurt) and afternoon hors d'oeuvres are served. The inn also boasts a first-rate spa with an exercise facility, sauna, hot tub, and a resistance indoor pool; massages can be arranged. The inn is around the corner from the rail trail and within walking distance of bay beaches. $$–$$$$.

❋ **Fort Hill Bed and Breakfast** (508-240-2870; forthillbedandbreakfast.com),

WHALEWALK INN & SPA

FORT HILL BED AND BREAKFAST

75 Fort Hill Road. This B&B has car-stopping street appeal, and I could live out the rest of my days here. Perched on a little knoll overlooking Nauset Marsh, Jean and Gordon Avery's two suites and cottage enjoy one of the Cape's best locations. The casual yet refined 19th-century Greek Revival farmhouse is a charmer with wonderful hosts (who have separate guest quarters). As for the guest rooms, the second-floor Lucille is sweet with slanted eaves, wide-pine floors, and a detached bathroom. The first-floor two-room Emma Suite features a little library, piano, and oversized tub. The *pièce de résistance*, though, is the ever-so-private Nantucket Cottage that boasts a secluded garden, distant marsh views, cathedral ceilings, and a sitting room with gas fireplace. Folks who stay tend to become serious repeat visitors. A delectable full breakfast might include zucchini quiche or piping-hot baked apples with "jammy" muffins. (The cottage has a self-catering option.) No credit cards. $$$–$$$$.

🍸 🚲 **700 Samoset** (508-255-8748; 700samoset.com), 700 Samoset Road.

Open May through October. The ever-resourceful Sarah Blackwell moved this abandoned 1870 Greek Revival farmhouse to its current location on the bay side of Route 6, on a quiet road near the bike trail. She also did a wonderful job restoring it, sanding floors and woodwork, and blending period pieces with contemporary accents like a painted checkerboard floor and tin lamps. It's all quite tasteful. Too bad for us: There are only two guest rooms, but Eastham could use a dozen of them! From the open country kitchen, guests enjoy an expanded continental breakfast. Plan your day from the front-porch rocking chairs. No credit cards. Rented by the week; call for rates.

🍸 🐾 **Inn at the Oaks** (508-255-1886; innattheoaks.com), 3085 Route 6. Open mid-March to late December. This big yellow Victorian house on the rail trail is hidden from Route 6 and across from the Salt Pond Visitor Center. Guests enjoy relaxing on the wide wraparound veranda or in the billiards room or parlor with velveteen curtains. All 10 guest rooms have lacy curtains and a smattering of antiques; some have a cathedral ceiling and skylight. The Garden Room, my favorite, has a private porch and fireplace. An adjacent carriage house has three family-friendly suites (and one that accepts pets), but in fact, the whole place is family-friendly: witness the playground and little kids' playroom. Afternoon tea or cider and cookies are included, as is an expanded continental breakfast. As a historical footnote, Henry Beston stayed on the property during bad weather while he was writing *The Outermost House.* $$–$$$.

COTTAGES 🐾 🐕 Fort Hill Cottages

(Cottage #1, 617-965-1002; Cottage #3, 202-320-8391; Cottage #4, 805-588-1341; forthillcottages.com), 45 Governor Prence, at the base of Fort Hill. Open January through November. I have great affection and admiration for this impressively designed and executed threesome. This cottage community is jointly owned by a group of old friends and is a place they enjoy visiting to connect with each other. Luckily for the rest of us, they're happy to share it when they're not there. Each cottage has been recently remodeled from head to toe, designed for comfort, and appointed with simplicity. Each reflects the owner's tastes and personalities, but all are in keeping with the charm of the Cape. Cottage 1 features a soaring beach stone fireplace and sleeping loft. Cottage 3 has clean lines, a modern design, an eclectic art collection, and a blue slate fireplace. Cottage 4 incorporates salvaged architectural pieces to give it a charm and warmth. I bet you won't want to leave. They're spacious, with well-appointed kitchens, large screened-in porches, private outdoor showers, and updated with air-conditioning and cable. Summertime weekly rates; nightly off-season rates.

🐚 🐾 **Cottage Grove** (508-255-0500; grovecape.com), 1975 Route 6. Open May through October. You can tell this is not your average cottage colony just by the unusually aesthetic fence that fronts Route 6. Although these are individually owned condos, they're expertly managed during the summer like rental units. No matter how you categorize them, I call them some of the most charming places to stay on the Outer Cape. The nine cozy cottages have been nicely renovated and are set back off the road on 3 acres. Cottages are rustic, with knotty-pine walls,

COTTAGE GROVE

but they have upgraded bathrooms and kitchens, firm new mattresses with cotton sheets, and a smattering of antiques. Nightly and weekly rates.

🐾 🏚 ✎ **Gibson Cottages** (508-240-7229; gibsoncottages.com), 80 Depot Road, off Samoset Road from Route 6. Open April through October. Some of the Cape's best lakeside cottages are down a little dirt road marked only with GIBSON. Amy and Mark Gibson take great pride in maintaining the seven neat and tidy cottages, which were established by Mark's parents in 1966. Each of the well-spaced one-, two-, and three-bedroom cottages has a screened porch or deck and fully equipped kitchen. A swimming dock, a sailboat, rowboats, a kayak, a canoe, and a BBQ area are shared by all. There are also two bike trails on the other side of the pristine lake, which boasts a private, sandy beach. This is a gem; call early. No credit cards. Summertime weekly rates; nightly off-season rates.

✎ **Midway Motel & Cottages** (508-255-3117; midwaymotel.com), Route 6. Open March to mid-October. Pine and oak trees shield this reasonably priced complex from the road. The tidy grounds, over which the Knisely family has presided since 1983, feature a nice children's play area, shuffleboard, badminton, horseshoes, picnic tables, grills, and direct access to the Cape Cod Rail Trail (see *To Do*). All rooms have refrigerators, microwaves, and coffeemakers. Rooms rented nightly, $; cottages weekly.

✎ **Hidden Village** (508-255-1140; hiddenvillageeastham.com), 1700 Bridge Road. Open June through September. Although some might think this place one step above camping, I happen to love these five, very rustic, two-bedroom units spread out over 18 acres. There's indoor plumbing and a very basic kitchen (already it's better than camping!), along with platforms in the room that serves as the living room, screened-in areas that serve as walls, and paper-thin real walls. You really feel like you're sleeping outdoors with a roof over your head (and a wood stove to ward against a chill). They're not for everyone, but they're a real find for kindred souls. And they're all about quiet and privacy. No TV, WiFi, or pets. Summertime weekly rates; nightly off-season.

RENTAL HOUSES & COTTAGES
William Raveis (508-255-4949; capecodvacation.com), 4760 Route 6.

HOSTEL 🐾 ✎ **Hostelling International Eastham** (508-255-2785; 617-536-9455 off-season; hiusa.org), 75 Goody Hallet Drive, off Bridge Road. Open mid-June to early September. Located in a quiet residential neighborhood off the Orleans rotary, this hostel has about 46 beds in seven coed, same-sex, and family cabins. The hostel boasts no lockout times, assorted summertime events, a fully equipped common kitchen, bike shelter, outdoor shower, volleyball, and BBQ area. It's about a mile to the nearest bay beach. Reservations are essential in July and August. Dorms and private rooms $.

❋ Where to Eat

There aren't many restaurants—good or bad—in Eastham.

❋ **Karoo Restaurant** (508-255-8288; karoorestaurants.com), 3 Main Street, Route 6. Open D. How do you follow a tiny, popular seasonal eatery (a "kafe" of the same name) in Provincetown? But of course: open a year-round one in Eastham, which is sorely lacking a variety of dining options. Chef Sanette Groenewald features her South African hometown cooking (like *bobotie*, a mild curry meat loaf, and Cape Malay stew, perhaps with mussels or chicken) alongside gluten-free, vegan, and vegetarian dishes. The overall buzz can be a tad loud, but most diners don't mind. (I don't.) Live music many early evenings in July and August. $$.

MAC'S SEAFOOD MARKETS

🦞 🐚 ♿ **Arnold's Lobster & Clam Bar** (508-255-2575; arnoldsrestaurant. com), 3580 Route 6. Open L, D, mid-May to mid-September. Arnold's, under the same stewardship for years, offers a raw bar, lobster clambake dinners, excellent local clams (without the sand), home-made ice cream, colorful salads, and the normal array of fried seafood baskets. Onion rings are excellent, too; they usually sell upward of 4,000 pounds of them during any given summer. Weekday lunch specials are an incredible bargain. Abutting the rail trail, the neat and tidy Arnold's has a nice fenced-off area with tables under pine trees and an open-air patio. Expect to wait. No credit cards. Dishes $–$$$.

❄ **Mac's Seafood Markets** (508-255-6900; macseafood.com), Route 6 near Brackett Road. Open L, D. Mac's, purveyors of take-home lobsters and all things seafood, has expanded into a beloved Outer Cape fiefdom. $–$$.

❄ **Red Barn Pizza** (508-255-4500; theredbarnpizza.com), 4180 Route 6. Open L, D. It may not look promising, being a big red barn and all, but these folks make one heck of a great pizza. I'm particularly partial to the buffalo chicken with broccoli, which costs $$$ for a large and also tastes great the morning after!

Seriously. (Slices are available, too.) For the rest of you, the Red Barn also offers salads, pasta dishes, subs, burgers, and kid-friendly sides. $–$$.

Friendly Fisherman (508-255-3009 market, 508-255-6770 restaurant; friendlyfishermaneastham.com), 4580 Route 6. Open L, D, mid-May to mid-October. This popular and rustic shack offers the requisite fish-and-chips, fried clams, and fish market, but I always gravitate to their truly excellent lobster rolls ($$). Portions are large.

Brackett Farms & Sam's Deli (508-255-9340; sams-deli.blogspot.com), 100 Brackett Road. Open L, D, mid-March through December. Right around the corner from Ben & Jerry's, these folks make great hot and cold sandwiches like the "Ringo Star": Swiss and provolone with pesto mayo, avocado, lettuce, tomato, roasted red peppers, and sprouts on a whole wheat wrap ($). Friday afternoon wine tastings expand the definition of a deli. $.

❄ 🐚 **Box Lunch** (508-255-0799; boxlunchcapecod.com), 4205 Route 6. Open L, D. If you've got a hungry family or have had enough fried food, stop at this inconspicuous strip mall. (In case you didn't know, they roll their sandwich meats in pita bread at this ubiquitous Cape franchise.) The "Jaws" rollwich with roast beef and horseradish has quite a bite. Rollwiches $; with lobster $$.

RED BARN PIZZA

✳ Entertainment

First Encounter Coffee House (508-255-5438; firstencounter.org), 220 Samoset Road. Open year-round except December and May. Performances (usually) on the second and fourth Saturday of each month. Acoustic, folk, blues, and bluegrass reign here, attracting musicians with national reputations—including Wellfleet's Patty Larkin and Vineyarder Livingston Taylor. Home to the 1899 Unitarian Universalist church (a.k.a. Chapel in the Pines) since 1974, the intimate venue has only 100 seats beneath its stained-glass windows. Off-season, it's a very local affair, where everybody knows your name and knows to arrive early to get a good seat. $$.

✳ Selective Shopping

✳ **Collector's World** (508-255-3616; collectorsworldcapecod.com), 4100 Route 6. Since 1974, Chris Alex has been selling an eclectic lineup of antiques, gifts, and collectibles like Russian lacquer boxes, scrimshaw, pewter, Civil War artifacts, and toy soldiers. It's one of the wackiest collections on the Cape.

✳ **Four Winds Leather** (508-240-7998), 5130 Route 6. You probably didn't come to the Cape in search of sheepskins and moccasins, but these are the real things. The store is piled high with Native American art, leather coats, wallets, and the like.

✳ Special Events

July–August: **Eastham Painters' Guild** (easthampaintersguild.com), at the Old Schoolhouse Museum, Route 6 at the Salt Pond Visitor Center. Outdoor art shows are held here most Thursdays and Fridays, as well as over the Memorial Day and Labor Day weekends.

Early to mid-September: **Windmill Weekend** (easthamwindmillweekend.org). This three-day community festival is staged for locals and features a road race, band concert, arts-and-crafts show, square dancing, and a parade.

FIRST ENCOUNTER COFFEE HOUSE

WELLFLEET

Although a whopping 70 percent of Wellfleet is conservation land, the town is perhaps best known as an art stronghold. Wellfleet's two principal thoroughfares, **Main Street** and **Commercial Street**, are dotted with 25 or so **galleries** representing a wide range of art: from souvenir works to images that transcend their media. Many artists and artisans who exhibit here call Wellfleet home, at least for a short time each year, gaining inspiration from pristine landscapes and an unrelenting ocean.

After art, Wellfleet's other main draw is nature. The outstanding **Wellfleet Bay Wildlife Sanctuary** offers practically unparalleled opportunities for observing marine and bird life through guided activities and self-guided walks. A mostly sandy, 8-mile-long **National Seashore trail on Great Island** yields solitude and commanding views of **Wellfleet Bay**. On the **Atlantic side**, dunes and cliffs back broad and uninterrupted beaches. Any of Wellfleet's meandering roads are perfect for cycling, leading you past ponds, salt marshes, heathlands, and scrub pines.

Wellfleet appeals to a distinct crowd, many of whom have returned year after year for decades. In fact, many nonnative families—wash-ashores—rent houses here for the entire summer. When shopkeepers and restaurateurs begin dusting off the shelves in early to mid-June, it feels like a real homecoming—old friends catching up over coffee in a café, neighbors renewing relationships as they tend their gardens.

And although Wellfleet is very popular with vacationing Freudian analysts, there's also a notable seasonal contingent of lawyers, professors, and writers. They've all come for the same purpose: to commune with their thoughts, recharge their batteries, and lead a simpler life (albeit only temporarily). Summer folks also venture out of their cocoons to dine on wonderful food in laid-back settings, to square dance outdoors, and to engage in lively conversation after a particularly spirited performance by the **Wellfleet Harbor Actors Theater**.

Wellfleetians are an independent bunch. Almost 30 percent of the 3,000 year-rounders are self-employed (proverbial Jacks and Jills of all trades), more than in any other Cape town, and almost 20 percent are unemployed in winter. (If you do visit midwinter, you'll find a few warm beds and the frozen bay—a romantic sight on an overcast day.) While most of the town rolls up its shutters from mid-October to mid-May, Wellfleet may also feel like a ghost town on a weekday in mid-June. But on any given summer day, about 17,000 folks will be overnighting in Wellfleet.

Wellfleet was most likely named for a town in England, which, like "our" Wellfleet, was also renowned for its oyster beds. As early as the 17th century, when Wellfleet was still a part of Eastham known as Billingsgate, the primary industries revolved around oyster and cranberry harvesting. Whaling, fishing, and other related industries also flourished until the mid-1800s. And by the 1870s, commercial markets had really opened up for littlenecks, cherrystones, and clams for chowder. Today, with the depletion of natural fish and shellfish stocks, year-round fishermen have turned to aquaculture. Currently more than 100 aquaculturists lease 120 acres of Wellfleet Harbor; you'll see them off **Mayo Beach** at low tide. Shellfish like **quahogs and oysters** are raised from "seed," put out in "protected racks," and tended for two to three years while they mature. Because as many as 2 million seeds can be put on an acre of land,

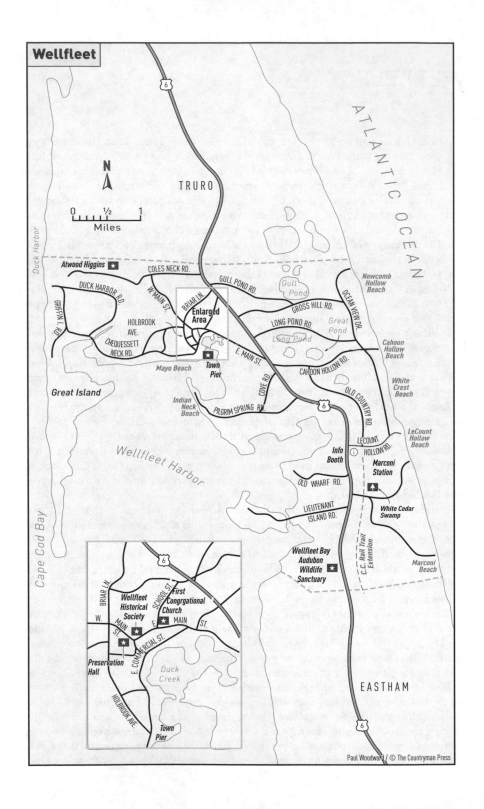

Wellfleet

TRURO

0   ½   1
Miles

ATLANTIC OCEAN

Duck Harbor

Atwood Higgins ★

COLES NECK RD.

GULL POND RD.

Gull Pond

Newcomb Hollow Beach

DUCK HARBOR RD.

W. MAIN ST.

BRIAR LN.

Enlarged Area

GROSS HILL RD.

OCEAN VIEW DR.

GRIFFIN I. RD.

HOLBROOK AVE.

LONG POND RD.

Great Pond

Long Pond

Cahoon Hollow Beach

CHEQUESSETT NECK RD.

Mayo Beach

Town Pier ★

E. MAIN ST.

CAHOON HOLLOW RD.

White Crest Beach

Great Island

Indian Neck Beach

COVE RD.

PILGRIM SPRING RD.

OLD COUNTRY RD.

6

LeCount Hollow Beach

Wellfleet Harbor

LECOUNT HOLLOW RD.

Info Booth ⓘ

Marconi Station ⚓

Cape Cod Bay

OLD WHARF RD.

White Cedar Swamp

LIEUTENANT ISLAND RD.

C.C. Rail Trail Extension

Marconi Beach

Wellfleet Bay Audubon Wildlife Sanctuary ★

EASTHAM

6

Enlarged Area (inset):

6

BRIAR LN.

SCHOOL ST.

Wellfleet Historical Society ★

First Congregational Church ★

W. MAIN ST.

E. COMMERCIAL ST.

E. MAIN ST.

Preservation Hall ★

Duck Creek

HOLBROOK AVE.

Town Pier

Paul Woodward / © The Countryman Press

A PERFECT (JAM-PACKED) DAY IN WELLFLEET

7:00	Dip into Long Pond before resident-only parking begins (by 8 AM).
8:30	Savor an omelet at Wicked Oyster.
9:30	Trek trails, identify birds, cross tidal creeks, and beach yourself on the sand at the Wellfleet Bay Wildlife Sanctuary.
12:00	Dine alfresco at Winslow's Tavern or indoors at PB Boulangerie Bistro.
1:30	Hike on the cool and primordial Atlantic White Cedar Swamp Trail.
3:00	Cruise the art galleries on Main and Commercial Streets.
5:00	Join the boisterous 30- and 40-something crowd for reggae and frozen drinks at the open-air, surfside Beachcomber.
6:30	Enjoy Chatham dayboat scallops from Moby Dick's or sushi from Mac's.
8:00	Catch a provocative show at Wellfleet Harbor Actors Theater.

this is big business. For those looking for fishing charters, though, the harbor and pier are still centers of activity.

GUIDANCE **Wellfleet Chamber of Commerce** (508-349-2510; wellfleetchamber .com), 1410 Route 6. Open spring through fall. The information booth is well marked right off Route 6 in South Wellfleet.

GETTING THERE *By car:* Wellfleet is 50 miles beyond the Cape Cod Canal via Route 6.

By bus: The **Plymouth & Brockton** bus line (508-746-0378; p-b.com) connects Wellfleet and South Wellfleet with Hyannis and other Cape towns, as well as with Boston's Logan Airport. The bus stops in front of Town Hall on Main Street in Wellfleet, and at Farrell's Market on Route 6 in South Wellfleet.

GETTING AROUND *By car:* From Route 6, take Main Street to the town center or veer from Main to Commercial Street to the colorful harbor. There is free parking at the Town Pier (at the end of Commercial Street) and behind Town Hall on Main Street. As the seagull flies, the town is anywhere from 2 to 5 miles wide.

PUBLIC RESTROOMS Seasonally at Bakers Field across from Mayo Beach (on Kendrick Avenue), as well as at the Town Pier and the marina (both at the end of Commercial Street). Year-round in the basement of Town Hall on Main Street.

PUBLIC LIBRARY ✳ ✎ ☂ **Wellfleet Public Library** (508-349-0310; wellfleetlibrary .org), 55 West Main Street. One of the Cape's best! Housed within the former Candle Factory, this outstanding library offers children's story hour and an impressive lineup of readings, screenings, and speakers.

OFF THE BEATEN PATH SECRET

Atwood Higgins House (508-255-3421), 269 Bound Brook Island Road, off Pamet Point Road from Route 6. Open for tours late June to late October (by reservation only). The pastoral 5-acre homestead, under the auspices of the CCNS, has a tour that focuses on the architecture and versatility of the 18th-century full Cape that was restored by its early-20th-century owners. Don't miss it. This is one of my favorite places on the entire Cape. Free.

ATWOOD HIGGINS HOUSE

MEDICAL EMERGENCY Outer Cape Health Services (508-349-3131; outercape.org), 3130 Route 6. Not an urgent-care facility.

✳ To See

Marconi Wireless Station, CCNS, off Route 6 at the Marconi Area. In 1901 Guglielmo Marconi began construction of the first wireless station on the U.S. mainland, in little old Wellfleet. Two years later the first U.S. wireless transatlantic message was transmitted between this station and England: President Roosevelt sent King Edward VII "most cordial greetings and good wishes." (Canada beat the U.S. in sending a wireless transatlantic message by one month.) A mere 14 years later, the station was closed for wartime security reasons; it was dismantled and abandoned in 1920 because of erosion and the development of alternative technologies. There are few remains today, save the concrete foundation of the transmitter house (which required 25,000 volts to send a message) and sand anchors that held guy wires to the 210-foot towers.

The Cape Cod peninsula is at its narrowest here, and from a well-positioned **observation platform** you can scan the width of it—from Cape Cod Bay, along Blackfish Creek, to the Atlantic Ocean. (See the Atlantic White Cedar Swamp Trail under *Green Space*.)

Wellfleet Historical Society Museum (508-349-9157; wellfleethistoricalsociety .com), 266 Main Street. Open June to mid-October. The society has collected photographs, toys, shipwreck detritus, marine artifacts, displays on Marconi and oystering,

SCENIC DRIVES

Ocean View Drive. Take LeCount Hollow Road to Ocean View (despite its name, it has only limited views) and head back to Route 6 via Gull Pond Road or Long Pond Road. You'll pass heathlands, cliffs, and scrub pines.

Chequessett Neck Road. Cross the dike at Herring River and head to the end of the road for magnificent sunset views. Although there is room for only a few cars at the very end of the road, you can park near the Great Island Trailhead and walk down to the beach (about 15 minutes).

Pilgrim Spring Road. Not to be confused with the Pilgrim Spring Trail in Truro, where the Pilgrims got their first taste of fresh water, this quiet road offers lovely inlet and cove views; at the end of the road, look back toward Wellfleet Harbor.

and household items to illustrate and preserve Wellfleet's past. Join one of their historical walks around town in the summer; meet at museum; $. (Self-guided audio walking tours are also available.)

First Congregational Church of the United Church of Christ (508-349-6877; wellfleetchurch.org), 200 Main Street. Although the church was organized in 1721, this Greek Revival meetinghouse dates to 1850. The interior is graced with a brass chandelier, eggshell-yellow walls, curved pews, and a Tiffany-style stained-glass window depicting a 17th-century ship similar to the *Mayflower*. The bell-shaped cupola, by the way, was added in 1879 after a storm destroyed the traditional one. (It was thought that a bell-shaped tower would be sturdier—perhaps it has been.) Select concerts feature a restored Hook and Hastings pipe organ. Check the church's website for myriad special events, including a summer concert series in July and August.

Town clock, First Congregational Church, 200 Main Street. According to the arbiter of strange superlatives, *Ripley's Believe It or Not*, this is the "only town clock in the world that strikes ship's time." Listen for the following chimes and try to figure out what time it is for yourself: Two bells distinguish 1, 5, and 9 o'clock; six bells signify 3, 7, and 11 o'clock; eight bells toll for 4, 8, and 12 o'clock. To make matters even more interesting, adding one chime to the corresponding even hours signifies the half hours. (After all these years of hanging out in Wellfleet, I still double-check my cell phone!)

Preservation Hall (508-349-1800; wellfleetpreservationhall.org), 335 Main Street. On the occasion of the country's 1976 bicentennial, two troubadours expressed their thanks to the town after a long celebration by donating the handsome painted carvings attached to the doors. More recently, the town purchased the former church and rechristened it as a nonprofit cultural center in the late 2000s. After years of renovations, the hall now houses live concerts, film screenings, art exhibitions, poetry readings, Vegas nights, oyster and strawberry festivals, and garden tours. A life-sized blue heron, created by local sculptor Del Filardi and symbolizing good luck, now proudly tops the reinstalled cupola.

Samuel Rider House, Gull Pond Road off Route 6. Although the house is not open to the public, it's a fine early-1700s Outer Cape farmstead.

✳ To Do

BICYCLING & RENTALS **Cape Cod Rail Trail**. It terminates in Wellfleet at LeCount Hollow Road (where there is parking), just east of Route 6.

Little Capistrano Bike Shop (508-349-2363; littlecapistranobikeshop.com), 1446 Route 6, South Wellfleet. Love this outfit, with a bigger location in Eastham.

Idle Times Bike Shop (508-349-9161; idletimesbikes.com), 2616 Route 6. Open June to early September. A full line of bicycles for the whole family. They will deliver bike rentals throughout the lower Cape.

BOAT EXCURSIONS & RENTALS Jack's Boat Rentals (508-349-9808; jacksboatrental.com), Route 6 at Cahoon Hollow Road. Open late June to early September. This friendly outfit rents canoes, pedal boats, sea cycles, surf bikes, kayaks, and Sunfish. If you want to paddle somewhere besides Gull Pond, pick up a boat at the shop (508-349-9808) on Route 6.

CAPE COD RAIL TRAIL

Funseekers (508-349-1429; funseekers.org) offers guided kayak and canoe tours through estuary marshes, along the tidal Pamet and Herring Rivers, and out to Great Island. Departures vary with the tides. Eric also offers instruction in surfing, kiteboarding, and windsurfing.

Wellfleet Marine Corp. (508-349-2233; wellfleetmarine.com), Town Pier. From mid-June to mid-September, you can rent Stur-Dee Cat sailboats, sloops, and fishing skiffs by the hour or by the day.

FISHING & SHELLFISHING Procure freshwater and saltwater fishing licenses and regulations online (www.mass.gov/eea/agencies/dfg/licensing/). Freshwater fishing holes include **Great Pond**, **Gull Pond**, and **Long Pond** (see *Green Space*). Shellfishing permits are required for the taking of oysters, clams, and quahogs. Wellfleet's tidal flats are wondrous places at low tide. Contact the **Beach Sticker Booth** (508-349-9818) on the pier from mid-June through August. Try your luck surf casting early in the morning or at night at the following Atlantic beaches: **Newcomb Hollow**, **White Crest**, and **LeCount Hollow**, or at **Duck Harbor** on the bayside.

Wellfleet Harbor Marina. My favorite boat and captain are no longer heading out, so please ask around the marina and trust your instincts.

GOLF Chequessett Yacht & Country Club (508-349-3704; cycc.net), 680 Chequessett Neck Road. Open April through October. This nine-hole, par-35 course offers beautiful views of Wellfleet Harbor.

MINI-GOLF ✺ **At the Wellfleet Drive-In** (508-349-2450; wellfleetcinemas.com), Route 6. Open late May through September. The only game in town is conveniently located next to the flea market, the drive-in, and a classic dairy bar.

SAILING ✺ **Chequessett Yacht & Country Club** (508-349-3704; cycc.net), 680 Chequessett Neck Road, offers junior and adult sailing late June to late August. Group instruction by the week for youths; individual instruction by the hour. Call ahead for availability.

SEAL CRUISES See the "Trails, Birds, Seals, & Classes" sidebar.

SPECIAL PROGRAMS See the "Trails, Birds, Seals, & Classes" sidebar.

🏊 **Summer recreation programs** (508-349-0314; wellfleetma.org), Baker's Field and Gull Pond. July to mid-August. Sports, arts and crafts, and swimming lessons; plus yoga on the beach ($), tennis courts ($$), and a skateboard park (free).

TENNIS Town courts are on **Mayo Beach**, Kendrick Avenue.

Oliver's Red Clay Tennis Courts (508-349-3330; oliversredclaytennis.com), 2183 Route 6. Open June through September. Seven courts; $$$ hourly; tennis lessons are available in July and August.

Chequessett Yacht & Country Club (508-349-3704; cycc.net), 680 Chequessett Neck Road. Open March through November. Five hard courts are available to the public; $$.

✳ Green Space

BEACHES **Marconi Beach**, CCNS, on the Atlantic. A boardwalk and steep staircase lead to the long, narrow beach backed by dramatic dunes. In-season amenities include lifeguards, outdoor showers, and changing facilities. Parking $$ (permit valid all day at any CCNS beach; no charge after 4 PM).

Cahoon Hollow Beach and **White Crest Beach**, town beaches on the Atlantic Ocean. Sandy shoals create shallow, warmish (i.e., not frigid) pools of water here. Although each beach is wide and sandy, local townsfolk favor the sea grass and dunes of White Crest, and hang gliders and surfers appreciate the surf. (Hang gliders are not allowed from mid-April to early October.) White Crest has more parking. Amenities include lifeguards and restrooms. Parking $$.

Mayo Beach, Kendrick Avenue. Parking is free, but the beach is nothing to e-mail home about. From here you can see some of the offshore areas—marked by yellow buoys—where modern aquaculture thrives in the form of constructed shellfish farms.

The following beaches require a town sticker: **Maquire Landing** and **Newcomb Hollow Beach**, both off Ocean View Drive on the Atlantic Ocean; **Burton Baker Beach** (the only place in town where sailboarding is permitted) and **Indian Neck Beach**, both off Pilgrim Spring Road on the bay side; **Powers Landing** and **Duck Harbor**, both off Chequessett Neck Road on the bay side. Cottage renters may purchase a sticker at the well-marked Beach Sticker Booth (508-349-9818) on the Town Pier from July to early September.

In late January 2008, after a fierce midwinter storm, a visitor washed ashore at **Newcomb Hollow Beach**: a mid- to late-19th-century schooner that had shipwrecked who knows when and had taken down who knows how many sailors with it (if any). The beached keel and ribs, upright in the sand, looked like the ribs

MARCONI BEACH

TRAILS, BIRDS, SEALS, & CLASSES

❊ **Wellfleet Bay Wildlife Sanctuary** (508-349-2615; massaudubon.org), 291 Route 6. This is one of my Top 10 places on Cape Cod. With almost 1,100 acres of pine, moors, freshwater ponds, tidal creeks, salt marsh, and beach, the Audubon sanctuary is one of New England's most active. Despite that, you'll appreciate the relative lack of human presence after a day of gallery hopping and sunbathing.

Three trails total more than 5 miles: Silver Spring Trail, a lovely, wooded walking trail alongside a long pond; Goose Pond Trail (an all-person accessible trail), past ponds, woodlands, a marsh, and heathland (a boardwalk leads to the bay from here); and Bay View Trail.

The sanctuary also offers a steady stream of activities throughout the summer (plenty year-round, for that matter): canoe trips, family seashore hikes, evening natural history talks, birding expeditions, and trips to Monomoy Island (see the sidebar under *Green Space* in "Chatham").

Call about their 90-minute seal cruises off the waters of Chatham, and don't miss one if your schedule jives with theirs. They also have a two-hour Sea Bird and Seal Cruise in late fall, which goes out on an open commercial fishing vessel. On-board naturalists will educate you about the habits and habitats of harbor and gray seals. Reservations required.

WELLFLEET BAY WILDLIFE SANCTUARY

Wellfleet Bay Wildlife Sanctuary **Natural History Day Camps** are offered June through August. Geared toward children, these excellent weeklong programs are designed to "expand curiosity about and respect for the environment through hands-on outdoor experiences . . . and to develop skill in discovering the natural world using the principles of scientific inquiry." Indeed.

The sanctuary's summertime **Adult Field School** incorporates multiday, hands-on courses. Topics include Cape Cod natural history, ornithology, marine life, nature photography, local endangered habitats, and sketching in the field. Instruction is expert.

Before departing, don't miss the eco-friendly **Esther Underwood Johnson Nature Center**, and especially don't miss the environmentally friendly composting toilets, which save 100,000 gallons of water per season. It's a beautiful example of green architecture, with solar heating and graywater planter beds. Exhibits feature Cape Cod natural history as well as two 700-gallon aquariums displaying life beneath the water of salt marshes and tidal pools. Trails are free to members, $ nonmembers. Members may tent in the wooded natural setting (call for fees and reservations).

of a 50-foot whale, and it captured the attention of locals and visitors from 100 miles away. The National Park Service suggested the ship was the largest to wash ashore in 15 years; another marine specialist suggested it could have been the *Logan*, a coal barge wrecked in 1920. What is known for sure is that 18 ships failed to navigate the treacherous shifting sand bars and shoals near the Cahoon Hollow Lifesaving Station between 1800 and 1927.

HANG GLIDING AT WHITE CREST BEACH

PONDS **Great Pond, Long Pond, and Gull Pond** offer freshwater swimming. If you're staying at an inn or cottage, you'll be eligible for the requisite parking sticker (available on the Town Pier; 508-349-9818). All ponds have lifeguards.

WALKS **Great Island Trail**, CCNS, off Chequessett Neck Road. About 8 miles round-trip, this trail is relatively flat, but soft sand makes for a challenging four-hour round-trip trek. Walk at low tide when the sand is firmer. (Besides, Jeremy Point, the tip of land farthest out to sea, is covered at high tide.) You'll be rewarded with scant human presence and stunning scenery. Great for birders; best on a sunny spring day or a crisp autumn one. Bring plenty of water and sunscreen.

This area was once an island, hence its name. Over time Cape Cod Bay currents deposited sandbars that eventually connected it to the mainland. Long ago, Great Island was home to various commercial enterprises—oystering, cranberry harvesting, and shore whaling—and the land was dotted with lookout towers used to spot whales. There was even a local watering hole and overnight hostelry, the Great Island Tavern, built in 1690 and used until about 1740. But as shore whaling died, so did the Great Island community. By 1800 the island was deserted and deforested. (Pines have been planted in an effort to keep erosion under control.)

Uncle Tim's Bridge, East Commercial Street. The often-photographed wooden footbridge connects Commercial Street to a small wooded island, crossing a tidal creek (Duck Creek) and marshland. Short, sandy trails circle the island.

Wellfleet Conservation Trust (508-349-2162; wellfleetconservationtrust.org) is constantly purchasing and opening up new trails and tracts of land—including Bayberry Hill, Fox Island Marsh and Pilgrim Spring Woodlands, and Box Turtle Woods. The easiest thing to do is go online and print trail maps.

See the "Trails, Birds, Seals, & Classes" sidebar.

AN UNUSUAL CAPE EXPERIENCE

Atlantic White Cedar Swamp Trail, CCNS, Marconi Area. One of the best Outer Cape trails, this swamp, navigable via a boardwalk, has a primordial feel. A dense overhead cover keeps it cool even on the most stifling of days. Nonetheless, the early and latter parts of this 1.2-mile trail traverse steep stairs and soft sand. This trail features one of the few remaining stands of white cedar on the Cape. Prized by settlers for its light weight and ease of handling, a century of overuse took its toll. While the swamp (in places, 24 feet deep with peat) has begun to recover, nature has its own cycles; red maples will eventually choke the white cedars out of existence. In August, trailside blueberries are ripe for the picking.

ATLANTIC WHITE CEDAR SWAMP TRAIL

✳ Lodging

Most summer visitors to Wellfleet stay in cottages and houses, rented by the week or, most probably longer, but there are plenty of places for short-term guests.

BED & BREAKFASTS 🦞 **Aunt Sukie's Bayside B&B** (508-349-2804; auntsukies .com), 525 Chequessett Neck Road. Open mid-June to mid-September. Hidden by a fence from a road less traveled, Sue and Dan Hamar's bayfront B&B is full of southward-facing picture windows. It takes just 30 seconds to walk from the shingled house, with a contemporary addition, across a boardwalk marsh to the inn's private bay beach. I'd live here all summer long if I could. As for the rooms, two contemporary ones boast private decks and splendid southward

bay views. The "antique" suite features wide-pine floors, Oriental carpets, a private patio, and a separate sitting room in the original 1830 section of the house. The common room, dotted with antiques, overflows with "Aunt Sukie's" history. Breakfast is self-serve (featuring Starbucks coffee and pastries from a local French bakery) and enjoyed from the bayside deck.

Run, don't walk, to their newly renovated adjacent cottage with just enough privacy and killer views: book right this minute to avoid disappointment. Rooms $$; cottage rented weekly.

✳ 🐚 **Oyster Cove B&B** (508-349-2994; oystercove.com), 20 Partridge Way. Hosts Sandy and Dick Nicholson, who built this spacious, three-story contemporary home in the late 1990s, offer great views of Indian Neck, Great Island, Chipman Cove, and Wellfleet Harbor.

And three levels of decks drink in those wonderful views. Further, the front beach is popular for walking or launching kayaks. At low tide you could even walk to town, although you have to watch it coming back! Guests have their choice of the romantic, upper Captain's Studio or the lower level Beach Suite (with three good-sized bedrooms). The latter can be rented in its entirety or as one or two bedrooms. The inn is quite well suited to families and reunions. Sandy makes muffins and scones for breakfast, while Dick is most helpful in arranging outdoor adventures. $$$ studio, $$$–$$$$+ suite.

❋ **The Wagner at Duck Creek** (508-349-9333; thewagneratduckcreek.com), 70 Main Street. About a mile from the town center and forever known as the Inn at Duck Creeke, The Wagner is undergoing a complete transformation that will continue through the 2017 season. I have every reason to believe it's going to be a winner, but do check its current progress online. $$–$$$$.

COTTAGES 🐾 **The Colony** (508-349-3761; colonyofwellfleet.com), 640 Chequessett Neck Road. Open late May to mid-September. This is not your average cottage colony. In fact, no place on the Cape remotely resembles it.

Well-traveled guests flock to these Bauhaus treasures, 1949 low-slung duplexes, for quietude (you'll be speaking in hushed tones before you know it), communing with nature (fresh flowers adorn each cottage), and daily maid service. Eleanor Stefani purchased the low-key place in 1963, but Nathaniel Saltonstall, a trustee of Boston's Institute for Contemporary Arts, built it as a private club in 1949. Scads of original artwork grace the cottages, which are furnished in mod 1950s style. Cottages also feature galley kitchens, glass-enclosed dining porches, and terraces with furniture for dining alfresco. Each of the 10 units has decks and lots of picture windows, which bring the natural surroundings indoors. For the right people who appreciate Bauhaus, it's a real retreat, without TV or WiFi (for a reason), and plenty of books, journals, and magazines in each cottage. No credit cards. $$–$$$ nightly; weekly rates, too.

🐾 🐾 **Surf Side Cottages** (508-349-3959; surfsidecottages.com), 45 Ocean View Drive. Open early April through November. These 1950s-style housekeeping cottages are within a minute's walk of the dunes and ocean. Nothing separates them from the ocean except other Surf Side cottages and scrub pines; a few of the 18 units have ocean views.

THE VIEW AT LOW TIDE FROM AUNT SUKIE'S BAYSIDE B&B

THE COLONY

Come for the quiet and a family-friendly atmosphere. Most larger cottages have a roof deck; each has a screened-in porch (with that classic wooden-door slamming sound), a wood-burning fireplace, and a private outdoor shower. Modern kitchens, knotty-pine paneling, and tasteful rattan furnishings are the norm. Bring sheets and towels and leave the cottage clean and ready for the next tenants. Reserve early. Since managers Armand and Lisa Audette took over in the late 2000s, they've helped owners remodel and upgrade (many) kitchens and bathrooms. Rented weekly, $$–$$$; otherwise daily off-season.

The Even'tide (508-349-3410; eventidemotel.com), 650 Route 6. Open late April to early September. These nine cottages, which rent weekly, are a cut above. Wooded and set back from Route 6, the complex has a nice children's play area, a big heated indoor pool, an exercise room, a billiard table, mini-golf, shuffleboard, table tennis, badminton, horseshoes, basketball, direct access to the rail trail,

and a walking trail to Marconi Beach. Phew! Is that enough for you? All cottages have fully tiled bathrooms and full kitchens (except Tern). They also have some above-average motel rooms and suites that rent nightly early May to mid-October. Inquire about the Kingfisher House, a five-bedroom place that rents weekly.

SURFSIDE COTTAGES

See also **Maurice's Campground** under *Campgrounds.*

CAMPGROUNDS ❀ ✔ **Paine's Camp ground** (508-349-3007; campingcapecod .com), 180 Old County Road. Open June to early September. At this tenter's haven there are designated areas for "quiet" campers, youth groups, and families, as well as sites to which you must lug your tent. Of the 150 or so sites, only a minority are reserved for big RVs. You can walk from the campground to the National Seashore. Freshwater swimming is found in nearby kettle ponds.

❀ ✔ **Maurice's Campground** (508-349-2029; mauricescampground. com), 80 Route 6. Open late May to mid-October. Maurice's has about 220 wooded sites for tents and trailers, a few cottages that can sleep four, and cabins that can sleep three with a cot. Ask about the duplex cabin that sleeps four to six people. Direct access to the Cape Cod Rail Trail is a real plus for folks.

See also the "Trails, Birds, Seals, & Classes" sidebar.

RENTAL HOUSES & COTTAGES **Kinlin Grover Real Estate**

(508-349-9800; kinlingrover.com/wellfleet), 2548 Route 6.

✳ Where to Eat

Wellfleet oysters are renowned: Legend has it that England's Queen Victoria served them at her state dinners (no others would do). According to aficionados, Wellfleet oysters taste better when harvested from the cooler waters in the off-season, but you'll have little choice if you vacation in July or August; order them anyway. Wellfleet is also known for its hard-shell quahog and steamer clams. In fact, these waters yield millions of dollars' worth of shellfish annually.

Although there are many restaurants reviewed here, *most are closed off-season.* Furthermore, most opening and closing *months* are wholly dependent on weather and tourist traffic.

DINING OUT ❀ ♈ **Winslow's Tavern** (508-349-6450; winslowstavern.com), 316 Main Street. Open L, D, May through October. Ahhh, alfresco dining overlooking a quiet town center in the summer. It's especially nice at

WINSLOW'S TAVERN

lunchtime, when the mosquitos aren't as fierce. This upscale bistro and tavern (resurrected in the mid-2000s) features New England classics, fresh fish, and imaginative specials. It's easy on the palate *and* the wallet. Start with perfection in a bowl (fire-roasted gazpacho) or a lightly dressed creative salad and move on to oven-roasted Chatham cod or pan-seared Colorado lamb chops with roasted artichokes and a mint crème fraîche. Within the casually elegant interior, meals are well paced and tables are well spaced. Come early for a drink upstairs in the cozy bar or wind up there for dessert and wine. L $$, D $$-$$$.

Ceraldi (508-237-9811; ceraldicape cod.com), 15 Kendrick Avenue. Open D May to mid-October. My biggest regret for this edition was not being able to indulge in Chef Michael Ceraldi's seven-course menus. Dining at the chef's table, with an open kitchen, allows Chef to interact with his guests and servers to share stories about local food purveyors and wine subtleties. "Amazing" is the most whispered adjective when folks try to describe Ceraldi. $$$$+.

✏ Wicked Oyster (508-349-3455; thewickedo.com), 50 Main Street. Open B, L, D, mid-January to late November (but no lunch in summer). This place, both casual and elegant, gets high marks for service and food. When new owners Ken Kozak and Eliza Fitts took over management in the late 2000s, they didn't miss a beat. For lunch in winter, try pan-seared scallops on a bed of spinach salad or fried haddock with chips. At dinnertime in-season, venture toward the catch of day in a light crème broth with littlenecks, leeks, bacon, and fingerling potatoes (for instance). And their oysters are deliciously buttery and soft. Feeling less adventurous? Order a "wicked" blue cheese and bacon burger or some fried seafood ($). Either way, top it off with a very sweet treat. Dress lightly in the summer, when it gets *really* hot in here. Four-course prix fixe

BOULANGERIE BISTRO

dinner off-season. Otherwise, B $, D $$-$$$.

PB Boulangerie Bistro (508-349-1600; pbboulangeriebistro.com), 15 Lecount Hollow Road, South Wellfeet. Open for B, L, D, depending. With its opening in 2010, you would have been forgiven assuming they were selling drugs or sex—it was that popular from the get-go—especially the orgasmic cheese sandwich. In fact, as the season progressed, a policeman had to start directing traffic off Route 6 because of traffic-flow issues. (Too bad someone can't fix the traffic flow inside the bakery.) What the bistro does offer is outstanding and authentic French pastries and breads, champagne cocktails, and for dinner, butternut squash risotto, slow-poached local codfish fillets, fricassee of summer vegetables, crème brûlée, and way more. All in a lovely, simple setting. And worth the inconveniences, a result of its own success. B, L $-$$, D $$-$$$$.

EATING OUT 🦞 ✏ Moby Dick's (508-349-9795; mobydicksrestaurant.com),

3225 Route 6. Open L, D, May to mid-October. My high season on Cape Cod begins and ends with a meal at Moby Dick's. Since 1983 Todd and Migs Barry and their team have provided the best and largest portions of area seafood. Pride of ownership and owner exuberance has its rewards. Although the place is always packed, would you really want to patronize an establishment that wasn't? Order off the blackboard menu, then take a seat surrounded by weathered nautical paraphernalia or at a picnic table on the open upper level. You know the fare (it's just not normally this fresh and tasty)—Chatham steamers (clams) caught off Monomoy Island, lobsters, Wellfleet oysters and scallops, seafood rolls (with barely a hint of mayo), lobster rolls with tail and claw meat, and "dayboat-hooked" cod. The chowder, loaded with big chunks of clams, really tastes like clam chowder should. BYOB. L $–$$, D $$–$$$.

❄ ❀ ✿ **Finely J.P.'s** (508-349-7500; finelyjps.com), 554 Route 6. Open D. With very good reason, loyal vacationers return to JP's again and again. Chef-owner John Pontius gussied up the place in 2007 with a two-level building, complete with a small bar, a rooftop deck for outdoor dining, and better soundproofing. He's been reelin' 'em in since, with large and satisfying portions of grilled scallops on linguine, almond crusted sole, and baked Wellfleet oysters. Call ahead and put your name on the waiting list, because if you arrive after 6 PM you'll be waiting. His off-season, three-course early dinner is one of the best deals on the Outer Cape; otherwise D $$–$$$.

Mac's Shack (508-349-6333; macsseafood.com), 91 Commercial Street. Open D, May to mid-October. If you want to know the definition of summer, visit Mac's Shack. Dine outside at the happenin' raw bar in a crushed seashell parking lot. Or join Wellfleetians in a long line to dine (just as casually) inside this big post-and-beam, colonial landmark. Order up some fresh sushi or other creative coastal cuisine brought to you by those who own Mac's Seafood on the harbor. $$–$$$.

MOBY DICK'S

MAC'S SHACK

Mac's Seafood & Market Grill (508-349-0404; macsseafood.com), Town Pier. Open D, late May to mid-October. Mac, who buys seafood direct from boats throughout the day, offers (among other seafood concoctions) smoked pâté and mussels or littlenecks with linguine in white wine sauce. You'll also find decent fried seafood, burritos, clambakes-to-go, and vegetarian dishes. Regardless of whether you eat in or take out, it's the harborside location and casual outdoor patio at sunset that draw folks; BYOB. He's been doing it since the mid-1990s, so you know something's right! Can't get enough of Mac's? Visit their online store for lobsters and clambakes shipped to your door. $$–$$$.

🍴 ✆ **Flying Fish** (508-349-7292; flyingfishwellfleet.com), 29 Briar Lane, between Route 6 and Main Street. Open B, L, D, mid-May to mid-October. This is a funky little place to eat, with modest tables, local art, and a partially visible kitchen. The café's vegetarian and ethnic menu is much more interesting than the simple decor suggests. For breakfast, try great omelets or a burrito. Keep dinner simple with a fancy pizza or a hot chicken Parmesan sub. B, L $–$$, D $$–$$$.

✆ **Marconi Beach Restaurant** (508-349-6025; marconibeachrestaurant .net), 545 Route 6. Open L, D, early April through November. You won't find better Southern-style, wood-fired BBQ on the Lower or Outer Cape. We're talking ribs, chicken, pulled pork, and beef brisket with all the fixin's. If you can't decide what to have, they'll help you with a BBQ platter. Look for the trail of smoke and follow your nose. L $–$$; D $$–$$$.

✆ **Catch of the Day** (508-349-9090; wellfleetcatch.com), 975 Route 6. Open L, D, mid-April to late October. This seafood market and no-frills eatery features fresh catch (grilled or blackened); buckets of local shellfish (Wellfleet littlenecks, Eastham mussels, and Chatham steamers); and daily specials like fish tacos, fisherman's stew, or baked Chatham scrod. Bring it to the beach, cook it at home, or dine on their patio. Cocktail lovers should try their "Paine's Hollow Painkiller." $–$$$.

✆ **Van Rensselaer's** (508-349-2127; vanrensselaers.com), 1019 Route 6. Open B, D, early April to late October. This longtime fixture packs in families with an all-you-can-eat breakfast buffet on weekends, early specials, seafood, prime rib, vegetarian dishes, and a half-portion bistro menu. They are also the brains behind Catch of the Day. B $–$$, D $$–$$$.

✆ **Bookstore & Restaurant** (508-349-3154; wellfleetoyster.com), 50 Kendrick Avenue. Open B, L, D, mid-February to late December. The owners raise oysters from family harbor shellfish beds, so I recommend you come simply for oyster appetizers, preferably raw, as they're so fresh. Lobsters are OK, too. If you can't get a table on the outside deck, dine elsewhere. B, L $–$$; D $$–$$$.

❄ 🍴 ✆ **Box Lunch** (508-349-2178; boxlunchcapecod.com), 50 Briar Lane. Open B, L. At proprietor Owen MacNutt's original branch of the ever-expanding chain, folks swear by "Porky's Nightmare." "Rollwiches" are perfect for the beach or to take on a Great Island hike. Rollwiches $, lobster rollwiches $$.

❄ **Wellfleet Market Place** (508-349-3156), 295 Main Street. An institution and a convenient in-town location for deli meats, wine, an array of groceries, and more.

See also **Beachcomber** under *Entertainment*.

COFFEE **The Juice** (508-349-0535; the juicerestaurant.com), 6 Commercial Street. Open B, mid-May to mid-October. This funky, archetypal Wellfleetian eatery (which looks like it's falling down but isn't) serves strong morning java and specialty organic smoothies. $.

❄ Entertainment

 ❖ **Wellfleet Harbor Actors Theater** (508-349-9428; what.org), 2357 Route 6. Performances March to November; matinees and kids' shows, too. Known locally as WHAT, it's clear why this serious and experimental theater company doesn't receive federal government funding from the National Endowment for the Arts. WHAT produces plays by new writers and directors, established folks like David Mamet, and radical interpretations of Chekhov, too. A fixture in the community since 1985, WHAT can always be counted on to be provocative. Don't worry; their kid's shows are tamer! If you consider yourself cool, do yourself a favor and check out one of their shows. $$–$$$$; half-price "student rush" just prior to curtain time.

Harbor Stage Company (508-514-1763; harborstage.org), 1 Kendrick Avenue. This intimate (90-seat) local landmark produces original and classic theater on the edge of the harbor. It's decidedly Wellfleet. If you treat yourself to a production here, you'll recall the experience for a coupla decades.

🦞 **Square dancing**, Town Pier or Mayo Beach parking lot. On Wednesday evening in July and August, the waterfront takes on a different tone. Dancing begins at 7 PM, and the steps get progressively more difficult until 9 PM or so. I found myself in the middle of families, callers, and klieg lights on a hot summer night in August and had a blast, I confess.

❄ 🦞 🍸 **Wellfleet Cinemas** (508-349-7176; wellfleetdrivein.com), 51 Route 6. Adjacent to the drive-in and showing first-run movies on four screens.

🍸 **Beachcomber** (508-349-6055; the-beachcomber.com), 1120 Cahoon Hollow Road. Open L, D, late May to early September. In its former incarnation, this 1890s structure was one of the Outer Cape's nine lifesaving stations. Today, perched on a bluff right above the beach, it's well known as a restaurant *and* a bar and club. By day, shuffle from the beach to hang out with a 30- and 40-something crowd on the outdoor deck, complete with a 40-foot-long, cabana-style raw bar. Burgers, seafood plates, and boneless buffalo wings also offered. Inside is dark, with wooden booths. Only appetizers and pizza are available after 9 PM. There's nothing else like it on the Cape, and

WELLFLEET HARBOR ACTORS THEATER

AN OPEN-AIR SCREEN WITH STARS

WELLFLEET DRIVE-IN

Wellfleet Drive-In (508-349-7176; 508-349-2450 to speak to a human being; wellfleetdrivein.com), Route 6. Shows early May to early September. One of the last holdouts of a vanishing American pastime, this drive-in has lured patrons since 1957, when the number of U.S. drive-ins peaked at 4,000. Today there are fewer than 800 left—only a handful in New England, no others on the Cape. Hence, it remains a treasured local institution. Late owner John Jentz, a former engineering professor at MIT, designed the 100-by-44-foot screen with his MIT pals; perhaps that's why it's withstood hurricanes with winds up to 135 mph. Double features are shown nightly at dusk. Movies change about once a week, and there's a play area behind the reasonably priced **Dairy Bar & Grill**. Films are generally family oriented. No credit cards. $.

it's simply amazing that it has survived this long, surrounded by National Park Service land. Be careful about wandering out onto the beach after a couple

BEACHCOMBER

of drinks; the first step is a doozy! Hip Boston bands and national blues artists perform in the evenings, but the club is perhaps best known for its Sunday afternoon concerts and reggae-filled happy hours (frozen mudslides are very popular). $–$$.

✳ Selective Shopping

Wellfleet Flea Market (508-349-0541 operator; 508-349-2520 automated assistance; wellfleetcinemas.com), at the Wellfleet Drive-In, 51 Route 6. Open early May to mid-October. With more than 300 stalls, there's more junk than treasure, but you never know what you'll find: name-brand clothing, a hat to ward off the summer sun, used and antique furniture, and trinkets, tea sets, and colored glasses. Wander in with the intention of spending a few minutes and a few dollars, and you'll probably find that hours have passed and you've bought more than you planned on! It's the Cape's biggest and best. $ per car.

WELLFLEET FLEA MARKET

ART GALLERIES Wellfleet is an art town. The **Art Gallery Association** publishes a complete list of galleries, some of which are excellent, others of which cater to souvenir art. Pick one up at the Wellfleet Chamber of Commerce. In July and August, many galleries host wine-and-cheese openings on Saturday evening.

Cherry Stone Gallery (508-349-3026), 70 East Commercial Street. Open by appointment only. This long-established gallery carries works by Abbott and Atget, Motherwell and Tworkov (and local Cape artists). Unpretentious and friendly, it's for serious collectors.

❋ **Left Bank Gallery** (508-349-9451; leftbankgallery.com), 25 Commercial Street. Audrey and Gerald Parent's gallery is arguably the most interesting in town. Don't miss the crafts-filled potter's room behind the wonderfully diverse main exhibition area.

❋ **Left Bank Small Works & Jewelry** (508-349-7939; leftbankgallery.com), 3 West Main Street. Works on paper, contemporary jewelry, and clothing are highlighted.

Berta Walker Gallery (508-383-3161; bertawalkergallery.com), 40 Main Street. One of my favorite Provincetown galleries, always bursting at the seams with expertly curated selections, opened a second primo spot in Wellfleet in 2015.

Blue Heron Gallery (508-349-6724; blueheronfineart.com), 20 Bank Street. Open mid-May to mid-October. Royal Thurston packs contemporary fine art, pottery, and sculpture into a seemingly endless series of small rooms. More than

LEFT BANK GALLERY

40 representational contemporary artists and artisans are shown.

Cove Gallery (508-349-2530; covegallery.com), 15 Commercial Street. Open late May to late-October. This gallery has featured oils, pastels, and a full range of media since 1968; it also has a lively sculpture garden overlooking Duck Creek.

ARTISANS ❄ **Salty Duck Pottery** (508-349-3342), 115 Main Street. You never know whom and what you're going to find in this community of tolerant eccentrics—perhaps potters shaping their lives and clay alongside a salt marsh. Check out potter Maria Juster's blue-green stoneware pottery, tiles, mirrors, and tables.

❄ **Narrow Land Pottery** (508-349-6308; narrowlandpottery.com), 2603 Route 6, adjacent to the service station. Joe McCaffery, who studied at the School of the Museum of Fine Arts, Boston, throws pots, vases, mugs, lamp bases, and plates. His glazes, porcelain, and stoneware come in a variety of colors.

BOOKSTORES ❄ **Herridge Books** (508-349-1323), 140 Main Street. Used books covering a wide range of subjects.

CANDY **The Chocolate Sparrow** (508-349-1333), 326 Main Street. Open mid-June to early September. As long as anyone can remember, Wellfleet has had a penny-candy store. The Chocolate Sparrow opened in 1990 to continue the tradition and added rich, hand-dipped chocolates.

CLOTHING Style-conscious women are in luck (in-season) in Wellfleet. Loose-fitting designs in cotton, linen, rayon, and earth tones reign. Try **Hannah** (508-349-9884; 234 Main Street) with "curated," comfortable, classic fashions from around the world; **Eccentricity** (508-349-7554, 361 Main Street) with ethnic designs featuring tactile fabrics; **Eccentricity's Off Center** (508-349-3634, across the street); and **Karol Richardson** (508-349-6378; karolrichardson.com), nearby at 11 West Main Street.

FARM STAND **Hatch's Fish Market/Hatch's Produce** (508-349-6734; hatchsfishmarket.com), behind Town Hall at 310 Main Street. Open mid-May to mid-September. Although you might find better prices at the supermarket, the fish and produce here are fresh and beautifully displayed, and the location can't be matched. Hatch's smokes its own fish, pâté, and mussels.

❄ Special Events

July 4: **Independence Day parade.**

Mid-October: **Oyster Festival** (wellfleetoysterfest.org). An instant tradition since it began in the early 2000s, this "aw shucks" weekend celebrates the famed local delicacy (and the men and women who make their livelihoods farming it) with oyster-shucking demonstrations, live music, an art auction, and more. Keep it simple with food and games, or get serious with shellfish education talks and demonstrations.

HATCH'S FISH MARKET

TRURO

onsidered to be the last vestige of "old Cape Cod," Truro has no stoplights, no fast-food outlets, no supermarket. It does have, though, the last working farm on the Outer Cape. And it has a lot of new construction—second homes that lie dormant during the off-season and lots of new year-round houses. Yes, Dorothy, the landscape is changing in Truro. Still, though, both Truro Center and North Truro consist of only a few shops. Nothing more, nothing less. And local folks, summer people (vacationing writers and urban professionals who have built large houses in the rolling hills and dunes), and even the newcomers are determined to keep it that way.

North Truro is also tiny but has blue-collar ties to Provincetown. Compare **Dutra's Market** (an institution) to **Jams** (a fancy food shop born in the '80s) and the differences are readily apparent. As you head toward Provincetown, the only real development—in a nod to the tourist industry—consists of hundreds of tiny cottages, motels, and houses lining a narrow strip of shore wedged between Cape Cod Bay and the dramatic parabolic dunes on Pilgrim Lake. It's an odd juxtaposition, but one I always look forward to.

There aren't many human-made sites to explore, except for **Highland Light** and the **Truro Historical Museum**, but there are plenty of natural ones. Almost 70 percent of Truro's 42 square miles (one of the largest towns on the Cape, in acreage) falls within the boundaries of the **Cape Cod National Seashore (CCNS).** There are hiking and biking trails as well as expanses of beach.

Rolling moors and hidden valleys characterize the tranquil back roads east and west of Route 6. Windswept dunes, lighthouses, beach grass, and austere shorelines will inspire you, as they did Edward Hopper. The painter built a summer home in Truro in the 1930s and worked there until 1967. In the late 2000s a land dispute erupted with the Klines, developer-owners who wanted to build a trophy house on 9 acres of what many view as sacred Hopper land and views. Neighbors wanted to preserve the landscape made famous by the artist. The Cape Cod Commission, arbiters of all things potentially contentious and historic, ruled that the Klines could go ahead and build their 6,500-square-foot house. Such is progress.

Truro, established in 1697, has endured many name changes. Originally it was called Payomet or Pamet, after the Native American tribe that inhabited the area before the Pilgrims. In 1705 it was known as Dangerfield because of the large number of offshore sailing disasters. Eventually it was named Truro, for a Cornish coastal town in England.

Although today Truro is sleepy and rural, it has been, at times during the past few centuries, a hotbed of activity. The *Mayflower*'s Myles Standish spent his second night ashore in Truro. His band of 16 fellow Pilgrims found their first fresh water in Truro, as well as a stash of corn (which belonged to the Native Americans) from which they harvested their first crop. And although you wouldn't know it today, since **Pamet Harbor** choked up with sand in the mid-1850s, Truro's harbor once rivaled neighboring Provincetown as a whaling and cod-fishing center. By the late 1700s, shipbuilding was thriving and the harbor bustling. Vessels bound for the Grand Banks were built here, and a packet boat sailed from Truro to Boston. The whaling industry also owes a debt to early Truro residents, one of whom (Ichabod Paddock) taught Nantucketers how to catch whales from shore.

In 1851 the population soared to a rousing 2,000 souls. But in 1860 the Union Company of Truro went bankrupt due to declining harbor conditions, and townspeople's

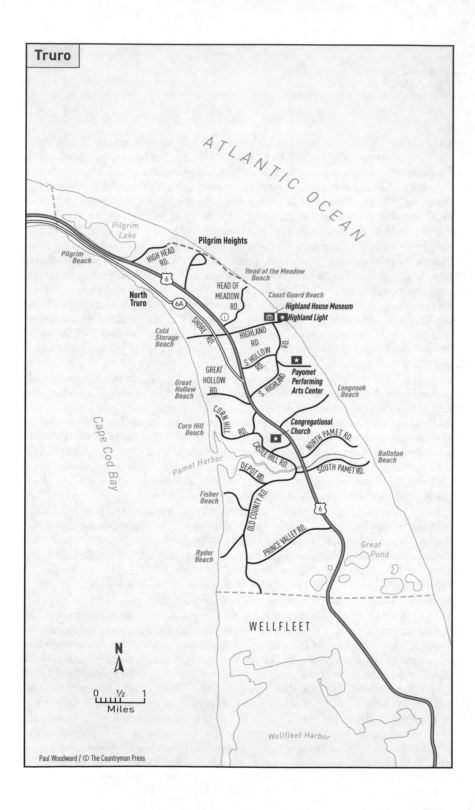

Truro

ATLANTIC OCEAN

Pilgrim Lake

Pilgrim Heights

Pilgrim Beach

HIGH HEAD RD.

Head of the Meadow Beach

North Truro

HEAD OF MEADOW RD.

Coast Guard Beach

Highland House Museum
Highland Light

Cold Storage Beach

SHORE RD.

HIGHLAND RD.

S. HOLLOW RD.

GREAT HOLLOW RD.

S. HIGHLAND

Payomet Performing Arts Center

Longnook Beach

Great Hollow Beach

CORN HILL RD.

Corn Hill Beach

Congregational Church

NORTH PAMET RD.

Ballston Beach

Cape Cod Bay

Pamet Harbor

CASTLE HILL RD.

DEPOT RD.

SOUTH PAMET RD.

Fisher Beach

OLD COUNTY RD.

Ryder Beach

PRINCE VALLEY RD.

Great Pond

WELLFLEET

Wellfleet Harbor

N

0   ½   1
Miles

Paul Woodward / © The Countryman Press

fortunes and livelihoods sank with it. Commercially, Truro never rebounded. Today, the year-round population is also about 2,100 (despite a recent housing boom); the summer influx raises that number tenfold.

GUIDANCE **Truro Chamber of Commerce** (508-487-1288; trurochamberofcommerce .com), Route 6. Open late May to mid-October.

GETTING THERE *By car:* The center of Truro is about 60 miles from the Cape Cod Canal via Route 6. Route 6A and Shore Road are synonymous.

By bus: The **Plymouth & Brockton** bus line (508-778-9767; p-b.com) connects Truro with Hyannis and other Cape towns, as well as with Boston's Logan Airport. The bus stops at Dutra's in North Truro and at the post office/Jams store in Truro Center.

GETTING AROUND *By car:* Beaches, sites, and roads are well marked off Route 6. Generally, the CCNS is east of Route 6. The Shore Road exit in North Truro takes you into North Truro and eventually to Beach Point, choked with motels as it approaches Provincetown. At its most narrow, Truro is only a mile wide, while it stretches for 10 miles north to south.

By shuttle: The excellent **Provincetown Shuttle** (508-385-1430; capecodtransit.org) operates late June to mid-September. The shuttles run from Horton's Camping Resort and Dutra's in Truro along Route 6A and up to the MacMillan Wharf in Provincetown. From there, another shuttle ferries folks to the Provincetown Inn, Beech Forest, and Herring Cove Beach. $.

PUBLIC RESTROOMS Stop at the Pilgrim Heights area in summer.

PUBLIC LIBRARY ❋ ✐ ☂ **Truro Public Library** (508-487-1125; trurolibrary.org), 7 Standish Way, North Truro. This contemporary library has programs for adults and kids. I often find myself here, working on the next edition of the *Explorer's Guide*.

MEDICAL EMERGENCY Call **911**.

A PERFECT DAY IN TRURO

8:00	Start with breakfast at Sweet Escapes.
9:00	Play the Scottish-style Highland Golf Links, the Cape's oldest course.
11:30	Tour the Cape Cod Light and historic Highland House Museum.
12:45	Assemble a picnic lunch from Jams.
1:00	Enjoy it at Truro Vineyards of Cape Cod, with tours and tastings.
2:00	Laugh at the irreverent Susan Baker Memorial Museum.
3:00	Catch afternoon rays at Head of the Meadow Beach on the Atlantic.
7:00	Indulge in consistently tasty gourmet-tavern cuisine at Blackfish.

ENTERING TRURO INC. 1709

❄ To See

Cape Cod Light, or **Highland Light**, CCNS, 27 Highland Road, off South Highland Road, North Truro. The original lighthouse that guarded these treacherous shores was erected in 1797. It was the first on Cape Cod and had to be rebuilt in 1853, the year that a whopping 1,200 ships passed by within a 10-day period. Almost as important to land-lubbers as mariners, the lighthouse provided shelter to Henry David Thoreau during one of his famous Outer Cape walks. The spot where he once stood and proclaimed that here a man could "put all America behind him" is thought to be 150 feet offshore now, thanks to erosion. One of only five working lighthouses on the Outer Cape, it was the last to become automated, in 1986. The original light shone with whale oil from 24 lamps, while later lamps were fueled with lard and kerosene. The modern light has a 110-kilowatt halogen bulb. Visible 21 miles out to sea, it's the brightest lighthouse on the New England coast. And at 120 feet above sea level, it's aptly named Highland.

In the mid-1990s the National Park Service, Coast Guard, Truro Historical Society, and the state joined forces to avert a looming disaster. Engineers cautioned that the lighthouse would crumble into the ocean. Erosion, at the rate of 3 to 4 feet per year, had chewed away the cliff upon which the lighthouse was built. (Thanks to ferocious storms in 1990, some 40 feet were lost in one year alone!) And when cliffs erode to within 100 feet of a lighthouse, it is too dangerous to bring in the heavy equipment needed to move it. So at a cost of $1.5 million, and over a period of 18 days, the 430-ton historic lighthouse and keeper's house was jacked up onto steel beams and pushed along steel tracks by hydraulic rams. At a rate of 25 feet per day, it was moved 450 feet west and 12 feet south (that is, inland), to a spot on the golf course. It should be safe for another 150 years, unless we get a lot of nor'easters.

Lighthouse tours (508-487-1121; trurohistorical.org and capecodlight.org), which include a short video and exhibit in the keeper's house, are offered mid-May through

HIGHLAND HOUSE MUSEUM

October; $. No children under 48 inches allowed. An observation deck, where the lighthouse recently stood, overlooks the ocean. Mark your calendar to ascend the lighthouse under the light of a full moon from April through December. It's quite something, watching the sunset and moonrise from here. Reservations are required and space is limited; donations.

❧ **Highland House Museum** (508-487-3397; trurohistorical.org), 6 Highland Light Road, North Truro. Open June through September. Operated expertly by the Truro Historical Society and housed in the circa-1907 Highland Hotel, this museum is wholly dedicated to preserving Truro's maritime and agricultural past. Permanent items on display include a pirate's chest, fishing and whaling gear, 17th-century firearms, photos of Truro residents and places, toys, and ship models. In essence, all 12 of the former hotel rooms are set up as mini-museums furnished with period pieces. One room is dedicated to Courtney Allen, the Truro Historical Society founder, artist, model maker, and wood-carver. Upstairs is reserved for rotating exhibits. The building is a fine example of the kind of fashionable, once prominent, turn-of-the-20th-century summer hotels that were common in Cape Cod. $.

TRURO CENTER FOR THE ARTS AT CASTLE HILL

❅ **Truro Center for the Arts at Castle Hill** (508-349-7511; castlehill.org), 10 Meetinghouse Road at Castle Hill Road, Truro. Classes and workshops year-round, although the majority are held in summer. A nonprofit educational institute, Castle Hill was founded in 1972 and has evolved into an important cultural voice on the Outer Cape art scene. Classes and workshops are offered in a converted 1880s barn to people of all ages in painting, drawing, writing, printmaking, book arts, photography, clay, and sculpture. Castle Hill also sponsors lectures, concerts, and artist receptions. Nationally renowned artists and writers lead weeklong (and longer) classes.

Truro Vineyards of Cape Cod (508-487-6200; trurovineyardsofcapecod.com), 11 Route 6A, North Truro. Tastings (which include five wines, $$) May through November. Free tours late May to early September. Feel free to bring lunch and enjoy a picnic amid the huge antique wine casks.

Jenny Lind Tower, CCNS, off Highland Light Road, North Truro. Between the Highland Golf Links and the former **North Truro Air Force Base**, this 55-foot tower of granite seems out of place. And in fact, it is. The short story goes like this: In 1850 P. T. Barnum brought Swedish singing legend Jenny Lind to America. When Barnum oversold tickets to her Boston concert, and when Lind heard the crowds were going to riot, she performed a free concert from the roof tower for the people in the street. When the building was to be destroyed in 1927, a Boston attorney purchased the tower and

TRURO VINEYARDS

brought it here (he owned the land at that time). The CCNS owns the property now and the entrance is blocked, but the granite tower still stands 150 feet above sea level, visible to passing ships and those of us on the ground.

Congregational church and **cemetery**, off Bridge Road, Truro. A marble memorial commemorates the terrible tragedy of the 1841 October Gale, when seven ships were destroyed and 57 crewmembers died. Renowned glassmakers of Sandwich made the church windows, and Paul Revere cast the steeple bell. Take Route 6 to Snow's Field to Meetinghouse Road to Bridge Road.

Payomet Performing Arts Center (508-487-5400; payomet.org), 29 Old Dewline Road, North Truro. Performances mid-April to mid-September. This outdoor tent space hosts worthy alternatives (comedians, plays, concerts, films, children's shows) to reading trashy novels. Note that in the off-season, the center sponsors additional performances through December at nearby venues such as Provincetown Hall. $$–$$$$+.

SCENIC DRIVES It's difficult to find an unpicturesque Truro road. Both North and South Pamet Roads, connected prior to a breach at Ballston Beach, wind past bayberry, beach plums, and groves of locust trees. From Truro Center, Castle Hill Road to Corn Hill Beach is lovely. In North Truro, take Priest Road to Bay View Road to the bayside Cold Storage Beach for great bay views.

HEAD OF THE MEADOW BIKE TRAIL

SCOTLAND COMES TO CAPE COD

Highland Golf Links (508-487-9201; highlandlinks.com), 10 Highland Light Road, off South Highland Road, North Truro. Open late April through November. Perched on a high windswept bluff, the Cape's oldest course (founded in 1892) is one of the country's oldest, too. At the turn of the 20th century, the course was part of the Highland House resort (now a museum; see *To See*), which drew Boston visitors by train. Today the museum sits between the eighth and ninth holes. The course exemplifies the Scottish tradition, with deep natural roughs, Scotch broom, heath, unirrigated open fairways, occasional fog, and spectacular ocean views. That's why golfers come to this nine-hole course. That, and for the dime-sized greens, whale sightings from the sixth tee in summer, and the view of Highland Light adjacent to the seventh hole. Avoid the crowds by playing on Sunday. It's the only public course between Orleans and Provincetown. $$$$; clubs $$.

HIGHLAND GOLF LINKS

✳ To Do

BICYCLING **Head of the Meadow Bike Trail**, CCNS, off Route 6, North Truro. Just south of Pilgrim Lake, this 2-mile (one way) bikeway runs from High Head Road, past salt marshes and dunes, to Head of the Meadow Beach up a fairly steep hill (see *Green Space*). Four-wheel-drive vehicles with proper stickers can enter the dunes here, too, depending on piping plover activity.

BOATING **Pamet Harbor**, at the end of Depot Road, Truro. If you have your own boat, contact the harbormaster (508-349-2555) for launching information.

FISHING & SHELLFISHING Procure freshwater and saltwater fishing licenses and regulations online (mass.gov/eea/agencies/dfg/licensing). Kids love fishing from the grassy shores off **Pond Road** (which leads to **Cold Storage Beach**); it's tranquil for picnicking and watching the sunset, too. Surf-fishing is good all along the Atlantic coastline. For freshwater fishing, try **Great Pond**, off Savage Road from Route 6 in southern Truro.

HEAD OF THE MEADOW BEACH

Charters can be arranged with Captain Mike of **Jigged Up Sportfishing** (774-200-1180; jiggedupsportfishing.com) and Captain Matt of **Tighten Up Charters** (203-414-6126; tightenupcharterscc.com). Both outfits boast state-of-the-art center consoles.

TENNIS **Pamet Harbor Yacht & Tennis Club** (508-349-3772; pametclub.com), 7 Yacht Club Road, on the harbor. When not reserved for club members, these three courts are available for rental to the public. $$.

✻ Green Space

BEACHES Town parking stickers are required from late June to early September. Cottage renters may purchase parking stickers ($$$$ weekly) at the Beach Program Office (508-487-6983), 36 Shore Road, Route 6A.

Head of the Meadow Beach, on the Atlantic Ocean. Half the beach is maintained by the town, half by the CCNS; both have lifeguards. The only difference is that the latter half has changing rooms and restrooms; otherwise, it's the same wide, dune-backed beach. Parking $$.

Corn Hill Beach, off Corn Hill Road on Cape Cod Bay. This is the only other town-managed beach where nonresidents

COAST GUARD BEACH

CORN HILL BEACH

can pay a daily parking fee ($$). Facilities include portable toilets and a large parking area. Backed by a long, low dune. The width of Corn Hill Beach decreases measurably as the tide comes in. There's good sailboarding, too.

Long Nook Beach, off Long Nook Road, on the Atlantic Ocean. Although this wonderful beach requires a town parking sticker, in the off-season anyone can park here. Lacking amenities, this beach offers a purer nature experience, which also extends to the steep walk down to the beach.

Coast Guard Beach, off Highland Road, and **Ballston Beach**, off South Pamet Road; both on the Atlantic Ocean. Each is owned by the town and requires a resident sticker, but anyone can bicycle in for free. (This Coast Guard Beach is not to be confused with Henry Beston's Coast Guard Beach in Eastham, under the auspices of CCNS.) Lifeguard and portable toilets. Note: Use caution because of the tricky undertow.

WALKS **Pilgrim Heights Area**, CCNS, off Route 6, North Truro. Two short walks yield open vistas of distant dunes, ocean, and salt marsh. As the name implies, the easy 0.75-mile round-trip **Pilgrim Spring Trail** leads to the spot where the Pilgrims reportedly tasted their first New England water. Or so historians say; it's debatable. One subsequently penned: "We . . . sat us downe and drunke our first New England

PILGRIM SPRING TRAIL

SMALL SWAMP TRAIL

water with as much delight as ever we drunke in all our lives." A small plaque marks the spot.

Small Swamp Trail (about the same distance as the Pilgrim Spring Trail, above) was named not for the size of the swamp or trail, but rather for the farmer (Mr. Small) who grew asparagus and corn on this former 200-acre farm. By August, blueberries are ripe for the picking. In spring look for migrating hawks. There's a wooded picnic area.

Pamet Area/Bearberry Hill, North Pamet Road, Truro. You won't want to pick this tangy and sour fruit come late September, but take the lovely walk to the top of Bearberry Hill for views of the Atlantic and the bog landscape. The trailhead is located at the parking lot below the youth hostel/education center.

❋ Lodging

COTTAGES & EFFICIENCIES

🌴 **Kalmar Village** (508-487-0585; 617-277-0091 in winter; kalmarvillage.com), 674 Shore Road, North Truro. Open mid-May to mid-October. On a strip chock-full of cottage colonies, Kalmar has been owned by the Prelacks since 1968 and it still stands out. It's particularly good for families, because Kalmar sits on 400 feet of private bay beach. Look for well-tended lawns around the pool, freshly painted chimneys atop the shingled cottages, and six newish waterfront cottages. All 45 cottages are roomy inside, with modern kitchens. Other perks include daily housekeeping and a coin-operated laundry; each unit has its own picnic table and grill. There are also large and small efficiencies, as well as three motel rooms. Rented weekly in season.

Days' Cottages (508-487-1062; day scottages.com), 271 Shore Road, North Truro. Open May to early September. These little green-and-white cottages, all

KALMAR VILLAGE

24 of them lined up like ducks in a row, are something of a local icon. When you see them, you know you're just about to the tip of the Cape. Although each is only 20 feet from the next, people love them. Perhaps because there's nothing between them and the ocean, except for a couple of lawn chairs (albeit on a cement slab). And perhaps because they face due west, toward the setting sun. Each cottage has a full kitchen. Linens provided. No credit cards. Rented weekly in season. $$.

MOTEL ✎ **Top Mast** (508-487-1189; top mastresort.com), 209 Shore Road, North Truro. Open late April to mid-October. Owned and operated by the Silva family since 1971, this nicely maintained 72-unit motel flanks Route 6A well before the congestion begins. Beachfront units are built right on sandy Cape Cod Bay, and each has a sliding glass door that opens onto an individual balcony with Adirondack chairs. Choose among motel rooms, one- and two-room efficiencies, and two-bedroom cottages with full kitchens. Poolside (gardenview) rooms rent by the night, even in high season. The indoor pool complex features a large heated saltwater pool, kiddie pool, hot tub, sauna, aromatherapy steam room, weight fitness room, big screen TVs, and cocktail area. Rented weekly in-season. $$.

RENTAL HOUSES & COTTAGES
Duarte/Downey Real Estate (508-349-7588; ddre.com), 12 Truro Center Road, in the center of town.

DAYS' COTTAGES

FOOD TRUCKS: RECENT ARRIVALS TO CAPE COD

My recent summer stay included some very good eats previously unknown to me on the Cape. I hadn't noticed a culinary void in 35 years of unfailingly joyous visits (which, by definition, requires a wide range of delicious meals). Between the ubiquitous and reliable Box Lunch, dozens of establishments righteously claiming the Cape's best lobster rolls or clam chowder, and restaurants preparing take-out orders to beach-ready perfection, what more could a hungry explorer want?

How could it not have occurred to me—a native of Brooklyn, where food trucks have been an integral part of my borough's renowned food scene for years—that food trucks and Cape Cod are as natural a union as sand and sea? In fact, my first food truck encounter was at **Head of the Meadow Beach**, where I was offered a free taco after the proprietor's black Lab unexpectedly leapt from his vehicle to surprise my cherished papillon-corgi mix. The ingredients were very fresh, and they hit the spot after a long walk on the beach. Read more about Kanguru Food Truck and its siblings at www.joeysfoodtruck.com.

Check out the annual late August **Cape Cod Food Truck Festival** (foodtruckfestivalsofamerica.com) for a listing of the 25 food trucks participating.

From a hot dog truck managed by four teenage boys (**Cape Cod Dawgs** in Hyannis) to upscale fare provided by Truro's acclaimed Blackfish restaurant (**Crush Pad**, which is parked at Truro Vineyards and offers charred broccolini, duck confit, egg, kale, and mozzarella sandwiches), my experiential guess is that you are likely to find something to please your palate.

—H. Laurie Yankowitz

CAMPGROUNDS 🦞 ⚓ **North of Highland Camping Area** (508-487-1191; capecodcamping.com), 52 Head of the Meadow Road, North Truro. Open late May to mid-September. On 60 acres of scrub pine forest within the CCNS, these 225-plus sites are suitable for tents and tent trailers only (no hook-ups, though) and are a 10-minute walk from Head of the Meadow Beach (see *Green Space*). There are strict quiet hours. From mid-July to mid-August, reservations must begin and end on a Saturday or Sunday. $.

🦞 🐾 **Adventure Bound Camping Resorts** (508-487-1847; abcapecod.com), 46 Highland Road, North Truro. Open April through October. Within the CCNS, these 22 acres of wooded sites accommodate about 325 tents and RVs. It's less than a mile to Coast Guard Beach (see *Green Space*), and only 6 miles to Provincetown.

HOSTEL 🦞 **Hostelling International, Truro** (508-349-3889; 888-901-2085 in-season reservations; hiusa.org), 111 North Pamet Road, Truro. Open mid-June to early September. Originally a U.S. Coast Guard station, the 42-bed hostel commands a dramatic location—amid dunes, marshes, and a cranberry bog. The hostel is within the CCNS and just a seven-minute walk from Ballston Beach (see *Green Space*). National Park Service interpreters host special programs each week; they're free to all and not to be missed.

✳ Where to Eat

EATING OUT **Blackfish** (508-349-3399), 17 Truro Center Road. Open D, mid-May to late October. This refreshed tavern place, resurrected from its longtime incarnation as the Blacksmith Shop, has

SAVORY AND SWEET ESCAPE PIZZA GRILL

been under the direction of chef-owner Eric Jansen since the late 2000s. Yay! The menu is heavy on meat (pork, rabbit, duck) and locally caught fish dishes that are strongly but not overpoweringly flavored (think truffle chips). The dining room can feel crowded, but the clientele thinks of it more like a buzz. All in all it reaches for (and hits) a high note: a gourmet-in-a-tavern. $$$–$$$$.

🦞 🍷 **Terra Luna** (508-487-1019; terralunarestaurant.com), 104 Shore Road, North Truro. Open D, mid-May to mid-October. Peaked ceilings, large canvases, shellacked wooden tables, and candlelight transform this otherwise unassuming roadside eatery with barn-board walls into a very desirable place to spend a couple of hours (except when it's really hot, since there's no air-conditioning). Chef-owner Tony Pasquale's dishes are rustic with a focus on fresh ingredients. The mouth-watering menu might feature dishes like roasted Chatham cod or pan-fried goat cheese with grilled figs, local honey, and fig balsamic. The cocktail menu is always creative. $$–$$$$.

❋ 🍷 **Savory and Sweet Escape and Pizza Grill** (508-487-2225), 316 Route 6. Open B, L, D. You can't miss this big red building, and I bet you'll stop more than once. From fabu ice cream choices like Lavender Fig and Wicked Mud Flats (a chocolatey concoction) to stone-fired pizzas, grilled burgers, chicken breast sandwiches, and hand-cut fries (with vinegar), this big place has the bases covered. Dine outside on Route 6 or at one of the long window stools. No credit cards. Dishes $–$$.

🦞 **Captain's Choice** (508-487-5800; captainschoicetruro.com), 4 Highland Road, North Truro. Open B, L, D, May to mid-October. This casual place with family-friendly prices offers something for everyone. While seafood is certainly a focus (the new owners are affiliated with Cape Tip Seafood Market on Route 6 in North Truro), they kept Portuguese kale soup and ice cream on the menu from the restaurant's previous

JAMS

incarnation. I'm partial to their sashimi tacos. $–$$$.

❄ 🎣 **Montano's** (508-487-2026; montanos.com), 481 Route 6, North Truro. Open D. This family restaurant serves dependable Italian favorites like seafood *shrimp Florentine* and Frutti di Mare with homemade pasta. Montano's gets big points in my book for serving hungry Explorers in the dead of winter. $$–$$$$.

Mac's Seafood (508-349-9409; macsseafood.com), 14D Truro Center Road. Open L, D, April to November. Mac's has seafood enterprises in Wellfleet and Eastham, along with this to-go place in Truro. Come here for fresh fish, cooked lobsters and clambakes, soups, chowders, and smoked-on-the-premises-fish. $–$$.

SNACKS, ICE CREAM, & COFFEE 🎣 **Jams** (508-349-1616), 14 Truro Center Road, off Route 6 in Truro Center. Open 6:30 AM–6 PM late May to early September. Jams caters to *New York Times* readers, G&T drinkers, truffle lovers, and pesto pizza prima donnas. And what a fine job they do. Coffee aficionados take note: Jams serves rich espresso and lattes. Basic groceries share the stage with sun-dried tomatoes, rotisserie-roasted chicken and ribs,

pizza-by-the-slice, and fresh mozzarella cheese. All the baked goods, including key lime pie and flan, are made from scratch. For those of you who don't live nearby, carry your picnic fixings to the small field across the street, perfect for bicyclists and the car-weary. $.

See also **Sweet Escapes** and **Captain's Choice** under *Eating Out*.

❋ Entertainment

Highlands Center at Cape Cod National Seashore/Payomet Performing Arts Center (508-487-5400; payomet.org), 78 Noons Heights Road, North Truro. The PPACT offers live music, original theater, film screenings, readings, and kids programs under their temporary summer tent on the CCNS grounds.

❋ Selective Shopping

Jules Besch Stationers (508-487-0395), 3 Great Hollow Road. Open April to late November. This gorgeous shop features products that will make you want to take pen (perhaps an antique 1880s pen or a quill) to paper (perhaps some handmade paper or a bound journal). It also sells

unique wrapping paper, collectible post-
cards, artsy boxed note cards, specialty
albums, and blank books. Parts of the
shop resemble a study, set up with writing tables, leather blotters, and stylish
desk lamps. Buy a blank card and ask
Michael Tuck (a.k.a. Jules) to personalize
it (overnight); he's known for his calligraphy and verse.

Susan Baker Memorial Museum
(508-487-2557), 46 Route 6A, Truro.
Open late May to mid-October. One of
the most irreverent painters on the Cape,
Baker is a humorist at heart. She has a
great body of work exploring the history
of Provincetown and a recent one of
European chapels and churches. She's
perhaps best known for her sculptural,
three-dimensional frames that take their
cue from the architecture of whatever
European building is in the painting.
It's hard to keep a good woman in one
medium.

SUSAN BAKER MEMORIAL MUSEUM

JULES BESCH STATIONERS

❋ **Atlantic Spice Co.** (800-316-7965;
atlanticspice.com), 2 Shore Road, North
Truro. Culinary herbs and spices, botan-
icals, make-your-own potpourri, teas,
spice blends, nuts, and seeds. They're
here, they're fresh, and they're in a
cavernous warehouse. Although this is
primarily a wholesaler, you can purchase
small quantities (less than the usual
1-pound increments) of most products.
You may also be tempted by an assortment of practical souvenirs, kitchen gadgets, spice jars, and such. $–$$.

❋ Special Events

Mid-September: **Truro Treasures** (truro
treasures.org). Since the early 1990s, this
folksy two-day weekend features a crafts
fair, antique car show, beach bash, treasure hunt, pancake breakfast, silent art
auction, and many more fun events, like
a grape stomp at the winery.

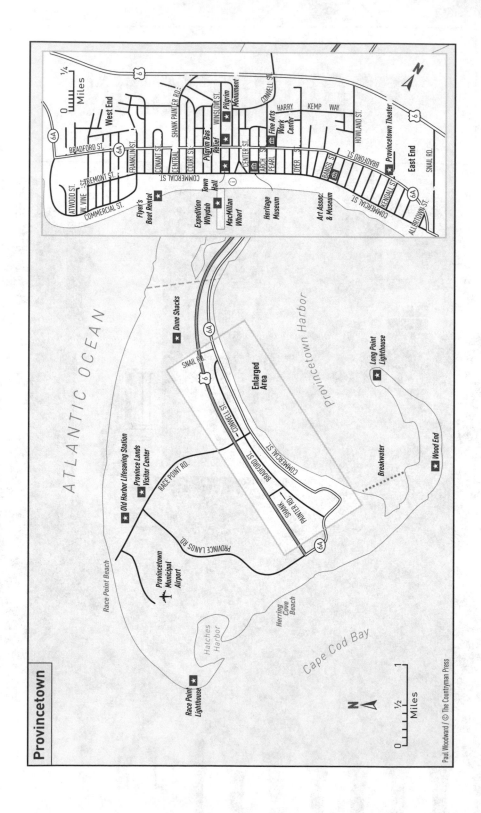

Provincetown

ATLANTIC OCEAN

Race Point Lighthouse ★

Race Point Beach

Hatches Harbor

Provincetown Municipal Airport ✈

Old Harbor Lifesaving Station ★

Province Lands Visitor Center ★

Dune Shacks ★

RACE POINT RD.

PROVINCE LANDS RD.

SHANK PAINTER RD.

BRADFORD ST.

COMMERCIAL ST.

SNAIL RD.

6

6A

Enlarged Area

Herring Cove Beach

Cape Cod Bay

Provincetown Harbor

Breakwater

Long Point Lighthouse ★

Wood End ★

N

0   ½   1
Miles

Paul Woodward / © The Countryman Press

West End

BRADFORD ST.

COMMERCIAL ST.

ATWOOD ST.
W. VINE ST.
TREMONT ST.
FRANKLIN ST.
CONANT ST.
CENTRAL
COURT ST.
WINSLOW ST.
ARCH ST.
PEARL
DYER ST.
BANGS ST.
KENDALL ST.
ALLERTON ST.
HOWLAND ST.
BRADFORD ST.

SHANK PAINTER RD.

Pilgrim Monument

Winslow St.

HARRY KEMP WAY

Fine Arts Work Center ⌂

Center St.

Cowell St.

East End

SNAIL RD.

6A

6

6

6A

Flyer's Boat Rental ★

Expedition Whydah ★

MacMillan Wharf ★

Pilgrim Bas Relief ★

Town Hall ⓘ

Heritage Museum ⌂

Art Assoc. & Museum

Provincetown Theater

0   ¼
Miles

N

PROVINCETOWN

A s you cross into Provincetown, where high dunes drift onto Route 6, you begin to sense that this is a different place. This outpost on the tip of the Cape, where glaciers deposited their last grains of sand, attracts a varied population. Whether seeking solitude or freedom of expression in the company of like-minded souls, visitors relish Provincetown's fringe status. (Although it's becoming less "fringey" every day, but more on that later.) P-town, as it's often referred to by nonlocals but not by locals, is perhaps best known as a community of tolerant individuals. The LGBTQ community, Portuguese fishermen and families, artists, writers—all call it home and welcome those who are equally tolerant.

Visitors parade up and down **Commercial Street**, the main drag, ducking in and out of hundreds of shops and galleries. The town has a carnival-like atmosphere, especially in July and August, testing the limits of acceptability. As you might imagine, people-watching is a prime activity. On any given Saturday, the cast of characters might include cross-dressers, leather-clad motorcyclists, barely clad in-line skaters, children eating saltwater taffy, and tourists from "Anytown, USA," some of whom can't quite figure out what they've stumbled into and some of whom have come to scope out (gawk or relish) the alternative scene.

Provincetown's history began long before the *Mayflower* arrived. It's said that Leif Eriksson's brother, Thorvald, stopped here in 1004 to repair the keel of his boat. Wampanoag Indians fished and summered here—the tiny strip of land was too vulnerable to sustain a year-round settlement. In 1620 the Pilgrims first set foot on American soil in Provincetown, anchoring in the harbor for five weeks, making forays down-Cape in search of an agreeable spot to settle. By the late 1600s and early 1700s, only 200 fishermen lived here.

But from the mid-18th to the mid-19th century, Provincetown was a bustling whaling community and seaport. After the industry peaked, Portuguese sailors from the Azores and Cape Verde Islands, who had signed on with whaling and fishing ships, settled here to fish the local waters. The Old Colony Railroad was extended to Provincetown in 1873, transporting iced fish to New York and Boston. Upward of four trains a day departed from the two-room station, located where the Duarte Motors parking lot is today, two blocks from MacMillan Wharf. But by the early 1900s, Provincetown's sea-driven economy had slowed. Trains stopped running in 1950. Today, although a small fishing industry still exists, tourism is the steam that drives the economy's train.

In 1899 painter Charles W. Hawthorne founded the Cape Cod School of Art. He encouraged his Greenwich Village peers to come north and take advantage of the Mediterranean-like light. By 1916 there were six art schools in town. By the 1920s, Provincetown had become as distinguished an art colony as Taos, East Hampton, and Carmel. Hawthorne encouraged his students to flee the studio and set up easels on the beach, incorporating the ever-changing light into their work. By the time Hawthorne died in 1930, the art scene had a life of its own, and it continues to thrive today.

Artistic expression in Provincetown wasn't limited to painting, though. In 1915 the Provincetown Players, a group of playwrights and actors, staged their works in a small waterfront fish house. In their second season they premiered Eugene O'Neill's *Bound East for Cardiff* before moving to 133 MacDougal Street in New York City, where they are still based.

Provincetown's natural beauty isn't overshadowed by its colorful population. **Province Lands**, the name given to the **Cape Cod National Seashore (CCNS)** within Provincetown's borders, offers bike trails and three remote beaches, where, if you walk far enough, you can find real isolation. Most summertime visitors venture onto the water—to whale-watch, sail, or sailboard in the protected harbor. A different perspective comes with a dune or aerial tour.

For all the history and natural beauty that doesn't change in Provincetown, the town itself is changing—like the rest of the U.S. Condos have sprung up on every empty strand of sand, turning Provincetown into a bedroom community for Bostonians. Nightlife isn't *quite* as vibrant as it once was; more visitors stay in, have dinner parties, and nest with their children. It's more expensive than ever for a new generation of gay youth, and the older generation is getting, well, older. Since gays moved into the mainstream and gay marriage was legalized across the country, it's no longer quite *the* gay destination it used to be. When *Queer Eye* brings its aesthetic into everyone's households, Ellen and Portia's wedding makes the cover of *People* magazine, and a different singer comes out as bisexual every week (it seems), it becomes a little easier for the LGBTQ community to vacation anywhere they want. Cisgendered folks are filling in around the edges and enjoying what gays and artists have long known: this is still one of the most special destinations in North America.

Provincetown is a delight in late spring and fall, when upward of 80,000 summer visitors return to their homes off-Cape. Commercial Street is navigable once again, and most shops and restaurants remain open. Tiny gardens bloom profusely well into October. From January to March, though, the town is given back to the almost 3,000 hardy year-rounders—almost half of whom are unemployed during this time. Although about 80 percent of the businesses close during January and February, there are still enough guest houses (and a handful of restaurants, especially on the weekends) open all winter, luring intrepid visitors with great prices and stark natural beauty. Steel yourself against the wind and take a walk on the beach, attend a reading at the **Fine Arts Work Center**, or curl up with a good book.

GUIDANCE ❄ **Provincetown Chamber of Commerce** (508-487-3424; ptownchamber
.com, provincetowntourismoffice.org), 307 Commercial Street at MacMillan Wharf
and Lopes Square. This is the most informative and helpful chamber on the Cape. They
offer free WiFi, but so do many cafés (see *Where to Eat*).

❄ **Provincetown Business Guild** (508-487-2313; ptown.org), 3 Freeman Street #2.
The guild, established in 1978 to support gay tourism, promotes about 275 mostly gay-
owned businesses.

🐾 ♺ **Province Lands Visitor Center** (508-487-1256; nps.gov/caco), Race Point Road,
CCNS. Open early May to late October. First things first: Climb atop the observation
deck for a 360-degree view of the outermost dunes and ocean. Second things second:
the center offers informative exhibits on Cape history, local flora and fauna, and dune
ecology, along with frequent short films. Organized summer activities include sunset
campfires and storytelling, birding trips, dune tours, and a junior ranger hour.

GETTING THERE *By car:* Provincetown is the eastern terminus of Cape Cod, 63 miles
via Route 6 from the Cape Cod Canal and 128 miles from Boston and Providence. It
takes almost 2½ hours to drive to Provincetown from Boston.

By boat from Boston: **Boston Harbor Cruises** (617-227-4321; bostonharborcruises
.com) operates daily fast boats (90 minutes) from Boston's Long Wharf to Provincetown from mid-June to mid-October. Round-trip $$$$$+.

Bay State Cruise Company, Inc. (877-783-3779 seasonally on MacMillan Wharf;
617-748-1428 on Boston's Commonwealth Pier, Northern Avenue; baystatecruisecom
pany.com) offers daily trips late May to mid-October. Round-trip $$$$$+.

By boat from Plymouth: **Plymouth-to-Provincetown Express Ferry** (508-747-2400),
State Pier (next to the *Mayflower*) in Plymouth and at Fisherman's Wharf in Provincetown. The ferry schedule is designed so that you leave Plymouth at 10 AM, spend five
hours in Provincetown, and are back in Plymouth by 6 PM. You even get a narrated
history of Plymouth Harbor as the boat pulls away from shore. Trips daily early June to
mid-September. Round-trip $$$$$, bicycles $$.

By bus: The **Plymouth & Brockton** bus line (508-746-0378; p-b.com) connects Provincetown with Hyannis and other Cape towns, as well as with Boston's Logan Airport.
The bus stops behind the chamber of commerce; purchase tickets on board. There are
five buses a day in summer, two in the off-season from early September to early May.
Travel time to Boston is 3½ hours and requires a bus change in Hyannis. $$$$ one-way.

FERRY DEPARTS PROVINCETOWN FOR BOSTON

By air: **Cape Air** (508-771-6944; flyca-peair.com) provides extensive year-round service from Boston to Provincetown Municipal Airport. The flight takes 25 minutes, and the airport is 3 miles north of town. Summer fares from around $200 round-trip.

GETTING AROUND *By car:* The first exit off Route 6 (Snail Road) leads to the East End. (Street numbers in the East End are higher than in the West End.) Take the second exit for MacMillan Wharf and Town Hall, where street numbers are in the 300s. Shank Painter Road, the third exit, leads to the West End. Follow Route 6 to its end for Herring Cove Beach. A right off Route 6 takes you to the Province Lands section of the CCNS.

PROVINCETOWN TROLLEY

Provincetown's principal thoroughfare, Commercial Street, is narrow, one-way, and 3 miles long. When you want to drive from one end of town to another quickly, use Bradford Street, parallel to Commercial. There are no sidewalks on Bradford, known as Back Street in the days when Provincetown had only a front and a back street. About 40 narrow cross streets connect Commercial and Bradford.

Finding free on-street parking is like that proverbial needle-in-a-haystack thing. There are municipal lots next to the Pilgrim Monument off Bradford Street; on Mac-Millan Wharf; off Commercial Street; off Bradford Street; and at the end of Commercial Street near the Breakwater.

🚍 *By shuttle:* The excellent **Provincetown Shuttle** (800-352-7155; capecodtransit .org) operates from late May to late September. Flag it down anywhere along the route: among other places, it stops at Herring Cove Beach, Beech Forest, the Provincetown Inn, and MacMillan Wharf before heading down Route 6A to Dutra's Market in North Truro. $.

🚍 *Getting across the harbor by boat:* **Flyer's Boat Shop and Rental** (508-487-0898; flyersboats.com), 131A Commercial Street. From mid-June to late September, a shuttle takes bathers and picnickers to and from remote, unspoiled Long Point (see *Green Space*). $$.

By trolley: **Provincetown Trolley, Inc.** (508-487-9483; provincetowntrolley.com), Commercial Street at Town Hall. These frequent 40-minute, narrated sight-seeing trips depart May through October. You can get on and off at the Provincetown Art Association & Museum (see *To See*); the Provincetown Inn next to the breakwater (see *Green Space*) at the western end of Commercial Street; and the Province Lands Visitor Center (see *Guidance*). $$.

Touring by foot: **Historic Walking Tour of Provincetown** (508-487-1310; pil-grim-monument.org). Led by a staff member from the Pilgrim Monument and Provincetown Museum (PMPM) and one from the CCNS, this 90-minute tour is a great introduction to art and architecture, to whalers and writers. Please, don't be too cool to take a walking tour in Provincetown. Call for the schedule in July through August. Reservations required. $$ (includes admission to the PMPM).

By taxi: Call **Cape Cab** (508-487-2222; capecabtaxi.com) to arrange a pickup. No, not that kind.

A PERFECT SUMMER DAY IN PROVINCETOWN

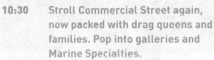

7:00	Stroll Commercial Street when everyone is still sleeping.
8:00	Flip a coin for breakfast at Devon's or Café Edwige.
9:30	Walk on the bayside flats during low tide.
10:30	Stroll Commercial Street again, now packed with drag queens and families. Pop into galleries and Marine Specialties.
12:30	Climb to the top of Pilgrim Monument or visit PAAM.
2:00	Enjoy a late brunch at Victor's or lunch at Ross' Grill.
2:45	Cruise the National Seashore backside dunes with Art's Dune Tours.
4:15	Get a delectable treat from Wired Puppy.
5:00	Circle the serene Beech Forest Trail, or go to the Boatslip Tea Dance (if you're a dancer like me or a gay guy).
7:30	Watch the sunset at Herring Cove Beach.
8:00	Enjoy a late dinner at Saki Sushi, the Mews, or Front Street, or catch a live show.

MEDIA The *Provincetown Banner* (508-487-7400; provincetown.wickedlocal.com) will give you a sense of the town's local, fascinating politics as well as the latest on what to do. The weekly *Provincetown Magazine* (provincetownmagazine.net) also has great information. Tune in to **Outermost Radio** at **92.1 FM** (508-487-2619; womr.org).

PUBLIC LIBRARY

MORE WEBSITES Check out province townforwomen.com and provincetown .com.

PUBLIC RESTROOMS ❄ Look behind the chamber of commerce, at the library (356 Commercial Street), at Whaler's Wharf (237 Commercial Street), and at Provincetown Town Hall (260 Commercial Street).

PUBLIC LIBRARY ❄ ✎ ⊤ **Provincetown Public Library** (508-487-7094; province townlibrary.org), 356 Commercial Street (at Center Street). This magnificent facility is housed in the former Heritage Museum; it's never looked so good!

MEDICAL EMERGENCY ❄ **Outer Cape Health Services** (508-487-9395; outer-cape.org), 49 Harry Kemp Way.

COMMERCIAL STREET, WHERE LIFE MEETS ART

Lyme disease. Ticks carry this disease, which has flulike symptoms and may result in death if left untreated. Immediately and carefully remove any ticks that might have migrated from dune grasses to your body. Better yet, wear long pants, tuck pants into socks, and wear long-sleeved shirts whenever possible when hiking. Avoid hiking in grassy and overgrown areas of dense brush.

✳ To See

Listings are organized from east to west.
Commercial Street. Until Commercial Street was laid out in 1835, the shoreline served as the town's main thoroughfare. Because houses had been oriented toward the harbor, many had to be turned around or the "front" door had to be reconstructed to face the new street. Some houses, however, still remain oriented toward the shore.

✳ ⛵ **Provincetown Art Association & Museum (PAAM)** (508-487-1750; paam .org), 460 Commercial Street. Under the forward-thinking stewardship of director Chris McCarthy, PAAM is basking in the glow of a stunning new building and exhibit spaces. One of the country's foremost small museums, PAAM includes five sparkling galleries that feature established and emerging artists. Organized in 1914 by artists to "promote education of the public in the arts, and social intercourse between artists and laymen," PAAM has included Ambrose Webster, Milton Avery, and Marsden Hartley among its members. Selections from the permanent collection of 2,000-plus works change frequently. Special exhibitions, juried shows, and other events

PROVINCETOWN ART ASSOCIATION MUSEUM

HISTORY WAS MADE HERE

Old Harbor Lifesaving Station (508-487-1256; nps.gov/caco), Race Point Beach. Open July and August. This 1898 structure, one of nine original Lifesaving Service stations on the Outer Cape, was floated by barge from Chatham to its present location in 1977—just in the nick of time. One year later the great nor'easter of 1978 blew through and wiped out its original location. The Lifesaving Service, precursor to the Coast Guard, rescued crews from ships wrecked by shallow sandbars and brutal nor'easters. The boat room contains the original equipment, but on Thursday at 6 pm (confirm the time before going), hourlong demonstrations are given using the old-fashioned techniques. "Surfmen" launch a rescue line to the wrecked ship and haul in the distressed sailors one at a time. Plaques lining the boardwalk to the museum explain how the service worked. In June and July there are also "breeches buoy rescue reenactments" conducted on Thursday evenings. Donation suggested, and you'll have to pay to park at Race Point Beach.

MACMILLAN WHARF

are sponsored throughout the year. The bookstore specializes in the local art colony. $; free on Friday evening.

MacMillan Wharf. By 1800 Provincetown was one of the country's busiest seaports; 50 years later it was the second-largest whaling port. By the 1880s, when cod fishing reached its peak and Provincetown boasted the Cape's largest population, MacMillan Wharf was just one of 56 wharves jutting into the harbor. (MacMillan Wharf, built in 1873, was originally called Old Colony Wharf after the railroad that met Boston packets, but was ultimately named for native son Adm. Donald MacMillan, who explored the North Pole with Adm. Robert Peary.) The town bustled with herring canning, cod curing, whaling, and fishing. Although only a few wharves are still standing, MacMillan Wharf remains true to its original purpose: Even though the fishing industry has recently suffered because of overfishing, some boats still unload their afternoon catch here. And instead of whaling ships, the wharf now is lined with whale-watching boats. The view of town from the end of the pier has always been expansive, and with its recent $2 million renovation, it's more impressive than ever.

✍ ⚓ **Expedition Whydah** (508-487-8899; whydah.com), 16 MacMillan Wharf. Open mid-May through October. This museum is devoted to chronicling the story of the *Whydah*, the only pirate ship ever salvaged. It sank 1,500 feet offshore from Wellfleet's Marconi Beach on April 26, 1717, and Cape Codder Barry Clifford discovered it in 1984. $$; children under 6, free.

They also have a new (in summer 2016) **Whydah Pirate Museum** that's more of an interactive science museum located at 674 Route 28 in West Yarmouth .

❋ **Provincetown Town Hall** (508-487-7000; provincetown-ma.gov), 260 Commercial Street. Constructed in 1886, the building serves as the seat of local government and community agencies. The wonderful auditorium is also used for concerts and lectures. Look for an art collection throughout and for the Works Progress Administration

EXPEDITION WHYDAH

(WPA)–era murals of farmers and fishermen by Ross Moffett and a portrait by Charles Hawthorne.

Pilgrim bas-relief, Bradford Street, behind Town Hall. Sculptor Cyrus Dalin's memorial commemorates the *Mayflower* Compact, which has been called the "first American act in our history." After traveling from England for almost two months, the *Mayflower* sat in the harbor until the compact was drawn up. No one was allowed to go ashore until William Bradford signed the document, attesting to his willingness to abide by laws. One relief memorializes the five Pilgrims who died before reaching Plymouth. (Three Pilgrims are buried near the center of town.) The other relief contains the text of the compact and the names of the 41 people who signed it

✳ ✄ ↑ **Pilgrim Monument and Provincetown Museum** (508-487-1310; pilgrimmonument.org), 1 High Pole Hill Road, off Winslow Street from Bradford Street. Open April through November. The 252-foot monument (the tallest all-granite U.S. monument) commemorates the Pilgrims' first landing in Provincetown on November 11, 1620, and their five-week stay in the harbor while searching for a good place to settle. President Theodore Roosevelt laid the cornerstone in 1907, and President Taft dedicated it in 1910. Climb the 116 stairs of the monument—modeled after the Torre del Mangia in Siena, Italy—for a panoramic view of the Outer Cape. On a clear day you can see 42 miles to Boston.

Photo by Lynette Molnar

PILGRIM MONUMENT

DUNE SHACKS

Dune shacks, beyond the end of Snail Road. In the dunes between Race Point and High Head in North Truro, along 2 miles of ridges and valleys, stand a line of weather-beaten dune shacks. Constructed between 1935 and 1950 of driftwood and scavenged materials, the shacks are the subject of local legend. Over the years, notable writers and artists have called them home for weeks, months, even years: among the tenants have been Jack Kerouac, e. e. cummings, Norman Mailer, Jackson Pollock, poet Harry Kemp, and Eugene O'Neill.

When the CCNS was created in 1961, the federal government set up 25-year or lifelong leases with squatters who were living in the shacks. (Only one of the inhabitants held a clear title to the land.) Some shacks are still occupied. In 1985, Joyce Johnson, a dune dweller since the early 1970s, founded the Peaked Hill Trust to oversee some of the shacks. Members of the trust can win stays through a lottery system; write to P.O. Box 1705, Provincetown, MA 02657, for membership information (or try thecompact.org). Since Province Lands was added to the National Register of Historic Places in 1989, the maintenance and fate of most of the historic shacks have fallen to the National Park Service. At this point, policies are decided from season to season. The park service still sets aside a few shacks, though, for an artist-in-residence program.

I've won weeklong stays in a shack owned by Hazel Hawthorne Werner. On my first visit, it took until the fifth day to shake the first thought that came to my mind after returning to the shack from a walk: I wonder who called while I was out? Remarkable. Remarkable that the shack felt so much like home and remarkable that it was such a deeply ingrained response to being away. I wrote many other impressions but didn't produce anything approaching Cynthia Huntington's *The Salt House*, which she wrote over many, many months of living in that shack. It's well worth reading.

There are a few off-road parking spots at the end of Snail Road. Take the short woodland trail and hike up the first steep dune, then over the next two crests; the shacks will appear in the distance. You can also reach the shacks by walking east from Race Point Beach. Remember, however, that most shacks are still occupied, and people live out there for privacy, to pursue the creative process uninhibited, to contemplate in isolation.

One wing of the museum is devoted to early Pilgrim travails: the *Mayflower*'s first landing, finding corn and fresh water, the unsuccessful search for a place to settle. The other wing contains dioramas and changing exhibits dedicated to a whaling captain's life ashore, the birth of modern theater, shipwrecks, dolls and toys, the Lower Cape and the Outer Cape, and local art. Parking fee of $$ includes one paid museum admission and is good for the day. Beware: Your car will be towed if you linger or park illegally. Check out their walking tours, too; see *Getting Around*. $–$$.

❋ **Universalist Meetinghouse** (508-487-9344; uumh.org), 236 Commercial Street. This 1847 Greek Revival church contains trompe l'oeil murals (by Carl Wendte, who painted similar murals for Nantucket's Unitarian Universalist Church), a Sandwich glass chandelier, and pews made with Provincetown pine. The pews are decorated with medallions carved from whales' teeth.

Pilgrim plaque, at the western end of Commercial Street. Provincetown's version of Plymouth Rock—a plaque in the middle of a landscaped traffic circle—commemorates the Pilgrims' landing.

SCENIC DRIVES You must drive out Race Point Road from Route 6 and around Province Lands.

✳ To Do

BICYCLING & RENTALS Province Lands. Eight miles of hilly paved trails—around ponds, cranberry bogs, and sand dunes—wind through Province Lands' 4,000 acres. Spur trails lead to Herring Cove and Race Point Beaches (see *Green Space*). Access is from Race Point Road near Route 6. There are parking areas at the Beech Forest Trailhead (see *Green Space*), Province Lands Visitor Center (see *Guidance*), and Race Point and Herring Cove Beaches. That covers the logistics. What it doesn't cover is this: Whatever you do, don't miss cruising around here. It's glorious and will be a highlight of your trip.

Rentals. Shops are open mid-April to mid-October, and bike rentals cost $$ for up to two hours, $$$ daily, depending on what kind of bike you get. **Ptown Bikes** (508-487-8735; ptownbikes.com), 42 Bradford Street, is my favored outfitter; **Gale Force Bikes** (508-487-4849; galeforcebikes.com), 144 Bradford Street Extension, is on the western edge of town.

BOAT EXCURSIONS & RENTALS Bay Lady II (508-487-9308; sailcapecod.com), 9 MacMillan Wharf. Trips mid-May to mid-October. These two-hour harbor sails into Cape Cod Bay are aboard traditionally gaff-rigged schooners. It's a really relaxing way to see the area. $$$.

Flyer's Boat Rental (508-487-0898; flyersboats.com), 131A Commercial Street. Open mid-May through September. Flyer's has been renting boats (hourly, daily) since 1965: Sunfish, sloops, kayaks, and powerboats. Sailing instruction is also offered by reservation.

See also **Provincetown Aquasports** under *Kayaks*.

FISHING Surf casting is great on **Race Point Beach** (see *Green Space*) in the early morning or after sunset. Nonresidents are not permitted to shellfish.

Beth Ann Charters (508-487-0034; nelsonsbaitandtackle.com; provincetowncharterfishing.com), MacMillan Wharf. Open daily late May to mid-October. The owners of Nelson's Bait and Tackle, who reluctantly closed in 2015, operate this charter business with enthusiasm. Their fishing excursions with Captain Rich

EXPLORING THE DUNES

Art's Dune Tours (508-487-1950; artsdunetours.com), 4 Standish Street at Commercial Street, offers trips mid-April to mid-November. The Costa family has expertly led tourists on these narrated, hourlong, off-road 4x4 trips through the CCNS dunes since 1946. I highly recommend taking one. The GMC Suburbans stop at least once (on the beach or atop a high dune) for photos, so you can take in the panoramic views. $$$; reservations necessary for sunset trips.

COMMERCIAL STREET

get rave reviews heading out for striped bass, fluke, or blue fin tuna. $$$$$+

See also **Flyer's Boat Rental** under *Boat Excursions*.

FOR FAMILIES ♂ **Playgrounds** are located at both ends of town: at Bradford and Howland Streets (East End) and at Bradford and Nickerson Streets (West End).

FITNESS CLUBS ✳ **Mussel Beach Health Club** (508-487-0001; musselbeach.net), 35 Bradford Street. The club has state-of-the-art equipment, free weights, and cardiovascular equipment. Day use: $$.

✳ **Provincetown Gym** (508-487-2776; ptowngym.com), 81 Shank Painter Road. The cardiovascular machines and free weights here might feel less intimidating for women than Mussel Beach. Day use: $$.

KAYAKS & PADDLEBOARDS **Provincetown Aquasports** (508-413-9563; ptown aquasports.com), 333 (rear) Commercial Street #1. Open seasonally. Enthusiastic renters of kayaks and paddleboards.

See also **Flyer's Boat Rental** under *Boat Excursions*.

BAY LADY II

SPECIAL PROGRAMS ✳ **Fine Arts Work Center** (508-487-9960; fawc.org), 24 Pearl Street. The center was founded in 1968 by a group of writers, artists, and patrons, including Robert Motherwell, Hudson Walker, Stanley Kunitz, and Myron Stout. And its intent was to provide a place for emerging artists to pursue independent work within a sympathetic community of their peers. In 1972 the center purchased Days Lumber Yard, where artists have worked in small studios since 1914. (Frank Days Jr., who had been concerned about the plight of artists, built 10 studios over his lumberyard. And Charles Hawthorne was one of the first tenants in 1914.) Writing and visual arts residencies, which include a monthly stipend and materials allowance, run October through April. Twenty candidates are chosen from a pool of about 1,000. Year-round readings, seminars, workshops, and exhibits are open to the public. There's also a great summer program for creative writing and visual arts, which offers weeklong and weekend workshops in printmaking, sculpture, fiction writing, and the like. Keep your eyes open for talks, presentations, and readings by visiting instructors like Kate Clinton. (File under fun trivia: Annie Dillard once completed a residency here.) Donations.

✳ ♂ **Provincetown Museum School** (508-487-1750; paam.org), 460 Commercial Street at Bangs Street. Programs run year-round; galleries open in summer. Printmaking, painting, monotypes, and watercolor are just some of the classes taught by notable artists at the Provincetown Art Association & Museum. Children's classes are also offered; some courses are accredited.

WHALE-WATCHING

For many people, seeing whales breech and frolic is one of the most exhilarating and sacred things they've ever done. There's something so inspiring about seeing these enormous and ancient creatures so close to the boat. If you've never done it, put it on your short list. On my most recent trip, the waters were thick with mothers and calves breeching in unison all around us. Even the naturalists were awed!

Located just 8 miles from Provincetown, the fertile feeding grounds of Stellwagen Bank attract migrating finback and humpback whales. Although the area was designated the country's first National Marine Sanctuary in 1992, the government's attempts to control the ocean's intricate ecosystem don't always work out as planned. For instance, whales feed on sand lance, which thrive when herring populations are small. (Herring eat sand lance larvae.) But since the government began protecting dwindling stocks of herring, the number of sand lance larvae has decreased. Some naturalists theorize that humpbacks are heading elsewhere in search of more abundant food supplies. Whale sightings vary each season. Some summers, sightings are a dime a dozen (although it never feels that blasé);

WHALE WATCHING

Photo by Lynette Molnar

other times, not so much. Although whale-watching outfits guarantee sightings (in the form of a free voucher for another trip), you may not have another afternoon to spare. Don't wait, as readers Doug and Lucyna Robertson did, until the last day of your trip. As they wrote to me, "d'oh!"

Most whale-watch cruises last about 3½ hours and have an on-board naturalist. Bring a sweater (even in summer) and seasickness pills if you think you'll need them. If you are prone

Center for Coastal Studies (508-487-3622; 800-826-9300 for whale-watching; coastalstudies.org), 115 Bradford Street. This independent, nonprofit, membership-supported institution is dedicated to research, public education, and conservation programs for the coastal and marine environments. Among other things, researchers study the endangered right whale (there are only about 350 to 400 in the world) and maintain the largest population database of humpback whales in the Gulf of Maine. They have raised important environmental questions about the overall health of Cape Cod Bay. The center is also the only East Coast organization authorized to disentangle whales trapped in fishing gear. Educational offerings include whale-watching aboard a Dolphin Fleet boat (see the "Whale-Watching" sidebar under *Beaches*).

❋ ✇ **Provincetown Community Center** (Provincetown Recreation Department, 508-487-7097; provincetown-ma.gov), 44 Bradford Street. In addition to holding classes sponsored by the Provincetown Recreation Department, the center has a weight room, martial arts classes, dance classes, and yoga classes.

to seasickness, do not stand out on the bow of the boat. Also, check the chamber of commerce brochure rack (see *Guidance*) or check with your lodging for money-saving coupons.

Dolphin Fleet Whale Watch (508-240-3636; whalewatch.com), MacMillan Wharf. Trips mid-April through October. On-board scientists, who will fill you with dozens of interesting facts, hail from the Center for Coastal Studies. $$$$.

Before or after your trip, stop by the **Stellwagen Bank National Marine Sanctuary** (781-545-8026; stellwagen.noaa.gov), 205 Commercial Street at Carver Street. There's a small exhibit with touch-screen computers offering images and information about local marine life, as well as two "video-scopes" that allow you to look into the underwater world of Massachusetts Bay. Free.

See also **Center for Coastal Studies** under *To Do*.

SWIMMING POOL ❉ **Provincetown Inn** (508-487-9500; provincetowninn.com), 1 Commercial Street. The outdoor, Olympic-sized pool is free and open seasonally (yes, the pool is free but you may spend some cash at the on-site bar and grill).

See also **Boatslip Beach Club** under *Entertainment*.

TENNIS Town courts are located at **Motta Field** off Winslow Street.

Provincetown Tennis Club (508-487-9574; provincetowntennis.com), 288 Bradford Street. Open May through October. Clay and hard courts.

❉ Green Space

BEACHES After you look at a map or take an airplane tour to see the long spit of sand arching around the harbor, you won't doubt there are about 30 miles of beach within the CCNS in Provincetown.

PROVINCETOWN HARBOR

Race Point Beach, CCNS, off Route 6. Race Point faces north and gets sun all day; it also has long breaking waves coming in off the Atlantic Ocean. Surrounded by dunes as far as the eye can see, Race Point feels as remote as it is. In spring, with binoculars, you might see whales spouting and breaching offshore. Facilities include lifeguards, showers, and restrooms. Parking late June to early September (and fall weekends) costs $$ daily (permit valid all day at any CCNS beach). The lot generally fills up by 11 AM in summer; there's rarely a charge to park after 5:30 PM.

Herring Cove Beach, CCNS, at the end of Route 6. The water here is calmer and "warmer" (it's all relative, isn't it?) than at Race Point. Because the beach faces due

Photo by Lynette Molnar

HERRING COVE

west, lots of folks gather for spectacular sunsets. (When I get a bonfire permit with friends it's always for Herring Cove.) Facilities include lifeguards, showers, and restrooms. Parking issues are identical to Race Point, above. The beach is also accessible by the Provincetown Shuttle. **Far Land Provisions** (see "Markets in the East and West" sidebar) provides an above-average menu in both quality and range of choices (salads, chowder, seafood, gourmet sandwiches, and more). Free concerts by talented locals on Wednesday and Sunday evenings attract a baby boomer crowd for folky/bluesy tunes and dancing to the oldies.

Photo by Lynette Molnar

LONG POINT LIGHTHOUSE FROM THE SHORE

Harbor Beach is about 3.5 miles long and parallels Commercial Street. Although there is little beach at high tide and few public access points, it's great to walk the flats at low tide. Really great.

Long Point. Long Point is easily accessible by boat in summer (see Flyer's Boat Rental under *Getting Around*), although relatively few people make the effort. You'll be rewarded if you do, but don't forget to pack a picnic and plenty of water. You can walk atop the breakwater (see *Walks*), but it takes about two hours. **Long Point Lighthouse**, at the tip of the spit, was built in 1826, two years before a community of fishermen began to construct homes out there. By 1846 there were 61 families on Long Point, all of whom returned to town during the Civil War. (Two Civil War forts were built on Long Point.) As you walk around town, notice which old houses sport a blue enamel plaque in the shape of a barge. This plaque identifies Long Point houses that were floated across the harbor on barges. (Locals call them "floaters.")

WALKS **Beech Forest Trail**, CCNS, off Race Point Road from Route 6. This sandy, 1-mile trail circles a freshwater pond before steep stairs cut through a forest of beech trees. Warblers migrating from South America pack the area from mid- to late May, but the trail is also beautiful in autumn. It's one of my all-time favorite Cape walks.

LONG POINT LIGHTHOUSE FROM THE HARBOR

WALKING ON WATER (SORTA)

Breakwater, at the western end of Commercial Street (at the Provincetown Inn) and Bradford Street Extension, is a mile-long jetty that serves as a footpath to the secluded Long Point Beach. Watch your footing. Even if you only walk out partway, it's a quintessential place to watch the tide roll in. Once you reach the beach, **Wood End Lighthouse (1872)** is to the north; **Long Point Lighthouse** is at the tip.

BREAKWATER

BEECH FOREST TRAIL

Hatches Harbor. From Herring Cove Beach, at the end of Route 6, walk about 10 minutes toward Race Point Light to the entrance of Hatches Harbor. There's a dike along the back of the salt marsh and tidal estuary that you can walk across.

See also **"Dune shacks"** sidebar under *To See* and **Province Lands** under *To Do*.

✳ Lodging

BED & BREAKFASTS & GUEST HOUSES ✳ ☙ 🐾 **Lands End Inn** (508-487-0706; landsendinn.com), 22 Commercial Street (West End). Run, don't walk, to the Web and make a reservation here. Lands End has some of the best ocean views in town. And it's easily Provincetown's most unusual place to stay. That'll be readily apparent as you

If you care about where you stay, don't go to Provincetown in summer without reservations. If you must wait until the last minute, there are often vacancies midweek in July. Most places have lengthy minimum-night stays during special events and holiday weekends—again, reserve early. (Rates for holiday weekends are always higher than I've reported.) Because the East End tends to be quieter than the West End, I've indicated where each lodging is located, unless it's in the middle of town. All guest houses included below welcome everyone, gay and straight, although there are always more gay visitors in the summer.

walk up the hidden path, catching glimpses of turrets and decks. (No description can really prepare you.) It's a visual feast, chock-full of Victoriana, woodcarvings, stained glass, and Oriental rugs atop floral carpets. Built in 1904, the inn offers 16 rooms and two apartments; the tower rooms and loft suite are spectacularly decorated and situated. Most theme rooms have access to decks; some rooms sleep four. It's all very tranquil and attracts a very diverse clientele. Be sure to return for wine, cheese, and beer in the afternoons; it's wonderfully relaxing since there is so much outdoor

space. Expanded continental breakfast. $$$–$$$$$.

❄ ☁ 🐾 **Gabriel's at The Ashbrooke Inn** (508-487-3232; gabriels.com), 102 Bradford Street. My other favorite place to stay in town, this well-established guest house has 17 units (individually owned condos, to be exact) in the heart of town. It's hard to beat them for quality of offerings and service. It's a first-rate place that features courtyards with five levels of deck and lush landscaping. Units are chock-full of amenities like flat-screen TVs, fireplaces, and Jacuzzis. Families and those traveling with pets

LANDS END INN

will be particularly happy here. Full or expanded continental breakfast, depending on the time of year. $$–$$$.

❋ **White Porch** (508-364-2549; whiteporchinn.com), 7 Johnson Street. This completely remodeled guest house and carriage house burst onto the scene in the late 2000s, and I couldn't be happier about it. The nine soothing and sophisticated rooms ooze a contemporary beach aesthetic and have been updated with iPod docking stations, flat-screen TVs, and luxe bedding. It's all quite stylin.' Although you might be tempted to cocoon here (at least you girls out there), gather for drinks with the gang on the front porch. In- and off-season, it's a very mixed guest house, with all welcome, of course. Expanded continental breakfast. $–$$$.

❋ **Sage Inn & Lounge Provincetown** (508-487-6424; sageinnptown.com), 336 Commercial Street. With a boutique-style intimacy, environmentally-friendly practices, luxurious and modern rooms, and farm-to-table small plates at their lounge . . . the Sage rules the roost—hands down. Super welcoming and centrally located, Sage delivers a lovely experience throughout. Hang out on the pleasant patio, borrow some beach chairs and sit in the bay as the tide goes out, or take advantage of amenities shared with and through other properties (like a pool, yoga, and bonfires). The Sage also operate a recommended 12-person culinary school in the off-season.

❋ 🐾 **Benchmark Inn** (508-487-7440; benchmarkinn.com), 6 Dyer Street. Hospitality has been redefined by the Swiss innkeepers who purchased the inn in the early 2000s. Their seven rooms and penthouse are welcoming and upscale. Service is supreme (think nightly turndown), amenities are top-notch (think marble bathrooms), and the aesthetic is simple but elegant with clean lines. Fireplaces, wet bars, outdoor space, and fresh flowers are the norm. Extended continental breakfast included. $$–$$$$.

The Brass Key (508-487-9005; brasskey.com), 67 Bradford Street. Open April through December. More like a luxurious private enclave—fenced in and gated—the Brass Key catapulted Provincetown accommodations to new heights when it opened. Purchased by the Crowne Pointe Inn in the late 2000s, all 43 rooms surrounding the enclosed pool and courtyard are completely different from one another. In addition to being elegant and sophisticated, rooms have vaulted ceilings, working fireplaces, whirlpool baths, upscale amenities, nightly turndown, and antiques. Some have balconies; all have access to a widow's walk and three living rooms. An expansive continental breakfast buffet is served in the country inn–style Gatehouse. No children. $$–$$$$+.

❋ **The Red Inn** (508-487-7334; 866-473-3466; theredinn.com), 15 Commercial Street (West End). Soothing and sophisticated, the Red Inn makes others green with envy. Not only is the waterfront location almost unequaled (sunrises are spectacular and there are semiprivate waterfront decks), but the accommodations (three rooms, two suites, and two residences) are worthy of design and comfort awards as well. A bed of down pillows (and 600–thread count sheets) will cradle your body as a tranquil color palette lulls your spirit. Two waterfront "residences" are absolutely stunning, if you can afford them. But as my friend Tim said after a multinight stay, "It can be noisy from 6 PM until 11 PM while the restaurant is in full swing, and it has relatively few amenities for the price point." Still, he would return for another stay. No children. Rooms $$$–$$$$, residences $$$$$+.

Eben House (508-487-0386; ebenhouse.com), 90 Bradford Street. Known as the Fairbanks Inn until 2015, when it was renovated from stem to stern, this centrally located, Federal-style 1770s sea captain's house was the first house in town to have indoor plumbing. In the 1800s it was owned by the town's

THE RED INN

wealthiest individual, David Fairbanks, who began Seamen's Bank. Today, its fine pedigree is still readily apparent. Although I was unable to peek inside the guest rooms during my summer research sojourn, I feel quite comfortable recommending it without hesitation. Breakfast included. $$–$$$.

❋ 🐾 **The Inn at Cook Street** (508-487-3894; innatcookstreet.com), 7 Cook Street (East End). Owners John Jay and Patrick operate a mixed house (gay, straight, men, women), which is just the way they like it. The gracious 1836 Greek Revival sea captain's house offers four rooms, two suites, and two cottages. They are all very tasteful and highly recommended. Pick your room based on its sleigh bed (Garden Suite), how much sun it gets (the Retreat is very bright), or its deck access (some have a private deck). Gas grills in the private, shady backyard are enticing and a rare amenity. Full breakfast. $$–$$$.

❋ 🐾 🐾 **Tucker Inn** (508-487-0381; thetuckerinn.com), 12 Center Street. This cozy eight-room B&B, dating to 1872, is one of the most comfy, welcoming, and well-priced places to stay in town, thanks to owner Howard Burchman. He's constantly upgrading the offerings with things like flat-screen TVs and little gardens. Rooms are both soothing and simply decorated. One of the big pluses: The inn also offers arguably the best full breakfast in town, including eggs any style any morning, served on the brick patio in warm weather. Take time to hang out in the hot tub or relaxing garden and I bet you'll return. Inquire about the nice little cottage, which rents weekly. The inn is a mixed house of gay, straight, men, women. (Still, like most other places, it's more gay than straight.) $–$$.

Inn at 7 Central (508-487-8855; innat7central.com), 7 Central Street. Open April to late October. This is a great spot. Centrally located, this completely renovated, contemporary guest house offers something that most do not: Each room has a private entrance and most have a private balcony. The shared courtyard deck is also relaxing and convivial. In-season guests are about two-thirds men, one-third women; off-season, it's evenly divided between LGBTQ and cisgendered folks. Breakfast included. $$–$$$.

APARTMENTS, COTTAGES, & STUDIOS ❄🐾 ❦ **Bay Shore, 77 Commercial Street, and Chandler House** (508-487-9133; bayshorechandler.com), 493 Commercial Street at Howland Street (East End). The six-building complex boasts 20 beachside units clustered around landscaped grounds. (Units across the street have access to the lawn and beach.) Most of the 25 units have a private deck or patio and a large picture window; all have a well-equipped kitchen; a few have a fireplace. The traditional exteriors belie individually and newly decorated interiors. I particularly like the Chandler House units, more contemporary and bright. All of these have a fireplace and "very good" or "spectacular" views. Although this is a condo complex, the managers keep standards consistent and high. Weekly rentals in summer; off-season $–$$ nightly.

❄ **Watermark Inn** (508-487-0165; watermark-inn.com), 603 Commercial Street at Wiley Street (East End). These 10 contemporary suites are right at the water's edge. They feature triangular gable windows, skylights, spacious living areas, and either a full kitchen or a kitchenette. (Two rooms have a fireplace.) Six suites have sliding glass doors that open out onto private decks—perfect for when high tide laps at the deck. It's a 20-minute walk from town, and they feature a rarity: on-site parking. Weekly and nightly rentals in summer; off-season $–$$$ nightly.

❄ ✑ **The Masthead** (508-487-0523; themasthead.com), 31–41 Commercial Street (West End). At the far end of the West End, about a 15-minute walk from the center of town, The Masthead offers a superb variety of distinctly "old Provincetown" apartments, cottages, and rooms. The neatly landscaped complex, operated by the Ciluzzi family since 1959, has a boardwalk with lounge chairs and access to the 450-foot private beach below. Each cottage has a large picture window facing the water. Units, in buildings more than 100 years old, have fully equipped kitchens, low ceilings, pine paneling, and Early American furnishings that

WATERMARK INN

THE MASTHEAD

are dated but nonetheless comfortable. Although most units can accommodate four people, one sleeps eight. It's a great place for families; children under 12 stay free. $$$–$$$$+.

Captain Jack's Wharf (508-487-1450; captainjackswharf.com), 73A Commercial Street at West Vine Street (West End). Open late May to late October. On a rustic old wharf, these 15 colorfully painted bohemian apartments (condos, actually) transport you back to Provincetown's early days as an emerging art colony. Many units have whitewashed interiors with skylights and lots of windows looking onto the harbor. Some first-floor units have narrow cracks between the planked floorboards—you can see the water beneath you! I particularly like Australis, a two-story unit with a spiral staircase and more than 1,000 square feet of space. The wharf is strewn with bistro tables, pots of flowers, and Adirondack chairs. Weekly rentals; $–$$$ off-season.

🐾 **White Horse Inn** (508-487-1790; whitehorseinnprovincetown.com), 500 Commercial Street at Daggett Lane (East End). Call to find out which months the inn is open. This low-key, artsy hostelry has been taking in guests since 1963,

intent on providing clean, comfortable rooms at good prices. Mary Martin presides over six studio apartments that have been individually decorated with an eclectic, bohemian flair. Some are light and airy; some are dark and cozy. All defy description—although one bathroom is truly "postmodern nautical." Suffice it to say each is a work of art in progress. Although the 12 guest rooms are basic (most with a shared bath), they are filled with local art from the past 30 years. They're a real find and are very popular with Europeans. No credit cards. $ rooms, $$ studios.

MOTELS 🐾 **The Foxberry Inn** (508-487-8583; thefoxberryinn.com), 29 Bradford Street Extension (West End). Open mid-April through October. You're in very good hands here: Owner John Gagliardi recently came out of retirement (you can't keep a good Provincetown man down) to restore this once-vacated motel. At the end of Bradford, within a stone's throw of sunset views over the magical moors, these 12 clean and very stylish rooms are a good value. $$.

👑 🐾 **Surfside Hotel & Suites** (508-487-1726; surfsideinn.cc), 543

THE FOXBERRY INN

Commercial Street at Kendall Lane (East End). Open mid-April through October. Of these two completely renovated buildings, one sits on a private harborfront beach and the other overlooks a large pool. After the complete transformation in 2008, visitors ended up with 88 summery and fresh rooms and three waterfront suites. Each has a small refrigerator and balcony. Inquire about two apartments, which sleep four to six people and have fully equipped kitchens. $$$–$$$$ rooms, $$$$+ suites.

🐾 **Inn at the Moors** (508-487-1342; innatthemoors.com), 59 Provincelands Road (West End). Open mid-May to late October. Perched at the edge of the moors, with unparalleled views of sand, sea, and sky, this 30-unit motel with unrealized potential enjoys a spectacular perch (albeit on the other side of the parking lot). Upper-deck rooms, as you might imagine, have better views. Amenities include a heated pool and parking at your front door. Summer $–$$.

LIGHTHOUSE & MORE 🐾 ✏ **Race Point Lighthouse** (855-722-3959; racepoint lighthouse.net). Open May through November. After the Coast Guard decommissioned this light in 1972, it stood empty for more than 20 years

before a nonprofit foundation took over. Now that it's renovated, overnight stays in the Keeper's House are wonderful for families and groups. It has three different-sized bedrooms (with a maximum occupancy of 11) that share 1½ baths as well as a living room. Solar energy powers appliances in the kitchen; bring your own food, water, and linens. It's glorious out here—with the Atlantic Great Beach on one side and Hatches Harbor, a tidal estuary with shallow warm water, on the other. First-time visitors tend only to come for one night, but those in the know come for two or three. When you arrive, a volunteer will drive you out to the Keeper's House. Make reservations as early as possible. $–$$.

The remodeled **Whistle House** opened in 2007 and can accommodate eight people in two bedrooms. The only trick? You have to have your own four-wheel drive to get there. Open late May to mid-September.

CAMPGROUNDS 🐾 ✏ **Dunes' Edge Campground** (508-487-9815; thetrustees .org/places-to-visit/cape-cod-islands /dunes-edge-campground.html), off Route 6. Open May through September. Look for a hundred wooded lots, mostly for tents, on the edge of the dunes and within earshot of the highway. As some friends said of a recent visit: "It's a clean, well-kept campground with a family atmosphere and overzealous night watchmen. The sites can feel small if you've got more than one tent. Bike access to downtown with kids is scary because of cycling on Route 6. Ask for sites along the dunes and/or the back of the campground; otherwise, you may hear road traffic."

🐾 **Coastal Acres Camping Court** (508-487-1700; coastalacres.com), West Vine Street Extension. Open April through October. Wooded sites on the western edge of town. No credit cards.

RENTAL HOUSES & COTTAGES **Across the Bay Real Estate** (508-487-8888), 132 Commercial Street. **Coldwell**

A FEW GENERALITIES ABOUT EATING IN PROVINCETOWN

The quality of Provincetown restaurants continues to impress me. In fact, Provincetown has the greatest concentration of fine restaurants of any town on the Cape. You'll have plenty of choices to suit your budget and taste buds. *Instead of listing places in order of preference (as I usually do), listings are from east to west relative to Commercial Street.* Opening and closing months listed here are only a guideline. If you have your heart set on a particular place, call ahead off-season to see if they are open. And always make reservations whenever and wherever you can, especially in summer.

Banker Pat Shultz Real Estate (508-487-9550; patshultz.com), 406 Commercial Street.

❋ Where to Eat

DINING OUT ❋ ✦ ⬩ **Ciro & Sal's** (508-487-6444; ciroandsals.com), 4 Kiley Court (at Commercial Street). Open D. The primary reason to eat here is historical, since it opened as a coffeehouse and sandwich shop for artists in the early 1950s. The ground floor still looks the same as it did back then—cozy with brick and plaster walls and chianti bottles hanging from the low rafters. Chef Larry Luster's extensive Northern Italian menu has traditional signature dishes like veal Marsala and seafood specials. My experiences here have always been "OK," but since Ciro & Sal's is open year-round, that almost qualifies it as a social service agency in my book. $$–$$$$.

❋ **Strangers & Saints** (508-487-1449; strangersandsaints.com), 444 Commercial Street. Open D. I like this place for specialty cocktails and creative apps at the bar before heading elsewhere for the main event (or for that matter, for heading out to nosh at a few places over the course of an evening—as long as it's not high season when that would be practically impossible). The atmosphere is super inviting, as it feels no money was spared on the handsome, warm, and cozy interior, right down to the gorgeous mural. New in 2016, and presided over by

Culinary Institute of America chef Fred Latasa-Nicks, the restaurant is certainly reaching and stretching. $$–$$$.

❋ ⬩ ⬩ **The Mews Restaurant and Café** (508-487-1500; mews.com), 429 Commercial Street (between Kiley and Lovetts Courts). Open D, Sunday brunch. One of Provincetown's most sophisticated restaurants, the beachfront Mews is elegant and romantic, awash in peach tones and bleached woods. Long-time chef Laurence deFreitas offers a popular mixed seafood grill and dishes like seared peppercorn-crusted tuna. Sauces are rich and delicious. Servers are very knowledgeable. The more casual upstairs café, with the same water views and lower prices, also has great burgers, appetizers, salads, and pasta. It's a great place for a before-dinner drink or after-dinner dessert and coffee. (The Mews stocks the largest selection of vodka in New England, by the way.) There's also entertainment in winter. Dine before sunset to better appreciate the water view. Brunch $$, D $$$–$$$$.

Devon's (508-487-4773; devons.org), 31 Bradford Street. Open B, D, mid-May to mid-October. Closed Wednesdays. This little place harbors a big gem of a kitchen. Romantic and cozy, the waterfront eatery excels in contemporary cuisine. Look for dishes like organic, grilled black pearl salmon with miso tamari glaze, soba noodles, and baby bok choy—most dishes nightly rise to this level of creativity and execution. Also come for one of the top three breakfasts in town.

DEVON'S

Sit outside on the enclosed front porch for a fancy omelet, tofu veggie scramble, organic vegan flax seed granola, or blueberry cornmeal pancakes. Arrive early or be prepared to wait. B $–$$, D $$$–$$$$.

🍴 **Edwige at Night** (508-487-2008; edwigeatnight.com), 333 Commercial Street (at Freeman Street). Open D, mid-May to mid-September. With sophisticated cuisine that even surpasses the lovely atmosphere, Edwige is easily one of Provincetown's top places to dine. By night it's one big romantic dinner party, with subdued lighting, solicitous service, and closely spaced tables. The eclectic menu, a fusion of Mediterranean, Asian, and Latin cuisines, changes seasonally. Think duck confit spring rolls, native seafood cake, and *moqueca*, a northern Brazilian dish of scallops, halibut, and shrimp in coconut milk over basmati rice. The food and presentation are fun, the staff colorful, and the salads creative. You can't go wrong here. Edwige also mixes a killer cosmopolitan, concocted from homemade vodkas. $$$–$$$$.

❄ 🦞 🍸 **Napi's** (800-571-6274; napisp-town.com), 7 Freeman Street (at Bradford Street). Open L, D. The important thing about Napi's is their unyielding commitment to year-round service, for which I commend them heartily! Chef-owners Helen and Napi Van Dereck opened this unusual restaurant in 1973 and have filled it chockablock with local art, plants, stained glass, and lively objects to stir your imagination. The eclectic, international menu includes dishes made with Portuguese sausage (linguiça), organic salads, a large selection of vegetarian dishes (try the coconut-crusted tofu), pasta dishes, and

NAPI'S

stir-fry. Health-conscious Napi's will go out of its way to accommodate no-fat, vegan, and low-salt diets. A favorite of local artists, townsfolk, and the "old guard," Napi's is even livelier off-season. Free parking on the premises. D $$–$$$.

♨ ⍋ **Saki Sushi** (508-487-4870; sakiptown.com), 258 Commercial Street (between Ryder and Gosnold Streets). Open D, April through January. If I didn't have to sample a wide range of places, I'd eat here every single night. Seriously. The sushi and Thai entrées are *that* great. The digs are super, too. Paired together, you basically have a culinary moment of Zen housed in a former Methodist church; the preacher's former pulpit is where cocktails are now served. Seems wonderfully fitting for Provincetown. $$–$$$.

♨ ⍋ **Front Street** (508-487-9715; frontstreetrestaurant.com), 230 Commercial Street (between Gosnold and Masonic Streets). Open D, May to early December. One of the Outer Cape's most consistent places, Front Street is often the best eatery in town for the money (depending on whom you talk to). Located in the cozy brick cellar of a Victorian house, it's a convivial place, made more so by small tables placed very closely together, antique booths, and local artwork. Service is provided by unobtrusive, attentive, and longtime waitstaff. Donna Aliperti, chef-owner since opening the restaurant in 1987, reigns over a kitchen creating much-lauded Mediterranean-American fusion. The repertoire of Italian, French, and Continental dishes changes weekly, but signature dishes include herb-crusted rack of lamb, tea-smoked duck, and Gorgonzola-stuffed filet mignon. The wine list is excellent. Leave room for pastry and sous-chef Kathy Cotter's delicious finales. $$$–$$$$.

❄ **Bistro at Crowne Pointe** (508-487-2365; crownepointe.com), 82 Bradford Street. Open D. This bistro (within a hotel-like inn) turns up the heat with excellent and refined dining. From filet mignon and seared duck breast to a specialty hot pot (with shrimp, scallops, and rice noodles) and a seafood stew, dining isn't fly by night. The wine list is excellent. For this kind of cash, I prefer dining inside rather than on the porch. $$$–$$$$.

❄ ⍋ **Victor's** (508-487-1777; victorsptown.com), 175 Bradford Street. Open for brunch, D. This is one hot and hoppin' restaurant; the tapas formula is a perfect concept for Provincetown. Mix and match little plates of stunning palate pleasers like lobster spring rolls, smoked ahi tuna pâté, herbed chicken quesadilla, braised short ribs, mini-burgers, and seafood cakes. We tried them all on repeated trips and registered euphoria each time. The open, airy, contemporary dining room is buzzy and convivial, and warm in the off-season thanks to a central stone fireplace. Kudos to owner Victor Depoalo and chef Christina Spencer. Start off with a specialty cocktail and something from the raw bar. "Sunday's a Drag" here; don't miss it. Brunch $$, D $–$$$.

♨ ✎ **Sal's Place** (508-487-1279; salsplaceofprovincetown.com), 99 Commercial Street (at Cottage Street). Open D, early May to late October. When Sal's reopened in 2016 with a pared-down menu, longtime patrons knew that all would be right with the world. Although the beloved and previous owner, Lora Papetsas, has moved on, Sal's still transports you to an earlier time and place, a space somewhere between Italy and Cape Cod. There's no better to way to spend a summer evening. Reserve a waterside table on the deck covered in grapevines, and enjoy Southern Italian dishes (or "healthy living dishes") while listening to waves lap at the deck pilings. Service is friendly and leisurely; portions are plentiful. $$–$$$.

⍋ **The Red Inn** (508-487-7334; theredinn.com), 15 Commercial Street. Open for brunch, D, April through December. This prime waterfront location is one of the hottest foodie destinations on the

THE RED INN

Cape. Decked out in white linens and soothing colors and perched on water's edge, the beautifully restored old house has sanded floors and huge picture windows—perfectly blending a contemporary aesthetic with a classic one. That about sums up the cuisine, too. The menu exudes finesse: pepper-crusted filet mignon with truffle mashed potatoes, and grilled duck breast with a passion fruit maple glaze. Then there's the specialty rack of lamb with a secret rub of spices. History buffs take note: this circa-1800 inn is a few steps from where the Pilgrims landed in 1620. D $$–$$$$+.

FANIZZI'S BY THE SEA

EATING OUT ❄ ✧ ✧ **Fanizzi's by the Sea** (508-487-1964; fanizzisrestaurant .com), 539 Commercial Street (between Hancock and Kendall Streets). Open L, D, and Sunday brunch. If you find yourself suffering from hunger pangs and lusting for a killer water view, fear not. Fanizzi's is also one of the rare places that serves throughout the afternoon. Enormous portions of comfort cuisine, seafood, and American dishes (from spinach salad to ribs and burgers) are offered at reasonable prices: Try the midday fish-and-chips and the evening buffalo chicken wings. When I consider the combination of price, offerings, execution, and its waterfront location, Fanizzi's is hard to beat. L $–$$, D $$–$$$.

✧ **Café Edwige by Day** (508-487-2008), 333 Commercial Street (at Freeman Street). Open B (call for specific days, like most places), May to mid-October. Proprietor Nancyann Meads has been working her magic since 1974, dishing up lobster Benedict, poppy seed cream Danish, specialty omelets (perhaps with Boursin and asparagus), fruit crêpes, steak and eggs, unbelievable French toast (covered with Fiji apples and toasted walnuts—think more along the lines of a baked casserole), spicy homefries, tofu casserole, and delectable Danish. High-backed booths and small tables fill the lofty second-floor space, bright with skylights. $–$$.

Y **Patio** (508-487-4003; ptownpatio .com), 328 Commercial Street (between Freeman and Standish Streets). Open throughout the day, May to mid-October. I like this "American Grill and Cocktail Bar" because it's outdoors and Provincetown has relatively little streetside dining (or drinking). It's a primo people-watching perch. Then I ate here—and was delightfully surprised at my sushi-grade tuna and my companion's perfectly prepared swordfish. Now I come as much for the food as the people-watching. Dishes $$$.

♨ **Lobster Pot** (508-487-0842; ptown lobsterpot.com), 321 Commercial Street (between Freeman and Standish Streets). Open L through D, April through November. This venerable waterfront institution, in the McNulty family since 1979, feels touristy and the service can be hurried. But the menu features a wide selection of fresh seafood, shore dinners, and truly great clam chowder. Look for the big, neon-red lobster sign and head down the long corridor, past the kitchens, and up the ramp. $$–$$$$.

❋ ♨ **Ross' Grill** (508-487-8878; rossgrillptown.com), 237 Commercial Street (within Whaler's Wharf). Open L, D. Overlooking the harbor from a second-floor vantage point, this casual American grill is a happening place, with good music, a structural steel ceiling, and an exposed kitchen. The menu is simple but very, very good: quite possibly the best burgers in town, duck à l'orange to die for, as well as shellfish risotto, a raw bar, and steak frites. There's also an impressive list of 75 wines by the glass and a dozen international beers. Because this place is tucked away, it feels like you need to be in the know to know, which is fun. L $$, D $$$–$$$$.

❋ **The Canteen** (508-487-3800; the canteenptown.com), 225 Commercial Street. Open L, D (and also B in winter).

From the backyard-style "patio" on the Bay to the wooden indoor tables, this is my kind of place because it feels like we're eating at a friend's house. Where we don't have to help with the dishes! From a miso Ceasar or BLT salad to side dishes like brussel sprouts and fried oysters to mains like a grilled PB&J, lobster roll or kale and linguica, the main question is: why didn't someone think of The Canteen sooner. Choose from a good wine and local beer list too—or sample their few (but primo) specialty cocktails. Dishes $-$$.

♨ **Nor'east Beer Garden** (508-487-2337; thenoreastbeergarden.com), 206 Commercial Street. Open L, D, seasonally. Because of the intersection of price point, delicious fish tacos from the bar menu, lush artisanal cocktails (and "mocktails"), craft beers, and sultry outdoor dining, this is a reliable favorite of mine. $$–$$$.

♨ **Café Heaven** (508-487-9639), 199 Commercial Street (at Carver Street). Open B, L, D, April through November. This very good storefront eatery with high ceilings is always lively, but sometimes it just feels noisy and cramped.

NOR'EAST BEER GARDEN

(Peek in and decide for yourself.) Deservedly popular for late-day breakfasts, Heaven's specialties include create-your-own omelets, sweet cornmeal scones, fluffy banana pancakes, garlicky home fries, and crunchy granola. An extensive lunchtime selection of cold salads and sandwiches reigns midday, while dinner offerings seem to change annually. You can expect build-your-own burgers and pasta dishes and friendly service. B, L $, D $$–$$$.

🦞❄ **Local 186 @ Enzo's** (508-487-7555), 186 Commercial Street. Open L, D. For great burgers and beer, on the outdoor porch or inside, this place is tough to beat. The creative menu features sublime choices like a lamb burger alongside feta tzatziki or Kobe beef alongside poached lobster and aioli. But you can also build your own from a multitude of choices (Kobe beef, turkey, veggie plus sautéed wild mushrooms, fried avocado, and smoked Gruyère—to name just a few). And forget pedestrian onion rings; these folks take it up a notch with onion strings. $–$$.

✑ 🍸 **Bubala's By The Bay** (508-487-0773; bubalas.com), 185 Commercial Street (at Court Street). Open L, D, May through October. Bubala's draws crowds because of its streetside tables and indoor bayside views. It's a moderately priced, fun, high-energy place with OK

CAFÉ HEAVEN

food. Live music, mostly jazz, almost every night. And free parking! L $–$$, D $$–$$$.

🍸 **Jimmy's Hideaway** (508-487-1011; jimmyshideaway.com), 179 Commercial Street (at Carver Street). Open D, mid-April to mid-February. This cozy, casual, and hopping place on the water always seems to draw a crowd. Comfort food reigns on the tavern menu: Think fish-and-chips and meat loaf. Also try the chef's specialty, bouillabaisse. Then again, you can always get a burger ($$). Those are just a few of the reasons that folks come back again and again. D $$–$$$$.

See also **Sage Inn & Lounge Provincetown**, under Lodging.

TAKE-OUT 🦞 ✑ **Mojo's** (508-487-3140), 5 Ryder Street, next to the MacMillan Wharf parking lot. Open L, D, May to mid-October. This clam shack/fry joint

LOCAL 186 AT ENZO'S

MARKETS IN THE EAST AND WEST (AND ONE IN THE MIDDLE)

❋ When you're in the middle of town, head to **Far Land Provisions** (508-487-0045; farlandprovisions.com), 150 Bradford Street (at Conwell Street). And when you need to see another human soul in winter, this is the hub. With or without hot coffee, lunchtime sandwiches with Boar's Head meats are killer. See also Herring Cove Beach.

In the West End, no one does it better than **Relish** (508-487-8077; ptownrelish.com), 93 Commercial Street. It's worth going out of your way for these higher-end sandwiches, prepared salads to go, and amazing desserts—especially cupcakes.

In the East End with parking (!) and open year-round, the upscale **Angel Foods** (508-487-6666; angelfoods.com), 467 Commercial Street, has gourmet fixings that'll cost a pretty penny.

LOCAL MARKETS

offers an extensive selection: fried mushrooms, baskets of fried shrimp or fish, chicken tenders, subs, burgers, Mexican dishes, salads, and vegetarian sandwiches. Take your enormous portions to the beach, pier, or, if you're lucky, to one of a few outdoor tables. Dishes $–$$.

🐟 🍴 **Aquarium Mall** (no phone), 207 Commercial Street. Open seasonally. This little mini-mall is a warren of diverse, inexpensive eateries: Come for quick and good burritos, gelato, Chinese, bagels, and breakfast sandwiches. There's a waterfront bar in the rear.

🍴 **The Red Shack** (508-487-7422), 315A Commercial Street, Lopes Square/MacMillan Wharf. Open L, D, mid-April to mid-October. New in 2008, from a family with longtime ties to Provincetown (see the Mayflower Café and Provincetown Portuguese Bakery), this take-out window offers sandwiches, slices of pizza, hot sausages smothered in sautéed onions and peppers, and very good lobster rolls. It's perfect when you want something quick before the ferry or when you want to keep cruising Commercial Street. Grab a seat in front of town hall or on the wharf. $–$$.

🍴 **Provincetown House of Pizza** (508-487-6655; ptownpizza.com), 50 Bradford Street. Open L, D, mid-April to late November. For fancy and plain pies, baked calzones, pasta, subs, and salads. You could feed an army here for less than most places in town. Two pluses: parking (free) and delivery. $$.

CAFÉS, COFFEE, DESSERT, & MORE
Connie's Bakery (508-487-2167; conniesbakery.com), 205 Commercial Street. Open May through October. Provincetown's morning hub makes unbeatable challah and other breads and pastries—as well as sandwiches and prepared foods to take home.

❋ **Purple Feather Dessert Café** (508-487-9100; thepurplefeather.com), 334

Commercial Street (at Freeman Street). Open for late-night dessert fixes. Just what Provincetown needed! It's a wonder no one thought of this satisfy-the-sweet-tooth idea sooner. Sure they have panini, mac and cheese, and soups when you want to be good. But most everyone gets swept in for the sweets: gelato, homemade chocolates, fancy pies and cakes, cannoli, truffles, specialty fudge . . . you get the idea. Skip dessert at most restaurants and make a beeline here. When the kids aren't looking, check out the XXX-rated adult candy.

Spiritus (508-487-2808), 190 Commercial Street (between Carver and Court Streets). Open really long hours, April to early December. Everyone comes to Spiritus at least once during their time here, and some come every day! If one of the front benches is empty, hang out and do some serious people-watching. This is *the* place to see and be seen after midnight (for guys anyway). Grab a slice of great thin-crust pizza, pop a pie, slurp an ice cream, or down a shake, an orgasmic brownie, or freshly squeezed orange juice. Wooden booths are perfect for rainy or chilly days.

❉ **Joe** (508-487-6656), 170 Commercial Street (between Winthrop and Central Streets). Consistently exceptional coffee. With this big new location (and

STEPPING BACK IN TIME

Provincetown may be filled with second homes and condos purchased by baby boomers dining on $35 entrées and homemade vodkas, but there are still vestiges where you can step back three and more decades. Let's do the time-warp again: head to the **Mayflower Café** (300 Commercial Street) for a quick meal; the **Portuguese Bakery** (299 Commercial Street; see above); **Sal's Place** (99 Commercial Street) for an outdoor, waterside Italian dinner; and the **Porchside Bar** at the Gifford House (9 Carver Street).

JOE

plenty of patio seating), Joe has taken its rightful place as *the* go-to beanery. Speaking of which, they're roasted by two women at Indigo, located in the tiny western Massachusetts town of Florence. There are fine pastries, too.

❉ **Wired Puppy** (508-487-0017; wired puppy.com), 379 Commercial Street (at Pearl Street). Open long hours. Come for strong coffee, sweet treats, and good people-watching.

Provincetown Portuguese Bakery (508-487-1803), 299 Commercial Street (between Standish and Ryder Streets). Open April through October. Short of hopping on a plane to Lisboa, you haven't

WIRED PUPPY

FOR THE BOYZ

The Boatslip Beach Club (508-487-1669; boatslipresort.com), 161 Commercial Street (between Central and Atlantic Streets), is known around the LGBTQ world for its packed, oh-so-gay summertime "Tea Dance" from 4 to 7 PM daily (May to mid-October). Every member of the LGBTQ community should experience the euphoria at least once. Last dance on Labor Day is particularly heady. If you like to dance, be here. You can also rent pool chairs and a towel ($) if you're not staying here, as long as you depart by tea time.

✳ **Atlantic House** (508-487-3821; ahouse.com), 6 Masonic Place, more commonly referred to as the A-House, has three diverse bars: the so-called Macho Bar (a nationally known men's leather bar); the nautically decorated disco Dance Bar; and the Little Bar (more intimate, with a roaring fireplace in the off-season). I'm confident that no other 18th-century house sees such action. Open 365 days a year until 1 AM. Seems like there isn't a gay guy in town who doesn't stop into the A-House off-season. Some credit the A-House with establishing Provincetown's "off-season" versus "closed for the season."

BOATSLIP BEACH CLUB

tried Portuguese breads and pastries unless you've dropped into this classic sense of place: *pasteis de coco*, meat pies, *pasteis de nata* (a custard tart), and *tarte de amêndoa* (almond tart). In summer the ovens are cranking 24 hours a day, and the *mallassadas* (fried dough) flies out faster than they can make it.

Farmers' Market, Ryder Street across from town hall. Great produce and more on Saturdays from mid-May to early December. It's about time that Provincetown got a market like this. Seems a no-brainer now that it's here.

✳ Entertainment

THEATER ✳ **The Provincetown Theater** (508-487-7487; provincetowntheater

PORTUGUESE BAKERY

✳ **Art House Theatre** (508-487-9222; ptownarthouse.com), 214 Commercial Street. This remodeled venue hosts some movies and a full lineup of entertainment, including drag queens.

MOVIES ✳ ✿ ⊤ **Water's Edge Cinema** (508-413-9369; watersedgecinema.org), 237 Commercial Street. Known as Whaler's Wharf (since forever . . . until it was sold and renovated in 2013), this cinema shows new releases, documentaries, and art films.

.com), 238 Bradford Street. Home to the Provincetown Theatre Company, this place has been a fixture since it opened its doors in 2006.

Provincetown Theater Co. (PTC), founded in 1963 to further the goals of the early-20th-century Provincetown Players, PTC is a collaborative of professional, semiprofessional, and amateur actors, writers, directors, technicians, teachers, and theater lovers. In addition to year-round theater, they also provide education for youth and adults and foster the development of emerging playwrights.

Ⴚ NIGHTLIFE Provincetown's after-dark scene can get rather spicy. There's something for everyone: gay, straight, and in between. Check the weekly *Provincetown Magazine* (provincetownmagazine.net). When the bars, clubs, and shows close at 1 AM, it seems like everybody ends up in front of the Provincetown Town Hall or Spiritus (see *Where to Eat*). It's rather extraordinary when you think about it: There can be 300 people hanging out in front of Spiritus in the middle of the night without any problems.

In addition to some of the places below, for live music head to **Bubala's By The Bay** (see *Eating Out*) for an eclectic lineup.

THE PROVINCETOWN THEATER

NATIONAL SEASHORE BONFIRES

A beach bonfire, with or without a clambake, defines the essence of summertime on the Outer Cape. Here's the process you need to follow to secure a permit: In July and August head to the Province Lands Visitor Center (508-487-1256; nps.gov/caco) on Race Point Road three days before you want a permit and request one. For instance, if you want it for Wednesday, go on Sunday. Be there *before* the center opens (there will be a line). On the day of your big event, be at the visitor center by 3:30 PM or you'll lose your permit to someone waiting in line. In the off-season, you can call three days ahead of your desired date without a problem. Fires are permitted year-round. During the off-season, permits must be obtained at the Race Point Ranger Station (518-487-2100).

✳ **Crown & Anchor** (508-487-1430; onlyatthecrown.com), 247 Commercial Street (between Gosnold and Masonic Streets). The diversity of entertainment is impressive here. The Crown features the town's largest nightclub (Paramount), the town's only video bar (Wave), a cabaret venue, a poolside bar with heated pool, a piano bar and an ever-popular leather bar (The Vault). It draws a mixed crowd. Check it out. It's home to some of the best entertainers in town, including the incomparable comedian Kate Clinton. You can't miss it: Drag queens will be strutting up and down Commercial in the late afternoon, handing out fliers for their shows. Their **Central House Bar** is "safe" for straight

CROWN & ANCHOR

ART HOUSE THEATRE

people. And FYI, their restaurant is open almost all day every day! Off-season brings all-you-can-eat Taco Tuesday.

Pied Piper Bar (508-487-1527; piedbar .net), 193A Commercial Street (between Carver and Court Streets). Open May to late October. This LGBTQ waterfront bar and club has been around since 1971. It's more geared to straight folks during the day, although there is very gay "after tea" dancing here when the Boatslip (see *For the Boyz*) breaks up.

PIED PIPER BAR

Enzo/Grotta Bar (508-487-7555; local186.com/grotta.html), 186 Commercial Street. Open mid-May through October. This spot successfully manages something for everyone: live entertainment, sports on a giant plasma TV, pinball, jukebox tunes, DJs, and a killer lineup of signature drinks. It's an easy place to hang with friends, made more so by the fireplace in winter.

Post Office Cabaret (508-487-0006; postofficecabaret.com), 303 Commercial Street (between Standish and Ryder Streets). Open seasonally. Although this long, narrow room has too many pew-style seats, it hosts big-name female impersonators like Jimmy James. (It hosts a bunch of other stuff, too, but I only recommend it for the above).

❄ **Governor Bradford** (508-487-2781), 312 Commercial Street (at Standish Street). To get a different but equally "real" flavor of Provincetown, stop into this townie and straight tourist tavern for a game of backgammon or to listen to live music. Head upstairs for karaoke. From the game tables, you can watch people on the streets watching each other.

Bingo at the Unitarian Universalist Meeting House (508-487-9344; uumh.org), 236 Commercial Street (near Winslow Street). When you need a dose of quirky Provincetown, nothing beats this mostly LGBTQ crowd at Wednesday night bingo.

Old Colony (508-487-2361), 323 Commercial Street. Open April through December. For a really classic, old Provincetown experience, belly up to a bar stool here. Don't be scared.

♉ **The Red Inn**, **Front Street**, and **The Mews Restaurant**, all under *Where to Eat*, all have nice little bars.

✳ Selective Shopping

Unlike other chapters, in which shops are arranged according to merchandise type, they're listed here from east to west along Commercial Street. (That's because there are upward of 300 shops on the strip.) Shops not on Commercial Street are inserted in the text where you would naturally detour to them from Commercial.

A few more notes before we start: Most shops are open mid-April to mid-October, although some galleries keep a shorter season (mid-June to mid-September). Many shops stay open until 11 PM in July and August, and a number of them offer sales in mid-October. Even the shops designated with an "off-season" icon are usually only open on winter weekends. And just to keep it interesting, other shops that aren't "supposed" to be open year-round may open without notice in winter, depending on the weather.

Provincetown Arts (provincetownarts .org), a 150-page annual published in July, is Provincetown's bible of visual arts, literature, and theater. Look for it around town.

Galleries hold Friday openings staggered between 5 PM and 10 PM, so patrons may stroll the street, catching most of the receptions, and meet with artists. Most galleries change exhibits every two weeks.

COMMERCIAL STREET ART GALLERIES

See also **Provincetown Art Associ-ation & Museum** under *To See* and **Fine Arts Work Center** and **Provincetown Museum School** under *Even More Things to Do*.

The Schoolhouse (508-487-4800; galleryschoolhouse.com), 494 Commercial Street. Located in a mid-19th-century Greek Revival schoolhouse, this venture features four galleries. Look for contemporary photography, paintings, and sculpture.

❊ **Julie Heller Gallery** (508-487-0955; juliehellergallery.com), 465 Commercial Street. In a little beachfront shack, Heller offers work by luminaries who established this art colony, including Milton Avery, Ross Moffett, and Charles Hawthorne.

Berta Walker Gallery (508-487-6411; bertawalkergallery.com), 208 Bradford Street (between Howland and Cook Streets). This excellent gallery represents Provincetown-affiliated artists

COMMERCIAL STREET ART GALLERIES

of the past, present, and future. Berta Walker also has digs in Wellfleet.

William-Scott Gallery (508-487-4040; williamscottgallery.com), 439 Commercial Street. This venue showcases contemporary art and preeminent regional artists like John Dowd and Will Klemm.

❋ **Simie Maryles Gallery** (508-487-7878; simiemaryles.com), 435 Commercial Street. Maryles's vibrant landscapes sold so well in local galleries that the artist decided to open her own shop. (Other contemporary artists are also featured.)

Rice/Polak Gallery (508-487-1052; ricepolakgallery.com), 430 Commercial Street. I always enjoy this gallery. Marla Rice represents more than 40 contemporary artists working in painting, photography, assemblages, graphics, and sculpture.

Albert Merola Gallery (508-487-4424; albertmerolagallery.com), 424 Commercial Street. You'll find very fine contemporary art here, as well as notables like Milton Avery and Michael Mazure. It's always worth dropping in.

Packard Gallery (508-487-4690; packardgallery.com), 418 Commercial Street. Gallery director Leslie Packard showcases paintings by her sister, Cynthia, and her mother, Anne. In fact, there are five generations of Packards who have painted in Provincetown: Anne's grandfather, Max Bohm, was an early member of the Provincetown Art Association. The gallery, by the way, is housed in a former Christian Science church, which Anne's grandmother used to attend. It's quite a family affair.

Utilities (508-487-6800; utilitieshome.com), 393 Commercial Street. They're purveyors of whimsical, colorful, summery, frivolous, and function items for the bath, home, and kitchen. Bed Bath & Beyond they are not!

❋ **Womencrafts** (508-487-2501; womencrafts.com), 376 Commercial Street. In addition to books and music, this Provincetown institution features handcrafted items made by and for women.

❋ **Song of Myself** (508-487-5736; songofmyself.com), 349 Commercial Street.

Brad Fowler's photographic studio is worth a visit regardless of whether you want a portrait. The walls are lined with his work, showcasing the diversity and pride of town residents and visitors alike.

❋ **141 Bradford Natural Market** (508-487-9784, the141market.com), 141 Bradford Street. They've got the market cornered for organic produce, homeopathic remedies, gluten-free this, dairy-free that, and much more.

❋ **Lands End Marine Supply** (508-487-0784; landsendmarinesupply.com), 337 Commercial Street. It's amazing that this old-fashioned two-story hardware store continues to thrive. But it does, by

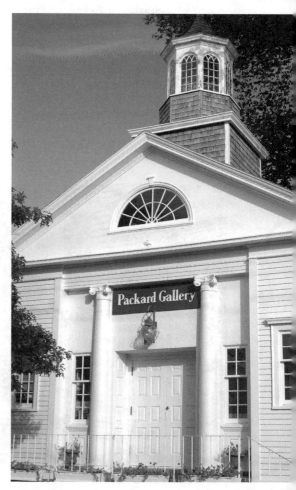

PACKARD GALLERY

selling beach chairs, umbrellas, coolers, suntan lotion, and more.

❋ **Hersheldon's Leather** (508-487-9046; hersheldonsleather.com), 317 Commercial Street. Hersh and Sheldon have a great knack for picking out just the right jacket (or briefcase or shoes) for your style and body type.

❋ **Shop Therapy** (508-487-9387; shoptherapy.com), 286 Commercial Street. This landmark, psychedelic-swathed building proclaims: "Monsters attack P-town. Shop Therapy blamed." No doubt. Merchandise revolves around current alternative lifestyles and the retro look. It's a head shop without the dope, and it was opened in 1972.

⚓ **Outer Cape Kites** (508-487-6133), 277A Commercial Street. There's no better place to fly a kite than the National Seashore dunes.

❋ ⚓ **Cabot's Candy** (508-487-3550), 276 Commercial Street. The Cicero family has made its own saltwater taffy here since 1969—it's the only shop on the Lower Cape or the Outer Cape to do so. Flavors range from peanut butter to piña colada to beach plum.

❋ **Provincetown Bookshop** (508-487-0964), 246 Commercial Street. A good selection of children's books, Cape titles, and cookbooks; established in 1932.

Whaler's Wharf, 237 Commercial Street. After a devastating fire in 1998 that burned the former building to the ground, this three-story open arcade brims with artisans, an artisan cooperative, shops, and a few restaurants. You're bound to find something interesting.

❋ **Marine Specialties** (508-487-1730), 235 Commercial Street. One of the Cape's most unusual shops stocks an odd jumble of Army-Navy items in a warehouse-like space: parachutes, wool blankets, candles, camel saddles, sand dollars, camping supplies, ship salvage, and other random military surplus items. You'll undoubtedly walk out with some strange gewgaw you hadn't even thought of buying but you just couldn't pass up for the price. My friend, May Lily,

SALTWATER TAFFY AT CABOT'S CANDY

always used to bang away on the piano here, offering passers-by impromptu and impressive concerts, and no one blinked an eye—just one more "expect the unexpected" at Marine Specialties.

Provincetown Human Rights Campaign Store (508-487-7736; shop.hrc .org), 209–11 Commercial Street. For all your Human Rights Campaign equality

MARINE SPECIALTIES

HUMAN RIGHTS CAMPAIGN STORE

T-shirt, jacket, jewelry, accessory, gift, and bumper sticker needs. And for those "Make America Gay Again" caps.

Roots (508-487-2500; shoproots. com), 193 Commercial Street. Beautiful accessories for the home: stained-glass lamps, kilims, handmade furniture (indoor and outdoor), antiques, ceramics, and frames.

❋ **Impulse** (508-487-1154; impulseart gallery.com), 188 Commercial Street. This contemporary American crafts shop offers a large selection of kaleidoscopes, wind chimes, wood objets d'art, fragile and colorful glass creations, jewelry, and signed celebrity photos and letters.

❋ **TJ Walton Gallery** (508-737-6697), 346 Commercial Street. Walton's large, bold canvases are a delight.

Provincetown Antique Market (508-487-1115; marketantique.com/province .htm), 131 Commercial Street. An engaging assortment of this and that: glass, toys, paper, books, tools, and ephemera.

❋ Special Events

Off-season there are dozens of special event weekends geared toward every segment of the LGBTQ and cisgendered world. If you want to be assured of a quieter off-season retreat, call the chamber of commerce (see *Guidance*) for an up-to-the-minute listing of events.

Mid-April: Whale-watching begins and seasonal shops begin to reopen.

Mid-May: **Single Women's Weekend** (provincetownforwomen.com). Although the title is self-explanatory, the weekend is filled with more events than you can imagine.

Late May: **Memorial Day** weekend kicks off the summer season.

Early June: **A Night at the Chef's Table** (508-487-9445; asgcc.org). An annual benefit for Provincetown's AIDS Support Group. This festive, multi-course gala dinner includes champagne and wine at many of the town's finest restaurants. More than 50 restaurants from Falmouth to Province town participate. It's a very local thing, but that doesn't mean you aren't welcome.

Women of Color Weekend (womenofcolorweekend.com). Finally, a few days devoted to diversity.

Mid-June: **International Film Festival** (ptownfilmfest.com). Established in 1999, with special screenings, features, documentaries, international selections, and LGBTQ shorts.

Late June: **Portuguese Festival and Blessing of the Fleet**, MacMillan Wharf. This four-day celebration was developed to coincide with the Blessing of the Fleet (when the bishop blesses a parade of fishing boats decked out with flags and families aboard). Festivities include a swing band concert, a kids' fishing derby, Portuguese menus at various restaurants, a food court and bazaar on Fisherman's Wharf, a parade, and competitions like lobster-pot pulls.

July 4: **Independence Day.** A spirited parade organized for and by the entire town, and a spectacular fireworks display.

Mid-July: **Secret Garden Tour** (508-487-1750). A popular annual benefit for the Provincetown Art Association & Museum.

Late July: **Girl Splash** (girlsplash.com). A full week of women's events during fine summer weather! Think Dinah Shore East.

Late July to early August: **Family Week.** At this popular event, the definition of *family* is expanded to include Heather and her two mommies as well as daddy-and-poppy nuclear families.

Mid- to late August: **Fine Arts Work Center Annual Auction** (508-487-9960; fawc.org). A benefit for the nationally recognized fellowship program for artists and writers (see *Even More Things to Do*). Since 1969, this has been an Art-with-a-capital-A event.

Carnival Week (508-487-2313; ptown.org). A weeklong gala sponsored by the Provincetown Business Guild (see *Guidance*), capped by a New Orleans Mardi Gras–style parade that's very gay and very flashy . . . and very popular. Folks from all over the Cape come to watch. Leave early and don't get stuck in traffic on the way.

Early September: **AIDS Support Group's Annual Silent and Live Auction** (508-487-9445; asgcc.org), at Fisherman's Wharf. It seems as if every artist in Provincetown donates work to this auction. Don't miss it.

Early September: **Provincetown Harbor Swim for Life & Paddler Flotilla** (swim4life.org). During this harbor swim from Long Point to the Boatslip Beach Club—to raise money for AIDS research—a "paddler flotilla" carries close to 300 swimmers across the bay so they can swim the 1.4 miles back to town. After the swim, the Boatslip holds a free "Mermaid Brunch" open to the public. The event often raises more than $150,000; since its inception it's raised more than $2 million. **The Great Provincetown Schooner Regatta** (province

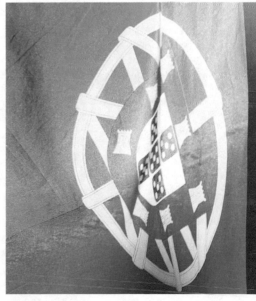

PORTUGUESE FESTIVAL

townschoonerrace.com). Two classes of sailing vessels parade along the waterfront (west to east) and then race.

Late September: **Tennessee Williams Theater Festival** (866-811-4111 for tickets; twptown.org). Four days of theater, dance, music, film, and fun sharing "the writer's vision of the healing power of love."

Mid-October: **Women's Week** (womeninnkeepers.com). It all started back in 1984 with a small weekend clambake on the beach. These days it spreads over a 10-day period with hundreds of events, including "Meet other women who . . ." mixers and dance parties at the Pied Bar. Hosted by Women Innkeepers of Provincetown, the weeklong extravaganza features women artists and entertainers.

Mid- to late October: **Fantasia Fair** (fantasiafair.org). This seven-day event brings cross-dressers, transgendered persons, and others to town.

Late October: **Halloween**. This is a big event, as you might imagine, with lots of costumes and contests. The children's parade starts at the Pilgrim Monument and ends at the Provincetown Community Center.

Late November: **Lighting of the Monument** (pilgrim-monument.org). The Wednesday before Thanksgiving. Nearly 5,000 white lights (4 miles' worth) illuminate the Pilgrim Monument and remain lit until early January.

Lighting of the Lobster Pot Tree (provincetownview.com). At Lopes Square in the center of town.

Early December: **Holly Folly Festival** (ptown.org). An annual LGBTQ festival featuring a concert by the Boston Gay Men's Chorus, seasonally decorated house tours, street caroling, shopping galore, special holiday menus, and general gay merriment and revelry.

December 31: **First Night**, ringing in the New Year.

MARTHA'S
VINEYARD

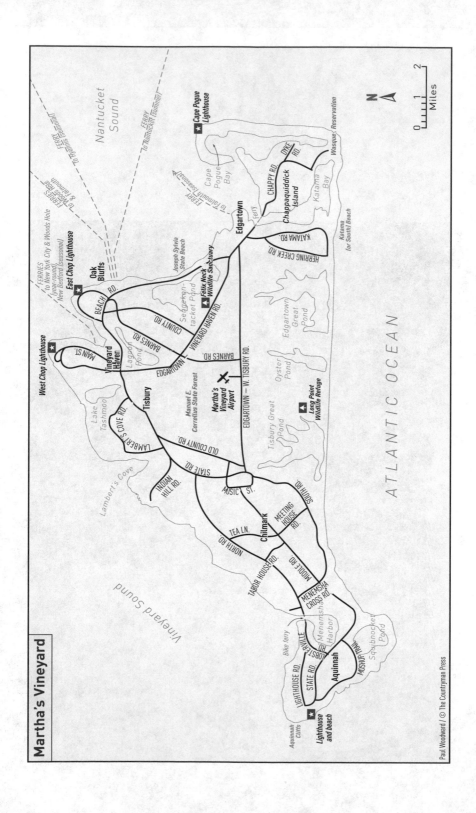

Martha's Vineyard

Paul Woodward / © The Countryman Press

MARTHA'S VINEYARD

Intrepid explorer Bartholomew Gosnold was the first European known to have visited Martha's Vineyard (in 1602), although Leif Eriksson may have done so earlier. Gosnold named the island for its bounty of wild grapes, but Martha's identity remains a mystery; she may have been Gosnold's daughter. The island was formally colonized in 1640, when a shipload of English settlers bound for Virginia ran short of supplies. They docked in Edgartown, found the resident Wampanoag friendly, and decided to stay.

The settlers converted the Wampanoag to Christianity with startling success, perhaps aided by the imported diseases that were killing Wampanoag by the thousands. A century after Edgartown was founded, the island's Native population had dropped from 3,000 to about 350. During that time, Vineyarders learned (from the surviving Wampanoag) how to catch whales. They also farmed in Chilmark and fished from Edgartown and Vineyard Haven.

During the American Revolution, islanders suffered extreme deprivation after British soldiers sailed into Vineyard Haven Harbor and looted homes and ships. Among their plunder were some 10,000 head of sheep and cattle from island farms. The island didn't fully recover until the 1820s, when the whaling industry took off. The Vineyard enjoyed a heyday from 1820 until the Civil War, with hundreds of whaling vessels sailing in and out of Edgartown. Whaling captains took their enormous profits from whale oil and built large Federal and Greek Revival homes all over the island. Many still stand today as gracious inns, renowned restaurants, and private homes.

After the Civil War, with the whaling industry in decline, tourism became the Vineyard's principal source of income. By 1878 the Methodist Campground of Oak Bluffs had become a popular summer resort, with 12,000 people attending annual meetings. Over the next 30 years, other travelers discovered the island and returned summer after summer to enjoy its pleasant weather, relatively warm water, excellent fishing, and comfortable yet genteel lifestyle. By the turn of the 20th century, there were 2,000 hotel rooms in Oak Bluffs alone—there aren't that many B&B or inn rooms on the entire island today! Summertime traffic was so high that a rail line was built from the Oak Bluffs ferry terminal to Katama. Daily ferry service ran from the New York Yacht Club to Gay Head (present-day Aquinnah).

Although the whaling industry rapidly declined, other sea-related businesses continued to reap healthy profits. In 1900, Vineyard Sound was one of the busiest sea-lanes in the world, second only to the English Channel. Heavy sea traffic continued until the Cape Cod Canal was completed in 1914. Tourism picked up again in the early 1970s. And when the Clintons began spending summer vacations here in the mid-1990s, they created a tidal wave of national and international interest in the island. As of late, the Obamas have continued the tradition with visits in 2009, 2010, 2011, and 2013.

Today the year-round population of 15,000 mushrooms in July and August to about 150,000. Grumpy year-round Vineyarders are fond of saying that the island sinks 3 inches when ferries unload their passengers.

The terms *up-island* and *down-island* are holdovers from the days when the island was populated by seafarers—as you travel west, you move up the scale of longitude. *Up-island* refers to the less developed, hilly western end, including West Tisbury,

EDGARTOWN HARBOR

Chilmark, the village of Menemsha (in Chilmark), and Aquinnah. Edgartown, Oak Bluffs, and Vineyard Haven, which are the most developed towns, are all *down-island*.

THE TOWNS

Elegant **Edgartown** is chock-full of grand, white Greek Revival ship captains' houses, with fanlights and widow's walks. Many of these private homes are clustered on North and South Water Streets, while elsewhere downtown you'll find chic shops, galleries, and restaurants.

Although it's less showy than Edgartown, **Vineyard Haven** maintains a year-round level of activity that Edgartown doesn't. It's the commercial center of the island, where

VINEYARD HAVEN HARBOR

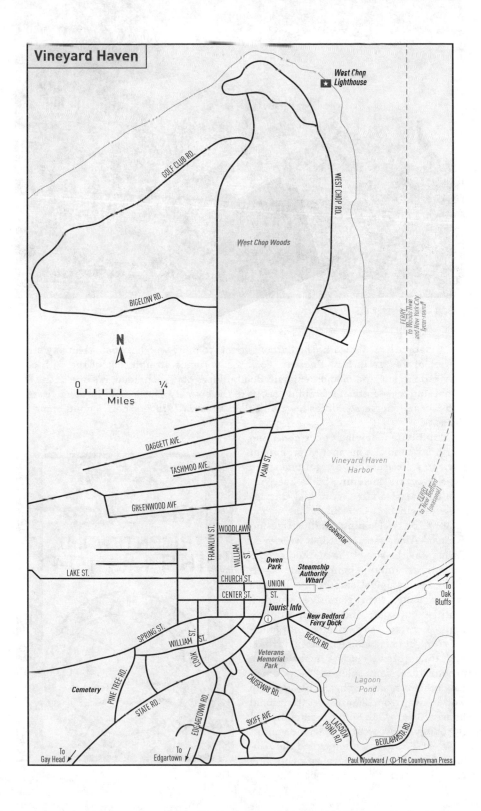

Vineyard Haven

West Chop Lighthouse

GOLF CLUB RD.

WEST CHOP RD.

West Chop Woods

BIGELOW RD.

N

0   ¼
Miles

DAGGETT AVE.

TASHMOO AVE.

GREENWOOD AVE.

MAIN ST.

FRANKLIN ST.

WOODLAWN

WILLIAM ST.

CHURCH ST.

CENTER ST.

LAKE ST.

Owen Park

UNION ST.

Tourist Info

Vineyard Haven Harbor

breakwater

Steamship Authority Wharf

New Bedford Ferry Dock

To Oak Bluffs

SPRING ST.

WILLIAM ST.

COOK ST.

PINE TREE RD.

Cemetery

STATE RD.

EDGARTOWN RD.

Veterans Memorial Park

CAUSEWAY RD.

SKIFF AVE.

BEACH RD.

Lagoon Pond

LAGOON PND. RD.

BEULAH ST. RD.

To Gay Head

To Edgartown

FERRY to Woods Hole and New York City (year-round)

FERRY to New Bedford (seasonal)

Paul Woodward / © The Countryman Press

GINGERBREAD HOUSES IN OAK BLUFFS

"real" people live and work. The harbor is home to more wooden boats than any other harbor of its size in New England. For an experience straight out of the 19th century, stop in at Gannon and Benjamin Boatbuilders on Beach Road; it's one of the few remaining wooden-boat rebuilding shops in the country. Dozens of big-name literary and journalistic personalities have all called Vineyard Haven their second home for decades.

Oak Bluffs today is at once charming and honky-tonk. A number of prominent African Americans have vacationed here over the years, including Spike Lee, Vernon Jordan, Dorothy West, and Charles Ogletree. In fact, Oak Bluffs has a long history of welcoming and attracting African Americans: In 1835, Wesleyan Grove was the site of the Methodist congregation's annual summer-camp meetings. The campers' small tents became family tents; then primitive, wooden, tentlike cottages; and finally, brightly painted cottages ornamented with fanciful trim. Cupolas, domes, spires, turrets, and gingerbread cutouts make for an architectural fantasyland. The whimsical, precious, and offbeat cottages are worlds away from Edgartown's traditional houses. So are Oak Bluffs' nightclubs and the baggy-pants-wearing, pierced youth.

West Tisbury is often called the Athens of the Vineyard because of its fine New England Congregational Church,

CHILMARK

Town Hall, and Grange Hall. Music Street, where descendants of the island's 19th-century ship captains still live in large houses, was so named because many of these families used whaling profits to purchase pianos. Over the years, West Tisbury summer residents have included *Washington Post* owner-publisher Katharine Graham, cartoonist Jules Feiffer, and historian David McCullough. Other A-list celebs clamoring for their place in the Vineyard sun (in Hollywood East) have included Ted Danson and Mary Steenburgen, Larry David, film mogul Harvey Weinstein, John Cusack, and Michael J. Fox.

Chilmark is a peaceful place of rolling hills and old stone fences that outline 200-year-old farms. You'll find dozens of working farms up-island, some still operated by descendants of the island's original European settlers.

Travel down North Road to **Menemsha**, a small, truly picturesque village and working harbor that you may recognize as the location of the movie *Jaws*. The surrounding area is crisscrossed by miles and miles of unmarked, interconnected dirt roads, great for exploring. (Alas, many are private.) Chilmark is sparsely populated, to the tune of 1,050 or so year-rounders, and they aim to keep it that way. In order to limit growth they issue the island's only 3-acre-minimum building permits.

Chilmark, which is among the 50 wealthiest towns in America (the average price of a single family home in 2016 was $2.1 million), has hosted such disparate personalities as photographer Alfred Eisenstaedt and John Belushi. (Belushi is buried on-island; "Eise's" photos are found in galleries and at his beloved retreat, the Menemsha Inn and Cottages.) Harvard Law School professor Alan Dershowitz is a denizen of Lucy Vincent Beach, one of the island's many residents-only beaches—and a nude one at that.

Aquinnah, a must-see destination, occupies the island's western tip. (If you haven't visited the Vineyard for a while, you may know Aquinnah as Gay Head. It was renamed Aquinnah, "land under the hill," in mid-1997 by a narrow 79–76 town vote.) Of the 1,100 members listed on the Wampanoag Indian tribal rolls, approximately 300 still reside on the Vineyard, half in Aquinnah. Tribal legend holds that the giant Moshup created the Vineyard, taught the Wampanoag how to fish and catch whales, and remains a protector. The Wampanoag own the brilliantly colored bluffs and the face of the Clay Cliffs of Aquinnah.

Martha's Vineyard has always attracted celebrity summer visitors. But in recent years many who visited decided they wanted to own a piece of it. Beginning in the late 1980s and continuing to this day, a tremendous building boom has changed the face of the Vineyard. While

MENEMSHA HARBOR

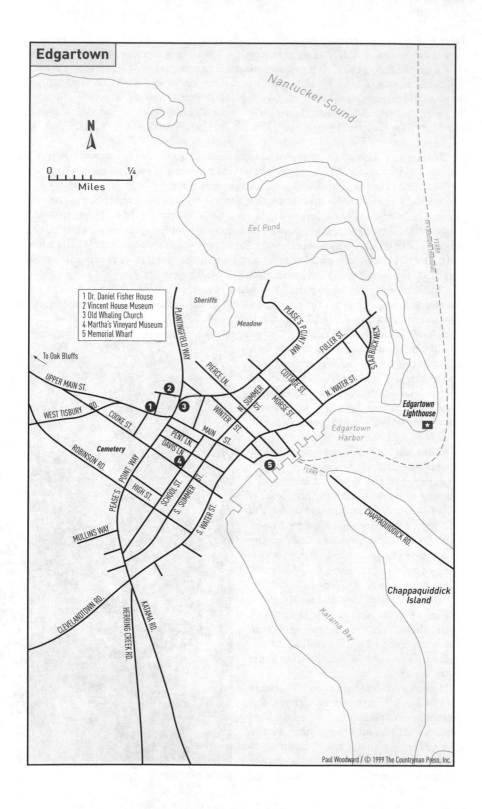

Edgartown

Nantucket Sound

1 Dr. Daniel Fisher House
2 Vincent House Museum
3 Old Whaling Church
4 Martha's Vineyard Museum
5 Memorial Wharf

Eel Pond

N

0   ¼
Miles

Sheriffs
Meadow

To Oak Bluffs

UPPER MAIN ST.

WEST TISBURY RD.

COOKE ST.

PLANTINGFIELD WAY

PIERCE LN.

PEASE'S POINT WAY

FULLER ST.

N. WATER ST.

COTTAGE ST.

N. SUMMER ST.

MORSE ST.

WINTER ST.

MAIN ST.

PENT LN.

DAVIS LN.

ROBINSON RD.

Cemetery

PEASE'S POINT WAY

HIGH ST.

SCHOOL ST.

S. SUMMER ST.

S. WATER ST.

MULLINS WAY

CLEVELANDTOWN RD.

HERRING CREEK RD.

KATAMA RD.

STARBUCK NECK

Edgartown
Lighthouse
★

Edgartown
Harbor

FERRY

CHAPPAQUIDDICK RD.

Chappaquiddick
Island

Katama Bay

Paul Woodward / © 1999 The Countryman Press, Inc.

the Vineyard had been a place where the well-heeled and well-off came to escape notice, today the celebrities and power brokers come as much to see and be seen. Although residents are generally unfazed by their celebrity neighbors—movie stars, authors, journalists, musicians, financial moguls—many locals and longtime visitors agree that the Vineyard is no longer the quaint, tranquil island it was prior to the mid-1980s.

Martha's Vineyard is unlike most of the rest of America; people tend to get along pretty well with one another. They work hard to maintain a sense of tolerance and community spirit. Most lengthy debates center on land use and preservation rather than on race or religion. (Of course, there are notable exceptions.) Everyone relies, to some extent, on the hectic summer season that brings in most of the island's annual income, though residents do breathe a sigh of relief when the crowds depart after mid-October.

To experience the Vineyard at its best and still have a dependable chance for good weather, plan your visit from May to mid-June or from mid-September to mid-October. From January to March, the Vineyard is truly a retreat from civilization.

GUIDANCE ❁ **Martha's Vineyard Chamber of Commerce** (508-693-0085; mvy.com), 24 Beach Road, Vineyard Haven. There are good, free street maps of Vineyard Haven, Oak Bluffs, and Edgartown available at all chambers.

Information booth (no phone), Steamship Authority terminal, Vineyard Haven. Open seasonally.

Information booth (no phone), at the foot of Circuit Avenue, Oak Bluffs. Adjacent to the Flying Horses Carousel, it's open seasonally.

❁ **Edgartown Information Center** (no phone), Church Street, Edgartown. Around the corner from the Old Whaling Church, this minor center has restrooms and a post office, and serves as a shuttle-bus stop (see *Getting Around*).

GETTING THERE ❁ *By boat from Woods Hole:* **The Steamship Authority** (508-477-8600 for advance auto reservations; 508-548-3788 in Woods Hole for day-of-sailing information only; no reservations accepted [don't count on getting lucky]; steamshi

STEAMSHIP AUTHORITY FERRY

ISLANDER FERRY DOCKING IN VINEYARD HAVEN

pauthority.com), 1 Cowdry Road. The Steamship is the only company that provides daily, year-round transport—for people and autos— to Vineyard Haven and Oak Bluffs. The Vineyard is 7 miles from Woods Hole, and the trip takes 45 minutes. About nine boats ply the waters daily.

The Steamship annually carries upward of 2 million people to the Vineyard. *Here's the best advice in the entire book:* Make car reservations as soon as possible. Call as soon as you know your dates. Auto reservations are mandatory/essential year-round. Otherwise, the Steamship has a standby policy that's first come, first served.

Round-trip tickets: $$ adults; $ bicycles; more than $150 for autos. Off-season, auto prices drop to just less than $100. If you are not taking your car, the Steamship Authority provides free, frequent buses between the parking lots and the ferry dock. Each bus has a bike rack that holds two bikes. Parking is $$ per calendar day.

By boat from Falmouth: **Island Queen** (508-548-4800; islandqueen.com), 75 Falmouth Heights Road. This passengers-only service (smaller and more comfortable than the Steamship Authority's boat) operates late May to mid-October and takes about 35 minutes; departures are from Falmouth Inner Harbor to Oak Bluffs. There is plenty of parking near the *Island Queen*'s dock ($$ per calendar day). Round-trip fares: $$ adults; $ bicycles.

Falmouth–Edgartown Ferry (508-548-9400; falmouthedgartownferry.com), 278 Scranton Avenue. From late May to mid-October, this service plies the waters three to five times daily between Falmouth and Edgartown (Memorial Wharf). Round-trip fares: $$$$ adults; $ bicycles. Parking is $$–$$$ per calendar day.

By boat from Hyannis: **Hy-Line Cruises** (508-778-2600; hylinecruises.com), 220 Ocean Street Dock. Two to five passenger boats (55 minutes) to and from Oak Bluffs from May to late October. If you haven't purchased advance tickets, it's wise to arrive an hour early in July and August. Round-trip, in-season fares: adults $$$$$+/high-speed ferry, traditional ferry less; bicycles $$. Parking $–$$.

By boat from New Bedford: **Seastreak Ferry** (866-683-3779; nefastferry.com) operates passenger boats from 49 State Pier to Vineyard Haven from late May to mid-October. The ferry crossing takes one hour. Round-trip fares: $$$$$+ adults, $$ bicycles. Parking is $$ per calendar day. For visitors coming from the south, New Bedford is a more convenient departure point than Woods Hole. Even those driving from points north may wish to consider taking the New Bedford ferry to avoid Cape Cod Canal bridge traffic.

By boat from Nantucket: **Hy-Line Cruises** (508-778-2600 Hyannis, 508 693-0112 Oak Bluffs; 508-228-3949 Nantucket; hylinecruises.com) offers interisland service between Oak Bluffs and Nantucket from mid-June to mid-September. The trip takes 1¼ hours; there is only one trip daily. One-way fares cost $$$$$ adults, $ bicycles.

By boat from New York City: **Seastreak Ferry** (866-683-3779; nefastferry.com) This five-hour voyage runs during the summer months.

See also **Patriot Party Boats** under *To Do* in "Falmouth and Woods Hole."

By bus: **Bonanza/Peter Pan** (888-751-8800; peterpanbus.com) provides daily year-round service to Woods Hole from Boston, New York, Hartford, and Providence. Buses are scheduled to meet ferries, but ferries won't wait for a late bus.

By air: With a booming increase in jet-setting visitors, it's no wonder a new terminal was built in the late 1990s. **Cape Air** (866-227-3247; capeair.com) flies to the Vineyard from Boston, Providence, Nantucket, New Bedford, Hyannis, and White Plains.

GETTING AROUND *By car:* The infamous Five Corners is the trickiest and most dangerous intersection on the island. It's also the first thing you'll encounter as you disembark from the Vineyard Haven ferry terminal. If you're going to Oak Bluffs, Katama, Edgartown, and Chappaquiddick, take the left lane. For West Tisbury, North Tisbury, Lambert's Cove, Menemsha, Chilmark, and Aquinnah, enter the right lane and turn right.

When making plans, consider these sample distances: Vineyard Haven to Oak Bluffs, 3 miles; Vineyard Haven to Edgartown, 8 miles; Oak Bluffs to Edgartown, 6 miles; Vineyard Haven to Aquinnah, 18 miles.

Unfortunately, summertime traffic jams are commonplace in down-island towns. Try to park outside of town and take shuttles into town (see below). Why would you want to stop and crawl in a picturesque village on a vacation day?

In-season, expect to pay more than $100 daily for the least-expensive rental car and upward of $200 daily for four-wheel drives and minivans. A word of note: Rates change according to weekday, weekend, and holiday rentals. Before heading out, invest a few bucks in the very detailed gold-and-orange Martha's Vineyard Road Map produced by Edward Thomas (508-693-2059). It's an excellent, accurate resource and even lists mileage between intersections. It's available at most bookstores, grocery stores, and liquor stores.

Car rental companies include **Budget Rent-a-Car** (508-693-1911; budgetmv .com), Edgartown, at the Triangle; 45

OAK BLUFFS

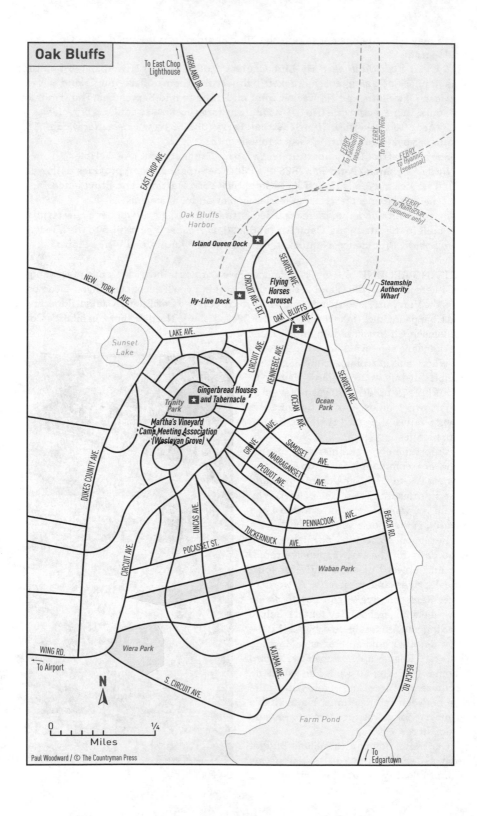

Oak Bluffs

To East Chop Lighthouse

HIGH LAND DR.

EAST CHOP AVE.

NEW YORK AVE.

FERRY to Falmouth (seasonal)

FERRY to Woods Hole

FERRY to Hyannis (seasonal)

FERRY to Nantucket (summer only)

Oak Bluffs Harbor

Island Queen Dock ★

Hy-Line Dock ★

CIRCUIT AVE. EXT.

SEAVIEW AVE.

Flying Horses Carousel

Steamship Authority Wharf

LAKE AVE.

Sunset Lake

OAK BLUFFS AVE. ★

CIRCUIT AVE.

KENNEBEC AVE.

OCEAN AVE.

SEAVIEW AVE.

Trinity Park

Gingerbread Houses and Tabernacle ★

Martha's Vineyard Camp Meeting Association (Wesleyan Grove)

Ocean Park

GROVE AVE.

SAMOSET AVE.

NARRAGANSETT AVE.

PEQUOT AVE.

AVE.

DUKES COUNTY AVE.

LINCAS AVE.

PENNACOOK AVE.

BEACH RD.

CIRCUIT AVE.

POCASSET ST.

TUCKERNUCK AVE.

Waban Park

WING RD.

To Airport

Viera Park

KATAMA AVE.

S. CIRCUIT AVE.

Farm Pond

BEACH RD.

To Edgartown

N

0   1/4
Miles

Paul Woodward / © The Countryman Press

Beach Road, Vineyard Haven; 9 Oak Bluffs Avenue (at the ferry dock), Oak Bluffs; and 71 Airport Road at Martha's Vineyard Airport. I've always found these outfits helpful: **Adventure Rentals** (19 Beach Road, Five Corners, Vineyard Haven, 508-693-1959); and **Island Hoppers** (23 Lake Avenue, Oak Bluffs, 508-696-9147; islandhoppersmv.com). By the way, gas is usually cheapest at the airport, but **Mobil** (North Line Road, Edgartown) and **Up-Island Automotive** (1074 State Road, West Tisbury) have decent prices, too.

MOPEDS FOR RENT

By moped: If most Vineyarders and emergency-room doctors had their way, mopeds would be banned. Once you've seen the face, arms, and legs of a fellow Explorer skinned, you'll know why. Sand, mopeds, winding roads, and speed do not mix. Take a look at the mopeds you might be renting; many of their plastic hulls have been cracked from accidents. Having said that and not wanting to appear maternalistic, here goes: Many rental agencies are located near the ferry terminals in Oak Bluffs and Vineyard Haven. **Adventure Rentals** has mopeds (often $100/day). Extra training, yellow diamond road signs (at notorious intersections), and maps (with danger spots and distances between points) should help reduce casualties.

❄ ❀ ♨ *By shuttle:* **Martha's Vineyard Transit Authority (VTA)** (508-693-9440; vineyardtransit.com) operates an excellent system of buses. Twelve buses travel among Vineyard Haven, Oak Bluffs, Edgartown, West Tisbury, Chilmark, Menemsha, and Aquinnah year-round. Buses seem to stop everywhere you want to go; you can also flag them down. They even have bike racks. Get a copy of the very helpful VTA map with stops and routes clearly listed. Carry it with you wherever you go. One-day passes cost $, three-day $$, seven-day $$$. Exact change is strongly suggested because change is given only in the form of credit vouchers for future trips. All routes run year-round except Edgartown Park & Ride and South Beach; the latter operates May to mid-October.

Of particular use are the following routes:

Edgartown Park & Ride. VTA has an alternative to wrangling for a parking place in Edgartown's car-choked streets. Leave your car at the Triangle (at the corner of Edgartown–Vineyard Haven Road and Oak Bluffs Road) and ride the shuttle. Parking and rides are free.

Tisbury Park & Ride, State Road (across from Cronig's Market). Avoid the parking nightmare in Vineyard Haven and let the VTA shuttle drop you off downtown. The free shuttle runs year-round. Parking is free for seven consecutive days; after that you must purchase tickets in advance at Town Hall (508-696-4200, William and Spring Streets) in Vineyard Haven. Seasonal passes available.

South Beach. This route runs from Edgartown's information building (near Church and Main Streets) to three points at South Beach.

Bus tour: **Gay Head Sightseeing** (508-693-1555) and **Martha's Vineyard Sightseeing** (508-693-4681) offer tours from mid-April to late October. The clearly marked buses meet incoming ferries. The Gay Head tour covers all six towns, but makes only one stop—at the Clay Cliffs of Aquinnah—where there are small food stands, souvenir shops, public restrooms, and a wonderful view of the cliffs and the ocean. The only potential drawback: You may tire of hearing the constant running commentary about which celebrities live down which dirt roads. They also offer charter tours for large groups. $$$.

Taxi tour: Most taxis conduct island sight-seeing trips for a price, but you don't want to go with just anyone. I highly recommend **Jon's Taxi** (508-627-4677). Trips with Jon or his drivers cost $$$$+ per hour for one to six people. Schedule these private trips at your convenience.

❋ **Adam Cab** (508-627-4462; adamcabmv.com) is also very good and gives a general 2½-hour tour twice daily from Edgartown from late May to early September (less often off-season) for $$$$ per person.

By taxi: Uber and Lyft are on-island, but I'd personally rather support local taxis.

🚲 *By bicycle:* Bicycling is a great way to get around, but it requires stamina if you're heading up-island (see *To Do*).

❋ 🚲 *On foot:* **Ghosts, Gossip, and Downright Scandals** (508-627-8619) is conducted by very knowledgeable folks from **Vineyard History Tours**. They take people by appointment any time of the year, except perhaps during a nor'easter. $$.

MEDIA *Vineyard Gazette* (508-627-4311; mvgazette.com), 34 South Summer Street, Edgartown. The newspaper, which first rolled off the press on May 14, 1846, is a beloved island institution. Although its year-round circulation is only 10,000, the paper is mailed to island devotees in all 50 states and internationally. There's no single better way for an Explorer to get a handle on island life.

Martha's Vineyard Times (508-693-6100; mvtimes.com), 30 Beach Road, Vineyard Haven. Celebrating its 30th birthday in 2014, the weekly publication and its corresponding website host up-to-date news as well as feature material on island life, arts, and entertainment. Their *Vineyard Visitor* publication and vineyardvisitor.com website have lots of travel tips and info on things to do.

MORE WEBSITES **mvol.com**. A complete guide.

A PERFECT DOWN-ISLAND DAY ON THE VINEYARD

8:00	Order everything on the menu at Art Cliff Diner.
9:30	Watch quiet morning harbor activity from Owen Park.
10:30	Feel the whimsy of the gingerbread houses in Oak Bluffs.
11:45	Sit for a minute in the solid Old Whaling Church in Edgartown.
12:00	Have a quick (sidewalk) lunch at Alchemy.
1:30	Head over to Chappy via the charming "On Time" ferry.
6:00	Walk out to the Edgartown Lighthouse with a camera.
7:00	Dine at The Dunes (Edgartown) or Sweet Life Café (Oak Bluffs).
10:00	Resolve to visit the Vineyard longer next time.

VineyardVisitor.com. Brought to you by the *Martha's Vineyard Times* (see *Media* above).

VineyardStyle.com. With articles about artisans, gardening, trends, home, cuisine, interiors, or shopping.

MVInfo.com. Billed as the original website for the Vineyard and established in 1985.

PUBLIC RESTROOMS In Vineyard Haven head to the top of the Stop & Shop parking lot (seasonal) and to the Steamship Authority terminal (year-round) off Water Street. In Oak Bluffs restrooms can be found at the Steamship Authority terminal on Seaview Avenue (seasonal); on Kennebec Avenue, one block from Circuit Avenue (seasonal); and next to Our Market (seasonal) on Oak Bluffs Harbor. In Edgartown, they're at the visitor center (year-round) on Church Street. Seasonal facilities are also located near the parking lot for the Clay Cliffs of Aquinnah, at Dutcher's Dock in Menemsha Harbor, and in West Tisbury at the Grange Hall next to Town Hall.

LAUNDROMATS **Airport Laundromat** (508-693-5005; takemmycleaners.com/airport laundramat, off the Edgartown–West Tisbury Road. Open daily 8 AM–7 PM.

PUBLIC LIBRARIES ✳ ✐ ⬆ Most of these libraries have story times and Internet access; call ahead or look online for hours and schedule vagaries:

Aquinnah (508-645-2314; aquinnahlibrary.org), 1 Church Street at State Road.
Chilmark (508-645-3360; chilmarklibrary.org), 522 South Road, Chilmark Center.
Edgartown (508-627-4221; edgartownlibrary.org), 26 West Tisbury Road.
Oak Bluffs (508-693-9433; oakbluffslibrary.org), 56R School Street.
Vineyard Haven (508-696-4211; vhlibrary.org), 200 Main Street.
West Tisbury (508-693-3366; westtisburylibrary.org), 1042 State Road.
See also **Martha's Vineyard Museum** under *To See*.

HERITAGE TRAILS **Aquinnah Cultural Trail** (508-645-9265; wampanoagtribe.net). For those interested in something other than beaches and shops, look for the excellent and informative map once you're on-island. You can always find it at the Aquinnah Cultural Center, 35 Aquinnah Circle, Aquinnah. It is full of interesting facts about the "first people of Noepe," place-name translations, Moshup legends, local government, and a schedule of events.

African-American Heritage Trail (508-693-4361; mvheritagetrail.org). Tours on request late May to early September. The brainchild of a Martha's Vineyard Regional High School history teacher and NAACP archivist Elaine Weintraub, this developing trail currently has about 16 sites devoted to telling the story of the island's strong association with African Americans. Weintraub researched the story of the Island's own African American whaling captain, William A. Martin, and two generations of his family, establishing an African American presence on Martha's Vineyard before the American revolution. Every town has sites, including abandoned graveyards; the home of Dorothy West, a Harlem Renaissance

BIKES FOR RENT

writer who lived on the island and died in 1999; a site dedicated to Rebecca Amos, an African woman enslaved on the Vineyard; and a decrepit Gospel Tabernacle. The book *Lighting the Trail: The African American Heritage of Martha's Vineyard* is sold in all the island bookstores. Choose from three different tours of varying durations and scopes.

MEDICAL EMERGENCY Martha's Vineyard Hospital (508-693-0410; mvhospital .com), 1 Hospital Road, off Beach Road, Oak Bluffs. Includes a 24-hour emergency room. In 2010 the hospital opened a new 90,000-square-foot building.

Lyme disease. Ticks carry this disease, which has flulike symptoms and may result in death if left untreated. Immediately and carefully remove any ticks that may have migrated from dune grasses to your body. Better yet, wear long pants, tuck pants into socks, and wear long-sleeved shirts whenever possible when hiking. Avoid hiking in grassy and overgrown areas of dense brush.

✳ To See

IN VINEYARD HAVEN

Sovereign Bank (508-696-4400), 75 Main Street. This distinctive 1905 beachstone building has lovely stained glass and great acoustics. On this site, incidentally, stood the harness shop where the Great Fire of 1883 started. The conflagration destroyed 60 buildings.

William Street. The only street in town that survived the devastating 1883 fire boasts some fine examples of Greek Revival architecture. The **Richard G. Luce House**, near the corner of William Street and Spring Street, is prime among the carefully preserved sea captains' homes. Captain Luce never lost a whaling ship or a crew member during his 30-year career, and apparently his good fortune at sea extended to life on land.

Jirah Luce House, near the corner of South Main and Main Streets. Built in 1804, this is one of the few buildings to survive the Great Fire of 1883.

Old Schoolhouse, Main Street at Colonial Lane. Built in 1829, the schoolhouse now houses a youth sailing program, but the Liberty Pole in front of it recounts the story of three courageous girls who defied British troops.

West Chop Lighthouse, at the western end of Main Street. Built in 1817 with wood and replaced with brick in 1838, the lighthouse has been moved back from the shore twice, first in 1848 and again in 1891. Today the lighthouse is inhabited and not open for touring.

WEST CHOP LIGHTHOUSE

Katharine Cornell Theatre/Tisbury Town Hall (508-696-4200; tisburyma.gov), 51 Spring Street. This 1844 performance center features murals by Stan Murphy depicting island scenes, whaling adventures, seagulls, and Native Americans. The 130-seat theater boasts no box office per se; event listings are best found at mvtimes.com or mvgazette.com.

IN OAK BLUFFS

East Chop Lighthouse (508-627-4441; mvmuseum.org/eastchop), Telegraph Hill, off East Chop Drive, Oak Bluffs. Open Sunday 90 minutes prior to sunset and 30 minutes after, June through August. This circa-1850 lighthouse was built by Capt. Silas Daggett with the financial help of prosperous fellow seafarers who wanted a better system of relaying signals from the Vineyard to Nantucket and the mainland. Up to that point, they'd used a complex system of raising arms, legs, flags, and lanterns to signal that ships were coming

EAST CHOP LIGHTHOUSE

in. In 1875 the government purchased the lighthouse from the consortium of sea captains for $6,000, then constructed the cast-iron structure that stands today. There are nice ocean views from here. $.

    ⚓ **Flying Horses Carousel** (508-693-9481), Circuit Avenue at Lake Avenue. Open mid-April to mid-October. The oldest operating carousel in the country, carved in

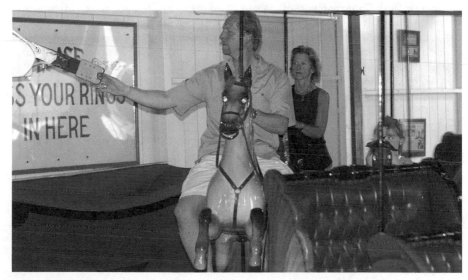

FLYING HORSES CAROUSEL

UNION CHAPEL

New York City in 1876, is marvelously well preserved and lovingly maintained. It was brought by barge to the island in 1884, complete with four chariots and 20 horses with real horsehair manes. Adults visit this national historic landmark even without a child in tow to grab for the elusive brass ring, which entitles the catcher to a free ride. (Here's a public service announcement: A few folks every year are not returning the brass ring when they grab it, and the carousel is getting precariously close to running out of them.) $.

Trinity Park Tabernacle, (508-693-0525; mvcva.org), behind Lake, Circuit, and Dukes County Avenues. The enormous, tentlike tabernacle was built in 1879 to replace the original meeting tent used by the Methodists who met here. Today the tabernacle is one of the largest wrought-iron structures in the country. There are community sing-alongs at 8 PM Wednesdays in summer.

Wesleyan Grove surrounds the tabernacle, which, in turn, is encircled by rows of colorful **"gingerbread" cottages**, built during the late 19th century to replace true tents. Owners painted the tiny houses with bright colors and pastels to accentuate the Carpenter Gothic architecture and woodwork. There are upward of 320 cottages today, still leased from the Camp Meeting Association. Visitors are welcome to wander around the mainly Protestant (but always ecumenical) community. No bicycles are allowed in Wesleyan Grove, and quiet time is strictly observed after 11 PM.

Union Chapel, 55 Narragansett Avenue, at the corner of Kennebec and Samoset Avenues. This 1870 octagonal chapel holds interdenominational services and hosts seasonal performing arts events.

Cottage Museum (508-693-7784; mvcma.org), 1 Trinity Park. Open seasonally. The interior and exterior of this 1867 cottage are typical of the more than 300 tiny cottages in Wesleyan Grove. Memorabilia and photographs span the ages from 1835 to present day. $.

IN EDGARTOWN

✳ ☙ **Martha's Vineyard Museum** (508-627-4441; mvmuseum.org), 59 School Street. This excellent collection is housed in several buildings. Perhaps the most interesting exhibit is the Oral History Center, which preserves the island's history through more than 1,400 interviews with some of the island's older citizens. (The project was begun in the mid-1990s.) Other facilities include a fine pre–Revolutionary War house which has undergone little renovation since the mid-19th century. Ten rooms at the Thomas Cooke House focus on various aspects of the island's history, including ethnic groups, architecture, natural history, and agriculture. The society also has a maritime gallery, a historical reference library, a tryworks replica, a carriage shed that houses boats and vehicles, and a historic herb garden. The enormous original Fresnel lens from the Aquinnah Lighthouse is here, too, and it's illuminated for a few hours after sunset every day. $.

FRESNEL LIGHT

Dr. Daniel Fisher House (508-627-4440; mvpreservation.org), 99 Main Street. The island's best example of Greek Revival architecture, this 1840 house has an enclosed cupola (perhaps more correctly called a "lantern"), roof and porch balustrades, a shallow hipped roof, large windowpanes, and a portico, all exquisitely preserved.

MARTHA'S VINEYARD MUSEUM

DR. DANIEL FISHER HOUSE

Dr. Fisher was a Renaissance man: doctor, whaling magnate, banker (he founded the Martha's Vineyard National Bank), merchant, and miller. He insisted that his house be constructed with the finest materials—with Maine pine timbers soaked in lime for two years, and brass and copper nails, for instance. The house is headquarters for the Martha's Vineyard Preservation Trust, which is charged with saving, restoring, and making self-sufficient any important island buildings that might otherwise be sold for commercial purposes or radically remodeled. Combination tours (45 minutes; $) with the Vincent House and the Old Whaling Church (see below) are offered May to mid-October.

Vincent House Museum (508-627-4440; mvpreservation.org), behind the Old Whaling Church. Open May to early September. Dating to 1672, the Vineyard's oldest residence was in the same family until 1941, and was eventually given to the Preservation Trust in 1977. Reproduction and antique furniture in three rooms depicts how the residence looked in the 17th, 18th, and 19th centuries. $.

Old Whaling Church (508-627-4440; mvpreservation.org), 89 Main Street. Built in 1843, this thriving parish church also serves as a performing arts center, hosting plays, lectures, concerts, and films. Owned by the Martha's Vineyard Preservation Trust, the building originally housed the Edgartown Methodist Church and was constructed with the same techniques used to build whaling ships. Free.

Memorial Wharf, adjacent to the Chappy Ferry on the water. This two-story landing is a terrific spot from which to watch harbor boat traffic in one direction and stately manses in the other.

North Water Street. Some of these fine Colonial, Federal, and Greek Revival houses may look familiar because many clothing companies, including Talbot's, have sent crews of models and photographers here to shoot their catalogs. Architectural detailing on these white houses trimmed in black is superb.

OLD WHALING CHURCH

OLD WHALING CHURCH

Edgartown Lighthouse (508-627-4441; mvmuseum.org), at the end of North Water Street. The first lighthouse to direct boats into and around Edgartown Harbor was built in 1828 on a small island. Shortly after a new lighthouse replaced it in 1938, the island became connected to the "mainland" of the Vineyard by a spit of sand. Today the lighthouse, renovated in 2007, is accessible by foot. Take note of the granite cobblestone foundation (dubbed the Children's Lighthouse Memorial), a tribute to Vineyard children who have died. Open to the public late May to mid-October. $.

UP-ISLAND

Mayhew Chapel and **Indian Burial Ground**, Christiantown Road, off Indian Hill Road, West Tisbury. This tiny chapel, burial ground, and memorial to the Praying Indians (who were converted to Christianity by the Reverend Mayhew Jr. in the mid-1600s) is a quiet place, owned by the Wampanoag tribe of Aquinnah.

Grange Hall (508-627-4440; mvpreservation.org), State Road, West Tisbury. Open seasonally. The original Agricultural Society Barn now hosts functions and events.

NORTH WATER STREET

CHERISHED INSTITUTION

Alley's General Store (508-693-0088; mvpreservation.org), State Road, West Tisbury. Alley's is a beloved Vineyard landmark. "Dealers in almost everything" since 1858, the store has a wide front porch where locals have gathered over the decades to discuss current events and exchange friendly gossip. In the early 1990s, though, economic conditions almost forced Alley's to close. In true island spirit, the Martha's Vineyard Preservation Trust stepped in to renovate the building and ensure its survival. Alley's continues to feel like a country store, selling everything utilitarian: housewares, mismatched cups and saucers, and locally grown produce.

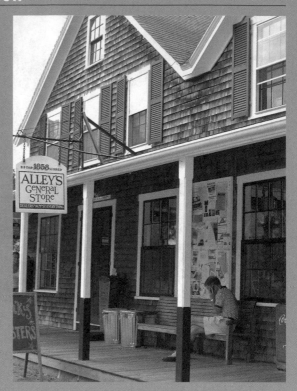

Beetlebung Corner, at the intersection of Middle, South, State, and Menemsha Cross Roads; the center of Chilmark. The intersection was named for the grove of beetlebung trees (the New England name for tupelos), which are unusual in this region. Tupelo is a very hard wood, an excellent material for making mallets (also called beetles) and the plugs (or bungs) that filled the holes in wooden casks and barrels during whale oil days.

Abel's Hill Cemetery, South Road, about ½ mile beyond Meeting House Road, Chilmark. John Belushi, of *Saturday Night Live* and Blues Brothers fame, was buried here after a drug overdose in 1982 at the not-so-ripe age of 33. He'd been partying with Robert DeNiro and Robin Williams at the Chateau Marmot in West Hollywood on March 5 when a mainline cocktail of heroin and cocaine did him in. According to legend, the only place Belushi ever said that he got a good night's sleep was on the Vineyard, where he and his wife had some property. You'll easily find the marked grave near the entrance of the cemetery, but his body lies in an unmarked grave about 11 feet north of where his original headstone was placed.

Quitsa Overlook, off State Road. At Beetlebung Corner, bear left onto State Road, heading toward Aquinnah. After a mile or so, you'll pass over a bridge; Nashaquitsa Pond (also known as Quitsa) is on your right and Stonewall Pond is on your left. Just beyond, a spot overlooks Quitsa and Menemsha Ponds. About half a mile farther locals fill water jugs from a fresh, sweet stream that's been siphoned off to run out of a pipe.

Local lore attributes various cures to the water—from stress relief, to a flu antidote, to a hangover remedy.

Aquinnah Community Baptist Church (508-693-1539; wampanoagtribe .net), 1 Church Street at State Road, Aquinnah. Turn left at the small red schoolhouse (now the town library). The lovely church is the country's oldest Indian Baptist church. It might have the prettiest location, too, overlooking windswept grassy dunes, stone walls, and the Atlantic Ocean.

Menemsha Harbor, at Menemsha Cross Road near Beetlebung Corner. This working fishing village is filled with small, sturdy docks and simple, weathered boathouses. Some islanders still earn a living from the boats of Menemsha's fishing fleet. For the rest of us, the harbor is a great location from which to

JOHN BELUSHI'S GRAVE ABEL'S HILL CEMETERY

watch the setting sun. It's one of several locations throughout the Cape and islands where the ritual of applauding the sun for its day's work is observed the moment it slips below the horizon. A few little shacks (shops and fast-food eateries) line the road to Dutcher's Dock.

Aquinnah Tribal Administrative Building (508-645-9265; wampanoagtribe.net), 20 Black Brook Road, Aquinnah. Housed inside this eco-friendly building (made almost completely of recycled materials and run by solar power) are a number of interesting small displays about the Wampanoag tribe. Look for an elders gallery with pictures of the tribal elders past and present, traditional native gardens, and a wetu, a traditional native home. When visiting, be aware that this is a working environment for the government of the tribe, not just a tourist destination.

Clay Cliffs of Aquinnah. The brilliantly colored clay cliffs, a designated national landmark, rise 150 feet above the shore and were formed 100 million years ago by glaciers. For a fine view of the full magnitude of this spectacular geological formation, and distant views of Noman's Land Island and the Elizabeth Islands, walk beyond the souvenir shops. A wooden boardwalk also leads to the beach, where you can appreciate the towering clay cliffs from sea level. It's important to note that the Wampanoag have lived here for more than 5,000 years and own most of this land, although most of the beach is public; only they may remove clay from the eroding cliffs.

Gay Head Lighthouse (508-627-4441; gayheadlight.org). This redbrick

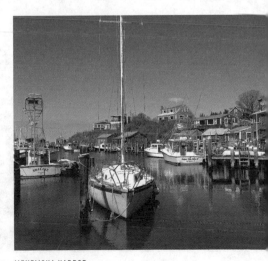

MENEMSHA HARBOR

lighthouse was built in 1844 to replace a wooden lighthouse that had stood since 1799. In 1856 a powerful Fresnel lens was mounted atop the lighthouse, where it warned ships away from the perilous Aquinnah coast; it was used for almost 100 years. The Gay Head light was named one of America's 11 Most Endangered Places by the National Trust for Historic Preservation in 2013, and in order to preserve it for generations to come, the "Keep on Shining" committee successfully raised funds to relocate the light away from the eroding cliffs; the committee continues its fund-raising efforts to complete restoration. From late June to mid-September, you can ascend the lighthouse to enjoy the sunset. It opens 90 minutes prior to sunset and closes 30 minutes after sunset; $.

CLAY CLIFFS OF AQUINNAH AND GAY HEAD LIGHTHOUSE

Aquinnah Cultural Center (508-645-7900; wampanoagtribe.net), Aquinnah. Open late June to early September. This 1880s homestead, which serves as the Indigenous Museum of the Aquinnah Wampanoag and community cultural center, enjoys some of the most wonderful windswept vistas on the island. It's no wonder that their 6 acres are leased for weddings. Donations.

Moshup Beach Overlook, on the northern end of Moshup Trail and south of the parking lot for the lighthouse, off State Road. This scenic coastal road has nice views of wild, low heathlands.

SCENIC DRIVES Instead of making a beeline up-island, detour onto Lambert's Cove Road from State Road out of Vineyard Haven. Take North, South, or Middle Roads up-island. I particularly like cutting between the roads on Tea Lane and Meeting House Road. As you approach Aquinnah, take a left onto Moshup Trail to the lighthouse and

AQUINNAH CULTURAL CENTER

circle back via Lighthouse Road and Lobsterville Road (but do follow Lobsterville to the very end, across the cut from Menemsha)

✳ To Do

AIRPLANE RIDES Classic Aviators (508-627-7677; biplanemv.com), off Herring Creek Road at the Katama Airfield, Edgartown. Open seasonally. Open-cockpit rides in a 1941 Waco biplane, solo or with a friend, with Snoopy-like leather caps and goggles. Rates start at $229 for one or two people for a 15- to 20-minute flight.

BICYCLING & RENTALS Several excellent (albeit crowded) bicycle paths connect the main towns: Vineyard Haven to Oak Bluffs, Oak Bluffs to Edgartown, Edgartown to West Tisbury, and Edgartown to South Beach via Katama Road. Because the roads from West Tisbury to Aquinnah are rather hilly, you need to be in pretty good shape to tackle the ride. A less ambitious but rewarding journey would entail taking your bike to Aquinnah and then pedaling the hilly but scenic up-island circular trail that begins at the Aquinnah Lighthouse: Take Lighthouse Road to Lobsterville Road and backtrack up Lobsterville Road to State Road to Moshup Trail. The Manuel E. Correllus State Forest (see *Green Space*), off Edgartown–West Tisbury Road, also has several bicycle paths.

    Rubel Bike Maps (bikemaps.com) are the best, most detailed maps available. Rubel produces a combination map that covers both the Vineyard and Nantucket ($), as well as another that includes the islands, Cape Cod, and the North Shore ($).

    The **Martha's Vineyard Commission** (508-693-3453; mvcommission.org) also produces a free map that tells you what to expect on major routes: for instance, narrow roadways (shared with cars), gently rolling terrain, steep rolling terrain, and so on. It does not give estimated times or exact mileage, though.

    Bike Ferry (508-645-3511). Operates 9 AM–5 PM (on demand) late May to early September. Some people riding out to Menemsha and Aquinnah will be thrilled to know about Hugh Taylor's little ferry, which takes cyclists across Menemsha Creek, which separates the picturesque harbor from Lobsterville Beach and Aquinnah beyond. This 150-yard ferry ride saves cyclists a 7-mile bike ride. $.

    Dozens of shops rent bikes, including **R. W. Cutler Bikes** (508-627-4052; marth asvineyardbike.com) on the harborfront at 1 Main Street in Edgartown; and **Wheel Happy** (508-627-5928), 8 South Water Street, and (508-627-5881), 204 Upper Main Street, both in Edgartown. Mountain bikes and hybrids are rented for one-, three- and seven-day periods. Most shops are open April through October; ask about delivery and pickup service. $$$ daily.

    ✳ **Cycle Works** (508-693-6966), at 351 State Road in Vineyard Haven, repairs bicycles. John Stevenson and his enthusiastic and helpful crew have the largest selection of cycling equipment (for sale and rent), accessories, and parts on the island. They've been here since 1975.

BOAT EXCURSIONS & RENTALS Magic Carpet (508-627-2889; sailmagiccarpet. com), Memorial Wharf, Edgartown. Departures June through October. This classic 56-foot wooden yawl comfortably accommodates 12 people on two-hour charters along Cape Poge. You'll learn some good island history and tales along the way.

    Sea Witch (508-650-0466; seawitchsailingcharters.com), out of Vineyard Haven, offers highly recommended private charters.

CHAPPAQUIDDICK

Accessible via the "Chappy ferry," *On-Time II* and *On-Time III* (508-627-9427; chappy ferry.com), at the corner of Dock and Daggett streets. The crossing between Edgartown and Chappy is completed in the blink of an eye. The ferry runs 6:45 AM–midnight in-season, but doesn't really have a schedule; it just goes when it's needed, and thus it's always "on time." Because it's the only method of transportation between the two islands and a surprising number of people live on Chappy year-round, the ferry runs daily. Round-trip for car and driver $$, walk-on passengers $, bikes $.

Chappaquiddick contains several lovely beaches and wildlife refuges, including the 516-acre Cape Poge Wildlife Refuge, the 14-acre Mytoi, and the 200-acre Wasque Reservation. Unfortunately, though, the beautiful island is perhaps best known because of Dike Bridge, the scene of the drowning incident involving Sen. Edward Kennedy in July 1969. To reach Dike Bridge, stay on Chappaquiddick Road after you get off the ferry until the road turns into Dike Road. When the road takes a sharp turn to the right (in about a mile), continue straight on the dirt road until you reach the bridge.

CAPE POGE LIGHTHOUSE

When the bridge was rebuilt in the mid-1990s, pedestrians once again had direct access to Cape Pogue, a thin ribbon of sand that stretches along the east side of Chappaquiddick and the remote Cape Poge Lighthouse. Four-wheel-drive vehicles can use the bridge when endangered shorebirds like the piping plover are not nesting. Cape Poge is also accessible by foot or by four-wheel-drive vehicle, over the sand of Wasque Point, several miles south of the beach.

✏ **Cape Poge Wildlife Refuge** and **Wasque Reservation** (508-627-7689; thetrustees.org). These adjoining tracts of land on the southeastern corner of Chappaquiddick—called Pogue or Poge, depending on whom you are talking to—are relatively isolated, so that even on summer weekends you can escape the crowds. This seaside wilderness contains huge tracts of dunes, the long and beautiful **East Beach**, cedars, salt marshes, ponds, tidal flats, and scrub brush. Overseen by the Massachusetts Trustees of Reservations, Cape Poge (516 acres) and Wasque (200 acres)

are the group's oldest island holdings. Half of the state's scallops are harvested each autumn off the coast near the **Cape Poge Lighthouse** (on the northern tip of the cape). The lighthouse was built in 1893 and automated in 1943. Note: It is dangerous to swim at Wasque Rip because of the forceful tide. Limited East Beach parking $, reservation entrance $ (late May to mid-October).

🖾 The outstanding three-hour natural history tours (508-627-3599; thetrustees.org) of Cape Poge are naturalist led, in an open-air four-wheel-drive vehicle, and depart from Mytoi garden (see below) daily, May through October. It'll be one of your best island adventures. $$$$.

🖾 **Cape Poge Lighthouse tours** (1½ hours), where you'll learn about the fascinating history of the light and the keepers who lived there, depart from Mytoi garden from late May to mid-October. Space is limited, so reserve early. Don't miss it. $$$.

Mytoi (508-627-7689; thetrustees.org), Dike Road. Open daily, sunrise to sunset. This 14-acre Japanese garden, built by Hugh Jones in 1958, has camellias, irises, a goldfish pond, and a picturesque little bridge.

🖾 **Poucha Pond Kayak Tour** (508-627-3599; thetrustees.org), Dike Bridge. Late May to mid-October. Only members of the Trustees of Reservations may take these self-guided tours; rentals available. Nonmembers must first purchase an introductory family membership. $$$.

MYTOI

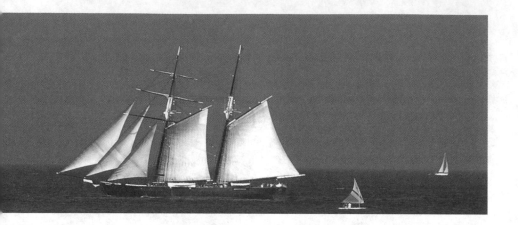

Sail Ena (508-627-0848; sailena.com), Vineyard Haven. Day, sunset, and sailing for women aboard a 34-foot classic Alden sloop.

Mad Max (508-627-7500; madmaxmarina.com), at the Seafood Shanty, Edgartown Harbor. This 60-foot catamaran sets sail on two-hour voyages from late May to September. They sure know these waters well. $$$$$+

Wind's Up! (508-693-4252; 508-693-4340; windsupmv.com), 199 Beach Road, at the drawbridge on Beach Road, Vineyard Haven. Rentals and instruction mid-May to late September (and possibly into October). This full-service outfit (on-island since 1962) rents Sunfish and small catamarans in addition to kayaks and stand-up paddleboards, and offers beginning, intermediate, and advanced instruction.

VINEYARD HAVEN HARBOR

CANOEING & KAYAKING 🐚 **Long Point Wildlife Refuge Tour** (508 627 3599; thetrustees.org), led by Trustees of Reservations in July and August. This two-hour tour is a great way to learn basic paddling techniques and about the local ecology and natural history of Long Point. If your visit is timed right, inquire about their (great) full moon kayak tours. $$$–$$$$$.

Chilmark Pond Preserve (Martha's Vineyard Landbank at 508-627-7141), access just before Abel's Hill Cemetery (where, incidentally, John Belushi and Lillian Hellman are buried) on South Road,

FISHING STORES

Chilmark. When you paddle across Chilmark Pond, you'll be rewarded with a small ocean beach on the south shore. This local secret (well worth the effort) is accessed only by canoe or kayak, which you must supply.

See also **Cape Poge Wildlife Refuge** under the "Chappaquiddick" sidebar and **Wind's Up** under "Boat Excursions/Rentals."

FITNESS CLUBS ❄ **Airport Fitness** (508-696-8000; airportfitnessmv.com), off Edgartown–West Tisbury Road, at the airport. A full-service center.

❄ **B-Strong** (508-693-5997; b-strong.com), 29 Kennebec Ave, Oak Bluffs. This small gym downtown has a good variety of equipment and the best hours on the island.

❄ **The Mansion House Health Club & Spa** (508-693-2200; mvmansionhouse.com), Main Street, Vineyard Haven. With a heated pool, spa, and sauna.

❄ **YMCA of Martha's Vineyard** (508-696-7171; ymcamv.org), off Edgartown–Vineyard Haven Road in Oak Bluffs. A great community center.

FISHING Fishing is excellent from most Vineyard **beaches and bridges**. The bridge between Oak Bluffs and Edgartown is perfect for anglers. There's also a wide area that hangs over the swiftly running channel between Nantucket Sound and Sengekontacket Pond. You're most likely to catch the island's prized striped bass and bluefish before sunrise. Surf casting is best from south-facing beaches and the beaches at Aquinnah. On Chappaquiddick, **East Beach** at Cape Poge Wildlife Refuge and **Wasque Point** (see the "Chappaquiddick" sidebar for both) are famed for fishing.

❄ **Coop's Bait & Tackle** (508-627-3909; coopsbaitandtackle.com), 147 Edgartown–West Tisbury Road, Edgartown. This is your basic one-stop shopping for bait, tackle, boat charters, and information on "hot spots" for catching the big ones.

Dick's Bait & Tackle (508-693-7669), 108 New York Avenue in Oak Bluffs; and **Capt. Porky's** (508-627-7117), Dock Street, Edgartown, rent fishing rods, tackle, and other necessary equipment. Capt. Porky's also arranges charters.

Great Harbor Sportfishing Charters (508-627-3122 land; 508-627-2128 cell; vineyardfishing.com), Edgartown Harbor. Trips May to late October. Captain Charlie uses light tackle, flies, and conventional means when he goes out sportfishing.

North Shore Charters (508-645-2993; bassnblue.com), out of Menemsha Harbor. May through October. Captain Scott McDowell takes anglers in search of bass and blues.

FOR FAMILIES ✐ There are so many family- and kid-friendly activities that I've interspersed them throughout this section. If I'd listed them under "For Families," the other headings would have been decimated!

GOLF **Farm Neck Golf Club** (508-693-3057; farmneck.net), off County Road, Oak Bluffs. Open April through December. Reservations are strongly suggested at this stately 18-hole course, but they're only taken two or three days in advance. A challenging course, but not long.

❋ **Mink Meadows** (508-693-0600; minkmeadowsgc.com), off Franklin Street, Vineyard Haven. A fairly long but very subtle nine-hole semiprivate course; more challenging than you might think. Just ask President Obama.

HORSEBACK RIDING ❋ **Red Pony Riding** (508-693-3788; redponyfarmmv.com), 85 Red Pony Road, off Edgartown–West Tisbury Road, West Tisbury. Private lessons and trails for experienced riders.

❋ ✐ **Nip-n-Tuck Farm** (508-693-1449), 39 Davis Look Road, West Tisbury. Hayrides are offered year-round.

ICE-SKATING **Martha's Vineyard Ice Arena** (508-693-5329; mvarena.com), Edgartown–Vineyard Haven Road, Oak Bluffs. Who brings skates to the Vineyard? No one, but you can rent them here. $.

MINI-GOLF **Island Cove** (508-693-2611; islandcoveadventures.com), 386 State Road across from Cronig's Market, Vineyard Haven. Open mid-May to mid-October. After golf, try your mountaineering prowess on the rock-climbing wall, then stick around for BBQ and ice cream.

PLEIN AIR PAINTING, EDGARTOWN

SAILBOARDING **Wind's Up!** (see above for practical details). Sheltered Lagoon Pond, where Wind's Up! has a facility, is a great place for beginners to learn sailboarding and sailing. The water is shallow and the instructors patient. Those more experienced can rent equipment, consult the shop's map, and head out on their own. Sailboarding is excellent all over the island, but experienced surfers should head to Menemsha, Aquinnah, and South Beach.

SPECIAL PROGRAMS ❋ **Vineyard Conservation Society** (508-693-9588; vineyardconservation.org), Wakeman Conservation Center, 57 David Avenue off Lambert's Cove Road, Tisbury. Since it was established in 1965, this nonprofit group has protected thousands of acres from commercial and residential development by engaging in conservation land acqui-sition and advocacy. The society also sponsors a wide range of public activities, most of them free, including the Winter Walks program, a summer environmental lecture series, educational seminars and workshops on such topics as alternative wastewater treatment and solar-powered building technology, and the annual Earth Day all-island cleanup.

❄ ♪ **Featherstone Center for the Arts** (508-693-1850; featherstoneart.org), Oak Bluffs, off Barnes Road half a mile north of Edgartown–Vineyard Haven Road. On 6 acres donated by the Martha's Vineyard Land Bank, this former horse barn and farm has been transformed into a community art center. **Classes** change seasonally but might include woodworking, stained glass, pottery, papermaking, printmaking, weaving, guitar lessons, and photography. Weekly summer art camps for kids, too. Continuously searching for ways to be more responsive to its community, from late June to late August the center also stages a **flea and fine-arts market**, an **open pottery studio**, an open **darkroom**, and **Musical Monday** evenings (with folk, country, jazz, blues, reggae . . . you name it). About 20 of the surrounding acres are criss-crossed with so-called **Featherstone Trails** for hiking.

♪ **Farm Institute** (508-627-7007; farminstitute.org), 14 Aero Avenue, off South Beach and Katama Road, Edgartown. By now you hopefully are aware of the Vine-yard's deep agricultural roots. Well, this is the place to milk goats, watch baby piglets or calves being born, explore vegetable gardens, or get lost in a multiacre corn maze (when they can pull it off)—for a day or a week or the whole season! This nonprofit educational center offers summer programs for kids, Saturday morning farm chores, adult workshops, tons of fresh produce and meats, and more special events. It's a rare opportunity for most of us to connect to the natural world.

A PERFECT UP-ISLAND DAY ON THE VINEYARD

7:45	Pick up fresh doughnuts from Humphrey's.
8:00	Take the scenic drive along Lambert's Cove Road.
9:30	Hike the crestline trail at Menemsha Hills Reservation.
11:30	Drive Tea Lane and Meeting House Road between North and South Roads.
12:00	Sit on the front porch of Alley's General Store with a sandwich.
1:15	Interact with the joyful sculptures at Field Gallery.
2:30	Explore Polly Hill Arboretum.
4:00	Visit Chilmark Pottery or Martha's Vineyard Glass Works.
5:30	Stroll the beach beneath the Clay Cliffs of Aquinnah.
7:30	Watch the dusky light change color at Menemsha Harbor.
8:00	Enjoy clam chowder or lobster rolls at The Galley or The Bite.
10:30	Split a Mad Martha's ice cream cone with your partner.

OPEN SPACE RULES

🔍 **Martha's Vineyard Land Bank** (508-627-7141; mvlandbank .com), 167 Upper Main Street, Edgartown. The Land Bank was established in 1986 in order to purchase open space with funds raised by a 2 percent tax on real estate transactions. I highly recommend getting this organization's map prior to your visit for a current look at the Vineyard's open land (more than 3,100 acres). Many of the island's conservation areas— ocean beach, moors, meadows, ponds, and woods—are free for all to enjoy. Maps are available at the six town halls, libraries, this office, and online. Don't forget to check out their guided walks.

SWIMMING POOL ❄ **Mansion House Health Club & Spa** (508-693-2200; mvman sionhouse.com), Main Street, Vineyard Haven. The 75-foot heated mineral spring pool also has lap lanes. $$.

YMCA of Martha's Vineyard (508-696-7171; ymcamv.org), off Edgartown-Vineyard Haven Road in Oak Bluffs, this community center has a 25-yard, six-lane pool, a large workout room, and a snack bar. $$$.

TENNIS Public courts are located at: **Church Street** (clay) near the corner of Franklin Street and Lake Street near the town landing, both in Vineyard Haven; **Niantic Avenue** (hard courts) in Oak Bluffs; **Robinson Road** (hard courts) near Pease's Point Way in Edgartown; **Chilmark Community Center** (508-645-3061) on South Road at Beetlebung Corner in Chilmark (available when members are not using them); and **Old County Road** (two hard) in West Tisbury.

❄ ☂ **Airport Fitness** (508-696-8000; airportfitnessmv.com), 22 Airport Road, off Edgartown–West Tisbury Road, West Tisbury. When it's raining, this full-service indoor facility arranges matches. Lessons, tennis camps for all ages, and ball machines, too.

❄ **Vineyard Youth Tennis** (508-693-7762; vineyardyouthtennis.org), 618 Barnes Road, just west of Edgartown–Vineyard Haven Road in Oak Bluffs. An inflatable bubble over the courts allows youngsters to play for free, year-round.

Farm Neck Golf Club (508-693-9728; 508-693-3057; farmneck.net), off County Road, Oak Bluffs. Tennis from mid-May to mid-October. Outdoor Har-Tru courts are available, reserved a few days in advance.

WATERSKIING **Martha's Vineyard Ocean Sports** (508-693-8476; mvoceansports .com), Dockside Marina in Oak Bluffs. Open mid-June to mid-October. Even if you're a self-described klutz, these folks can teach you how to waterski, Jet Ski, kneeboard, tube, wakeboard, and parasail.

✳ Green Space

Manuel E. Correllus State Forest (508-693-2540; mass.gov/eea/agencies/dcr/mass parks), off Edgartown–West Tisbury Road or Barnes Road. Comprising almost 5,400 acres of woodland and meadows in the center of the island, the forest's trails are used regularly by bikers, joggers, picnickers, and hikers. Park near the Barnes Road entrance.

IN OAK BLUFFS

Ocean Park, along Ocean Avenue. Fringed with some of Oak Bluffs' best-preserved gingerbread cottages, the park's centerpiece is a large white gazebo that serves as a bandstand for summer-evening concerts.

IN AND NEAR EDGARTOWN

✐ **Felix Neck Wildlife Sanctuary** (508-627-4850; massaudubon.org), off Edgartown–Vineyard Haven Road, Edgartown. The Vineyard is populated by many species of birds that flock to the island's forests and wildlife sanctuaries. This 219-acre preserve, affiliated with the Audubon Society, has 4 miles of easy trails that traverse thick woods, open meadows of wildflowers, beaches, and salt marshes. The interpretive exhibit center has turtles, aquariums, a gift shop, and a library. Year-round activities for children and adults include guided nature walks and bird-watching trips for novices and experts alike. Inquire about weeklong children's day camps. $.

See also **Mytoi, Cape Pogue Wildlife Refuge** and **Wasque Reservation**, and **natural history tours** under the "Chappaquiddick" sidebar.

IN WEST TISBURY AND UP-ISLAND

Menemsha Hills Reservation (508-693-3678; thetrustees.org), off North Road, Chilmark. This exceptional Trustees of Reservations property makes for a great two-hour hike. The 3-mile crestline trail, part of which runs along the island's second highest point, leads down to a rocky beach. This point was used during World War II as a military lookout. No swimming allowed.

Cedar Tree Neck Sanctuary (508-693-5207; sheriffsmeadow.org), off Indian Hill Road from State Road, West Tisbury. The 400-acre sanctuary, owned and managed by the Sheriff's Meadow Foundation, has trails through bogs, fields, and forests down to the bluffs overlooking Vineyard Sound.

Long Point Wildlife Refuge (508-693-7392; thetrustees.org), off Edgartown–West Tisbury Road, West Tisbury. A long, bumpy, dirt road leads to a couple of mile-long trails, Long Cove Pond, and a long stretch of the south shore. Parking is limited at this 632-acre preserve, maintained by the Massachusetts Trustees of Reservations, so get there early. $ per person, parking $$ per vehicle.

Peaked Hill Reservation (mvlandbank.com), off Tabor House Road from Middle or North roads, Chilmark. Turn left on the dirt lane opposite (more or less) the town landfill and then keep taking right-hand turns until you reach the trailhead. This 149-acre Land Bank property is the highest point on the island, at a whopping 311 feet above sea level. Good for hiking, picnicking, and mountain biking, this reservation also offers vistas of Noman's Land Island, Aquinnah peninsula, and Menemsha Bight.

Waskosim's Rock Preservation (mvlandbank.com), North Road, just over the Chilmark town line. At almost 200 acres, this is one of the largest and most diverse of the

Land Bank properties, with great hiking, bird-watching, picnicking, and mountain biking. The Waskosim boulder marks the start of a stone wall that ran down to Menemsha Pond, separating the English and Wampanoag lands in the mid-17th century.

Allen Farm Vista (mvlandbank.com), South Road, Chilmark. On the south (or the left side) about 1 mile beyond Beetlebung Corner as you head toward Aquinnah. Practically the entire stretch of South Road in Chilmark once looked like this striking 22-acre field and pastureland, protected as a Land Bank property. Lucy Vincent Beach is just beyond the pond, grazing sheep, and moorlands.

Cranberry Acres, West Tisbury. This cranberry bog, on the southside of Lambert's Cove Road from Vineyard Haven, has walking trails.

❋ **Polly Hill Arboretum** (508-693-9426; pollyhillarboretum.org), 809 State Road, West Tisbury. Grounds open year-round; visitor center open late May to mid-October; tours during the summer, and winter walk program during the off-season. This is a magical place. Now totaling 70 acres, this former sheep farm was brought under cultivation by legendary horticulturist Polly Hill in order to preserve it as native woodland. The arboretum, opened to the public in the late 1990s, is a not-for-profit sanctuary devoted to a mix of almost 3,100 native and exotic plants, many threatened by extinction. The arboretum is tranquil and beautiful from early spring well into fall. Wandering visitors will discover an extraordinary range of plants. Lecture series, too. Donations gratefully accepted.

Fulling Mill Brook Preserve, off Middle Road, about 1½ miles east of Beetlebung Corner, Chilmark. Biking and foot access from South Road. Hiking trails pass through 49 acres of forests, fields, and streams.

See also **Featherstone Meetinghouse for the Arts** under *To Do*.

BEACHES Unlike Nantucket, many Vineyard beaches are private, open only to homeowners or cottage renters. (By law, though, anyone has the right to fish from any beach between the high- and low-water marks. So if you want to explore where you otherwise aren't allowed, make sure you're carrying a fishing pole!) Many innkeepers, especially those in the up-island establishments, provide walk-on passes to their guests. (A much-coveted Chilmark pass will get you access to Lucy Vincent Beach off South Road, the island's prettiest.) And just to keep you in the loop, two other private beaches in Chilmark—Quansoo and Hancock—require a key to gain entry. It's *always* locked and sometimes guarded. If you don't summer in Chilmark, you might consider purchasing a key, which sells for hundreds of thousands of dollars. (File under: if you have to ask the price, you probably can't afford it.) The following are public beaches.

IN VINEYARD HAVEN

Lake Tashmoo (or Herring Creek), at the end of Herring Creek Road, off Daggett Avenue from Franklin Street. This small beach offers good swimming, surf-fishing, and shellfishing. No facilities; limited parking; lifeguard.

⌁ **Owen Park Beach**, on the harbor just north of the ferry. Good for small children and swimming. Public restrooms; lifeguard. Limited parking.

IN WEST TISBURY

⌁ **Lambert's Cove Beach**, off Lambert's Cove Road. Although it's restricted to town residents and inn-goers in-season, you can park here off-season to enjoy one of the island's top beaches. The sand is fine and the waters calm.

ISLAND MYSTERIES

Vineyard mystery novelist Philip R. Craig writes page turners that are perfect for beach getaways. In one of my favorites from this 20-plus-book series, *The Double Minded Men*, we first meet J. W. Jackson, a retired Boston cop, and his future wife, Zee, who tangle with a potentate, stolen necklace, and murder—all of which threaten their idyllic island home.

A big Craig fan who visited the Vineyard frequently, I always looked forward to the next installment of J. W.'s escapades, ones that took him to every nook and cranny of the island. When visiting, I'd always know with certainty that I'd just passed a little road that led to one of his character's homes or a favorite fishing beach where he and Zee would catch blues when they were running. I recognized places from every page: street corners, shops, summertime traffic, Alley's General Store, or a specific beach on which we'd search for shells. The Vineyard becomes even more real to anyone who's read Craig's books.

J. W.'s friends and family are sometimes helpful in solving these cozy mysteries, but at other times he must protect them as he becomes involved in schemes by land developers, old-time gangsters, entertainers, environmentalists, and old pals. The characters who pop up become old friends we look forward to meeting in subsequent books. Sprinkled throughout, his love of cooking also becomes apparent with recipe riffs for smoked bluefish, clam cakes, and striped bass ("delish"). When reading the last sentence of his last book—*Vineyard Chill*, which was completed just before his death—I felt a sadness that I'd not read another J. W. case that would bring Martha's Vineyard even more to life than it already is.

—Martha Grant

IN OAK BLUFFS

⚓ **Oak Bluffs Town Beach**, on both sides of the ferry wharf, Oak Bluffs. This calm, narrow beach is very popular with Oak Bluffs families and seasonal visitors with small children. No facilities. Public restrooms next to the ferry dock.

⚓ **Joseph Sylvia State Beach**, along Beach Road between Edgartown and Oak Bluffs. The Edgartown end of this 2-mile-long barrier beach is also called Bend-in-the-Road Beach; this part of the gentle beach has lifeguards but no facilities. Park free along the roadside. Kids will like jumping into the water from Big Bridge, famous from the movie *Jaws*. Good shore fishing and crabbing along the jetties, too.

Aquinnah Beach, just south of the Clay Cliffs of Aquinnah. Take the boardwalk and path through cranberry and beach plum bushes down to the beach, about a 10-minute walk. Resist the temptation to cover yourself with mud from the cliff's clay baths; the cliffs have eroded irreparably over the past century. (If that doesn't dissuade you, perhaps the law will: it's illegal to remove or use the clay.) Instead, walk along this 5-mile beach, called, from north to south, **Moshup Public Beach**, Moshup (the shuttle bus drops off here—otherwise, it's a 10-minute walk from paid Aquinnah parking), Philbin, and Zack's Cliffs. The cliffs are to the north, but the

JOSEPH SYLVIA STATE BEACH

beaches are wider to the south. **Philbin** and **Zack's Cliffs** beaches are reserved for residents, but if you stick close to the waterline, you might not have a problem. Zack's fronts Jacqueline Kennedy Onassis's former estate. The farther south you walk, the fewer people you'll see. But those people you do see, you'll see more of—people come here specifically to sunbathe nude. It's not legal, but generally the authorities look the other way. Swimming is very good here; the surf is usually light to moderate, and the shore doesn't drop off as abruptly as it does along the island's south shore. Facilities include restrooms and a few small fast-food shops at the head of the cliff. Parking is plentiful; $$.

⚓ **Eastville Beach**, Beach Road (at the drawbridge), Oak Bluffs. This county-owned public beach has gentle surf and good views of the ferries coming and going in Vineyard Haven Harbor. No facilities.

IN EDGARTOWN

Lighthouse Beach, at the end of North Water Street, adjoining Fuller Street Beach. From Lighthouse Beach you can watch boats going in and out of the harbor. Rarely crowded with bathers because of seaweed, but always crowded with picture-takers; gentle waves. No facilities. **Fuller Street Beach** is a short bike ride from town and generally quiet.

Katama (or South) Beach, off Katama Road, is a favorite among college students. A shuttle runs from Edgartown to this popular, 3-mile-long barrier beach, which has medium to heavy surf, a strong undertow, and high dunes. Children can swim in the calm and warm salt water of Katama Bay. There are lifeguards, but not along

UP-ISLAND

the entire beach. Facilities at the end of Katama Road and Herring Creek Road. This beach becomes the Trustees of Reservations' **Norton Point Beach** when you are traveling east.

See also **Cape Pogue Wildlife Refuge** and **Wasque Reservation** in the "Chappaquiddick" sidebar, and **Long Point Wildlife Refuge**, above.

UP-ISLAND

Long Point Wildlife Refuge, off Waldron's Bottom Road from Edgartown–West Tisbury Road, West Tisbury. Owned by the Trustees of Reservations, this wide beach is isolated and beautiful, with good surf. From here you can also follow nature trails to **Tisbury Great Pond**. Limited parking. $.

✒ **Menemsha Beach**, Menemsha Harbor. This calm, gentle beach is also pebbly. Nearby restrooms. Sunsets from here can't be beat.

✒ **Lobsterville Beach**, off State and Lobsterville Roads, Aquinnah. This beach is popular with families because of shallow, warm water and gentle surf. Limited parking along the road. Popular for fishing, too.

Lucy Vincent Beach, off South Road, is arguably the island's nicest beach. Although it's open only to residents and Chilmark inn-goers (which is reason enough to stay in Chilmark), you can enjoy the wide, cliff-backed beach off-season. The farther east you walk, the less clothing you'll see. The farther west you walk, the more trouble you'll get in, because that stretch of beach is as private as they come.

Squibnocket Beach, also off South Road in Chilmark, has the most reliable surfing on the island.

✒ **Uncle Seth's Pond**, off Lambert's Cove Road. A tiny (but public) freshwater pond on the side of the road. Good for children. Limited parking.

PICNICS **Owen Park**, off Main Street, north of the ferry dock, Vineyard Haven. This thin strip of grass runs from Main Street down to the harbor beach. It's a great vantage point for watching boats sail in and out of the harbor. Swings for the kids. Limited parking.

Mill Pond, West Tisbury. This wonderful place to feed ducks and swans is next to the simple, shingled West Tisbury Police Department.

✳ Lodging

With a few exceptions (primarily smaller B&Bs noted by our special value [✿] symbol), it is very expensive to stay on the Vineyard. Room rates have soared well, well beyond the rate of inflation since the late 1990s. Of all the towns, Edgartown is the most expensive by far; Oak Bluffs tends to draw younger visitors; and Vineyard Haven and West Tisbury are the most sensibly priced towns.

Reservations, made well in advance of your visit, are imperative during July and August and on weekends from September to mid-October. The *height of high season* runs, of course, from late June to early September, but many innkeepers define high season as mid-May to mid-October. In addition, many up-island inns are booked months in advance by hundreds of bridal parties, many with no ties to the island, who want meadows, stone walls, and spectacular ocean views as the backdrop for their photographs.

So many inns require a two- or three-night minimum stay in summer (and two nights on weekends in autumn)

WINNETU OCEANSIDE RESORT

amenities—two heated pools, a kiddie pool, a first-rate tennis club and fitness center with an array of classes and massages, plenty of teen and children's programs (including a complimentary one in the mornings in-season), oversized chess pieces for playful fun, poolside bingo, a little pond with turtles, outdoor table tennis, a putting green, antique fire truck rides, weekly clambakes, a library with fireplace, and a sublime restaurant (see **The Dunes** under *Dining Out*). A variety of accommodations suit a multitude of vacationer configurations: studios; one-bedroom suites with a combo living/dining area and a deck or patio (sleeping a family of five); and larger suites. Full kitchens are available. Furnishings are summery, contemporary, and upscale but not so precious that you can't enjoy the place after the beach. In the end, it's hard to say what's better—the facilities or the services, but they do go hand in hand. Tons of organized trips make it easy to relax here: kayak tours of Poucha Pond, private charters to Nantucket, whale watching, lighthouse and dune trips, and sunset water taxis to Edgartown. Concierges are ready to help with any and all requests and nary a staff member passes without a huge smile on their face and a ready hand. Rooms $$–$$$$$+; off-season packages offer a great value.

that I have omitted this information from the individual reviews. Assume it's true. Although there are quite a few year-round lodging choices, the island is incredibly quiet from January to March. Rate ranges listed below are for high season.

RESORT

IN EDGARTOWN

🛶 **Winnetu Oceanside Resort** (508-310-1733; winnetu.com), South Beach, Edgartown. Open mid-April to late October. The Winnetu is easily one of the best family resorts on the Eastern Seaboard. But it also offers plenty of ways for romantics and more active folks to have a stellar holiday, too. It has no rivals on the Vineyard or Cape Cod. (It's rival on Nantucket—the **Nantucket Hotel & Resort**—isn't really a rival; it's their sister property!) Three miles from Edgartown proper, and abutting South Beach (via a private pathway), this 11-acre resort offers tip-top service and plentiful

NOBNOCKET BOUTIQUE INN

INNS & BED & BREAKFASTS

IN VINEYARD HAVEN

✳ **Nobnocket Boutique Inn** (508-696-0859; nobnocket.com), 60 Mt. Aldworth Road. No indulgence was spared in this 2016 top-to-bottom renovation; no detail within the Arts & Crafts manor house was too small to overlook. It's the signature work of innkeeper–owners Simon and Annabelle Hunton, who most-immediately hail from an extraordinary property on Cape Cod. They tackled this seven-room boutique property with the same aplomb. The result? Just the balance of soulful rejuvination and visual excitement. Just the right aesthetic for modern travelers with a respectful nod to its historic bones. And of course, what truly sets Nobnocket apart is its concierge-level services. $$-$$$$.

✳ 🐾 **Crocker House Inn** (508-693-1151; crockerhouseinn.com), 12 Crocker Avenue. With each return visit, I remain impressed by the value that Jynell and Jeff Kristal offer at their turn-of-the-20th-century B&B on a quiet side street near the center of town. And to boot, they're one of the few inns that takes one-nighters (although I certainly

THORNCROFT INN

suggest staying longer). Each of the eight guest rooms has a fresh summer charm, retiled bathroom, and an iPod docking station. The primo third-floor loft, tucked under the eaves with a gas fireplace and Jacuzzi, also has harbor views. Room 5 has good cross breezes and a private feeling; Room 7 is larger, with a gas fireplace and strong morning sun; Room 3 is good for three people traveling together and boasts a private entrance. A word of caution: The intimate size of the inn allows sound from the common areas to carry into the downstairs rooms. If you're a light sleeper, opt for a room on the second or third floors. A full breakfast, served daily in the small combination living/dining room, is included. But many guests linger over a second cup of coffee and the newspaper on the front wraparound porch set with rockers. You can't go wrong here. Also check out the first-rate, fabu "cottage" that Jynell and Jeff offer! $$-$$$$.

✳ **Thorncroft Inn** (508-693-3333; thorncroft.com), 460 Main Street. Under the meticulous care of Karl and Lynn Buder (veteran hospitality gurus presiding here since 1980), this elegant and conservative Craftsman-style bungalow sits on a 3½-acre wooded estate about a mile out of town. All nine guest rooms are decorated with Victorian and Colonial-period antiques and have plush carpeting. There is also a private cottage with a king bed. Amenities include thick

CROCKER HOUSE INN

robes, air-conditioning, and the morning paper delivered to your door. Some rooms have hot tubs or Jacuzzis for two; many have wood-burning fireplaces. A complimentary full country breakfast is served at two seatings in the inn's two intimate dining areas, or you may opt for a continental breakfast in bed. It's all very sedate and harks back to another era. $$$–$$$$$.

❄ ♨ **Kinsman Guest House** (508-693-2311), 278 Main Street. This shingled summer home is located a 10-minute walk from the center of town and a 20-minute walk to the West Chop Lighthouse. Built in 1880 as the original manse to the church across the street, it boasts high ceilings and an elegant staircase. It has only three guest rooms, two of which share a newly tiled bath with modern fixtures. All rooms are gussied up with Laura Ashley accents, and two

OAK BLUFFS INN

have four-poster beds. Breakfast is not included, but the front porch is so inviting many people pick up something in town to enjoy here. $.

IN OAK BLUFFS

✐ **The Oak Bluffs Inn** (508-693-7171; oakbluffsinn.com), 64 Circuit Avenue at Pequot Avenue. Open May through October. You can't miss the inn—it's the marvelously detailed pink building with an enormous third-floor cupola. It also has a great location: at the tip of Circuit Avenue, on the edge of the "campground," three blocks from a beach, and a 10-minute walk to the ferry. And it completely reflects the ethos of Oak Bluffs: laid-back casual. The friendly innkeepers, Erik and Rhonda Albert, have done a great job freshening the place up. All 10 guest rooms have small but newly redone baths, air-conditioning, cottage-style bedroom sets, and views of colorful neighboring cottages from every window. Make a beeline for the soothing and contemporary two-bedroom apartment ($$$$) on the third floor; you could easily settle in for a week, especially given the balcony and kitchenette. Families are welcome in the carriage house or the first-floor room. An expanded continental buffet breakfast, enjoyed at individual tables, is included; guests may also eat on the wraparound porch. $$–$$$$$+.

❄ **Isabelle's Beach House** (508-693-3955; isabellesbeachhouse.com), 83 Seaview Avenue. This turn-of-the-20th-century guest house was resurrected in 2008 by the namesake innkeeper, who has been associated with in-town inns for some time. Most of the 11 simply and tastefully decorated rooms have ocean views; all have air-conditioning and refrigerators. Although the house sits on the main drag heading out of town and toward Edgartown, the traffic isn't a problem for city dwellers (who are at the beach and exploring during the day anyway). Two big pluses: It's across the street from the expansive town beach and it's just a five-minute walk to town from here. The wide front porch is also perfect for sunset cocktails. Buffet breakfast included. $$$–$$$$$.

❄ 🐾 🏠 **Brady's NESW Bed & Breakfast** (508-693-9137; sunsol.com/bradys), 10 Canonicus Avenue. A 10-minute walk from the center of town and one block from the water, this refreshingly friendly place has been Brady Aikens's family home since 1929; he summered here in the 1940s and opened it as a B&B in the early 1990s. Guest rooms are named according to direction: north, east, south, or west (hence the NESW appellation). The summery, whitewashed rooms have wood-slat walls and are decorated in soothing colors and designer linens. West (with sunset views) is the largest and nicest room. Two rooms boast a private balcony; one has a private bath; all have a ceiling fan. Start your day with an outdoor shower, followed by a continental breakfast on the wraparound porch with rockers, and end up back here with Brady as the sun sets. (He's here at 5 PM sharp every afternoon.) The comfy living room, decorated with southwestern influences, has a large video and CD collection. $–$$.

❄ 🐾 **Nashua House** (508-693-0043; nashuahouse.com), Kennebec Avenue. The 1873 Nashua House has 17 breezy and simple rooms, all of which share five bathrooms. I particularly like the corner rooms (Room 11 included). This guest house is perfectly situated in the thick of the action. $–$$.

🐾 **Attleboro House** (508-693-4346; attleborohouse.com), 42 Lake Avenue. Open mid-May through September. This authentic gingerbread cottage faces Oak Bluffs Harbor and sits on the outer perimeter of the Methodist Camp Meeting Association. It's been taking in seaside guests since 1874, and it hasn't changed much since then. In Estelle Reagan's family since the 1940s, the guest house has 10 simple but tidy guest rooms that share five bathrooms. (Some rooms have a sink.) Most rooms have a porch, but if yours doesn't, there's a wraparound porch on the first floor. $ $$.

IN EDGARTOWN

🏠 **The Christopher** (508-627-4784; thechristophermv.com), 24 South Water Street. Formerly the Victorian Inn, and now completely renovated and operated by the delightful duo of Julie and Marla, this boutique property is a two-minute walk from the harbor and a world away when you are sitting by the backyard patio fire pit. The inn manages to walk a casual-chic line straddling contemporary, breezy and comfy. Attention to detail reigns in their 15 rooms, right down to black out shades, iPads for use during your stay, Apple TV for the flat screen TVs, waffle robes and luxe bedding. Full breakfast and afternoon snacks are included, as you might expect with this level of service. $$–$$$$.

🐾 🐕 **Edgartown Inn** (508-627-4794; edgartowninn.com), 56 North Water Street. Open mid-April to mid-October. You don't find these kinds of places anymore because usually they've been gutted and gussied up. But this is the real deal, with an honest sense of place. A hostelry since the early 1800s, the inn has hosted such notables as Daniel Webster, Nathaniel Hawthorne, and then-senator John F. Kennedy. Sandi, the inn's manager since 1985, has worked hard at maintaining and upgrading the inn's 15 (generally large) rooms with firm mattresses and homey antiques. The spick-and-span rooms are simply but nicely decorated and represent perhaps the best value in town. Bathrooms are nicely retiled. Three light and airy (but somewhat spartan) rooms in the Garden House have private entrances. A full country breakfast ($)—including homemade muffins, griddle cakes, and the like—is served in the old-fashioned, charming period dining room or on the back patio. No credit cards. $$–$$$.

EDGARTOWN INN

❋ **Hob Knob Inn** (508-627-9510; hobknob.com), 128 Main Street. This boutique property exudes a haughty sense of self and prides itself on attentive services and eco-friendliness. Just a few minutes' walk from the center of town (request a room off Main Street if you like to sleep in—otherwise you'll be awakened by truck traffic), this Gothic Revival house has 17 spacious guest rooms (and two private houses) with down bedding, king-sized beds, fine antiques, and a very soothing and tasteful ambience. Afternoon tea and a full, local, organic breakfast, served at small tables, are included. Or have breakfast in bed. During inclement weather, you'll appreciate the enclosed porch, a private back patio, two sitting rooms, and a front porch with rockers. Exercise hounds will appreciate the fitness room. $$$–$$$$$+.

❋ **The Charlotte Inn** (508-627-4751; thecharlotteinn.com), 27 South Summer Street. The Vineyard's highbrow grande dame is owned by Gery and Paula Conover, ardent Anglophiles who make frequent trips to the United Kingdom to purchase antiques. Without an ounce of hyperbole, it's fair to say that it has few equals in the U.S. Equestrian prints, elegant armchairs, and collections of beautifully bound classic novels have turned each of the 17 rooms (and two suites) into a luxuriously inhabitable museum. The Conovers' taste for all things English reveals itself on the inn's grounds,

HOB NOB INN

CHARLOTTE INN

too: ivy-edged brick sidewalks, small croquet-quality lawns, impeccable flower beds. Continental breakfast included; full breakfast available for an additional charge. $$$–$$$$$+.

※ ✈ **The Lightkeepers Inn** (508-627-4600; thelightkeepersinn.com), 25 Simpson's Lane. Within a short walk of Lighthouse Beach and just a block from the harbor, the five suites in the main house each have a separate sitting room and kitchen or kitchenette, and they share a covered patio with a BBQ grill. (The East Chop suite boasts its own deck.) None is fancy, but they sure are comfortable. The separate cottage sleeps four. $$–$$$.

UP-ISLAND

※ **Lambert's Cove Inn & Restaurant** (508-693-2298; lambertscoveinn.com), 90 Manaquayak Road, West Tisbury. This place is quite something. The secluded country inn has a setting that couldn't be more picturesque. The farmhouse estate once belonged to an ardent horticulturist, and the impressive formal gardens (and ancient rock walls) are nicely preserved. Common rooms, straight out of a magazine shoot, have the feel of a private gentleman's club; everything is just so, right down to the gilded mirrors and hunting prints. That said, service is quite friendly rather than haughty. Fifteen guest rooms are scattered throughout the inn and two outbuildings. They vary considerably, but each is distinctive and highly recommended. The grounds boast a heated outdoor pool and hot tub, around which are plenty of chaises and teak furnishings. Guests also receive parking passes to nearby Lambert's Cove, one of the island's prettiest beaches. In addition, the secluded and beautiful Ice House Pond is within walking distance. Tennis court, too, and a full breakfast featuring farm-fresh eggs laid from 50 hens and goat products from their "future cheese makers." The **restaurant** (see *Dining Out*) is outstanding. $$–$$$$$.

Beach Plum Inn (508-645-9454; beachpluminn.com), 50 Beach Plum Lane (off North Road), Menemsha. Open May through October. Secluded amid 7 wooded acres overlooking Menemsha Harbor in the near distance, the Beach Plum offers 11 luxurious guest rooms with fine bedding, first-class bathrooms (many with deep soaking or whirlpool tubs), stylish but unpretentious furnishings, and high-quality craftsmanship. A few inn rooms have small but private balconies with harbor views, and most rooms have some sort of water view. Practical in-room amenities like umbrellas, beach chairs, playing cards, and flashlights are not overlooked, either. The six cottages are each decorated with a simple but fresh style and grace. Facilities include beach access, a croquet court, and a tennis court. Don't be alarmed if you see some alpaca grazing on the grounds; they are gentle and soft creatures. Because this is such a popular place for weddings, you'll find a large white lawn tent between the inn and the harbor in spring and fall. The inn also offers **dinner** (see *Dining Out*). Off-island innkeepers Sarah and Bob Nixon (of soap opera Agnes Nixon fame) have owned the inn since the mid-2000s. Full breakfast and afternoon wine and cheese included. $$–$$$$.

Outermost Inn (508-645-3511; outermostinn.com), Lighthouse Road, Aquinnah. Open early May to mid-October. Hugh and Jeanne Taylor's 20-acre parcel of land has the island's second-best ocean view. (The best view is just up the hill from the Aquinnah Lighthouse, where Jeanne's great-great-grandfather was born.) The inn's seven rooms (one with a whirlpool, two with views of the lighthouse) and one suite feature natural fabrics, wool rugs, and down duvets. Subdued colors and unpainted furniture emphasize the seaside light. Rooms are named for the wood used in each: beech, ash, hickory, oak, and cherry. (Speaking of wood, don't miss the outdoor bar made from one long, impressive hardwood tree.) Inquire about the adjacent lighthouse suite. In keeping with the family's musical tradition, guitars, pianos, and other instruments are placed in the common areas. (You might get lucky and wander into an impromptu living-room concert given by Hugh's brother James.) There's also a full-service restaurant on premises; see *Dining Out*. $$$–$$$$.

❄ 🐾 ✐ **The Duck Inn** (508-645-9018; duckinnonmv.com), 10 Duck Pond Lane, off State Road, Aquinnah. A throwback to the '70s in that it feels like a hippie retreat, The Duck Inn is arguably the most unusual place to stay on the island. It's also only a five-minute walk to Philbin Beach, one of the island's top two or three strands. You may be sleeping in a sleigh bed with a silk, hand-painted, feather duvet (in my favorite room, which also boasts a balcony). Another room has a brass bed, freestanding marble basin, a little balcony, and one French door to the water closet. Ask longtime proprietor Elise LeBovit for a complete description of the eclectic rooms. The whole open first floor is a communal-style gathering space, complete with wax-covered candlesticks on the dining table, a central fireplace and Glenwood stove, and kilims and Native American carpets. There is a well-used

game area and special breakfast table for kids, not to mention a hot tub and masseuse. A full organic breakfast is included. Ask about the sauna in the "Flintstone" room. $–$$.

COTTAGES & EFFICIENCIES

IN OAK BLUFFS

🐾 ✐ ⛄ **Island Inn** (508-693-2002; islandinn.com), Beach Road. Open late March through November. If you want to avoid in-town crowds or let the kids (or dogs) run around, this is a decent choice. Situated between Oak Bluffs and Edgartown, this 7-acre resort is right on a bike path, within walking distance of two beaches, and adjacent to Farm Neck Golf Course. In all there are 51 units with kitchenettes (in the form of **studios**, one- and two-bedroom **suites**, **town houses**, and a **cottage** that can sleep up to four) in several low-slung buildings. For a quieter stay, choose a room in a one-story building. Town-house units have a fireplace, a spiral staircase to the loft bedroom, and a separate bedroom. Facilities include three well-maintained tennis courts, a swimming pool, playground, and plenty of space to picnic and barbecue. There is also a **restaurant and bar** on premises; see *Dining Out*. $$–$$$$.

IN EDGARTOWN

✐ **Edgartown Commons** (508-627-4671; edgartowncommons.com), Pease's Point Way. Open May to mid-October. These 35 efficiencies—from studios to two-bedroom apartments—are near the center of town and great for families. Most of the individually owned units are in very good condition; these are rented first. Units in the main building have high ceilings and thus feel more spacious. Many units surround the pool, all are comfortably furnished, and most feature newish kitchens. Outside there are grills, picnic tables, and a nice enclosed play area. $$–$$$.

UP-ISLAND

🦞 **Menemsha Inn and Cottages** (508-645-2521; menemshainn.com), North Road, Menemsha. Open May through October. This secluded 25-acre parcel of forest has some lovely views of Vineyard Sound, a four-minute wooded path to Menemsha Beach, and a friendly atmosphere. Over the years (it was actually opened in 1923) it has been continuously upgraded and maintained with pride. There's an emphasis on peace and quiet, rather than fussy interior decorating. The complex boasts six luxurious and crisp rooms in the carriage house (with a great room and fieldstone fireplace); nine smaller but first-rate "regular" rooms with freshly retiled bathrooms; 11 tidy seascape cottages; and one elegant, two-bedroom suite. Cottages have a screened-in porch, fully equipped kitchen, outdoor shower, barbecue, and wood-burning fireplace. Walk-on passes to Lucy Vincent and Squibnocket Beaches are provided. Reserve cottages as far ahead as February if you can; this well-manicured place has a loyal, repeat clientele. Facilities include a fitness center, bike rentals, basketball court, table tennis, croquet, and a tennis court. Expanded continental breakfast with smoked salmon quiche and the like included. $$$$–$$$$$+; inquire about weekly cottage rates.

MENEMSHA INN AND COTTAGES

See also **Island Inn** under *Cottages & Efficiencies*.

HOTELS

IN VINEYARD HAVEN

❋ ♂ **Mansion House Inn** (508-693-2200; mvmansionhouse.com), 9 Main Street. This professionally operated four-story hotel, located just a few blocks from the ferry, features 40 rooms and suites that range from cozy to spacious—with prices to match. Deluxe rooms have soaking tubs, fireplaces, and balconies that afford views of Vineyard Sound (or Main Street). The basement health club and spa, with a 75-foot mineral spring pool, pampers guests with a wide array of services, including clay cliffs **Moshup Mud Wraps**. The roof deck is a quiet place to escape. Continental breakfast included. $$$–$$$$$.

IN OAK BLUFFS

❋ 🦞 🐚 **Surfside Motel** (508-693-2500; mvsurfside.com), 7 Oak Bluffs Avenue. One of the few Oak Bluffs places open through the winter (with limited availability), the Surfside has above-average motel-style rooms near the ferry. The area can get a bit boisterous on summer evenings, but room rates reflect that. Each room has a queen, two double beds, or two twin beds, air-conditioning, and a small refrigerator; cribs and roll-away beds are available for a fee. Corner rooms are particularly nice and spacious. $$–$$$$.

IN EDGARTOWN

❋ ♂ **Harbor View Hotel and Resort** (508-627-7000; harbor-view.com), 131 North Water Street. This is one privileged perch. Overlooking a lighthouse, grass-swept beach, and Chappaquiddick, the 1891 Harbor View Hotel is Edgartown's best-situated hostelry. This grande dame boasts 114 rooms and 21 suites. (Suites, by the way, are privately owned condos

Most restaurants are open May to mid-October; some are open through Christmas. Each year more and more operate year-round. Opening and closing days vary considerably from week to week, largely dependent on the weather and number of visitors, so it's impossible to tell you reliably which days any given restaurant will be open. Always call ahead after Labor Day and before Memorial Day.

There are a few more generalizations I can make. Vineyard Haven and up-island towns are "dry," so BYO wine or beer. West Tisbury is now "half wet," so beer and wine are sold in some establishments. (Some/most restaurants charge a nominal corking fee.) I've tried to note when there is a chef-owner because generally these places provide the most reliable food. Many Oak Bluffs establishments are family oriented and casual, though there are a few sophisticated options. The dress code in Edgartown is a bit more conservative. Dining options are scarcer up-island and require reservations well ahead of time. Otherwise, reservations are highly suggested at all *Dining Out* establishments.

but available for rent. They feature deep soaking tubs and kitchenettes with granite countertops.) Tranquil harbor views from the hotel's spacious veranda (lined with rocking chairs) are reason enough to patronize the place. Some guest rooms enjoy these views; other rooms have porches overlooking the pool. The upscale guest rooms are generally large and appointed with antique prints and watercolor landscapes by local artists. Facilities include room service, summertime children's programs, a swimming pool, and concierge. Because of its size, the hotel caters to large groups. $$$$$+.

⌔ **Harborside Inn** (508-627-4321; theharborsideinn.com), 3 South Water Street. Open mid-April to early November. This seven-building place—half time-share and half conventional hotel—is one of the few waterfront (harborfront, no less!) accommodations on the island. And it's the only one on Edgartown Harbor. Practically all rooms have some sort of water view; most have a porch or patio. The 90 rooms and four suites are well appointed with standard hotel-issue furnishings. Facilities include a heated pool overlooking harbor boat slips. $$–$$$$.

RENTAL HOUSES & COTTAGES *⌔*
Mattakesett Properties (508-310-1733;

mattakesett.com). South Beach, Edgartown. Open mid-May to mid-October. These exceptional properties, privately owned and located all along South Beach, will not disappoint. They're fully equipped and offer access to their sister property, the Winnetu Oceanside Resort (see *Resort*) and The Dunes (see *Dining Out*). Town houses, duplexes, and three- to five-bedroom homes rent weekly.

Seacoast Properties (800-388-1855; mvseacoast.com), 261 Upper Main Street, Edgartown. Dozens of agencies handle thousands of rentals, which vary from tiny cottages to luxe waterfront homes, from dismal and overpriced units to great values. I like this one.

CAMPGROUND *⌔ ⌔* **Martha's Vineyard Family Campground** (508-693-3772; campmv.com), 569 Edgartown Road, Vineyard Haven. Open mid-May to mid-October. In addition to shaded tent and trailer sites, the island's only campground also has rustic one- and two-room cabins.

YOUTH HOSTEL *⌔ ⌔* **Hostelling International—Martha's Vineyard** (508-693-2665; 888-901-2087 for in-season reservations; hiusa.org/marthasvine yard), Edgartown–West Tisbury Road, West Tisbury. Open mid-May to mid-October. This saltbox opened in 1955, and it remains an ideal lodging choice for cycling-oriented visitors. The hostel is at the edge of the Manuel E. Correllus State Forest (which is full of bike paths; see *Green Space*) and next to the path that runs from Edgartown to West Tisbury. The large kitchen is fully equipped, and the common room has a fireplace. Reservations strongly recommended, especially from mid-June to early September, when large groups frequent the hostel. Linens, pillows, and blankets provided free of charge. Accommodations are single-sex, dormitory-style bunk beds, with the exception of one private room ($–$$) available.

❋ Where to Eat

DINING OUT

IN VINEYARD HAVEN

❋ ✎ **Black Dog Tavern** (508-693-9223; theblackdog.com), 21 Beach Street Extension. Open B, L, D. Longtime Vineyarder Bob Douglas became frustrated when he couldn't find good chowder within walking distance of the harbor, so he opened this place in 1971, naming it for his dog. These days the restaurant—and its ubiquitous T-shirts—are synonymous with a Vineyard vacation. And although the portions are smaller now that Bob's son is running the place, it's a fair place to eat. While you'll have to wait an hour for dinner, lunch won't be much of a problem. Interior decor is simple, with pine floors, old beams, nautical signs, and shellacked wooden tables packed close together. Best of all, this shingled saltbox is cantilevered over the harbor. And you can now sit outside. Fresh island fish and locally grown vegetables dominate the menu. Although staff are often eager to hustle you out the door, don't be shy about finishing your meal. B $, L $–$$, D $$–$$$$.

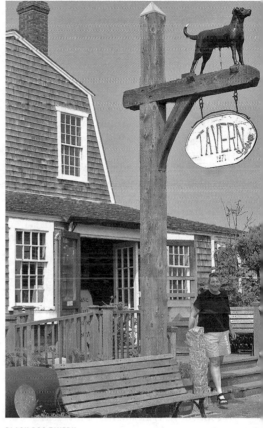

BLACK DOG TAVERN

IN OAK BLUFFS

Sweet Life Café (508-696-0200; sweetlifemv.com), 63 Circuit Avenue. Open D, May through September. In 2013 Sweet Life was purchased by Kevin and Suzanna Crowell, owners of the acclaimed Edgartown establishment Detente. Though Kevin has taken over as chef, Sweet Life retains a classical gourmet menu of fresh island seafood within a restored and airy Victorian house or outside on the twinkling garden patio. During my most recent dinner, their seared halibut with sweet pea risotto rose above my expectations. The wine list is exemplary. The café was a must for the Obamas when they vacationed on the Vineyard. After leaving, you'll muse about how sweet life is, indeed. $$$$.

✳ **Park Corner Bistro** (508-696-9922), 20 Kennebec Avenue, in the square off Circuit Avenue. Open D, Sunday brunch. This cozy, 10-table find has a rustic, European, and intimate feel. Featuring a wide range of New American dishes and a well-versed staff, Park Corner serves seasonal dishes like steak frites, chicken Marsala, and grilled pork. $$–$$$.

✳ 🍸 **M.V. Chowder Company** (508-696-3000; mvchowder.com), 9 Oak Bluffs Avenue. Open L, D. The venerable *Yankee Magazine* claims this is the best chowder in New England—and I heartily agree: Their chowder rules. Beyond that, come for classic burgers and BLTs or Asian fusion dishes like pork dumplings and tempura nuggets. The ambiance is classy but dark. They also specialize in cocktails, particularly martinis. L $–$$, D, $$$–$$$$.

🍸 **The Red Cat Kitchen at Ken 'n' Beck** (508-696-6040; redcatkitchen.com), 14 Kennebec Avenue. Open D, April through September. Don't let burly, tattooed chef and co-owner Ben deForest fool you; he has a delicate way with food. The menu features robust items like buttermilk fried chicken and waffles, "Big-Ass Scallops," and PBR/BBQ-braised pork shank, but changes daily; the flavors, sides, and desserts are divine and imaginative. $$$–$$$$.

IN EDGARTOWN

🍴 🍸 **Atria** (508-627-5850; atriamv.com), 137 Upper Main Street. Open D, April through October. Atria specializes in elegant, hip dining with a global flair. It's the kind of quiet and sophisticated place where celebs like to hang out. It's classy but casually romantic; tables are closely spaced and there's a rose garden patio, too. Fish is a big deal here; look for rare ahi tuna tempura as a starter and pan-seared Georges Bank scallops and cauliflower-goat cheese purée. The menu changes daily, but it's always

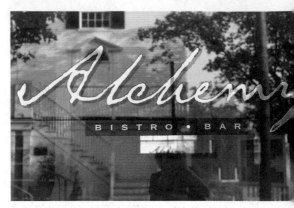

ALCHEMY

worth asking about a vegetarian risotto. (The burgers with onion rings are also great.) Natural flavors come through loudly and clearly. As for dessert, think along the lines of gooey chocolate molten cake or traditional thin pecan tart. The bar (which hosts live jazz, folk, and blues on many nights) is a great place for solo diners and an even better place for a nightcap—try their martinis. $$$$–$$$$$.

🍸 **Alchemy** (508-627-9999; alechemy edgartown.com), 71 Main Street. Open L, D, February through December. Owners Scott and Charlotte Caskey, so successful at Savoir Faire for so many years, have struck gold in this larger and more visible casual American space. Chef Giordano Smiroldo (new to Alchemy in 2015) is their bullion, keeping the inspired food focus loosely on French and Italian. If you're lucky, you'll get one of a few sidewalk tables. Fish and seafood specialties at dinner change regularly, but with luck you'll find seared salmon with creamed lentils or halibut meunière with lemon. The wine list is quite well chosen. In the evening, the open, rotunda-like, two-story bistro and bar is loud and energetic; it's a great place for singles to nosh at the bar. L $$, D $$$–$$$$$.

l'étoile (508-627-5187; letoile.net), 22 North Water Street. Open D, late April to late November. After all these years (since 1986, to be exact), chef-owner

Michael Brisson is still the go-to guy for that singularly spectacular meal. Check out his impressive resume on the website; it's a dishwasher-to-young-prodigy-chef story. There isn't a more elegant dining room on the island, nor more perfect contemporary French cuisine in New England. Although the garden patio is romantic too, I'm always bowled over by the soothing main dining room. Nothing short of spectacular, dishes like Dover sole, rack of lamb, and étuvée of native lobster are meticulously prepared and artistically presented. Michael uses local fish and produce whenever possible, and you can taste the difference. If your wallet and appetite aren't quite up to the main event, a lighter bar menu has venison burgers, cheese paninis with roasted tomato soup, and the like. Look for biweekly wine tastings and tapas on the lawn. Bar menu $$–$$$$, D $$$$–$$$$$, tasting menu $$$$$+.

❦ **Detente** (508-627-8810; detentemv .com), 15 Winter Street. Open D, May through October. This intimate and stylish restaurant, tucked back in Nevin Square, feels like a real find. Especially when you're inside with white linens and dark furniture. Especially when you dine on the summertime terrace. Especially when you grab a bite at the soapstone bar. It doesn't matter where you dine: It's candlelit, refined, romantic, and tickling to a modern palate. Owners Kevin and Suzanna Crowell get my warm thanks for superb New American cuisine. The menu, which features locally procured ingredients, is thankfully limited to about six entrées, all executed with aplomb. Try the harpooned swordfish with sweet pea raviolis on spiced carrot slaw. The wine list is excellent. $$$$–$$$$$+.

❦ **The Dunes** (508-627-3663; winnetu .com), 31 Dunes Road (Katama Road). Open B, L at the pool, D, mid-April through October. The Dunes, emphasizing the freshest of island ingredients, is a centerpiece of the outstanding **Winnetu Oceanside Resort** (see Resort under *Lodging*). It successfully walks the tightrope of feeding regulars multiple times a week and pushing the envelope for foodies. Although I didn't get to dine here on my most recent visit, based on island contacts I'm comfortable with wholeheartedly endorsing the new (in 2016) chef Noel Middleton. Katama Bay oysters (plucked from waters just a stone's throw away) and sea scallops prepared in any manner of ways remain divine. To give you as many reasons as possible to return, children have their own menu and families have their own dining room. Snag a seat on the second-floor deck and enjoy the sunset during dinner. Snag their free sunset water taxi to the restaurant from Edgartown at 5:30 PM in the summertime. It's a lovely way to arrive. L $$–$$$, D $$$–$$$$$.

❦ **Chesca's** (508-627-1234; chescas mv.com), 38 North Water Street. Open D, early April to mid-October. Chef-owner Jo Maxwell offers a reliable menu of eclectic Italian-inspired seafood and pasta specials. She features a diverse menu where you can either eat affordably or drop a bundle. Try the grilled salmon with sweet Thai chili BBQ glaze, or lobster ravioli and seared sea scallops. It's noisy here—not good or bad noisy, just loud. Because reservations are accepted only for large parties, expect to wait (preferably at the sceney bar). $$$–$$$$.

❋ **Lattanzi's** (508-627-8854; lattanzis .com), Old Post Office Square, off Main Street behind the brick courthouse. Open D. Chef Albert Lattanzi and his wife, Catherine, offer sophisticated and traditional Italian cuisine in conservative but not stuffy surroundings. Tables are candlelit, covered with bistro paper and linen; the staff is professional. As for the food, it's prepared with flair: from wonderfully crusty Tuscan bread and handmade pastas to lobster and wood-grilled steaks and chops. In a nod to modern preferences, you'll also find gluten-free selections. Of course the tiramisu is great, but so is the *gianduja* (flourless chocolate hazelnut cake). There is some alfresco dining, too. $$$–$$$$.

❄ **Square Rigger** (508-627-9968; squareriggerrestaurant.com), at The Triangle. Open L, D, February through December. You can tell right away that this place is by and for locals: Patrons and servers are friendly well into September! It's a meat-and-potatoes kind of place; actually, it's a char-grilled meat, seafood, and lobster kind of place—with an emphasis on lobster. There's nothing surprising—just good and casual, with plenty of parking and a publike atmosphere. $$$–$$$$.

UP-ISLAND

Lambert's Cove Inn & Restaurant (508-693-2298; lambertscoveinn.com), 90 Manaquayak Road, West Tisbury. Open D; call for opening months. Dine on exceptional New American cuisine far from the crowds in a rarefied world that epitomizes genteel elegance. Wall sconces, floor-to-ceiling bookcases, fireplaces, and well-spaced tables set a deeply romantic tone. Tinkling piano music in the summer furthers it. Chef James McDonough is deft at menu creation and execution. The inn serves beer and wine. $$$–$$$$.

Beach Plum Inn (508-645-9454; beachpluminn.com), 50 Beach Plum Lane, off North Road, Menemsha. Open D, May through October. Although you're probably drawn here for its country location and distant sunset views of Menemsha Harbor, the chef would probably prefer the focus to be their locally caught seafood and locally grown produce from Chilmark's Beetlebung Farm. With good reason. Although the menu at this minimalist dining room changes nightly, portions tend toward nouvelle (read: small). And unless you're allergic to chocolate, you'd be crazy not to order the chocolate quad cake. Service, by the way, is friendly and low-key but professional. BYOB. $$$$$.

Outermost Inn (508-645-3511; outermostinn.com), 81 Lighthouse Road, Aquinnah. Open D; call for opening months. Take the inn on its terms—or don't. It draws patrons because it's exclusive (there are a limited number of tables), because they do things their own funky way out here, and because of dramatic sunsets over the ocean. As for the New American menu, it highlights fresh island ingredients. There are usually four or five appetizer and entrée choices, perhaps including Edgartown oysters and roasted halibut. Two seatings; reservations required. $$$$$+.

❄ 🐟 **Home Port** (508-645-2679; homeportmv.com), 512 North Road, Menemsha. Open D. New ownership in 2009 saved this institution by retaining the menu and improving the quality. It's an efficient surf-sun-and-turf kind of place, with long wooden tables and lobster cooked lots of different ways, thick swordfish, jumbo shrimp, and a raw bar. The servings are large and the clientele a bit older. Dine on the outside deck for the best sunset views of Menemsha Creek. Or get take-out from the back door and sit at the harbor. BYOB. $$$$.

Chilmark Tavern (508-645-9400; chilmarktavern.com), 9 State Road, Chilmark. Open D. If you're stationed up-island, the haul to Edgartown, Vineyard Haven, or Oak Bluffs for dinner can be daunting. Chilmark Tavern is one of the few up-island options, but it's a good one. The food is simply but classily presented, like the establishment itself. Perhaps not surprisingly, crowds can slow down the service in summertime. BYOB. $$$–$$$$$.

❄ **State Road Restaurant** (508-693-8582; stateroadrestaurant.com), 688 State Road, West Tisbury. Open B, L, D. Special attention has been paid to interior design craftsmanship at this local favorite off-season; but it's an upper-class outing during the summer. Reservations are hard to come by, but the food—contemporary American cuisine by chef Austin Racine—is exquisite.

ART CLIFF DINER

Brunch is a good option if you have kids in tow or if you want to enjoy State Road without the wait. Wine and beer only. $$$–$$$$$.

EATING OUT

IN VINEYARD HAVEN

✳ 🦞 🗡 **Art Cliff Diner** (508-693-1224), 39 Beach Road. Open B, L. Great things come from this little package. Although it's not much to look at and the parking is limited in summer, the buzz is resounding and the dishes stellar. Chef-owner Regina Stanley, a whirlwind of energy who was the pastry chef at Blair House, the guest house of the White House, meets and greets patrons. She works alongside Teddy Diggs, who has brought success to island restaurants like Home Port and The Beach Plum. Breakfast is out of this world: fancy frittatas, daily scone and eggs Benedict specials, tofu scramble, almond-crusted French toast, breakfast tacos, and the Bayou Bundle. Anything-but-prosaic meat loaf is a terrific lunch choice. It's also family friendly, with crayons available for the kids. $$.

✳ 🗡 **Waterside Market** (508-693-8899; watersidemarket.com), 76 Main Street, Vineyard Haven. Open B, L. Stop by these spacious and casual digs for quick but filling lunchtime sandwiches and salads, as well as breakfast dishes like hash, croissant sandwiches, and buttermilk pancakes. There's always something appealing on the huge blackboard menu. Watch the street scene through large, street-front picture windows. Sandwiches are huge. You can usually get away with splitting one, but the fresh ciabatta bread will make you want to eat the whole thing. $–$$.

✳ **The Black Dog Bakery Café** (508-696-8190; theblackdog.com), 509 State Road. Open B, L. The Black Dog began as a cottage industry, but now it's more like an industrial complex (figuratively speaking). About a mile out of town, you no longer have to fight traffic to fork over money for Black Dog pastries. Look for the vintage 1914 rail car outside the café, as it makes a fine backdrop for a picnic. $.

🦞 **Sandy's Fish & Chips** (508-693-1220), 5 Martin Road. Open mid-May to mid-September. Located within John's Fish Market, this family-operated, no-frills place has great fried fish sandwiches and fried clams. The fish market opened in the 1960s and the restaurant started in 1978. $–$$.

✳ **Net Result Fish Market** (508-693-6071; mvseafood.com), 79 Beach Road. Sushi, lobsters, shellfish, smoked fish, and bay scallops (in-season) purchased on the spot or shipped home as a nostalgic reminder. $–$$.

✳ **Rocco's** (508-693-1125; marthas vineyardpizza.com), 79 Beach Road in Tisbury Marketplace. Open L, D. Though hidden in the back corner of a plaza, Rocco's is a local favorite for pizza and one of the only spots to get a good pie off-season. In addition to New York–style cheese and pepperoni slices, they offer inventive meat and veggie specials daily. Full pizzas come with all the usual toppings. Skip the rest of the offerings—only because the pizza rules. $.

✳ **Little House Café** (508-687-9794; littlehousemv.com), 339 State Road. Open B, L, D. This easy-to-miss, tiny gem next to Cronigs puts a Mediterranean twist on breakfast, lunch entrées, and

THE NET RESULT

salads. Regulars and I dive into their fish tacos and shawarma. $$.

IN OAK BLUFFS

Nancy's Restaurant and Snack Bar (508-693-0006; nancysrestaurant.com), 29 Lake Avenue. Open L, D, late May to mid-October. Nancy's is another sought-after spot of the Obama family.

SLICE OF LIFE

Classic lobster rolls, a nice raw bar, and the Dirty Banana mudslides at Donovan's Reef, the downstairs bar, drive the success of this busy location. Not to mention, you can almost pull your boat right up to the window. $$–$$$.

❊ ❀ **Slice of Life** (508-693-3838; sliceoflifemv.com), 50 Circuit Avenue. Open B, L, D. This wonderful and casual place offers savory and sweet treats to eat in or take out. Don't miss it. It's always one of the friendliest places on-island. Try the chowder and a fried green tomato BLT for lunch. Dinner is fancier with, perhaps, roasted cod with sundried tomatoes or any number of nightly specials. You can always keep it simple with a thick burger, too. B, L $–$$, D $$–$$$.

20ByNine (508-338-2065; 20bynine .com/mv), 16 Kennebec Avenue. Open L, D mid-April to mid-October. This isn't just a fun craft beer and whiskey bar *for the Vineyard*; it could compete with the best of the breed within 300 miles. The vibe is cool but not hipster-haughty, warm but not too intimate. The small plates are way better than simply providing a little something to soak up the drinks! Try their diverse cheese board, mini-burgers, and lobster fritters, and by all means, do leave room for the s'mores. $$-$$$.

❄ ☙ ♪ **Linda Jean's** (508-693-4093; lindajeansrestaurant.com), 25 Circuit Avenue. Open B, L, D. Established in 1976, this is a classic American diner without the chrome. It's a pleasant storefront eatery serving old-fashioned meals at old-fashioned prices. Breakfast is still the best meal of the day here: Pancakes are thick but light, for instance. But the fish sandwich is quick and good, and the onion rings are crispy. Kids are happy with burgers and PB&J. And the waitstaff is friendly. What more could you ask for? If you haven't tried that famed New England "delicacy," Grape-Nuts custard, this is the place to do it. Expect a wait for breakfast even in the dead of winter! $$.

❄ ☙ ♪ ♈ **Offshore Ale Co.** (508-693-2626; offshoreale.com), 30 Kennebec Avenue. Open L, D. Not only is the food good—crispy, wood-fired, brick-oven pizzas, hefty burgers, grilled fish, fried calamari, and beer-batter fish-and-chips—but the place is fun, too. The front door is marked with a big barrel full of peanuts, and patrons toss the shells onto the floor. But freshly fermented beer is reason enough to frequent this dark, two-story barn—as is the homemade root beer. Check the blackboard for what's fresh from the shiny copper vats, and try to come in the afternoon for a brewery tour before eating. Frequent entertainment off-season. L $$, D $$-$$$.

☙ ♪ **Giordano's** (508-693-0184; giosmv.com), 18 Lake Avenue. Open L, D, May through September. This classic, family-style restaurant is run by fourth-generation Giordanos who pride themselves on serving value-packed portions. Giordano's serves some of the best fried clams on-island (head to the takeout window), but I tend to stick to pizzas here. The cocktails are also big. $$.

♪ ♈ **Oak Bluffs Harbor Boardwalk**, Circuit Avenue Extension. Among the

COOPE DE VILLE

many eateries that line the boardwalk, two places deserve particular mention:

Coop de Ville (508-693-3420; coop devillemv.com), 12 Circuit Avenue Extension. Open L, D, late April to late October. This place is the best fry joint and raw bar. The oysters are excellent and fish-and-chips very good. Otherwise, you know the menu: seafood by the pint or quart; steamed lobster with corn; wings. But the wings . . . the hot wings are arguably the best on the island. With picnic tables and counters, this is a great location for fast food and people-watching. $$-$$$.

Lobsterville Bar and Grille (508-696-0099; lobstervillemv.com), 8 Circuit Avenue Extension. Open L, D, mid May to mid-October. The big turquoise tower has run-of-the-mill offerings (lots of seafood and fried appetizers), but you can always get a reliable burger here. The real kicker: sit on the second-story deck for an unbeatable view of the harbor. $$-$$$.

☙ ♪ **Farm Neck Café** (508-693-3560; farmneck.net), at the golf club off County

Road. Open B, L, D, early April to late November. When I ask locals to recommend a great, inexpensive lunch place, this place inevitably pops up. Yes, it's crawling with golfers, but the setting is lovely—with views of long, manicured fairways. While the atmosphere is clubby, it's public and very comfortable. You can get grilled shrimp and other seafood, soups, Cobb salad, sesame chicken wrapped in a flour tortilla, a burger, or a roast beef sandwich Philly style. L $–$$, D $$–$$$$.

Lookout Tavern (508-696-9844; lookoutmv.com), 8 Seaview Avenue. Open L, D, April through December. This aptly named pub looks out over the ferry terminal and into Vineyard Sound. Most folks come for super-fresh sushi, but they also offer de rigueur American fare and fried seafood. It's a great place to have a draft while watching a Sox game.

Ocean View Restaurant (508-693-2207; oceanviewmv.com), 16 Chapman Avenue. Open L, D. Sink into a seat and watch TV and nosh from a bar menu,

or try the tavern. Wherever you sit, the servers make bustling summer OB feel like a small town where everyone knows your name. The combination of a surf-and-turf-oriented menu and crayons for kids keep all familiy members happy. If you haven't had your fill of fried food for the week, don't miss this guilty pleasure: the hodgepodge of fried wings, ravioli, and mozzarella sticks. $$.

Bangkok Thai Cuisine (508-696-6322; bkkcapecod.com), 67 Circuit Avenue. This authentic, spicy, and welcome diversion makes a mean peanutty pad thai. Servers are prompt and polite, and the atmosphere is casually romantic, especially outdoors on the brick patio. $$–$$$.

IN EDGARTOWN

Among the Flowers (508-627-3233), Mayhew Lane, off North Water Street. Open B, L, D, May through October. This small, friendly café has some of the most reasonable prices in Edgartown. It's a good choice for healthier options, and

AMONG THE FLOWERS

THE NEWES FROM AMERICA

the lunch specials always feature unique flavor combos. There aren't many indoor tables, but there is an outdoor patio, enclosed and heated during inclement weather. Look for excellent omelets, lobster rolls, PB&J for the kids, crêpes, salads, quiches, corn chowder, and clam chowder. L $–$$, D $$–$$$$.

❋ ☙ ✎ ♈ **The Newes From America** (508-627-4397; kelley-house.com), 23 Kelley Street. Open L, D. Occupying the basement of the Kelley House, the food here is surprisingly good for pub grub—renowned burritos and fish-and-chips, as well as burgers and sandwiches. Stick to pub mainstays and don't order anything too fancy. At about $15 per person, lunch here is one of the better island values. The atmosphere is cozy, too: exposed beams, red brick, and a wood floor. Check out the selection of micro-brews, or try the beer sampler rack and receive a wooden nickel souvenir (collect at least 500 and you'll get a named bar stool). When it's cold outside, this place will warm you to the core. $$.

❋ ☙ ✎ **Edgartown Diner** (508-627-9337; edgartowndinermv.com), 65 Main Street, Old Post Office Square. Open B, L, D. This nostalgic 1950s-style diner is a fun place for kids because there's plenty to look at—from old signs to a jukebox. As for the actual dining, you've got your basic comfort foods: eggs, pancakes, grilled cheese, meat loaf, PB&J, burgers,

and some Italian. Parents won't mind the prices either. L $–$$, D $$

✎ ♈ **Seafood Shanty** (508-627-8622, theseafoodshanty.com), 31 Dock Street. Open L, D, mid-May through September. So you just want to nibble on something and have drinks on the water? Head here for lobster cakes, something from the raw bar or sushi bar, and a beverage of your choice. If you can't get a table on the rooftop deck, don't bother, though. They also have DJs, reggae nights, and the like in the summer. L $$, D $$$–$$$$.

Right Fork Diner (508-627-5522; rightforkdiner.com), 12 Mettakesett Way. Open B, L, D, mid-May to mid-October. Parked at the edge of the airfield on Katama's right fork, this diner is a fun spot to enjoy a hearty breakfast while watching classic biplanes putter around. $$.

❋ **Dock Street Coffee Shop** (508-627-5232), 2 Dock Street. Open B, L, D. A hole-in-the-wall with an old-timey breakfast counter, the joint's menu is straightforward, the service is quick, and they stay open late a few nights a week to satisfy those milkshake cravings.

UP-ISLAND

Fella's (508-693-6924; fellacaters.com), 479 State Road, West Tisbury. Open B, L, D, May through October. Stop by this tiny, low-key take-out place for breakfast sandwiches, hearty sandwiches, hot pressed paninis, chili, and pizza. You can always count on them when you're hungry and heading up-island. $–$$$.

✎ **Aquinnah Shop** (508-645-3867, theaquinnahshop.com), 27 Aquinnah Circle, Aquinnah. Open B, L, D, mid-April to mid-October. Come for the island's best sunset views rather than decent food and unbearably slow service. The Vanderhoop and Madison families, native Wampanoag, operate this homey restaurant, located near the Aquinnah Cliffs. Try the Tomahawk Special at breakfast: homemade fish cakes covered with salsa atop poached eggs. Lunch is more prosaic: burgers, sandwiches, and salads. I'd go elsewhere for dinner, but just so you know, they dress up the place with sautéed shrimp, lobster with béarnaise sauce, fresh fish daily, and buffalo short ribs braised in cabernet. L $$, D $$$–$$$$.

❋ **Plane View** (508-693-1886; mvyairport.com), 71 Airport Road, West Tisbury. Open B, L. If you're flying in, this airport diner is a good first stop—especially at breakfast. Lunches revolve around sandwiches and burgers. $.

LIGHT MEALS, SNACKS, & SWEETS

IN VINEYARD HAVEN

❋ **Black Dog Bakery** (508-693-4786; theblackdog.com), 11 Water Street. At the Five Corners intersection near the Steamship Authority parking lot, the Black Dog is well positioned to accommodate the hungry hordes that arrive each day. Indeed, it is many visitors' first stop—for a cup of strong coffee and a sweet pastry, muffin, or other goody.

❋ 🍴 **Humphrey's** (508-693-6518; humphreysmv.com), 455 State Road,

MOCHA MOTT'S

West Tisbury. Pick up homemade soups and enormous sandwiches made with homemade bread, and save room for their jelly- or cream-filled doughnuts, affectionately called "belly bombs." Find two other seasonal operations at Dippin Donuts (508-627-7725; 241 Edgartown-Vineyard Haven Road, Edgartown) and Woodland Center (508-693-6518; 455 State Road, Vineyard Haven).

❋ **Tisberry Frozen Yogurt** (508-693-1125; tisberry.com), 29 Main Street. Stop for a real fruit smoothie or a low-fat and no-fat froyo with more than 30 fruit, nut, and candy toppings. They also do soups and salads.

❋ **Not Your Sugar Mamas** (508-338-2018; notyoursugarmamas.com), Tisbury Market Place. Look for Chilmark Coffee and healthier baked goods using cacao and coconut rather than junk ingredients.

IN OAK BLUFFS

❋ **Mocha Mott's** (508-696-1922; mochamotts.com), 10 Circuit Avenue. This tiny, aromatic basement café has rich espresso that keeps me going well into the evening, plump bagels, and newspapers that keep me in touch. In Vineyard Haven they're at 15 Main Street (508-693-3155).

❋ **Tony's Market** (508-693-4799; tonysmarketmv.com), 119 Dukes County Avenue. Doubling as a small grocer, this is a good pit stop for caffeine, baked goods, and sandwiches.

M.V. Gourmet Café & Bakery (508-693-3688; mvbakery.com), 5 Post Office Square. Open mid-April through October. Sure, stop during the day, but when the sun goes down they fling open their back door for a late-night crowd. Apple fritters the size of your head, doughnut sundaes . . . there's a reason the line sometimes fills the entire parking lot behind the building.

See also **Slice of Life Café** under *Eating Out* and **Humphrey's** under *In Vineyard Haven*.

IN EDGARTOWN

✣ **Soigné** (508-627-8489), 190 Upper Main Street. A connoisseur's deli just outside town, Soigné has all the makings for a gourmet picnic: the island's best take-out sandwiches, soups, myriad cold salads, and boutique wine from around the world. Owners Ron and Diana, who have been at this since 1986, also sell "designer" pastas, pâtés, pastries, mousses, excellent clam chowder, dried fruits, imported cheeses, sauces, and select wines. It's a bit pricey, but worth every penny. By the way, something like "millions and millions" of brownies have been gobbled up here.

Espresso Love (508-627-9211; espressolove.com), 17 Church Street, Edgartown. Open B, L, March through December. Tucked back off Main Street, these folks make strong cappuccino and sweet pastries. If you're a big breakfast eater, their small egg sandwiches will leave a hole in your stomach. A limited selection of soups and sandwiches is offered at lunch, when you can enjoy the outdoor patio.

See also **Morning Glory Farm** under *Farm Stands* and **Humphrey's** under *In Vineyard Haven*.

UP-ISLAND

✣ **Scottish Bakehouse** (508-693-6633; scottishbakehousemv.com), 977 State Road, Tisbury. Be prepared for summertime waits that are well worth it. Baking scones, meat pies, sweetbreads, and more since the mid-1960s. Double-egg sandwiches and lunch entrées are just as good as the sweets. It's also a good choice for vegan or gluten-free options.

🦞 *∂* **The Galley** (508-645-9819; menemshagalley.com), 515 North Road, Menemsha. Open mid-May to mid-October. This tiny place has the best chowder on the island and great lobster rolls. Burgers and soft-serve ice cream, too.

🦞 *∂* **The Bite** (508-645-9239), 29 Basin Road, Menemsha. Open May to late September. This tiny shack serves arguably the best fried clams on-island. Don't miss the chance to decide for yourself.

MENEMSHA SUNSET PICNICKING

Chilmark Store (508-645-3739; chilmarkgeneralstore.com), 7 State Road, near Beetlebung Corner, Chilmark. Open mid-May through September. This general store offers great pizzas and baked goods (especially the pies) in addition to conventional general-store items. Do some people-watching from the front-porch rockers before you leave.

❅ **7a Foods** (508-693-4636; 7afoods .com), 1045 State Road, West Tisbury. Behind Alley's General Store, this busy spot sells killer baked goods, gelato, and filling sandwiches. The Liz Lemon—pastrami, turkey, Swiss, coleslaw, Russian dressing, and potato chips on rye—is a favorite, as are the jalapeño-cheddar biscuits. Lots of ingredients come straight from 7a Farms in Aquinnah.

❧ **Larsen's Fish Market** (508-645-2680; larsensfishmarket.com), Dutcher's Dock, Menemsha. Open early May to late October. Down some oysters and cherry-stones at the raw bar while you wait for

FARM STANDS

Despite summer traffic, $45 dinner entrées, chichi boutiques, and a building boom, the Vineyard is an agricultural island at heart. With little effort you'll find farms with produce so fresh you can almost taste the earth. Stop often; it will be one of the things most cherished about a Vineyard holiday.

Morning Glory Farm (508-627-9674; 508-637-9003; morninggloryfarm.com), 120 Meshacket Road, off West Tisbury Road, Edgartown. Open late May through December. Although their business card says "Roadside Stand," this is a full-fledged farm with a large, rustic barn-board building. You'll find farm-fresh eggs, a great salad bar, home-baked pies and breads, and homemade jellies, including especially tasty white grape jelly.

your lobsters to be boiled. Or pick up some stuffed quahogs and head to the beach.

❅ **Menemsha Fish Market** (508-645-2282; menemshafishmarket.net), 56 Basin Road, Menemsha. This little place smokes its own fish and has a small raw bar, which is convenient for appetizers while you wait for your lobsters-to-go.

AROUND THE ISLAND

Mad Martha's has irresistible homemade ice cream (with island specialties like lobster ice cream!) and many locations

DECIDE BETWEEN TWO MENEMSHA FISH MARKETS

MAO MARTHA'S

in all the right places (near the ferries, on Main Streets, and the like).

✳ Entertainment

ARTS & MUSIC ✳ ♪ **Vineyard Playhouse** (508-693-6450; box office 508 687-2452; 508-696-6300; vineyard playhouse.org), 24 Church Street, Vineyard Haven. This small, community-based professional theater produces well-done plays and musicals; the main stage is within a former Methodist meetinghouse. They also host many special events; keep your eyes peeled. Summer performances are scheduled most nights. Look for a varied and entertaining lineup at the troupe's Tisbury Amphitheater, Tashmoo Overlook, State Road, Vineyard Haven. The playhouse also offers educational programs, theater for young audiences, summer outdoor productions, and a theater arts camp. $$$$.

♫ **The Yard** (508-645-9662; dance theyard.org), Middle Road, near Beetlebung Corner, Chilmark. May through October. Founded in 1973, this colony of performing artists in residence is always engaging and appreciated. The choreography and dance are spirited. If you have a chance to go to one of their performances, by all means go. The Yard is one of those special organizations that makes the Vineyard uniquely the Vineyard. Most shows $$$; some are free.

✳ **Martha's Vineyard Chamber Music Society** (508-696-8055; mvcms .org). Mid-July to mid-August. Monday concerts are held at the Old Whaling Church in Edgartown; Tuesday concerts are at the Chilmark Community Center. $$$$.

The Vineyard Sound band concerts (886-846-7686; vineyardsound.org). Check the website for locations, days, and times around the island.

Ⓨ NIGHTLIFE
✳ **The Newes From America** (508-627-4397; kelley-house.com), 23 Kelley Street, Edgartown. This colonial-era basement tavern is atmospheric and cozy, with hand-hewn beams. The Newes features microbrews; try the specialty Rack of Beers, a sampler of five brews from the outstanding and unusual beer menu (see *Eating Out*).

Atlantic (508-627-7001; atlanticmv .com), 2 Main Street, Edgartown. Open April through October. The setting at this waterfront restaurant and bar couldn't be better, especially if you get an outdoor table on the porch. It's hip, urban, and loud, with live bands and DJs. It's owned by Charlotte Inn proprietor Gery Conover (see Inns & Bed & Breakfasts under *Lodging*), who also developed the oh-so exclusive and private Boathouse (above the Atlantic).

✳ ♪ **Sharky's Cantina** (508-693-7501; sharkyscantina.com), 31 Circuit Avenue. Always packed and hopping, Sharky's is a fun place for wildly inauthentic Mexican food and margaritas—the watermelon version is a local legend. Dishes $–$$. (There's another location in Edgartown if you're headed that way.)

✳ **The Ritz** (508-693-9851; theritzmv .com), 4 Circuit Avenue, Oak Bluffs. Mostly middle-aged locals hang out at this funky blues bar, which, according to the *Improper Bostonian,* is: "seedy," "smokin'," "scary," "disgusting," "hilarious," and "a blast."

Lampost/Dive Bar (508-696-9352; lampostmv.com, divebarmv.com), 4 Circuit Avenue, Oak Bluffs. On the second floor, the Lampost features dancing from early April to late October. The Dive Bar, open late May to early September, is a smaller lounge with nightly summer entertainment and a young partying college crowd. It has the most diverse beer selection on the Vineyard.

✳ **The Wharf** (508-627-9966; wharf pub.com), Lower Main Street, Edgartown. A popular pub with a cozy, sports bar feel.

✳ **Henry's Hotel Bar** (508-627-7000; harbor-view.com), 131 North Water

Street, at the Harbor View Hotel. When you're in the mood for a sedate drink, there's no place better for a signature martini or mojito.

See **20ByNine** and **Offshore Ale Co**. under *Eating Out* in "Oak Bluffs," and **Atria** under *Dining Out* in "Edgartown."

MOVIES ❋ ⛲ **Capawock Movie Theater** (508-627-6689; fandango.com), 43 Main Street, Vineyard Haven. Built in 1912, the Capawock was the oldest continuously operating movie theater in Massachusetts until its closure in the mid-2000s for about three years. As entertaining as movies can be, though, you might be just as entertained by conversations before the film begins.

❋ **Martha's Vineyard Film Center** (508-696-9369; mvfilmsociety.com), 79 Beach Road, Tisbury Market Place, Vineyard Haven. Richard Paradise is the man behind this elegant little theater, established by the nonprofit Martha's Vineyard Film Society in 2002. They play some blockbusters, but mostly fine independent and foreign films. Many screenings for the Martha's Vineyard

International Film Festival are held here in early September.

⛲ **Entertainment Cinemas** (508-627-8008; entertainmentcinemas.com), 65 Main Street, Edgartown.

❋ Selective Shopping

These entries are truly "selective," for they do not begin to scratch the surface of what's available shopping-wise on the Vineyard.

ART GALLERIES For a super-complete listing of artists and galleries, look for the free and excellent *"Arts Directory"* available in many galleries.

Alison Shaw Gallery (508-693-4429; alisonshaw.com), 88 Dukes County Avenue, Oak Bluffs. Open seasonally. This prolific photographer started in abstract black-and-white imagery (for the *Vineyard Gazette*) before moving to highly graphic color imagery. Her work these days is more painterly than postcardy. Alison also leads excellent workshops and mentorship programs.

OLD SCULPIN GALLERY

❋ ♠ **Craftworks** (508-693-7463; craft worksgallery.com), 42 Circuit Avenue, Oak Bluffs. These folks have a mixed but usually affordable selection of contemporary American crafts that's worth a look and always visually interesting. Clay, metal, glass, paper, and wood. Fun and colorful.

Old Sculpin Gallery (508-627-4881; marthasvineyardartassociation.org), 58 Dock Street at corner of Daggett, Edgartown. Open late May to mid-October. Operated by the nonprofit Martha's Vineyard Art Association, the building was originally Dr. Daniel Fisher's granary, then a boatbuilder's workshop. Look for the long, wide depression in the main room where boatbuilder Manuel Swartz Roberts's feet wore down the floor as he moved along his workbench during the early 20th century. Paintings, photographs, and sculpture of varying degrees of quality are exhibited. Classes for all ages are offered throughout the season.

❋ **North Water Gallery** (508-627-6002; northwatergallery.com), 27 North Water Street, Edgartown. Regional and national artists emphasizing Vineyard landscapes, seascapes, maritime scenes, figurative works, photography, and still lifes are represented here.

❋ **Granary Gallery at the Red Barn** (508-693-0455; granarygallery.com), 636 Old County Road, West Tisbury. In addition to folk art and landscape paintings, this gallery carries old and new photography. Look for classic photos by the venerable photographer Alfred Eisenstaedt, who came to the island on assignment for *Life* in 1937 and vacationed here until his death in 1995. Most artists represented here have some affiliation with the island.

Field Gallery (508-693-5595; fieldga llery.com), 1050 State Road, West Tisbury. Open seasonally. Tom Maley's field of joyfully dancing figures, which seem to be celebrating the surrounding beauty, is an icon of the Vineyard's cultural life. Other Vineyard artists are exhibited

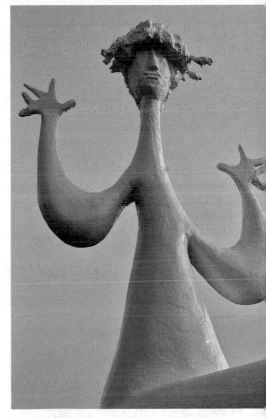

A FIELD GALLERY SCULPTURE

during summer months; receptions are held 5 PM–7 PM on many Sundays June through August.

See also **Featherstone Center for the Arts** under *To Do.*

ARTISANS ❋ **Tuck & Holand Metal Sculptures** (508-693-3914; tuckand holand.com), 275 State Road, Vineyard Haven. Although Travis Tuck died in 2002, his partner and former apprentice Anthony Holand carries on as the exclusive maker of Tuck's famed weather vanes. Holand also creates wonderful original designs of his own. Despite the prices ($12,000 and up) and time required to painstakingly produce one (weeks and weeks), the wait times are long. The client list includes Steven Spielberg, who owns an animated velociraptor, and Bill and Hillary Clinton. You can see examples of their work around the island, too. Check out the weather vanes atop the new Agricultural Hall in West Tisbury (a Holstein cow); Cronig's Market on State Road (a grasshopper, as a public market symbol); the Tisbury and Edgartown Town Halls (a whale tail and whaling ship, respectively); and the *Vineyard Gazette* building (a quill pen). A short video with striking images of notable vanes on the website offers a glimpse into this extraordinary enterprise.

❋ **Chilmark Pottery** (508-693-6476; chilmarkpottery.wixsite.com/ chilmarkpottery), 145 Field View Lane, off State Road, opposite Nip-n-Tuck Farm, West Tisbury. In 1982 artist Geoffrey Borr established his studio in a weathered shingled barn where he and his staff transform thoughtfully designed, wheel-thrown creations into hand-painted pottery with distinctive seascape, oxblood, and copper red hues. You'll find functional and sculptural mugs, vases, and plates, as well as more unusual sculptural pieces.

Martha's Vineyard Glass Works (508-693-6026; mvglassworks.com), 683 State Road, West Tisbury. Open April through January. Many designers share this dynamic studio, a colorfully bold visual feast where you can watch the artists and apprentices at work.

BOOKSTORES ✑ **Edgartown Books** (508-627-8463; edgartownbooks.net), 44 Main Street, Edgartown. Open February through December. This charming independent bookshop has everything from travel and local fiction to books and activities for children.

❋ **Bunch of Grapes Bookstore** (508-693-2291; bunchofgrapes.com), 35 Main Street, Vineyard Haven. This beloved island establishment continues its 40-plus year tradition as the Vineyard's best year-round, independent, locally ownedgeneral bookstore.

CLOTHING ❋ **Black Dog General Store** (508-696-8182; theblackdog.com), behind the eponymous bakery, 5 Water Street, Vineyard Haven. The Black Dog rakes in tens of thousands of dollars daily in merchandise (sweatshirts, towels, caps, and so on). And they have all the bases covered with a lot of stores scattered around the island.

Bryn Walker (508-693-8340; bryn walker.com), 21 Kelly Street, Edgartown (open April through December), and 16 Main Street, Vineyard Haven (open year-round). Upscale but affordable, mix-and-match women's linen and cotton clothing in updated styles and colors.

❋ **The Great Put-On** (508-627-5495; thegreatputonmv.com), 1 Dock Street at Mayhew Lane, Edgartown. One of the island's most fashionable clothing

EDGARTOWN BOOKS

MUST SEE SUMMER EVENTS

Fourth of July Weekend: July Fourth. One of the busiest weeks of the summer. Edgartown puts on a family-friendly parade followed by fireworks in the harbor.

Late July/Early August: Possible Dreams Auction (mvcommunityservices.com), Winnetu Oceanside Resort, Edgartown. Given the celebrity involvement, it's not surprising that national publicity surrounds this event. Celebrities offer to fulfill "dreams" that vary from predictable to unusual. High bidders in the past have won a tour of the *60 Minutes* studios with Mike Wallace; a sail with Walter Cronkite on his yacht; a seat at a Knicks game with Spike Lee; a tour of Carnegie Hall with Isaac Stern; a walking tour of the Brooklyn Bridge with David McCullough; a song and a peanut butter sandwich from Carly Simon; and a lesson in chutzpah at the Five Corners intersection in Vineyard Haven with Alan Dershowitz. Longtime island celebrities see the auction as their chance to give back to the Vineyard—the auction raises hundreds of thousands of dollars for Martha's Vineyard Community Services. That's a far cry from the $1,000 raised in 1979, when it began and folks bid in $5 increments for the privilege of helping lobstermen set out their pots. More than 1,000 people usually attend the event, and to date it has raised more than $11 million.

Mid-August: Illumination Night. Usually held the third Wednesday in August, the evening always begins with a community sing and is followed by an Oak Bluffs resident (usually the oldest) lighting a single Japanese lantern after all the electric lights in town are turned off. Then the rest of the "camp" residents illuminate their gingerbread cottages with lanterns and candles.

Mid-August: Fireworks. Usually held the third Friday in August, these fireworks in Ocean Park, set to the music of the Vineyard Sound, are far more spectacular than the Fourth of July display.

Mid-August: Agricultural Fair (508-693-9549; marthasvineyardagriculturalsociety.org). Held at the Ag Hall and Fairgrounds on State Road in West Tisbury, this is arguably the island's most beloved summer event. It's certainly one of the oldest: It began during the Civil War! $.

stores stocks an impressive selection of dressy clothing for women, more shoes for women than for men, and unisex accessories like leather backpacks, loose jackets, and sweaters.

Pandora's Box (508-645-9696), 4 Basin Road (off North Road), Menemsha. Open May to mid-October. The emphasis here is on comfortable, contemporary women's clothing.

HOME FURNISHINGS ❊ **Midnight Farm** (508-693-1997; etsy.com/shop/midnightfarm.com), 44 Main Street, Vineyard Haven. Carly Simon's home furnishing store has some well-chosen items.

LeRoux (508-693-0030; leroux kitchen.com), 62 Main Street, Vineyard Haven. This store is devoted to kitchen items, home goods, and furnishings.

CB STARK JEWELERS

Their gourmet shop across the street is a foodie's dream.

JEWELRY ❊ **C. B. Stark** (508-693-2284; cbstark.com), 53A Main Street, Vineyard Haven. Goldsmiths Cheryl Stark and Margery Meltzer have designed gold and silver jewelry with island motifs since 1966. Cheryl created the original grape design that has become so popular on the island. The shop also carries locally made wampum from quahog shells. Look for their shop on North Water Street, Edgartown, too.

SPECIALTY SHOPS **Allen Farm Sheep & Wool Company** (508-645-9064; allen farm.com), 421 South Road, Chilmark. Call ahead for hours or take your chances. Engaging in sustainable and organic farming practices, the Allen family has been raising black and white Corriedale sheep on these rolling fields for more than 200 years. Their wool is custom spun and hand dyed and used by islanders to make sweaters, scarves, mittens, and the like.

❊ **Island Alpaca** (508-693-5554; islan dalpaca.com), 1 Head of the Pond Road, off Edgartown–Vineyard Haven Road, Oak Bluffs. These gentle creatures, more than 80 in this herd at last count, are raised for breeding, sales, and for their fleece. It's as soft as cashmere, four times warmer, comes in more than 20 natural colors, and is hypoallergenic. The farm store sells all things alpaca. Inquire about spinning and knitting classes and Alpaca Jr. Discovery Days, on Sunday mornings in the summer, for children ages 8 and up. Follow the alpacas on their very own webcam.

Seaside Daylily Farm (508-693-3276; seasidedaylily.com), Great Plains Road, off Old County Road, West Tisbury. Open seasonally with limited hours; call ahead. These lilies are grown without the use of harmful chemicals that disrupt the ecosystem's natural balance.

Chilmark Chocolates (508-645-3013), 19 State Road, near Beetlebung

Corner, Chilmark. Open in summer and around Christmas and Valentine's Day. Good deeds and good products make an unbeatable combination. Not only will you love the creamy truffles and mouthwatering chocolates, it's nice to know that this chocolatier believes all members of society should be given a chance to be productive. They hire people with disabilities to make and sell the chocolate. Try their Tashmoo Truffles, West Chomps, or Squibnuggets.

❊ **Mosher Photo** (508-693-9430; mosherphoto.com), 25 Main Street, Vineyard Haven.

❊ Special Events

The Vineyard has hundreds and hundreds of charming—great and small—special events throughout the year. A sampling of the larger, predictable, annual events follows. Contact the chamber of commerce (508-693-0085; mvy .com) for specific dates unless an alternative phone number is listed below.

Mid-May through November: **Antiques at the Old Grange Hall**. On most Fridays, but also on some Tuesdays and Saturdays.

Throughout the summer: **Vineyard Artisans Summer Festivals** (508-693-8989; vineyardartisans.com). Shows May to December. Don't have time to pop into two dozen galleries? Then check this out. These excellent shows are held indoors and outdoors, rain or shine at the Grange Hall in West Tisbury. Look for furniture, ceramics, book arts, fiber arts, glass, jewelry, mixed media, painting, photography, printmaking, and sculpture.

Mid-June–mid-October: **West Tisbury Farmers' Market** (508-693-8989; thewesttisburyfarmersmarket.com), at Grange Hall, late June to mid-October.

Mid-June: **Oak Bluffs Harbor Festival** (508-693-3392). Since 1991.

July–August: **Community Sing** (508-693-0525). Singing and more at the Tabernacle at the Methodist "camp-ground" in Oak Bluffs every Wednesday at 8 PM. **Band concerts** every Sunday evening, alternating between Owen Park in Vineyard Haven and Ocean Park in Oak Bluffs.

Mid-July: **Edgartown Regatta** (508-627-4361; edgartownyc.org). Racing since the mid-1920s.

Late July: **Book Sale** (508-693-3366). A benefit since the late '50s for the West Tisbury Library, held at the West Tisbury Elementary School on Old County Road.

Early August: **Edgartown House Tour** (508-627-7077). This event, sponsored by the Federated Church of Martha's Vineyard, opens up five antique houses in downtown Edgartown for tours every year. Tea and refreshments are served in the Old Parsonage at the end of the tour. $$$$.

Mid-September: **International Film Festival** (mvfilmsociety.com). A laid-back but passionate, four-day celebration of films.

Early to mid-September–early to mid-October: **Striped Bass and Bluefish Derby** (mvderby.com). When dozens of surf casters begin furiously fishing from your favorite beach, you'll know it's derby time. Prizes are awarded for the largest fish caught each day, with a grand prize for the largest fish caught during the monthlong tournament. Weighing is done in Edgartown Harbor, just as it's been done every year since the mid-1940s.

Mid-September: **Tivoli Day.** A lively street fair on Circuit Avenue in Oak Bluffs.

Mid-October: **Food & Wine Festival** (mvfoodandwine.com), Edgartown. A three-day fete of food and wine with cocktail parties, chef demonstrations, tastings, seminars, and a Sunday farmer's brunch.

Early–mid-December: **Christmas in Edgartown.** The town and its lighthouse get dressed up for the occasion. There's also a parade, chowder contest, horse and carriage rides, and more.

Vineyard Artisans Holiday Festival (508-693-8989; vineyardartisans.com), at the Grange Hall, West Tisbury. More than 50 crafters and artists have gathered for this event since the mid-1960s.

NANTUCKET

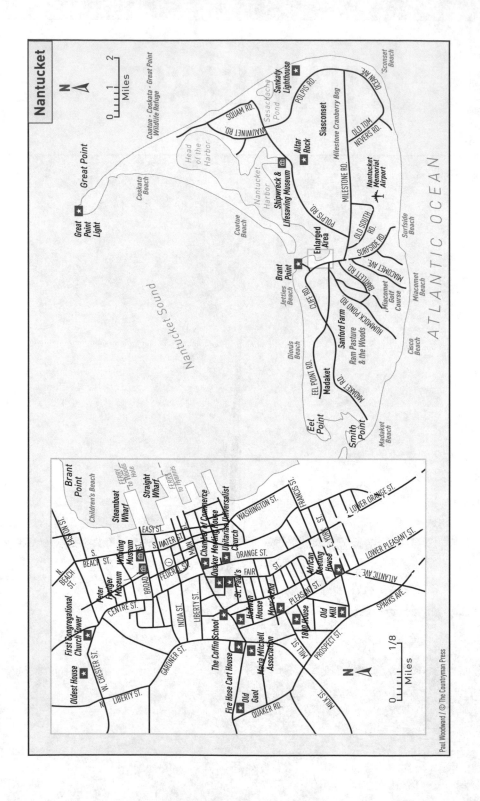

Nantucket

N

Miles
0 1 2

Great Point

Great Point Light

Coatue - Coskata - Great Point Wildlife Refuge

Coskata Beach

SQUAM RD.

Sesachacha Pond

Sankaty Lighthouse

POLPIS RD.

'Sconset Beach

Head of the Harbor

Nantucket Harbor

MADAKET RD.

Siasconset

Milestone Cranberry Bog

OLD TOM NEVERS RD.

OCEAN AVE.

Altar Rock

MILESTONE RD.

Nantucket Memorial Airport

Coatue Beach

Shipwreck & Lifesaving Museum

Brant Point

Enlarged Area

CLIFF RD.

POLPIS RD.

OLD SOUTH RD.

SURFSIDE RD.

Surfside Beach

Jetties Beach

BARTLETT RD.

MIACOMET AVE.

Miacomet Beach

Sanford Farm
Ram Pasture
& the Woods

Miacomet Golf Course

HUMMOCK POND RD.

EEL POINT RD.

Dionis Beach

Cisco Beach

Eel Point

Madaket

MADAKET RD.

Smith Point

Madaket Beach

ATLANTIC OCEAN

Nantucket Sound

Brant Point

Children's Beach

Steamboat Wharf

FERRY to Hyannis

FERRY to Hyannis

Straight Wharf

EASTON ST.

S. BEACH ST.

N. BEACH ST.

Whaling Museum

Peter Foulger Museum

EASY ST.

S. WATER ST.

MAIN ST.

Chamber of Commerce

Unitarian Universalist Church

Quaker Meeting House

WASHINGTON ST.

FRANCIS ST.

LOWER ORANGE ST.

CENTRE ST.

BROAD ST.

FEDERAL ST.

ORANGE ST.

First Congregational Church Tower

Oldest House

W. CHESTER ST.

N. LIBERTY ST.

GARDNER ST.

LIBERTY ST.

INDIA ST.

St. Paul's

FAIR ST.

Hadwen House

PLEASANT ST.

African Meeting House

E. YORK ST.

LOWER PLEASANT ST.

ATLANTIC AVE.

The Coffin School

Maria Mitchell Association

Fire Hose Cart House

Old Gaol

QUAKER RD.

MILL ST.

1800 House

Old Mill

PROSPECT ST.

MILK ST.

SPARKS AVE.

N

Miles
0   1/8

Paul Woodward / © The Countryman Press

NANTUCKET

Thirty miles out to sea, Nantucket was called "that far away island" by Native Americans. Just 14 by 3.5 miles in area, Nantucket is the only place in America that is simultaneously an island, a county, and a town. In 1659 Thomas Mayhew, who had purchased Nantucket sight unseen (he was more interested in Martha's Vineyard), sold it to Tristram Coffin and eight of his friends for £30 and "two Beaver Hatts." These "original purchasers" quickly sold half-shares to craftsmen whose skills they would require to build a community.

When Mayhew arrived, there were more than 3,000 Native American residents, who taught the settlers which crops to farm and how to spear whales from shore. By the early 1700s, the number of settlers had grown to more than 300, and the number of Natives had shrunk to less than 800, primarily because of disease. (The last Native descendant died on-island in 1854.)

In 1712, when Captain Hussey's sloop was blown out to sea, he harpooned the first sperm whale islanders had ever seen. For the next 150 years, whaling dominated the island's economy. The ensuing prosperity allowed the island's population to climb to 10,000. In comparison, there are also about 10,500 year-rounders today.

Nantucket sea captains traveled the world to catch whales and to trade, and they brought back great fortunes. By the late 1700s, trade was booming with England, and in 1791 the *Beaver*, owned by islander William Rotch, rounded Cape Horn and forged an American trade route to the Pacific Ocean. Fortunes were also made in the Indian Ocean—hence, Nantucket's India Street. Speaking of place names, the nearby village of 'Sconset takes its name from the native Indian for "near the great whale bone." It was first settled three centuries ago as a whaling outpost, around a lookout tower used for spotting whales.

BRANT POINT LIGHTHOUSE

In its heyday, Nantucket Harbor overflowed with smoke and smells from blacksmith shops, cooperages, shipyards, and candle factories. More than 100 whaling ships sailed in and out of Nantucket. But when ships grew larger to allow for their longer voyages at sea, they couldn't get across the shallow shoals and into Nantucket Harbor. The industry began moving to Martha's Vineyard and New Bedford.

At the height of the whaling industry in 1846, the "Great Fire," which began in a hat shop on Main Street, ignited whale oil at the harbor. The catastrophic blaze

NANTUCKET HARBOR

wiped out the harbor and one-third of the town. Although most citizens began to rebuild immediately, other adventurous and energetic souls were enticed to go west in search of gold in 1849. When kerosene replaced whale oil in the 1850s as a less expensive fuel, it was the final blow to the island's maritime economy. By 1861 there were only 2,000 people on-island.

MODERN DAY TOURISM

Although tourism began soon after the Civil War and picked up with the advent of the railroad to 'Sconset, the island lay more or less in undisturbed isolation until the 1950s. Perhaps it was the sleepiness of those 100 years that ultimately preserved the island's architectural integrity and community spirit, paving the way for its resurrection. In the late 1950s and early 1960s, islander and S&H Green Stamp heir Walter Beinecke Jr. organized a revitalization of the waterfront area, replacing decrepit wharf buildings with cottages. He also declared the premise that guides tourism to this day: it is preferable to attract one tourist with $100 than 100 tourists with $1 each. In accordance with the maxim, strict zoning laws were adopted, land-conservation groups were launched, and Nantucket's upscale tourism industry began in earnest.

By the late 1990s, the well-to-do set was foregoing the Hamptons and similar enclaves for Nantucket. By 2000 it had become too popular for its own good and was placed on the list of Most Endangered Historical Places, as decreed by the National Trust for Historic Preservation. In contrast to the Vineyard's showy excess and celebrity allure, Nantucket is a restrained haven for behind-the-scenes power brokers.

In the recent past, mammoth multimillion-dollar trophy houses (and to be fair, some of the more understated ones, too) have belonged to people like the Gambles of Procter & Gamble, the Du Ponts, R. H. Macy, R. J. Reynolds, Bill Blass, David Halberstam, Graham Gund, Jack Welsh, Tommy Hilfiger, John Kerry, and Russell Baker. And now, downtown properties like the former Harbor House Hotel are being converted into one- to three-bedroom residences (a.k.a. condos) with hefty price tags.

It was only a matter of time, I suppose, although many islanders are up in arms with dismay at what their island is fast becoming: a gated theme park for the rich. It's no longer enough to be a millionaire on Nantucket. Billionaires are the new millionaires.

In 1966 Nantucket was declared a **National Historic Landmark**: It boasts more than 800 buildings constructed before 1850—the largest concentration of such buildings in the U.S. The historic district is picture-perfect: paved cobblestone streets, brick sidewalks, electrified "gas" street lamps. Gray-shingled houses are nestled close together on narrow lanes, which wind as you amble beyond the downtown grid of streets. Elegant white residences are trimmed with English boxwood hedges, white picket fences, and showcase flower gardens.

NANTUCKET HUMOR

With a daily summer population that swells to about 50,000, today's tourist industry is about as well oiled as the whale industry once was. It's difficult to find a grain of sand or a seashell that hasn't been discovered.

Most sites in Nantucket are within a mile of the **historic center**—you might walk more than you're accustomed to. In addition to historic houses and museums, Nantucket prides itself on offering world-class dining. Although there are little pockets of settlements around the island, the only real "destination" is **'Sconset**, an utterly quaint village with rose-covered cottages. Elsewhere on the island, more than 45 percent of the island's 10,000 acres are held by conservation trusts; you'll be able to explore places where most tourists don't venture. The island boasts excellent bicycle paths and almost limitless public beaches.

Nantucket is a year-round destination. Hundreds of thousands of daffodils blanket the island in yellow as the earth reawakens each April. The weather in May and June is slightly less predictable than in fall, but if you hit a nice stretch, you'll probably muse

BRANT POINT LIGHTHOUSE AND FERRY

that life just doesn't get any better. Gardens are brightest in May and June. Where once there were whaling ships, yachts now fill the harbor in summer. Warm ocean water and beach barbecues beckon, wild roses trail along picket fences, and many special events are staged. Come September (my favorite month on-island), the crowds recede a bit. You can swim in the still-temperate ocean by day and not have to wait for a table at your favorite restaurant at night. Skies turn crisp blue, and cranberry bogs, heathlands, and the moors blaze red, russet, and maroon.

Many restaurants that close in mid-October (at the end of Columbus Day weekend) reopen for the long Thanksgiving weekend. The first three weeks of November are very quiet indeed. Before the monochrome days of winter set in, there is one last burst of activity: Nantucket Noel and Christmas Stroll (see *Special Events*). In January, February, and March you'll discover why whaling captains called the island the "little gray lady"—she is often shrouded in fog. It's a time of reflection and renewal for year-rounders and visitors alike.

GUIDANCE ✸ **Nantucket Visitor Services & Information Bureau** (508-228-0925; nantucket-ma.gov), 25 Federal Street. The bureau also maintains seasonal kiosks at Straight Wharf and Nantucket Memorial Airport.

✸ **Nantucket Island Chamber of Commerce** (508-228-1700; nantucketchamber .org), 0 Main Street. For sure (!), get their glossy book, *The Official Guide: Nantucket*, which is free on-island (and can also easily be downloaded in sections) but costs $ to mail in advance of your visit.

Nantucket Historical Association (NHA) (508-228-1894; nha.org), 15 Broad Street. The NHA owns 23 historic properties, 10 of which are open to the public, representing island life from its farming beginnings to its prosperous whaling days, and is a fabulous source of historical information. Generally, NHA properties have "normalish" hours late May to mid-October and shortened winter hours; they change from year to year. A Historic Sites ticket ($) is valid for admission to Hadwen House, the Oldest House, the Old Mill, and the Quaker Meeting House. Guided tours are available at the Hadwen House, Oldest House, and Old Mill. The combo ticket, which includes the Whaling Museum (see *To See*), is a good deal ($$).

WHALING MUSEUM

GETTING THERE With high-speed ferry service, day-tripping to Nantucket from Hyannis is more feasible than ever. Although I still recommend spending a few days on Nantucket, you are no longer shut out if you can't.

By bus: **Peter Pan/Bonanza** (800-343-9999; peterpanbus.com) travels from points south to Hyannis, where you can catch the boats. **Plymouth & Brockton** (508-746-0378; p-b.com) runs from Boston to Hyannis.

✳ *By boat from Hyannis:* **The Steamship Authority** (508-477-8600 for information and advance auto reservations; 508-771-4000 for day-of-sailing information—no reservations—in Hyannis; 508-228-0262 for day-of-sailing

WAITING FOR THE STEAMSHIP AUTHORITY FERRY

information—no reservations—on Nantucket; steamshipauthority.com), South Street Dock, Hyannis. The steamship, established in 1948, carries autos, people, and bikes to Steamship Wharf year-round. Make car reservations in the spring for the summer if you can; no reservations are needed for passengers. There are six high-season sailings daily and three off-season. Parking in Hyannis is $$ per calendar day. The voyage takes 2¼ hours. Round-trip fares: $$$$; bicycles $$. Cars cost a whopping $450+ mid-May to late October, about $320 off-season—but you really don't need one. Take it from me, a my-car-is-my-home-when-I-travel nut.

The Steamship Authority's **high-speed passenger boat**, *Iyanough* (508-495-3278 for reservations; 508-477-8600 for information) sails dock-to-dock in one hour, early May through December, and makes four to five trips daily; $$$$$+. Reservations strongly suggested.

✳ **Hy-Line Cruises** (800-492-8082; hylinecruises.com), Ocean Street Dock, Hyannis. Passengers and bicycles to Straight Wharf, late May to mid-October. There are three summertime boats daily, one to three daily off-season. Round-trip fares are $$$$$, bicycles $$. Parking in Hyannis is $$ per calendar day.

✳ **Hy-Line's high-speed passenger boat**, *Grey Lady* (800-492-8082; hylinecruises .com), Ocean Street Dock. This high-speed luxury catamaran costs a bit more, but it operates year-round. Reservations are strongly recommended. There are five to six boats daily.

By boat from Harwich: **Freedom Cruise Line** (508-432-8999; nantucketisland ferry.com), Saquatucket Harbor in Harwich Port, provides daily passenger service to Nantucket, early June to late September and during the Christmas Stroll (see *Special Events*). During the summer, two of the three trips are scheduled so that you can explore Nantucket for about 6½ hours and return the same day. In spring and fall, there is only one morning boat daily. Reservations are highly recommended; make them three to four days in advance. Round-trip prices: $$$$$+, bicycles $$. Free parking for day-trippers; $$ daily thereafter. The trip takes 80 minutes each way.

By boat from Martha's Vineyard: **Hy-Line Cruises** (508-778-2600 in Hyannis; 508-228-3949 on Nantucket; 508-693-0112 in Oak Bluffs, Martha's Vineyard; hylinecruises .com). One daily, interisland departure from mid-June to mid-September. The trip takes 75 minutes. (There is no interisland car ferry.) One-way: $$$$, bicycles $.

By air: **Cape Air/Nantucket Airlines** (508-771-6944; flycapeair.com; nantucke tairlines.org) offer dozens of daily flights direct from Boston, Hyannis, New Bedford, Providence (T. F. Green), and Martha's Vineyard. Frequent-flier coupon books for 10 one-way trips are available.

GETTING AROUND *By shuttle:* 🚲 **NRTA Shuttle** (508-228-7025; nrtawave.com). WAVE information aides and other amenities are available at the Greenhound Building at 10 Washington Street. Buses daily, late May to early October. This is an economical, relatively convenient (if you pay attention to departure times), and reliable way to travel to 'Sconset (two routes) and Madaket, but the schedule is too complicated to disseminate here. Pick up a route map on-island. Shuttles have a bike rack, so you can take the bus out to 'Sconset, for instance, and ride back. The Surfside Beach and Jetties Beach buses run on a shorter season, from mid-June to early September. Tickets cost $, depending on the route; exact change required. Ask about multiday passes at the NRTA office at 3 East Chestnut Street.

By car or four-wheel drive: There isn't a single traffic light in Nantucket, and Nantucketers intend to keep it that way. You don't need a car unless you're here for at least a week or unless you plan to spend most of your time in conservation areas or on outlying beaches. Even then, a four-wheel-drive vehicle is the most useful, as many of the stunning natural areas are off sandy paths. Nantucket is also ringed by 80 miles of beaches, most of which are accessible via four-wheel drive. Four-wheel drives are rented faster than the speed of light in summer, so make reservations at least a month in advance. And lastly, parking is severely restricted in the historic center. Rent from my favorite company, **Affordable Rentals** (508-228-3501; affrentals.com), 6 South Beach Street, early April to late December. Expect to pay $125+ for a compact during the summer, $250+ for a four-wheel-drive Jeep. **Nantucket Windmill Auto Rental** (508-228-1227; nantucketautorental.com) is based at the airport but also offers free pickup from the ferry; **Hertz** (800-654-3131; hertz.com) is also based at the airport. Prices drop by almost half off-season.

GOING ON THE WHALE

If you get stuck in the sand, call **Harry's 24-Hour Towing** (508-228-3390). Once you do call him, though, wait with your vehicle so he doesn't make the trek out to fetch you, only to find that you've been helped by a friendly local.

Contact the **Police Department** (508-228-1212), South Water Street, for **overland permits**, which are required for four-wheel, over-sand driving. Expect to pay $100+ off-season and $150+ in season. The Coatue–Coskata–Great Point nature area (see *Green Space*) requires a separate permit, available from the **Nantucket Conservation Foundation** (508-228-2884 information; 508-228-0006 Wauwinet gatehouse, where permits are purchased; nantucketconservation.com),

WALKING TOURS

A PERFECT DAY TRIP TO NANTUCKET

8:15	Board a high-speed ferry in Hyannis.
9:30	Get fresh-squeezed concoctions and treats from The Juice Bar.
10:00	Take a walking tour with the Nantucket Historical Association.
11:45	Learn the island's rich history at the Nantucket Whaling Museum.
1:15	Split an oversized sandwich from Provisions with your companion.
2:00	Take an island driving tour with Nantucket Island Tours.
3:15	Shop and stroll along cobblestone streets; pop into the Atheneum.
6:15	Enjoy regional cuisine at the Boarding House or Centre Street Bistro.
8:40	Take the last high-speed ferry back to Hyannis.

mid-May through October. Most beaches are open to four-wheel-drive traffic, except when terns are nesting.

By taxi: Taxi fares can add up, but cabs are a useful way to get to the airport or to an outlying restaurant.

Try **All Point Taxi** (508-228-5779) or look for one when you disembark from the ferry. Taxis usually line up on lower Main Street and at Steamboat Wharf. Flat rates are based on the destination: $$$ to 'Sconset, $$ to the airport, and $ within town, for instance. Rates are for one person; add a coupla bucks for each additional passenger. As for Uber or Lyft: personally, I'd rather support local taxis.

By bicycle: Bicycling is the best way to get around (see *To Do*).

By moped: **Nantucket Bike Shop** (508-228-1999; nantucketbikeshop.com), Steamboat Wharf, rents scooters April through October. $$$$$+ daily.

On foot: 🚲 **Architectural Walking Tours** (508-228-1387; nantucketpreservation.org), 55 Main Street, by the Nantucket Preservation Trust. June through September. $$.

🚲 See the Nantucket Whaling Museum for great walking tours sponsored by the **Nantucket Historical Association.**

By van or bus tours: ❄ **Ara's Tours** (508-228-1951; 508-221-6852; arastours.com) offers a 90-minute island tour for $$$ that makes stops for photography. On a clear day you can see all three lighthouses. For those who have more time and money, ask about the three-hour barrier beach tours of Great Point (see *Green Space*).

🦞 **Trustees of Reservations** (508-921-1944; thetrustees.org) offers excellent 3½-hour natural history tours from mid-May to mid-October. Tours depart from the Nantucket Shipwreck & Lifesaving Museum, where a guided tour of the museum is followed by a tour of the Coskata-Coatue Wildlife Refuge. $$$$$; reservations strongly recommended.

Barrett's Tours (508-228-0174), 20 Federal Street, and **Nantucket Island Tours** (508-228-0334), 34 Straight Wharf, offer 90-minute narrated mini-bus tours May through October. $$$.

MEDIA The venerable *Inquirer and Mirror* (ack.net) has been published on Thursday since 1821 and is also available online.

The free weekly *Yesterday's Island* (yesterdaysisland.com) is useful for entertainment listings.

On-island, tune into **Channel 22** and **Channel 17** to learn more about the island.

WNAN 91.1 (508-548-9600; wgbh.org) is the NPR affiliate.

MORE WEBSITES **Mahonabouttown.wordpress.com**. You wanna know about this island, you gotta know about this "Mahon About Town" blog.

Artsnantucket.com. Look for their free color guide to the island's visual and performing arts.

Nantucketonline.com. Look for their glossy publication, *Only Nantucket,* which is also viewable online.

Nantucket.net. A complete guide.

PUBLIC RESTROOMS Visitor Services & Information Bureau at 25 Federal Street (open year-round); Children's Beach (see *Green Space*) and Straight Wharf (both open seasonally).

PUBLIC LIBRARY See **Atheneum** under the "Quiet Time" sidebar.

ATM Short on greenbacks? In town, look for automatic teller machines at the Pacific National Bank (15 Sparks Avenue), Bank of America (15 Main Street), the Steamship Authority terminal (Steamboat Wharf), and Nantucket Bank (2 Orange Street).

MEDICAL EMERGENCY **Nantucket Cottage Hospital** (508-825-8100; nantuckethospital.org), 57 Prospect Street. Open 24 hours.

Lyme disease. Ticks carry this disease, which has flulike symptoms and may result in death if left untreated. Immediately and carefully remove any ticks that may have migrated from dune grasses to your body. Better yet, wear long pants, tuck pants into socks, and wear long-sleeved shirts whenever possible when hiking. Avoid hiking in grassy and overgrown areas of dense brush.

✳ To See

ON THE HARBOR **The wharves** (from north to south). The Steamship Authority is now based at **Steamboat Wharf**, but from 1881 to 1917, steam trains, which met the early steam-powered ferries and transported passengers to Surfside and 'Sconset, originated here. **Old North Wharf** is home to privately owned summer cottages. **Straight Wharf**, originally built in 1723 by Richard Macy, is a center of activity. It was completely rebuilt in the 1960s (except for the Thomas Macy Warehouse; see below) as part of a preservation effort. The wharf is home to Hy-Line, a few T-shirt and touristy shops, restaurants, a gallery, a museum, a nice pavilion area, and charter boats and sailboats. Straight Wharf was so named because folks could cart things from here "straight" up Main Street. **Old South Wharf** houses art galleries, crafts shops, and clothing shops

STRAIGHT WHARF

in quaint little one-room "shacks" (see *Selective Shopping*). **Commercial Wharf**, also known as Swain's Wharf, was built in the early 1800s by Zenas Coffin.

Thomas Macy Warehouse, Straight Wharf. Built after the Great Fire of 1846, when the wharves were completely destroyed and more than 400 houses burned, the warehouse stored supplies to outfit ships.

MAIN STREET

The lower three blocks of Main Street were paved in 1837 with cobblestones, purchased in Gloucester, which proved quite useful—they kept carts laden with whale oil from sinking into the sand and dirt as they were rolled from wharves to factories. After

OLD SOUTH WHARF

MAIN STREET

the Great Fire swept through town, Main Street was widened considerably to prevent future fires from jumping from house to house so rapidly. In the mid-1850s Henry and Charles Coffin planted dozens of elm trees along the street, but only a few have survived disease over the years. The former drinking fountain for horses, which today spills over with flowers, has been a landmark on Lower Main since it was moved here in the early 1900s.

Pacific Club, Main Street at South Water Street. This three-story, Georgian brick building was built as a warehouse and countinghouse for shipowner William Rotch, owner of the *Beaver* and *Dartmouth*, two ships that took part in the Boston Tea Party. In 1789 it served as a U.S. Customs House. In 1861 a group of retired whaling captains purchased the building for use as a private social club, where they swapped stories and played cribbage. Descendants of these original founders carried on the tradition of the elite club until the 1980s.

Pacific National Bank, 61 Main Street at Fair Street. This 1818, two-story, Federal-style brick building is one of only four to survive the Great Fire. It's no coincidence that the two important buildings anchoring Main Street are named "Pacific" for the fortunes reaped from the Pacific Ocean: This bank almost single-handedly financed the wealthy whaling industry. Step inside to see the handsome main room, original teller cages, and murals of the port and street scenes.

Thomas Macy House, 99 Main Street. Many think this is Nantucket's most attractive doorway, with its silver doorplate, porch railing that curves outward, and wooden fanwork. This Nantucket Historical Association (NHA) property is open to the public on special occasions.

"Three Bricks," 93, 95, and 97 Main Street. These identical Georgian mansions were built in 1836 for the three sons (all under the age of 27) of whaling-ship magnate Joseph Starbuck. Joseph retained the house titles to ensure that his sons would continue the family business. When the sons approached age 40 (firmly entrenched in the business), Joseph deeded the houses to them. One house remains in the Starbuck family; none is open to the public.

Hadwen House (508-228-1894; nha.org), 96 Main Street. Taken together, 94 Main (privately owned) and 96 Main are referred to architecturally as the "Two Greeks." Candle merchant William Hadwen married one of Joseph Starbuck's daughters and built the Greek Revival house at No. 96. Starbuck's two other daughters also ended up living across the street from their brothers—at 92 and 100 Main Street, creating a virtual Starbuck compound. Docents point out gas chandeliers, a circular staircase, Italian marble fireplaces, silver doorknobs, and period furnishings. Don't overlook the lovely historic garden in back. The "other" Greek (No. 94) was built in the mid-19th century for Mary G. Swain, Starbuck's niece; note the Corinthian capitals supposedly modeled after the Athenian Temple of the Winds. This is an NHA property (see *Guidance* for hours and fees).

Henry Coffin House and **Charles Coffin House**, 75 and 78 Main Street. The Coffin brothers inherited their fortunes from their father's candle-making and whaling enterprises and general mercantile business. They built their houses across the street from each other, using the same carpenters and masons. Charles was a Quaker, and his Greek Revival house (No. 78) has a simple roof walk and modest brown trim. Henry's late-Federal-style house (No. 75) has fancy trim around the front door and a cupola. Neither is open to the public.

John Wendell Barrett House, 72 Main Street. This elegant Greek Revival house features a front porch with Ionic columns and a raised basement. Barrett was the president of the Pacific National Bank and a wealthy whale oil merchant, but the house is best known for another reason. During the Great Fire, Barrett's wife, Lydia, refused to leave the front porch. Firefighters wanted to blow up the house in order to deprive the fire of fuel. Luckily for her, the winds shifted and further confrontation was averted. Not open to the public.

NORTH OF MAIN STREET

✺ **Whaling Museum** (508-228-1894; nha.org), 13 Broad Street. This 1846 brick building, another NHA property (see *Guidance* for hours), is a must-see on even the shortest itinerary. It began life as Richard Mitchell's spermaceti candle factory, and as such, it now tells the story of the candle factory and preserves Nantucket's whaling history. Spermaceti, by the way, is a substance found in the cavity of a sperm whale's head; it was a great source of lamp and machine oil. During the restoration of the original candle factory in 2004, the NHA discovered an original beam press and the base of the factory triworks. (It's the only one in the world still in its original location.) So, the story the museum can tell grows even richer. You can also see the lens from the

ONE OF "THREE BRICKS"

WHALING MUSEUM

Sankaty Head Lighthouse, as well as an entire exhibit about the *Essex* whaling ship. **Gosnell Hall** houses a 46-foot sperm whale skeleton and a fully rigged whale boat, which will help you envision the treacherous "Nantucket sleigh ride." When the small boat harpooned a mammoth whale and remained connected by a rope, the boat was dragged through the waves until the whale tired. **Peter Foulger Gallery** is named for one of the island's first settlers who acted as an interpreter when the settlers purchased the island from Native Americans in 1659. Peter's daughter, Abiah, was Ben Franklin's mother. $$; History Tickets with guided walking tours are additional. Combo pass for the museum, Hadwen House, the Oldest House, the Old Mill, and the Quaker Meeting House is $$$.

Centre Street was referred to as Petticoat Row during the whaling era, when men went out to sea and women were left to run the shops and businesses. It's still chock-full of fine shops.

First Congregational Church Tower (508-228-0950; nantucketfcc.org), 62 Centre Street. Church open mid-May to mid-October; tower open mid-June to mid-October. This church is known for its 120-foot steeple, from which there are 360-degree panoramic views of the island and ocean. The climb to the top is 94 steps—not that I've counted or anything. On a clear day you can see from Eel Point to Great Point (see *Green Space*) and all the moors in between. Serious photographers shouldn't get too excited, though, because they'll have to shoot through dirty storm windows.

MAIN STREET

✳ ✐ ⬥ **Nantucket Atheneum** (508-228-1110; nantucketatheneum.org), 1 India Street. This fine Greek Revival building with Ionic columns was designed by Frederick Coleman, who designed the "Two Greeks" (see Hadwen House under *To See*). When the library and all its contents were lost in the Great Fire of 1846, donations poured in from around the country and a new building replaced it within six months. The Great Hall on the second floor has hosted such distinguished orators as Frederick Douglass, Daniel Webster, Horace Greeley, Henry David Thoreau, Ralph Waldo Emerson, and John James Audubon. (The hall seats about 100 people; there are numerous free readings and lectures here.) Maria Mitchell (see Maria Mitchell Association sidebar under *To See*) was the first librarian. Since then there have been, amazingly, only seven other librarians in its long history. In addition to comfortable reading rooms on both floors, the Atheneum has an excellent children's wing and a nice garden out back. Some of the more than 50,000 volumes include town newspapers dating from 1816, early New England genealogy, and ships' logs. Portraits of whaling captains grace the space, while display cases are filled with scrimshaw and other historical artifacts. This is one of the island's most special places. It's a quiet refuge from the masses in the height of summer, as well as a delightful place to spend a rainy day. Call for information about special events and story hours.

The current steeple was built in 1968; the previous one was dismantled in 1849, when it was deemed too shaky to withstand storms. The church was built with whaling money at the industry's apex in 1834. Note the things money could buy: a 600-pound brass chandelier and trompe l'oeil walls. The rear wing of the church contains the simple vestry, the oldest church building on the island (circa 1720). Donation suggested for climbing the steeple $.

🏛 **Oldest House** (508-228-1894; nha. org), 16 Sunset Hill Lane. Also known as the **Jethro Coffin House**, this 1686 home was built as a wedding present for Jethro Coffin and Mary Gardner by their parents. Peter Coffin cut and shipped timbers from his land in Exeter, New Hampshire, for the house. The marriage joined two prominent island families—the Coffins were "original purchasers," while the Gardners were "half-share men." Features include small, diamond-shaped, leaded windows, sparse period furnishings, and a huge central chimney decorated with an upside-down horseshoe. When lightning struck the house in 1987, the Nantucket Historical Association decided it was time to restore it. To provide visitors with a better understanding of what everyday life was like three centuries ago, a kitchen garden and a small orchard of old-variety apple trees was planted in 2007.

Brant Point Lighthouse, off Easton Street. In 1746 the island's first "lighthouse" (and the country's second oldest,

FIRST CONGREGATIONAL CHURCH TOWER

BRANT POINT LIGHTHOUSE

after Boston Light) guarded the harbor's northern entrance. It was rather primitive, consisting of a lantern hung on rope between two poles. The lighthouse standing today is small in size but large in symbolism. Folklore and tradition suggest that throwing two pennies overboard as you round the point at the lighthouse ensures your return. Many throw two pennies, and many return. Don't pass up the chance to catch a sunset from here; it's the reason you came to Nantucket in the first place.

NEAR OR OFF UPPER MAIN STREET

Quaker Meeting House (508-228-1894; nha.org), 7 Fair Street. Open late April to mid-October. This small, simple building with wooden benches and 12-over-12 windows began as a Friends school in 1838. NHA property (see *Guidance* for hours and fees).

❄ **Nantucket Historical Association Research Library** (508-228-1894, ext. 4; nha .org), 7 Fair Street. This library contains Edouard A. Stackpole's collection of manuscripts, photographs, ships' logs, and other items. $.

St. Paul's Episcopal Church (508-228-0916; stpaulschurchnantucket.org), 20 Fair Street. Stop in to admire this granite church's Tiffany windows.

❄ **Unitarian Universalist Church** (508-228-5466; unitarianchurchnantucket.org), 11 Orange Street. Open July and August, or by appointment during the rest of the year. This 1809 church, also called **South Church**, is known for its tall spire (quite visible at sea and a distinct part of the Nantucket "skyline"); a wonderfully illusory trompe l'oeil golden dome; and a mahogany and ivory 1831 Goodrich organ. Orange Street was once home to more than 100 whaling captains, and for years a town crier watched for ships (and fires) from this tower.

🐚 **The Coffin School** (508-228-2505; eganmaritime.org), 4 Winter Street, one block off Main Street. Open for seminars and presentations only. The school was founded in 1827 by Adm. Sir Isaac Coffin, English baronet and a descendant of Tristram Coffin, one of the island's first settlers. It was established to provide a "good English education" for Coffin descendants. (In the early 19th century, more than half of Nantucket's children were Coffin descendants.) The impressive brick Greek Revival building now serves as home for the **Egan Maritime Institute**, displaying special exhibits related to Nantucket history. A fine collection of 19th-century paintings portraying significant Nantucket events is featured, including works by Elizabeth R. Coffin, a student of Thomas Eakins. Historical lectures on the school and maritime subjects are given year-round. Admission $; price also includes admission to the Nantucket Shipwreck and Lifesaving Museum (see *Around the Island*).

See also **Lightship Basket Museum** under the "Lightship Baskets" sidebar.

BEYOND UPPER MAIN STREET

Fire Hose Cart House (508-228-1894; nha.org), 8 Gardner Street. This small 1886 neighborhood fire station is the only one of its kind remaining on-island. As you can imagine, lots of stations were built after the Great Fire. On display are leather buckets and an old hand pumper used more than a century ago. NHA property (see *Guidance* for hours); self-guided.

The Old Gaol (508-228-1894; nha.org), 15R Vestal Street. This 1806 penal institution, built of logs bolted together with iron, was used until 1933. It had only four cells. The first incarcerated felon escaped (a 15-year-old climbed out the chimney), but others weren't so lucky. Well, perhaps they were—it's said that the last prisoners got to sleep at home rather than on the planks that served as beds. NHA property (see *Guidance* for hours); self-guided.

Old Mill (508-228-1894; nha.org), 50 Prospect Street. Reputed to be made with salvaged wood, this 1746 Dutch-style windmill has canvas sails and a granite stone that still grinds corn in summer. A reminder of when the island's principal activity was farming, this windmill is the only remaining of the four originals. (It's in its original location, too.) NHA property; tours offered. (See *Guidance* for hours and fees.)

African Meeting House (508-228-9833; afroammuseum.org), 29 York Street. Open June through October. Built as a church and a schoolhouse in the 1820s, when black children were barred from public school, this house is thought to be the second oldest such building in the country. Boston's Museum of Afro-American History presents cultural programming and interpretive exhibits on the history of African Americans on Nantucket. It also publishes a very good pamphlet with a walking tour of the island's black heritage sites. The Florence Higginbotham House (at Pleasant Street), also at the center of the thriving 19th-century African American community on the island, has recently been acquired. The pre-Revolutionary War building has a fascinating history. Thanks to federal funding, the meetinghouse is being restored to its 19th-century state. $.

Moor's End, 19 Pleasant Street. This large 1830s Georgian house—the first island house made with brick—belonged to Jared Coffin. Although today it's among the island's finest, Mrs. Coffin was not satisfied with its location. She wanted to be closer to town, so Jared built another at 29 Broad Street (see **Jared Coffin House** under *Lodging*). A beautiful garden lies behind the tall brick wall, but unfortunately for us, like the house, it's private.

AROUND THE ISLAND

Great Point Light, Great Point, is accessible by four-wheel-drive vehicle, by boat, or by a difficult 5-mile (one-way) trek through soft sand. A 70-foot stone structure guarded

HOMAGE TO A LOCAL, 19TH-CENTURY HERO

❄ ✐ **Maria Mitchell Association (MMA)** (508-228-9198; mariamitchell.org), 4 Vestal Street. Founded in 1902, the association owns six properties that celebrate the life and continue the work of Maria (pronounced *mar-EYE-a*) Mitchell, born on-island August 1, 1818. At age 13 she helped whaling captains set their navigational devices with the aid of astronomical projections. At 18 she became the librarian at the Atheneum, where she served for the next 20 years. At 29 Mitchell was the first woman to discover a comet (which was dubbed Mitchell's comet)—from atop the Pacific National Bank, where her father (bank president and an amateur astronomer) had set up an observatory. She was also the first woman admitted to the American Academy of Arts and Sciences and the first woman college professor of astronomy. (She taught at Vassar from 1865 until her death in 1888.)

The association hosts a number of children's programs that foster an appreciation of the connection between science and "beauty and poetry." Also, look for postings of special lectures and walks sponsored by the group; I've never been to one that was less than excellent. And, in July 2009, the association received the ultimate seal of approval when President Obama announced that the Maria Mitchell Association had been selected to receive the Presidential Award for Excellence in Science, Mathematics, and Engineering Mentoring.

A combination ticket to the birthplace, observatory, and museum (available at any of the properties) costs $$. Tickets may also be purchased separately for the aquarium. To whet your appetite, enjoy free tours of the Vestal Street campus most days during the season, meeting in the Science Library Courtyard.

❄ ✐ **Maria Mitchell Science Library** (508-228-2896; mariamitchell.org), 2 Vestal Street. This library, which has a children's section, houses 19th-century science books, current scientific periodicals, Maria's own papers, and natural history and astronomy books. Maria's father taught navigation by the stars in this former schoolhouse. Appointments available for research.

the island's northeastern tip for 166 years, until a ferocious storm destroyed it in 1984. This new one was built to withstand 20-foot waves and 240 mph winds.

Madaket. When Thomas Macy landed here in 1659, he found poor soil and didn't stay long. Today there is a large summer community and many rental houses. On the western coast, Madaket is a great place to enjoy a sunset, do some bluefishing, or get a boat repaired in the boatyard. The picturesque creek is best viewed from the little bridge to the right of the main road.

✐ ⛱ **Nantucket Shipwreck & Lifesaving Museum** (508-228-1885; eganmaritime.org), 158 Polpis Road on Folger's Marsh. Open late May to mid-October. This building replicates the original 1874 Surfside Lifesaving Service station that survives today as the Nantucket

NANTUCKET SHIPWRECK & LIGHTSAVING MUSEUM

Maria Mitchell Birthplace (508-228-2896 in summer, 508-228-9219 rest of year; maria mitchell.org), 1 Vestal Street. Open mid June to mid October. Built in 1790, Mitchell's birthplace contains family memorabilia and the telescope she used to spot her comet. Tour the house and check out the island's only public roof walk. See above for ticket.

Maria Mitchell Vestal Street Observatory (508-228-9273; mariamitchell.org), 3 Vestal Street. Call for tour times.

✒ Natural Science Museum (508-228-0898; mariamitchell.org), Hinchman House, 7 Milk Street. Open late May to mid-October. See displays of Nantucket's natural history and visit the live animal room to meet frogs, turtles, snakes, spiders, insects, fish, and other island creatures. There's also a popular, well-stocked museum shop; a new high-tech scavenger hunt; and kids can learn how to (theoretically) save Nantucket Harbor with a Jenga-style game and learn more about wider ecological issues.

❋ Loines Observatory (508-228-9273; mariamitchell.org), 59 Milk Street Extension. Open June through December (see website for dates and times, and call to confirm weather conditions), when lectures and telescope viewings are held. Climb a ladder to the eyepiece of a fine, old telescope and sample the sights of the distant heavens. You'll also have the opportunity to see the MMA's new, 24-inch research telescope. $$.

✒ Maria Mitchell Aquarium & Museum Shop (508-228-5387; mariamitchell.org), 28 Washington Street. Open early June through August. Once a railroad station ticket office for the Nantucket Railroad, the aquarium has grown into a much-loved island resource. Visitors have the opportunity to learn about Nantucket's marine ecology through firsthand experience with many of the organisms that inhabit our coastal areas. The expanded aquarium complex contains 20 saltwater tanks in three buildings, an orientation area for dry exhibits and small group instruction, and two large "touch tanks" for curious hands. Visitors might count the eyes of a scallop, watch a channeled whelk feeding on a mollusk, or see baby squid hatching. Call about the popular marine ecology walks, whale watches, and seal cruises. $; see combo ticket details above.

Hostel (see *Lodging*). Instead of being at water's edge, however, it's scenically situated on a salt marsh—perfect for a picnic. Dedicated to humanity's dramatic efforts against the relentless sea—treacherous shoals and inclement weather led to more than 700 shipwrecks in the surrounding waters of Nantucket—this museum houses equipment used in the daring rescues of sailors stranded offshore in their sinking boats. Treasures include one of only three Massachusetts Humane Society lifesaving surfboats and the only surviving beachcart still used for demonstration drills. You'll also find photographs, accounts of rescues, Nantucket's three Fresnel lighthouse lenses, and artifacts from the *Andrea Doria*, which sank off Nantucket almost half a century ago. $.

❋ To Do

BIRD-WATCHING **Maria Mitchell Association** (508-228-9198; mmo.org), 1 Vestal Street, offers birding field trips June to early September. $$; binoculars available for hire. Some people think that Nantucket offers the best wintertime bird-watching on the East Coast. I wouldn't argue.

See also **Eco Guides** under *Outdoor Adventure*.

BOAT EXCURSIONS & RENTALS Endeavor (508-228-5585; endeavorsailing.com), Slip 1015, Straight Wharf. May through October. Capt. Jim Genthner and his wife, Sue, operate a 31-foot Friendship sloop that departs on at least three daily 90-minute harbor tours and a sunset cruise. Custom sails may include pirating for children and an on-board fiddler or storyteller. $$$$+.

Island Boat Rentals (508-325-1001; boatnantucket.com), Straight Wharf, Slip 1001. You don't have to be macho to handle one of these little runabouts or powerboats that can take you across the harbor to Coatue, where you can sunbathe and picnic in relative quiet. Leave in the morning when there's less wind. Rentals start at $385.

✐ **Nantucket Island Community Sailing** (508-228-6600; nantucketcommunity sailing.org), Jetties Beach. Rents Windsurfers, Sunfish, kayaks, and large sailboats, and it holds youth, sailboard, sailing, and racing classes. For a really unique thing to do, take a class in how to sail a replica 19th-century whaleboat. Mid-June to early September.

COOKOUTS Contact the **Fire Department** (508-228-2324), 131 Pleasant Street, for the requisite (nominally-priced) permits for charcoal cookouts.

FISHING & SHELLFISHING Permits for digging clams, mussels, and quahogs are obtained from the Marine Department and shellfish warden (508-228-7261), 34 Washington Street. Or try online (mass .gov). Scalloping season opens October 1, after which you'll see fishermen in the harbor and off nearby shoals of Tuckernuck Island; local scallops harvested from mid-October through March are delicious.

Try your luck freshwater fishing at **Long Pond** (see *Green Space*). Nantucket blues, which run in schools from May to October, are caught from the southern shore. Fishing isn't as good in July and August when the waters are warmer,

BICYCLING & RENTALS

Excellent paved, two-way bicycle paths lead to most major "destinations." If you're riding on the street, ride in the direction of traffic or you'll be fined. Or walk your bike.

Madaket Bike Path begins on Upper Main Street. This 6-mile (one-way) road takes you to the western end of Nantucket in 45 minutes. Although the route is a bit hilly and winding, it's beautiful. There are rest areas along the way, a water fountain at the halfway point, picnic tables at Long Pond (see *Green Space*), and usually elegant swans, too.

Dionis Bike Path is a 1-mile spur trail off the Madaket Bike Path that runs to Dionis Beach. Getting to the beach has never been easier.

'Sconset (or Milestone) Bike Path begins at the rotary east of the historic district. This 6.5-mile (one-way) route with slight inclines parallels Milestone Road; it takes about an hour to get to 'Sconset. (Visually, the ride is a bit dull.) There's a water fountain at the rotary.

Surfside Bike Path. Take Main Street to Pleasant Street, then continue straight and bear right onto Atlantic Avenue to Surfside Road. This flat 2.5-mile (one-way) path is very popular in summer; it takes about 20 minutes to get to the beach.

Polpis Road Path. The loop from the 'Sconset Bike Path to Polpis Road and back to town is about 16.5 miles. It's definitely worth the detour, especially in springtime, when it's lined with thousands of daffodils.

Cliff Road Bike Path begins on Cliff Road from North Water Street. This 2.5-mile, slightly hilly road passes large summer homes.

Rental Shops. With more than 2,500 rental bikes on-island, companies offer competitive rates. Average daily adult prices: $$$; kid's bikes, trailers, zipper strollers, and trail-a-bikes, too. Inquire about discounts for family rentals. The following shops rent bicycles: **Young's Bicycle Shop** (508-228-1151; youngsbicycleshop.com), 6 Broad Street, Steamboat Wharf, one of the best in town, a third-generation, family-owned bike shop since 1931); **Nantucket Bike Shop** (508-228-1999; nantucketbikeshop.com), 4 Broad Street, Steamboat Wharf; and **Cook's Cycles** (508-228-0800; cookscyclesnantucket.com), 6 South Beach. Young's has the longest season, but Cook's is often a bit less expensive.

See also **Eco Guides** under *Outdoor Adventure.*

but if that's the only time you're here, toss out a line anyway. No fishing licenses are needed for Nantucket.

Bill Fisher Tackle (508-228-2261; billfishertackle.com), 127 Orange Street, rents a full line of equipment, supplies daily fishing reports, and provides guide service.

Most charters in search of striped bass and bluefish are located on Straight Wharf, including *Herbert T* (508-228-6655; fishnantucket.net), *Slip 14*, and *Just Do It Too* (508-228-7448; justdoittoo.com), Slip 13.

GOLF **Siasconset Golf Club** (508-257-6596), 260 Milestone Road. Open late May to mid-October. This nine-hole public course, encircled by conservation land, dates to 1894.

✳ **Miacomet Golf Course** (508-325-0333; miacometgolf.com), 12 West Miacomet Road. This flat, 18-hole course is the island's only 18-hole public golf facility. It's owned by the Land Bank and has views of Miacomet Pond, heathland, and the coastline.

Sankaty Head Golf Club (508-257-6655; 508-257-6629; sankatyheadgc.com), 100 Polpis Road, 'Sconset. Although this links-style, 18-hole course is private, the public may play off-season from October to May. There are magnificent lighthouse views. This course operates one of the last remaining caddy camps in the U.S. (for boys), and it has done so since the early 1930s.

Nantucket Golf Club (508-257-8500; nantucketgolfclub.org), 250 Milestone Road (there's no sign, nor is entry allowed for tourists). One of the most exclusive clubs anywhere. Many members, like gazillionaire Bill Gates, do not own property on-island, but rather jet in, play golf, and jet out. Memberships cost hundreds of thousands of dollars, plus annual dues. The membership list is closely guarded, of course, but it has its share from the Forbes 400 Wealthiest Americans list. As for the golf, the par-72, links-style course rolls with the naturally undulating landscape, within sight of Sankaty Head Light, on the moors with scrub oak and pitch pine. Generally appreciated by island conservationists, who realize that it could have been developed in less favorable ways, the 350-acre course was designed by Rees Jones.

IN-LINE SKATING Summertime skating is prohibited in town. You can skate on bike paths and at the skateboarding park at Jetties Beach; helmets and pads are required.

OUTDOOR ADVENTURE ❋ ⚓ **Strong Wings Eco Guides** (508-228-1769; strong wings.org). Casual, customized adventure instruction and guided group trips, for novices and experts, in birding, climbing, mountain biking, sea kayaking, and natural history. After settling on a trip, price, and meeting time with them, be absolutely sure that you confirm and reconfirm your trip. There is also a large youth organization geared toward year-rounders, but vacationing kids can participate, too.

SCUBA DIVING ❋ **The Sunken Ship** (508-228-9226; sunkenship.com), 12 Broad Street. Perhaps because the *Andrea Doria* sank off Nantucket's treacherous shoals in July 1956, the island attracts Atlantic Ocean divers. This full-service dive shop has the market cornered with charters, lessons, rentals, and even fishing referrals.

SEAL CRUISES ❋ **Shearwater Excursions** (508-228-7037; shearwaterexcursions .com), Straight Wharf, Slip 1011. Daily departures, weather permitting, to see lounging seals on the outer island of Muskeget. Tours are 2½ hours. $$$$$+.

SURFING **Force 5 Watersports** (508-228-0700), 6 Union Street, a retail surf shop with a knowledgeable staff, is a good source of information, too. Surfing is best on the southern beaches. Open May through December.

TENNIS Free, public courts are open at **Jetties Beach** (see *Green Space*) from early September to mid-June; from mid-June to late August there is a fee. Sign up at the **Parks and Recreation Building** (508-228-7213), North Beach Street, for one of six courts. Clinics and lessons are offered for adults and children.

✳ Even More Things to Do

FITNESS CLUB ✳ **Nantucket Health Club** (508-228-4750; nantuckethealthclub.com), 10 Young's Way. A full array of machines, free weights, classes, and personalized training sessions.

FOR FAMILIES ♂ **Strong Wings Summer Camp** (508-228-1769; strongwings.org), late June to late August. Choose from weekly action-filled day and half-day camps for kids. These might include sea kayaking, rock climbing, snorkeling, biking, ghost stories, crafts, and nature exploration.

✳ ♂ **Nantucket Babysitters Service** (508-228-4970; nantucketbabysitters.com) provides parents a respite. Ronnie Sullivan-Moran assesses your needs, matches a sitter to your kids (all ages), and then sends the sitter to wherever you're staying. The company also offers grocery shopping services, event planning, and meal preparation assistance.

SPECIAL PROGRAMS ✳ ♂ **Nantucket Island School of Design and the Arts** (508-228-9248; nisda.org), 23 Wauwinet Road. Founded in 1973, NISDA presents an extraordinary range of classes and lectures for adults and kids. Summerlong, weeklong, or daylong classes might include drawing, design, textile, folk art, floorcloth painting, puppet making, garden tours, yoga, modern dance, clay and sculpture, painting, and photography. Affiliated with Massachusetts College of Art in Boston, the school offers college graduate and undergraduate summer sessions in a converted dairy barn. Individuals attending classes may rent the school's studios and one-bedroom cottages on the harbor.

✳ ♂ **Artist's Association of Nantucket** (508-228-0722; nantucketarts.org), One Gardner Perry Lane. Offering seasonal workshops and classes in a variety of disciplines for adults and children, the association also maintains a fine art library on Gardner Perry Lane and a gallery at 19 Washington Street (see *Selective Shopping*).

✳ ♂ **Nantucket Community School** (508-228-7285, ext. 1571; nantucketcommunityschool.org), 10 Surfside Road. Offers adult-education classes and programs and camps for kids.

SWIMMING POOL ✳ ♂ **Nantucket Community Pool** (508-228-7285, ext. 1578; nantucketcommunityschool.org), Atlantic and Surfside Avenues. An Olympic-sized pool at the Nantucket High School is open for swimming and offers lessons both for a fee.

WINE, BEER, & SPIRITS ✳ **Nantucket Vineyard, Cisco Brewers, and Triple Eight Distillery** (508-325-5929; ciscobrewers.com), 5 Bartlett Farm Road, about 2.5 miles south of town off Hummock Pond Road. Imagine a warm summer afternoon, sitting at

'SCONSET

This charming village on the eastern shore is the island's only real "destination," 7 miles from town. (Well, for the adventuresome, Great Point—see *Green Space*—is the other "destination.") The village is renowned for its tiny rose-covered cottages, all a few feet from one another. Some of the oldest are clustered on Broadway, Centre, and Shell Streets. You won't have any problem finding them since the town consists of only a post office, a liquor store, a market, and a few restaurants. Of course, 'Sconset also has its share of grand summer homes—along Ocean Avenue and Sankaty and Baxter Roads (on the way to Sankaty Head Lighthouse; see below). Recently, the combination of severe winter storms and the absence of offshore shoals to break incoming waves has created extreme beach erosion. Beachfront homes have been moved after several were engulfed by the sea.

Siasconset, which means "land of many bones," was probably named after a right whale was found on the beach. The 17th-century village was settled by and used as a base for fishermen in search of cod and whales. When wives began to join their husbands here in summer, the one-room shanties were expanded with additions called warts. (Perhaps early summer visitors wanted to escape the oil refineries in town, too.) When the narrow-gauge railway was built in 1884, it brought vacationing New York City actors who established a thriving actors' colony. Today 200 hardy souls live here year-round.

TELLING TIME WITH THE SUNDIAL IN 'SCONSET

an outdoor café in the interior of the island, surrounded by Bartlett farmland, sipping a frosty beer or icy vodka. Well, imagine no longer: It's a fun diversion. Come to sample fresh, traditionally brewed ales, porters, stouts, and seasonal concoctions like Celebration Libation. Look for the excellent Cisco beer at island restaurants and package stores. It's more satisfying (and cheaper) than most bottles of restaurant wine. And look for the clean tastes of 888 vodkas, flavored with vanilla, cranberry, and orange. (In tastings, the pure 888 outscored Kettle One.) I didn't get a chance to sample their boutique Hurricane Rum, Gale Force Gin, or Nor'Easter Bourbon (hey, someone has to be clear-eyed for long research days!), but I encourage you to sip to your heart's content. As for wine, because grapes don't grow particularly well on Nantucket, this vineyard imports grapes for its wines.

A few "sites" in 'Sconset include the 'Sconset Pump, an old wooden water pump dug in 1776, and the 'Sconset Union Chapel, the only place of worship in town. Despite its name, the Siasconset Casino, built in 1899 as a private tennis club, has never been used for gambling. Turn-of-the-20th-century actors used it for summer theater; movies are now shown in summer (see *Entertainment*).

Sankaty Head Light, 'Sconset. Partially solar powered, this red-and-white-striped light stands on a 90-foot-high bluff about 300 feet from the shoreline—it was relocated in 2007 thanks to community action and should be safe for the foreseeable future. Its light is visible 24 miles out to sea.

Nantucket is renowned for the amount of open, protected land on the island. In fact, thanks to the efforts of various conservation groups, about half the island is protected from development. Two organizations deserve much of the credit: Nantucket Conservation Foundation (508-228-2884; nantucketconservation.org), 118 Cliff Road; and the Nantucket Land Bank (508-228-7240; nantucketlandbank.org), 22 Broad Street. The Conservation Foundation was established in 1963 to manage open land—wetlands, moors, and grasslands. It's a private, nonprofit organization that's supported by membership contributions. Because the foundation is constantly acquiring land, call for a map of its current properties, published yearly; free. The Land Bank was created by an act of the state legislature in 1983, granting permission to assess a 2 percent tax for all real estate and land transactions. With the tax receipts, property is purchased and kept as conservation land.

✳ Green Space

🐚 **Maria Mitchell Association** (508-228-9198; mmo.org) leads informative field trips around the island (see *To See*). $$.

Coatue–Coskata–Great Point, at the end of Wauwinet Road, accessible only by four-wheel-drive vehicle and on foot. The narrow strip of very soft sand leading to Great Point is about 5 miles long. Note the "haulover," which separates the head of the harbor from the Atlantic Ocean. This stretch of sand is so narrow that fishermen would haul their boats across it instead of going all the way around the tip of Great Point. During severe storms, the ocean breaks through the haulover, effectively creating an island. (Sand is eventually redeposited by the currents.) The spit of sand known as

THE MOORS

Coatue is a series of concave bays that reaches all the way to the mouth of Nantucket Harbor.

There's a wealth of things to do in this pristine preserve: birding, surf casting, shellfishing, sunbathing, picnicking, and walking. Because the riptides are dangerous, especially near the Great Point Lighthouse (see *To See*), swimming is not recommended. These three adjacent wildlife areas, totaling more than 1,100 acres, are owned by different organizations, but that doesn't impact visitors. The Conservation Foundation owns both Coatue and the haulover. But the world's oldest land trust, the Trustees of Reservations, also manages part of the land. Ara's Tours and the Trustees of Reservations offer tours of Great Point; see *Getting Around* for tours and for information on getting your own four-wheel-drive permits.

Eel Point, off Eel Point Road from the Madaket Bike Path (see *To Do*), about 6 miles from town. Leave your car or bicycle at the sign that reads 40th Pole Beach and walk the last ½ mile to the beach. There aren't any facilities, just unspoiled nature, good birding, surf-fishing, and a shallow sandbar. Portions of this beach are often closed to protect nesting shorebirds. For in-depth information, pick up a map and self-guided tour from the **Nantucket Conservation Foundation** (see *Getting Around* in "Nantucket").

Sanford Farm, **Ram Pasture**, and **the Woods**, off Madaket Road. These 700-plus acres of wetlands, grasslands, and forest are owned and managed by the Conservation Foundation and the Land Bank. Ram Pasture and the Woods were one of the foundation's first purchases (for $625,000) in 1971. Fourteen years later, Sanford Farm was purchased for $4.4 million from Mrs. Anne Sanford's estate. A 6.5-mile (round-trip) walking and biking trail goes past Hummock Pond to the ocean, affording great views of heathlands along the way. Interpretive markers identify natural and historic sites. There is also a popular 45-minute (1.6-mile) loop trail as well as the Barn Trail (1½ hours, 3 miles), which affords beautiful expansive views of the island's southern coastline.

Milestone Bog, off Milestone Road on a dirt road to the north, about 5 miles from town. When cranberries were first harvested here in 1857, there were 220 acres of bogs. Today, because of depressed prices and a worldwide cranberry glut, very few bogs are still harvested. The land was donated to the Conservation Foundation in 1968. It's not open to the public, but it's interesting to know it's here.

Windswept Cranberry Bog, off Polpis Road to the south. This 40-acre bog is also completely owned by the Conservation Foundation.

BEACHES Nantucket is ringed by 50 miles of sandy shore, much publicly accessible. In general, beaches on the south and east have rough surf and undertow; western and northern beaches have warmer, calmer waters. There is limited parking at most beaches; NRTA (508-228-7025) provides a special beach bus to Jetties Beach and Surfside Beach from mid-June to early September, and regular buses to Madaket and 'Sconset Beaches.

NORTHERN BEACHES

Children's Beach, off South Beach Street on the harbor. A few minutes' walk from Steamboat Wharf, this is a great place for children (hence its name). Facilities include a lifeguard, restrooms, bathhouse, playground, food, picnic tables, bandstand, and a grassy play area.

Brant Point, off Easton Street. A 15-minute walk from town and overlooking the entrance to the harbor, this scenic stretch is great for boat-watching and surf-fishing. Swimming conditions aren't great: there's a strong current and a beach that drops off suddenly.

Jetties, off Bathing Beach Road from North Beach Road. Shuttle buses run to this popular beach—otherwise it's a 20-minute walk. (There is also a fairly large parking lot with lots of bike racks.) This is a great place for families because of the facilities (restrooms, lifeguards, showers, changing rooms, a snack bar, chairs for rent) and the activities (volleyball, tennis, swings, concerts, a playground, an assortment of sailboats and kayaks). The July Fourth fireworks celebration is held here. Look for the skateboarding park, for which helmets and pads are required.

CHILDREN'S BEACH

Francis Street Beach, a 5-minute walk from Main Street at Washington and Francis Streets. This harbor beach is calm. There are kayak rentals, portable restrooms, and a small jungle gym.

Dionis, off Eel Point Road from the Madaket and Dionis bike paths (see *To Do*). Nantucket's only beach with dunes, Dionis is about 3 miles from town. The beach starts out narrow but becomes more expansive (and less populated) as you walk farther east or west. Facilities include a bathhouse.

SOUTHERN BEACHES

Surfside, off Surfside Road; large parking lot. Three miles from town and accessible by shuttle bus, this wide beach is popular with college students and families with older kids because of its proximity to town and its moderate-to-heavy surf. Kite flying, surf casting, and picnicking are popular. Facilities include restrooms, lifeguards, showers, and a snack bar.

Nobadeer, east of Surfside, near the airport and about 4 miles from town. There are no facilities at Nobadeer, but there is plenty of surf.

Madaket, at the end of the scenic Madaket Bike Path (see *To Do*). About 5 miles west of town (served by shuttle bus), Madaket is perhaps the most popular place to watch sunsets. This long beach has heavy surf and strong currents; there are lifeguards, portable restrooms, and very little parking.

🏄 **Cisco**, off Hummock Pond Road from Milk Street. About 4 miles from town, this long beach is popular with surfers. There are lifeguards and surfing lessons for kids, but very little parking.

"Nude Beach," an unofficial beach, certainly, is unofficially located between Miacomet and Cisco.

EASTERN BEACHES

'Sconset (a.k.a. Codfish Park), at the end of the 'Sconset Bike Path; turn right at the rotary. About 7 miles from town and accessible by shuttle bus, this long, narrow beach takes a pounding by heavy surf. Seaweed lines the beach when the surf whips up. Facilities include lifeguards, a playground, and very limited parking.

PONDS **Long Pond.** Take Madaket Road from town and, when you reach the Hither Creek sign, turn left onto a dirt road. This 64-acre Land Bank property is great for birding. A mile-long path around the pond passes meadows and a cranberry bog.

Miacomet Pond, Miacomet Avenue (which turns into a dirt road), off Surfside Road. This long, narrow, freshwater pond next to the ocean has a sandy shore and is surrounded by grasses and heath. This Land Bank property is a pleasant place for a picnic, and the swans and ducks make it more so.

Sesachacha Pond. Take Polpis Road to Quidnet Road. A narrow barrier beach separates the pond and ocean. There's a nice view of the Sankaty Head Lighthouse from here. Makes a nice afternoon with the kids.

WALKS **The Moors and Altar Rock**, off Polpis Road, to the south, on an unmarked dirt road. When you want to get away from the summertime masses, head to the moors (preferably at dawn or dusk, when they're most magical). From Altar Rock, the third-highest point on the island (rising a whopping 103 feet above sea level), there are expansive views of lowland heath, bogs, and moors. It's stunning in autumn. The moors are also crisscrossed with trails and deeply rutted dirt roads.

Lily Pond Park, North Liberty Street. This 6-acre Land Bank property supports lots of wildlife and plant life, but the trail is often muddy. You may find wild blackberries, grapes, or blueberries.

✳ Lodging

Consider making summertime reservations in February. No kidding. Also keep in mind that the historic district, while convenient, has its share of foot traffic (and boisterous socializers) late into the evening and that houses are also very close together. A 10-minute walk from Straight Wharf will put you in quieter surroundings. Most lodgings require a two- or three-night minimum stay in-season; I indicate only minimum-night-stay policies that go beyond that norm.

I also only indicate high season rates (and an abstract range at that!). You can also reasonably deduce that places are relatively lower, relative to one another, off-season.

Much to my chagrin, many places charge more for weekends than weekdays. Lastly, most places are not appropriate for small children. More and more folks are renting houses rather than staying in guest houses. Which means that, even though the number of B&B rooms dwindles every year, it's worth calling at the last minute to check on availability—even at the primo places.

IN A CLASS BY THEMSELVES

ON THE OUTSKIRTS OF TOWN

✐ **Cliffside Beach Club** (508-228-0618; cliffsidebeach.com), 46 Jefferson Avenue. Open late May to mid-October. *Stylish simplicity, understated elegance,* and *breezy beachside living* are the watchwords at this low-key luxe inn. You can't get a bed closer to the beach than this: Decks sit on the beach, and a boardwalk over the sand connects the low-slung, weathered-shingle buildings. A private club when it opened in 1924, it has been in Robert Currie's family since 1958. Family pride of ownership knows no bounds here. Improvements are constant. The lobby is large and airy, decorated with white wicker furniture, local art, and quilts hanging from the rafters. The dedicated breakfast room is sunny and window-filled. The 22 contemporary guest rooms (most with ocean views) feature handcrafted woodwork and granite bathrooms. Five newer suites, with outstanding views of dunes and sunsets, offer the most privacy. There is also a luxuriously simple three-bedroom apartment that almost defies description. If it were possible, I'd live in this unit forever. For meals, shuffle to the excellent **Galley Beach** (see *Dining Out*), the rustic-chic **Bob's Bar** (open to resort guests only), or walk 15 minutes into town. For exercise, nothing on-island compares to their impressive health club, an oh-so-private 60-foot lap pool, leisure pool, Jacuzzi, and saunas. If you get the impression that I'm smitten with this place, you are correct. It's pricey but it's worth every penny. $$$$$+ rooms and suites.

AROUND THE ISLAND

&. **The Wauwinet** (508-228-0145; 508-426-8718; wauwinet.com), 120 Wauwinet Road. Open mid-May to late October. When privacy and extraordinary service are of utmost concern, this Relais & Châteaux property is *the* place. Nine miles from town, it occupies an unparalleled location between oceanside dunes and a beach-rimmed harbor. The 28 guest rooms and six cottages feature luxe linens and toiletries, pine armoires, Audubon prints, and sophisticated decorating touches. Public rooms are awash in chintz, trompe l'oeil, fresh flowers, and bleached woods. There's practically no reason to leave the enclave. Facilities include tennis courts, a spa, boating, mountain bikes, croquet, a DVD library, lobstering demonstrations, afternoon port and cheese in the inn's library, and Great Point nature trips. All are included in the room rates. **Topper's** (see *Dining Out*) offers truly outstanding dining. In the morning, enjoy as much from the complimentary breakfast menu as you'd like. $$$$$+.

THE WAUWINET

HOTELS

IN TOWN

✳ ♪ **The Nantucket Hotel & Resort** (508-228-4747; 508-310-1734; thenantuckethotel.com), 77 Easton Street. The owners of the top-notch Winnetu Oceanside Resort on Martha's Vineyard have definitely outdone themselves. To say they have completely rehabbed this former hostelry does not come close to explaining the depths of their efforts and extraordinary execution. The grand, historic property is my new favorite place to stay on-island. It feels authentic and real; it caters to couples as ferociously as families; and it redefines the intersection of luxury and comfort. Oh, and the service—it artfully walks the fine line between attentive and giving guests their space. It almost has too many sweet spots to call out, but I'll at least whet your appetite. In no particular order: two heated swimming pools, a full children's program (free), a spa/fitness center, the excellent **Breeze Restaurant** (see *Dining Out*), an in-town/central location, super-sophisticated but oh-so-relaxed decor, a sense of whimsy throughout, rocking chairs lining the 1891 wraparound porch, and an appealing mix of hotel rooms, suites, and cottages. $$$–$$$$$+.

White Elephant Hotel (508-228-2500; whiteelephanthotel.com), Easton Street. Open late April to early November and during Stroll. After recent total renovations, the sedate White Elephant is more sedate than ever. A 10-minute walk from the center of town and on the edge of the harbor, many of the spacious 65 rooms, suites, and garden cottages have prime water views framed by shuttered white windows. Most have a balcony or deck; many suites have a fireplace. Decor is a sophisticated blend of leather armchairs and white wicker; crisp linens and textured, neutral fabrics; antique prints and contemporary artwork. Bathrooms boast fine toiletries, lots of white tile, and marble counters. Common space includes a

THE NANTUCKET HOTEL AND RESORT

handsome library, a fitness room, extensive spa, and broad lawns that reach a harborside dock. Inquire about their two in-town lofts (three-bedroom places that sleep eight with fully equipped kitchens, one of which includes use of a BMW). $$$$$+.

NEAR THE AIRPORT

Nantucket Inn (508-228-6900; 800-321-8484; nantucketinn.net), 1 Miller Lane. Open mid-May to mid-October. The main reason I'm including this tasteful but undistinguished motor inn near the airport is because it has 100 rooms, which is a lot of rooms for this small island. Other amenities include an indoor pool, tennis courts, and a complimentary full breakfast. $$$.

INNS & BED & BREAKFASTS

IN TOWN

Union Street Inn (508-228-9222; unioninn.com), 7 Union Street. Open April through October. The island's best run B&B, a circa 1770 hostelry, is run by innkeepers Ken and Deb Withrow with a sense of understated hospitality. You want to know perfection? Stay here. There are a variety of rooms, many with fireplace and all with air-conditioning and TV. The two-room suite and Room #3 (with pine-paneled wall and wing chairs in front of the fireplace) are the premier rooms, but smaller chambers aren't slighted in any way. (Value-conscious shoppers should inquire about the inexpensive room with a detached bath.) After a new round of redecorating and renovating, the 12 rooms are more luxurious than ever, with fine linens, plush bathrobes, and fluffy duvets. On my last visit the full breakfast, served on the side patio, was a choice between an omelet with goat cheese and dill or bagel and smoked salmon. (It's the only B&B that's allowed to serve a full "B.") The art of providing attentive service remains a strong suit here. $$$$–$$$$$+.

✐ **The Veranda House Hotel Collection** (508-228-0695; theverandahouse .com), 3 Step Lane. Open mid-May to mid-October. This consortium consists of three properties where concierge and personalized service are hallmarks. The

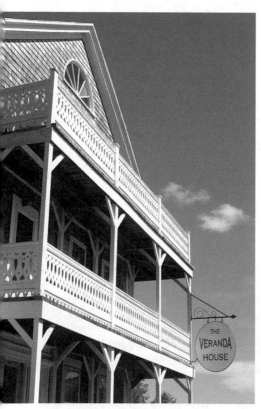

THE VERANDA HOUSE

Veranda House, with 15 guest rooms and three suites, reflects a "retro chic" vibe—awash in black, white, and neutral tones with a splash of red here or there. No expense seems to have been spared, and it could certainly hold its own in SoHo. Gracious "extras" are the norm here: Balconies overlooking the harbor, goose down comforters, spanking new bathrooms with hip tile, and Frette linens make for a most hospitable stay. Fortunately, the owners kept one of the best features: three wraparound porches that offer spectacular views of Nantucket Harbor. For this reason and more, they're to be seriously applauded. An ultrasophisticated continental breakfast is served on the patio by oversolicitous servers, and the terraced garden is a welcome respite. The three-room **Arbor Cottage** next door is all about a sense of calm, style, and privacy. Rooms have a fresh summery feel, with clean lines, a pale palette of whites, and a liberal dose of sisal and linens; amenities are top notch. You'll long remember tucking into a decadent bed dressed in Frette linens and the epicurean breakfast across the lane at the Veranda. $$–$$$$$+.

❉ **Anchor Inn** (508-228-0072; anchor-inn.net), 66 Centre Street. This friendly B&B, one of the best values in town, has been innkeeper owned and operated since 1983. Charles and Ann Balas and their crackerjack staff offer 11 guest accommodations in a historic 1806 house; the most spacious rooms are corner ones with a queen canopy bed. All have tiled bathrooms, TV, air-conditioning, and comfortable period furnishings. One has a private porch. The less expensive rooms are snug but inviting, tucked under the eaves in the back of the house. A continental breakfast is served on the enclosed porch or carried to the tranquil side garden. Beach towels and ice packs are available in-season. $–$$.

Pineapple Inn (508-257-4577; pine appleinn.com), 10 Hussey Street. Open late April to late October and on

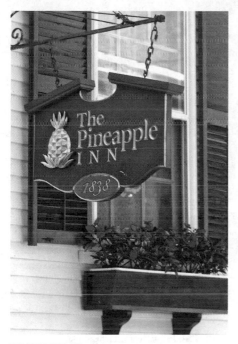

THE PINEAPPLE INN

Christmas Stroll weekend. This 1838 whaling captain's house led the surge toward luxury B&B renovations in 1997 with a refined and understated elegance. Six years later it was acquired by the Summer House in its march toward the acquisition of fine properties around the island. Historic grace and modern conveniences (like air-conditioning) coexist comfortably in this 12-room inn. Except for the lack of an on-site innkeeper, first-rate touches surround you, including white marble bathrooms and custom-made four-poster beds fitted with Ralph Lauren linens and down comforters. I particularly like the enclosed back patio, complete with trickling water fountain; it makes for a nice respite from the crowds. Complimentary use of the Summer House Beach and Pool Club is included. $$–$$$.

Ship's Inn (508-228-0040; shipsinn nantucket.com), 13 Fair Street. Open May through October. Beyond the bustle of Main Street and a 10-minute walk from Straight Wharf, the Ship's Inn is known for its fine dining (see *Dining Out*) but is a largely unsung, very comfortable choice for lodging. The three-story 1831 whaling captain's house was completely restored in 1991. Its 13 large guest rooms, named for Capt. Obed Starbuck's ships, all have refrigerator, air-conditioning, and TV. Many are bright corner rooms. Like the living room, they're large, airy, and sparsely furnished to create a summery feel. Expanded continental breakfast included. $$–$$$, single with shared bath $.

❄ **Vanessa Noel Hotel** (508-228-5300; vanessanoelhotel.com), 5 Chestnut Street. The VNH—a chic but cozy boutique property by the noted, eponymous shoe designer—is often confused with the Vanessa Noel Green Hotel, which feels to me like overflow for VNH. Because there is so much confusion when visitors book online through various agencies, please be careful if you book. $$$–$$$$.

❄ **Martin House Inn** (508-228-0678; martinhouseinn.com), 61 Centre Street. A resident innkeeper presides over this 1803 mariner's house, an elegantly comfortable and relaxed place that consistently gets rave reviews. The side porch is decked out in white wicker; on cooler days you can curl up in front of the fire or

MARTIN HOUSE INN

in a window seat in the large living room. Many of the 13 guest rooms (four with shared bath) have canopy bed, period antiques, and fireplace. Some bright third-floor singles are tucked under the eaves. A continental buffet breakfast is served at one long table, or you can take a tray table to the porch or your room. $$–$$$; single rates, too.

Centerboard Guest House (508-228-9696; centerboardinn.com), 8 Chester Street. Open April through December. A five- to 10-minute walk from the ferry, Centerboard is a restored 1886 former whaling captain's home with a generally light Victorian sensibility. You'll find pleasing contemporary touches throughout, including an outdoor fire pit. The second-floor rooms are romantic, with feather beds, luxurious linens, stripped floors and woodwork, and gleaming bathrooms. The two-room master suite features inlaid floors, rich woodwork, a working fireplace, marble bathroom, deep Jacuzzi tub, and pencil-post canopy bed. Two garden rooms are decidedly different. One is reminiscent of a houseboat, with built-in carpentry, a galley kitchen, a matching pair of raised double beds, and a snug twin berth; it can sleep five. Modern amenities include mini-refrigerators and flat-screen TVs. Expanded continental breakfast included. $$–$$$$.

Century House (508-228-0530; centuryhouse.com), 10 Cliff Road. Open mid-May to mid-October. The oldest continuously operating inn on Nantucket, dating to 1835, has 16 rooms and suites that are just far enough from the center of town to be quiet and just close enough for a pleasant walk. Innkeepers Gerry Connick and Jean Ellen Heron, hands-on owners since 1984, have created a homey and luxurious getaway, complete with an abundant Berry Buffet Breakfast enjoyed on the wraparound veranda or garden patio. Beach towels and tote are provided for the nearby sands. $$–$$$$$+.

❄ ✐ **The Chestnut House** (508-228-0049; chestnuthouse.com), 3 Chestnut Street. Not many old-fashioned guest houses remain, and this one has been in the Carl family since the early 1980s. The family-friendly place is busy and eclectic, with local art taking up almost every inch of wall space. (See Hawthorn House, below, for more about familial contributions to decor.) Two-room suites can sleep four people if they are good friends, or a family. Otherwise, they are nice and roomy for two people. One suite is particularly quiet, and there is only one "regular" guest room. All have TV, a small refrigerator, air-conditioning; most have a DVD. The freestanding cottage is more like a suite, with a Murphy bed and separate kitchen. You'll find added value in the additional bathrooms, which allow for a final post-beach shower and late departures. Rates include a daily breakfast voucher, valid at two good restaurants. $$–$$$; cottage more.

❄ **The Hawthorn House** (508-228-1468; hawthornhouse.com), 2 Chestnut Street. A guest house since the mid-1940s, this simple B&B was built in 1849, so the rooms are small. Seven of nine guest rooms and suites are upstairs off a casual common area; all rooms have a private bath. Because the B&B is in the historic district, the two ground-floor rooms can be a tad noisy in the evening. Innkeepers Mitchell and Diane Carl came to Nantucket on their honeymoon and loved it so much they returned three years later to purchase the inn and have operated it since. Mitchell's father made the hooked rugs; Diane made the needlepoint pillows; and his mother did most of the paintings. Mitchell is responsible for the lovely stained-glass panels. Inquire about the efficiency cottage and two-room suite. Rates include a daily breakfast voucher, valid at two good restaurants. $$.

❄ **21 Broad Hotel** (508-228-4749; 21broadhotel.com), 21 Broad Street. Open when. This complete overhaul, restoration, and rehab (in 2014) bears zero resemblance to its former incarnation as the Nesbitt. If you're a repeat visitor to

Nantucket, you'll probably walk by shaking your head, thinking, hey wait a minute... Restoration was painstaking—and worth every second. Modern and almost urban in feel, this lively and breezy 27-room hotel suits travelers to a tee. From Vitamin C-infused showerheads (!) to loaner iPads to black out shades, they've overhauled the place with a fresh appeal—right down to a flickering fire housed in a concrete vessel in the living room to a back deck where you BYOB to add to their mixers. $$-$$$$$$+.

Jared Coffin House (508-228-2400; jaredcoffinhouse.com), 29 Broad Street. The island's first three-story house, topped with a cupola and slate roof, was built in 1845 by a wealthy ship owner for his wife. Made of brick, it was also one of the few buildings to survive the Great Fire of 1846. One year later, after Coffin's wife refused to live here, it was converted to an inn. (I simply note it here for its historical value.)

AROUND THE ISLAND

Summer House Cottages (508-257-4577; thesummerhouse.com), 17 Ocean Avenue, 'Sconset. Open late April to late October. The brochure's photograph is almost too idyllic to believe: Honeysuckle vines and roses cover a shingled cottage with tiny windows; the double Dutch door opens to a white, skylit interior that's cozy and simple. But it's true! Dating to the 1840s, these enchanting cottages surround a colorful garden set with Adirondack chairs. The munchkin-like cottages have been updated with marble Jacuzzi bathtubs, English country-pine antiques, and hand-painted borders; some have a fireplace and kitchen. All have off-season heat. Shuffle across the street to the eastern beach or to the inn's pool, nestled in the dunes just below the bluff. Drinks and lunch are served in their dining room, as well as pool- and oceanside. Continental breakfast included. $$$$$+, more for two- and three-bedroom cottages.

COTTAGES

IN TOWN

🐾 **The Cottages** (508-325-1499; thecottagesnantucket.com), 24 Old South Wharf. Open early May through November. These 29 snug cottages are fun for a change, although they'll cost a pretty penny for all that fun! Occupying a unique location—jutting out on wharves in the midst of harbor activity—most have private decks and water views; all have fully equipped kitchens, TVs, and daily maid service. Although the cottages are small and rather rustic by Nantucket standards, they're efficiently designed and crisply decorated in yellows, whites, and blues. It can be noisy on the pier, but that's part of the fun of staying here. Complimentary daily shuttle to Surfside Beach, and guests have access to the new spa at the White Elephant Hotel (see above). Several of the cottages, known as the Woof Cottages, are also pet-friendly. $$$$$+.

See also **The Chestnut House, Hawthorn House**, and **Anchor Inn** under *Inns and Bed & Breakfasts*.

JARED COFFIN HOUSE

AROUND THE ISLAND

⚓ **Wade Cottages** (508-257-1464; wadecottages.com), 37 Shell Street, 'Sconset. Open early May to early October. There's nothing between the property and the ocean here except a broad lawn and an ocean bluff. Parents will appreciate the wide-open lawns and the play area and swings for kids. The five apartments have from one to three bedrooms. A portion of this private estate is still used by Wade family members. Rented weekly.

See also **Summer House 'Sconset** under *Inns and Bed & Breakfasts*.

RENTAL HOUSES Many islanders are opposed to the residential building boom that began in earnest in the mid-1990s because the island's infrastructure just can't handle it. But there's no going back. There are thousands of new three- to seven-bedroom rental houses on the market. Expect a nice two-bedroom house to rent for $2,000 to $4,000 weekly in August.

Congdon & Coleman (508-325-5000; congdonandcoleman.com), 57 Main Street.

Jordan Associates (508-228-4449; jordanre.com), 8 Federal Street.

✴ **Barntucket** (508-228-4835; barntucket.com), 73 North Liberty Street. A five-bedroom, three-bath beauty built in the early 1800s, with prices that are actually quite reasonable if you're splitting them among five other couples or individuals.

TimeAndPlace.com. A stellar site with premier homes for rent.

CAMPGROUNDS Camping is not permitted.

HOSTEL 🏠 ⚓ **Hostelling International Nantucket** (508-228-0433; hiusa.org/hostels), 31 Western Avenue. Open mid-May to early October. Originally built in 1873 as the island's first lifesaving station, and now on the National Register of Historic Places, this hostel is 3 miles from town on Surfside Beach (see *Green Space*) and steps from the NRTA beach shuttle. Facilities include a kitchen, BBQ and picnic area, and volleyball. Dormitory-style, gender-separated rooms accommodate about 50 people; inquire about private rooms. Reservations are essential in July and August and on all weekends. Continental breakfast included.

✴ Where to Eat

The dining scene here is highly evolved. Enough Nantucket diners are so passionate about haute cuisine that the island supports one of the densest concentrations of fine-dining establishments in the country. And one of the most expensive: $50 entrées are commonplace. Some restaurants offer less expensive, bistro-style fare in addition to their regular menu.

Prices aside, many of Nantucket's 60-some restaurants would hold their own in New York or San Francisco. It's rare to be served a bad meal in Nantucket, but some restaurants do offer more value (note the v symbol for value) than others.

A few more details: Unless otherwise noted, reservations are highly recommended at all *Dining Out* establishments. In addition, you might need to reconfirm your reservation on the day of or you'll lose it. There are perhaps 10 restaurants (not all are reviewed here) that serve the year-round community. Generally, you can assume that all places below are open daily late June to early September.

Because dining particulars (which meals are served on which days) change with lightning speed, I simply indicate which meals are served. Never assume a particular meal is offered on any particular day or month. It's best to pick up the phone.

By the way, don't pass up the opportunity to have bay scallops after mid-October (when the scalloping season begins). The experience might explain why Nantucketers are so passionate about food.

DINING OUT

IN TOWN

❄ ▼ **Boarding House** (508-228-9622; boardinghousenantucket.com), 12 Federal Street. Open D and brunch, May through December. Chef-owners Seth and Angela Raynor's contemporary, sexy, Euro- and Asian-inspired cuisine stands center stage at one of Nantucket's most consistent and superior restaurants. An award-winning wine list and organic ingredients from local farms are featured. As for atmosphere, with brick and plaster arched walls, the main dining room is cozy. At street level, there's a lively bar packed with locals and 30-something visitors; it's a real scene and has an extensive appetizer menu. But in good weather, the patio—surrounded by flowers and a white picket fence—is the place you'll want to be. It's common for folks to line up in summer at 4 PM for one of these seats. D $$$–$$$$, brunch $$.

▼ **The Pearl** (508-228-9701; thepearlnantucket.com), 12 Federal Street.

THE PEARL

Open D, May through October. From the attitude to the oh-so-trendy-cocktail bar to the whole scene, don't look now: You just might be in Miami's South Beach. Executive chef-owner Seth Raynor (see Boarding House, above) has furthered his winning formula of coastal cuisine prepared with an Asian flair. The atmosphere and cuisine here are sophisticated, relaxing, and dramatic. (Note the onyx bar, huge fish tanks filled with brilliant fish and coral, pearl-shaped ceiling, and pale blue lighting.) Although the menu changes frequently, you can always count on creatively prepared native seafood and local fish. Patrons are particularly fond of tuna martinis (non-alcoholic) and Chef Seth's wok-fried lobster. After dinner the pearl transforms into a late-night lounge. $$$$–$$$$$.

Company of the Cauldron (508-228-4016; companyofthecauldron.com), 5 India Street. Open D, late May to mid-October and on Christmas Stroll weekend (see *Special Events*). Peer through ivy-covered, small-paned windows and you'll see what looks like an intimate dinner party. Sure enough, since the tables are so close together,

COMPANY OF THE CAULDRON

THE BREEZE BAR & CAFÉ

you'll probably end up talking to your neighbors before the night is over. It's a warm and inviting place, with low-beamed ceilings and plaster walls illuminated by candlelight and wall sconces. Classical harp music wafts in the background three evenings of the week. The New American menu is set a week in advance (check on Friday by 5 PM), but it might go something like this: a trio of crab, lobster, and salmon cakes with three luxurious sauces; a mesclun salad with caramelized shallot vinaigrette; ginger- and herb-crusted rack of lamb with blackberries and pine nut couscous; and a pear almond tart to top it all off. One or two seatings; prix fixe $$$$$+.

American Seasons (508-228-7111; americanseasons.com), 80 Centre Street. Open D, April to mid-December. While inspired by America's regional traditions, Chef Neil Ferguson's menu is both inviting and innovative. The ever-changing menu might feature venison saddle with red cabbage and rutabaga purée or black pearl salmon with an apple-bacon compote, sunchoke puree, and hazelnuts. Portions are

balanced with savory and sweet tastes, crunchy and smooth textures. Not up to a full-on meal? Sip a cocktail, dine from the (light) bar menu, and add a fanciful dessert. The candlelit dining room is as tasteful as they come. $$$–$$$$.

🍸 **Cru** (508-228-9278; crunantucket .com), 1 Straight Wharf. Open L, D, mid-May to mid-October. Night or day, try to get a chic outdoor patio table at Nantucket's only harborside (yachtside might be more apt) restaurant. If you can't, though, don't worry; the upscale interior is open to sea breezes and rolling fog banks. Lunchtime is a bit less of a scene than dinner, but no matter the time of day, drinks are super-pricey. I prefer to come for lobster rolls and oysters from the raw bar; I stay away from the clams. The super-bustling (read loud and buzzy) Cru occupies the former perch of the longtime Ropewalk. Oh, and they take reservations for the best seats; try your luck! $$$–$$$$.

❄ 🌿 🦞 **Breeze Bar & Café** (508-228-4730; thenantuckethotel.com), 77 Easton Street. Open B, Sunday brunch, L, D. Within the Nantucket Hotel & Resort, this welcome addition to the local dining scene excels in so many important ways: personalized attention, great cuisine at good prices, and a lack of pretense. It's a breath of fresh air and a downright pleasure. (And it doesn't feel like a hotel restaurant.) Start with super-tasty lobster bisque or perfectly light calamari rings and move to utterly satisfying crabcakes (with practically no filler) or a big bowl of clams. Oh yeah, and then there are those incredible truffle fries and that lunchtime lobster-stuffed burger. Desserts are homey: think brownie sundaes and other treats that hark back to simpler times. Throughout the deep winter, the café is open for light bar meals most nights and full dinners on weekends. $$$–$$$$.

♣ ♈ **Ship's Inn Restaurant** (508-228-0040; shipsinnnantucket.com), 13 Fair Street. Open D, May through October. Longtime chef-owner Mark Gottwald, who graduated from La Varenne in Paris and apprenticed at Le Cirque and Spago, serves California-French-style cuisine in a romantic, subterranean, bistro-style space. He often catches his own seafood, too. I always leave here very satisfied. Many dishes are healthful (that is, sans butter or cream) without sacrificing taste or creativity. I particularly like the signature sautéed halibut with a cognac lobster ragout. Save room for the chocolate soufflé. They have an award-winning wine list; sit at the old dory boat bar and enjoy a glass. $$$–$$$$.

♈ **Straight Wharf Restaurant** (508-228-4499; straightwharfrestaurant.com), 6 Harbor Square. Open D, June through October, as well as lunch and brunch in July and August. When given the choice, I prefer the more casual dining, reasonable price points, and first-come, first-served nature of the bar. It's also pleasantly upbeat and zippy (despite no air-conditioning). No matter where and when you dine, though—whether it's on the deck overlooking the harbor or in the lofty main dining room with exposed rafters—the New American dishes are

well prepared and elegantly presented. Look for the likes of wood-grilled sirloin or a clambake with buttered lobster, sweet corn, chorizo, and potatoes. Other dishes might overwhelm some palates and totally tantalize others: pumpkin chowder with cranberries, fennel, and shoestring potatoes; dayboat scallops with royal trumpets, kumquats, butternut squash, and vadouvan-cauliflower purée; and chèvre cheesecake with Concord grapes, walnut crust, and quince sorbet. L $$–$$$, D $$$–$$$$$.

❄ ♈ **Lola 41** (508-325-4001; lola41 .com), 15 South Beach Street. Open L, D. This is one hip eatery. I mean, really. Walk through the doors and you'll forget you're on Nantucket. Along with boasting a "global bistro menu," Lola 41 specializes in sushi, sashimi, and designer rolls. Try the excellent gnocchi Bolognese, or go for one of the house specialties: sesame-crusted calamari with Korean chili dipping sauce or a house-ground rib eye served on an English muffin. Bring a fun attitude and live it up. No reservations taken in summer. D $$$–$$$$.

♈ **Brant Point Grill** (508-325-1320; whiteelephanthotel.com), at the White Elephant Hotel, 50 Easton Street. Open B, L, D, seasonally. There's no more pleasant place to have an alfresco luncheon than this harborside terrace. (Heaters and awnings keep it warm well into autumn.) The handsome grill with attentive service specializes in steamed and grilled lobsters and thick, juicy steaks. Nothing is too fussy or overdone. On Friday afternoons check out the raw bar, too. B $–$$, L $$–$$$, D $$$$–$$$$$, Sunday brunch $$$$.

♈ **Club Car** (508-228-1101; theclubcar .com), 1 Main Street. Open L, D, mid-May through October. The kitchen has been churning out the same Continental cuisine since 1972, and its off-season beef Wellington Sunday-evening specials are still classic—best enjoyed in the elegant and haughty dining room, set with linen and silver. I prefer to come simply for a seafood salad and chowder at lunch—and to enjoy the only remaining club car from the narrow-gauge train that used to run between Steamboat Wharf and 'Sconset. Depending on the time of night, be prepared for sing-alongs at the piano bar. L $$, D $$$$–$$$$$.

❉ **Fifty-Six Union** (508-228-6135; fiftysixunion.com), 56 Union Street. Open D. Since they opened in 2003, chef-owners Peter and Wendy Jannelle have succeeded in creating a friendly find away from tourists roaming the more well-known haunts downtown. It's one of the more playful and lighthearted "serious" restaurants in town—to wit, you can't miss the mannequins out front. Seasonal menus reflect what's fresh in the world of global cuisine: Curried mussels and dayboat summer fluke are personal favorites. There are two seatings (at 5:30 PM and 8:15 PM during peak season; open seating rest of year) at banquettes as well as patio dining. Inquire about the outdoor table "#56." $$$–$$$$$.

ON THE OUTSKIRTS OF TOWN

♿ **Galley Beach** (508-228-9641; galleybeach.net), 54 Jefferson Avenue. Open L, weekend brunch, D, late April to late October. At the Cliffside Beach Club (but with no relation to it), you'll literally dine beachside, drinking in sunsets along with your cosmos. But this isn't a sand-in-your-shoes kind of place—it's elegant, candlelit dining on Nantucket Sound, thanks to a multimillion-dollar renovation in 2009, complete with a zinc bar. The coastal cuisine menu features sea scallops, other local seafood, and organic greens. A restaurant with this kind of location might be content to pass, but the Galley Beach is absolutely stellar in all ways. L $$–$$$, D $$$$–$$$$$+.

♨ ❉ **Island Kitchen** (508-228-2639; nantucketislandkitchen.com), 1 Chin's Way. Open B, L, D. This super-pleasant place is owned by the former chef of famed Le Languedoc, Patrick, and features locally sourced New American

cuisine. It's a great find and value. Even better? It's not "a scene," and it's heavily patronized by old Nantucket folks rather than newcomers. Dress down, appreciate a limited menu (knowing that they concentrate on doing a few things well), and sit back and enjoy. It's across the street from Stop & Shop, so there's plenty of parking. L $–$$, D $$–$$$.

AROUND THE ISLAND

♨ **Topper's** (508-228-8768; wauwinet.com), 120 Wauwinet Road, Wauwinet. Open for L, D, and Sunday brunch, May through October. You could break the bank here and Topper's would still be worth every penny. All the superlatives in the dictionary just can't do the place justice. The setting and service are luxurious, indulgent, and sophisticated yet relaxed. Regional dishes are downright sublime: New American cuisine is matched by outstanding pairings from a French and California wine list. (Topper's consistently wins the just-about-impossible-to-win *Wine Spectator* Grand Award). And to quote myself in *National Geographic Traveler*, "Their wine pairing is unrivaled on the Eastern Seaboard.") On my most recent visit, I splurged on the off-season six-course degustation menu *with* wine pairing. Each dish and wine comes into its own when paired with the other: one plus one equals three. It's pricey, but it's an uncommonly rare dining experience. Dishes and wines ascend in boldness, telling a story exuberantly, then come back down to earth. For lunch, served on the bayside porch, Topper's offers a two-course menu ($$$). Topper's offers complimentary van service from town, as well as transportation aboard the *Wauwinet Lady*, which takes guests from Straight Wharf to the restaurant's private dock in-season. Kudos to chef Kyle Zachary and the whole staff. Brunch $$–$$$$, L $$$, D $$$$$, multi-course prix fixe, too.

'Sconset Café (508-257-4008; sconsetcafe.com), 8 Main Street, 'Sconset.

'SCONSET CAFÉ

Open L, D, mid-May to mid-September, breakfast in summer. This tiny place is always great. It's known for its chowder with herbs, but you'll also find creative salads and sandwiches at lunch. Chef-owner Rolf Nelson's dinners really shine and tend toward sophisticated New American dishes. The menu changes constantly, but chocolate volcano cake is often the dessert specialty. Reservations accepted for 6 PM seating only. No credit cards; BYOB. Rolf owns the wine shop next door, where he recommends wines that go with his menu. Customers typically buy their wine there for dinner. B $, L $$, D $$–$$$$.

♿ **The Chanticleer** (508-257-4499; thechanticleer.net), 9 New Street, 'Sconset. Open L, D, May through October. This venerated institution features a modern French menu emphasizing New England and artisan ingredients. Meals are served in the courtyard of a rose-covered cottage, in small dining rooms overlooking the courtyard through small-paned windows, or in the more formal main dining room with low ceilings. Local fish, local produce, and game birds are highlighted. I suspect that dining here will live on in your memory for years. The wine list is outstanding. Jackets preferred. L $$$–$$$$, D $$$–$$$$$.

EATING OUT

IN TOWN

❄ ⚲ **Centre Street Bistro** (508-228-8470; nantucketbistro.com), 29 Centre Street. Open B, L, D. Chef-owners Ruth and Tim Pitts, who have been cooking on-island since 1989, have cultivated a deservedly

THE CHANTICLEER

loyal following. Perhaps it's because they serve exceedingly good food at even better prices. Their ever-evolving menu might include dishes like cheeseburger tortilla, but I often revert to their signature smoked salmon taco. Or start your day with their "Nantucket Breakfast"—scrambled eggs, bacon, potato pancake, and blueberry pancake. There are only a couple of dozen seats (and a small bar) within this Mediterranean-style space, but that's fine, as people enjoy the summertime patio. BYOB. B, L $; D $$–$$$.

Black-Eyed Susan's (508-325-0308; black-eyedsusans.com), 10 India Street. Open for brunch, D, seasonally. This small place with no air-conditioning and with pickled walls is part bistro, part glorified lunch counter with open kitchen. Hip, funky (in a good way), mellow, and homey, the downscale decor belies the stylishly presented plates. The global menu changes frequently, but look for complex fish preparations and dishes like North African spiced chicken with seasonal veggies. Breakfasts run the gamut from bagels and grits to Pennsylvania Dutch pancakes and a veggie scramble with pesto (made with eggs or tofu). BYOB. No credit cards. B $–$$, D $$–$$$.

❅ ✿ ✐ ⛾ **Brotherhood of Thieves** (508-228-2551; brotherhoodofthieves .com), 23 Broad Street. Open L, D. The 1840s former whaling tavern feels like an English pub: brick walls, beamed ceilings, and few windows. It's a convivial place—helped along by an extensive coffee and drinks menu—frequented by locals chowing on good chowder, burgers, cheddar cheese soup, shoestring fries (long and curly), and thick sandwiches. Open until late at night. Expect a line in summer; patio dining available until mid-October. L $$, D $$–$$$.

❅ ✿ ✐ **Fog Island Café** (508-228-1818; fogisland.com), 7 South Water Street. Open B, L, D. Anne and Mark Dawson preside over one of the top two or three breakfast joints on-island. Casual and inviting with wooden tables and booths,

BLACK-EYED SUSAN'S

they offer food that you can relate to: burgers, quesadillas, and specialty sandwiches at lunchtime, and grilled salmon and roasted pork loin at dinner. I love the thick-cut brioche French toast and Nantucket fishcakes in the morning (as long as I'm skipping lunch). They also do breakfast and lunch to go. B $–$$, L and D $$.

❅ **Sushi by Yoshi** (508-228-1801; sushibyyoshi.com), 2 East Chestnut Street. Open L, D. When you tire of eating fancy gourmet preparations, this small place offers fresh sushi and sashimi, Aloha rolls with yellowtail tuna from Japan, dynamite rolls, and noodle dishes. For dessert, consider banana tempura or green tea ice cream. They do a brisk take-out business. BYOB. Dishes $–$$$.

❅ ✐ ⛾ **Rose & Crown** (508-228-2595; theroseandcrown.com), 23 South Water Street. Open L, D, mid-April through

September. This hopping place serves OK American fare—sandwiches, pastas, chicken wings, steak, and seafood—in a traditional pub atmosphere. Formerly a carriage livery, the large, barnlike room is decorated with signs from old Nantucket businesses. Dishes $–$$.

✼ ⌖ **Starlight Café** (508-228-4479; starlightack.com), 1 North Union Street. Open L, D. I like to come to this low-key spot for live music in the summer, a glass of wine, and their house specialty: lobster macaroni and cheese. The arbor patio is perfect on a warm summer night. Look for Italian Nights and late-night menus, too. L $–$$, D $$–$$$.

⌖ **Nantucket Lobster Trap** (508-228-4200; nantucketlobstertrap.com), 23 Washington Street. Open D, May through September. If you've got a hankering for lobster, *plain and simple*, head to this casual eatery with barn-board walls and booths. (I recommend only the basic lobster here.) Other pluses include a large patio and outdoor bar; Tuesday "Buck-a-Shuck" with bluegrass and folk music; delivery and take-out packed with dinnerware with beach picnicking

in mind; and a food truck parked outside Cisco Brewery starting at noon. $$$–$$$$.

ON THE OUTSKIRTS OF TOWN

✼ **Sea Grille** (508-325-5700; theseagrille.com), 45 Sparks Avenue. Open L, D. Despite having plenty of parking, this attractive restaurant is overlooked by nonlocals (except in winter, when it's one of a handful open). Every kind of seafood and fish is prepared practically every way: as bouillabaisse (a specialty), grilled, blackened, steamed, fried, and raw (there's an extensive raw bar). Light meals at the bar are a good alternative. The wine list is excellent. L $$–$$$, D $$$–$$$$.

LIGHT FARE & COFFEE

IN TOWN

Provisions (508-228-3258; provisionsnantucket.com), 3 Straight Wharf at Harbor Square. Open early May to mid-October. Even in the height of summer, when this island institution is cranking, they make excellent

BROTHERHOOD OF THIEVES

sandwiches (big enough to feed two people), salads, and soups. Hot and cold vegetarian dishes, too. Since 1979.

❄ **The Bean** (508-228-6215; nantuck etcoffee.com), 4 India Street. This funky little café has strong coffee, specialty teas, and baked goods. Grab a local newspaper, play some board games, and watch this rarefied world go by.

✐ **Henry Jr.** (508-228-3035), 129 Orange Street. Open mid-May to mid-October. Downright excellent sandwiches with fast, efficient service.

✐ **"The Street."** The first block of Steamboat Wharf is lined with fast-food shops appreciated by families and those catching ferries. Take-out eateries are generally open May to mid-October.

The Juice Bar (508-228-5799), 12 Broad Street. Open late May to mid-October. Yes, they offer fresh juices like carrot, lemonade, and orange, but they also make their own low-fat ice cream, nonfat yogurts, and breakfast baked goods. In fact, they make everything from scratch.

❄ ✐ **Congdon's Pharmacy Soda Fountain** (508-228-0180), 45 Main Street. This old-fashioned drugstore soda fountain, complete with swivel stools at Formica counters, offers egg creams, milk shakes, inexpensive soups, sandwiches, and New York City–style hot dogs.

ON THE OUTSKIRTS OF TOWN

✐ **Downy Flake** (508-228-4533; the downyflake.com), 18 Sparks Avenue. Open April through February. Order justifiably famous doughnuts (there are only three kinds, but who cares?) and pancakes (but not on the same morning, please) from this island institution. Light lunches, too.

Nantucket Bake Shop (508-228-2797; nantucketbakeshop.com), 17½ Old South Road. Open April through November. Its advertisement claims more than 100 different items baked daily, including Portuguese breads, desserts, muffins, croissants, quiches, cakes, and pastries. You can take Jay and Magee Detmer's word for it; they've been baking the goodies since 1976.

❄ **Pi Pizzeria** (508-228-1130; pipizze ria.com), 11 West Creek Road. Excellent wood-fired, thin-crust pizza for take-out and dining in. Someone in your group not a pizza fan? Nightly seasonal alternatives include roasted cod, beet salad, chicken piccata, and New York strip. Large pizzas $$, other dishes $$–$$$.

AROUND THE ISLAND

Claudette's, (508-257-6622), 10 Main Street at Post Office Square, 'Sconset. Open mid-May to mid-October. Known primarily for catering (perhaps the best catered clambakes on Nantucket), this tiny shop's raisons d'être are box lunches and lemon cake. Although there are a few indoor tables, most people take their sandwiches to the beach or ice cream to the front deck.

THE JUICE BAR

✳ Entertainment

MUSIC 🎻 **Band concerts** (508-228-7213) at the Children's Beach bandstand off South Beach Street. They're mostly held on Thursday and Sunday early evenings in July and August.

Noonday concerts (508-228-5466), 11 Orange Street at the Unitarian Universalist Church. These concerts, featuring ensembles, soloists, and an 1831 Goodrich pipe organ, are held on Thursday in July and August. Donations.

Nantucket Musical Arts Society (508-228-1287; nantucketmusicalartssociety.org), 62 Centre Street at the First Congregational Church. Look for concerts with world-renowned musicians on most Tuesday evenings in July and August. On the night before the concert, there is a meet-the-artist event hosted at the Unitarian Universalist Church, 11 Orange Street. $$.

THEATER ✳ **Theatre Workshop of Nantucket** (508-228-4305; theatreworkshop.com), Methodist Church, 2 Centre Street. Since 1956, this community-based group has staged a variety of plays, musicals, and comedy nights.

See also **Dreamland Theater** under *Movies/Films*, below.

🎭 🍸 MOVIES & FILMS **Dreamland Theater** (508-332-4822; nantucketdreamland.org), 17 South Water Street. This institution has a long and beloved history. It began as a Quaker meetinghouse, was converted to the Atlantic Straw Company, and was eventually moved to Brant Point to serve as part of a hotel before it was floated back across the harbor in 1905 on a barge. More recently it shuttered its doors to first-run movies in 2005 and was headed for demolition. But thanks to a powerhouse of locals (hedge fund managers, the wife of Google's CEO, the former CEO of Starwood Hotels, and more), it was purchased for almost $10 million in the late 2000s and reopened in fall 2010 after an enormous renovation. It's just another little example of summer folks pitching in to help preserve a little of Nantucket's history. Year-round movies, children's theater, speaker series, and wide-ranging collaborations for visual and performing arts programming.

✳ **Starlight Theatre and Café** (508-228-4435; starlightack.com), 1 North Union Street, shows first-run movies. Drop by the café for a drink before or after the show. See *Eating Out*.

🍸 NIGHTLIFE **Chicken Box** (508-228-9717; thechickenbox.com), 16 Dave Street, off Lower Orange Street. This divey, boxy bar and music club is very laid-back. When things quiet down in town, take a cab out to "The Box" to extend your night—if you're into pool tables, table tennis, and live tunes. No, you can't get chicken here, but you could in 1948 when it opened as a restaurant-club.

The Muse (508-228-6873; 508-228-1471 for take-out; 44 Surfside Road). This roadhouse has DJs, techno music, live bands (the Dave Matthews Band cut its teeth here), pool tables, table tennis, and a big screen TV. It's on the shuttle circuit and has take-out pizza, too.

Many *Dining Out* restaurants have bars that, when diners depart for the evening, become happenin' places to socialize. Look for the 🍸 symbol.

✳ Selective Shopping

ANTIQUES **Nina Hellman Antiques** (508-228-3857; nauticalnantucket.com). Nautical items, folk art, Nantucket memorabilia, and work by scrimshander Charles A. Manghis, who gives scrimshaw demonstrations on premises.

The J. Butler Collection (508-228-8429; butlersoffarhills.com), 12 Main Street in rear courtyard. Open June to mid-October. Antiques and reproduction furnishings, collectibles, and dishware in a homey setting.

Antiques Depot (508-228-1287; nan tucketantiquesdepot.com), 2 South Beach Street. An interesting collection of furniture and fine decorative arts.

ART GALLERIES **Cecilia Joyce & Seward Johnson Gallery (Artists Association of Nantucket)** (508-228-0294; nantucketarts.org), 19 Washington Street. Open April through December. This association of 200 artists was founded in 1945 to showcase members' work. Changing AAN member exhibits, juried shows, demonstrations, and special events conspire to make this a vital venue for the local arts scene. *See Special Programs*.

Old South Wharf. Generally open mid-May to mid-October. Lined with small galleries, clothing stores, artisans, and a marine chandlery, Old South is located in the boat basin just beyond the Grand Union parking lot. Definitely wander over.

Art Cabinet (508-325-0994; artcab inet.com), 18 Dukes Road. Open May to late September. Owner Doerte Neudert showcases European contemporary artists; the relocated studio and sculpture garden are delightful.

Dane Gallery (508-228-7779; dane gallery.com), 28 Centre Street. An outstanding shop with a dazzling array of sophisticated glass sculpture by artists like shop owner Robert Dane.

BOOKSTORES ✎ **Nantucket Bookworks** (508-228-4000; nantucketbook partners.com), 25 Broad Street. This shop has a very well-chosen selection of travel books, literature, children's books, and biographies—along with an incredibly helpful staff.

Mitchell's Book Corner (508-228-1080; mitchellsbookcorner.com), 54 Main Street. This icon, which has anchored Main Street since the late 1960s, was sold in early 2008 to Wendy Schmidt, a philanthropist, wife of Eric Schmidt (Google CEO), and seasonal visitor to the island. The former owner, Mimi Berman, a descendant of astronomer Maria

OLD SOUTH WHARF

LIGHTSHIP BASKETS

Although it is thought that Nantucket's first famed baskets were made in the 1820s, they didn't get their name until a bit later. When the first lightship anchored off the Nantucket coast to aid navigation around the treacherous shallow shoals, crewmembers were stationed on board for months at a time. In the spare daylight hours, sailors created round and oval rattan baskets using lathes and wooden molds. Stiff oak staves were steamed to make them more pliant; the bottoms were wooden. They were made to withstand the test of time. There are perhaps 20 stores and studios that sell authentic lightship baskets, which retail for hundreds to thousands of dollars and require at least 40 hours of work to produce. Among the shops that make them and take custom orders are Michael Kane Lightship Baskets (508-228-1548; michaelkaneslightshipbaskets.com), 18A Sparks Avenue, and Bill and Judy Sayle (508-228-9876), 112 Washington Street Extension.

Make it a point to visit the Nantucket Lightship Basket Museum (508-228-1177; nantucketlightshipbasketmuseum.org), 49 Union Street. Open late May to early October. This informative little museum has re-created a workshop with simple tools that helps visitors understand the simple techniques artisans employed to make exquisite baskets. With baskets from the 1850s to the present, the museum certainly helps promote the art form. $.

If you want to try making lightship baskets on your own, purchase kits and materials from Peter Finch Basketmaker (508-332-9803; bracklet.com), 5 Polliwog Pond. Because it's a long walk to the shop, take the South Loop shuttle in summer.

The Golden Basket (508-228-4344; ackgoldenbasket.com), 18 Federal Street, sells miniature gold versions of the renowned baskets.

Mitchell, vowed to stay on for matchmaking (books to people, that is). There's a great selection of maritime, whaling, and naturalist books. Sit and browse titles in the small "Nantucket Room," which features all things Nantucket.

CLOTHES **Hepburn** (508-228-1458), 3 Salem Street. Open April through January. A chic boutique with designs for women executed in crushed velvet, satin, silk, and wool.

Johnston's Cashmere (508-228-5450),4 Federal Street. Scottish cashmere, with a nice selection of classic women's sweaters, dresses, and scarves.

Pollack's (508-228-9940; pollacksnantucket.com), 5 South Water Street. Open mid-May through December. The personable proprietor, Bob Pollack, stocks comfortable, sophisticated clothing for men and women.

Murray's Toggery Shop (508-228-0437; nantucketreds.com), 62 Main Street. This shop "invented" and owns the rights to Nantucket Reds, all-cotton pants that fade to pink after numerous washings—almost as "Nantucket" as lightship baskets. This is the only shop that sells the real thing, and has since 1945.

Peter Beaton Hat Studio (508-228-8456; peterbeaton.com), 16½ Federal Street and on Straight Wharf. Open April through December. Down a little walkway, this fun little shop has finely woven straw hats. Custom fitting and trimming, of course.

Zero Main (508-228-4401), 34 Centre Street. Formerly located at 0 Main Street, this shop is now known as Zero Main on Centre. It still sells classic and contemporary women's clothes and shoes.

CRAFTS SHOPS **Stephen Swift Furniture** (508-228-0255; stephenswiftfurnituremaker.com), 23 Federal Street. Beautifully handcrafted chairs, benches, stools, beds, dressers, and other furnishings.

Erica Wilson Nantucket (508-228-9881; ericawilson.com), 25-27 Main Street. Wilson, an islander since 1958, is known worldwide for needlework and has taught the art to numerous celebrities. The store also sells jewelry and clothing.

Nantucket Looms (508-228-1908; nantucketlooms.com), 51 Main Street. Features weavers at work on their looms and their creations. Although customers are not allowed into the work area, they can watch the weavers through a window in the shop.

Claire Murray (508-228-1913; clairemurray.com), 11 South Water Street. Murray came to Nantucket in the late 1970s as an innkeeper and began hooking rugs during the long winter months. She has since given up the B&B business to concentrate on designing and opening more stores; her staff now makes the rugs. She sells finished pieces as well as kits.

Four Winds Craft Guild (fourwindscraftsguild.com), 15 Main Street, off Fair Street. Baskets, lightship purses, scrimshaw, and marine items.

FARM PRODUCE **Main Street at Federal Street**. Local produce is sold from the backs of trucks daily except Sunday, May through October. It doesn't get any fresher than this.

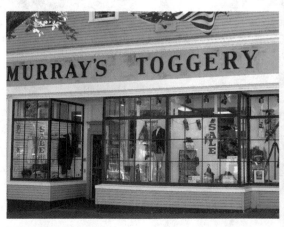

MURRAY'S TOGGERY SHOP

Nantucket Farmers and Artisans Market (they're always downtown, often at Cambridge and Union Streets, but constantly on the move). From 9 AM to noon on Saturdays, June to mid-October, weather permitting. Run by Sustainable Nantucket (sustainablenantucket .org), all products offered here are either grown or made on the island.

Bartlett's Farm (508-228-9403; bartlettsfarm.com), 33 Bartlett Farm Road, off Hummock Pond Road. Bartlett's boasts a 100-acre spread run by an eighth-generation islander family. Its market carries thousands of different food and nonfood items for any eating-related occasion, plus a kitchen selling paninis, deli items, and all kinds of food to go.

SPECIAL SHOPS **Sweet Inspirations** (508-228-5814; nantucketchocolate .com), 0 India Street. Purveyor of Nantucket Clipper Chocolates, displayed in luscious mounds in the glass cases. Of particular note are cranberry-based confections such as cranberry cheesecake truffles and chocolate-covered cranberries.

Nantucket Natural Oils (508-325-4740; nantucketnaturaloils.com), 12 Straight Wharf. A treat for the senses, this shop deals in essential oils and perfumes and looks like an old apothecary. Take a seat at the bar and let master perfumer John Harding custom-mix you an original fragrance. Gorgeous handblown glass perfume bottles, too.

Vanderbilt Gallery (508-325-4454; vanderbiltgallery.com), 18 Federal Street #B. Open April through December. An eclectic assemblage of paintings, sculpture, and classic custom jewelry.

✤ **The Toy Boat** (508-228-4552; thetoyboat.com), Straight Wharf 41. An old-fashioned children's toy store selling great wooden boats, a wooden ferryboat and dock system, rocking boats, cradles, handmade toys and puzzles, marbles, and books.

NANTUCKET FARMERS' MARKET

✳ Special Events

Contact the chamber of commerce (508-228-1700; nantucketchamber.org) for specific dates unless an alternative phone number is listed below. Also, remember that this is *just a sampling* of the larger, predictable annual events. The chamber produces an excellent events calendar.

Late April: **Daffodil Festival** (daffodil festival.com). In 1974 an islander donated more than a million daffodil bulbs to be planted along Nantucket's main roads. It is estimated that after years of naturalization, there are now more than 3 million of these beauties. The official kickoff weekend to celebrate spring includes a vintage-car parade to 'Sconset, a tailgate picnic in 'Sconset, and a garden-club show. *This is a Very Big Weekend.*

May: **Historic Preservation Month** (508-228-1387; nantucketpreservation .org). This celebration of Nantucket's rich local history and heritage includes discussions about preservation and education efforts. **Wine Festival** (617-527-9473; nantucketwinefestival.com). Look for Grand Tastings at the Nantucket Yacht Club, as well as winery dinners at local restaurants.

Late May: **Figawi Sailboat Race** (508-221-6891; figawi.com). A famed race over

Memorial Day weekend that goes from Hyannis to Nantucket; since 1972.

Mid-June: **Nantucket Film Festival** (646-480-1900; nantucketfilmfestival .org). It's been an intimate and important venue for new independent films and filmmakers since 1996. Screenings, Q&A seminars, staged readings, as well as panel discussions on how screenplays become movies and the art of writing screenplays. The festival has attracted the Farrelly brothers and Natalie Portman and included readings by Rosie Perez and Jerry Stiller.

July 4: **Independence Day** (508-228-0925). Main Street is closed off in the morning for pie- and watermelon-eating contests, a 5K run, a dunk tank, puppets, face painting, fire-hose battles, and more. Festivities are capped off with fireworks from Jetties Beach off Norton Beach Road.

Late July–early August: **Billfish Tournament** (508-228-2299; nantucketangler sclub.com). A weeklong event on Straight Wharf since 1969.

Mid-August: **House Tour** (508-325-5239; nantucketgardenclub.org). Sponsored by the Nantucket Garden Club since 1955 and featuring a different neighborhood every year; preregistration is required. **Sandcastle & Sculpture Day**. Jetties Beach off Norton Beach Road, since 1974.

Mid-September: **Island Fair** (508-228-7213). At the Tom Nevers Recreation Area, a two-day event with puppet show, flea market, music, food, pumpkin weighing contest, and more.

Late November–December: **Nantucket Noel** begins the day after Thanksgiving with a Christmas tree–lighting ceremony. Live Christmas trees decorated by island schoolchildren line Main Street, and special concerts and theatrical performances heighten the holiday cheer and merriment.

Early December: **Christmas Stroll**. Begun in 1973 and taking place on the first Saturday of December, the Stroll includes vintage-costumed carolers, festive store-window decorations, wreath exhibits, open houses, and a historic house tour. Marking the official "end" of tourist season, like the Daffodil Festival this is a *Very Big Event*. Make lodging reservations months in advance.

INDEX